D1217312

The Politics of Advanced Capitalism

This book serves as a sequel to two distinguished volumes on capitalism: *Continuity and Change in Contemporary Capitalism* (Cambridge, 1999) and *Order and Conflict in Contemporary Capitalism* (1984). Both volumes took stock of major economic challenges advanced industrial democracies faced, as well as the ways political and economic elites dealt with them. However, during the last decades, the structural environment of advanced capitalist democracies has undergone profound changes: sweeping deindustrialization, tertiarization of the employment structure, and demographic developments. This book provides a synthetic view allowing the reader to grasp the nature of these structural transformations and their consequences in terms of the politics of change, policy outputs, and outcomes. In contrast to the major existing approaches, the book advocates and contributes to a return of electoral and coalitional politics to political economy research.

Pablo Beramendi is Associate Professor of Political Science at Duke University. He is the author of *The Political Geography of Inequality* (Cambridge, 2013), winner of the 2013 APSA Best Book Award from the European Politics and Society section and 2014 Honorable Mention recipient of the APSA Luebbert Best Book Award.

Silja Häusermann is Professor of Political Science at the University of Zurich. She is the author of *The Politics of Welfare Reform in Continental Europe: Modernization in Hard Times* (Cambridge, 2010).

Herbert Kitschelt is George V. Allen Professor of International Relations at Duke University. His recent publications include *Latin American Party Systems* (coauthored; Cambridge, 2010) and *Patrons, Clients, and Policies* (coedited; Cambridge, 2007).

Hanspeter Kriesi holds the Stein Rokkan Chair in Comparative Politics at the European University Institute in Florence. He previously served as director of a Swiss national research program on the "Challenges to Democracy in the 21st Century" from 2005 to 2012.

The Politics of Advanced Capitalism

Edited by

PABLO BERAMENDI
Duke University

SILJA HÄUSERMANN
University of Zurich

HERBERT KITSCHELT
Duke University

HANSPETER KRIESI
European University Institute

CAMBRIDGE UNIVERSITY PRESS

CAMBRIDGE
UNIVERSITY PRESS

32 Avenue of the Americas, New York, NY 10013-2473, USA

Cambridge University Press is part of the University of Cambridge.

It furthers the University's mission by disseminating knowledge in the pursuit of education, learning, and research at the highest international levels of excellence.

www.cambridge.org
Information on this title: www.cambridge.org/9781107492622

© Cambridge University Press 2015

First published 2015

A catalog record for this publication is available from the British Library.

Library of Congress Cataloging in Publication Data
The politics of advanced capitalism / [edited by] Pablo Beramendi, Silja Häusermann, Herbert Kitschelt, Hanspeter Kriesi.
    pages   cm
Includes bibliographical references and index.
ISBN 978-1-107-09986-9 (hardback) – ISBN 978-1-107-49262-2 (paperback)
1. Economic history – 1990–   2. Economic policy.   3. Capitalism – Political aspects.   4. Economics – Political aspects.   I. Beramendi, Pablo, editor of compilation.   II. Häusermann, Silja, editor of compilation.   III. Kitschelt, Herbert, editor of compilation.   IV. Kriesi, Hanspeter, editor of compilation.
HC59.15.P655   2015
330.12'2–dc23   2014044224

ISBN 978-1-107-09986-9 Hardback
ISBN 978-1-107-49262-2 Paperback

Cover image: The façade of Puls 5, a complex of offices, galleries, shops, and restaurants in Zurich-West, Switzerland. Located in the former production sheds of the Escher Wyss foundry, which operated until 1975, Puls 5 is a prime example of postindustrial transformation that is at the heart of this book. Photo by Dieter Möckli.

Contents

v

Figures

Tables

Contributors

Melina Altamirano, Duke University
Christopher Anderson, Cornell University
Ben Ansell, Nuffield College, University of Oxford
Pablo Beramendi, Duke University
Carles Boix, Princeton University
Rafaela Dancygier, Princeton University
Gøsta Esping-Andersen, Universitat Pompeu Fabra
Jane Gingrich, Magdalen College, University of Oxford
Anke Hassel, Hertie School of Governance
Silja Häusermann, University of Zurich
Jason Hecht, Cornell University
Evelyn Huber, University of North Carolina, Chapel Hill
Gregory Jackson, Free University in Berlin
Herbert Kitschelt, Duke University
Hanspeter Kriesi, University of Zurich
Daniel Oesch, University of Lausanne
Jonas Pontusson, University of Geneva
David Rueda, Nuffield College, University of Oxford
John Stephens, University of North Carolina, Chapel Hill
Kathleen Thelen, Massachusetts Institute of Technology
Stefanie Walter, University of Zurich
Erik Wibbels, Duke University

Preface

The present volume is a sequel to two distinguished predecessors. Sixteen years have gone by since the publication of *Continuity and Change in Contemporary Capitalism* (1999), itself a follow-up to the earlier *Order and Conflict in Contemporary Capitalism* (1984). Both volumes took stock of major economic challenges advanced industrial democracies faced, as well as the ways political and economic elites understood and dealt with them by building institutions and enacting policies that ultimately shaped citizens' quality of life. But capitalism and democracy have not stood still. During the last decades, the structural environment of advanced capitalist democracies has undergone profound changes, linked most importantly to sweeping deindustrialization, accelerated tertiarization of the employment structure, and demographic developments. These changes have been accelerated and accentuated by the Great Recession, but their implications for the politics, policy strategies, and outcomes across advanced capitalist democracies can only be understood in a longer time horizon, which is the perspective we have adopted in this volume. Along the way, the analytical toolkit to understand these changes has gained in sophistication, complexity, and precision since the earlier volumes on which we build. New realities ask for new analytical tools and a periodic revision of the basic framework to understand cross-national differences and changes over time.

The present volume sets out to analyze the dynamics of contemporary advanced capitalism in the footsteps of the two earlier volumes. Our goal as editors has been to provide a synthetic view allowing the reader to grasp the nature of the current transformations. The volume is guided by a heuristic framework that takes as its point of departure the context of the structural transformations and proceeds to the politics of change, which, in turn, account for the governments' policy outputs and, ultimately, lead to outcomes that, on their part, contribute to the transformation of society. In developing this framework, this volume is intended to advocate and contribute to a return of politics to political economy research. We put an emphasis on electoral and coalitional *politics* – understood as the dynamics of constrained policy choices. We understand policy choices (and changes thereof) as the fundamental tool to form and sustain political coalitions in a multidimensional policy space against the background of changing voter preferences. We believe that our model of constrained partisanship sheds light on the complexity of partisan coalition formation in advanced capitalist democracies.

This book has been long in coming. It was more than five years ago, in September 2009, that the four of us met for the first preparatory meeting in a small and remote mountain village in the Grisons, Switzerland, where we brainstormed about our heuristic scheme and drew up an agenda for this volume. We then invited scholars whose work has focused on these issues to join us in our endeavor to study the politics of advanced capitalism. Two conferences, one organized at the University of Zurich in June 2011 and a follow-up conference at Duke University in October 2012, drew together the prospective contributors to this volume. On several other occasions, the draft chapters have been discussed with a large number of colleagues, in particular at the CES conference in June 2013 in Amsterdam, where the organizers generously granted us two sessions to present and discuss chapters from the project. Finally, the four of us met for a last round of work at the European University Institute (EUI) in Florence in May 2013 to discuss what has now become the long Introduction to this volume.

This endeavor would not have been possible without the seed money provided for the organization of the preparatory workshop by the Centre for Comparative and International Studies (CIS) of the University of Zurich. The Hochschulstiftung der Universität Zürich, the NCCR-Democracy, the Swiss National Science Foundation, and the Institute of European Studies at Cornell University generously provided financial support for the Zurich conference. At Duke, we were generously supported by the Department of Political Science and by the Provost office. The Stein-Rokkan Chair of the EUI provided the funding for our final get-together in Florence.

Many colleagues have helped us clarify our ideas along the way. In addition to the contributors to this volume, who have always been very generous in discussing with us the overall orientation of the project, we would like to thank Pepper Culpepper, Peter Gourevitch, Martin Höpner, Swen Hutter, Edmund Malesky, Layna Mosley, Jonas Pontusson, Damian Raess, Armin Schaefer, David Soskice, and Jürg Steiner for highly valuable input and suggestions. Special thanks are due to Suzanne Berger and Torben Iversen for hosting a discussion of a draft of the introduction as part of the Harvard-MIT "State and Capitalism since 1800" seminar in the fall of 2014. Their comments and criticisms, as well as those offered by several participants in the session, have proved very influential in our revisions and improved the final product a great deal. Finally, we thank Matthias Enggist and Alexander Frind for their excellent research assistance in preparing the final manuscript.

Introduction: The Politics of Advanced Capitalism

Pablo Beramendi, Silja Häusermann, Herbert Kitschelt,
and Hanspeter Kriesi

In the concluding chapter of the 1999 volume *Continuity and Change in Contemporary Capitalism*, the then-editors affirmed that the most challenging part of the characterization of contemporary capitalism is to determine "how the cross-sectional patterns of variation, locked in through intricate pathways of industrialization and democratization, are shaped by growing global interdependence and domestic political and socioeconomic change" (Kitschelt et al. 1999: 427). Today, almost two decades later, the task at hand seems even more daunting, as advanced capitalism is caught up in an accelerating flux, induced by both external constraints as well as the internal dynamics of its political forces and institutional reforms.

In a process accelerated by the Great Recession, virtually every essential aspect of advanced political economies is undergoing fundamental, and potentially far-reaching, transformations. From the demographic tenets of society, through partisan loyalties or the organization of labor markets and economic institutions, to education, tax, and social protection systems, everything seems to be in a process of fundamental change and in need of either adaptation or radical reform. The cross-national variation in institutional arrangements seems to have shifted from frozen landscapes to a complex, hybrid, and morphing configuration of elements taken from different places and "models." What were previously understood as stable and rather self-contained "models" of economic growth, distribution, and risk management are now giving way to unprecedented combinations across such models with unanticipated consequences for economic performance as much as individual citizens' life chances.

A full understanding of these processes requires revisiting existing accounts of the cross-national variation among advanced political economies. While the current reconfiguration may no longer conform to any of the models highlighted in the previous literature on the post–World War II past of today's most affluent democracies, and while current developments may even make us reconsider how these models need to be characterized in the first place, the stream of new evidence does not, however, warrant the conclusion that current transformations are either random or a signal of convergence on a single institutional equilibrium. The challenge is to theorize structured diversity in a world with changing policy preferences, policy options, and exogenous constraints. Moving away from some earlier approaches, we aim to incorporate the following considerations to capture these movements:

1. We recast the constraints and institutional conditions that shape the feasibility set in which partisan politics explains policy strategies. Thereby, we consider both the changing *supply and demand sides of politics*, that is, politicians' political-economic policy proposals and commitments, but also citizens' policy preferences.

2. We operate with a two-dimensional policy space that considers (1) the scope of public policy efforts to shape economic processes, but adds (2) the differential emphasis of such policy efforts devoted to either *investment or consumption oriented policies*. The former (in particular investments in education, child care, or research and development) prioritize long-term returns; the latter (most notably welfare transfers) prioritize short-term direct economic returns to voters.

3. *Agency and decisions* matter: We theorize how politicians can move beyond the status quo and embrace genuine innovation that breaks with political continuity. Pursuing their own survival in office, politicians experiment with building winning coalitions backed by alignments of constituencies with specific preferences over the two dimensions of public policy. But in each polity constraints still matter, both as policy legacies of past coalitions and sunk costs of policy, as well as limited capabilities of states to realize new policies.

4. We place *politics*, in the sense of partisan competition and electoral accountability, and hence the actions of vote- and office-seeking politicians, at center stage, more so than interest groups as the associational representatives of economic factors, sectors, or occupations.

5. Policy outputs and outcomes then emerge from the interaction between political supply (politicians offering policy prospects) and demand (citizens with preferences regarding the two dimensions of political economy), restricted by political constraints (i.e., legacies of coalitions and institutions, state capacities).

We refer to our analytical framework as a *model of constrained partisanship*. We build on the premise that parties' preferences and strategies are a joint function of two hierarchically ranked goals: First, parties seek to gain and retain office for as long a period as feasible. Second, we assume that they do so in pursuit of a particular policy portfolio, and not just for the mere purpose of extracting personal rents (Dixit and Londregan 1996, 1998). As a result, parties must often sacrifice ideological goals for the sake of electoral viability. This is no new dilemma (Przeworski and Sprague 1986; Kitschelt 1994), and the fundamental premises in this account remain true today. There is no reason to believe that political parties today seek less to gain and retain office than they did before. However, the crafting of electoral coalitions has become more complicated. The dimensionality of the political space has increased and electorates are more fragmented. As a consequence, models built around dichotomous constituencies (Left vs. Right, labor vs. capital) in one dimension provide limited analytical leverage. Politicians have to build electoral coalitions in an at least two-dimensional space. In fact, the openness and possibility of innovation in the constrained partisanship model may derive from the condition that competing parties cannot find stable, coalitional equilibrium strategies in a more than unidimensional world. The possibility of party entry, voter abstention, and differential time horizons of interest maximization, among other behavioral complications, may further subvert the stability of coalitions.[1]

The structural transformations of the past decades have promoted this two-dimensionality and complexity of coalition formation. On the side of preference formation, even stylized accounts can no longer plausibly build on a "democratic class struggle" model that dichotomizes the world of political economy between rich and poor or trichotomizes it among rich, middle, and poor, with one side wanting less scope of public intervention and the other more. The transformation of the workforce through technological change, globalization, and the stratification effects of welfare states themselves has created a more complex set of divides that involves divisions of sectors, occupations, and skills, as well as among different gradations of labor market integration. These complications force politicians to assemble electoral coalitions in a more ad hoc manner and to propose and pursue polices in an at least two-dimensional policy space.

But in choosing policy options, politicians are hemmed in not only by citizens' preference distributions on the *demand side*, but also by *supply-side constraints*, that is, by the differential capabilities of incumbents across political economies to offer an adequate response to changes in policy demand. This is key to our model of constrained partisanship. With respect to the political supply side, our analysis emphasizes constraints induced by previous policy decisions, and the feedback effects deriving from existing institutional arrangements. The strategic adaptation of actors and the institutional feedback from the context in which they operate mediate the ways in which political demands are actually articulated, and ultimately the responses in terms of political supply by collective actors and governments. Moreover, in some polities, state capacities – for tax extraction and policy implementation requiring professionalized bureaucracies – may simply be too limited to make credible policy commitments.

---

[1] We are relying here on Laver's (2005) critique of the precariousness and fragility of equilibrium results in formal models of party competition.

The emphasis on *electoral politics* – understood as the dynamics of constrained coalition formation in a two-dimensional policy space against the background of changing voter preferences – sets our approach apart from much of the literature that has focused on interest groups, in particular producer groups, as the key actors of the politics of advanced capitalism. We certainly do not argue that these actors are irrelevant. However, the recent literature has tended to neglect the electoral arena, precisely because most of it still assumes a unidimensional conceptualization of partisan competition between Right (capital) and Left (labor), which – indeed – is not very helpful to understanding current dynamics of coalition formation and policy choice. By contrast, explicitly conceptualizing the two-dimensionality of partisan competition and policy strategies allows us to shed light on the complexity of partisan coalition formation in advanced capitalist democracies. In our view, an updated electoral-partisan approach regains analytical leverage. This volume is intended to advocate and contribute to an "electoral turn" in current political economy research.

Let us point out one more important analytical premise that frames our argument before proceeding. In agreement with much of the established political economy literature, almost all contributions to this volume treat advanced capitalist democracies as an object of theoretical analysis sui generis, separable from a treatment of political challenges of economic development and distribution more generally. We focus on advanced industrial democracies: countries whose democracies have been in operation for more than one generation, whose purchasing power parity assessed affluence (per capita GDP) according to World Bank data exceeded $25,000 international dollars in 2011, and whose population is greater than 4 million inhabitants.[2] While there are significant differences among them in terms of the legal and fiscal capacity of the state and development indicators (Besley and Persson 2011), advanced industrial societies are separated by a surprisingly wide gulf from most middle-income countries.[3] They industrialized and democratized significantly earlier than the rest and as a result have enjoyed, with the partial exception of Southern Europe, much higher levels of institutional stability. Two chapters in the volume (those by Boix and by Rueda, Wibbels, and Altamirano) reinforce this point by situating this group of countries within a global and historical context.

---

[2] We are relying here on the World Development Indicator databank, as last updated on April 16, 2013, accessed on June 4, 2013. http://databank.worldbank.org/data/home.aspx

[3] The only larger democracies with per capita incomes in 2011 between $15,000 and $25,000 and more than 10 million inhabitants were Hungary ($22,000); Poland ($21,000); Chile, Turkey, and Mexico (all around $17,000); and Romania ($16,000). Taking all large countries – regardless of regime and regime legacy – into account, our list excludes only two affluent countries (Korea and Taiwan) and a handful of upper middle-income nondemocratic countries (Russia at $22,000 and Malaysia at $16,000). The majority of populous middle-income countries – democratic or not – have well below half of the income level chosen as the lower cutoff point of our affluent group, $25,000.

Our delineation of the observational universe is more than an inconvenient pragmatic choice of focus due to data or length restrictions. Rather, it is only this set of countries that exhibits an institutional integrity and stability, and a cumulative experience of collective action and interest aggregation, that hold constant many fundamental variables that shape policy making and policy outcomes elsewhere all over the world. Whereas elsewhere the fragility and variability of the rule of law and citizens' and politicians' basic compliance with universal, institutionalized rules and civil liberties are precarious and account for much of the variance in observed patterns of policy and outcomes, such matters can be taken for granted in advanced capitalist democracies. Moreover, all of the polities we are dealing with have a long history of collective mobilization of economic interest groups. For this reason, explaining variance across policy and outcomes within the restricted group and across the entire global universe of cases would face a problem of causal heterogeneity. In other words, the relevant set of drivers of policy and outcomes is conditional on the level of development: The factors accounting for differences among developed societies either do not explain differences between developed and developing democracies or work differently in the latter.[4]

The rest of this introductory chapter is organized as follows: Section 1.1 begins with a selective overview of major structural changes, policy strategies, and outcomes observable in advanced capitalist societies over the last decades. It provides the empirical and conceptual background against which we then develop the elements of our model of constrained partisanship in section 1.2: We introduce the supply and demand side of politics, including a justification of focusing on parties and elections more than interest groups, before developing in section 1.3 how their combination and interaction shape and restrict the feasibility sets for governments in different countries. This will allow us to generate an alternative interpretation of the evolution of advanced capitalism over the last three decades. Section 1.4. follows up on the exposition of our approach with a brief consideration of existing alternatives. Section 1.5. closes this chapter by outlining the organization of the rest of the book.

1.1. Advanced Capitalism Twenty Years Later: Patterns and Puzzles

For several decades advanced capitalist democracies have undergone massive structural transformations in the domestic and international divisions of

---

[4] An early empirical example in the political economy literature illuminating this causal heterogeneity is Harold Wilensky's (1975) analysis of global social expenditure patterns. In global comparison, all that accounts for expenditure variance are demand side factors (percentage of the elderly, sanitation/hygiene levels), whereas political processes and divisions come into view only when Wilensky turns to the variance among the advanced capitalist democracies alone. For more recent evidence on causal heterogeneity between the developed and the developing world, see Wibbels (2006).

labor. The connection between the transition from a manufacturing to a service economy and the size of the welfare state is a well-established finding. Whether the major engine of the transition lies in endogenous productivity changes (Rowthorn and Ramaswamy 1997, 1999), increasing international competition (Wood 1995), or an interaction between the two continues to be an object of debate among labor and international economists. The facts remain, however, that advanced capitalism has *deindustrialized and tertiarized*, thus producing significant changes in its occupational structure and the demand side of the welfare state (Iversen and Cusack 2000). While routine and medium-skilled occupations, especially in the industrial sector, are shrinking massively, employment in some countries is expanding strongly in the low-skilled service sector, and – throughout advanced capitalist countries – strong job growth is observable in the high-skilled high-quality professions of the private and public service sectors (Goos and Manning 2007; Oesch and Rodriguez Menés 2011; Oesch 2013). Alongside these processes of generalized upgrading and differential polarization of the employment structure, advanced capitalism has become *more integrated* for capital and labor alike (Rodrik 2011) with differential migration in- and outflows contributing to major transformations in the employment structure.

The first few chapters in this volume lay out and explain the dynamics of this postindustrial transformation of advanced capitalism, as well as its consequences for the structural and institutional context of the politics of advanced capitalism. In his chapter, Boix points to sectoral shifts as the main determinants of cross-country and longitudinal developments of economic growth and productivity. He finds substantial cross-country variation in the extent to which countries have adapted to the decline of the manufacturing sector, that is, to deindustrialization, but he also emphasizes that the loss of employment in the manufacturing sector is universal across advanced capitalist economies: From about 20 percent of the total working age population, employment in the manufacturing sector declined to around 10 to 15 percent on average in Europe and the United States, whereas the service sector provides employment for about 50 to 70 percent of people of working age.[5] This sectoral shift has entailed a substantial slowdown in growth and brings about a number of political-economic consequences that are likely to challenge existing postwar capitalist arrangements fundamentally. The most straightforward consequence is a more severe constraint on public finances, especially in countries that have not managed to readjust to deindustrialization through service sector growth – both low- and high-skilled – and suffer from poor productivity in the remaining industrial sector, notably the Southern European countries. As Rueda, Wibbels, and Altamirano (this volume) argue, the distributive implications of

---

[5] These numbers are calculated over the entire working age population (active population), not only the employed. Since several countries have rather low employment rates, the numbers do not add up to 100 percent.

these sectoral shifts in terms of labor market performance and inclusiveness differ strongly among countries depending on their historical pathway of industrialization. Countries with a record of economic openness and interdependence have developed institutions that allow for a more flexible adaptation to structural shifts, while those countries that industrialized via protectionism institutionalized strong elements of employment protection. Over time, this has led to increasing dualization of their labor markets with a growing share of politically and economically marginalized labor market outsiders.

Deindustrialization is induced by technological innovation in competitive markets, as well as by the globalization of production, often in interaction with each other. Dancygier and Walter (this volume) argue that low-skilled labor is increasingly threatened not only by such a globalization of production and the threat that jobs can be moved abroad, but also by the globalization of labor. The inflow of substantial numbers of low-skilled migrant workers, most notably into nontradable service sector occupations, has led to globalization pressures both from abroad and from within. As a result, low-skilled labor in manufacturing and service sector jobs constitutes a group of "globalization losers." These workers not only voice increased needs and demands for protection and compensation by regulative and redistributive public policies; they also form an important (electoral) segment of antiglobalization and antiimmigration voters, further constraining politics in advanced capitalism.

But the increasing scarcity of low-skill jobs is not the only feature of postindustrial occupational structures. At the other end of the skill distribution, deindustrialization has gone hand in hand with a massive growth in service sector employment, much of it in medium- and high-skilled professions. Oesch (this volume) examines this process of "upgrading" of the employment structure, which affects mostly the expansion of employment in the high-skilled financial business sector, and in creative businesses, as well as in public and private social services, notably education, health, and welfare state services for families, the unemployed, and the youth more generally. Job creation in high-skilled employment has outnumbered the decline in low-skilled manufacturing jobs across Europe. This development in turn changes the electoral landscape governments face in advanced capitalist countries, as it produces a large segment of (public and private) highly educated managerial, technical, and client interactive professions, while it erodes employment prospects of production workers and office clerks. As with deindustrialization, this process impacts the needs and electoral demands governments face. On the one hand, much of the upgrading job growth is tied to the public sector and strengthens the support for and demand for extensive public services in times of fiscal constraint. This development is partly driven by the female educational revolution and the massive entry of women into the labor force. The incorporation of women into the labor market has produced a revolution across firms, public sectors, and households (Esping Andersen 2009; Iversen and Rosenbluth 2010). Oesch explains why and how female employment changes the occupational structure of advanced capitalism, while Esping-Andersen (this volume) points to the consequences of this development in terms of household formation and distribution. Esping-Andersen argues that occupational upgrading and changing gender roles in the society will eventually lead to a reconfiguration of household composition around more educational homogamy. He calls this process the "return of the family." The political consequences are obvious: Increases in the number of homogeneous dual earner households lead to increasing household income inequality, and to increasing social policy demands for policies that support labor market participation.

This brief overview has shown that the politics of advanced capitalism unfold in a context that differs deeply from the context of the politics of industrial capitalism, in terms of its economic, sociostructural, and institutional features. How have governments coped with the changing context? We present here some simple empirical results, distinguishing two dimensions to motivate our theoretical treatment in the next section of the Introduction. Consider as the roughest measure of government response the total "effort" governments are making to address citizens' quest for income, measured in terms of the financial resources extracted from the private economy and channeled back into society, as a percentage of GDP, through a myriad of programs for social transfers and services. A large social policy–related resource flow through the government sector does not characterize a specific policy program structure or profile of distributive effects on society, but it does make possible certain effects, whether they concern equality, (un)employment, earnings, or quality of life.

Then, as a second dimension, divide up these state expenditures into two categories, those that empower people to earn a living in the labor market – with policies classified under the rubrics of education, child care, labor market activation, research and development, and public infrastructure – and those that help people cope with the loss of income, whether due to old age (pensions), skill redundancy (unemployment insurance), or illness (disability benefits and sick leave from employment, medical diagnostics and therapy). We refer to social expenditures aimed at immediate income restoration as "consumption" and to policies aimed at increasing people's capacity for future earnings as "investment."

Let us begin with an inspection of countries' efforts to dedicate funds to social investments and consumption (Figure 1.1.). Overall, countries spend more money on social consumption than on economic and social investment policies. While consumption expenditures account for between 6 and 18 percent of GDP, investment expenditures for education, public and private research and development, child care services, and active labor market policies only total between 2 and 8 percent of GDP. The second point of interest in Figure 1.1 concerns the considerable stability of investment-oriented spending over the past two or three decades (investment-oriented data are available only from the early 1990s onward and unavailable for Norway and Switzerland). Nevertheless, there are more countries above the diagonal line,

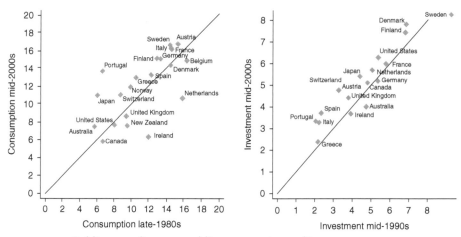

FIGURE 1.1. Public expenditure on public consumption and investment as a percentage of GDP over time.

Note: Consumption refers to the sum of per GDP expenditures on old age pensions, survivors' pensions, unemployment benefits, and incapacity pensions, 1983–1987, 2003–2007, OECD data; investment refers to the per GDP expenditures on public and private research and development, tertiary education, child care services, and active labor market policies, 1992–1995, 2003–2007, OECD data. Investment data are lacking for Switzerland and Norway for the 1992–1995 period.

indicating that, over time, a greater share of countries managed to increase their investment expenditure. The intertemporal continuity of expenditure is similarly high on consumption, although some countries exhibit substantial changes: The Netherlands has strongly reduced consumption-oriented social spending, together with Ireland, whereas countries such as Portugal, Greece, Japan, Switzerland, and Norway have increased consumption spending. Both the Anglo-Saxon and the Southern European countries cluster at the lower end of consumption spending generosity. Overall, there does not seem to be a uniform trend; nor is there convergence or group clustering. Regarding investment,[6] the distribution of countries is rather stable over time, but there is wide variation of levels across countries: The Southern European countries are clearly the lowest spenders on investment, whereas the Nordic countries spend the highest part of their GDP on investment. In the middle, however, we have a heterogeneous mixture of countries.

We turn now to the analysis of the relationship between the overall spending effort (the sum of spending on both investment and consumption) and its composition, measured by the relative importance countries attribute to investment versus consumption. Figure 1.2 shows roughly four groups of countries. In the

---

[6] Since we do not have data on public expenditure on infrastructure, we include expenditure on private research and development in our measure of investment, with the idea that investments in infrastructure attract private investments in R&D.

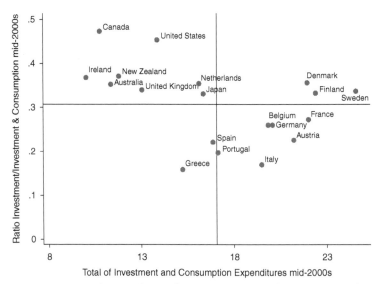

FIGURE 1.2. Total expenditures for consumption and investment in the mid-2000s and the weight of spending on investment in total expenditure (2003–2007, OECD data).

upper right-hand quadrant of the graph, we see the Nordic countries Denmark, Finland, and Sweden with high overall levels of expenditures as well as a strong accent on investment (investment-related expenditures account for about 30–40 percent of total expenditures). In their emphasis on investment-related expenditures, these countries resemble the liberal market economies in the upper left-hand quadrant. In Canada and the United States, investment counts for about half of total expenditures. We also see the Netherlands and Japan in this quadrant: In combination with Figure 1.1 earlier, it appears clearly that the Netherlands has "moved" over time to the upper left-hand quadrant by reducing its consumption expenditures while maintaining a strong emphasis on investment. Japan, by contrast, has expanded both consumption and investment expenditures jointly. In the lower right-hand quadrant we see two groups of countries: The continental countries France, Austria, Germany, and Belgium are "big" and generous welfare states, but investment accounts for only about 20 to 30 percent of their efforts. Finally, the Southern European countries Greece, Spain, Portugal, and Italy have both the lowest levels of overall spending among the continental countries and the most consumption-oriented pattern of expenditure.

Critically, Figure 1.2 shows that advanced capitalist democracies are highly different in terms of their profile of public spending. These patterns have been relatively stable over time, even though some countries have shifted their emphasis, but we do not see signs of convergence in these data.

Finally, let us consider employment protection as an important aspect of consumption policy in capitalist democracies. Employment protection

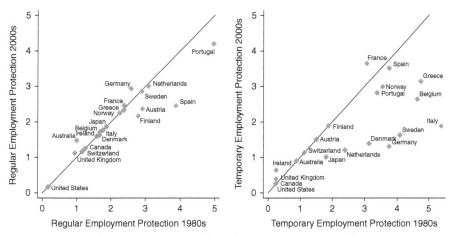

FIGURE 1.3. Employment protection of regular and temporary employment contracts in the mid-1980s and mid-2000s.

Note: OECD regular and temporary employment protection indicators (1985–1989 and 2003–2007).

indicators are possibly best suited to evaluate the extent of convergence and regime stability, as they directly reflect the way governments attempt to coordinate the functioning of labor markets. The left-hand panel of Figure 1.3 focuses on regular employment protection. Once again we find a pattern that defies expectations of convergence, as levels of protection of regular employment contracts are mostly stable. Only Portugal and Spain have considerably lowered the level of employment protection between the 1980s and 2000s, although they did so from very high levels, which they by and large retain. All other countries have maintained preexisting levels. Overall, we again face a strong divergence among the various polities and very limited support for convergence. The right-hand panel of Figure 1.3 completes the analysis of regulation. It shows the level of protection of temporary employment by country, which reflects the degree of the employers' difficulty in hiring temporary workers. The pattern of this panel provides evidence for convergence toward the liberalization of temporary employment in most coordinated market economies, most notably in Germany, Sweden, Italy, Denmark, Belgium, and Greece. The resulting disjuncture of the regulations for regular and temporary work has been interpreted as a sign of a trend in coordinated market economies toward "dualization," that is, the liberalization of conditions for the marginally employed and the preservation of existing levels of regulation for the core workforce (Emmenegger et al. 2012). But a careful look at the way different countries combine both types of protection shows no uniform pattern of convergence: While some countries combine high levels of regular employment protection with a move toward the deregulation of temporary employment (e.g., Sweden), other countries combine very high levels of protection for both types of workers (e.g., Spain, Portugal). Accordingly, the extent to which insiders manage to capture economic opportunities and secure their consumption levels in the labor market continues to vary considerably from one country to another.

The motivating evidence presented here does not reveal an obvious simple pattern, say a convergence of all countries over time or a clustering into two clearly distinct sets of countries. We now explore whether we can nevertheless discern principles that may govern the distribution of cases and the dynamics within polities over time. We home in on certain exogenous constraints on the supply side (legacies, state capacities), but then focus on the interplay of political partisan supply of policy options and citizens' demands that sets the stage for winning political coalitions to make policy choices, albeit under conditions of constraint, therefore "constrained partisanship."

1.2. A Model of Constrained Partisanship: Two-dimensional Policy Options, Preferences, and Institutional Constraints

Observable patterns of variation in terms of policies and outcomes reflect the nature of the different responses of advanced capitalist polities to the structural transformations of demography, technology, and globalization. These responses are conditioned by certain constraints that result from the trajectory of past decisions and political coalitions, congealed around policies and institutions enacting them. At the same time, actors choose among alternative policy responses with some degrees of freedom. We need first to understand what range of policy options is relevant in the feasibility sets of political parties competing for office in the various democracies (the supply side of policy alternatives). We then consider the distribution of political demand, as reflected in citizens' political preferences over different policy options. Supply and demand then meet and produce binding policy choices. Our approach puts a deliberately strong focus on political parties, governments, and electoral politics, because the electoral arena is the locus where institutional and structural constraints meet public demands.

1.2.1. Constraints Imposed on the Political Space: Past Choices and Agency Loss

Government choices and strategies in advanced capitalism face two sets of constraints. First, there are the sunk costs of past policy choices that have solidified around legal codes, bureaucratic institutions, and political coalitions. Moreover, past policy choices indirectly affect contemporary preference distributions, and thus the current political demand side, by shaping the profile of production regimes and thus the occupational and social structure (Pierson 1994; Häusermann 2010; Gingrich and Ansell 2012; Beramendi and Rehm 2013). At any given moment, except during profound social crises and catastrophes, political choices, therefore, evolve as an incremental modification of the status quo. As we show later when discussing feasibility sets and political dynamics in four specific institutional settings, the starting point from which political coalitions attempt to innovate matters tremendously. It restricts what types of policy outcomes are available within the space of theoretical alternatives. Only in the long run, through trajectories involving multiple steps, may all points in a policy space become available, regardless of the starting point *status quo ante*. Concretely, polities that start with social policies emphasizing social consumption and devoting scant resources to social investment cannot reverse these priorities from one electoral term to the next. Established policies involve lock-in effects, often operating through power asymmetries between supporters and opponents of the effective policy. These asymmetries may be reinforced over time through institutional feedback effects.

Second, also on the supply side, the size and capacity of the state restrict the political "feasibility set" of choices at any moment in time. State capacity is also conditioned by past policy choices and cannot be undone quickly. It constrains the available policy options of politicians who attempt to build winning coalitions (Besley and Persson 2011). We understand state capacity as a set of administrative, fiscal, and legal capabilities that allow politicians to effect the translation of policies into binding and authoritative public policies. Weak state capacity involves "agency losses" that undermine politicians' programmatic credibility in the electoral game, as they lack the possibility of offering and then implementing policies in a uniform and impartial way.[7] Polities with high agency loss in the state apparatus have weaker capacity to intervene in the capitalist economy. The implications of this divide have been largely overlooked in the comparative political economy of advanced capitalism. Our approach in this book helps bridge this increasingly important gap, especially in light of the extensive scholarly attention issues of state capacity continue to attract within the political economy of development.

In theorizing policy legacies and capacity as different sources of agency loss, the crucial distinction is between situations in which the political intervention in the economy reflects political *choices* and situations in which the lack of intervention reflects the *incapacity* to decide effectively the allocation of resources in society. When a new incumbent takes power in a context of strong state intervention, a high level of state capacity is implicit. This is not the case in situations of weak state intervention, as it may result from the *choice* to pursue a market oriented policy strategy (which we will refer to as a *competitiveness model* in Figure 1.4) even in the presence of high

---

[7] Among other features, low state capacity is characterized by civil servants who are ill trained; appointed and promoted for reasons other than qualification and professional skill, such as nepotism and partisan patronage; rely on nonsalarial forms of compensation; and have to act on an incomplete and contradictory web of statutes and legal regulations.

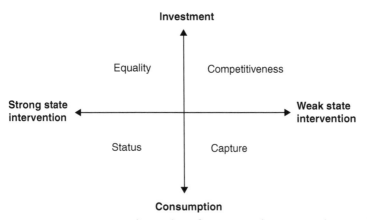

FIGURE 1.4. Dimensionality and configurations of institutional constraints.

state capacity. These are states that might potentially intervene strongly in the economy but have decided not to do so. By contrast, incumbents in low state capacity contexts do not have the necessary institutional leverage to regulate the economy more strongly. In these cases, low state intervention reveals inability, not choice. Low state capacity precludes a number of policy choices for institutional reasons, which may be feasible (though politically unlikely) in countries that have weak state intervention as a result of political choice. This distinction between low state capacity and low state intervention (by choice) is important in determining the feasibility set of countries, that is, the range of potential policy choice.

Policy legacies and state capacities both involve political institutions, such as electoral systems, executive-legislative relations, subnational delegation of jurisdictions (federalism), and other rules of the game. In order not to lose sight of the more basic argument about policy dimensions and political coalitions that act on such constraints, however, we deliberately deemphasize such institutions in this Introduction.

1.2.2. The Two-dimensional Space of Supply Side Policy Options

We propose to conceptualize key political choices over questions of political economy to take place in a two-dimensional space. Our conceptualization of the first dimension is on rather familiar ground: It refers to the scope of public policies designed to affect the income flow of market participants, whether they derive income from wages or profits, and of all citizens in their capacity as past or future labor and capital market participants. Taxing, spending, and regulatory policies affect these income flows, as compared to spontaneous market allocation. Since markets have a tendency to assign benefits in a skewed, unequal fashion that makes some highly vulnerable to existential crises due to low and/or uncertain income flows – for many reasons that are related to people's capacities, skills, endowments, and plain fortune – public policy intervention empirically has a tendency to further equality. Those who pursue broad market intervention, therefore, often do so under the banner of equalizing policy goals, even though the scope and precise shape of distributive effects of strong state intervention differ substantially depending on the specific policy instruments at stake.

On the second dimension, we distinguish whether government policy affects the size and certainty of citizens' resource flows either *immediately*, as a consequence of current transfers and consumer services, or *in the future*, as the payoff accruing to individuals from public policies that help them gain the capacity to participate in markets, where they can earn an income. Add to this public policies advancing research and development and infrastructure through direct state funding/procurement of goods and services, or indirectly through incentives to invest, and not all future-directed effort is going to individuals, but also to companies.

In terms of spending, the government must choose how much to emphasize *consumption* compared to future returns via *investments* in education, research and development, and services such as child care. The distinction between consumption- and investment-oriented policies is substantiated in the recent welfare state literature on social investment, which analyzes the determinants and effects of transfers (consumption) as opposed to investment-oriented public transfers and services (Esping-Andersen 1999; Bonoli and Natali 2012; Morel et al. 2012; Hemerijck 2013; Gingrich and Ansell, this volume). We build on these contributions, but conceive of the distinction between consumption and investment in a more comprehensive fashion. Ultimately, this distinction links back to different growth strategies. An innovation based strategy builds on skills upgrading in the medium run and aspires to increase productivity levels and to sustain growth through "leading edge innovations," in Aghion and Howitt's (2006) terms. In contrast, for countries behind the technology frontier growth occurs primarily via capital investments, the import of technologies developed elsewhere, and consumption oriented policies aimed at sustaining high levels of aggregate demand (Acemoglu et al. 2006). Accordingly we define "investment" not only in relation to social policy, but more widely as public expenditures that increase the productivity of the economy overall and of labor and capital in particular. The term "investment" refers to the future orientation of these expenditures. On the other hand, we define "consumption" as a function of both measures of regulatory protectionism (such as employment protection) and social transfers to beneficiaries who use them in order to cover current needs and demands. The balance between these two sets of policy instruments is critical to the understanding of policy effects, economic performance, and distributive outcomes in the postindustrial world (Beramendi, this volume).

In combination, the preexisting *balance*[8] between policies promoting consumption and investment, on the one hand, and the inherited level of state intervention, on the other, constitutes the set of constraints governments face in designing and implementing policy in different contexts. Let us discuss different analytical configurations in the quadrants of Figure 1.4 as ideal types of policy settings.

In an institutional setting as in the lower right-hand quadrant, public policy operates on a selective case-by-case base to compensate the losers of the process of market allocation. It has very little forward-looking capacity but responds to the immediate demands of particular social groups. Because intervention occurs case by case, chances are great that small, well-organized groups capture parts of the state and carve out preserves that cater to their interests. Both the fragmentary social policy as well as the selective regulation of industries and occupational groups illustrate this process of policy formation. We are dealing here with a situation of "state capture" in public policy and regulation, which was common at the beginning of democratic politics in most capitalist countries. New incumbents assuming office in these societies encounter medium to low levels of state intervention and capacity with a strong accent on consumption expenditures and regulatory insider protection.

Countries belonging to the lower left-hand quadrant in Figure 1.4 are characterized by stratifying and status-oriented patterns of state intervention. Welfare states are comprehensive, including a variety of consumption benefits and the codification of differential access to such benefits (pensions, health care, unemployment), but also systematic policies to regulate whole industries and organize their access to capital, their methods of skill formation, their certification of products, and their exposure to foreign competitors. We use the shortcut of policy making as awarding "status" to groups through a complex array of measures. Continental European countries such as France, Germany, or Austria correspond most typically to this type of policy legacy, as they combine an emphasis on consumption expenditure (cf. Figure 1.2) with high regulatory density that protects well-organized business and labor interests, but provides little for the poorest tier of the population and creates limited capabilities for innovation.

Investment-oriented polities involve a relatively higher public effort in education and skill formation, measures to stimulate research and development directly or indirectly through an infrastructure of basic research and professional excellence, as well as investment in the logistical infrastructure

---

[8] As argued previously, we conceive of the investment-consumption dimension in terms of the *relative weight of investment and consumption* in the inherited, institutionalized allocation of public resources, that is, in terms of policy priorities rather than absolute levels of policy implementation. This implies that strong state intervention is not a precondition for a particular profile regarding investment or consumption. Incumbents in settings of both strong and weak state intervention are equally constrained by the legacy of policy priorities.

of communication and transportation. Furthermore, investments in families (notably work-care conciliation policies) are investments in the future viability of postindustrial economies facing demographic transition. In settings where investment-oriented policies are combined with limited state intervention, it is likely that such policies fuel and intensify a competitive struggle for scarce resources and marketable assets. Actors compete for a relatively small pool of resources, and policies tend to concentrate resources on individuals and organizations whose marginal productivity promises to be very high. Hence, the outcomes of this policy pattern are likely to be highly unequal and driven by a competitive mode of resource allocation; that is why we refer to this quadrant as a "competitiveness"-oriented model. It is mostly the Anglo-Saxon countries, which combine an overall weak state effort (see Figure 1.2) with a relative accent on investment, a combination that suggests a conscious policy choice. It is important to stress that this accent on investment is a relative one. Indeed, "status"-oriented polities may spend similar amounts on investment to competitiveness-oriented ones, but what counts here is that the *relative* weight of consumption expenditures, which constitute the preponderance of past policy constraints for governments, will be much higher in the status-oriented polities.

Finally, in settings where investment-oriented policies are pursued within a framework of rather strong state intervention, new incumbents confront a different set of constraints. Previous policy distributed benefits across a broad spectrum of groups, and individuals receive the opportunity to improve their capacities to acquire economic resources (e.g., through early, universal, affordable, and high-quality schooling or generous work-care policies). Such a policy configuration is thus more likely to result in a more equal distribution of wealth than in a configuration where future-oriented investments accrue only to relatively small groups. The equalizing effect is further enhanced by the long time horizon of investment policies, which creates uncertainty about the ultimate beneficiaries of the policy. For these reasons, we refer to the combination of strong state intervention and investment orientation in policy making as "equality"-enhancing policies, with the Nordic countries providing instances where policy legacies correspond most closely to this ideal type.

Our basic premise is that in any particular polity, not all conceivable policy options are available to the political actors to respond to challenges, given the nature of the political supply space, that is, the institutional policy legacies. These institutional legacies shape future policy dynamics through several feedback mechanisms: on the levels of state capacity over time; on the social structure, that is, on the relative weight of different social groups in a society (Oesch 2013); and on their political predispositions and preferences regarding alternative policy proposals. Through these channels, policy legacies endogenously prestructure power relations at a later point. However, the actual policy trajectories within the two-dimensional continuum opened up by the combination of weak or strong state intervention with more consumption- or more investment-oriented policy options reflect not only institutional legacies, but also the relative size and preferences of different groups of actors in a society, to which we turn now.

1.2.3. *The Demand Side: Mapping Citizens' Political Preferences on the Space of Political-Economic Policy Alternatives*

In this section we focus on the preferences of and electoral demands on incumbents and their connection with the political economy space (as in Figure 1.4). We do so by mapping the location of relevant sociostructural groups in the political preferences space. Moreover, we claim that political-economy relevant parts of the citizens' preference space directly map on the two-dimensional policy space we have outlined previously.

Building on a large body of public opinion survey research, we characterize the structure of political preferences as two-dimensional (see Figure 1.5). A first dimension refers to considerations of material gains. People are concerned about the amount and the security of resources that now or in the future accrue to them through markets and the state. They tend to opt for markets when their endowments and capabilities make them expect strong market revenues. They demand state intervention when their prospects and payoffs in the market are weaker.

The analytical characterization of the second dimension of political preferences has been more diverse in the literature. This second dimension combines concerns for sociopolitical governance ("libertarian" versus "authoritarian" positions, Kitschelt 1994) with concerns for group identity and diversity in an increasingly open, multicultural world (national demarcation vs. supranational integration, Kriesi et al. 2008). For our purposes, it is sufficient to settle on a single second dimension, orthogonal to the state-market dimension, that distinguishes preferences for a "universalistic" conception of social order[9] in which all individuals enjoy and support a wide and equal discretion of personal freedoms to make choices over their personal lives, from preferences for a "particularistic" conception that sees the individual as embedded in a collective heritage and tradition that command compliance, including a clear demarcation of boundaries between those who are members and those who are not (see Bornschier 2010; Häusermann and Kriesi and Kitschelt and Rehm, this volume). The polarity of universalism versus particularism, in our terminological use, thus relates to the role of the individual, as the locus of rights and the origin of choices and with the basic equality of all individuals. It therefore reflects a preference for the procedural treatment of all individuals as equal and endowed with personal autonomy to make decisions about their own lives and participate in collective decision making, regardless of their particular tastes, beliefs, and social affiliations.

---

[9] Bornschier (2010) characterizes this pole of the second dimension as "universalistic-egalitarian."

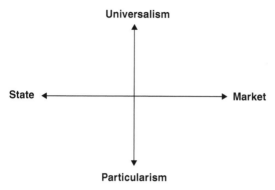

FIGURE 1.5. Dimensions of the preferences space.

The critical challenge now is how to theorize the link between these two preference dimensions and the two policy dimensions. In which regard can it be claimed that the preferences "map" on the policy alternatives? We establish this link by identifying the experiential anchors that explain people's preferences about positions in the two-dimensional preference space. The determinants driving preference dynamics are developed in greater detail, both theoretically and empirically, in the chapters by Oesch and by Häusermann and Kriesi in this volume. For now, consider basic sociodemographic and political economic endowments and faculties shaping political preferences.

On the first policy dimension, scope of state intervention, the link between preferences and the policy space is straightforward. Individuals try to maximize their flow of material benefits. Hence, capacities and endowments that command a high market income are likely to poise people to endorse a limited scope of economic intervention: Capital ownership, high income and/or wealth, high education, self-employment, and managerial or professional occupational status in competitive private sector corporations come into play here. Because prevailing cultural norms thrust upon women the majority of family care responsibilities, which often enough restrict their labor market opportunities, they tend to be more supportive of expansive policies to hedge labor market risks. Low-skill, low education wage earners, more generally, endorse broader state intervention with insurance and redistributive effects. Highly educated sociocultural professionals in social service professions, especially education, health and well-being, culture, and personal counseling services, also tend to support broader scope of state intervention. Most importantly, such professionals tend to work in organizations insulated from hard budget constraints of bankruptcy, as they are funded by governments or run as non-profits. Even as profit-oriented enterprises, they typically are not competing beyond local or national frontiers and thus face less competition. Many of their salaries depend on a broad scope of the state, and strong tax extraction by the state does not endanger the competitiveness of their organizations in a global market. Moreover, such occupations are immersed in client-interactive service processes that may encourage a greater understanding of and sympathy with the less well-off and thus induce support for more state intervention in the market economy.

The second dimension of preference formation – universalism versus particularism – is, on the face of it, harder to associate with political-economic orientations toward investment or consumption, because many of the political issues around which this dimension crystallizes in actual party competition appear to be very weakly related to questions of political economy (cultural liberalism, multiculturalism, etc). However, we claim that there is a link between universalistic preferences and support for investment, and a link between particularistic preferences and support for consumption. We establish this link via two mechanisms: through joint sociostructural determinants of these preferences, as well as – analytically – through the distributive effects of investment- versus consumption-oriented policies.

So first, we note that the same sociodemographic capacities and endowments that predict (noneconomic) universalistic versus particularistic preference orientations also by implication predict preferences over the second economic policy dimension, dividing policies with high ratios of investment to consumption at one extreme from those with low ratios. The most clear-cut link between universalistic preferences and investment works through education. The most powerful predictor of universalism on questions of political governance and collective identity is education. But in political-economic terms, highly educated people also have more cognitive capacities and material resources to put a high value on policies of investment that yield a stream of income only in the more distant future. Most importantly, their own advantageous market location is a result of long-term investment policies in education. After all, pursuit of lengthy courses of general education or professional training is a long-term strategy to boost one's labor market returns. Gender, as a second predictor of preferences over universalism and particularism, may also have a political-economic implication: With the role of primary caregiver thrust upon them for long-term dependents, particularly children, and being themselves often more precariously inserted in labor markets than men, women tend to express a stronger emphasis on policies of investment than men.

Beyond these sociodemographic, experiential bridging mechanisms, universalistic orientation, as a belief in the procedural equality and autonomy of all individuals, may be epistemically linked to investment policies more directly. The magnitude and beneficiaries of investments, which pay off in the distant future, are more uncertain than the distributive effect of more immediate consumption policies. Their distributive consequences can less easily be targeted to specific groups and individuals in the here and now than current consumption expenditures. Because of this veil of ignorance over future distributions resulting from current investment policies, people with universalistic preferences are more likely to embrace investment strategies than advocates of particularistic preferences.

Having established the congruence of the political economy space and the political preference space, we are able to locate specific sociostructural groups in the respective quadrants of the two-dimensional space. The definition and location of these groups will allow us to theorize coalitional potentials and dynamics. Conventional unidimensional political economy models usually distinguish among the poor, the middle, and the rich only. In the two-dimensional space, there is greater differentiation between the characteristics that affect the political preferences of social groups. For the purposes of our analytical framework, we define the relevant social groups with a special focus on occupational profiles. Occupational task structures are strong correlates of income, education, gender, and employment status (Oesch 2006; Goldthorpe and McKnight 2006). They are also independent causes of preferences through the work experience they generate for individuals, and, finally, occupational groups or classes form relevant sociostructural categories with distinct political preferences and voting behavior. We propose a stylized model with four main groups, based on the criteria of occupation and market situation, building on Oesch's (2006) class scheme. The preference profiles of these groups can be located in the respective quadrants of the two-dimensional space. In this Introduction, we cannot elaborate fully on the mechanisms that link these occupational groups and their sociostructural correlates to political preference profiles. A large body of research on class politics has obviously done precisely that (Evans 1999; Knutsen 2004). More recent studies theorize the links between labor market experiences and preferences for a transformed, typically postindustrial structure of occupations. We build here on this growing body of literature to identify both the relevant groups and the determinants of their specific preference profiles (e.g., Kitschelt 1994; Kriesi 1998; Oesch 2006; Häusermann 2010; Schwander and Häusermann 2013; Häusermann et al. forthcoming; Kitschelt and Rehm 2014; and Häusermann and Kriesi, this volume):

- Business-finance professionals, technical experts, and managers: Individuals with high education, high earnings, and capital assets in financial industries and at the peaks of managerial hierarchies or liberal professionals who assist people in these positions (legal and business consultants) tend to prefer market-based resource allocation with a minimally invasive state, but, when pressed, prefer government investment to consumption expenses (services and transfers to groups with little market income). On the universalism-particularism dimension, they take more universalist positions given their high level of education.
- Sociocultural professionals: Individuals with high education in social and cultural services, typically working in nonprofit or public organizations with flat hierarchies and with extensive work autonomy and client interaction, are characterized by decisively universalistic positions but are somewhat conflicted on questions of economic distribution. Their high income and human capital make them somewhat more critical toward state intervention, but given their universalistic-egalitarian value profile, their often

atypical employment biographies (many of them being women), and their reliance on (para-)public sector employment, they are in favor of strong state intervention.

- Petty bourgeoisie: Individuals with low education, but relatively high incomes and capital assets who are typically self-employed and run small enterprises, whether in agriculture, retail and general services, or custom crafts production, tend to be predisposed toward free markets, opposed to state intervention other than enterprise subsidies, and thoroughly rooted in a culture of political particularism, rejecting multiculturalization of society and libertarian governance.

- Low-skill clerical, service, and manufacturing wage earners: On the basis of their low human capital assets, this group tends to be committed to strong state intervention in the economy. Low-skilled workers have a propensity to embrace particularistic positions, and here both economic considerations as well as education and cultural interpretations come into play as explanatory factors (see Dancygier and Walter, this volume). Lower-skill workers, particularly in manufacturing, tend to favor consumption expenditure over investment, as they share a strong preference for answering current needs. We want to point here to a differentiation between lower-skill workers in manufacturing and lower-skill service sector workers. These two groups differ strongly not only in their gender ratio (the group of service workers being mostly female and manufacturing workers predominantly male) and the type of employment relationship they are typically in (with service workers being frequently exposed to atypical and interrupted employment biographies and precarious employment), but also to some extent with regard to their preference for consumption versus investment. Because of their more fragile employment situation, lower-skilled service workers have a stronger interest in investment-oriented policies of activation and human capital development. The literature on insider-outsider divides and dualization theorizes precisely this divide within the working class (e.g., Rueda 2005; Häusermann 2010; Schwander and Häusermann 2013; Emmenegger et al. 2012). Lower-skilled service workers, however, have so far been only weakly mobilized politically in terms of turnout and representation; that is why they matter less as a group for the theorization of electoral coalitional dynamics.

Figure 1.6 projects these groups onto the two-dimensional political economy space. Note that the "middle class" is fragmented among sociocultural professionals, business-finance professionals and managers, and the petty bourgeoisie.[10]

---

[10] We are aware that our stylized simplification leaves out many considerations that most certainly impact on individuals' political preferences, as well. Gender, as discussed earlier, overlaps with insertion in the occupational structure, but gender roles *sui generis* leave an imprint

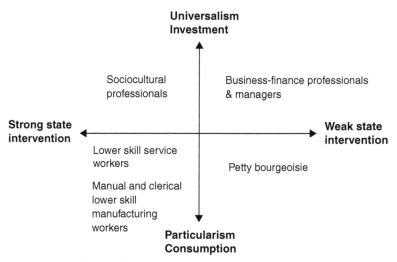

FIGURE 1.6. Electoral constraints: Socioeconomic groups in the political economy space.

The two-dimensional space suggests that politicians have considerable opportunities to devise electoral appeals that craft diverse coalitions for government majorities (Evans and De Graaf 2013). And such electoral coalitions are not entirely bound by structural or institutional constraints. Rather, they have opportunities to change the trajectory of a certain polity. Hence, our two-dimensional account of politics stresses the possibilities of change and the opportunities for political choice. In the postindustrial context, "coalitional flexibility" (Häusermann 2010: 87) is further enhanced by the ongoing process of electoral realignment and dealignment: On the one hand, the vote is still structured by societal experiences, but the relevant dimensions of these societal experiences are more complex than in industrial societies. Simple unidimensional class-based models like Erikson and Goldthorpe's (1992) or those of Moene and Wallerstein (2001) fail to capture these essentials. On the other hand, the differentiation and diversification of life experiences also weaken the socioeconomic roots of political preferences and contribute to the growth of unaffiliated electorates and electoral volatility (Dalton 2004).

on preferences that is not reflected in the political-economy scheme. Labor market outsiders' interests cannot be exactly mapped onto the occupational groups. However, even though their integration in our analytical scheme is perfectly possible, they are not a powerful electoral group in contemporary capitalist democracies; that is why we do not fully conceptualize them in the context of demand side constraints governments face. The same applies to migrant minorities. Likewise, the nonworking do not appear here.

However, coalitional flexibility is not absolute and the opportunities for governments seeking to build majorities are constrained. First and foremost, they are constrained by the *relative size of the groups* displayed in Figure 1.6. None of the groups has a majority by itself. Low- and intermediate-skill wage earners together, for instance, account for between 30 and 40 percent of the society when taking all advanced capitalist economies together (around 50 percent of the workforce, i.e., excluding pensioners). The relative size of the different groups is an important constraint on the reform strategies governments can pursue (what we will call the "feasibility set"). It is most relevant to notice that this relative size varies across countries, partly endogenously to the institutional legacies. Indeed, the production regimes and welfare states themselves have contributed to shaping the occupational structure and thereby have prestructured the opportunities and limits of coalitional strategies in the postindustrial era. Hence, the particular configurations of policy legacies (as conceptualized in Figure 1.4) are also characterized by the relative size and importance of specific sociostructural groups and their political potentials. The equality model builds on a very strong public sector and massive investment in education and public services, which have generated not only a politicized, but also a particularly large category of sociocultural professionals as one of the core coalitional potentials in electoral dynamics. Similarly, status-oriented models have fostered the organized working class mostly in manufacturing as one of the key coalitional actors. The same goes for business-finance professionals and managers in the competitiveness-oriented model and for the petty bourgeoisie in those countries characterized by consumption-oriented policies and weak state capacity overall. Hence, every set of institutional legacies and constraints is also characterized by a core group, on whose support the traditional model relies politically. Just to illustrate this idea of long-term, endogenous institutional effects on the occupational structure and relative size of groups,[11] consider that sociocultural professionals, for instance, represent almost 20 percent of the workforce in the Nordic countries, as opposed to about 15 percent in continental Europe, 10 percent in the United Kingdom, and only 7 percent in Southern Europe. Conversely, small business owners, that is, the petty bourgeoisie, represent almost 25 percent of the workforce in Southern Europe, as opposed to only around 10 to 15 percent in continental Europe and the United Kingdom and less then 10 percent in the Nordic countries on average. Such differences in the relative sizes of these groups are no coincidence. They reflect the institutional structure of capitalism, which in turn reflects the (historically accumulated) power resources of different societal interests. For this reason, past policy choices codefine the set of feasible coalitional strategies on which governments can build. Democratic politics is coalitional politics across preference divides.

---

[11] These numbers reflect calculations based on ESS 2008 data.

1.2.3. Collective Mobilization through Parties and Elections as the Critical Democratic Link

What is the organizational link between preference distributions and political action? How are preferences primed and mobilized in the political process to crystallize around collective actors that pursue policies corresponding to their constituencies' preference profiles? We posit that for the foreseeable future the prime organizational vehicle to make the link between citizens and market participants, on one hand, and policy formation, on the other, is political parties and elections. Parties represent segments of the popular preference distribution. But there is no one-to-one relationship. Politicians have a limited freedom to carve out different profiles of support groups, contingent upon how they stage their appeals. They operate under different institutional rules that at the margin will modify their strategies and capacities to reach voting blocs and craft coalitions among political parties. The "electoral turn" in political economy means for us that parties are not just treated as direct representation of producer (labor, business, etc.) or income groups. Rather, they may form complex alignments of economic interests both within their own ranks as well as through interparty coalitions, where institutional rules make the formation of government executives and legislative majorities dependent on interparty cooperation.

At first sight, it might appear that our account of transformation in the political economies of advanced capitalist democracies is devoid of economic producer interest groups, a core concern in much of the political economy literature over the past two generations, and instead puts all the emphasis on electoral competition. Let us offer here a few clarifications to dispel this inference. We are not arguing that economic producer groups are unimportant. Instead, we are arguing that producer group politics *alone* is insufficient to account for the politics of advanced capitalism, and that electoral politics has become *increasingly* important for the transformation in the political economies of advanced democracies. But we certainly do recognize that producers, particularly those with capital to threaten exit from a polity, have "outside options" to influence the policy-making process and further constrain the feasibility set of likely policy outcomes.

First of all, then, we would not deny that the degrees of business and labor organization, and the change of such organization over time, are important constraints affecting parties' strategies of constructing electoral alignments, and parties' degrees of freedom to modify the institutional and policy legacies with which they are working in each polity. However, the institutional setup of labor market relations and economic coordination is itself dependent on distributive politics and shifts along with the development of political coalitions (Beramendi and Rueda 2014).

Second, however, and demonstrated in the contributions to this volume by Hassel and, to a lesser extent, Jackson and Thelen, there has been at least a *partial atrophy of the organizational capacity of labor*, manifested in sometimes catastrophic membership decline of labor unions. This decline is most visible where labor has always been weak, particularly in the United States, but it has extended to a rather large swath of countries with the partial exception of Scandinavia. The decline of labor has given more prominence to electoral partisan competition. Ironically, whereas the theorists of corporatism in the 1970s saw electoral politics only as a marginal contributor to the choice of political-economic strategies, parties have become central mediators of political-economic change now. Parties are not simply ratifying the balance of power among economic interest groups. Taking off from the Jackson-Thelen chapter on industrial relations change, this could be fleshed out for the calculations of German social democrats in 1998–2004 in accepting and promoting corporate governance reform, or of Danish conservatives in transforming industrial relations systems.[12]

Third, while labor unions have declined in organizational capacity more than business, the electoral perspective, however, qualifies a seemingly plausible implication, namely, that with the weakness of labor, it is *business alone* that prevails in policy making. While this appears to be by and large true in the United States (cf. Hacker and Pierson 2010; Gilens 2012),[13] for many other contemporary capitalist democracies, one may find instances where politicians have the incentives to pursue policies not favored by business, for reasons of their own electoral survival. Examples in this volume are supplied in the chapters by Gingrich and Ansell, and by Huber and Stephens on social policy development.

Fourth, finally, we should not forget that the economic interest group literature ignores large and electorally influential occupational groups that traditionally have weak associational mobilization, but that are nevertheless substantial electoral forces able to shape partisan strategies and policy choice. Across a broad range of countries, this applies especially to the growing numbers of sociocultural professionals who are not the main, traditional constituencies of labor unions, but who organize through specialized professional associations or even public interest groups, few of which have any direct national weight in policy making. We made the point that these socioeconomic groups are electorally

---

[12] Recent electoral politics in Germany may also serve as an example: Schröder's Agenda 2010 was a form of "government by commission" (Czada 2005: 177), implemented by a social-democratic government that felt abandoned and immobilized by status-preserving, progressively weaker labor unions. After all the attempts to reach a consensus with the unions had failed, the only way out appeared to be a reform against instead of together with the unions (Streeck 2005: 163). Even though this strategy backfired electorally and subsequent governments had to reorient policies toward the demands of labor to some extent, key elements of the Agenda 2010 that were implemented against the will of the trade unions have remained in place.

[13] However, the autonomous weight of shifting public opinion and "second dimension" politics about sociocultural governance should not be counted out (cf. McCarty et al. 2006; Kitschelt and Rehm 2013).

important earlier; now let us emphasize, however, that particularly for these politically aware and interested citizens the mediation of their concerns through electoral partisan vehicles is absolutely crucial, as their associational vehicles are unsuitable to deliver much bargaining power over policy making. In a similar vein, the petty bourgeois self-employed in crafts, retail, and increasingly social service sectors still constitute a vocal force in a number of advanced democracies, particularly in the Mediterranean countries, although they have never produced strong national interest associations. Lacking powerful associational articulation, petty bourgeois tend to mobilize above all in the form of electoral populist parties. Both sociocultural professionals and petty bourgeois together with their families may well account for 40 percent or more of national electorates in most democracies, but in different proportions (sociocultural professionals dominant in some, petty bourgeois in others). The traditional fixation in the political economy literature on big corporate capital and organized wage labor tends to ignore these large categories of citizens and the vital importance of electoral mediation for the pursuit of their interests.

1.3. Constrained Partisanship at Work: Feasibility Sets and Political Dynamics in Advanced Capitalism

We turn now to the final stage in our analytical account, which involves using the theoretical framework to analyze the likely politico-economic dynamics in advanced capitalist societies. The presence of news shocks that actors have to work through and the two-dimensionality of the competitive policy space and options call for a dynamic analysis of coalition building, political choice, and change that does not (yet?) result in equilibria.

As the shocks of occupational change, demographics, and globalization put pressure on incumbents to devise new policies and find new budgetary resources, they face tough choices. Our framework predicts that governments – depending on the electoral coalition they are based on – have opportunities for innovation, but the range of options available to them is limited by both electoral and institutional constraints: There are paths of institutional reform and adjustment that are outside the feasibility set for newly elected leaders, whereas others are within the range of feasible strategies. More precisely, we argue that governments in different polities start out in a configuration of institutional legacies regarding both the profile of state intervention (consumption vs. investment) and its level, which puts certain policy strategies at the forefront. Moreover, they also start out in a political-electoral configuration of preferences and power relations that makes particular interests and groups pivotal politically.

Analytically, we consider three possible types of policy reform:

- *Marketization*: policy reforms that make access to or levels of either consumption or investment policies dependent on the individual's

situation in the labor market. The reduction of minimum, noncontributory
unemployment benefits or pension benefits and the privatization of education are examples of marketization in consumption and investment
policies. In terms of expected outcomes, marketization leads to more
inequality.

- *Segmentation*: policy reforms that stratify the access to consumption
  benefits or investment services across different groups of the population
  via regulation. Access to particular benefits, such as pension rights and
  health benefits, and educational opportunities, by type of contract or
  other legal-regulatory markers, are examples of segmentation. In terms
  of expected outcomes, segmentation also leads to more inegalitarian outcomes as it exacerbates divisions between different types of insiders and
  outsiders (core workers vs. marginal workers, natives vs. immigrants, etc.)
  with respect to consumption and investment policies.

- *Inclusion*: policy reforms undertaken to broaden the pool of beneficiaries
  in either investment or consumption policies. Removal of barriers to access
  to basic pensions between contributors and noncontributors, expansion
  of access to child care to all, and removal of restrictions to access higher
  education for low income families are all policies that exemplify the idea
  of inclusion. Inclusion is in large part the antithesis of segmentation. At
  the extreme, universalist policies are the most inclusive of all.

From any given *status quo ante* the combination of reforms undertaken by
incumbents shapes the transition toward possible alternative policy states. Our
analysis of the dynamics of advanced capitalism rests on three claims, to be
substantiated in the following:

1. In addition to all the common challenges associated with postindustrialism, political conflict revolves around a number of issues that are specific
   to each preexisting equilibrium. Policy legacies generate effects and constituencies of their own. Hence, a certain degree of specificity in the type
   of problems to be confronted is to be expected.

2. What parties can do depends in turn on the *feasibility set* of policy
   reforms for each quadrant. Conceptually, this implies that there are policy reforms inside the feasibility set (i.e., available for different partisan
   coalitions to choose from) and paths of policy reform that are out of
   reach. The feasibility set depends upon state capacity, past policy legacies, and the electoral constraints they face by virtue of the composition
   of their coalition of support. Figure 1.7 maps out the feasibility sets for
   different politico-economic configurations in advanced capitalism.

3. While political coalitions can undertake horizontal and vertical movements toward adjacent cells, so to speak, as "incremental" change of
   policy from respective *status quo ante* starting points, we consider distant diagonal moves across the entire policy space to lie beyond the policy feasibility set of any coalition. Put simply, governments lack either

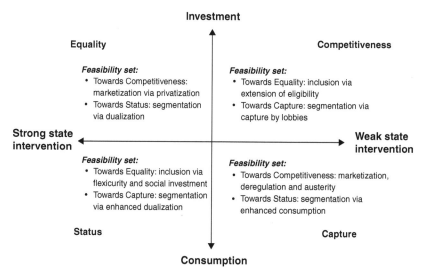

FIGURE 1.7. Political contention and feasible reform paths in advanced capitalism.

political support or the institutional capacity to pursue them. An important caveat is in order: We are talking about policy reforms to be enacted within one electoral term. In the long run, governments can shift their policy regimes in any direction of the political space. Our argument simply states that direct transitions along the diagonal are unfeasible within the limits of one legislative term.

In what follows, we substantiate these claims on the basis of an in-depth analysis of the political dynamics in each of these quadrants. For each quadrant, we provide the same sequential analytical treatment: (1) status quo equilibrium (policy and supporting coalition), (2) challenges, (3) potential coalitional strategies and feasible paths, (4) illustration of actual policy moves on the basis of relevant country experiences. We conclude by drawing together the core lessons from the analysis of each quadrant.

1.3.1. Equality-Oriented Capitalism: Challenges and Evolution

Status Quo Equilibrium

Equality-oriented political economies are characterized by encompassing welfare states, with a strong component of social services. These configurations reflect the long term dominance of Social Democracy[14] (Castles 1978;

---

[14] The dominant position of the Nordic Social Democrats can be explained by a combination of structural advantages: On the one hand, because of the absence of both a religious cleavage and a strong communist challenge, they did not face significant competition for the working-class

Stephens 1979) and rest upon three pillars: (1) a cross-class compromise by which strong unions (Hassel, this volume) facilitate wage compression at the top in exchange for generous consumption and investment policies and large levels of private investment; (2) an institutional system of coordination, both in the economic and in the political arenas (Iversen and Soskice 2006, 2009), that allowed unions, employers, and political coalitions to overcome commitment problems in the short run and develop long-term economic strategies; and (3) a rapid expansion of the public sector as a way to develop investment policies and absorb the employment surplus of deindustrialization. As a result, equality-oriented welfare states have achieved both low social inequality and high investment ratios.

Over time, the expansion of the public sector altered the balance among different occupational groups, increasing the relative weight and sociopolitical importance of sociocultural professionals. who have become the core electoral constituency in these countries (Esping-Andersen 1996; Oesch, this volume). The erstwhile dominant working-class organizations have transformed over time by nurturing an electoral constituency of sociocultural professionals that is partly supportive of their goals, but partly transcends their objectives. These (mostly state-affiliated) groups press for investment-oriented social policies, particularly in the realms of education and family policies, and they clearly support overall strong state intervention. Hence, the dominant electoral coalition in these economies is one of sociocultural professionals and organized labor. The policy package that has held them together historically is a combination of generous universal social insurance and large-scale efforts devoted to innovation and human capital formation. Business in this model was de facto subsidized with relatively lower tax burdens and a highly trained labor force willing to undertake major skill investments.

By virtue of this particular solution to the democratic class struggle, these societies were typically characterized by a policy legacy of large budgetary commitments, a very inclusive set of both consumption and investment policies, and, accordingly, very low levels of either labor market segmentation or marketization.

Challenges

Yet it is the very inclusiveness of the system, arguably one of its core strengths, that came to be perceived by many political actors as a potential source of weakness. Three developments put the traditional policy strategies under pressure. First is a very high and growing fiscal burden that is effectively narrowing the room to increase consumption taxes further or reduce the progressivity in income tax returns (Mares 2006; Beramendi and Rueda 2007).

vote (Przeworski and Sprague 1986); on the other hand, the traditional divisions on the Right (with a farmers' party complicating the classic opposition between liberals and conservatives) weakened their main competitors.

Second, at the same time some businesses and high wage earners, namely, those with a strong earnings potential in the international economy, may find tax levels and wage binding agreements too straight a jacket and start to mobilize against them.

These tensions have built up over a long period, as illustrated, for instance, by the Swedish experience. After its golden age in the fifties and sixties, the Swedish model ran into increasing difficulties as a result of the changing structure of the national economy (deindustrialization/tertiarization, technological change in industrial production, feminization of the workforce), which implied an increasingly heterogeneous risk profile in the workforce. This reflected in large part a changing international context (1973 oil crisis, deregulation and integration of financial markets, multinationalization of Swedish corporations) that made Swedish business less dependent on the national economy (Pontusson and Swenson 1996) and undermined the financial instruments (national credit controls and devaluations of the national currency) that had traditionally been used to stabilize the Swedish model (Huber and Stephens 1998).

These developments threatened directly the stability of the cross-class coalition between low and high wage earners, on the one hand, and business, on the other. In an effort to protect the relative position of low-skilled workers, the LO turned to the Social Democrats to legislate a series of measures to democratize working life and to control investments by other means. The most radical element of this program was the wage earner funds, which were conceived "as a mechanism to socialize the economy and reverse the trend toward the concentration of economic power in private hands" (Steinmo 1988: 431). This move of the unions toward an accentuation of the equality model provoked a massive counteroffensive by the business community that not only led the Social Democrats to abandon the wage earner funds (1982), but eventually induced the Swedish employers' association (SAF) to withdraw from the key institutions of the Swedish model of corporatism (1990) and, supported by the neoliberal ideas of allied think tanks and academic economists, to contest the legitimacy of the Swedish model altogether (Blyth 2001). The erosion of the Swedish industrial relations system went hand in hand with the Swedish Social Democrats' loss of power in the 1991 elections. This example illustrates the extent to which fiscal sustainability exercises pressure to redraw the coalitional map in equality-oriented capitalism.

Third, the policy inclusiveness built in the model has in more recent years opened yet another political divide within the original coalition: A growing inflow of immigrants and their access to universal services and insurance policies have fed resentment throughout the labor force. For low-wage earners, immigrants are competitors in access to transfers and services. Sociocultural professionals, business professionals, and managers perceive immigrants as a lesser competitive threat and express more tolerance toward diversity, even though a proper integration of immigrants may increase their very significant fiscal burden. Immigration thus becomes a major political divide among

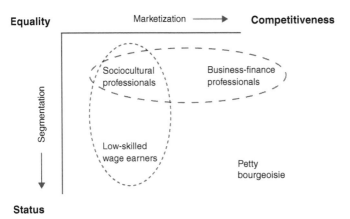

FIGURE 1.8. Coalitional politics in equality-oriented capitalism.

workers not only in identity or cultural terms but also, critically, in purely distributive ones.

Coalitional Options

In the face of these challenges, what can office-seeking parties do to succeed in building or preserving governing coalitions? Given the transformations in the structure of political demand outlined above, political parties articulate their platforms around two issues: calls for ensuring the fiscal viability of the state and, closely linked, demands for introducing some degree of segmentation in the labor market. Figure 1.8 displays the possible coalitional strategies available to parties.

The urgency to respond to the pressures posed by a growing fiscal burden and immigration triggers two possible coalitional realignments. The first one would involve an alliance of sociocultural professionals, business and managerial professionals, and large employers. This strategy would open up opportunities for private supplementary insurance (pensions, health care) or defined contributions plans for high wage earners, relieving them of redistributive burdens in the public social insurance pools. This policy would be carried by a coalition of all high-skilled professionals, moving the political status quo from equality toward competitiveness via marketization. In strategic terms, the existence of this opportunity for center-right parties may force Social Democrats to adjust their preferences and offer, for the sake of political survival, policy changes aimed to retain high wage earners as part of their core constituency.

A second, potentially concurrent shift in the coalitional strategy would concentrate primarily at the lower end of the wage distribution. The idea is to respond to the challenges of immigration by increasing segmentation in the labor market. This would imply a move toward status via segmentation. The goal is to preserve the stability of the coalition of sociocultural professionals and low wage earners by introducing a clearer distinction – or dualization – between those who are both contributors to and recipients from the system and those, such as lower-skilled immigrants, whose labor market trajectories may put them in a position to extract net benefits. These reforms, fiercely advocated by new challengers, such as radical Right populist parties, force incumbents to accede to reforms in order to preempt massive political losses among core members of their coalition.

These two sets of reforms are gradually transforming the nature of equality-oriented capitalism. But none of them should be interpreted as a full-scale transition to a different politico-economic model. Full dualization, for instance, would imply a model in which insiders enjoy high levels of protection via consumption policies and a sharp decline in investment levels via public services, both strongly opposed by sociocultural professionals, business, and parts of labor alike. Such a move is clearly outside the political realm of feasible reforms, as is a nearly impossible transition to a regime built around the ability of organized interests to capture rents. In terms of political coalitions, this implies that the *petit bourgeois* cannot be the core building block of any feasible political coalition in equality-oriented capitalism. Its unwillingness to contribute to the common pool of resources via taxes and its antagonistic approach to both consumption and investment policies alienate them from both business and organized workers.

Empirical Illustrations: Sweden and Denmark

Sweden and Denmark provide prominent examples of the type of coalitional moves our argument suggests. In 1992, Sweden, together with Finland, was hit by a dramatic financial and economic crisis – the deepest and most complicated crisis in its modern history. The fact that this crisis had hit when the center-right was in power gave the Social Democrats the chance for a fast comeback. Constrained by the employers' associations' neoliberal positions and the fiscal consequences of the crisis, Social Democrats reconstructed the industrial relations system and reformed the Swedish social and economic policy. The reemerging industrial relations system was clearly a step in the direction of marketization. Central collective agreements became thinner, establishing a set of principles and procedures for predominantly local bargaining and wider discretion at the firm level (Baccaro and Howell 2011: 29). In addition, the new Social Democratic government consolidated a sharp reduction in income tax progressivity, taking another step in the direction of marketization (Bengston et al. 2012). These reforms provided a favorable context for export-oriented growth by combining a hard currency and price stability policy with a balanced budget (Benner and Vad 2000: 426ff.), which in turn fed back into growing tensions between high- and low-skilled workers, slowly eroding the Social Democratic coalition.[15] These tensions exacerbated electoral trade-offs for center-left parties in Sweden. In their analysis of Swedish

---

[15] This reorientation was underpinned by the decision to join the EU, a move seen as a way to lock in these policy changes.

elections between 1994 and 2010, Lindvall and Rueda (2014) show that if center-left parties emphasize the interest of insiders (as in the 1998 election),[16] low-skilled, low wage outsiders tend either to abandon politics altogether or to switch to radical Right parties. By contrast, when center-left parties reform policy in a more inclusive way to retain outsiders (as in the 2006 and 2010 elections),[17] high wage earners shift their support in favor of center-right parties and their platform of promarketization reforms. Eventually, the electoral success of the Swedish Social Democrats declined, too, reaching a historic low of only 30.7 percent in the 2010 elections. From 2006 to 2014, Sweden was governed by a center-right coalition, as Denmark was from 2001 to 2011.

The strength of the challenges and their coalitional implications are even more extreme in the Danish case. In 1993, under the pressure of unemployment peaking at 10 percent, the incoming Social Democratic government, in cooperation with its social partners, introduced key labor-market policy reforms, including an emphasis on activation and a regionalization of the implementation of labor-market policy (tripartite regional boards that strengthened the role of the social partners). Subsequently, given their minority status after the 1994 elections, the Social Democrats had to make compromises with the support of various reform partners (Green-Pedersen 2001). Eventually, in 2001, they lost power and for the next ten years, a center-right coalition stayed in power, supported by the radical populist Right Danish People's Party (PF). Against the resistance of both the Left and the unions, and aided by the exogenous shock of the financial crisis of 2008, this cohesive government pushed through a series of far-reaching social reforms based on a program combining tax freezes (highly effective in limiting the growth of social expenditures), welfare chauvinism (segmentation through dualization, introducing targeted cuts for social assistance, immigrants, and young unemployed), and antiunionism (exclusion of social partners from the implementation of labor-market policy and breakup of the Ghent system of administrating unemployment insurance) (Rathgeb 2013). Even if the amount of money spent on activation is still comparatively large in Denmark, these reforms turned the preexisting "flexicurity" model into something very different – a "work-first" regime in which sanctions are at least as important as incentives (Jørgensen and Schulze 2012) and that excluded the unions from both legislation and implementation.

This program catered to the preoccupations of a coalition composed of the business-financial professionals (clearly in favor of marketization) and a significant share of low-skilled wage earners (clearly in favor of segmentation and dualization of them and the growing population of immigrant workers). The center-right coalition succeeded in interpreting the coalitional

---

[16] In this election, the incumbent Social Democrats put a low cap on the fees to be paid to access child-care services, a measure that clearly benefited high-wage earners.

[17] Social Democrats, Greens, and the Left party objected to tax cuts and reductions in benefits for the long-term unemployed, a core subgroup among outsiders.

implications of the changes in Danish society. As a consequence of immigration and individualization, Denmark is no longer the homogeneous society it used to be. Therefore, pressures for marketization at the upper end of the wage distribution and pressures for segmentation at the lower end of the wage distribution jointly undermined the traditional ideal of social partnership (Katzenstein 1985; Campbell and Hall 2009). This is particularly the case among the constituents of the "traditional Left." In a powerful analysis, Sniderman et al. (2012) show that these voters long for the time when Denmark was a culturally homogeneous and religious country and feel marginalized in the contemporary world, which has lost "a feeling of community." It is this group, which combines particularistic preferences with preferences for strong state intervention, that is very sensitive to the sirens of the radical populist Right.

These two cases illustrate the scope of changes in equality-oriented capitalism in the last two decades. As Thelen (2012, 2014) suggests, these societies have followed their own path of liberalization – the path of "embedded flexibilization," which involves a combination of lower levels of coordination, market-promoting labor market policies, and still-egalitarian social programs designed to ease the adaptation of especially weaker segments of society to changes in the market. Marketization and segmentation have taken place but have not completely unraveled the core features of the preexisting equilibrium (Schneider and Paunescu 2012). The emerging hybrid policy regimes reconciling equality (solidarity) and market efficiency continue to show considerable success (Emmenegger et al. 2012; Martin and Swank 2012; Häusermann and Palier 2008; Pontusson 2011), but it is too early to tell how much egalitarianism will change as the inherent tensions within the model continue to exacerbate.

1.3.2. Status-Oriented Capitalism: Challenges and Evolution

Status Quo Equilibrium

The dominant equilibrium in these societies features encompassing, but status-preserving social insurance security nets with relatively limited redistributive capacity. Status-oriented polities are typically "premised on segregated risk pools" (Palier and Thelen 2010: 122). Coverage has become inclusive over time but has remained fragmented, stratified, and often indirect, especially for spouses and dependent family members. The core electoral constituency both social-democratic and moderate right-wing (often Christian-democratic) parties have been competing for in these party systems is labor, more specifically the core workforce of the main manufacturing industries. The pivotal electoral position of this class is one of the key reasons why status-oriented polities have been built around the consumption needs and demands of the industrial male breadwinner workers and their employers. Labor in these countries tends to be organized in different political parties and in both sectorally and ideologically fragmented unions. Therefore, the cross-class policy compromises that have emerged from this structure of interest representation are segmented, as well.

The preeminence of the actuarial insurance principle draws together labor as the key sociostructural constituency favored by such strong, stratified, and consumption-oriented welfare states, with the petty bourgeoisie and business. By virtue of their design, these political economies generate a lower share of sociocultural professionals in the labor force than equality-oriented political economies. In contrast to equality-oriented capitalism, the key characteristic of the allocation of rights and benefits in these countries is a tight link between employment and entitlements, which is reflected in the strong reliance on financing state activities through contribution payments, that is, payroll taxes. For instance, until the 1990s, social insurance contributions increased to more than 40 percent of total taxation in France and Germany (Manow 2010: 292). Unsurprisingly, these regimes have a much weaker redistributive impact. Insofar as these welfare states have supplied redistribution, it proceeds from families in the upper middle to the lower middle of the income distribution, rather than through highly progressive benefits targeted to the very poorest.

Challenges

Much as in the case of equality-oriented capitalism, the structural transformations reshaping advanced capitalism since the early 1980s adopted the form of some specific challenges in these political economies. As the labor market surplus of deindustrialization required responses, governments decided to fight unemployment by shedding labor (through early retirement, the discouragement of female employment, or easier access to disability pensions), thus entering a seemingly vicious circle of declining state revenues, soaring consumption social expenditures, and increasing contribution rates, which just discouraged employment performance further. By the late 1990s, status-oriented countries such as Germany and France were considered "frozen landscapes" (Esping-Andersen 1996: 24), suffering from the symptom of very high levels of consumption expenditures with an eroding tax basis. The growing gap between rapidly increasing budgetary demands and a shrinking revenue base was particularly intense in status-oriented capitalism. These tensions are only exacerbated by increasing levels of immigration. Immigration matters for two reasons: It increases the budgetary burden, and it increases the within-class heterogeneity, thus weakening the support for the defense of the status quo among wage earners, particularly at the lower end of the wage distribution (Shayo 2009). These trends in turn shape directly the evolution of coalitional politics in these political economies.

Coalitional Options

In terms of preferences, the risk of excessive generosity to consumption demands, particularly pension systems requiring high payroll taxes, jeopardizes the viability of export-oriented industries, and therefore higher income classes may support reforms oriented to more public sector efficiency. On the other hand, organized labor strives for the maintenance of the status quo in terms of protection and consumption, particularly in the case of low-wage earners in declining manufacturing sectors, while perceiving economic globalization and immigration as sources of the increasing threat to their labor market conditions.

Given this map of preferences and institutional legacies, what are the options in terms of coalition formation? Governments may form an alliance between organized labor and especially small and medium-sized business to increase further the levels of labor market segmentation, meaning that the core maintains the status quo, whereas the outer buffer becomes exposed to tougher conditions, in terms of both salaries and social insurance packages. This allows business to secure fiscal solvency and a lesser tax burden, whereas organized insiders achieve what could be called welfare protectionism (Häusermann 2012: 117). The obvious losers of this strategy, labor market outsiders in weakly organized sectors, tend to be marginalized politically. This move would effectively imply an increase in the degree of budgetary capture by a more selected group of insiders, limiting consumption benefits to themselves, and the *petit bourgeoisie*, limiting their tax contributions to the common pool. Thus, Figure 1.9 depicts this movement toward capture through higher levels of segmentation (implying effects of marketization for the outsiders). The end point of this move is a large yet highly segmented welfare state, composed of a protected core of wage earners and a growing belt of lesser-paid and more weakly protected workers. These marginal workers usually have only restricted levels of access to regular social insurance and are instead relegated to (more or less generous) means-tested social security programs.

Alternatively, incumbents (or challengers) may opt for a strategy more oriented toward sociocultural professionals, seeking an alliance between the latter and organized labor. This would be a move from Status towards Equality, as captured in Figure 1.9, via higher levels of inclusion through the extension of consumption or investment policies. Such a move is more likely in status-oriented political economies with more moderately organized labor and more flexible labor markets to begin with. The end point along this path is a flexicurity-oriented model of flexible labor markets, high rates of labor market participation, and inclusive social protection for atypical workers.

What seems politically unfeasible, however, when starting from a status quo of segmented, consumption-oriented social policy is a drastic move toward a deregulated, market driven, competitive model of allocation of economic resources. The preferred option for top managers and some businesses, this option meets the resistance of both organized labor and sociocultural professionals, and even of petit bourgeois. Given the relative size of these different groups, we regard such a transition as politically and electorally unfeasible in the short run.

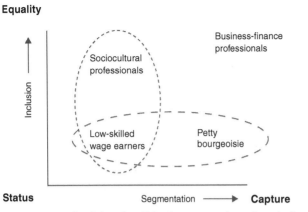

FIGURE 1.9. Coalitional politics in status-oriented capitalism.

Empirical Illustrations: France, Germany, and the Netherlands

In response to the challenges outlined earlier, French, German, and Dutch governments have, from the 1990s onward, defied the picture of inertia and implemented a series of "ambitious" (Vail 2010: 83) and even "path-breaking" (Hemerijck 2013: 183) reforms aimed at fiscal balancing and employment creation. The politics of this attempted turn toward both activation as well as lowering the preponderance of consumption expenditures is highly revealing with regard to our analytical model, because it shows the range of feasible coalitional options governments have had in these countries. A brief discussion of the main reform strategies of different governments in France and Germany in the next paragraphs reveals that the manufacturing working class has remained a pivotal constituency in these status-oriented polities: The turn toward more investment-oriented strategies of activation and job creation generally did not occur at the expense of the formerly privileged core workers. Rather, governments to a large extent preserved the rights of the core workforce but pursued segmentation by liberalizing, activating, and retrenching at the margin, that is, among service sector employees, atypically employed workers, the young, and others. This strategy of segmentation and dualization (Emmenegger et al. 2012) exacerbates the fragmented and stratified nature of these systems with the support of a coalition of the core workforce and industrial employers (Palier and Thelen 2010). In sharp contrast with these two experiences, the Dutch case, arguably a traditionally status-oriented polity, has successfully engaged in a more investment-oriented path of more egalitarian activation and universal welfare (inclusion through flexicurity).

French governments started in the late 1980s to move from labor shedding to encouraging employment growth by liberalizing and increasing nonstandard work, and in particular by expanding state-subsidized employment (Palier and Thelen 2010: 130). As far as this strategy of publicly subsidized job creation was supposed to generate stable and profitable employment in the longer run, it can be seen as an increase in investment-oriented expenditures. The accent of all French governments' reforms since the late 1980s, however, was not on investment or (de)regulation, but on consumption welfare policies, that is, on reforming the distribution of social insurance benefits and their financing, to preserve the model of the French social insurance welfare state for the core workforce, while relegating the nonstandard employed to a separate area of tax-financed, means-tested welfare (Palier 2010). Such a dualizing strategy relied on the support of organized labor and (strongly subsidized) business but further exacerbated the segmented, particularistic, and inegalitarian aspects of the French welfare state. Left-wing governments, typically reliant on a coalition of labor and sociocultural professionals, have thus put stronger accents on the creation and reinforcement of rather generous universal minimum income schemes, which to date have managed to prevent the rise in income inequality that we observe in the other continental European countries.

Hence, while both left- and right-wing governments segmented the French labor market, broadening the gap between insiders and outsiders, Left governments expanded consumption benefits to prevent outsider poverty, starting most markedly with the introduction of the *revenu minimum d'insertion* (RMI) in 1988 by the socialist Rocard government. The conservative governments in the 1990s then continued to encourage employers to expand part-time and fixed-term work by exempting these contracts from social contribution payments. On the expenditure side, the Juppé government famously failed to curtail pension and health benefits in the mid-1990s: These reform proposals were purely retrenchment-oriented, mobilizing a massive and unified labor protest against them in the streets (Häusermann 2010). The failure of the Juppé reforms showed that despite weak union density, the core workforce's full opposition could not be circumvented.

The socialist Jospin government that took power in 1997 attempted a more fundamental redesign of the French labor market and welfare financing from consumption to investment (Levy 1999: 246–252), without, however, even touching the hot potatoes of pensions and health care. Regarding the labor market, the government introduced massive subsidization of employment for young labor market entrants, created a negative income tax for low-paid employment, attempted to distribute employment by reducing the regular work time and – most importantly – broadly increased the fiscalization of social security charges. The Jospin government increased the *contribution social généralisée*, a tax levied on all forms of income, from 3.4 to 7.5 percent, thus widening the tax base and alleviating wages. This tax reform managed to reduce the cost of labor, but it also served the goal of generating tax-financed revenues to finance the "noncontributory" benefits for social insurance outsiders. It thus deepened the "social protection dualism" (Palier 2010) of the reformed French welfare state, at the same time alleviating some of the exclusionary social policy consequences of labor market segmentation.

The right-wing governments that assumed power after 2003 followed the path of expanding low-wage employment (e.g., the *contrat première embauche* by the Villepin government in 2005), while reinforcing the accent on negative activation and workfare by transforming the RMI into a conditional benefit with higher benefits for in-work individuals. In addition, they retrenched pension levels significantly, watering down the cuts, however, for core workers with long employment careers (Häusermann 2010).

In sum, this brief overview shows that none of the French governments significantly lowered consumption benefits and rights of the core workforce. Rather, they differed in the extent to which they expanded specific benefits and services for the marginal workforce. For business, the model of dualizing both the labor market and the welfare state (Palier and Thelen 2010) was acceptable, because it provided employers with flexibility in terms of regulation and wages (Vail 2010: 91).

A similar story of segmentation by design, that is, preserving employment protection for the core workforce while liberalizing and expanding a low-wage sector of nonstandard work, applies to the German trajectory (Palier and Thelen 2010). Both the Conservative Kohl government in the 1990s and subsequently the Social Democratic and Green Schröder government around 2000 lowered the restrictions on the use of agency workers and fixed-term employment and encouraged the spread of "marginal employment" exempt from social contributions (Vail 2010). In consequence, as in France, the distinction between social insurance and assistance was sharpened in Germany. Another similarity appears in the fact that the Conservative Chancellor Kohl attempted radical retrenchment against labor in the mid-1990s with his 1996 pension reform and failed. The pension reform backfired at the polls and put the Left in power after sixteen years of Christian-Democratic rule. As with the failure of the Juppé reforms in France, this failure of retrenchment against organized labor demonstrates the pivotal role of organized labor in status-oriented polities.

The years of the red-green government, however, deviated from the more timid French reform trajectories by the ambition and scope of the reforms. The German red-green government that lasted between 1998 and 2005 is the only government that seriously attempted to reallocate resources from consumption and insider privileges toward investment, activation, and flexicurity. In coalition terms, it is fair to say that the Schröder government tried to shift reform efforts from the consumption- to the investment-oriented axis, attempting almost a diagonal move toward competitiveness, with the support of a coalition of business and sociocultural professionals. Indeed both groups worried about the financial unsustainability of the consumption-heavy profile of the German welfare state and were open to measures of financial consolidation. The Schröder agenda involved a mixture of competitiveness-oriented elements of tax cuts, retrenchment, and liberalization, with equality-oriented investment and some improvement through universal minimum protection. Most instructively, this attempt ultimately failed. Such a move would have required a strong alliance of sociocultural professionals, parts of business, and parts of labor. Against such an alliance worked the fact that precommitted consumption expenditures continued to impose strong constraints on the expansion of investment.

In terms of retrenchment, the 2001 pension reform was probably the most significant project. The reform lowered regular pension replacement rates substantially, while introducing a new voluntary pillar of private, capitalized pension saving. At the same time, minimum pensions for people with discontinuous employment careers were improved and major financial incentives were introduced for low-income workers to take up supplementary insurance. This mixture of retrenchment, privatization for the higher-income classes, and subsidization for the outsiders proved successful politically, but it was possible only against labor, that is, in direct confrontation with the trade unions (Häusermann 2010). This split between German Social Democrats and trade unions intensified around the Hartz labor market reforms. While the unions had supported the early reforms of the government in favor of youth employment (JUMP reform 1998) and activation and retraining (Job AQTIV law 2002), the Hartz reforms of 2002–2005 drove a deep split between the government and organized labor. The most consequential reform was the Hartz IV legislation, which merged long-term unemployment benefits (after twelve months) and social assistance into a new, tax-financed unemployment benefit II (which could also be paid as an in-work benefit), combined with stronger activation requirements. The distributive consequences of the reform are somewhat controversial (Palier and Thelen 2010: 138), but it clearly and most drastically cut the benefits for well-insured labor market insiders, while it actually provided a boost for an estimated one-third of those who were previously in the lowest tier of the old social assistance system, such as single mothers. However, as the unemployment benefit II was set very low and regular employment protection remained intact, the reform still negatively affected large parts of low-wage earners. Finally, regarding activation and investment, the Schröder government reinforced training and retraining programs, supported a large-scale reorientation of the higher education system toward more competitiveness, and initiated a profound reorientation of family policy toward child care and the encouragement of parental employment (Häusermann 2006; Bleses and Seeleib-Kaiser 2004).

Ultimately, the reforms of the Schröder government tried to circumvent the core working class as the key electoral constituency, a strategy that backfired. The government lost its majority in 2005, and a new radical left-wing party (die Linke) entered the party system with a program emphasizing traditional consumption demands of the working class. During the following years of the grand coalition of CDU-CSU and SPD between 2005 and 2009, the government basically pursued the competiveness- and investment-oriented agenda of the social-democratic government (e.g., by increasing the age of retirement to sixty-seven, lowering options for early retirement, and expanding child care options for middle-class women), while the radical Left continuously grew in strength. In reaction, both SPD and CDU/CSU reoriented their electoral and programmatic focus to some extent back to the interests of labor. Unemployment benefit regulations were, for example, upgraded for elderly unemployed adults and family policy was reoriented toward more conservative male breadwinner concerns under the CDU/FDP coalition. Overall, the reform trajectory initiated by the SPD/Green government was an experiment appealing to an alliance of professionals of all stripes (sociocultural and business-finance), but given the strong pivotal electoral and organizational position of labor in this country, the strategy was not viable politically. Agenda 2010 was an attempt to override labor, but by the mid-2000s, both Social Democrats and Christian Democrats had realized the limits of such a coalitional strategy in a polity marked by a status-oriented institutional and electoral legacy.

The one country that arguably has managed a turnaround from a status-oriented model to an investment- and activation-oriented polity, which is a significant shift along the vertical axis in Figure 1.9, is the Netherlands (see also Figure 1.2). It must be noted, however, that the Dutch welfare state had also traditionally deviated from the social insurance model by providing basic public pension and tax-financed minimum assistance. Also, the Dutch unions already decided in the 1980s to support the activation strategy by the then-conservative CDA/VVD government (Levy 1999: 259), which may have been the pivotal point for the feasibility of a long-term strategy of equalization and inclusion in terms of combining a flexibilized labor market with social security. When Labor entered a coalition with the conservatives in 1989, they asked for a stronger accent on equalization in the competitiveness-oriented activation strategy of the Lubbers government (Hemerijck 2013: 182). The deal was to make consumption expenditures conditional on activation: Full indexation of minimum wage and social benefits was conditional on a certain threshold of the ratio between the active and inactive population. From 1994 onward, successive social-democratic-led governments massively expanded (female) employment in the service sector, introduced targeted tax breaks for low-income workers, made consumption exit options such as disability pensions more costly for employers, and improved employment conditions for atypical workers (Visser and Hemerijck 1997). A "flexicurity agreement" with the social partners in 2000 granted part-time workers explicit right to equal treatment in all areas of social security and equal wages. Hence, Dutch employers hire part-time workers as a means of gaining organizational flexibility, not as a means of evading taxes and benefits paid to regular workers (Levy 1999: 262). Combined with efforts in the field of child care to support female employment, this long-term activation strategy resulted in the inclusion of nonstandard work.[18] This reform was possible only because Dutch organized labor supported a transformative shift toward encompassing and

---

[18] Hemerijck refers to this process as "labor market desegmentation" (2013: 183).

investment-oriented interest representation already in the 1980s. Over time, the support base of the new policy strategy increased with the transformation of the occupational structure itself.

These three cases illustrate the evolution of status-oriented capitalism over the last two decades. Attempts to transition toward competitiveness via a combination of marketization and investment have backfired because of the continuing pivotal position of organized labor. The dominant response by governments has been an increase in the levels of segmentation at the expense of outsiders. Only in the case of the Netherlands is there systematic evidence of a transition to an investment-oriented strategy around flexicurity. That this is the case where the institutional legacies of status-oriented polities were least present illustrates the long shadow of organized labor in coalitional politics within this subset of political economies.

1.3.3. Competitiveness-Oriented Capitalism: Challenges and Evolution

Status Quo Equilibrium

The status quo in competitiveness-oriented capitalism is a selective welfare state, with highly redistributive programs targeted to the very poorest, thereby implying a very high level of marketization from the start. Traditional partisan alignments pitting mildly redistributive reformist parties against often militantly conservative free-market parties have geared public policy toward only restrained market intervention without a strong commitment to either large-scale consumption or investment policies, thus limiting the level of state intervention overall. Political coalitions collect and use revenues at less than full capacity and therefore provide less extensive safety nets and public services.

Given the weaker level of public services generally, the growth of professional occupations in the interpersonal social service sector, particularly those serving the poorer tiers of the population, is more limited in this configuration. Rather, the centerpiece of governments' support coalition has typically been big business and professionals, particularly in financial industries. The fragmented and uncoordinated nature of the labor movement, along with the dominant position of financial capitalists and business organizations, renders the transition to any form of full-grown state led investment or consumption regime a political chimera.

Traditionally the conservative partisan coalition has been supplemented with support from small business and intermediate-level wage earners, whereas reformist parties have drawn on organized labor and a wide range of intermediate occupational groups, as long as they walked a fine line not to antagonize business. More recently, with the erosion of small business and of low-skill wage earners in the voting population, both sides have vied for the support of the growing segment of sociocultural professionals. As we discuss in the following in detail, failure to win majorities in this group spells defeat for the moderate Left.

Challenges

The major challenge of efficiency-oriented capitalism lies in the increasing polarization of income and wealth resulting from the shocks of technology. By rewarding those with very high and adaptable education, and globalization, and further penalizing citizens with low occupational skills and general education, efficiency-oriented capitalism nurtures an extremely skewed distribution of fortunes. At the other end of the 1 percent, there emerges a tier of very low-income, low-education immigrants, most starkly articulated – and already politically consequential – in the United States (cf. McCarty et al. 2006; Picketty 2014: 291–303). Even with relatively strong aggregate investment policies, the distribution of beneficiaries, for example, in the education system, is so skewed to the well-off that major groups of the population are left behind, whether these are low-skilled citizens in the dominant ethnic group or the much larger proportion of low-skilled individuals among minorities and immigrants. Here more than in other capitalisms, the middle-income tier is hollowed out by the increasing restriction of economic opportunities at the upper tier of the income distribution.

Among the key challenges of efficiency-oriented capitalism is the incorporation of a growing proportion of practically illiterate young labor market entrants, unfit to compete for jobs in a postindustrial economy that could deliver a working wage. At the same time, there are also growing poverty and destitution among the elderly, now increasingly also affecting the retirement prospects of the ethnically indigenous majority. This is setting up a deep divide between those who want to invest more and broaden the scope of education and training (enabling young labor market entrants of diverse backgrounds to enjoy a more promising occupational career) and those who prioritize improving the lot of older low-skilled wage earners and the self-employed (either by more defensive social insurance schemes or by lower income and payroll taxes).

Coalitional Options

This polarization of fortunes has direct implications for the prospects of political coalition formation, as captured in Figure 1.10. Conflicts tend to center around extensions of the *level* of public investments on the horizontal dimension (a leftward horizontal move toward equality via inclusion) and tolerance toward the ability of organized interests and lobbyists to shape policy (a downward vertical move toward capture via an increasingly unequal access of lobbies, resulting in enhanced segmentation).

Parties and/or governments oriented toward the support of a coalition of professionals both in sociocultural services and in the large-scale corporate business and finance sectors in these polities would aim for a business- and employment-friendly coalition in favor of equality of opportunity-enhancing investments. This will be the dominant strategy by left-wing forces in this type of political economy. By contrast, a coalition of predominantly large-scale corporate business and finance, together with small business in consumer and

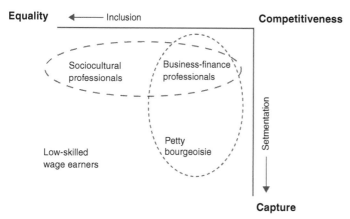

FIGURE 1.10. Coalitional politics in competitiveness-oriented capitalism.

service economies, would support lower levels of state intervention and regulation and strive to maintain their policy influence through lobbying, seeking special interest group rents. This will be the dominant strategy among conservative parties and coalitions.

Sharp inequality compels conservative parties that favor only minimal social insurance or redistribution to attract support from portions of downwardly mobile low-skilled wage earners of the dominant ethnic group (cf. McCarty et al. 2006; Kitschelt and Rehm 2013), for example, by appeals to oppose immigration and by emphasis on national identity (Shayo 2009). This creates the possibility of an electoral coalition of low-skilled wage earners and petty bourgeois, both belonging to the dominant indigenous ethnic group and confronting an alliance of professionals and ethnic minorities and immigrants at the other pole of the political spectrum. The former coalition converges on support for narrowly circumscribed and segmented social benefits and minimal overall scope of state intervention, undercutting public social investments, particularly in education. The latter emphasizes public investment policy, but, given the realities of policy constraints and makeup of the coalition, has little momentum to mobilize a grand push for more equalization.

Empirical Illustrations: The United Kingdom and the United States

In Britain, the transition towards efficiency-oriented capitalism took place under the Conservative governments of Thatcher and Major (1979–1997). The cabinets pushed systematically promarket, antiredistributive policies with little additional investment in education or health care. In their political-economic strategies, as well as with their positions on questions of sociocultural particularism, Thatcher and Major captured the petty bourgeois strata, intermediate groups, at least initially business, as well as even unorganized elements of labor, but clearly antagonized organized lower-skill wage earners, particularly with a brutal retrenchment of the unemployment insurance and especially of the earnings-related component of the pension system, as a consequence of which Britain faces the prospect of massive old-age poverty in future decades (see Pierson 1996; Galasso 2008: 160–163; Seeleib-Kaiser et al. 2012: 162). In terms of investment policies, the Conservative governments added little to the existing mix. True, enrollment in higher education was broadened, particularly to the upper middle class, but at the price of steeply declining quality, as no new public spending was forthcoming (Ansell 2010: 198–200). Thatcher's Conservatives disliked the British National Health Service but were politically unable to touch it, with the exception of creating more options for choice by higher income users. Overall, in terms of our two-dimensional scheme, the Thatcher-Major governments stayed close to, or sharply accentuated, political legacy features, that is, limited redistribution paired with restraint on investments, implementing an ideologically conservative program (Huber and Stephens 2001).

Against this background, Tony Blair's subsequent Labour government provides a good example of a successful coalition between business and sociocultural professionals toward higher levels of equality via public investments. Blair's government reversed the redistribution toward the wealthy that had taken place under the Conservatives and significantly increased investments in education and health care. Most importantly, Blair once again reformed the pension system in order to boost minimum pensions, achieved through a sharper redistributive design of the program benefits that provides relatively more for those with the lowest benefit levels. Nevertheless, public pension benefits for the less well-off remain very low and further deteriorated as the new century wears on (Galasso 2008: 171).

Blair's government doubled spending on the National Health Service but sustained efforts to create more quasi-market competition among providers and personal choice among users in the spirit of market liberalization (Gingrich 2011b). British education spending, finally, increased by a quarter between 2000 and 2009, that of tertiary education alone by 30 percent (OECD 2012: 244), although the Labour government did not reverse the Conservatives' tuition policy.[19] Overall, the Labour administration moved to a new course toward slightly more redistribution and a great deal more social investment. This thrust was particularly designed to attract sociocultural professionals who had been antagonized by the party in previous decades to Labour's electoral coalition, while still providing a business-friendly environment (especially among the City's financial centers).

Relative to the United Kingdom, the United States better illustrates a move from efficiency to capture by the increasing role of specialized interest lobbies

---

[19] They actually extended it to make the affluent pay more for their children's higher education (Galasso 2008: 166).

over the last three decades. While partisan differences remain prominent, significantly more so than in Britain, the large number of institutional veto points have traditionally given business a lopsided advantage in Washington. Since the 1980s, the U.S. Republicans built a powerful backward-looking, if not nostalgic coalition of white (and male) America, configured around small business, parts of big business, and broad strands of the white working class antagonized by the Democrats' efforts to reach out to sociocultural professionals, women, and especially ethnocultural minorities.[20] In the spirit of this coalition, Republican congressional majorities and presidents worked to enact cutbacks in means-tested welfare support and health care benefits for the poor (Medicaid). A major watershed was the 1996 welfare reform in which a Democratic president relented and made substantial concessions in the face of a Republican onslaught.

Subsequent efforts by Republicans to engineer an erosion of social security programs by converting parts of them into defined contributions private savings accounts, however, failed, in part because they divided their own coalition. The U.S. social security system hence remained mildly redistributive toward the worse off (cf. Galasso 2008: 187–189). The 2002 Bush Medicare drug benefit expanded social policy along the consumption dimension by bestowing a new benefit on pensioners, a core group of the Republican support coalition, albeit with the greatest windfall being reaped by the pharmaceutical industry. The Republican coalition opposed higher public investments other than to research and development funneled through military defense. Nevertheless, a bipartisan majority passed the No Child Left Behind education act of 2002, which added a great deal of standardized testing, as well as substantial public educational funding (cf. OECD 2012: 232). This majority pushing the educational investment agenda was supported by corporate business, on the moderate Republican side, and by sociocultural professionals, as well as the African-American minority, aligning with moderate Democrats. It was primarily opposed by a radical populist wing of the Republican Party, whose members even wish to abolish the U.S. Department of Education and whose mass following is particularly strong among white low-skilled men and the self-employed. A similar coalition under the Bush administration (2001–2009) also passed tax legislation with Democratic Senate supporters and budgets that were designed to shift the income distribution in favor of the wealthy and to move policy tasks out of the public realm into the market.

Against this legacy, President Obama was elected by a coalition of sociocultural professionals, minorities of all sorts of occupational backgrounds, and considerable white working-class support, all shocked by the financial crisis of 2008 and the large loss of manufacturing jobs it caused. He has developed since several policy initiatives to expand inclusive investments in an egalitarian

---

[20] These efforts date back at least to McGovern's 1972 presidential bid.

direction. The Affordable Health Care Act of 2010, as a strategy of inclusion, has prospectively shifted the benefits in a redistributive direction, benefiting uninsured younger citizens most. At the same time, the Democratic president did not tire of advocating more educational effort but could not gain support in the face of a hostile legislature and the financial crisis.[21] Overall, with divided government and powerful business interests, activist, interventionist Democratic governments made more headway building policy coalitions around investment-oriented policies than redistributive consumption policies. Even the Affordable Health Care Act fits this bill, as it focuses on children and working-age adults without health insurance who can be productive economic contributors, not retirees. Investment-oriented reforms not only are supported by large sectors of the Democratic coalition (sociocultural professionals, minorities, women), but also are negotiable with large sectors of large corporations that rely on qualified labor, that is, the core constituency of the competitiveness-oriented model. Redistributive-consumption policies, by contrast, fail to rally a winning coalition, when it comes to expanding existing benefits, with the glaring exception of the 2002 Medicare drug benefit act. Conversely, it has been all but impossible to turn back the clock on universal benefits once enacted, such as basic Social Security and Medicare programs for the elderly (cf. Pierson 1996).

In sum, partisan politics has moved policy making in different directions in both the United Kingdom and the United States. In terms of our analytical scheme, conservatives in both countries opted for an accentuation of the competitiveness model through a withdrawal from market intervention and disinvestment as well as retrenchment of consumption expenditure. By contrast, center-left governments, while trying to restore a modicum of redistribution, particularly in health care and sometimes pension systems, focused their strategy on expanding social investments, particularly in education and training. Around the latter, Left governments managed to rally a broad coalition of parts of low-skilled wage labor (albeit divided by ethnic loyalties) and parts of big business, most of the sociocultural professionals, and, in the United States, ethnic minorities regardless of occupational and market experiences. Policy, by and large, has remained sensitive to partisan alternatives.

These alternatives are crystallized primarily in the area of investment. While they may pass narrow, focused targeted redistribution to the very poor in brief moments of political-economic crisis, our analysis suggests that the feasible coalitional options preclude instituting broad-ranged, encompassing policies with strong insurance and redistributive objectives. Hence, the remains of organized labor, low wage earners, linger outside the space of feasible winning coalitions.

---

[21] Federal educational effort made much more progress under Obama's Democratic predecessor Clinton and even some under Bush.

1.3.4. Capture-Oriented Capitalism: Challenges and Evolution

Status Quo Equilibrium

The status quo equilibrium in capture-oriented capitalism carries a heavy legacy from late industrialization and late democratization. Late industrialization implies typically a reliance on import substitution strategy. As cogently argued by Rueda, Wibbels, and Altamirano (this volume), state led import substitution industrialization processes generated a core of well-organized manufacturing workers who enjoyed the state's insurance and protection even prior to democratization. With the arrival of the new regimes, these organized sectors of the labor force were in a privileged position to protect their interests and became a central constituency for political parties, particularly those on the left of the political spectrum. On the other hand, small business owners, the chief beneficiaries of the spread of economic informality, became a natural focus of attention for conservative parties. The legacy of autocratic forms of social paternalism implies an insurance system tailored to the interests of insiders: Large, expensive, and quasi-regressive pension and unemployment insurance systems eat up most of the welfare budget. As a result, welfare states are deeply segmented and stratified, and effectively regressive in their distributive incidence. There is little to no redistributive solidarity toward the poor. And while public spending on consumption may be sizable, it is directed to relatively narrow sets of interests.

In terms of coalitional potential, sociocultural occupations have remained a marginal part of the workforce. Instead, the pivotal position belongs to two groups: small businesses and organized insiders (Rueda 2007). The former resist any sort of systematic expansion of state involvement in the economy that would require the increase of governments' capacity to tax. The latter push for consumption policies tailored to their interest, whereas the upper end of the wage distribution rather supports the expansion of public services (investment). With few exceptions, such as health care in Spain or Italy, public services are generally low in quality and transfers benefit mostly a core of well-organized insiders. In such contexts, the lack of effective fiscal capacity finds its correlate in practices of organized patronage and even vote buying at national and local levels (Ferrera 1993, 1996).[22] With services provided with small scope and quality, the family becomes a functional alternative for the purposes of income maintenance and provision of services and care.

Challenges

Capture-oriented polities confront the challenges of deindustrialization and international economic integration from the worst possible footing. Their

---

[22] As recently assessed by Hemerijck (2013: 197), "the combination of extended households, high rates of self-employment, large informal economies, tax evasion, and an institutionally weak administrative apparatus has created infertile grounds for the modernization of social safety nets based on criteria of quasi-universal coverage."

relatively weaker revenue collection capacity magnifies the political trade-offs associated with the push for austerity. Given the highly segmented nature of both labor markets and welfare states, the tensions between the insider core and the outsiders' ring are bound to exacerbate and expand to a conflict between different political generations (the excluded young vs. the protected elderly).

These tensions breed a second, more political challenge, directly linked to the push for austerity. Low administrative capacities and the regressive nature of the welfare state (Beramendi and Rehm 2014) translate into fewer differences across political ideologies, further shrinking the realm of programmatic politics. The lack of effective fiscal capacity reduces the scope for political contentions between parties over the scope of the state intervention in the economy. In times of austerity, incumbents of both Left and Right are forced to pursue reductions in both consumption and investment policies,[23] with direct consequences for the evolution of potential coalitions.

Coalitional Politics

Figure 1.11 outlines the coalitional space in capture-oriented capitalism. Historically, left-oriented parties sought a coalition between organized labor and the emerging sociocultural professionals around the expansion of services (health, education) and at the expense of the consumption options of those at the lower end of the wage distribution. Such was, for instance, the coalitional strategy of Gonzalez's Socialist government in Spain (Boix 1998; Maravall 1996b). Right-wing parties, by contrast, sought a very different alliance: one including the petit bourgeois, business owners, and liberal professionals. This coalition would rest on the reduction of consumption benefits for workers, the regulatory protection of organized interests (in particular, small business), and the purposeful limitation of the state's tax capacity.

Over time, the legacy of limited state capacity in an era of austerity undermined the feasibility of both these strategies. The sustainability of a coalition of sociocultural professionals and organized labor over the expansion of public services requires resources that are simply not available to incumbents. As a result, the Left must choose between alienating the sociocultural professionals by limiting investments or alienating labor by limiting (regressive) consumption. Against a backdrop of weak state capacity, governments will hardly be able to implement policies that deliver more inclusive redistribution or forward-looking investment-oriented policies. Hence, the core supporters of large-scale investment fall out of any of the feasible policy coalitions. While a short-term move in the direction of inclusion is theoretically possible, it requires significant tax increases and a reallocation of benefits at the expense of

---

[23] In most instances this limitation of the policy space reflects the constraints imposed by the Eurozone. The common currency constrains monetary policy directly, through the ECB, and fiscal policy indirectly, by imposing macroeconomic thresholds in terms of public deficits that need to be observed at all costs.

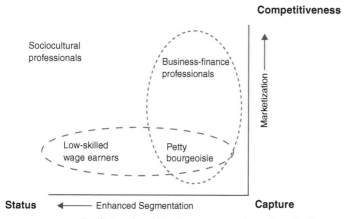

FIGURE 1.11. Coalitional politics in capture-oriented capitalism.

more privileged constituencies. Accordingly, the lack of support by core groups renders these reforms unfeasible. With increasing economic strain, these countries operate under the imperative to reduce fiscal debt and deficits at the peril of declaring bankruptcy. A direct move toward equality via inclusion is out of the short-term feasibility set.

This leaves incumbents and challenging parties with a very limited set of alternatives in the era of austerity. At first, conservative parties can ride the wave of austerity and orchestrate a promarketization coalition of the petit bourgeois and large businesses. This alliance rests on the reduction of taxes and, importantly, the reduction of labor market protection and consumption transfers to insiders. The political feasibility of such an approach has its limits, though: Proausterity wage policies (internal devaluations) and welfare cuts progressively alienate a large share of wage earners, putting proausterity incumbents at risk of electoral overhaul.

These dynamics should open up an opportunity for established Left parties. Yet the latter are in an odd position to profit from it, for three reasons. First, the push for austerity caught many of them in office and with no room to resist (due to the weak fiscal capacity in their state). Second, any attempt to regain organized labor via enhancing consumption policies favoring insiders would alienate outsiders, high-wage earners, and sociocultural professionals. And they lack sufficient government resources to craft a stable coalition across these subgroups. Finally, building those resources through tax increases in the short run is not an option because the medium-term gains will not overcome the short-term costs across employers and high-wage earners to make the proposition electorally feasible. Therefore, the shift from capture to status via increased levels of consumption toward insiders is within the feasibility set, but remains unlikely to provide a successful, stable coalitional strategy in these societies. As a consequence, partisan conflict over distributive issues becomes blurred.

Empirical Illustrations: Italy and Spain

The fate of major attempts at policy reform in Italy and Spain from the early 1990s until today illustrates the political dynamics of capture-oriented economies. Particularly illustrative are the failures of conscious political attempts to develop a move toward equality via expansions of investment policies in both countries.

Pushed by the EMU and the Maastricht requirements, successive Italian governments faced the challenge of correcting the skyrocketing fiscal burden, mostly driven by pensions directly paid by the Treasury (Jessoula and Alti 2010). Ideological differences among incumbents made them embrace the new context differently. During the early 1990s Berlusconi's failure to impose a comprehensive program of reform (including reductions in seniority pensions and revisions in reference earnings and indexation mechanisms) contributed to his cabinet's fall in December 1994. The opposition of insiders and current pensioners, articulated around a massive general strike, blocked the reform. Since the need to meet the Maastricht criteria did not end, Dini's cabinet tried a more moderate strategy: He successfully managed to disconnect pensions from previous earnings and link them to contributions actually paid, and, via tax incentives, to complementary pension funds. Informed by Berlusconi's experience, Dini only managed to get these reforms through by introducing a significant time lag for their actual implementation: The reforms would only apply to workers entering the system after 1996, thus sheltering current insiders from any negative implications. The fate of the Italian pension reform is illustrative of the veto power of insiders. However, from the standpoint of our predictions about the dynamics of different forms of capitalism, the (failed) attempts to pursue an investment-oriented strategy by left-leaning governments (Prodi most prominently) are even more revealing.

By the end of the 1990s, scholars and practitioners alike were aware of the unbalanced nature of the Italian welfare state: It overprotected old age and privileged labor market insiders at the expense of outsiders (Ferrera and Hemerijck 2003; Ferrera and Gualmini 2004). To correct these imbalances, left-leaning cabinets pushed forward a series of reforms to reduce the transfer dependency in labor market policy and boost the size and scope of active labor market policies. These included a tighter targeting of antipoverty benefits, the elimination of the public monopoly of placement services, and an expansion of services dedicated to ease labor market transition. The logic, very much inspired by the antiexclusion and activation focus emerging from the European Employment Strategy, consisted in combining deregulation, activation, and a combination of universal services (in the realm of family policies, for instance) with noncontributory means-tested transfers, such as the minimum insertion income. Seen in the light of our theoretical framework, the driving motive behind these policy packages implies a shift from consumption to investment. As Jessoula and Alti (2010: 172) point out, "if fully accomplished, [the reform plan] could have led the Italian welfare state and labor market clearly beyond Bismarck" – except that the program was never fully implemented. The political weakness of Left cabinets vis-à-vis organized interests and insiders, the inability of governments to overcome the budgetary pressures around the convergence criteria, and the eventual return of more conservative cabinets targeting the core basis of insiders stalled the experiment. The net outcome is one of stasis amid budgetary pressures. The elements of the reform pursuing budgetary stabilization remained in place, but by and large the fundamental parameters of a capture-oriented welfare state did not change. Dualization remains largely unchanged, as does the system of unemployment insurance, in an illustrative failure to overcome labor market segmentation. Deregulation stopped and so did the efforts to shift the balance between active and passive labor market policies. During the first half of the 2000s, Berlusconi drastically cut social policy spending, closed the minimum insertion income, and restored a traditional family based welfare state articulated around community networks (Hemerijck 2013). The latter operated as an important device in his success as a political entrepreneur of the politics of capture. The eventual return of the Left to office for two years did not allow enough time to reattempt a feasible shift toward investment policies before the constraining impact of the Great Recession contributed to reducing observable differences across the parties in Italy's political spectrum.

The evolution of the welfare state in Spain presents a similar picture. The big push toward universalism in education and health during the 1980s, with significant success in health care provision, helped bridge the gap with other European economies by the early 1990s (Maravall 1996b). The push was far less forceful in terms of social security transfers, which were only boosted after the general strike in 1988. Social effort as a percentage of GDP peaked at 23 percent immediately before the economic recession of 1993. Overall, total revenue collection and welfare effort have consistently remained below those of more advanced welfare states. The push to close the investment gap in education did not translate either to social security or to labor market regulations. As extensively analyzed by the specialized literature (Rueda 2007; Guillén 2010) the system was in part an achievement of organized insiders that made the most of its design. Several labor market reforms (1984, 1994, 1996) allegedly designed to increase flexibility in the labor market have only increased the levels of dualization in terms of economic opportunities between insiders and outsiders (Espina 2007). In recent years, conservative administrations have made an effort to reduce the level of regular employment protection, as partially reflected in Figure 1.3, whereas the level of protection of temporary workers has remained stable.[24] Along the way, the decentralization of health, education, and social assistance has created a complex institutional environment where reform has become harder to implement (Moreno 1997; Beramendi 2012). The need to fulfill the Euro convergence criteria allowed the Conservative cabinets (1996–2004) to justify austerity and freeze the expansion of social provision relative to needs, while pushing for flexibilization without investment.

It is against this background that Zapatero's attempt to develop, even if partially, a move toward equality through inclusive investment took place. The two pillars of his strategy were a reinforcement of the scope of research and development and the introduction of a publicly funded comprehensive program of social services for dependent relatives (Ley de Dependencia), along with regulatory changes to ease the conciliation between work and family for women (Moreno 2007). In Spain, families and especially women remain the main service providers in case of need, preventing an effective incorporation of the latter into the labor market. The ultimate goal was to rebalance the sectoral weights of the economy in favor of skill intensive sectors and erase some of the constraints imposed by the family-oriented welfare regime that had developed since the transition to democracy. But Zapatero proved unable to modify labor markets to reduce dualization and introduce measures of positive activation for outsiders. The reforms stalled for a number of reasons. Before the crisis, Zapatero lacked the political and institutional capacity to fund and implement them. By virtue of the decentralization process he had to rely on the regions as the executors of the legislation. He did so, *yet without increasing their resources to meet the cost*. He lacked the resources to reform fiscal federal arrangements in a way that would allow the regions to implement this legislation effectively. Unsurprisingly, this created an implementation deadlock that was only exacerbated after 2007–2008. The crisis also forced him to resort first to short- term transfer packages for the benefits of insiders (reelection took place in mid-2008) that depleted his fiscal buffer, effectively doing away with the possibility of implementing an investment strategy.

As was the case in Italy, after 2010 the two main parties became hardly distinguishable in terms of economic policy platforms. Zapatero first, in a remarkable change of course in May 2010 imposed from Brussels, and Rajoy later became champions of austerity. State weakness erased differences between the Left and the Right in terms of economic policy. Before the crisis, both countries saw attempts to eliminate labor market dualization blocked or distorted by organized insiders and governments without the budgetary clout to alter the balance between negative and positive activation in labor markets. Finally, postcrisis reforms appear primarily oriented toward the protection of

---

[24] More recently, the conservative government in Spain has enacted a major reduction in the level of employment protection of regular workers, in a clear move toward the creation of a deregulated labor market. It is too early to evaluate the substantive implications of these reforms at this stage.

patronage driven politics, creating a political deadlock on needed institutional reform. Unsurprisingly, this poor institutional and economic performance fed large increases in political disaffection and historic "high(s)" in levels of distrust of programmatic politics, ultimately casting a shadow on the actual functioning of democracy across these political economies.

These two experiences illustrate the difficulties of programmatic politics in capture-oriented capitalism. The deadlock of programmatic politics paves the way for alternative political organizations to undertake the mobilization of those groups left out by the politics of austerity. A common strategy across these neopopulist (both Left and Right) forces is to portray a conflict between "the people" and the political class (or *casta*, or elite, according to various formulations). The left-wing version of this strategy proposes a generalization of consumption benefits to both insiders and outsiders, an expansion of investment, and a significant increase in taxation, along with a refusal to underwrite most of the current national debt. The Right version also endorses a expansion of consumption toward status but with a clear antiimmigrant message and a lesser emphasis on investment. Our argument suggests that, however appealing, these messages contain policy paths of limited feasibility in the short run. Whether their initial appeal translates into a stable realignment of political coalitions and what the implications are for political stability in these societies remain to be seen.

1.3.5. Summary: The Political Space in Advanced Capitalism

Our analysis of the dynamics of policy making in advanced capitalism suggests that the space for partisan politics over the last three decades across political economies has been at least two-dimensional, making possible multiple options for political alignments. It also suggests that the way the strategies of successful reform coalitions have shifted depends largely on past policy legacies, as captured by the four corners in Figure 1.12, constraining policy shifts along two dimensions: the scope of the state's intervention in the economy and the inherited balance in terms of investment and consumption policies. These two parameters shape the relative size of different social groups and their core policy claims, thus giving birth to a new set of feasible versus unfeasible political alliances. Figure 1.12 maps out the set of feasible coalitions across social groups emerging from our analysis. The political viability of these coalitions depends on the status quo equilibrium, as explained in detail earlier. Also, these coalitions may be mobilized by different partisan actors, depending on the patterns of party competition in different countries. A thorough analysis of the parties mobilizing these coalitions is, however, beyond the scope of this chapter (see, however, the chapters by Kitschelt and Rehm and by Häusermann and Kriesi, this volume).

1. *Sociocultural professionals and organized labor* (wage earners) remain, together, the core political coalition leading to outcome equality. Both

groups agree on strong and redistributive state intervention, but they must compromise on investment and consumption. To some extent, labor must accept the sociocultural professionals' emphasis on investments, whereas the sociocultural professionals have to compromise with labor's preference for status-segmented consumption. If these compromises become untenable, the proequality coalition unravels.

2. A second coalition involves *sociocultural professionals and business-finance professionals*: in this coalition, both parties agree on the emphasis on investment but must compromise with regard to the size and the redistributive scope of the state. Our analysis suggests that this coalition is likely to be pursued by left-wing parties in market-oriented societies.

3. The third potential coalition is that between small and large businesses, between the *petit bourgeois and the business and finance professionals*. In this coalition, both agree on limiting state intervention in markets that benefits primarily organized labor. In turn, they must compromise on investment, necessary for industry development but disliked by the self-employed. If the tax burden associated with investment becomes too contentious, this typically conservative coalition will unravel, opening opportunities for the Left.

4. Finally, the fourth potential coalition highlighted by our analysis includes elements of organized labor (wage earners) and the petit bourgeois. Both sides agree on prioritizing consumption over investment but must compromise on the scope of taxation and state intervention/regulation. This alliance of strange bedfellows emerges particularly in contexts where both groups develop a strong antiimmigrant sentiment and is most likely to be pursued by right-wing populist partisan forces.

Figure 1.12 places each of these coalitions around the coordinates of our theoretical framework. Critically, our analysis also rules out as implausible in advanced capitalism two other alliances:

a. *An alliance between the sociocultural professionals and the petit bourgeois:* they disagree on both the scope of state policy (taxation and social benefits schemes) as well as priorities over intertemporal resource allocation (investment/consumption): taxes and equality and the policy priorities.

b. *An alliance between business and organized labor (wage earners and, in particular, low-wage earners):* This suggests that such cross-class coalitions around which post–World War II capitalism was configured, particularly in what are today the status-oriented political economies, are hardly feasible anymore. Put simply, unions representing low-wage earners want an emphasis on consumption that creates too high an opportunity cost in terms of investment and competitiveness for business and sociocultural professionals. The alternative alliance with sociocultural

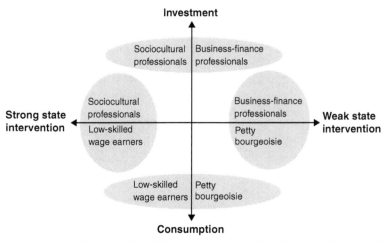

FIGURE 1.12. Coalitional configurations in the political space of advanced capitalism.

professionals in favor of investments (item 2 above) at the expense of consumption is a more attractive option for business, even in PR systems (Iversen and Soskice forthcoming).

1.4. Relationship to the Existing Literature

In a stylized fashion, we see at least two approaches at variance with the proposal we have drawn up in this Introduction. The first essentially posits a convergence of advanced capitalist politics and policy making across all political units, and it is clearly far from our diagnosis. The second sees a path-dependent evolution of different varieties of capitalism and is closer to our analysis.

The convergence perspective that was also in the crosshairs of criticisms in this volume's predecessor (Kitschelt et al. 1999) has received a strong second wind through the financial crisis followed by the Great Recession. It essentially argues for convergence in at least two ways: (1) All incarnations of advanced capitalism develop in the same direction: convergence Mark I, parallel development; and (2) where there were differences across polities and regions, these "varieties" are being whittled away to a common political economic practice of "just capitalism" without adjectives (cf. Streeck (2009, 2011, 2014a and b): convergence Mark II, homogenization around a common "best" practice. This strong conception of inequality convergence, combining Mark I and Mark II, is also consistent with Piketty's (2014) purely economic analysis of long-term patterns of inequality: The West's reductions of inequality in the aftermath of World War I, the Great Depression, and especially World War II were idiosyncratic exceptions, induced by exogenous shocks of war and economic dislocation, that tempered inequality differentially and temporarily. Capitalism, described in its crudest terms, is now returning to its steady state.

We have no doubt that there are powerful tendencies that increase inequality in contemporary capitalism (convergence Mark I). But we challenge the proposition that these forces effectively generate a homogenization of capitalism (convergence Mark II). The cursory evidence displayed in this Introduction, as well as the more detailed evidence provided by the many contributions to this volume, overwhelmingly speak against this hypothesis. Moreover, we tend to disagree on the mechanisms of convergence. Whereas in the evolutionary political (Streeck) and economic (Piketty) approaches it is purely (global) markets that drive these changes, our approach highlights the continuing importance of politics as a source of diversity.[25] In the convergence theory, it is the power of footloose capital, alone, that compels politicians and ultimately voters to accept the fate of convergence Mark II.

We beg to differ on a number of counts. On the one hand, we disagree with the analysis of mechanisms. Globalization is a force that constrains politics, but it is technology, mediated by the changes in occupational structures, that has far more influence on the movement of relative prices of capital and different skill and task profiles of labor. European and North American peasants and miners, printers and longshoremen, bank tellers and telephone switching operators did not lose their livelihood because their jobs went abroad or were taken away by immigrants. They vanished, supplanted by machines and increasingly "code." About half of all jobs are highly likely to fall victim to "code" in the remainder of the twenty-first century (Frey and Osborne 2013). Also demographics, together with changes in family structure that, themselves, are intertwined with occupational and technological changes calling for new techniques of socialization and skilling of young people, are powerful forces that have no room in the convergence narrative. We see no compelling reason why family structures and occupational clusters should become uniform across space, even though they respond to similar fundamental technological challenges.

More importantly, however, the convergence perspective entirely discounts politics. Piketty says as much and delegates the task to explore the modifying role of politics to other researchers. Streeck's analysis is a return to the models of late-capitalist state theories that saw state functionaries – out of their own interests to survive and thrive, not by taking direct orders from capitalist bosses – enact the imperatives of capital accumulation (cf. Offe 1972, 1985; Poulantzas 1973). Relying on Peter Mair's theory of cartel parties and party systems, Streeck sees a "hollowing out" of politics (Mair 2006) in which democratic accountability to electoral interests and preferences vanishes either by politicians of all parties colluding to ignore them or by politicians (and the mass media) manipulating citizens so that popular preferences are no longer exogenous to the strategies of capital and party politicians seeking to secure

---

[25] To be fair, Piketty (2014: part IV) agrees that democratic politics may modify outcomes, but that is not part of his analysis.

their survival in political office. Politics becomes a handmaiden to international capital markets instead of responsive to genuine popular interests.

We document in this book that substantial evidence contradicts this general perspective. Parties remain differentiated in their electoral appeals, do represent constituency groups, and act on their electoral alignments in public policy making. And if politicians do not implement the kind of redistribution contemporary Marxians would postulate for the working class to demand, it is not because they defy the preferences of large publics, but because these publics express more complicated, differentiated preference schedules. These observations contradicting structuralist neo-Marxism do not, of course, exclude that business interests under many conditions have substantial leverage over policy formation outside the circuit of electoral partisan accountability. We are the last to deny that there are other ingredients to policy formation than electoral politics. Nevertheless, understanding the operation of electoral democracy is constitutive in order to account for variance over time and across space in policies and quality of life outcomes delivered by postindustrial democracies.

Compared to structuralist neo-marxism, our perspective is much closer to the varieties of capitalism literature, which goes back at least as far as Shonfield (1965), then the corporatism literature (e.g., Cameron 1984; Katzenstein 1985; Lange and Garrett 1985), and finally what has explicitly called itself the "varieties of capitalism" (VoC) approach (see Soskice 1999; Hall and Soskice 2001; Iversen 2005; Iversen and Stephens 2008; Iversen and Soskice 2009). Let us first sketch how our approach is steeped in the VoC literature before we specify where we depart from its postulates.

We align with VoC in accounting for the development of political-economic institutions (e.g., industrial relations regimes, corporate governance), actors (producers, political parties), and endowments (technology, skills) as a path-dependent process in which starting points matter and the options for change follow from distinctive constraints and capacities encountered in the choice process. Both VoC and the constrained partisanship framework observe that actors' basic political preference schedules are largely exogenous to the game of party competition, rooted in political-economic, occupational, and social experiences. Democracy does operate as an accountability mechanism in which competing party politicians must pick up on (some of) their constituencies' preferences in order to win and stay in office. While globalization of products/services, labor, and capital imposes restrictions on polities' domestic domain of maneuver, it remains quite large, as can be traced in the differential responses of party governments to similar exogenous technological and demographic shocks (cf. Hall and Thelen 2009).

Our endeavor, however, also parts company with VoC in some regards. First of all, in the distinction of variety types, as clusters of institutional and political attributes (mainly corporate governance, industrial relations, skill formation, and research and development on the production side; profiles of redistribution and risk hedging in social policy on the welfare state side), we think it to be less useful for most explanatory purposes to operate with two main types – coordinated and competitive market economies (CME and LME) – and then many "mixed" types and "sub" types than straightforwardly with the four types introduced earlier that crystallized in the post–World War II decades in today's advanced capitalist democracies. The welfare state literature always had to operate with a minimum of three rather than two types that required a distinction based on partisan politics alone (Esping-Andersen 1990; van Kersbergen 1995; Kitschelt et al. 1999). Cross-class Christian Democratic parties whose unique role could not be characterized in terms of production systems were introduced to account for major differences in social policy formation and inequality outcomes that broke the CME/LME conceptual dualism. A further limitation of VoC's conceptual dualism was its treatment of the Mediterranean countries by either excluding them from analysis or relegating them to the "mixed" types hard to accommodate with the existing conceptual strategy.

Second, we accord a different theoretical status to political-economic types than the VoC theorists might suggest. For us, types are shorthand for empirical clusters of the scores on continuous variables that appear historically and bring about different effects, depending on circumstances. For VoC, by contrast, the empirical approximation of types activates specific "complementarities" of institutions and policies that yield particularly desirable macroeconomic performance. Clusters of traits reinforce each other both in the production system (Hall and Soskice 2001) as well as between production and social policy (Estevez-Abe et al. 2001; Iversen 2005; Iversen and Soskice 2009) according to the economic interests of all producers – both capital and labor – and make them particularly efficient and competitive compared to "mixed" types in macroeconomic terms (Hall and Gingerich 2009). Moreover, complementary institutions and policies constitute Nash equiibria among actor strategies that make it costly for any single actor to diverge from them.

Empirical research has shown that the association of polities with particular types of production systems has been in flux for some time (Schneider and Paunescu 2012). We challenge that at least currently, under the impact of the technological, demographic, and globalization "shocks," it is possible for theory to identify efficient equilibria of political-economic "packages" of policies and institutions that deliver superior performance. Likewise, political actors, such as party (coalitions), grounded in different political-economic interest alignments, experiment into an open horizon, often driven by myopic conceptions of group interests, without anyone's being able to predict today whether the path pursued will actually pay off in the longer run either for (1) the political actors and their constituencies advancing the reforms right now and/or for (2) the macroeconomic performance of the polities (or regions) in which these reforms prevail.

We have not investigated here whether the past record of political-economic development since World War II ever produced time windows in which empirical clusters of political-economic institutions and policies became complementarities that were particularly high performing. In recent decades, however, under the impact of the new shocks – technology-induced occupational change, demographics, and globalization – partisan governments and coalitions appear to have adopted policy and institutional experimentation that move them away from the complementarity and equilibrium conditions even in the historical cases that once were closest to the two CME/LME types of capitalist varieties (Ahlquist and Breunig 2012; Schneider and Paunescu 2012; Thelen 2014; in this volume, see especially Jackson and Thelen, as well as Hassel).

Beyond pure description, all that is currently possible in political-economic explanation is to delineate feasibility sets of policy options that are reachable from certain status quo institutions and policies and trace the partisan coalitions that dominate the political agenda within these feasibility sets. Because of high uncertainty about economic consequences and efficiencies of alternative policy pathways, however, such partisan alignments express pure politics, unfettered by clear economic signals of "best" and "inferior" policy practices, and it remains uncertain whether the emerging partisan and policy coalition strategies may enact lasting equilibria, let alone equilibria with collectively beneficial positive-sum outcomes.

Recent work by key proponents of VoC is close to this very perspective (Iversen and Soskice forthcoming). For CMEs, they see new technological conditions undermine the producer coalitions that achieved superior economic performance with CME institutions and policies in the past. Technology undercuts the coordination among different components of the working class, broadly conceived as consisting of an ascending ladder of skills, with an increasingly narrow band of high-skilled workers in CMEs still supporting the continued coordination with business that once marked this type, but now at odds with low-skilled wage earners' interests. How policy making treats the mass of less-skilled labor, then, is a matter of pure partisan politics in the Iversen-Soskice analysis, just as it would be within the framework of "constrained partisanship." According to them, where cross-class parties prevail in systems of proportional representation, the pathway of policy reform will be different, and less favorable, for the worst-off, than where pure bourgeois parties with strong liberalization agendas make it more likely that center-left and Left parties rally in coalitions protecting even the poorest against the onslaught of market liberalization promoted by parties of business and professionals.

Setting aside questions about empirical claims in Iversen and Soskice's paper,[26] let us draw attention to a theoretical move toward what we consider essential for the electoral turn in political economy: The presence of cross-class parties does not reflect specific producer interests, but is a purely electoral, political phenomenon. As in our approach, parties themselves shape economic

---

[26] For example, Iversen/Soskice do not focus on social policies – particularly pension reform – where party systems with pure market-liberal parties have prompted even center-left coalitions to embrace stronger market liberalization than governments produced by cross-class parties, e.g., through defined-contributions components within the public pension system or raising the criteria of eligibility for full pension benefits.

policy coalitions with distributive consequences.[27] We would add: And the actors (and scholarly observers!) do not know whether or not they contribute to an ensemble of strategies ultimately generating a set of policies and institutions that might again deserve to be labeled "types" in political-economic analysis, because they persist over time and may yield superior economic performance. It is this supremacy of electoral partisan politics, acting into an uncertain future of reform, but constrained by the existing institutions, state capacities, and party system configurations, that should drive explanatory accounts of policy choice in political economy right now and that deserves the label of "constrained partisanship" approach.

This leaves one feature to be highlighted on which VoC and the constrained partisanship approach sketched here may or may not agree: the need for a two-dimensional characterization of the space of political controversy that builds on citizens' diverging economic interests. Economic actors disagree not only about the allocation of resources and capabilities at any given point in time, but also about the intertemporal distribution of chances to acquire resources and capabilities: Some want to discount the future more than others. In the constrained partisanship approach the wager is that (1) preference disagreements over the level of state intervention are orthogonal to (2) the targeting of more policy resources to current consumers (however these resources may be distributed among claimants) or more heavily to future consumers, by making investment efforts right now that pay off for the chances of future citizens to earn a good income.

Our insistence on the two-dimensional nature of the policy space is intimately associated with the different characterization of relevant economic occupational groups highlighted in the "constrained partisanship" approach, when contrasted to VoC. Whereas VoC – all the way to Iversen and Soskice's recent paper – makes do with what is essentially a unidimensional characterization of social structure, rising from unskilled, via high-specifically skilled to very high/generally skilled professional/business operatives (or from low to middle to high incomes), we propose a two-dimensional field of occupational groups, market locations, and economic interests as the "raw material" for politicians' creative efforts to craft winning electoral coalitions and novel public policies.

1.5. Organization of the Book

This chapter has outlined the fundamental elements of our reinterpretation of the politics of advanced capitalism. In the rest of the volume contributors take on the task of analyzing in detail specific preconditions, dynamics, and

---

[27] Note that it is not electoral systems, and economic producer interests standing behind the choice of electoral systems, that explain the difference of party systems with or without cross-class parties in Iversen and Soskice's article.

consequences of the general process described in this Introduction. The volume is organized in four sections.

We begin by situating our cases of interest in space and time and by analyzing the key structural transformations putting pressure on advanced industrial democracies and delimiting the context in which the dynamics of our model of constrained partisanship play out. The determinants and constraints on productivity and prosperity are such key factors shaping the larger macroeconomic context. Carles Boix offers a *longue dureé* perspective on the relationship between sector composition and economic growth and contextualizes current developments in advanced democracies within these long-run processes of structural transformations in the composition of economic sectors. Rueda, Wibbels, and Altamirano complement this view on structural determinant with a focus on institutions. They argue that differences in the timing and type of industrialization between a "core" of advanced capitalist democracies and the "periphery" have led to very different institutional configurations of labor market regulation, resulting in the patterns of dualization we observe today, especially in the countries of Southern Europe and Latin America. These two chapters situate advanced capitalism in a broader context and help calibrate the scope of our conclusions.

Thereafter, the volume turns to three major sources of social structural change: the occupational structure (Oesch), changing household patterns and gender roles (Esping-Andersen), and international pressures, with a particular focus on the pressure migration puts on the working class (Dancygier and Walter). Oesch argues that technological change has eroded lower-skill occupations in advanced capitalist democracies and reduced social and occupational mobility, because of stronger educational stratification. The chapter by Esping-Andersen then shows that these occupational trends are reinforced by changing household patterns, in particular, increasing sociostructural homogamy, a trend that also increases stratification and reduces social mobility. Moreover, as Dancygier and Walter show, globalization and migration flows further threaten the jobs and social status of the lower-skill classes in society, thereby changing the political preference space governments are confronted with.

In the second step, we go on to analyze the impact of these structural changes on politics. Kitschelt and Rehm start with a defense of realignment theory, showing that in most advanced capitalist democracies, political parties still present voters with alternative programmatic choices and represent their constituencies rather well. Häusermann and Kriesi then analyze these constituencies in more detail. They investigate the preference profile Rueda (2007); Häusermann (2010); Schwander and Häusermann (2013); Emmenegger et al. (2012) of party electorates, as well as the sociostructural determinants of these preferences with regard to the state-market and universalism-particularism dimension. The upshot is that the class profile of left- and right-wing parties has profoundly changed: While the Left has largely become the representative of a universalist-statist middle class, working class and low-income voters increasingly vote for particularistic parties. These changes clearly transform the coalitional opportunities for constrained governments even further, especially on the state-market dimension. Furthermore, the chapter by Hassel shows that the Left is losing the working class not only in terms of its parties, but also in terms of organized labor: Union density is not only declining, but highly unequal in all but the "universalist" Nordic countries. Despite relatively stable levels of institutional coordination, this erosion of organized labor further complicates the coalitional choices constrained governments have in terms of their policy choices.

The first two sections lay the foundations for the analyses of the political and institutional responses to transformed supply- and demand-side constraints. The third section on policies then analyzes coalitional dynamics and government choices with regard to particular key distributive policy areas. In line with our analytical framework, we focus on consumption (Huber and Stephens), investment (Gingrich and Ansell), as well as the evolution of labor market regulation and corporate governance, two policy areas for which our focus on electoral dynamics needs to be complemented by a close analysis of producer group politics and its interaction with partisan strategies (Jackson and Thelen). Both chapters on consumption and investment show that partisanship continues to matter within altered structural and institutional constraints. All three chapters account for a growing hybridization of the institutional policy setup of advanced capitalist countries, and for complex coalitional dynamics in which governments engage.

Finally, we turn to analyzing the outcomes of the constrained partisanship politics of advanced capitalism, broadly understood. We focus first on economic and distributive outcomes of different sets of constraints (Beramendi), to analyze then the determinants of self-reported happiness across political economies (Anderson and Hecht). The Conclusion by the editors summarizes our key results and discusses the impact of the economic crisis on politics and policies.

PART I

STRUCTURAL TRANSFORMATIONS

2

Prosperity and the Evolving Structure of Advanced Economies

Carles Boix

During the last century and a half economic growth has been formidable in the North Atlantic basin. As shown in Figure 2.1, in 1870 per capita income (in constant dollars of 2000) ranged from around $1,100 in Portugal to about $3,500 in New Zealand and the United Kingdom. By 2007 it had multiplied by about twelve to fourteen times to more than $35,000 in the United States, about $25,000 in France and Germany, and $16,000 in Portugal. Such a shift in income levels implied an average annual growth rate of about 1.8 to 2.0 percent.

Within this explosive secular trend, growth rates exhibited considerable variance over time. OECD countries (defined here following the old membership criteria restricted to Western Europe, North America, Japan, and Australasia) grew at below that average rate before 1914 (at 1.7 percent) and between 1929 and 1939 (at 1.2 percent). By contrast, their growth rates exceeded the historical average right after World War I and especially after World War II. From 1945 to 1960 their growth rate, at 6.6 percent, tripled the average rate, and, although it slowed down in the period 1960–1980, it still more than doubled it, at 4.8 percent. A similar story can be told about Europe as a whole: It underperformed (relative to its historical average) during the belle époque yet it overperformed after the two world wars over the period aptly labeled the Golden Age (Crafts and Toniolo 1996; Toniolo 1998) that ended with the stagflation crisis of the mid-1970s and early 1980s. By the early 2000s, growth rates were around or below 2 percent.

Growth rates also varied substantially across countries. Before 1914, growth took place mainly in the European industrial core and the North

Two previous versions of this chapter were prepared for the meetings on "The Future of Democratic Capitalism" held in Zurich in June 2011 and at Duke University in October 2012. I thank Elena Nikolova for her research assistance and the editors of this current volume and the participants in the Zurich and Durham meetings for their comments.

67

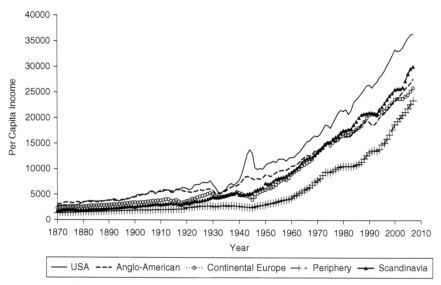

FIGURE 2.1. Per capita income, 1870–2007.

American Atlantic seaboard. Then, after the nineteenth-century period of industrial take-off, poor economies grew faster than wealthy ones – in line with the predictions of standard growth models (Solow 1956; Barro 1997).[1] Nonetheless, that long-run process of economic catch-up only narrowed cross-country differences moderately. Up until the 1920s, the United Kingdom had a per capita income higher than or similar to the American one, continental European countries had a per capita income equivalent to between 60 and 80 percent of the U.S. income and the Scandinavia/United States and Southern Europe/United States income ratios were 0.6 and 0.4, respectively. By 1975 the average per capita income in all regions except Southern Europe had risen to about 80 percent of the American per capita income, but then it did not change afterward. In Southern Europe it stood at 55 percent in 1975 and rose to about 65 percent by 2007.

Economic convergence hardly altered the initial economic ranking of each country. Figure 2.2 plots the per capita income of advanced countries in 1901 and 2007. The correlation coefficient is around 0.5. In fact, it becomes much higher, at around 0.75, when we include non-OECD countries: The fitted line

[1] In an unconditional-convergence estimation – with the function form $\Delta y_p = \alpha + \beta \log y_o$, where p stands for the period under analysis, o the initial year, and y is per capita income, the ß-convergence coefficient was −1.6% during the interwar period, a very high −7.2% between 1950 and 1980, and −3.3% between 1980 and 2007. In all cases it is statistically significant. For the period 1980–2007 the ß-coefficient fell to −3.3% – and to −1.34% once we exclude the two outliers of Ireland and Luxembourg.

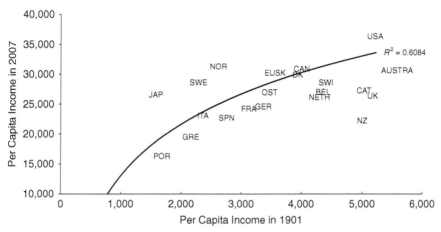

FIGURE 2.2. Historical continuities in development.

is estimated with OECD and non-OECD countries. Relatively wealthy nations at the turn of the twentieth century remain at the top of the economic ladder one hundred years later. The declining economies of the United Kingdom and New Zealand appear to be rather exceptional cases.

In the rest of this chapter I explore the nature and causes of the varying economic performance across countries. In the first section I link the different trajectories of the industrial core (Northwestern Europe and North America) and the industrial periphery (mainly Southern Europe) to their internal sectoral composition. In the second section I trace those differences back to both long-run pre-nineteenth-century growth patterns and the industrialization path taken by each economy after 1870. In the third section of the paper I suggest that, as a result of the impact of new labor-saving technologies and of trade competition from emerging markets, the gap between core and periphery (within the advanced world) will not shrink and may even widen significantly in the future. In the last section I conclude by reflecting on the impact that these findings may have for the political economy of advanced countries.

2.1. Growth and Sectoral Composition of the Economy

2.1.1. *Standard Convergence Dynamics*

To explore what is behind such a moderate degree of economic convergence and relatively stable cross-national economic rankings, I first examine the process of economic growth using standard conditional convergence models in Table 2.1. I employ a panel data structure with five decades: 1960–1969, 1970–1979, 1980–1989, 1990–1999, and 2000–2009. All models include country and time fixed effects. For the sake of comparison, Model 1 shows

TABLE 2.1. *Conditional convergence models, 1960–2009*

	Model 1	Model 2	Model 3	Model 4
Constant	0.739***	0.7418***	0.792***	0.9060***
	(7.60)	(7.17)	(7.82)	(7.70)
Log y_0	−0.0715***	−0.0740***	−0.0802***	−0.0918***
	(7.51)	(7.26)	(7.48)	(7.43)
Population growth		0.0080	−0.468	−0.5267*
		(0.03)	(1.56)	(1.78)
Investment share of GDP		0.0006	0.0007	0.0005
		(1.17)	(1.58)	(1.04)
Percentage of population with some secondary education		0.0003	0.0005	0.0006**
		(0.96)	(1.62)	(2.08)
Trade openness			0.0004***	0.0004***
			(3.31)	(3.54)
Social security transfers (percentage GDP)			−0.0001	−0.0001
			(0.16)	(0.18)
Wage coordination			0.0001	−0.0002
			(0.55)	(0.13)
Employment protection			0.0025	0.0022
			(1.16)	(1.08)
Percentage population older than 65			−0.0020*	−0.0027**
			(1.74)	(2.26)
Percentage industrial sector				0.1333*
				(1.82)
Period dummies	Y	Y	Y	Y
Country dummies	Y	Y	Y	Y
R^2	0.4811	0.4829	0.5126	0.4927
No. observations	111	110	108	108

Notes: Estimation: OLS with panel data structure.
T-statistics within parentheses.
Statistical significance: *** $p < 0.01$; ** $p < 0.05$; * $p < 0.10$.

the unconditional convergence model. Model 2 then tests the basic conditional convergence framework. The initial log of per capita GDP has a strong and statistically significant negative effect on the growth rate of per capita income: Poorer countries grow faster. Population growth does not reduce growth. As predicted in the theoretical literature (Barro 1997; 2008), the investment share over GDP and the quality of human capital (measured as the proportion of the population with at least some secondary education) have a positive effect on growth. However, the coefficients are not statistically significant. Model 3 in Table 2.1 adds several independent variables to probe for some institutional and economic dimensions specific to the advanced world. Trade openness (measured as the sum of exports and imports over GDP) is statistically significant, but its effect on growth rates is very small. Social security transfers as a percentage of GDP have no effect on growth. A separate model, not reported here, shows that public consumption does not either. Labor market institutions (measured through both Kenworthy's index of wage coordination and Blanchard and Wolfers's index of employment protection) do not matter. The level of central bank independence (not reported here because its inclusion leads to a small loss of observations) has a negative but statistically not significant effect. Finally, a larger share of an older population is negatively related to growth: Naturally, the causal relationship may work both ways.

The standard conditional-convergence framework models the economy as having a single, aggregate production function. Consider, however, the possibility that the economy has several sectors, each one with an idiosyncratic production function, and that there are intersectoral barriers that prevent the allocation of all capital and labor to the most efficient sectors. Those barriers may range from pure demand factors (world demand for any given product is not unlimited) to financial market imperfections or to particular industrial traditions that make the transfer of know-how across sectors very costly.[2] The economywide growth rate, which will be a composite of every sector's growth rate, will shift as a function of both the share in the economy and the marginal productivity of each sector. To approximate this scenario, Model 4 in Table 2.1 includes a control for the size of the industrial sector. The coefficient is statistically significant and has a substantial impact on the growth rate. A decline of 10 percentage points in the size of the industrial sector corresponds to a drop of 1.33 points in the growth rate. A 10 percent reduction in the weight of the industrial sector matches the average reduction across OECD countries in the last few decades – and therefore it may explain the decline in the growth rate since the 1960s. The 10 percent share is also close to the difference between heavily industrialized countries and nations with a small manufacturing sector.

2.1.2. *Sectoral Composition of the Economy*
To examine the structural composition of advanced economies, which appears to shape growth performance, in more detail, Table 2.2 reports the employment

---

[2] Along similar lines, recent models on the generation and persistence of inequality characterize the economy as having several households (sectors in our case) with different factor endowments making allocation decisions in the context of imperfect credit markets and some investment threshold separating low-value-added from high-value-added investments. See Kahhat's (2007) excellent survey of the literature modeling the persistence of inequality.

TABLE 2.2. *Sectoral composition of advanced economies in the mid-1990s*

A. Employment Share (Percentage)

	Primary	Manufacturing	of Which:		Construction, Tourism	Finance	Public Goods
			Low VA	High VA			
United States	1.5	9.8	21.4	78.6	19.2	3.8	18.1
Scandinavia	3.8	11.1	27.2	72.8	11.5	1.7	25.7
Germany	2.3	15.2	60.1	39.9	14.0	2.3	18.0
Benelux	2.3	10.0	40.4	59.6	14.8	2.3	18.2
France	2.9	9.4	45.9	54.1	13.1	1.9	19.6
Italy	3.5	13.0	75.3	24.7	10.3	1.6	13.4
Spain	4.2	9.2	94.2	5.8	10.6	1.3	11.9
Portugal	9.9	14.9	100.0	0.0	12.4	1.4	12.9

B. Share of Total Value Added (Percentage)

	Primary	Manufacturing	of Which:		Construction, Tourism	Finance	Public Goods
			Low VA	High VA			
United States	2.3	18.3	21.4	78.6	28.1	6.6	20.5
Scandinavia	9.6	17.8	14.1	85.9	24.1	4.1	21.6
Germany	1.7	22.9	50.7	49.3	29.7	4.1	17.4
Benelux	4.3	17.3	27.9	72.1	27.2	6.1	20.8
France	3.3	16.5	36.7	63.3	33.9	5.1	22.5
Italy	3.2	21.6	66.9	33.1	28.0	4.4	17.0
Spain	4.3	17.8	87.0	13.0	31.2	3.9	17.1
Portugal	5.4	17.4	100.0	0.0	26.7	4.4	22.3

Source: For European countries, EUROSTAT's NACE data set; for the USA, Bureau of Labor Statistics and Bureau of Economic Analysis.

and value added shares of the main sectors of several economies in the mid-1990s. The data are taken from EUROSTAT's NACE data set for Europe and from the Bureau of Labor Statistics and the Bureau of Economic Analysis for the United States. The reported sectors are primary (agriculture, fishing, and mining), low-value-added manufacturing, high-value-added manufacturing, services in real estate and tourism, financial services, and provision of public goods (public administration, education, and health). Manufacturing industries are classified into low or high value added, depending on whether their per capita value added is below or above the average per capita value added in the manufacturing sector in the whole data set. Scandinavian and Benelux countries have been clustered by region because their particular profiles do not differ much.

In employment terms, Germany has the largest industrial sector, followed by Italy and the small European countries. The United States and France are next, with a sector that employs one-tenth of the working population. Cross-country differences narrow down, however, in terms of share of value added. In any case, the crucial difference across countries results from the weight of high-value-added and low-value-added industries.

High-value-added industries dominate in the United States, Scandinavia, and the Benelux countries. The United States leads in at least three industries: the chemical sector, which includes the pharmaceutical industry; the electrical and electronics industry, which includes the production of personal computers; and the financial sector. In all the other industries, American and German value added per capita are similar or slightly higher in the United States. The high-value-added industrial sector in small European countries is concentrated in very few sectors – from one to three. In Sweden, for instance, the electrical industry had a value added per person of about €250,000 and the chemical industry of about €210,000 by 2007, but the remaining sectors such as the auto and metal industries remained modest or suffered important setbacks over time.[3] In the large economies of continental Europe, France and Germany, the high-value-added and low-valued-added industries are relatively similar in size. France is closer to Scandinavia: In terms of share of value added, 63 percent of its industrial sector falls into the high-value-added sector. This is the result of having an extraordinarily productive chemical industrial and a solid electronics sector. All the other sectors perform at the OECD average at best. Finally, the European South relies on low-value-added industries: 67 percent of Italian industry, 86 percent in Spain, and 100 percent in Portugal. Generally speaking, per capita incomes correlate well with the size of high-value-added sectors across countries: Wealthier countries have a sizable high-value-added industrial sector.

[3] As noted in Spence and Hlatshwayo (2011), the rapid increase in value added per person in the electronics industry may be a statistical artifact, reflecting the construction of value added data using a recent year as its benchmark – personal computers were highly prized in the early 1990s, yet their input costs and prices have fallen quickly since then.

Table 2.2 shows that advanced economies differ in their sectoral composition in three additional ways. First, Scandinavian countries have a large public goods sector in employment terms. In value added terms, however, that sector is similar across all countries – reflecting relatively low public salaries in generous welfare states and, on the other extreme, the key role of the private health industry in the United States. The only exception is the European periphery – with a small public goods sector in employment and value added. Second, the American economy relies heavily on real estate and direct services (hotels, restaurants, etc.) and finance. Third, Southern European economies have a much lower participation rate – due to their underdeveloped '"public goods"' sector.

2.2. The Shadow of the Past

The sectoral composition of national economies and their income level (and growth performance) seem to be the result of two long-run variables: a long-run period of protoindustrialization preceding the Industrial Revolution and the nature of the (second) industrial revolution.

2.2.1. *Long-Run Growth*

Constructing a comprehensive spatial and temporal data set of the geography, institutions, urbanization, and location of protoindustries in medieval and modern Europe, Abramson and Boix (2014) show that a substantial part of the variation in contemporary economic development across Europe can be traced back to the growth of population, the emergence of cities, and the formation of protomanufacturing sectors that took place in highly productive agricultural lands after the introduction of the heavy plow and other technological innovations from about 1000 onward.

As Nicholas (1997) writes, "cities could not develop until the rural economy could feed a large number of people who, instead of growing their own food, compensated the farmer by reconsigning his products and later by manufacturing items that the more prosperous peasants desired. The 'takeoff' of the European economy in the central Middle Ages is closely linked to changes in the rural economy that created an agricultural surplus that could feed large cities" (p. 104). In those new urban clusters, specialized in textile and metal protoindustries, technological change proceeded at a faster pace than in less populated areas. In addition, geography itself contributed to accelerate the process of urban agglomeration and technological innovation in the European core: Proximity to cheap transportation means such as waterways augmented trade. As trade flourished, both the size of markets and the volume of population engaged in commercial and intellectual exchanges increased, leading to a higher rate of technological progress. In fact, because of the

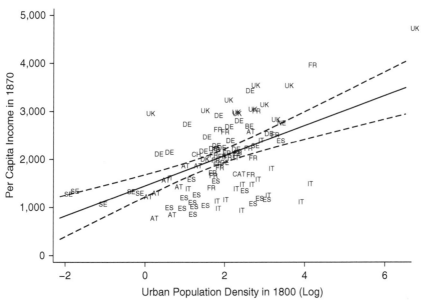

FIGURE 2.3. Modern urban population and nineteenth-century development.

presence of increasing returns to scale to knowledge and positive agglomeration externalities, that initial (and probably modest) variation in soil fertility – triggered or "unearthed" by the heavy plow – and low transportation costs across European regions resulted in much faster growth in initially urbanized areas.

To show the extent of historical continuity in economic fundamentals, Figure 2.3 plots urban population density in 1800 and per capita income in 1870 for European regions (defined at the NUTS2 level) as well as the fitted regression line and the 95 percent confidence intervals of the bivariate relationship. Those areas that were relatively urbanized before the industrial take-off and that, broadly speaking, occupied the European corridor that broadly runs from southern England to northern Italy, had much higher levels of per capita income by the end of the century. By contrast, thinly urbanized regions in 1800 were still lagging behind a century later.

2.2.2. The Second Industrial Revolution

Although the long-run process of urbanization and the formation of a protoindustrial base in medieval and modern Europe explain part of the divide between the European core and the Southern and Eastern European peripheries, the type of industrialization was shaped also by two main factors: (1) the emergence of specific economic sectors (and the corresponding productivity gains) in each industrialization wave and (2) the nature of the second

Industrial Revolution and the role of the state – processes examined first by Gerschenkron (1962) and, to some extent, Kurth (1979), but then marginalized by the most recent neoinstitutionalist literature on growth.

The first industrializers, particularly the United Kingdom, could not extend their leading position during the first Industrial Revolution into the second industrial revolution and fell behind in the following decades. As shown in Figure 2.2, Britain's current per capita income is about 25 to 30 percent lower than its predicted value given the income level of 1901. As partially explored in Landes (2003), Britain's relative failure was probably related to the structure of the financial sector, which made it difficult for companies in new industries to gain enough economies of scale; to the role of colonial possessions, which may have attracted investors; and to cultural changes in the value attached to entrepreneurship. Several of the small continental countries (Belgium, Netherlands, Switzerland) that industrialized early have also experienced slower than expected growth. Their income per capita is about 15 to 20 percent lower than their predicted estimate.

Long-run economic growth was consistently stronger in those countries, such as the United States and (to some extent) Germany, that succeeded in creating the financial institutions, mobilizing the capital, and establishing the right kind of industrial corporations to exploit the technologies and economies of scale associated with the second industrial revolution (Chandler 1990).

In Southern and Eastern Europe, industrialization took place with a substantial temporal lag – with several regional exceptions such as the Italian Lombardy, Catalonia, or the Basque Country. Its dynamics then tended to vary as a function of the political economy of each country. At different points in time during the twentieth century, the French, Italian, and Spanish state elites attempted to forge strong industrial conglomerates and to pick national champions to overcome their weaker political and economic position vis-à-vis Britain, Germany, and their own regional peripheries. French postwar planners succeeded at destroying the small and medium size industry based in the eastern arch (especially around Lyon and the Rhone) (Shonfield 1965; Piore and Sabel 1984), and, in the process, they consolidated some high-value-added industries. The northern Italian business elite mostly neutralized Rome's and ENI's role in the Italian economy. In Spain, where both Catalonia and the Basque Country industrialized early, control over industrial policy evolved to the advantage of central elites – particularly after the civil war. From an economic point of view, the Spanish state-led industrial strategy was unsuccessful. Spain's performance (at the peak of the last economic cycle in 2007) was below its predicted income and its "high-value-added" sectors of the 1990s and 2000s (financial intermediation and utilities) have proved insufficient to create a stable and truly competitive economy.

2.2.3. The Role of Institutions

The institutional framework of the economy has been said to affect growth (North 1990) and comparative advantage (Porter 1990; Hall and Soskice 2001). An alternative story stresses the impact of pure technological variables on the sectoral structure of the economy and the performance of its sectors. Naturally, technology and institutions may be endogenous. To explore their possible effect, as shown in Table 2.3, I regress several types of variables on the level of value added per capita and on the level of employment (as a proportion of working population) in 2008: sector dummies to capture any common technological structure across countries; country dummies to approximate any national institutional configuration; binary variables classifying countries as either liberal market economies (LMEs), coordinated market economies (CMEs), or Southern market economies (SMEs); interactive variables of the latter with manufacturing sectors (bundled in four categories: food, textiles, and leather; paper, petroleum, et al., chemicals; plastic, other nonmetallic minerals, metals; machinery, electrical, and transportation); the energy sector; and those sectors engaged in the production of public goods (public administration, education, health).

Model 1 (on levels of value added per capita) reports the model with sector dummies and the three variables measuring types of economies. The point estimate for SMEs is $-33,251 and statistically significant at the 90 percent level. Five sector dummies are statistically significant: extraction of coal, oil, and so on; transformation of coke and petroleum; electrical equipment; electricity, gas, and water supply; and financial intermediation. In estimations that include country dummies and that are not reported here, only a few countries are statistically significant. Likewise, the variables for types of sectors (manufacturing organized in four categories, energy, or public goods), alone or in interaction with type of capitalism, are not significant – results are not reported here either. There seems to be little evidence of a national regulatory framework sustaining some particular competitive advantage – a result that is at variance with the results presented in the next chapter by Rueda et al.

Model 2 runs the same variables as Model 1 now regressed on level of employment in 2008. The only sectors that are statistically significant are wholesale retail and those related to the provision of public services. Being an LME is also related to higher employment levels. Otherwise there is no effect of the type of institutional structure (alone or in interaction with type of sector) on employment.

2.3. Technological Change, Globalization, and Growth

Until the stagflation crisis of the mid-1970s and early 1980s, economic convergence among countries was fast and income gaps (across and within countries) narrowed considerably. In the last four decades, however, intercountry equalization has slowed and intracountry inequality has widened in several

TABLE 2.3. *Institutions and the sectoral composition of advanced economies*

	Value Added per Capita 2008	Employment (in Thousands) in 2008
Constant	17,284.3	180.5
	(0.47)	(0.3)
Agriculture	20,795.4	63.4
	(0.44)	(0.08)
Fishing	41,756.0	−287.8
	(0.86)	(0.37)
Mining of energy producing materials	328,449.5***	−291.9
	(6.4)	(0.37)
Other mining	71,663.7	−289.9
	(1.48)	(0.37)
Food products, beverages, and tobacco	32,743.4	−100.4
	(0.71)	(0.13)
Textiles	31,566.8	−321.6
	(0.68)	(0.42)
Leather	27,780.8	−278.3
	(0.54)	(0.36)
Wood industry	27,441.3	−363.2
	(0.59)	(0.47)
Paper and paper products	53,521.2	−246.7
	(1.15)	(0.32)
Coke, refined petroleum products	335,577.2***	−453.7
	(7.04)	(0.58)
Chemicals	107,123.5	−290.7
	(2.3)	(0.38)
Rubber and plastic	47,271.2	−314.4
	(1.01)	(0.41)
Other nonmetallic mineral products	47,850.8	−336.3
	(1.03)	(0.44)
Basic metals and fabricated metal products	45,339.3	−41.5
	(0.97)	(0.05)
Machinery and equipment	48,465.3	−157.2
	(1.04)	(0.2)
Electrical and optical equipment	87,847.6*	−145.0
	(1.89)	(0.19)
Transport equipment	44,605.3	−176.8
	(0.96)	(0.23)
Other manufacturing.	26,623.0	−261.5
	(0.57)	(0.34)
Electricity, gas, and water supply	178,023.5***	−340.4
	(3.82)	(0.44)
Construction	24,092.7	964.4
	(0.52)	(1.25)
Wholesale and retail trade	33,565.3	2,567.5***

	Value Added per Capita 2008	Employment (in Thousands) in 2008
	(0.72)	(3.34)
Hotels and restaurants	13,030.4	858.2
	(0.28)	(1.11)
Transport, storage, and communication	60,425.6	673.9
	(1.3)	(0.88)
Financial intermediation	99,804.0***	265.8
	(2.18)	(0.35)
Real estate	69,433.1	2,353.6***
	(1.49)	(3.06)
Public administration	34,220.9	1,878.4***
	(0.73)	(2.44)
Education	23,803.8	438.6
	(0.51)	(0.57)
Health and social work	16,860.4	1,747.8**
	(0.37)	(2.27)
Other community and personal services	29,700.9	586.2
	(0.64)	(0.76)
CMEs	9,324.4	−124.2
	(0.53)	(0.42)
SMEs	−33,251.0*	125.0
	(1.68)	(0.38)
LMEs	9,143.5	2,072.3***
	(0.34)	(5.52)
Observations	378	413
R^2	0.316	0.258

Notes: T-statistics in parentheses.
Significance levels: *** $p < 0.01$; ** $p < 0.05$; * $p < 0.10$.

countries (particularly in Anglo-American economies). In this section I first relate these trends to the evolution of employment and value added per person per economic sector. I then suggest that those changes have been shaped by both technological change and trade competition – in different proportions depending on the sector at hand.

2.3.1. Employment Trends

Between 1995 and 2009, the American manufacturing sector lost about 5 million jobs – a 1.6 percent drop every year. The manufacturing sector suffered similar losses in Europe: about 5 million jobs in Germany and France between 1991 and 2009, more than 3 million in Italy between 1980 and 2009, 740,000 jobs in Scandinavia between 1980 and 2005, and 1.8 million in Portugal and

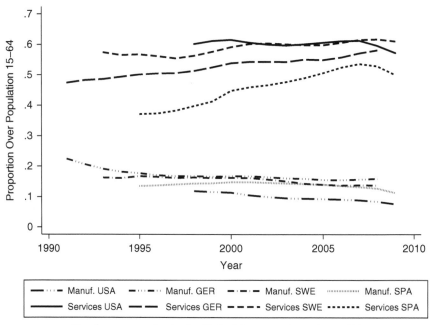

FIGURE 2.4. Employment ratios in the United States and continental Europe.
(Own elaboration based on EUROSTAT's NACE data set for Europe and from the
Bureau of Labor Statistics and the Bureau of Economic Analysis for the United States.)

Spain between 1995 and 2009 – losses equivalent to a 1.5 percent annual
decline. As a fraction of the economy, the manufacturing sector fell from around
20 percent of the working population in Germany to slightly above 15 percent and to about 10 in Europe and below 10 percent in the United States. In
Northern Europe, for which there are much longer time series, historical trends
for manufacturing were broadly similar to those in the United States and continental Europe. In 1970 the primary and secondary sector employed between
a fourth and three-tenths of the labor force. By 1990 they had declined to less
than 20 percent. By 2009 they employed 15 percent of the labor force – a proportion very similar to Germany's. Figure 2.4 plots the evolution of employment shares for selected countries.[4]

Because losses in the manufacturing sector were picked up by the service
sector, all economies added jobs in net terms. However, the rate of expansion
of the service sector varied considerably across countries. The American service
sector experienced a net gain of about 25 million jobs, or about a 1.65 percent
increase, every year from 1991 to 2009. The rate was lower in Europe. Whereas
the United States created about five net service jobs for each manufacturing

---

[4] For an analysis of employment trends by sector, see Oetsch, this volume.

job it lost, Europe only generated two on average.[5] As a share of the working population, the service sector increased from 45 percent to close to 70 percent in the Netherlands, 60 percent in the United States, and 55 percent in France. Most European jobs were generated in those areas not producing "public goods." According to the Dutch historical series, which stretches back to 1980, most of the rise in non-public-goods service jobs happened from the late 1980s onward. The "public goods" sector grew moderately in continental Europe to less than 25 percent of the labor force. It remained flat in the United States. By contrast, public employment rose sharply in Scandinavia. In Denmark, for example, it almost tripled to more than 30 percent of the working population in 2009.

Southern European countries' employment trajectory sets them apart from the rest of the advanced economies. In manufacturing trends they were similar. Italy experienced a fall in the manufacturing sector from above 25 percent in 1970 to 15 percent by 2009. Spain and Greece show similar trends over a shorter period. The only exception is Portugal, where more than 20 percent of the working population was still employed in manufacturing in 2007. As shown later, this is directly related to dismal productivity rates. Yet Southern European countries were clear laggards in the generation of service jobs: The proportion in that sector was 30 percent in 1970 (six-tenths of the Danish proportion that same year) and 50 percent in 2009 (about 20 percentage points below Denmark and the Netherlands). Sectors engaged in the generation of "public goods" employed a much lower proportion of the workforce than the rest of the OECD countries: about 15 percent of the labor force. As a result, employment ratios had remained much lower than in other countries.

2.3.2. *Trends in Value Added*
In addition to a shift in the sectoral composition of employment, all OECD economies have witnessed a substantial change in value added per sector and person. The extent of that change has varied across sectors, however, and constitutes a main (accounting) source of differential growth rates and arguably of the growth of pretax inequality. Figures 2.5 and 2.6 reproduce the evolution of value added per person employed in manufacturing, public-goods-producing sectors, and other service sectors in the United States, Germany, Sweden, and Spain.

Growth in value added per person was strong in most manufacturing industries – and stellar in a few economic sectors. Value added per person in the manufacturing sector grew by about 40 percent from €70,000 in 1990 to €100,000 in 2009 in the United States. This growth in value added was

---

[5] EUROSTAT does not reported data on employment for the United Kingdom. However, in total value added, the British manufacturing sector declined from representing more a third of total value added in the economy in 1970 to about one-sixth 35 years later.

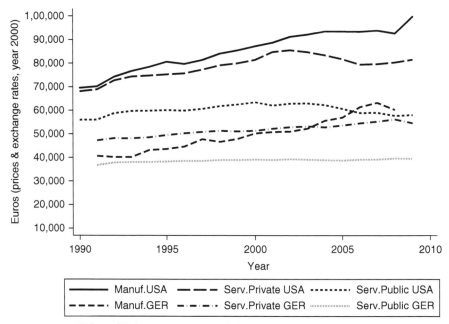

FIGURE 2.5. Value added per capita, United States and Germany.
(Own elaboration based on EUROSTAT's NACE data set for Europe and from the Bureau of Labor Statistics and the Bureau of Economic Analysis for the United States.)

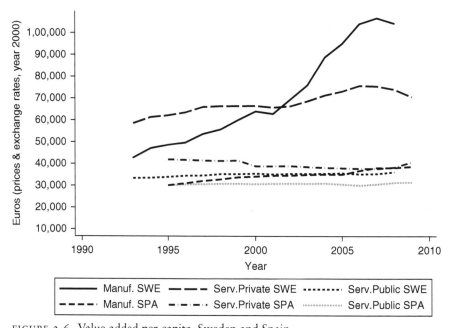

FIGURE 2.6. Value added per capita, Sweden and Spain.
(Own elaboration based on EUROSTAT's NACE data set for Europe and from the Bureau of Labor Statistics and the Bureau of Economic Analysis for the United States.)

concentrated in three main sectors: the chemical sector, which includes the pharmaceutical industry; the electrical and electronics industry, which includes the production of personal computers; and the financial sector. Growth in value added in the financial sector moderated and then became negative in the late 2000s – reflecting the economic crisis and increased regulation. All other sectors' value added per person did not change – although in some cases it remained at levels as high as or higher than that of the same sector in other countries. Value added per person in Germany increased by 50 percent although at overall lower levels – from around €40,000 to €60,000. The German chemical, electronics, and auto industries went through sharp increases in value added per person – from 100 percent in the first case to about 50 percent in the latter. The metal and machinery industry also became more productive, although at a slower pace.

Value added in the French industry grew by 25 percent after 2000 to €66,000, slightly ahead of Germany. The French chemical industry now has a value added per person identical to the American one, and both its electrical and auto industries are at the German level. But, with the exception of finance, all other sectors have seen limited increases in value added per person. In small countries such as the Netherlands and Sweden, the increase was spectacular – by 70 percent in the former and by about 145 percent in the latter – but extremely concentrated in a few sectors or subsectors. The remaining sectors, however, have experienced moderate or no gains: In fact, the Swedish auto and metal industries suffered dramatic declines after 2006. In contrast to that in the United States and Northern Europe, value added growth was more moderate in the European periphery and completely absent in Portugal.

The change in value added has occurred hand in hand with a clear-cut fall in jobs. The chemical industry now employs less than 0.8 percent of the labor force in Germany and 0.4 percent in the United States. The figures for the electrical and electronics sector are only slightly larger. As a result, total value added in the tradable sector (primary and manufacturing industries) has grown slowly in real terms: In Germany it rose from €504 billion in 1991 to €522 billion in 2008; in France from €252 billion in 1999 to €258 billion in 2008; in the United States it was around €1,200 billion in both 1990 and 2008. Smaller economies have done better: In the Netherlands it went up from €66 billion in 1991 to €93 billion in 2008; in Finland from €24 billion in 1990 to €54 billion in 2008.

In contrast to the manufacturing sector, value added in the public goods services has remained effectively flat for the last thirty years. The non-public-goods service sector diverged across countries, tracking the gains of the manufacturing sector in the United States up until 2000 – basically because of the performance of the American financial sector. But this has been the exception to the rule. Value added per person in the public goods sector has remained unchanged at around or below €40,000 in both the big and the small European economies.

In Italy, for which we have long temporal series starting in 1970, value added per person in the public goods sector rose until the early 1990s and then stayed put in the following fifteen years. This rather poor performance is due to the fact that public goods sectors are labor intensive and not readily amenable to capital-labor substitution processes, and to a corresponding low wage growth among public sector employees.

2.3.3. Interpreting the Data
Most of the slowdown in overall growth rates across OECD economies can be explained by an overall shift in the sectoral allocation of jobs: Employment growth has occurred in service sectors with low (often negative) growth rates in value added per person; jobs have actually shrunk in highly productive sectors; and the net creation of jobs has not been enough to sustain the growth rates of the Golden Age. The relatively better performance of some countries (such as the United States, Luxembourg, and Ireland) after 1980 may be attributed to the better performance of a few American service sectors (such as finance), the containment of publicly provided jobs (resulting in a much higher value added in some sectors in the United States), and the relocation of industries in the case of Ireland and Luxembourg.

The very different trajectories in value added per capita in the manufacturing and service sectors have resulted in a growing divergence across sectors. In the Netherlands, for example, the ratio between value added per person in manufacturing and in non-public-goods services rose from 1 in 1987 to 1.34 in 2009. This heterogeneity should have fundamental consequences for wage bargaining institutions, electoral politics, and the foundations of the welfare state (since it moves the underlying structure of interests away from an insurance logic accepted by sectors with similar returns and risk variance).

The evolution of the manufacturing sector, with strong improvements in continental Europe and the United States but not in Southern European countries, implies that the latter (perhaps including Italy) face strong limitations in their path to economic convergence. Since productivity is low across all sectors, their steady state should remain below that of the rest of the advanced world. It also explains the divergent performance of each economy in the aftermath of the last crisis. Germany and Scandinavia still rely on core industries that can export successfully. Southern European countries, which replaced part of their declining low-value-added industries with real estate, are now adjusting their economies downward to their "true" steady state.

The shift in employment shares and in value added levels results from two broad forces: the introduction of labor-saving techniques in standardized routine tasks and the corresponding decline of intermediate clerical and administrative positions (Autor 2010; see also Chapter 4) and the international integration of labor markets through trade, the emergence of new industrial competitors, and offshoring (Spence and Hlatshwayo 2011; Krugman 2008; see also Chapter 5).

The impact of each factor has varied with economic sector – as a function of the latter's tradability and of the competition of a similar industry in emerging economies. To explore the impact of each factor at the sectoral level, Figures 2.7a, 2.7b, and 2.7c examine the annual change in value per capita from 1995 to 2008 and employment levels from 1995 to 2007 per sector in the United States, Germany, and Italy. Agriculture, fishing, and mining are referred to by their abbreviations. Manufacturing sectors are marked with their standard coding (DA to DN). Service sectors are denoted with NT – with the exception of construction ("Con"), education ("Edu"), finance ("Fin"), government ("Gov"), health ("Hea"), real estate ("RealE"), and utilities ("Util"). The introduction of labor-saving technologies should result in declining or stagnant levels of employment *yet* increasing levels of value added per capita. By contrast, the rise of competitors in emergent economies and the process of outsourcing should lead to *both* job losses and a stagnant value added per capita.

Mining plus a subset of manufacturing sectors, normally in the low-value-added side (DA – food, DB – textiles, DC – leather, DD – wood), have declined in both value added per capita and employment – a strong indication of sharp competition from emerging economies. The remaining manufacturing sectors (from plastics to the auto industry) fall into the category of sectors that have implemented labor-saving technologies that have resulted in higher value added number but lower levels of employment. However, except two sectors (DG – chemical and pharmaceutical; DL – electrics and electronics), the annual change in value added has been generally low – below the 2 percent growth rate. The German auto industry (DM) is the only manufacturing sector where both jobs and value added have risen. The generation of net employment has concentrated in the service sector. Finally, most U.S. nontradables have experienced positive growth rates in value added per capita, whereas few sectors have in Europe. In short, new technologies and foreign competition have eroded the industrial base of those economies with a high concentration of low-value-added manufactures. By contrast, globalization has affected countries with high-value-added sectors much less.

2.4. Concluding Thoughts

Economic growth in democratic capitalist economies peaked in the so-called Golden Age. Part of that growth was due to the political and institutional conditions prevalent during the postwar period: a stable monetary and trade system at the international level; peace at the domestic level. Part of it was a function of strict technological progress (Craft and Toniolo, eds. 1996). Helped by high growth rates, economic convergence was also substantial, especially for periphery countries that moved away from an agricultural order. Still, even that high degree of catch-up did not erode long-run differences across countries rooted in their corresponding protoindustrialization processes and their timing of industrialization.

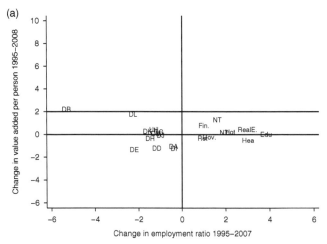

FIGURE 2.7a. Change in value added per capita and employment share in the United States. (Own elaboration based on EUROSTAT's NACE data set for Europe and from the Bureau of Labor Statistics and the Bureau of Economic Analysis for the United States.)

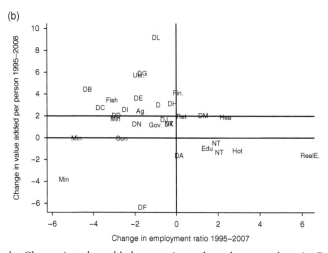

b. Change in value added per capita and employment share in Germany.
(Own elaboration based on EUROSTAT's NACE data set for Europe and from the Bureau of Labor Statistics and the Bureau of Economic Analysis for the United States.)

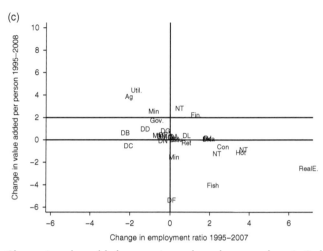

c. Change in value added per capita and employment share in Italy.
(Own elaboration based on EUROSTAT's NACE data set for Europe and from the Bureau of Labor Statistics and the Bureau of Economic Analysis for the United States.)

After the economic crisis of the 1970s, growth slowed, traditional manufacturing tradable sectors declined, and employment shifted to the service sector. Although some industrial sectors experienced very high growth rates in value added per capita, their overall weight in the economy hardly changed and in some cases it even fell – in part because they shrank in employment terms and in part because they hardly grew in total value added. The response to a declining manufacturing sector varied as a result of political and institutional factors. Some European countries (Scandinavia and, later, France) expanded the public sector. In the United States and the United Kingdom, by contrast, lower regulatory barriers and a more flexible labor market resulted in the expansion of private jobs in the service sector.

The decline of the manufacturing sector was basically driven by technological factors (plus the impact of global competition). Countries as diverse in institutional infrastructure and political traditions as the United States, Germany, or France experienced similar losses in employment and gains in value added per person in overall terms. However, the impact of those changes has varied with the sectoral composition of each country, which was, in turn, an outcome of its particular industrialization path. England and some European regions that industrialized early on succeeded only partially in adjusting to the second (and third) industrial revolution(s) – their historical trajectory may explain why their manufacturing sector has experienced a sharp fall. By contrast, Germany and the United States generated a strong industrial base during the second industrial revolution (in France, that happened later). Although they have also witnessed a strong employment shift, they have seen substantial improvements in value added per person and, particularly in the American case, have added new subindustries (in information technology and biotechnologies) in the last decades. Finally, the transformations of the last decades have taken the heaviest toll among the European laggards of the periphery. Their low-value-added industries have been eroded by both technological change and new global competitors, but they have been unable to develop high-value-added industries. As the following contributions to this volume will show, the implications of the different trajectories of the successful core industrializers and the European laggards of the periphery for domestic politics, for the future of the welfare state, and for the current state of the European integration process have been quite dramatic.

The parallel shift toward low growth and increasing economic divergence across sectors and regions in the last thirty years have several important political and institutional implications. First, slower growth makes it much harder to finance welfare states under the expectation (born during the Golden Age) that future growth would absorb current spending: the shock of the recent economic crisis has been enough to send public debt up to wartime levels. Second, as national economies become more heterogeneous and some sectors perform consistently better than the rest over time, the political consensus around high taxes and high levels of transfers and the welfare state as an insurance mechanism may unravel. Likewise, nationwide wage bargaining institutions will become weaker. As national economies become more heterogeneous, risk differentiation will be generally facilitated, while risk pooling will become generally more difficult to achieve. Third, with the Southern European countries lagging behind, fiscal and political convergence will be harder to achieve at the European level. Finally, and from a more theoretical point of view, the economic developments of the last decades call for an amended version of the claim that globalization sparks a "race to the bottom" that jeopardizes the postwar settlement of embedded liberalism. Globalization may be undercutting the position of periphery countries (in the Mediterranean basin) that combine weakly competitive industries with relatively generous welfare systems. But economic interdependence does not yet seem to threaten the position of those countries with high-value-added sectors.

3

The Origins of Dualism

David Rueda, Erik Wibbels, and Melina Altamirano

From Spain and Greece to Brazil and South Africa, dualized labor markets are a worldwide phenomenon. In many countries, workers are divided between those with permanent contracts that include valuable benefits and extensive labor market protections and those who work under contingent contracts or no contracts at all. This latter group receives few or no labor market protections and lower levels of social benefits. They are the world's labor market outsiders. Recent research has suggested that this pool of outsiders has important implications for the nature of democratic politics in the twenty-first century,[1] an argument that is perfectly in line with the core idea of this book, namely, that coalitional alignments among different labor market groups are at the heart of postindustrial reform strategies.

Yet the extent of dualization varies hugely across countries. Data on the size of the informal sector around the world (from Schneider et al. 2010) show that while there is clearly a negative association between the wealth of societies and the extent of dualization, there is also huge variation both within and across rich and developing nations. In the OECD context, the process of dualization has been linked to a number of political and economic processes: increasing competition in manufacturing, the rise of the service sector, the decline of unionization, political choices by Left governments, and others. Echoes of these arguments are present in work on developing countries, where dualization is closely linked to the informal sector and has received a lot of attention from economists and sociologists (if not political scientists). Indeed, a long tradition of models in development economics emphasize the stark income and productivity gaps inherent in "dual economies" and the uneven growth that characterizes broad swaths of the developing world (Rosenstein-Rodan 1943;

---

[1] See, for example, Mares (2006), Martin and Thelen (2007), Rueda (2007), Iversen and Stephens (2008), Palier and Thelen (2010), and the contributions to Emmenegger et al. (2012).

Ray 2010). Yet while all of these arguments emphasize important features of dualization, they often focus on the consequences rather than the causes of labor market dualism. Most existing analyses understand dualization as an exogenous factor (some countries have more of it; some countries have less of it) and explore its political and economic implications. They therefore provide little leverage for explaining why dualization varies so much among rich and middle-income countries.

We seek to explain the political origins of dualization. We argue and show that there are affinities among the nature of industrialization in the aftermath of World War II, the emergence of labor market regulations, and the extent of labor market dualism across the world today. Industrialization produces a demand for protection and insurance (called "consumption policies" in the Introduction of this book). As recognized by authors such as Katzenstein (1985), industrialization in an open economy is consistent with either very modest protection/compensation, as in the United States, or very significant compensation, as in the small states of Northern Europe. While this last benign combination of openness and social compensation (and its resulting flexibility and competitiveness) has received a lot of attention in the literature, we argue that both in the OECD and in developing countries the combination of internally oriented industrialization, stark risk differentiation in favor of insiders, and dualized labor markets has been more common. It is this set of outcomes that interests us most. Indeed, the inflexible economies of Southern Europe represent a much more general model than the rather unique flexicurity arrangements of Northern Europe.

More specifically, we argue in the following that policies developed with an eye toward internally oriented industrialization left a powerful imprint on labor market regulations aimed at protecting labor market insiders. Those labor market policies have survived the last several decades of economic liberalization thanks to a series of advantages that insiders have in electoral and interest group politics. Yet by increasing employment protection legislation and protecting workers in some of the least productive sectors, those labor market policies then become a significant determinant of labor market dualization today. Ours is a story of continuity within countries and tremendous diversity across them. We argue that this variation helps explain why some economies have generated good jobs and produced more equitable societies, while others have produced large pools of labor market outsiders.

By focusing on the origins of dualization and its temporal stability, this chapter substantiates the analytical framework of this book as developed in the Introduction. Our chapter explains how institutional legacies in the area of labor market regulation have emerged, developed, and solidified over time. These institutional legacies have become important supply side constraints on partisan politics and government choices today, as they structure an allocation of resources in favor of the consumptive needs and demands of labor market insiders. More specifically, our argument helps explain why the feasible set of reforms in contemporary Southern European countries is so restricted both institutionally and in terms of coalitional realignments. These countries indeed seem "captured" in a logic of dualization and risk differentiation.

The organization of the chapter is as follows: In the following section we provide a more detailed explanation of our main argument and explore the implications for alternative and complementary views in the existing literature. We present two claims: one connecting the process of industrialization to employment protection and the second connecting employment protection to labor market dualization. In the second section, we provide some suggestive evidence showing the link between autarkic industrialization and insider employment protection around the world. We show how resilient insider protection levels have been even in a context of general financial and economic liberalization, and we explore the relationship between insider employment protection and labor market dualization. We show that high levels of insider protection are an impressive predictor of subsequent dualization; once insiderness emerges, outsiderness follows. The final section includes our conclusion and a discussion of the implications of our argument for insider-outsider politics around the world.

3.1. Protectionism, Insiders, and Dualism

There are several ways of thinking about dualization. They represent different emphases on factors including employment status, access to benefits and protection, political representation, and citizenship.[2] For the purpose of this chapter, we follow Rueda (2005, 2006, and 2007) in understanding the division between insiders and outsiders to be essentially related to the unemployment vulnerability of different actors in the labor market. We understand insiders to be workers with highly protected jobs. They are sufficiently protected by the level of security in their jobs not to feel significantly threatened by unemployment. Outsiders, on the other hand, are unemployed, are working in the informal sector, or hold formal jobs characterized by low levels of protection and employment rights, lower salaries, and precarious levels of benefits.[3]

Because low vulnerability to unemployment is the key distinction between insiders and outsiders, the emergence of insider employment protection is the first outcome we need to explain. In the following, we argue that labor market

---

[2] For a more detailed analysis of these distinctions in industrialized democracies, see Davidsson and Naczyk (2009).

[3] To be clear, this definition distinguishes dualism that emerges from government regulation of the labor market (as in Spain, Portugal, Brazil, and others) from segmented labor markets that result primarily from the distribution of skills and labor market demand (as in the U.S. and UK). While the latter cases have seen considerable growth in low-wage, high-turnover work, it is not the result of unequal legal treatment of different classes of workers.

regulations have their roots in processes of industrialization, and we relate this claim to alternative explanations in the existing literature. We then explain what happens subsequently in countries with highly protected insiders and provide an argument for the relationship between insider employment protection and the emergence of dualized labor markets.

3.1.1. *Protectionism and the Origins of Labor Market Regulations around the World*

Industrialization exposes large numbers of market participants to a dizzying array of risks: physical injury, unemployment and business failure as a result of downturns in the business cycle or technological innovation, aging in a social context marked by the decline of traditional family networks, and others. Some of these are the direct result of industrial production while others are the result of the economic specialization that is the hallmark of industrialization. In the face of these dislocations, citizens often demand social solutions, and history shows that the widespread demand for social policy is closely associated with labor market specialization, wage labor markets, and urbanization that are inherent to the process of industrialization. Those solutions involve the use of the fiscal and regulatory power of the state to reallocate risks and the costs of mischance. Whether through spending programs for the displaced, diseased, or otherwise debilitated or regulations that make displacement less likely, social policy serves to ease the risk of participating in an industrial economy.

Key to our argument is a recognition that policy can *compensate* workers after they have suffered mischance, or it can *protect* them from mischance in the first place. While compensatory measures protect workers from ill health, aging, and unemployment *ex post,* labor market regulations are designed to protect them *ex ante.* The former set of policies can facilitate adjustments to market forces, while the latter are aimed at resisting them. This distinction is essential to the rest of this chapter because different experiences with industrialization have resulted in quite different weights on compensatory and protective social approaches to risk, and, as we discuss in the next section, the two have starkly different implications for the extent of dualization in today's globalized markets.

History shows that there is more than one path to industrialization. While some countries developed industry in the context of open markets, others pursued import substitution industrialization (ISI). In the open economy cases, policies seek to promote international competitiveness and generate foreign exchange by exporting manufactures. Complementary policies typically included export incentives, low trade barriers (with some exceptions for imports), and weak exchange rates. Import substitution industrialization, with its emphasis on heavy industry to service domestic demand, reflects a very different policy mix: trade protection, the creation and subsidization of infant industries, overvalued exchange rates to promote the importation of capital goods, and the extraction of surplus from commodity exports in order to finance the industrialization project.

While the focus of this chapter is the consequences of internally oriented industrialization, a prominent literature in political economy has emphasized the relationship between openness and compensation. In economies dependent on international markets, the costs of industrialization can be met with social compensation. As a long line of work suggests, this compensatory approach to market risks plays a prominent role in work on the development of the welfare state in Northern Europe. Whether the welfare state is seen as an efficient compromise in the face of open markets (Cameron 1978; Katzenstein 1985; Garrett 1998; Rodrik 1998; Adserá and Boix 2002) or a reflection of varieties of capitalism (Iversen 2005), social policy compensation supposedly provides the linchpin between democratic politics and open markets. In the former set of arguments, there is an affinity among democracy, open markets, and insurance from labor market risks. Adserá and Boix summarize the dynamic well: "In closed economies, politicians have few incentives to engage in substantial public spending. In open economies, a large public sector emerges as the price that the tradable part of the economy has to pay to ensure the acquiescence and cooperation of both the sheltered economy and declining tradable industries."[4] The larger the tradable sector and the greater the international economic competition, the greater the compensation. In the VoC version, high minimum wages and social insurance transfers compress the income distribution.[5] By constraining wages in those sectors where the marginal product of labor is highest, labor market insurance serves as a subsidy to investment in the most competitive sectors of the economy (even as it increases wages in nontradable sectors). These are benign accounts that emphasize how compensation, competition, and democracy can go together.

Yet, as recognized by Katzenstein (1985), *ex post* compensation is only one means of insuring against the risks of an industrial economy. By comparative standards, *ex ante* protective measures are much more common, and as we show in the following it is the most internally oriented economies that generated the most extensive *ex ante* protections for labor market insiders. Consistent with the need to respond to dynamic market signals, the most externally oriented economies promoted low levels of employment protection. They combined these with high levels of social compensation in the Scandinavian cases and low levels of compensation in the non-OECD export-led industrializers.[6]

---

[4] Adsera and Boix 2002: p.246.

[5] One might reasonably ask why some workers are willing to forgo higher wages for social insurance. The answer, as discussed in Moene and Wallerstein (2001) and Iversen and Soskice (2001), is that given some level of risk aversion, workers are willing to forgo higher income now for greater income security in the future.

[6] Katzenstein (1985) makes a distinction between social and liberal variants of corporatism (unlike the Scandinavian one emphasized previously, the liberal one is characterized by strong outward-oriented employers but weak labor). We address the role of labor in inward-oriented industrializers later.

The most extensive *ex ante* labor market protections did not develop in the smallest, most open economies; their chief constituents were not in the most trade-exposed or competitive sectors of the economy; and they have not facilitated productive dynamic labor markets in today's globalized economy. Quite the contrary, labor markets were most protective in the most closed economies, and their chief supporters were in the most internally oriented portions of the economy. In these countries, employment protections were explicitly designed for the advantage of industrial workers who benefited from trade restrictions (and public sector workers who faced no external competition). Why?

While industrialization in an open economy made market actors sensitive to the need for competiveness, adaptability, and the costs of insuring against the risks of industrialization, protectionism provided an easy means for actors in the insulated industrial sector to pass them on. Import-substituting economies allocated risks in a very particular way that produced a shared interest among capital and labor in trade and labor market protections.[7] In ISI countries, capital and labor shared a preference for limiting competition, and they coordinated to capture the rents associated with protection.[8] Capital benefited from these economic rents directly through subsidies, trade protection, and anticompetitive regulations on the domestic market; labor benefited through high wages and employment protection, which were the cost of labor peace in the protected industrial sectors.[9]

The greatest threat to labor in an industrializing economy is unemployment, and its interest vis-à-vis any prospective social policy is to protect jobs and increase wages. One can imagine workers as maximizing their expected wage income, that is, the probability of finding an industrial sector job times the industrial wage plus 1 minus that probability times the reservation wage (e.g., farm labor income). Risk is the *ex ante* probability that the worker will not be employed in the industrial labor force. This *ex ante* preferred level of insurance holds for *all* workers, not just those who hold well-paying industrial jobs. A worker's preferred level of insurance will be increasing not just in the risk of not holding an industrial job, but also in the difference between

---

[7] The argument does not necessarily imply that development strategy choices preceded social policy implementation. They can be chosen jointly, e.g., Perón's promise of substantial benefits to workers while also promoting ISI policies, or they can be chosen sequentially, as what appears to have happened in Mexico and Korea.

[8] Economic rents occur in uncompetitive product markets and are due to the market power of producers vis-à-vis consumers. Such power allows producers to charge a price for their products in excess of the price that would prevail in competitive market conditions.

[9] A link between the competitiveness of product markets and the employment conditions of employees is strongly supported by the labor economics literature. For example, a well-established empirical finding in the OECD is that employees in economies or sectors with relatively low levels of competition enjoy higher wages than those employed in companies operating in more competitive markets (Jean and Nicoletti 2002: 4). There also exists a strong cross-country association between levels of product market competition and levels of employment protection (Conway et al. 2005: 31).

industrial and nonindustrial wages and the worker's aversion to risk (Moene and Wallerstein 2001). *Ex post*, well-paid industrial workers will still want insurance to the extent that the probability they continue in that job is uncertain, and their demand for insurance will *increase* with income (Moene and Wallerstein 2001).

The severity of labor's *ex ante* and *ex post* risks was shaped by the nature of industrialization. Particularly at early stages of Fordist industrialization, manufacturing utilizes unskilled workers whose counterfactual wage in agriculture is very low. This was particularly true in import-substituting countries, which typically industrialized faster and later than their open economy counterparts. In such settings the wage gap between industrial and traditional employment tended to be very high. The high levels of inequality between manufacturing wages and farm incomes, in combination with government policies that limited the arbitrage of urban and rural wages, implied that the actuarial value of a good industrial job was higher in inward-looking industrializers; in the event of job loss, injury, sickness, and so forth, workers in such settings had farther to fall.[10]

If labor's primary interest is job stability, the interests of capital in industrializing societies center on labor peace. Since Marx, work on the sociology of industrialization has noted that urbanization and the industrial workplace serve to harmonize the interests of workers, facilitate collective action, and promote unionization (Silver 2003). In this regard, Collier and Collier's account of labor mobilization in Latin America characterizes industrialization processes more generally. They write that labor stability was most important and most threatened in the dynamic sectors of the urban industrial economy:

> The paralysis of this latter sector through strikes is therefore an important economic and political event, and the use of repression to control strikes may be especially problematic because of its effect on the skilled labor force in this sector and the greater difficulty of replacing skilled workers. (1991: 41)

Generous labor market protections, steep seniority pay, and severance payments are potential means to appease the working class and reduce the risk of labor unrest.[11] These labor market regulations had the obvious effect of insulating workers from being laid off, increasing barriers to entry into the formal industrial labor market, and increasing industrial wages.

The problem, of course, is that such policies increase costs for business. They do so by increasing the barriers to firing urban blue- and white-collar

---

[10] One can imagine labor as maximizing its expected return from current wages and its alternatives in the labor market. Where the alternatives are sufficiently poor (conditions of high inequality), it prefers spending on insurance at the expense of human capital. When the alternatives are sufficiently good (conditions of low inequality), it prefers spending on human capital that will permit increased wages in a context of an open development strategy.

[11] Indemnities are a more common policy tool than unemployment insurance in the developing world.

workers while reducing the incentives to hire additional workers from the traditional sectors. Once in place, they increase labor turnover costs and provide substantial obstacles for rural workers seeking to break into the modern sector, thereby constraining the supply of skilled workers and limiting the arbitrage between urban and rural incomes. These costs are easier to address in a closed economy than an open one. In ISI countries, product markets were both highly protected and concentrated. Protectionism ensured that producers did not have to compete with foreign companies, and concentrated markets (a typical by-product of protection, monopolistic state-owned enterprises, and economies of scale) ensured that capital did not face domestic price competition. With captured product markets, capital was free to raise prices, serving to externalize the costs of labor market regulations onto all of society. No such option was available to firms in open economy industrializers as they faced prices set on global markets.

Thus, labor colludes with capital to share the rents of protection in inward-looking industrializers. As in the open economies, unions grow in strength in ISI countries because they act as a buffer against the increasing uncertainties brought about by industrialization. Although referring to an earlier process of industrialization, Agell's (2002) explanation of organized labor's role resonates with the late industrialization of inward-looking countries. In these cases, union strength develops as a response to the specialization-related insecurities inherent to industrialization. Unions provide employment provision services, unemployment benefits, and union member protection (through pressure on employers for bans on overtime work, "short time" work arrangements as a substitute for lay-offs, etc.).[12] Unlike in open economies, however, the consequence of this increased labor power is *ex ante* protection in inward-looking industrializers. It could be argued that *ex ante* protection should be equivalent to *ex post* compensation for insiders if they are indifferent between severance pay and unemployment benefits for the same value.[13] Nevertheless, immediate *ex ante* protection is more attractive than the more conditional possibility of *ex post* compensation, particularly if the latter is subject to the give and take of budgetary and partisan politics. These protections, in turn, have important implications for competitiveness and the development of labor markets. While *ex post* compensation is associated with the positive developments mentioned – it can subsidize investments in the most competitive sectors of the economy, allows workers to invest in specialized skills, and so on – *ex ante* protection promotes labor market segmentation.

Our argument implies a specific historical development of employment protection as a consequence of post–World War II economic development.

---

[12] In the OECD countries, in this period inward-looking industrialization coincides with other factors magnifying the influence of organized labor (full employment, labor unrest, Keynesian macroeconomic management, etc).

[13] See Fernandez-Albertos and Manzano (2008).

Empirically, this is clearer in OECD countries (where the data are more readily available). First, starting in the late 1960s, firms accepted highly restrictive tenure and severance pay arrangements – see Blanchard and Summers (1986) and Bentolila and Bertola (1990). In many respects, the creation of a significant degree of "insiderness" (defined as protection for those in standard employment) starts at this point in most OECD countries. This explanation of the development of employment protection in the OECD is consistent with that emerging from the work of Allard (2005). Allard has created a historical series based on the OECD's employment protection legislation indicator (OECD 1999, chapter 2). Her indicator provides a picture of "fairly unregulated labor markets in the OECD overall during the 1950s and early 1960s, with sharp increases in regulation clustered in the 1964–1978 period" (p. 8). We will show in the following that these highly diverse cross-national levels of employment protection are, in fact, strongly correlated with the nature of industrialization.[14]

3.1.2. Employment Protection and Labor Market Dualization

By the end of the 1970s a substantial share of labor in many countries around the world had become significantly insulated from unemployment by restrictive legislation. Our second claim is that where the advantages of insiders dominate, labor market policies built for an era of protectionism have persisted and served to block the labor market adjustments needed in a world of increasingly open markets. In these cases, proinsider labor market policies have become a source of social exclusion and segmented labor markets even as they are a robust political equilibrium.

In our account, just as insiderness established itself in those countries that had experienced protectionistic industrialization, a new set of challenges was developing. A large body of work has described the economic shocks associated with the liberalization of the global economy beginning in the 1980s. A common result across all of these cases – developed and developing, open market and import-substituting industrializers alike – was a pronounced process of deindustrialization. A fairly extensive literature in economics has examined the extent of deindustrialization across the world (Pieper 2000; Rowthorn and Coutts 2004). Explanations range from the technological bias of contemporary manufacturing, to the diminishing marginal returns, to the consumption

---

[14] Our argument is not that the nature of industrialization is the only factor that matters. Blanchard et al. (1986) argue that this process was influenced by a pattern of stability and growth that allowed firms to consider employment protection as relatively costless. Esping-Andersen (1999) argues that Catholic political culture is one of the sources of strict job security regulations (but Emmenegger 2011 finds no evidence for this). Bentolila and Bertola point out that the post–oil shock crises contributed to a further reinforcement of legislation in France and the UK, among other countries, around 1975 (Bentolila and Bertola 1990: 394). And many analysts agree that these later developments were influenced by social unrest and union activism. We are unable to arbitrate among these competing arguments in our analysis later.

of manufactured goods as incomes increase. More important for the focus of this chapter is the challenge that deindustrialization represents for insider protection.

Since many of the factors emphasized by standard explanations of deindustrialization are common across countries, they provide limited leverage to explain cross-country variation in the extent of labor market dualization. The fact that industry had shrunk and production changes demanding flexibility were more common did not imply that outsiderness had to grow. Indeed, the proponents of market reforms argued that while the reallocation of labor and capital inherent in liberalizing policy would certainly destroy some jobs, they would produce new ones in more efficient sectors. Yet, while the transition from an industrial to a postindustrial economy proceeded relatively smoothly in some countries, it did not in others. In the former cases, relatively flexible labor markets facilitated the transition; in the latter cases, labor market protections complicated the transition by protecting insiders and promoting the growth of a large pool of labor market outsiders.

We argue that even where they are large in number, labor market outsiders face stark disadvantages in the democratic process when compared with their insider counterparts. While labor market insiders benefit from concentrated interests and impressive powers of collective action, outsiders have heterogeneous preferences and face severe limitations on collective mobilization. Thus, outsiders tend not to share a programmatic orientation that would enable them to serve as a key constituency for political parties. Unlike traditional classes or even coherent interest groups, the pool of outsiders is composed of a large number of individuals with few shared interests and even fewer incentives and capabilities to organize around them.

In economies where insiders are well protected, therefore, the logic of policy change becomes a profoundly dualizing one. When insiders are sufficiently powerful, the need for flexibility to achieve international competitiveness will not result in lower employment protection. The relationship between insider-outsider differences and employment protection can therefore be best understood as a reinforcing loop playing itself out since the late 1970s. Once insider employment protection is high, it allows insiders to direct adjustment strategies by facilitating the emergence of an outsider sector, which allows for the continuation of high levels of insider protection. Thus, where the advantages of insiders dominate, labor market policies built for an era of protectionism have persisted as institutional legacies (cf. Chapter 1, this volume), constrained reform strategies, and slowed economic adjustments to a world of open markets.

In developing countries, instead of a boom in new employment opportunities afforded by liberalized markets, millions of workers and small businesses had to fend for themselves in a burgeoning informal sector. Though there are important debates about what exactly constitutes the informal sector, the crucial characteristic for our purpose is that it is defined by work that occurs outside the legal system of taxing, spending, and regulation. Informal work spans a broad range of activity ranging from small manufacturing firms, to pirates of intellectual property, house cleaners, and everything in between. Informal sectors have become a permanent feature of many developing economies, and a huge body of work has emerged in response (Turnham et al. 1990; Centeno and Portes 2006; de Soto 1989; Gerxhani 2004; Tokman 1992; Maloney 1999; Levy 2008). Generally speaking, informal sectors grow as a result of coping strategies on the part of workers without alternative employment opportunities and the desire of firms to avoid regulations.[15]

In a similar way, the need for flexibility did not result in lower employment protection in many OECD countries. Instead, the flexibilization of labor market legislation that took place in the 1980s affected entry into (not exit from) the labor market (see, for example, Bentolila and Bertola 1990). One of the consequences of this process was a dramatic increase in part-time work and temporary contracts (Maier 1994). The great majority of part-time work and temporary contracts, however, pay poorly, are concentrated in low-skilled activities, and offer a precarious level of benefits and employment rights.[16] Moreover, the precariously employed and the unemployed are the main, if not the only, group to suffer the consequences of economic fluctuations (being hired in good times and fired in downturns).[17]

3.2. Evidence on the Links among Industrialization, Labor Market Protections, and Dualization

Unfortunately, all of the key concepts discussed previously – internally orientated industrialization, labor market protections, and dualization – are difficult to measure across a broad cross section of countries, and there is almost no means of measuring them in a common way as one goes further back in history. That being the case, we present three waves of highly preliminary evidence bearing on our argument. With each wave, we present evidence for as large a sample of countries as possible, albeit using data that only partially capture the key concepts, and then present results for the OECD sample for which we have

---

[15] The World Bank defines coping strategies in terms of casual jobs, temporary jobs, unpaid jobs, subsistence agriculture, and multiple job holding. It defines illegal business activity in terms of tax evasion, avoidance of labor regulation and other government regulations, and failure to register companies. See: http://lnweb90.worldbank.org/eca/eca.nsf/0/2e4ede543787a0c085256a94 0073f4e4?OpenDocument

[16] See, for example, Maier (1994) for an analysis of part-time legislation and Mosley (1994) for a description of temporary employment in Europe. See also the contributions in Gregory et al. (2000).

[17] Immigration also plays an important role in buffering insiders. In fact, it could easily be argued that immigrants are the ultimate outsiders. Immigrant labor is not emphasized in this chapter, but see King and Rueda (2008) for a more detailed analysis of this issue taking the insider-outsider model as its starting point.

better data. First, we show the cross-country association between trade distortions in the 1960s–1970s and subsequent labor market regulations; we have to rely on more modern labor market regulatory data because there are very few data for the developing world that date to even the 1980s. Second, we show that labor market regulations are extremely stable through time. In light of the data constraints discussed, we provide results only for Latin America and the OECD, the two regions where we have a reasonably long time series that is comparable. Third, we show that labor market regulations are associated with larger pools of outsiders. We do so with a measure of the size of the informal workforce for a large cross section of countries and then show more refined results for the OECD. The results are only suggestive, but they are broadly consistent with our argument.

3.2.1. Industrialization and Labor Market Protections

To test our argument on the link between internally oriented industrialization and labor market protections, we would like to have a measure of internal-orientation circa the 1960s and for the initial decades when labor market reforms are passed. It is not obvious how to measure internal orientation during industrialization (Gibson and Ward 1992; Nomi 1997; Balassa 1981; Aitken 1992). In this section, we understand industrialization to take place during the 1960s and 1970s, and we measure outward-looking orientations as trade openness. As a proxy that covers as many cases as possible, we rely on Hiscox and Kastner's (2004) data on trade distortions. They use fixed country-year effects in a gravity model to produce an index of trade distortions. This measure has the important advantage over traditional trade ratios of internalizing the impact of country size and distance from markets on trade patterns. To maximize country coverage, we take the average for all countries over the course of the 1970s.

Cross-national data on labor market regulations are very hard to come by, particularly for the years before 2000. That being the case, we rely on more recent data that are reasonably close to approximating our desire to measure obstacles to hiring and firing workers on fixed contracts. The first is a summary measure of "labor freedom" produced by the Heritage Foundation on the basis of the World Bank's *Doing Business* report. The measure equally weights data on six dimensions: hindrance to hiring additional workers, rigidity of regulations on working hours, the ratio of minimum wage to the average value added per worker, difficulty of firing redundant employees, the legally mandated notice period for firing an employee, and mandatory severance pay. The measure is scaled from 0 to 100, with labor regulations falling across the scale. The second, more focused measure is on the cost of firing a worker. Botero et al (2004) collect data on the cost of firing a worker by calculating the sum of the notice period, severance pay, and any mandatory penalties established by law or mandatory collective agreements for a worker with three years of tenure with the firm. Figure 3.1a plots each of these measures against the trade

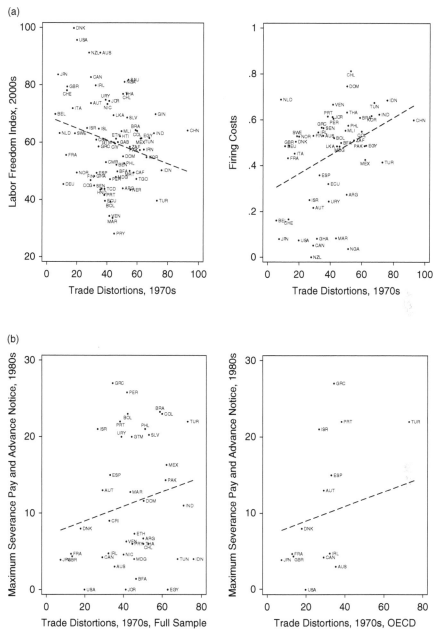

FIGURE 3.1. Early trade distortions and labor market policies. (a.) Trade distortions and general labor market regulations. (b.) Trade distortions and severance costs, full sample (left panel) and OECD.

distortions measure discussed. Though there is obviously considerable noise, there is clearly a negative relationship between labor "freedom" and a history of import substitution (as proxied by trade distortions). Likewise, the costs of firing workers increase with such a history. Obviously, one would like to see whether these relationships hold in the face of multivariate analysis and alternative measures of labor protections, but the initial findings are broadly consistent with our hypothesis, even if the results with regard to the cases in the developing world are less clear. As discussed in Wibbels (2014), deviations from gravity-model trade predictions as per Hiscox and Kastner (2004) mask important variations in trade policy. While export-led industrializers (such as Korea) and import-competing industrializers (such as Brazil) look very similar on the trade distortions data, they do so for different reasons. While the export-led cases subsidized exports and limited imports (of consumer manufactured, if not capital, goods), import substituters subsidized the importation of capital goods and taxed exports. Wibbels (2014) shows that the link between import substitution and labor market policies is clearer in the developing world when using a measure of the share of manufactures *not* exported, even if such a measure is hard to make comparable across years and a sample that includes the OECD.

We can complement the analysis in Figure 3.1a with data produced by the IMF on employment protection legislation in low-, middle-, and high-income countries. To ensure comparability across different groups of countries (as well as over time), the IMF extends the OECD methodology for collecting and coding the information to the non-OECD countries in the sample. The data in Figure 3.1b reflect the maximum legally mandated severance payments and advanced notice period in months (see Aleksynska and Schindler 2011 for details). Severance pay is measured as monthly salary equivalents and coded according to the OECD methodology. The picture emerging from Figure 3.1b is quite similar to that in Figure 3.1a. The left panel contains all the countries in the sample while in the right panel there are only OECD countries. In the OECD, countries where trade distortions were high in the 1970s (e.g., Greece, Portugal, Spain, Israel, and Austria) have high levels of insider employment protection in the 1980s. Countries where trade distortions were low in the 1970s (e.g., the United States, Japan, or Switzerland) have low levels of insider employment protection in the 1980s. While the relationship is not perfect, both panels in Figure 3.1b are broadly supportive of our claims.

3.2.2. *The Stability of Labor Market Regulations through Time*
We argue that ISI is linked to contemporary rates of dualization via labor market regulations, which we hypothesize have proven highly resilient in the face of the political power of labor market insiders. As noted previously, beginning in the late 1970s and running through the following decades, politicians and the private sector in many countries, including many former import

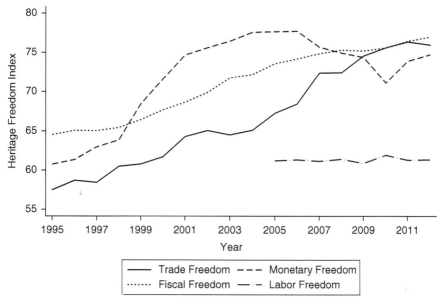

FIGURE 3.2. Economic policy through time in developing and OECD countries.

substituters, fundamentally reoriented their economies, and the era of "state-led development" came to a halt. Trade liberalization, macroeconomic discipline, capital account liberalization, privatization of state-owned enterprises, and the like, swept across the globe. Given that labor markets in import substituters had been built around a dated vision of economic policy, one might have expected labor market policies to follow the common liberalizing trend. As explained earlier, we expect otherwise – the power of insiders should produce tremendous persistence in labor market policies, despite the sea change in other policy spheres.

Keeping in mind how difficult it is to find comparable time-series data Figure 3.2 provides some initial, suggestive evidence. The figure displays Heritage Foundation data on trade, fiscal, monetary, and labor market policies from 1995 to 2011 for both the OECD and developing worlds. Though the data on labor markets are available for only half of this period, they evince a very different trend from those bearing on trade, fiscal, and monetary policies. While the macroeconomic policy tools have undergone a steady process of liberalization, labor market policies have barely moved at all.

We can further explore the stability of labor market regulations by looking back at the IMF data described in Figure 3.1b. Figure 3.3a captures the maximum of both the legally mandated severance payments and notice periods for workers with nine months, four years, or twenty years of experience (see Aleksynska and Schindler 2011 for details). The figure compares these levels of employment protection (measured as monthly salary equivalents) in two periods: the 1980s and

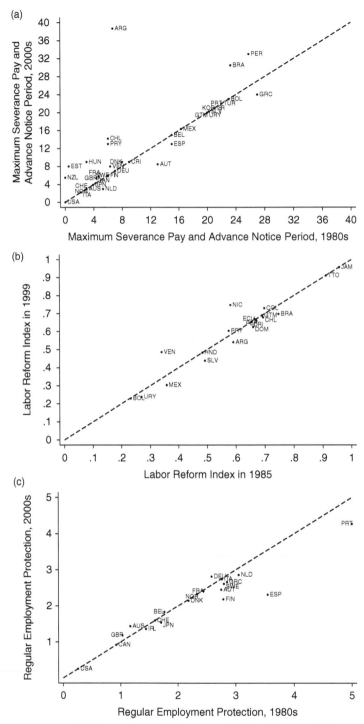

FIGURE 3.3. Labor market policies across the decades around the world, Latin America and the OECD. (a.) Severance pay around the world in the 1980s and 2000s. (b.) Labor market reform index in 1985 and 1999 in nineteen Latin American countries. (c.) Labor market policies in the 1980s and 2000s in OECD countries.

the 2000s. The 45-degree line in the figure denotes no change at all, and, remarkably, most cases fall quite close to (if not on) the line.

Moving beyond comparable measures for OECD and non-OECD countries, the two exceptions to the paucity of cross-sectional, time-series data on labor market regulations are from Lora (2001), who report annual data on various reform indices for nineteen Latin American countries from 1985 through 1999 and an OECD measure on regular employment protection available from the early 1980s. Latin America is interesting because many of its countries pursued a particularly aggressive version of market liberalization; it is also a region with a high concentration of countries that have a history of import substitution. The OECD, on the other hand, is the region where there has been the most research on insider-outsider labor markets and politics. For the OECD cases, we can use a better measure of insider employment protection. We analyze an indicator summarizing the main aspects of dismissal protection for workers with regular contracts. The OECD indicator incorporates three aspects of dismissal protection: "*(i)* procedural inconveniences that employers face when starting the dismissal process, such as notification and consultation requirements; *(ii)* notice periods and severance pay, which typically vary by tenure of the employee; and *(iii)* difficulty of dismissal, as determined by the circumstances in which it is possible to dismiss workers, as well as the repercussions for the employer if a dismissal is found to be unfair (such as compensation and reinstatement)" (Venn 2007: 6).

Figures 3.3b and 3.3c show that the picture that emerges in the Heritage data in Figure 3.2 and in the IMF data in Figure 3.3a is not the result of averaging across countries. Figure 3.3b shows that most of the countries in Latin America pursued basically the same labor market policies in 1999 as they did in 1985. Again, most cases fall quite close to the 45-degree line denoting no change at all. Though deviations from the line are very limited, it is worth noting that the former import substituters, including Mexico, Argentina, and Brazil, have, if anything, made policy more restrictive rather than more liberal over the fifteen-year period. At least in the Latin American sample, it seems that labor markets have seen much less reform than other areas of public policy. Figure 3.3c presents a very similar picture for the countries in the OECD. Cases are again concentrated along the 45-degree line. Only in Spain and Portugal have extremely high levels of insider employment protection in the 1980s become less high in the 2000s (but these two countries remain within the group characterized by the highest levels of insider employment protection).[18]

Given the historical link between ISI and proinsider labor market regulations, it seems reasonable to expect that restrictive labor market policies would have gone the way of other policies that characterized the internally

---

[18] In the case of Spain, the attack on the employment protection of insiders (even if marginal) was one of the consequences of conservative governments starting in 1996. This chapter does not emphasize the connection between insider protection and Left government, but see Rueda (2007) for an analysis of this topic.

oriented development model. Yet while differential exchange rates, high tariffs, state-owned enterprises, industrial subsidies, and the like, have disappeared, proinsider labor market policies have persisted. The power of insiders has been born of their continued organizational strength in the nontradable service and state sectors, where for various reasons, employers can pass on high costs to the entire domestic market of consumers. These groups are the political legacy of the era of import substitution. Their privileged economic and organizational position stands in stark contrast to the heterogeneous interests and weak capacity for action among the outsiders. In many cases, the economic and organizational strength of insiders makes them privileged constituents for political parties and provides them influence when governments consider social policy reforms. Given the centrality of labor market regulations for the very survival of insiders, they have spent considerable resources blocking microeconomic reforms, even as they passed on various macroeconomic ones that, while painful, did not strike at their very survival (Murillo and Schrank 2009).

3.2.3. Labor Market Regulations and Dualization

Finally, we turn to our last explanandum: labor market dualization. An ideal measure of dualization would include the unemployed, the involuntarily underemployed, those on contingent contracts, and those in the shadow economy. But, again, there are no such data for a large cross section of countries (indeed, there are not even comparable unemployment data). As a first cut we rely on an indicator of the size of the informal labor market. Measuring the size of this pool of labor market outsiders is a daunting task complicated by the fact that much of the work and production take place outside the purview of tax authorities, regulators, and many survey firms (La Porta and Shleifer 2008). Neither workers nor firms declare earnings to the government, and both firm and income surveys have a hard time reaching individuals in the informal sector. We therefore use a measure provided by the *Global Competitiveness Report 2006–2007* based on a survey of business leaders in which they were asked to estimate the amount of business activity that is unregulated (Lopez-Claros et al. 2006).

For the OECD and non-OECD sample, our key independent variables are assorted measures of labor market regulations that proxy for proinsiderness. We rely on the measure of labor market freedom from the Heritage Foundation and the measure of severance costs from the IMF described earlier. We then add three measures provided by the Frasier Institute. The first is a product of the World Competitiveness surveys, which ask respondents whether the hiring and firing of workers are impeded by regulations or flexibly determined by employers; it is scaled from 1 to 8, with regulations declining across the scale. The second measure is the cost of dismissing workers and is calculated by the Frasier Institute on the basis of the World Bank's *Doing Business* data. The measure includes information on the advance notice, cost, and penalties for firing a worker, with regulations again falling across the scale. Finally, we also rely on

TABLE 3.1. *Labor market regulations and the size of the informal sector*

	Model 1	Model 2	Model 3	Model 4	Model 5
Hire/fire	−0.704 (0.446)				
Dismissal		−0.677*** (0.227)			
Labor freedom			−0.103** (0.0435)		
Collective relations				13.63** (6.177)	
Severance costs					0.141 (0.0874)
GDPpc (logged)	−9.108*** (0.746)	−7.887*** (0.843)	−8.396*** (0.778)	−9.626*** (1.035)	−5.969*** (0.817)
Constant	115.5*** (7.383)	104.3*** (7.556)	111.9*** (6.915)	110.3*** (10.23)	78.75*** (7.401)
Observations	67	63	68	47	54
Adj. R^2	0.695	0.720	0.708	0.660	0.513

Notes: Standard errors in parentheses.
*$p < 0.1$, **$p < 0.05$, ***$p < 0.01$.

the Fraser Institute's data on collective bargaining, with the expectation that peak level bargaining will produce proinsider policies. The Frasier Institute produces an index scaled from 1 to 7 designed to capture the extent to which wages are set at the firm-level (=7) or by a collective bargaining process (=1).

Probably the only standard finding in the small cross-national quantitative literature on informality is that there is an inverse relationship between societal wealth and informality. Because of this, we run a series of simple models that control for logged per capita income. The key independent variable in each model is one of the indicators of labor market regulations discussed. We limit the sample to countries that have had some history of industrialization and have populations that exceed 2 million people.[19] Table 3.1 reports the results of the five models described. The findings suggest that protective labor regulations are associated with a larger informal sector (different signs reflect different codings of the labor market regulation variables). While the relationship is less clear for some indicators, the overall results show that informal employment is climbing in the restrictiveness of labor regulations.

Our OECD sample allows us once more to use a measure for the dualization of labor markets that better addresses our theoretical claims. In Figure 3.4 we again

[19] We operationalize a history of industrialization as an industry to GDP ratio in excess of 20 percent at some point since 1980.

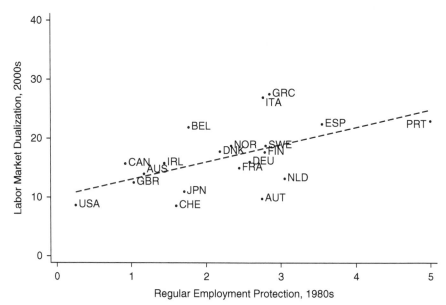

FIGURE 3.4. The relationship between employment protection and labor market dualization in the OECD.

use the OECD index of insider protection as country averages for the 1980s used in Figure 3.3c. We then use a measure of labor market dualization in the 2000s that includes individuals who are unemployed, in fixed-term employment, and in involuntary part-time employment as a percentage of the civilian labor force.

Given the importance of secure employment to the definition of insiders, including the unemployed within the category of outsiders is not controversial. The classification of fixed-term and part-time employment is perhaps not as straightforward. There are two aspects to employed "outsiderness." The first is related to the precarious nature of employment. Fixed-term and part-time jobs are not simply insider contracts with added flexibility; they are, in fact, characterized by low wages, protection, and rights (see, for example, OECD 1998). The second relates to the involuntary nature of outsider employment. Most outsiders would like to have insider jobs. This is particularly the case when looking at fixed-term employment (most workers holding fixed-term contracts in the OECD do so involuntarily), but it is also the reason why we focus on involuntary part-timers.[20]

Figure 3.4 again presents some evidence in support of this chapter's arguments. In the OECD, countries with high levels of insider employment

---

[20] Because of missing data, labor market dualization is measured only as unemployment and involuntary part-time employment in Australia and New Zealand and only as unemployment in the U.S.

protection in the 1980s developed high levels of labor market dualization in the 2000s. It is, in fact, the case that this relationship would also be present if we used labor market dualization data from the 1990s. Notoriously dualized countries such as Spain and Portugal are an example of this combination of high insider employment protection and high labor market dualization, but so are Finland, Sweden, and the Netherlands. Countries such as the United States, the United Kingdom, Australia, Switzerland, Ireland, and Denmark are examples of very limited insider employment protection in the 1980s, which then promoted low levels of labor market dualization in the 2000s.

3.3. Conclusions

While protections from labor market risks might have facilitated skill investments, helped overcome labor market failures, and increased overall productivity in a small handful of European countries, they have led to bifurcated, unproductive labor markets across many other OECD countries and most of the developing world. Built as they were for the demands of autarkic economic policies, systems of social protection built upon *ex ante* protections have proven poorly adapted for a world of open economies. Such systems limit the capacity of workers to enter the formal economy, reduce their incentives to gather human capital (the returns of which are low in the informal sector), and encourage investments in low-productivity sectors. As a result, labor regulations that date to protectionist processes of industrialization have contributed to the growth of informal sectors, weak labor productivity, and income inequality.[21]

Above and beyond the economic costs associated with bifurcated labor markets, our account of their origins and effects speaks to the overall framework of this volume and has implications for further related literatures in at least three ways. First, although not one of the goals of a volume that mostly focuses on advanced capitalism, it provides a framework for unifying the study of the welfare state and labor markets in developed and developing countries. A host of recent contributions have provided rich insight into the link between global markets and changes in social priorities, innovations in targeted poverty relief, and social policy reform in the developing world. In the OECD, an equally significant literature has emphasized the changing nature of the welfare state (and the role of conditionality and workfare).[22]

---

[21] The claim that insider-oriented labor market protections are inefficient does not necessarily conflict with Boix's finding in this volume. In his chapter, Boix shows that Kenworthy's index of wage coordination and Blanchard and Wolfers's index of employment protection are not correlated with economic growth. It is the nature of economic growth that is of interest to our argument. We contend that ex ante labor market protections tend to encourage low productivity growth with limited human capital investment.

[22] See, for example, Rueda (forthcoming).

But most of these literatures are focused on *changes* in social policy, even if researchers draw on different theoretical traditions, develop distinct causal claims, and use diverse empirical methods. Clearly, by emphasizing insider employment protection and uniting OECD and non-OECD cases, we tend to see continuity where others see considerable change. More generally, we believe there is considerable room for unifying the study of welfare states and social protection across the developing and developed world around a set of simple factors – labor market risks, the competitiveness of markets, interest organization and representation, and partisan politics – that characterize democratic capitalism the world over.

Second, we place a specific set of actors, policies, and institutions – those relating to labor markets – at the center of the analysis and link them to the emergence and extent of bifurcated labor markets. This approach is not entirely new, but our findings do call into question the generality of an influential claim in research on advanced industrial democracies. In some European countries, extensive systems of social insurance that broadly share risks coexist with highly productive economies. In some accounts, social policy, labor market regulations, educational systems, and other factors constitute an equilibrium political outcome that promotes economic competitiveness; this is a virtuous story in which many good things go together. We diverge from such accounts by describing an equilibrium in which social insurance persists despite huge negative effects on economic efficiency. Efficient *ex post* compensation is much less common than inefficient *ex ante* protection in most developing countries, but also in some OECD countries. In the introductory chapter of this book, the political economy of countries with such an institutional legacy has been referred to as a model of "capture," because weak state capacity is combined with strongly consumption-oriented institutional legacies. Structuralist or functionalist accounts cannot explain the persistence of such an institutional arrangement, which is clearly economically inefficient and limits occupational change and adaptation. Such regulations also severely constrain the range of political reform strategies. A reorientation of consumptive to investive state expenditures and regulations is politically difficult because institutional constraints and the configuration of preferences and power relations all but preclude the emergence of an investment-oriented reform coalition.

Third and finally, our account speaks to the sustainability of markets and democracy in a globalized world. An enormous body of work on the OECD suggests that social policies have served a key role in mediating the relationship between capitalism and democracy. Absent the security provided by social insurance, citizens would reject the creative destruction inherent in the market and fail to make productivity enhancing investments that generate returns over the long run. Fueled by the democratic power to vote and organize, citizens have demanded insurance as compensation for the costs of open economies. If *ex post* social compensation has played a key role in smoothing citizen participation in markets in a handful of OECD countries, *ex ante* employment protection across much of the rest of the world would seem ill equipped to fill such a role. It benefits too few citizens located in the least propitious portions of the economy and does so while generating distortionary economic incentives and limiting opportunities for many entrepreneurs and workers. The political consequences of the failure of social insurance to be the glue binding democratic politics and market participation can be quite damaging.

4

Occupational Structure and Labor Market Change in Western Europe since 1990

Daniel Oesch

Observers of social change have been fascinated for a long time by the question of how the employment structure evolves: toward good jobs, bad jobs, or increasing polarization? Three issues are at stake. At the microlevel of single jobs, the concern is with the quality of new employment created. The question raised is to know whether jobs are becoming better paid, more highly skilled, and endowed with greater autonomy. At the macrolevel of social structure, the debate evolves around the question whether occupational change transforms affluent countries into large middle-class societies or, on the contrary, into increasingly divided class societies. The two levels of analysis are bridged by the concern for social mobility. Here, the question is as to whether change in the employment structure allows forthcoming generations to move to more rewarding jobs than those held by their parents – or whether downward mobility is the more likely outcome. The direction of change has then manifest implications for parties' electoral constituencies and citizens' political preferences.

This chapter strives to shed light on some of these issues by analyzing the pattern of occupational change in Western Europe since 1990. It does so by examining the evolution of the employment structure with large-scale microlevel data for Britain, Denmark, Germany, Spain, and Switzerland. The central question is to know what kind of occupations have been expanding and declining over the last two decades: high-paid jobs, low-paid jobs, or both?

Our analysis shows that the five countries under study underwent a process of major occupational upgrading. The only ambiguity concerns the question whether the process is clear-cut or has a polarizing twist to it. The labor market created ample opportunities at the high-skilled end of the occupational structure but made perspectives bleak in the lower-middle range of jobs held by clerks and production workers. Depending on whether low-end services expanded or not, countries find themselves with a more or less polarized version of upgrading. In order to make sense of the pattern of occupational change, we examine how the class structure and the sectoral distribution of employment evolved since 1990. In parallel, we discuss how it is possible that large numbers of low-skilled jobs vanished over the last two decades without leading to a significant rise in low-skilled unemployment. The key lies in massive educational expansion: Not only low-skilled jobs, but also the low-skilled workers themselves have become more rare over the last two decades.

By analyzing occupational change in postindustrial economies, this chapter contributes to the overall framework of this book by shedding light on the demand side constraints of government choices. The introductory chapter to this volume argues that the feasible reform strategies of governments depend – among other factors – on the availability of potential sociostructural support coalitions. In this vein, occupational upgrading may alter the political balance of power among different classes and political concerns.

This chapter is structured as follows. Section 4.1 presents a snapshot of the long-running debate in the social sciences on occupational change. Section 4.2 moves on to the empirical analysis and presents the data and analytical strategy. Section 4.3 documents change in the employment structure since 1990 and looks at the evolution of the class structure over the same period. Section 4.4 retraces the evolution of low-skilled unemployment and examines the increase in the workforce's educational attainment. Section 4.5 tentatively discusses the social and political implications of upgrading: its potential influence on social inequality and political preferences. Section 4.6 concludes with a summary and an outlook.

4.1. The Debate in the Literature on Occupational Change

The debate about the direction of occupational change is as old as the social sciences. Karl Marx, and Marxists after him, held a deeply pessimistic view of the impact of capitalism on the employment structure. Employers were expected to use technology in the struggle between antagonistic classes as a means to fragment work tasks, reduce work autonomy, and increase supervision. Workers would become deskilled and the occupational structure downgrade as self-employed artisans were gradually transformed into wage labor, craft workers into machinists, and clerks into operatives (Braverman 1974; Wright and Singelmann 1982).

This gloomy expectation contrasts with the optimistic view of Industrialism that North American social scientists developed in the postwar decades partly as a response to Marxist immiseration theory (Kerr et al. 1960; Blauner 1964). Industrial society and its corollary of a rationally developed technology were seen as leading to growing differentiation within the workforce and hence to an increased demand for skilled labor. From the late 1960s onward, industrialism gives way to the theory of postindustrial society and the expectation that economic activity would be dominated by knowledge workers (Fuchs 1968; Bell 1973). Scientific progress and service sector expansion were expected to increase the need for professional and managerial expertise constantly at the expense of routine production tasks. In the early 1990s, this optimistic account of technology-driven upskilling became widely accepted in economics under the name of skill-biased technological change (SBTC). SBTC posits that technology is complementary to high-skilled labor but substitutes for low-skilled labor (Berman et al. 1998). While the occupational structure upgrades, the employment prospects of low-qualified workers deteriorate.

In parallel to the expanding literature on SBTC, several authors maintained that the impact of technology on the employment structure is not stable over time: While electrification and, more recently, computerization had increased the demand for skilled relative to unskilled labor, mechanization in the nineteenth century had shifted employment away from skilled artisans toward unskilled factory workers (Katz 1999: 236, Manning 2004: 603). This argument led to the routinization thesis of technological change: The idea is that computers have taken over routine production and clerical tasks – yet these tasks are typically done in intermediate jobs. In contrast, computers cannot substitute for many interpersonal service tasks such as restaurant waiting, caregiving, or cleaning that are done in jobs set at the bottom of the occupational hierarchy. Modern technology may thus complement both high-skilled analytical and low-skilled interpersonal service jobs, but hollow out the middle of the employment structure, occupied by industrial workers and office clerks (Autor et al. 2003).

The polarization argument was already put forward in the 1970s and 1980s by proponents of dual labor market theories who argued that the workforces were divided into a primary (or internal) segment of well-paid and stable jobs occupied by insiders and a secondary (or external) segment of low-skilled and insecure jobs left to outsiders (Doeringer and Piore 1971; Lindbeck and Snower 1986). This division between a protected core and a vulnerable periphery was explained either by firms' response to technological change (Doeringer and Piore 1971) or by labor market institutions such as job protection legislation and collective bargaining rights (Lindbeck and Snower 1986) – a strand of research revived in recent years under the name of dualization (Emmenegger et al. 2012).

The focus on institutions has the advantage of explaining country differences in occupational change: Unlike technology, institutions vary across economically advanced countries. Institutional accounts such as the varieties of capitalism approach thus expect occupational upgrading to take place in countries with strong vocational training systems, an equal skill structure, and coordinated wage bargaining – typically coordinated market economies such as the German-speaking and Nordic countries. In contrast, the more unequal skill distribution of liberal market economies such as Britain or the United States should translate into a more polarized pattern of occupational change (Tåhlin 2007: 46).

A key issue in the analysis of occupational change is unemployment. Institutions such as extensive bargaining rights and high minimum wages may channel technological change into occupational upgrading. But if upgrading implies that a growing proportion of low-skilled workers are priced out of the labor market, a new social divide emerges – not based on unequal earnings, but on unequal access to jobs. Countries may thus have the choice between two undesirable outcomes: occupational upgrading at the cost of unemployment or labor market integration of the low-skilled with the drawback of a polarized earnings structure (Krugman 1994; Iversen and Wren 1998; Scharpf 2000). The central issue of the debate on occupational change thus concerns the prospects that postindustrial labor markets offer to low-skilled workers.

What does the empirical evidence tell us about the pattern of occupational change? From the 1960s up to the 1990s, three trends have been common to economically advanced countries: first, the phasing out of agricultural employment and the spectacular drop among farmhands; second, the steady decline of manufacturing jobs, most notably among operatives; third, the rise of business, health, and social services, mainly creating jobs for (associate) managers and (semi)professionals (Castells and Aoyama 1994; Berman et al. 1998; Juhn 1999). The seemingly continuous shift away from lower toward higher skilled work is all the more spectacular if one adopts a longer time horizon and accepts the argument that the majority of preindustrial labor was low-skilled, backbreaking, monotonous, and unrewarding (Attewell 1987: 334).

While much of the international evidence points toward occupational upgrading, this consensus view was shattered in the early 2000s by two studies finding a trend toward polarization in the United States (Wright and Dwyer 2003; Autor et al. 2008). In a large-scale analysis covering four decades, Erik Wright and Rachel Dwyer (2003) document the shift in the American job structure from unequivocal upgrading in the 1960s and 1970s to relatively even job growth in the 1980s and finally to polarization in the 1990s. Large employment gains in business services and public administration explain the expansion at the top, whereas retail trade and personal services provided the jobs at the bottom – jobs largely filled by the growing immigrant Hispanic workforce (Wright and Dwyer 2003: 309). As evidence on the American labor market accumulated, a new consensus emerged: The U.S. employment structure had become subject to an unbalanced – *polarized* – pattern of growth in the 1990s, with strong job expansion at the top, stagnant employment in the middle, and small growth in occupations at the bottom (Ilg and Haugen 2000; Autor et al. 2003, 2008; Rehm 2010: 381).

The controversial question is to know to what extent the American pattern of occupational change also applies to Western Europe. Findings are most ambiguous for Britain. In terms of skills, a battery of different measures points to substantial upskilling of the British labor market over the period 1986–2006 (Felstead et al. 2007). In contrast, an influential study defining occupations' quality not based on their skill requirements, but their median earnings, finds a clear polarizing trend for the period 1979–1999 (Goos and Manning 2007). Two occupational groups account for this simultaneous expansion at the extremes: low-paid welfare state occupations such as nursing aides and educational assistants as well as high-paid business service occupations such as consultants, treasurers, and computer programmers (Goos and Manning 2007: 124).

Polarization does not describe well the evolution of the employment structure in other European countries. Three comparative studies report a tendency toward occupational upgrading in most Western European countries (Fernández-Macías 2012: 15, Hurley and Fernández-Macías 2008: 12, Tåhlin 2007: 71). Particularly small affluent countries such as Denmark, Sweden, or Switzerland seem to have witnessed a significant and linear upgrading of their employment structure (Åberg 2003: 203, Korpi and Tåhlin 2009: 192, Skaksen and Sørensen 2002; Sheldon 2005). More controversial are findings for Spain and Germany. In Spain, both the number of professionals and – albeit more weakly – that of low-skilled service workers have increased over the last thirty years (Bernardi and Garrido 2008). In Germany, high-paid and high-skilled occupations grew substantially over the 1980s and 1990s. But at the same time, midrange jobs disappeared more quickly than those at the bottom end of the labor market (Dustmann et al. 2009: 871, Spitz-Oener 2006: 262). Unlike the American experience, the German occupational structure may thus have polarized not because low-end jobs expanded – they probably did not – but because intermediary jobs decreased to a greater extent.

This overview suggests that up to the end of the 1980s, labor market researchers agreed in their verdict of occupational upgrading. This consensus no longer holds for the period after 1990. While the finding of polarization for the United States seems well established, the evidence for Western Europe is inconclusive. Accordingly, this chapter examines these two areas of uncertainty: the pattern of occupational change in Western Europe in the 1990s and 2000s.

4.2. Country Selection, Data, and Strategy of Analysis

Our empirical analysis focuses on five West European countries: Britain, Denmark, Germany, Spain, and Switzerland. We thus choose the "most similar systems design" (Przeworski and Teune 1970) with the objective to compare countries that differ little on a range of explanatory factors such as economic affluence and technological advancement. This makes it more likely that observed changes in the phenomenon to be explained are caused by those explanatory factors by which these countries do differ, notably labor market institutions. Our group of countries provides us with four different sets of institutions governing social policy and the labor market (Esping-Andersen 1990): a liberal Anglo-Saxon welfare regime (Britain), a social democratic Scandinavian regime (Denmark), a conservative Mediterranean regime (Spain), and a conservative continental regime (Germany, Switzerland). We select two

TABLE 4.1. *Key features of the data sets used*

	British Labor Force Survey	Danish Labor Force Survey	German Socio-Economic Panel	Spanish Labor Force Survey	Swiss Labor Force Survey
	LFS	EU-LFS	SOEP	EPA	SAKE
Period covered in study	1991–2008	1992–2007	1990–2007	1990–2008	1991–2008
Sample size,* early 1990s	54,760	10,965	7,977	58,582	8,490
Sample size,* end of 2000s	41,402	51,062	9,400	62,697	23,351
Information on occupation	soc90 3-digit soc2000 3-digit	isco88 2-digit + nace industry	isco88 4-digit	cno94	isco88 4-digit
Earnings included	Yes (after 93)	No	Yes	No	Yes
Other database used for earnings	No	EU-SILC	No	CIS 1989, 1990, 2006	No

Note: *Our samples include individuals aged 18 to 65 years who spend at least 20 hours per week in employment.

continental countries to account for the fact that this group of welfare regimes is both largest and internally most heterogeneous. For these five countries, changes in the occupational structure are examined for the two decades since German reunification, the period between 1990/1 and 2007/8. The two cutoff points constitute the end of long cyclical upswings that were then followed by OECD-wide recessions (1991–1993 and 2008–2010).

Our empirical analysis is based on large-scale microlevel data sets that contain detailed information on individuals' occupation, earnings and education: the national labor force surveys for Britain (UK-LFS), Spain (EPA), and Switzerland (SAKE); the Danish labor force survey stemming from Denmark's cooperation with Eurostat (EU-LFS); and the German Socio-Economic Panel (SOEP). Danish EU-LFS, German SOEP, and Swiss SAKE are annual surveys, whereas Spanish EPA and – beginning in 1993 – British LFS are carried out on a quarterly basis. For these two surveys, we choose the spring quarter. Table 4.1 gives an overview of the key features of these datasets.

We examine occupational change with the analytical strategy developed by Erik Wright and Rachel Dwyer (2003), which is based on the following three steps. First, we restrict our sample to people aged 18 to 65 years who spend at least twenty hours per week in paid employment. For these individuals, occupations are distinguished as precisely as possible given the data at hand (isco88 at the four-digit level or comparable codes). Occupations containing fewer than ten individuals reporting wages are merged with similar occupations to increase the accuracy of our estimates. Since occupations are coded at a more aggregated level in the Danish survey, we combine them with information on the economic sector in order to obtain a more fine-grained measure of occupations.[1] Depending on the country, we distinguish among 108 (Denmark), 120 (Spain), 145 (Germany), 161 (Switzerland), and 171 (Britain) different occupations.

Second, we determine an occupation's quality on the basis of its median earning – in our view the most consequential and most reliably measurable indicator of what is a good or bad job. We thus equate occupational upgrading with an expansion of occupations with a comparatively high median earning at the expense of occupations with a low median earning.[2]

Third, once we have calculated the median earning of each occupation over the period of interest, we rank-order the occupations from the lowest- to the highest-paid. These rank-ordered occupations are then grouped into five equally large quintiles, containing as close as possible to 20 percent of total employment at the beginning of the period under study. The bottom quintile 1 thus holds the 20 percent of employment in the occupations with the lowest median earnings and the top quintile the 20 percent of employment in the occupations with the highest median earnings. The occupational hierarchy looks surprisingly similar in the five countries under study. Sales assistants, waiters, and farmhands are found in the bottom quintile 1, bricklayers and truck drivers in the lower-middle quintile 2, secretaries and machine mechanics in the middle quintile 3, nurses and police officers in the upper-middle quintile 4, and senior officials, computer professionals, and doctors in the top quintile 5.

These five quintiles constitute the building block of our analysis: We determine the pattern of occupational change on the basis of how occupations in

---

[1] Unlike Wright and Dwyer (2003), we explicitly integrate the industry-part of an occupation only for Denmark. For the other four countries, information on the sector of employment (industry) is only used for a few large and indeterminate occupations such as senior officials, managers, secretaries and elementary occupations in the Swiss database and business owners, mid- and low-rank office clerks, operators of mobile machinery, truck drivers and cleaners in the Spanish dataset.

[2] An occupation's median earning is calculated as the average of its standardized hourly median earning at the beginning and end of the period under study, weighted by the number of individuals employed in the occupation at a given moment. The Danish EU-LFS and the Spanish EPA surveys do not include information on earnings. For Denmark, we determine occupations' median earnings based on combined data stemming from the three Danish EU-SILC surveys 2004, 2005 and 2006. The Danish case is particular in our analysis insofar as occupations' rank-ordering (based on their median earnings) reflects the situation at the end of the period under study. For Spain, we calculate occupations' median earnings by relying on three surveys performed by Spain's Centre for Sociological Research (1989, 1990, 2006). The 1990 survey was combined with the 1989 survey to provide single estimates of occupational earnings for the beginning of the period analyzed. These calculations were carried out by Jorge Rodriguez Menes at the University Pompeu Fabra, Barcelona.

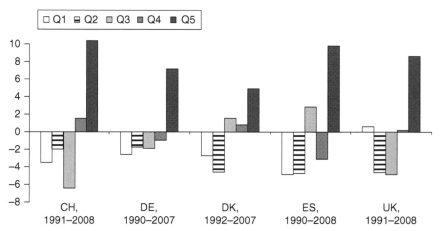

FIGURE 4.1. Relative employment change in job quality quintiles (in percentage points). *Q1* stands for *quintile 1*, which held – at the beginning of the period under study – the 20 percent of employment in the occupations with the lowest median earnings. *Q5* stands for *quintile 5*, which comprised – at the beginning of the period under study – the 20 percent of employment in the occupations with the highest median earnings. (The analyses for Spain were generously provided by Jorge Rodriguez Menes, University Pompeu Fabra, Barcelona.)

these quintiles evolve in terms of employment. Rather than representing the current distribution of jobs, we thus measure *net* change by taking into account both job destruction and job creation (for more details on the analytical strategy, see Oesch 2013: 37–42).

4.3. Empirical Evidence of Occupational Change since 1990

What has occupational change looked like over the last two decades? Figure 4.1 shows that in all five countries under study, employment expanded most at the top of the occupational hierarchy. The occupations set in quintile 5 increased their employment share by 5 percentage points in Denmark (from 20 to 25 percent), by 7 in Germany, by 9 in Britain, and even by 10 percentage points in Spain and Switzerland. While employment tended to decrease everywhere in the lower half of the occupational hierarchy, there is substantial cross-country variation. In relative terms, Germany and Spain witnessed the largest job losses in the lowest-paid occupations of quintile 1, Denmark in quintile 2, and Britain and Switzerland in the middle quintile 3.

The hypothesis of occupational downgrading can clearly be rejected for the period under study. On the contrary, for Germany and Spain the evidence points toward unambiguous upgrading. The same finding applies to Denmark and Switzerland – although midrange jobs declined somewhat more than low-end jobs. In contrast, results for Britain suggest a pattern of polarized upgrading with very strong employment growth at the top of the occupational hierarchy, substantial losses in the middle, and modest growth in the bottom-end quintile. Britain's pattern of occupational change closely resembles that found for the polarizing U.S. employment structure over the 1990s (Wright and Dwyer 2003; Autor et al. 2008).

The evidence presented earlier suggests that West European labor markets have created a disproportionate share of job opportunities in high-paid occupations of quintile 5 and thus provided labor market entrants with improving occupational prospects over the last two decades. Intergenerational mobility should thus have risen as older birth cohorts working in menial occupations leave the labor force and retire, while younger generations enter the labor market and take on more qualified occupations. We examine this hypothesis by comparing how age cohorts were distributed across quintiles in 1990/1 and 2007/8. For this reason, we distinguish four age cohorts (25–29, 30–34, 35–39, 40–44 years), compute the distribution across quintiles of workers in a given age cohort in 1990/1 and 2007/8, and then calculate relative change in employment across quintiles between 1990/1 and 2007/8 for the same age cohort.

The results are shown in Figure 4.2 for four countries (these analyses were not run for Spain). The most interesting finding concerns the two youngest cohorts no longer in full-time education, workers aged 25–29 and 30–34 years. Everywhere, workers in these two age brackets were much more likely to obtain a job in a top-end occupation of quintile 5 in 2007/8 than had been the case for young cohorts in 1990/1. Young people thus were, on average, entering the labor market in more advantageous occupations in the mid-2000s than in the early 1990s. Occupational change over the last two decades provided succeeding cohorts with greater opportunities for upward mobility. Yet Figure 4.2 also reveals that age cohorts did not experience a linear pattern of occupational upgrading. In the four countries analyzed, young workers were in 2007/8 both more likely to have a job in the top-end quintile 5 *and* in the bottom-end quintile 1 than were young workers in 1990/1. In other words, entering cohorts in the mid-2000s strongly expanded their relative employment in well-paid occupations of quintile 5 at the expense of the intermediate quintiles, but employment in the low-end quintile 1 also increased moderately (except in Switzerland). Moreover, the largest decline of employment opportunities over time occurred everywhere in the two lower-middle quintiles 2 and 3. The rise in occupational polarization of successive cohorts is particularly marked in the United Kingdom, but also evident for Germany and, to some extent, Denmark and Switzerland.

What did occupational change look like in terms of class locations? We examine this issue by using a detailed measure that discriminates *hierarchically* between more or less privileged employment relationships and *horizontally* between different work logics (see Oesch 2006). Combining the two dimensions provides us with the eight-class schema shown in Table 4.2, which reveals

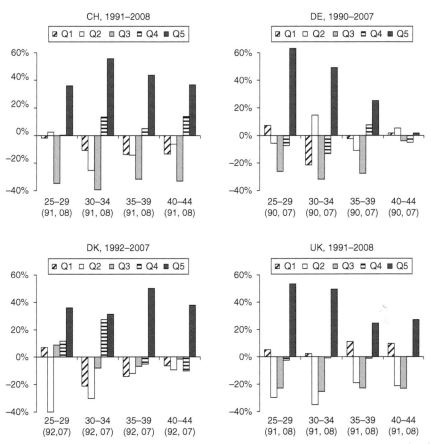

FIGURE 4.2. Change in the distribution of relative employment across quintiles for identical age cohorts.

Note: vertical columns show for Switzerland that workers aged 25–29 were 36 percent more likely to be employed in quintile 5 in 2008 than were workers aged 25–29 in 1991.

that occupational upgrading was driven by two categories: managers and sociocultural professionals. Together with technical professionals, they constitute the strongly expanding salaried middle class. At the beginning of the 1990s, only 32 to 35 percent of the labor force belonged to the salaried middle class, as compared to 42 to 45 per cent at the end of the 2000s.

In contrast, primarily two categories lost out from occupational change: office clerks and production workers. The former shrank dramatically in Denmark and Switzerland; the latter declined most strongly in Britain and Germany. Since clerks cluster in the middle of the earnings distribution, their decline contributed to the hollowing out of the job structure. In comparison, the decrease among production workers was more evenly distributed across the lowest four quintiles (Oesch and Rodriguez Menes 2011: 524). Production workers,

TABLE 4.2. *Change of workforce in eight occupational classes (share in percentage), 1990/1–2007/8*

	Interpersonal Service Logic	Technical Work Logic	Organizational Work Logic	Independent Work Logic
	Sociocultural (semi) professionals	Technical (semi) professionals	(Associate) managers	Liberal professionals and large employers
	Medical doctors Teachers Social workers	Engineers Architects Technicians	Administrators Consultants Accountants	Entrepreneurs Lawyers Dentists
CH	11 → 14	10 → 11	11 → 18	3 → 5
DE	10 → 14	10 → 10	13 → 18	1 → 3
DK	15 → 17	8 → 8	11 → 18	2 → 3
UK	9 → 13	8 → 8	17 → 23	2 → 2
	Service workers	Production workers	Office clerks	Small business owners
	Assistant nurses Waiters Shop assistants	Mechanics Carpenters Assemblers	Secretaries Receptionists Mail clerks	Shop owners Independent artisans Farmers
CH	13 → 13	24 → 19	17 → 10	11 → 11
DE	10 → 11	36 → 23	13 → 13	6 → 7
DK	18 → 18	24 → 21	13 → 8	9 → 7
UK	11 → 15	25 → 16	16 → 12	12 → 11

Notes: Values in gray/in boxes indicate an employment share in 2007/8 that is 20 percent higher/20 percent lower than in 1990/1. The shares refer to a target population of individuals aged 18–65 years who spend at least 20 hours per week in paid employment.
Source: Own computation based on the data sets presented in Table 4.1.

service workers, and clerks occupy the twilight zone below the middle class, made up of working-class and lower-middle-class positions. Taken together, the employment share of these three occupational classes decreased from 60 to 47 percent in Germany, from 55 to 48 in Denmark, from 54 to 42 per cent in Switzerland, and from 52 to 43 percent in Britain over the last two decades. As a result, the working- and lower-middle classes combined account today for about the same proportion of the labor force as the salaried middle class in all four countries.

A widely echoed expectation in the political economy literature of the 1990s was that employment growth in the age of globalization would have to arise mainly from low-paid private services (e.g., Iversen and Wren 1998; Scharpf 2000). Table 4.3 disaggregates occupational change according to the economic sector and shows that, contrary to popular perception, the share

TABLE 4.3. *Employment across sectors in 1990/1 and 2007/8 (in percentage)*

	Agriculture	Manufacturing	Construction	Sales, Hotels and Restaurants, Personal Services	Business Services Including Transports	Social Services and Public Administration
CH	4 → 4	24 → 18	7 → 7	25 → 22	22 → 25	18 → 25
DE	4 → 1	37 → 27	8 → 6	14 → 18	13 → 18	23 → 30
DK	5 → 3	21 → 16	6 → 7	32 → 20	12 → 20	24 → 32
ES	12 → 4	23 → 17	10 → 13	17 → 18	27 → 29	11 → 20
UK	2 → 2	27 → 16	9 → 9	20 → 16	20 → 26	22 → 32

Notes: Values in gray/in boxes indicate an employment share in 2007/8 that is 20 percent higher/20 percent lower than in 1990/1.
Source: Own computations based on the data sets presented in Table 4.1; Jorge Rodriguez Menes for Spain. The sample has been restricted to individuals aged 18–65 years who work at least 20 hours per week.

of employment in private consumer services such as retail trade, restaurants, and hotels decreased (in Denmark, Britain, or Switzerland) or increased very little (in Germany and Spain). While private consumer services stagnated and manufacturing continued to lose jobs in all countries, strong employment growth took place in two areas: in social services mainly set in the public sector and in business services mainly set in the private sector (IT and communication, banking and real estate). This pattern of sector shifts also explains why the problem of stagnant productivity in services (known as "Baumol's disease") is overstated: Growth has taken place in highly productive service sectors, among computer programmers and legal consultants, rather than among domestic aides and waiters.

Where does the tendency toward polarization originate? Not from McJobs in retail trade and restaurants, but from social services. Jobs in health care, social work, and education expanded not only at the top of the employment structure, but – albeit to a lesser extent – also at the bottom end. Growth of social services in the low-end quintile 1 was not only significant in the United Kingdom, but also in Denmark and Spain. In the United Kingdom, polarization of the occupational system is driven by the evolution in social service jobs, which were created in great numbers both at the top and at the bottom, but not in the middle of the employment structure (Oesch and Rodriguez Menes 2011: 526).

4.4. Upgrading at the Cost of Unemployment?

The upgrading thrust may not warrant excessive optimism if it occurs at the cost of unemployment – if the low-skilled have simply been pushed out of the labor market. In this case, governments face a difficult trade-off: They can protect their wage structure and hence smother the growth of low-wage services.

Thereby, they limit wage inequality and achieve occupational upgrading but have to cope with growing unemployment among the low-skilled who are priced out of the labor market (Krugman 1994; Scharpf 2000).

The trade-off between upgrading and full employment should play itself out at the labor market's bottom end. Accordingly, we examine in Table 4.4 low-skilled workers' unemployment rates.[3] They are averaged over five-year periods in order to smooth out the business cycle effect. Still, low-skilled unemployment closely trails the cyclical evolution of general unemployment – when general unemployment rose or fell, low-skilled unemployment followed suit. Over the period under study, low-skilled unemployment thus increased substantially in Germany and more moderately in Switzerland, while it gradually declined in Britain and Denmark prior to the global financial crisis in 2008. In Spain, low-skilled unemployment embarked – like general unemployment – on a spectacular roller-coaster journey, with a steep hike in the early 1990s, an even more massive fall between 1995 and 2007, and a staggering rise thereafter.

Did occupational upgrading ruin low-skilled workers' labor market prospects? Table 4.4 throws doubts on this gloomy expectation: In 2008, the low-skilled unemployment rate was below 7 percent in Britain, Denmark, and Switzerland – and thus moderate despite an ongoing process of occupational upgrading. Most notable is the evolution in the two small countries in our sample, Denmark and Switzerland. Neither country witnessed a polarization of its employment structure. In effect, job losses in the bottom-end quintile 1 were substantial in both countries (–42,000 jobs in Denmark between 1992 and 2007, –53,000 in Switzerland between 1991 and 2008) – yet low-skilled unemployment did not skyrocket. On the contrary, in Denmark it continuously declined over the 1990s and 2000s and fell below 4 percent prior to the Great Recession.

Unemployment rates paint a too-optimistic picture of low-skilled individuals' employment opportunities if involuntary labor market withdrawal takes other forms such as disability or early retirement. We check this possibility by computing in Table 4.4 the low-skilled employment rate, which measures the proportion of low-skilled working-age adults (aged 25 to 64 years) who are in gainful employment – and are thus neither unemployed nor economically inactive. Table 4.4 shows that over the last two decades, Denmark and Spain succeeded in significantly raising the employment rate of their low-skilled working-age population. In Britain, the low-skilled employment rate remained at a comparatively high level of 65 percent between 1997 and 2008. In contrast, Germany and Switzerland's low-skilled employment rate rose and fell in unison with the business cycle, all the while showing a slight downward trend. Interestingly, country differences became smaller over time but did not

---

[3] The low-skilled are defined as having an educational attainment of lower-secondary school or less, that is no more than 9 to 10 years of formal education (ISCED levels 0–2).

TABLE 4.4. *Low-skilled unemployment and employment rates averaged over five-year periods (in percentage)*

	Low-Skilled *Unemployment* Rate				Low-Skilled *Employment* Rate			
	91–95	96–00	01–05	06–08	91–95	96–00	01–05	06–08
CH	4	6	6	7	68	68	67	66
DE	11	15	17	18	53	48	51	50
DK	11	8	7	4	62	61	62	65
ES	18	17	11	10	47	50	57	60
UK	12	10	6	6	61	65	66	65

Note: The low-skilled employment rate measures the employment-to-working-age population ratio for low-skilled individuals aged 25–64 years. Low education is defined as ISCED levels 0–2 (preprimary, primary, and lower secondary education).
Source: OECD, Education at a Glance Database.

disappear. Britain, Denmark, and Switzerland feature substantially higher employment rates among the low-skilled than Germany and Spain.

Table 4.4 points out two interesting conclusions. First, there is no clear-cut trend toward reduced labor market participation of low-skilled adults in the five European countries under study. Rather than showing a secular decline, low-skilled workers' employment rates reflect the underlying business cycle, strongly expanding during Spain's labor market boom 1995–2007 and contracting during Germany's economic recessions. Second, countries with comparatively low wage inequality and a strong trend toward upgrading such as Denmark and Switzerland seem at least as successful in integrating low-skilled workers into the labor market as Britain, where high wage inequality and a polarizing occupational structure should have stimulated the creation of low-paid jobs to a greater extent than elsewhere. Evidently, the trade-off argument continues to fare badly in empirical scrutiny (see also Nickell and Bell 1996: 307; Card et al. 1999: 870; Glyn 2001: 701; Bosch 2009: 349).

How is it possible that large numbers of low-skilled jobs have vanished over the last two decades without leading to a significant rise in low-skilled unemployment or to a massive drop in low-skilled workers' labor market participation?[4] The answer is strongly related to the evolution of skill supplies: Not only have jobs for the unqualified become more rare, but so have the unqualified people themselves. Goldin and Katz (2007) argue that labor markets evolved in the twentieth century as the result of a race between education and

---

[4] Nor has there been a significant widening in *lower-tail* wage inequality. Over the period 1990–2005, the gap between the median wage and the wage at the 1st decile (p50/p10) seems to have remained stable in the majority of OECD countries, notably in Britain, Switzerland and the U.S. (OECD 2007: 128). An exception is Germany where lower-tail wage inequality has been on the rise since the mid-1990s (Antonczyk et al. 2009: 9).

technology: Permanent technological change increased firms' demand for skills and massive educational expansion increased workers' supply of skills. In this race, educational advance seems to have kept up with technological progress in the countries under study.

In Western Europe, educational expansion began in earnest in the 1950s with the strong growth of educational enrollments in upper secondary schooling. It took up speed in the following decades when universities and technical colleges were opened to significantly larger sections of the population. This process continued over the last two decades. Between 1990 and 2008, the proportion of the labor force with a tertiary degree increased from less than a fourth to more than a third in Britain, Denmark, and Switzerland and from less than a fifth to a fourth in Germany and Spain. In parallel, the share of the workforce without upper secondary schooling declined everywhere and dropped below 20 percent in Britain, Denmark, and Spain and below 15 percent in Germany and Switzerland.[5] Moreover, statistics of educational attainment probably underestimate the real extent of upskilling, as the qualifications of those with upper secondary schooling – still the majority of the population – increased at the level of both general education (A-Levels and Abitur instead of O-levels and Mittlere Reife) and vocational training (longer and more qualifying apprenticeships).

A more difficult question is to know whether this upward shift in skills has taken place in unison with occupational change. Causality between educational expansion and occupational upgrading may run in both directions. On the one hand, industrial automation, the spread of computers in services, and the massive decline in semiskilled jobs provided incentives for young people to stay on in school longer and invest in their education. On the other hand, abundant skill supplies may also have led employers to adapt their production techniques and to create high-skilled jobs in order to benefit fully from the educational profiles available on the labor market.

A counterfactual analysis run on our data suggests that the pattern of occupational change predicted on the sole basis of skill evolution closely mirrors the observed pattern (Oesch and Rodriguez Menes 2011: 521). Educational expansion and occupational upgrading seem to have gone hand in hand in all five countries. However, the correspondence between educational upskilling and occupational upgrading is stronger in Denmark, Germany, and Switzerland, where vocational training dominates, than in Britain and, above all, Spain, where educational expansion over the last two decades was particularly strong and outpaced occupational upgrading.

In effect, the skill evolution in Britain and Spain would lead us to expect a larger decline in low-paid occupations than the one observed in Figure 4.1. One key element is immigration: Both Britain and Spain experienced strong surges in immigration between the late 1990s and the crisis of 2007/8. While immigrants

---

[5] Own computations based on data shown in Table 4.1.

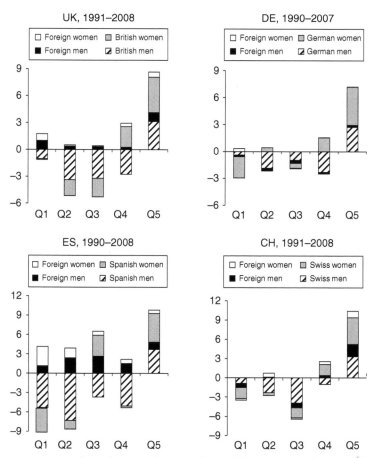

FIGURE 4.3. Contribution of nationality-gender groups to the pattern of occupational change (relative change in employment in percentage points).

were mostly low-skilled in Spain, they had a bimodal skill distribution in Britain, with disproportional shares among both the least and the most highly educated (OECD 2008: 83). We analyze the role of immigration by disaggregating relative change in employment for four nationality-gender groups: national women, foreign women, national men, foreign men. Figure 4.3 shows the contribution that these four groups make to the observed pattern of occupational change for Britain, Germany, Spain, and Switzerland (results for Denmark not shown here). Two findings are noteworthy.

First, occupational upgrading between the early 1990s and the late 2000s was strongly fostered by national women. While the share of national women working in the low-paid jobs of quintile 1 decreased considerably, their proportion expanded massively in quintile 5 in all five countries under study. Accordingly, women's catch-up process in educational attainment has everywhere translated into higher occupational attainment.

Second, in Britain and Spain expansion in low-paid occupations of quintile 1 was exclusively due to job growth among foreign workers. In the United Kingdom, the relative employment decline in quintile 1 among British men and women was overcompensated by the employment rise among foreign men and women. In Spain, foreign workers – above all, women – also increased their employment in quintile 1, whereas relative employment among Spanish men and women strongly fell. In Germany and Switzerland, employment shifts were similar for nationals and foreigners.

The U-shaped skill profile of immigration contributed to occupational polarization in Britain. Comparable to Hispanics in the United States, East European immigrants in Britain supplied the manpower necessary to fill the gaps at the bottom end of the labor market (Wright and Dwyer 2003: 308; Oesch and Rodriguez Menes 2011: 531). Without the large surges in immigration between the late 1990s and the mid-2000s, Britain and Spain would probably have experienced a stronger trend toward occupational upgrading – simply because employers would not have found as abundant a labor supply for low-paid jobs.

4.5. What Implications for Inequality and Politics?

What are the social and political implications of an occupational structure that expands massively at the top, declines in the middle, and stagnates at the bottom end? Clearly, the labor market creates new opportunities at the high-skilled end of the occupational structure, but makes perspectives in the (lower) middle range of jobs bleaker. Bleaker prospects primarily affect clerks and production workers. Their numbers have dropped and led to a thinning out of the twilight zone between the working and the middle class. Secretaries, tellers, craft workers, or plant operators are all occupations at the fringes of the lower-middle class that – while not requiring high levels of education – used to secure middle-range incomes and a steady rise in living standards. Today, people in these occupations do not face a bright future. In the case of plant closure, organizational downsizing, or career interruptions, they are exposed to a serious risk of social downgrading.

The drop in clerical and manufacturing jobs also means that workers who have limited education have fewer opportunities for upward mobility. Unlike the situation prevailing when industrial plants and organizational bureaucracies expanded, it probably has become more difficult for people working in the least-paid jobs to move up in the employment structure. Large industrial firms, financial conglomerates, or public utilities in postal services, telephone, and energy no longer provide ample job opportunities for semiskilled workers. Without higher education (advanced vocational degrees or schooling at the tertiary level), it probably becomes increasingly difficult to secure a job – or to move to a senior position over the career – that provides a middle-class lifestyle (Wright and Dwyer 2003: 322).

Ironically, future demand for low-skilled jobs may depend on the expansion among managers and professionals. Personal services such as cleaning, home delivery, babysitting, or private security are determined by the geographic proximity of wealthy customers and the extent of income inequality: The greater the difference between the customers' purchasing power (the wealthy individual's income) and the price of the personal service (the poor individual's wage), the greater the demand (Manning 2004: 588). Combined with increasing marital homogamy (see Chapter 6 by Gøsta Esping-Andersen, this volume) and the time constraints afflicting dual-earner households, occupational upgrading may thus generate the consumer demand for services supplied by low-paid workers.

In this context, Wright and Dwyer (2003: 323) raise the question whether polarization in the U.S. labour markets leads to a rise of master-servant relationships – to a new cultural reality of social inequality where a growing share of the people at the bottom provide personal services to the people at the top: cleaning their house, ironing their clothes, delivering their groceries, babysitting their children. Table 4.2 does not show a significant increase among interpersonal service workers except in Britain. A possible explanation may be that higher wage floors – set directly by collective agreements and indirectly by the welfare state – make McJobs economically less viable in Denmark, Germany, and Switzerland than in Anglo-Saxon countries. However, since our analysis only includes people spending at least twenty hours per week in formal employment, our results are likely to be lower-bound estimates. Part-timers working few hours and illegal immigrants make up a sizable (and probably growing) share of the workforce in low-end personal services.

What are the political implications of unbalanced occupational upgrading? To begin with, there is the paradox that class divisions deepen, but class mobilization weakens (Kohli forthcoming). Most available indicators suggest that the gap in earnings between the salaried upper-middle classes and the lower classes has widened over the last two decades. At the same time, the political mobilization of social class – notably of the working class, not the very upper class (Hacker and Pierson 2010) – has dwindled, be it in terms of strike activity, wage bargaining, or collective organization. A central piece in this puzzle is the decline among production workers. Once the backbone of labor parties and trade unions, the industrial working class shrank by another third since the early 1990s and today accounts even in Germany – the most industrial West European country – for less than a fourth of the labor force (see Table 4.2). Outside the Scandinavian countries, union movements have been incapable of substituting their declining core constituency of male blue-collar workers with female employees in expanding social services, education, and health care. The results are lower union density, less inclusive collective bargaining, and increasingly flexible employment relationships (Bosch 2009; see also Chapter 9 by Anke Hassel, this volume, on the decline of trade unions).

In terms of political preferences, the implications are more difficult to grasp. Occupational upgrading has contributed to the increasing heterogeneity of the social structure, adding to the sectoral heterogeneity that is shown in Chapter 2 of this volume. More fundamentally, it has provided new opportunities for some groups, while making life more difficult for others. The winners benefited from the opening up of tertiary education to new social categories and the growth of highly qualified positions in the professions and management. Thanks to the democratization of higher education and the expansion of business and welfare services, large proportions of the population have obtained comfortable positions within the salaried middle class. The losers are primarily found among blue-collar workers, semiskilled clerks, personal service workers, owners of small stores, and independent artisans who have lost out from both educational and occupational upgrading and find themselves at the gradually less populated lower end of the social structure. The evolution toward a more skill-intensive and competitive service economy has worsened their job and mobility prospects. In addition, they are more vulnerable to economic openness than the high skilled, either because their jobs can be offshored, or because the immigrant inflow in their occupations tends to be larger (see Chapter 5 by Dancygier and Walter, this volume).

This widening gap in life chances spills over into political and partisan preferences (see Chapter 8 by Häusermann and Kriesi, this volume). The winners of upgrading have embraced libertarian and universalistic values – among others strongly supporting parties of the New Left, notably the Greens – and are firm supporters of liberal democracy. In contrast, the losers have disproportionately rallied around right-wing populist parties (Kitschelt 2007; Kriesi et al. 2008; Oesch 2012). This has happened in part because deindustrialization and educational expansion eroded working-class culture and organizations, leaving an organizational void readily filled by right-wing populist movements. The populist Right's angry resistance to cultural change, its solitary opposition against the political elites, and its pointed defense of national preference seems to strike a chord with the losers. In West European countries with a sizable right-wing populist party, production and service workers form the core of the party's electorate (Bornschier and Kriesi 2012; Ivarsflaten 2005; Oesch 2012).

The cleavage between losers and winners of social modernization overlaps with a new geographical divide of which we only see first contours. The winners – high-paid dual-earner couples working in management and the professions – primarily expand in the metropolitan centers and transform European cities into increasingly exclusive commercial and residential areas. West European capitals are thus undergoing a much faster process of occupational upgrading than the suburbs, small towns, or countryside. A prime example is London. In 1981, inner London used to be more working class than the rest of England, but in 2001 it had a much greater concentration of the middle and upper classes than outer London, the South East, or the rest of England (Butler et al. 2008: 77). In Paris, the expansion of the professional middle classes was even more pronounced. Its metropolitan area is increasingly segmented into three socially distinct spaces: The salaried upper-middle classes live in the center; the working poor are relegated to the suburban sprawl; and the old (and lower-) middle classes settle in the periurban area of detached houses (Donzelot 2004). A similar evolution can be observed in Southern European cities such as Barcelona, Lisbon, Madrid, Milan, or Rome, where the rising concentration of the upper-middle classes in the center contrasts with the peripheral settlement pattern of the working class and notably of immigrants (Arbaci and Malheiros 2010).

4.6. Conclusion

In debates about society in the twenty-first century, two notions hold great sway over both the academic and the general public: labor market dualization and the end of the middle class. Both ideas make reference to significant phenomena – the destandardization of employment and the increase in income inequality. However, another evolution in the labor market, namely, the pervasive upgrading of the occupational structure, has affected our societies to a much greater extent. This chapter examined how the occupational structure of five advanced industrial democracies evolved since the beginning of the 1990s and produced four main findings.

First, the different labor force surveys make a clear case for occupational upgrading. Employment expanded much faster in high-paid occupations in management and the professions than in mid- and low-paid jobs in production, menial services, and the back office. This shift in employment has fundamentally redrawn – and is still redrawing – the face of European societies. As professional and managerial jobs expanded at the expense of the lower-middle class and the industrial working class, the class structure moved upward in all five countries under study. Contrary to what newspapers like to claim, technological change has not eroded the middle class, but the ranks of production workers and office clerks.

Second, occupational upgrading did not lead to major disequilibria in the labor market because it was accompanied by a major increase in the educational attainment of the workforces. By supplying greater numbers of mid- and high-educated school leavers, educational systems successfully met the increasing skill demands of firms. Occupational upgrading thus did not occur at the cost of low-skilled workers' labor market prospects: Their employment rates did not significantly decline in any of the five countries studied. The growth in the numbers of tertiary-educated people and the parallel decline in those of people with only compulsory schooling explain why low-paid jobs could decline without causing a rise in low-skilled unemployment. Moreover, in countries with strongly growing low-end services such as Britain, Spain, or the

United States, the large inflow of low-skilled immigrants provided the labor supply to fill these jobs.

Third, unlike studies on the American labor market, our analysis of European surveys produces, at best, lukewarm support for a trend toward employment polarization. It would be tempting to overplay the result of polarization – because it makes for such a spectacular story (Goos et al. 2009). Yet our data make a much stronger case for occupational upgrading. Keeping this reservation in mind, several elements suggest that polarization may nonetheless become more consequential for the future of European labor markets. To begin with, employment dropped more in intermediary than in bottom-end occupations in Britain and, to a lesser extent, Denmark and Switzerland, as firms' falling demand for production and back-office staff led to a decline in lower-midrange jobs. Moreover, the comparison of age cohorts between the early 1990s and the late 2000s suggests that the employment structure evolved in a j-shaped pattern, with strong job creation at the top of the occupational hierarchy, a decline in the middle and relative stability at the bottom end. In addition, low-skilled workers' employment rates heavily depend on the underlying business cycles; that is, they have been particularly heavily hit by the Great Recession.

Fourth, our evidence does not support the assumption, popular in the early 2000s, that postindustrial economies could only achieve full employment if they opened their wage structure downward and created low-paid service jobs (Krugman 1994; Iversen and Wren 1998; Scharpf 2000). Nothing in our analyses indicates that Scandinavian and Continental European countries need to travel down this desolate road. On the contrary, if governments want to support occupational upgrading, they seem well advised to take action at both ends of the labor market. At the upper end, public investment in tertiary education allows firms to hire high-skilled workers in sufficient numbers and thus to take full advantage of technological advance. At the lower end, a strengthening of upper secondary education – notably vocational training – and the establishment of a minimum wage incite firms to invest in workers' productivity rather than to rely on a stagnant low-wage sector.

The central political implication of unbalanced occupational upgrading – whether accentuated by polarization or not – is the relative decline of originally powerful social-structural groups. The trend toward a more skill-intensive and competitive service economy worsened the job and mobility prospects of production workers, semiskilled clerks, owners of small stores, and independent artisans, who find themselves at the gradually less populated lower end of the social structure. As a result of this decline, we observe a decrease of the political clout of the organizations that have defended the interests of these groups in the past, notably trade unions (see Chapter 9), and a gradual shift of the representation of their interests to new organizations, notably the parties of the new populist Right (see Chapter 8).

5

Globalization, Labor Market Risks, and Class Cleavages

Rafaela Dancygier and Stefanie Walter

Advanced capitalist democracies face important challenges in the modern age. In addition to the domestic changes on national labor markets (see in particular the introductory chapter of this volume, as well as Chapter 2 on the long-term consequences of structural change and Chapter 4 on occupational change in the service economy), they are also embedded in a worldwide process of increasing economic and cultural integration. This process of globalization has not only created new opportunities and considerable constraints for policy makers in democratic capitalist states. Globalization has also produced new lines of division among voters. The deep and wide-ranging processes of economic liberalization and cultural exchange have been shown to reorder preferences and priorities among the electorate and, in doing so, have shaken up existing cleavage structures (e.g., Rogowski 1989; Kitschelt and McGann 1995; Mughan and Lacy 2002; Kayser 2007; Kriesi et al. 2008; Häusermann and Walter 2010; Margalit 2011).

In this chapter, we focus on the impact of globalization on voter preferences. Similarly to the chapter by Daniel Oesch in this volume (Chapter 4), we thus contribute to the general analytical framework of the book – as developed in the introductory chapter – by explaining how structural change affects the demand-side constraints policy makers face in advanced capitalist democracies. More specifically, we consider the consequences of trade, foreign direct investment, and immigration, which have had immediate effects on both the structure of labor markets and– thereby – voter preferences in advanced capitalist democracies.[1] As previous scholars have argued and as we discuss later,

---

[1] For reasons of space, we do not consider the impact of the globalization of finance other than foreign direct investment on individual preferences in this chapter (see, for example, Frieden 1991; Jupille and Leblang 2007; Hobolt and Leblond 2009; Leblang et al. 2011; Walter 2013). We also do not discuss how globalization may influence voter preferences for redistribution and the welfare state more generally (for a discussion of these issues see, for example, Rehm 2009; Hays 2009; Häusermann and Walter 2010; Walter 2015).

the globalization of production and the international flow of labor generate gains and losses in ways that cut both along and across traditional class cleavages, especially when such globalization has uneven sectoral effects. To identify who benefits and who loses from globalization, scholars have investigated effects on the basis of skills, industries, and occupation. As we sketch out in the following, more recent research has developed increasingly complex models that take into account differences in the productivity of firms, in the skill and cultural profiles of domestic and migrant labor, and in economic conditions across and within countries. The first part of this chapter provides an overview of this literature.

In the second part of this chapter we contribute to this literature by reexamining the role of class. Though the scholarship we review paints an increasingly complex picture of globalization's distributional consequences and its ensuing effects on preferences, we contend that class remains significant in ordering preferences: Low-skill workers have often been identified as the group most likely to voice its discontent about economic liberalization and cultural opening.[2] This finding is in line with skill-based economic models that predict that low-skill workers in high-skill economies should suffer most from globalization. As we will illustrate, however, it can also be consistent with accounts that focus on the sectoral and occupational threats posed by the global flow of goods and labor. By examining exposure to trade, foreign direct investment (FDI), and immigration together, we show that low-skill workers in advanced industrialized democracies cannot easily escape the labor market pressures that globalization generates. Those low-skill workers who are relatively sheltered from the threats associated with outsourcing and trade are most vulnerable to competition arising from immigration, and vice versa. Further, the labor market pressures experienced by low-skilled workers occur alongside and are inseparable from exposure to cultural diversity. More than their high-skill counterparts, low-skilled workers experience economic and cultural threats jointly.

While the chapter by Oesch in this volume emphasizes the beneficial effects service sector expansion has had on job growth for medium- and high-skilled workers, our chapter looks at the low-skilled workers, who are threatened by both globalization and immigration and whose political preferences are driven by the fear of losing their economic, social, and political status. Even though both occupational upgrading in the service sector, as well as the effects of globalization and immigration on low-skilled voters, seem to strengthen traditional, skill-level-driven class divides rather than blurring them, these

---

[2] Low skill levels have been consistently linked to opposition to immigration and to support for antiimmigrant parties (see later discussion). Skill has also been found to correlate positively with support for trade (e.g., Scheve and Slaughter 2001a; O'Rourke and Sinnott 2002). Note, however, that it is often not clear whether skill – often measured as educational attainment – or unobservable characteristics related to skill (e.g., cosmopolitanism, tolerance) help explain attitudes toward various facets of globalization (Hainmueller and Hiscox 2006; Mansfield and Mutz 2009).

processes of occupational change stir up the configuration of political interests policy makers are confronted with (what was called the "demand-side constraints" in the introductory chapter). While in the past, low-skilled vulnerable workers were a natural electoral constituency of the Left, these voters have also become an electoral segment with decidedly particularistic, antiuniversalist, and antiimmigrant preferences. Even though our chapter shows that globalization negatively affects low-skill workers across the board and thereby potentially reinforces class-based politics, the confluence of economic dislocation and cultural diversity prompts many of these voters to opt for the Far Right (see Chapter 7 by Kitschelt and Rehm, as well as Chapter 8 by Häusermann and Kriesi, this volume).

The rest of this chapter proceeds as follows. We first review how the globalization of production and the free flow of labor influence the economic welfare of natives across skill groups, concentrating on labor market effects. We next present data on occupational offshorability risks and on the concentration of foreign-born labor across industries and occupations in Western European countries. These data reveal that, more so than the highly skilled, low-skilled natives are likely to face globalization pressures on all fronts. An empirical analysis of globalization-related attitudes further shows that low-skill workers are united in their opposition against the globalization of labor (i.e., immigration), whereas we find that occupational offshorability – and the associated economic benefits – conditions the support for globalization among the highly skilled. The last section summarizes our findings and briefly discusses their implications for the formation of political cleavages.

5.1. Trade and International Production

It has long been recognized that international trade and the internationalization of production more generally have strong distributional consequences. Even though they raise aggregate welfare in open economies, the globalization of production generates winners and losers *within* these economies (for an overview see Frieden and Rogowski 1996). Despite years of research, however, no consensus has emerged among political economists about how best to model these distributional effects, and whether such effects influence policy preferences at all (e.g., Scheve and Slaughter 2001a; Beaulieu 2002; Kaltenthaler et al. 2004; Hays et al. 2005; Mayda and Rodrik 2005; Hainmueller and Hiscox 2006; Mansfield and Mutz 2009; Rehm 2009; Ehrlich and Maestas 2010; Wren and Rehm 2013). Research in international political economy has traditionally relied on two distinct trade models to identify these effects: the sectoral Ricardo-Viner models, which predict a cleavage between winners and losers either between comparatively disadvantaged and advantaged industries (e.g., Gourevitch 1986) or between the exposed tradables and the sheltered nontradables sector (e.g., Frieden and Rogowski 1996; Hays et al. 2005). In contrast, factor-endowments models, most notably those in the

Stolper-Samuelson tradition, suggest that in advanced economies, high-skilled individuals are beneficiaries of globalization, while low-skilled workers lose out (Findlay and Kierzkowski 1983). Unequivocal empirical evidence about which of these models is best suited to identifying winners and losers of globalization is still lacking. Many microlevel studies test the implications of the two models simultaneously and frequently find at least partial support for both sectoral and factoral lines of conflict (e.g., Beaulieu 2002; Mayda and Rodrik 2005; Mayda 2008; Hays et al. 2005; Hays 2009; Rehm 2009) – a surprising result, given that these models build on contradictory assumptions about the level of factor mobility.

Recent empirical work in economics shows that the distributional effects of trade are more heterogeneous than these traditional models predict (e.g., Wagner 2007; Schank et al. 2007). The latest generation of trade models pioneered by Melitz (2003) model this heterogeneity explicitly. These models emphasize variation in firm productivity and argue that more productive firms benefit from free trade, because they gain new customers abroad, whereas less productive firms suffer. The latter cannot survive in the face of global competition and are therefore forced to close down. Moreover, since workers differ in their "ability" to work productively, their chances of being employed by productive firms differ as well (Helpman et al. 2008), with more productive firms hiring workers with a higher average ability and paying them higher wages. When the economy opens up to international trade, the most productive firms, who now sell their products both abroad and at home, receive higher revenues, which they at least partly redistribute to their high-quality workforce. Workers in less productive firms in the same industry, who are on average less skilled, fare less well: Their employers face stronger competition, a lower market share, and lower revenues. These workers therefore are confronted with both lower wages and a higher risk of unemployment. These labor market risks are particularly high for "low ability" workers who do not fulfill the hiring requirements of the productive firms. As a result, the distribution of wages in an internationally exposed industry is more unequal and the risk of unemployment is higher in an open economy than in autarky – despite overall gains from trade (Helpman et al. 2008).

This intuition can be extended to workers in nontradable industries as well (Walter 2015). The professional life of workers in industries and professions that produce nontradable goods and services is relatively sheltered from global competition: Doctors, teachers, hairdressers, or bus drivers are therefore much less affected by globalization than their counterparts in exposed industries and occupations. For these individuals, the inequality of wages should be smaller than in industries in which some firms export, because the variation in profits is smaller than it is among firms in tradable sectors. This suggests that on average, high-skilled workers in the sheltered industry receive lower wages than those working in firms exposed to international competition. At the same time, low-skilled workers sheltered from global competition receive higher wages

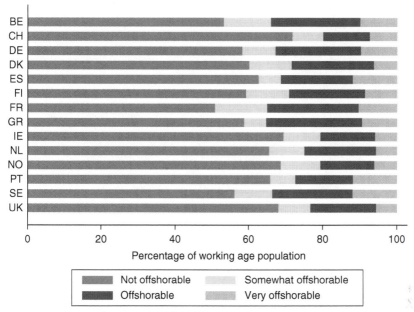

FIGURE 5.1. Distribution of offshorable occupations across countries.

and enjoy more job security than their counterparts in more exposed firms. Note, however, that these accounts do not consider the role of immigration, which, as we will see later, complicates this picture.

Furthermore, as (relatively) free trade has become the norm rather than the exception in recent years, an additional facet of globalization has received increasing attention: the growing ability of firms to offshore certain parts of the production chain. As technology has progressed, it has become increasingly easy to provide services from geographically distant locations. This has increased the offshorability, that is, the degree to which jobs in a given occupation can be substituted by jobs abroad, of many jobs previously sheltered from global competition, especially in the services sector.

Figure 5.1 displays the distribution of offshorable jobs across fourteen European countries based on Blinder's (2007) "offshorability-index."[3] This ordinal index measures a job's potential to be moved abroad, that is, whether the service the job provides can theoretically be delivered over long distances with little or no degradation in quality; it ranges from 1 (no offshoring potential) to 4 (high offshoring potential) and is available for approximately eight

[3] The data are aggregated from survey data from the European Social Survey 2008, for which information on respondents' occupations was matched with information about the offshorability of each individual occupation (for a detailed discussion of this procedure see Walter and Maduz 2009).

hundred occupations. Individuals who have jobs that can be readily offshored – such as seamstresses or IT programmers – are much more exposed to international competition than are individuals whose jobs cannot be substituted with jobs abroad, such as janitors or doctors. Nonoffshorable professions are typically occupations in which personal services are provided or that require a physical presence (Blinder 2007). Figure 5.1 shows that while the majority of occupations is still not substitutable with services from abroad, a substantial fraction of jobs is indeed offshorable, although the extent and distribution of offshorable jobs vary across countries. On average, about 38 percent of all respondents work in at least somewhat offshorable occupations.

This tendency not only has resulted in an increasing international interdependence of production processes, but also has significant consequences for domestic workers and firms. Several studies show that workers employed in industries with high levels of foreign direct investments or in occupations that can readily be offshored report higher levels of job insecurity (Scheve and Slaughter 2004; Walter 2015, 2010). Offshoring and individuals' risk to lose their job to offshoring processes thus constitute an important aspect of the political economy of the internationalization of production.

The impact of the globalization of trade and production on the individual is thus determined by two factors: first, whether the individual is exposed to international competition or not (either in the form of trade or in the form of offshoring, or both), and, second, the individual's skill level. In combination, these two factors allow us to rank-order the risk profile of different groups of workers: Low-skilled individuals exposed to international competition experience the highest risk of losing their job and receiving low wages, making them the losers of globalization (Walter 2015, 2010). Low-skilled individuals working in sheltered industries or professions (e.g., cleaning personnel) are better off than their counterparts in the exposed industry, because they can enjoy the benefits of globalized production regimes – lower product prices and a higher variety of goods – without the employment risks associated with this development. Nonetheless, they receive lower wages than equally sheltered but highly skilled workers such as doctors or teachers. Finally, highly skilled workers exposed to international competition (such as engineers or business consultants) benefit most from globalization. They receive the highest wages and have the lowest risk of becoming unemployed because they can sell their output and labor at home and abroad.

In terms of policy preferences, this suggests that low-skilled and exposed individuals should be most opposed to a further opening of economic borders, whereas highly skilled individuals exposed to international competition should be the major supporters of further economic integration. Individuals sheltered from global competition should hold a more intermediate position, with low-skilled individuals more opposed than high-skilled individuals, although both benefit from the lower prices and higher product variety that the unfettered flow of goods and services generates.

The globalization of trade and production might thus generate preferences that cut across skill. However, this internationalization of commerce does not occur in isolation, but rather alongside another facet of globalization: the internationalization of labor. After a brief review of the pertinent literature, the next section will show that many low-skilled workers who do not have to compete with workers abroad because the goods and services they produce cannot easily be outsourced or imported will instead find themselves competing with immigrant labor.

5.2. Immigration Patterns and Preferences

Over the past few decades, immigration has fundamentally altered the social and demographic fabrics of many advanced industrialized democracies. In countries that never perceived themselves as nations of immigrants, such as Germany or Austria, foreign-born residents now constitute a sizable share of the population, on par with traditional immigration countries, such as the United States (see Figure 5.2).

At the low end of the skill spectrum, migrant workers may be recruited because they are willing to take menial and physically challenging jobs that natives deem undesirable. Migrant workers may also be willing to perform these tasks more cheaply than do native workers. At the high end of the skill spectrum, foreign workers are often recruited to meet domestic skill shortages. Immigrants arrive also for noneconomic reasons. Over the past two decades, domestic and international conflicts have produced a steady flow of refugees who flee their home countries in search for a better life. Moreover, primary economic migrants may be joined by their spouses and children, who are often not in the labor force.[4]

These seismic demographic changes have left their mark on domestic politics: Parties campaigning on antiimmigration platforms are credible contenders in a number of European countries, and they have siphoned off support from mainstream parties on both the Right and the Left. Parties in the center in turn feel pressure to respond to voters' discontent surrounding issues of immigration (e.g., Kitschelt and McGann 1995; Norris 2005; Mudde 2007; Arzheimer 2009; as well as Chapter 7 by Kitschelt and Rehm, this volume).

However, just as we have seen with other aspects of globalization, not all native workers are equally exposed to foreign labor, and, moreover, scholars disagree about the forces that shape preferences over immigration. Existing research presents conflicting evidence on whether and how economic considerations influence attitudes toward immigration. Though there is strong and consistent evidence that skill matters in shaping views about immigration, there

---

[4] For a review of the economic consequences of immigration, see Hanson (2009). See Constant and Zimmermann (2005) on the link between immigration policies and immigrant economic performance.

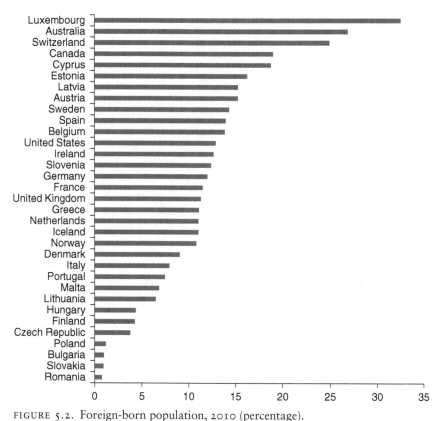

FIGURE 5.2. Foreign-born population, 2010 (percentage).
(OECD (2012a, 2012b) and Eurostat (2012a, 2012b). Note that data for Canada are from 2006; data for Slovakia and Romania are from 2009; and data for Switzerland are from 2011.)

is less agreement about the mechanisms driving this association. Some argue that the relationship between skill and immigration preferences is based on economic interests. In terms of predictions derived from the Heckscher-Ohlin framework, native workers are said to fear that immigrants with similar skills to their own will drive down their wages and take their jobs. Examining attitudes in the United States (Scheve and Slaughter 2001b) and across countries (Mayda 2006), scholars have indeed found that in settings where low-skilled immigrant labor is prevalent, low-skilled natives are more opposed to the inflow of immigrants than are natives with higher skill levels. Moreover, low-skilled natives prefer more highly skilled migrants to those with fewer skills (Hainmueller and Hiscox 2007; 2010). These patterns are consistent with the idea that economic interests and, specifically, the potentially adverse effects that immigration may have on wages play a role in shaping preferences over immigration policy.[5]

---

[5] The authors also find, however, that more highly skilled individuals prefer immigrants with more advanced educational qualification, a result that does not fit this line of argument.

Yet, as Hainmueller and Hiscox (2007; 2010) argue, skill levels – measured by educational attainment – can proxy for individuals' social tolerance, rather than measure their economic interests. Individuals who are more highly educated are also more likely to view the impact of immigration and the ethnic and cultural diversity it produces in a positive light. As a result, high-skilled natives more readily accept immigrants (even if migrants are highly skilled and therefore potential competitors in the labor market) than do their low-skilled counterparts. Opposition to immigration on the part of the less educated, less skilled workers is in turn largely a function of their xenophobic attitudes. A large body of research has in fact documented strong links between individuals' ethnocentrist attitudes and their positions on immigration. Fears that immigration may undermine national unity, endanger valued social norms, and threaten religious traditions are often at the forefront of antiimmigrant campaigns, and they are also important in shaping individuals' assessment of immigration (e.g., Sniderman and Hagendoorn 2007; Sides and Citrin 2007; Brader et al. 2008; see also Chapter 8 by Häusermann and Kriesi, this volume, for an analysis of the determinants of attitudes toward universalism vs. particularism).

Though we may think of accounts that stress the significance of economic sources of opinion formation on immigration, on the one hand, and those that insist on the primacy of cultural concerns, on the other, as representing two distant poles, it is also plausible that these two mechanisms overlap and interact. For the individual worker grappling with the consequences of immigration, separating cultural from economic effects in a clean and unambiguous way may not be feasible. Furthermore, the economic pressures of globalization itself – including those brought about by immigration – may help engender ethnocentrist attitudes. Economic losers of globalization can be particularly susceptible to nationalistic, ethnocentrist appeals (Kriesi et al. 2008). Others have similarly found that individuals who express uncertainty or dissatisfaction with respect to their own economic circumstances are more wary of immigration (O'Neil and Tienda 2010; Helbling 2011; Helbling and Kriesi 2012).[6]

This importance of individuals' positions in the economy suggests that varying economic conditions should lead to varying assessments of immigration. Depending on the economic context, natives may view immigration as benefiting or harming their economic welfare. It is not necessarily the case, for example, that natives encounter immigrant coworkers as economically threatening. In practice, immigrants often move to growing sectors and when the economy is booming, in which case downward wage pressures may be muted.[7] If

---

[6] By contrast, Citrin et al. (1997) argue that personal economic circumstances do not account for views on immigration but rather evaluations of the state of the national economy and taxes. See Dancygier (2010) for an account that links local economic conditions to antiimmigrant mobilization.

[7] See Card (2001) on how native outflows as well as positive demand shocks may influence immigration's labor market effects across cities. Note that the wages that a native worker would have earned in the absence of immigration may very well have been different.

immigrants seek employment in sectors that experience growth, they may provide the necessary reinforcement to meet rising demand, ensuring that firms remain competitive. Native workers may not be displaced from their jobs and their wages may not decline as a result of immigration.[8] This will be especially true if immigrant workers are not perfect substitutes for native labor, but are complements. For example, as Peri and Sparber (2009) note, immigrants who have imperfect language skills may specialize in manual labor, allowing natives to shift from manual to communication tasks.[9] When immigrants enter his sector, a native construction worker may thus move up to being a foreman.[10] In this scenario, natives may view immigrants as beneficial to their own economic situation.

Furthermore, migrant workers may actually protect native labor from the vagaries of the economy. When economic activity declines, employers often choose to lay off migrant workers ahead of native employees: During the Great Recession of 2007–2008, the unemployment rate among migrants increased twice as fast as that of natives in the EU-15 (OECD 2011: 74). Natives who observe the departure of migrant labor during slowdowns might therefore actually associate immigration with job security, though the opposite would be true if migrants continued to arrive and be hired once economies slowed down.

When investigating how the inflow of immigrant workers in natives' sector of employment influences preferences over immigration policy, evidence suggests that economic contexts do operate in this fashion. Focusing on migrant labor from outside Europe before and during the global financial crisis and the recessions it spawned, Dancygier and Donnelly (2013) find that the arrival of these migrant workers at the industry level dampens support for immigration, but only during economic downturns and in settings where public confidence about the future state of the economy is low. Conversely, during good economic times, additional arrivals of immigrants in their sectors do not trigger such negative reactions. Moreover, natives who are employed in sectors that experience growth are more likely to approve of immigration, while employment in shrinking sectors reduces support for open borders.

To gain a sense of how migrant workers are distributed, Table 5.1 presents the share of the foreign-born workforce in the five sectors with the highest share of immigrant labor across Western European countries (averaged

---

[8] Such dynamics have been said to characterize much of the low-skilled immigration occurring in the United States during the 1990s and 2000s (see Massey 2008).

[9] See also Ottaviano and Peri (2008). Note that Borjas et al. (2008) are critical of the empirical evidence supporting complementarity in the U.S. case.

[10] For a similar argument, see Hoffmann-Nowotny (1973).

TABLE 5.1. *Sectors with the highest shares of immigrant workers, by country*

Country	Sector	Percentage Immigrant Workforce		
		All	non-EU	EU
Austria	Accommodation and food	28.8	22.2	6.6
	Real estate	24.9	20.3	4.5
	Food manufacturing	20.1	16.5	3.6
	Arts, culture, and recreation	18.4	9.4	8.9
	Construction	18.1	14.5	3.6
Belgium	Accommodation and food	25.8	16.2	9.6
	Other business activities	14.2	7.0	7.2
	Arts, culture, and recreation	12.5	6.2	6.3
	Information technology	12.1	5.0	7.1
	Construction	12.0	5.0	7.0
Switzerland	Accommodation and food	41.5	24.8	22.6
	Household goods and service production	32.0	12.2	19.9
	Manufacturing related to natural resources	31.4	16.6	19.2
Greece	Household goods and service production	74.9	67.7	7.2
	Construction	29.1	27.1	2.1
	Accommodation and food	12.8	10.8	2.0
	Manufacture of consumer and other goods	12.2	11.3	0.9
	Manufacturing related to natural resources	9.7	9.1	0.6
Ireland	Accommodation and food	29.1	11.1	18.0
	Information technology	23.7	6.7	17.1
	Food manufacturing	21.4	5.5	15.9
	Other business activities	15.2	4.0	11.3
	Health and social services	15.0	6.5	8.5
Italy	Household goods and service production	66.7	54.4	12.3
	Construction	15.5	11.5	4.1
	Accommodation and food	15.5	11.5	3.9

(continued)

TABLE 5.1. (continued)

Country	Sector	Percentage Immigrant Workforce		
	Food manufacturing	29.1	20.8	12.5
	Construction	27.1	13.9	17.1
Denmark	Accommodation and food	15.5	13.5	2.1
	Land transportation	7.9	6.9	1.0
	Food manufacturing	7.5	6.2	1.3
	Education	7.5	4.8	2.6
	Other business activities	7.4	5.2	2.1
Spain	Household goods and service production	49.0	43.4	5.6
	Accommodation and food	26.1	21.4	4.7
	Construction	19.8	16.2	3.7
	Agriculture, fishing, and logging	14.6	12.3	2.3
	Food manufacturing	12.0	9.6	2.4

Country	Sector	Percentage Immigrant Workforce		
	Other services	13.8	10.5	3.3
	Manufacturing related to natural resources	10.4	8.3	2.0
Luxembourg	Household goods and service production	88.2	7.4	80.8
	Accommodation and food	77.4	17.9	59.5
	Construction	74.1	6.6	67.6
	Financial auxiliary activities	64.0	9.0	55.0
	Other business activities	59.7	7.8	51.9
Netherlands	Accommodation and food	17.2	14.3	2.9
	Food manufacturing	15.9	13.4	2.6
	Other business activities	13.7	10.8	2.9
	Manufacturing related to natural resources	13.0	10.6	2.4
	Manufacture of consumer and other goods	12.6	10.4	2.2

Country	Sector			
Finland	Accommodation and food	6.1	5.0	1.1
	Retail	2.9	1.4	1.5
	Wholesale	2.9	1.5	1.4
	Other business activities	2.9	1.8	1.1
	Automotive	2.8	2.0	0.9
France	Household goods and service production	23.5	11.7	11.8
	Accommodation and food	19.1	15.2	3.9
	Construction	17.1	9.1	7.9
	Real estate	15.9	7.4	8.5
	Other business activities	14.2	10.7	3.5
Great Britain	Accommodation and food	21.6	14.8	6.8
	Information technology	16.6	12.6	4.0
	Food manufacturing	15.8	8.5	7.3
	Finance	13.9	9.6	4.3
	Land transportation	13.3	10.5	2.8
Norway	Accommodation and food	18.5	14.7	3.8
	Food manufacturing	9.5	6.9	2.7
	Land transportation	9.0	6.9	2.2
	Health and social services	8.5	5.4	3.1
	Postal and courier activities	7.7	6.3	1.4
Portugal	Household goods and service production	12.3	11.7	0.6
	Accommodation and food	11.5	10.0	1.5
	Other business activities	10.8	8.8	2.0
	Other services	10.8	9.2	1.6
	Construction	10.3	8.9	1.4
Sweden	Accommodation and food	29.1	24.3	4.8
	Research and development	15.4	8.8	6.6
	Land transportation	15.4	11.1	4.4
	Food manufacturing	15.0	10.8	4.2
	Health and social services	14.0	9.2	4.8

over the period 2002–2009).[11] We observe remarkably similar trends: Across countries, immigrant labor is most heavily represented in a small set of industries. The accommodation and food industry (comprising jobs in hotels and in food services) is one of the most common employers of migrant labor cross-nationally. In seven of the sixteen countries listed here, more than a quarter of workers in this industry hail from abroad. Likewise, household services are often performed by immigrant workers in many countries, especially in Southern economies. The construction industry is another popular destination for immigrant workers. If we take these countries as a whole, it emerges that 38.3 percent of all workers employed in the household services industry are foreign-born. The same is true for 21.7 and 14.2 percent of workers in the accommodation and food and in the construction industry, respectively.

5.3. Globalization Pressures and Individual Policy Preferences

The high concentration of foreign-born workers in predominantly low-skill-intensive industries implies that although many of the workers in nonoffshorable professions do not have to compete with workers abroad, they will instead find themselves competing with migrant labor at home. As Table 5.1 shows, the share of immigrant workers is highest in industries that predominantly employ low-skilled labor and whose goods cannot be outsourced or imported. Most jobs in the hotel and restaurant industry, in households, and in construction have to be performed locally. Native low-skilled workers who find shelter from international trade and offshoring are thus exposed to migrant labor.

A similar picture emerges when we examine the relationship between offshorability and immigration across occupations[12]: Workers with the lowest risk of having their jobs shipped abroad are most likely to compete with migrants domestically. Across West European countries, 13 percent of the workforce employed in occupations that cannot be offshored is foreign-born, with the majority of workers originating outside the EU (see Table 5.2). This share is almost 4 points lower in occupations that do have offshoring potential (p = .000), and the difference is especially pronounced among the low-skilled. Native workers who did not complete lower secondary education and whose

---

[11] The table includes the EU-15, plus Norway and Switzerland. Germany is excluded because German labor force surveys do not contain information about workers' country of birth. The data derive from European labor force surveys that typically identify respondents' industry of employment and country of birth, and industry designations are based on the Classification of Economic Activities in the European Union (NACE). Note that industry classifications changed in 2008. In order to make NACE version 1.1 (2000 to 2007) compatible with version 2 (implemented in 2008) we rely on the classification of Dancygier and Donnelly (2013), which identifies 31 mutually exclusive industries across versions. This allows us to track sectoral employment patterns over time. For more details on the industry coding procedure and on the resulting data set, see Dancygier and Donnelly (2013).

[12] Note that while offshorability data are based on four-digit ISCO codes, Eurostat only provides data on the concentration of foreign-born in occupations at the three-digit level. We must therefore interpret the exposure to immigrants as pertaining to the larger occupational grouping.

TABLE 5.2. *Concentration of foreign-born labor force in occupations by offshorability and skill (percentage), among natives*

		All	< Lower Secondary	Lower Secondary	Upper Secondary	Postsecondary and Tertiary	N
Overall average		11.52	13.85	13.70	10.95	9.51	19,979
By offshoring potential							
none	0–24	13.03	15.99	15.45	12.22	10.15	12,165
low	25–49	8.85	7.83	9.26	9.09	8.69	2,036
medium	50–74	8.85	10.00	10.22	8.99	9.13	4,016
high	75–100	8.97	8.05	11.84	9.60	7.92	1,762
Difference (none vs. low, medium, high)		3.86	6.90	5.15	3.09	1.45	
T-statistic		29.73	19.55	15.73	13.25	8.17	

Note: These data are based on weighted responses from the fourth round of the European Social Survey. The concentration of foreign-born labor is based on responses gathered in European Labor Force Surveys and provided by Eurostat.

jobs cannot be offshored can be found in occupations where the average share of foreign-born workers is 16 percent, which is almost 7 points higher than the exposure to foreign-born labor that their low-skill counterparts in offshorable occupations encounter. These differences decline monotonically across the skill spectrum: As skill rises, overall immigrant exposure at the occupational level declines, and it varies less by offshorability. On average, native high-skill workers employed in occupations that cannot be offshored are only slightly more likely to work with migrant workers than are those employed in occupations that cannot be offshored.[13]

Figure 5.3 provides additional information on how these differences are distributed across skill and immigrant groups. It displays that the gap in exposure to migrant labor that we observe when comparing offshorable to nonoffshorable occupations is largely driven by immigration from outside the EU. To illustrate, the share of non-European housekeeping and restaurant service workers in France is 16 percent, but only 2.5 percent of workers in these nonoffshorable occupations are from an EU member state. Similarly, 20 percent of messengers, porters, and doorkeepers in France originate outside the EU while 12 percent hail from within the EU. By contrast, French workers employed in easily offshorable data entry occupations face a share of non-EU/EU labor of 6 and 3 percent, respectively.

In other words, workers with few skills who are employed in occupations that are safe from offshoring are much more likely to compete with migrant labor in general and with foreign workers whose ethnic backgrounds,

---

[13] With very few exceptions, the data do not indicate that specific occupations and sectors are entirely dominated by immigrants. The argument that immigration benefits low-skilled natives because they are able to move up to more desirable jobs (Hoffmann-Nowotny 1973) is therefore likely to play out only in areas with a very high concentration of immigrants.

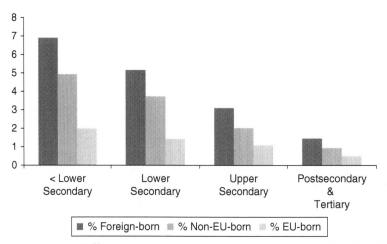

FIGURE 5.3. Difference in exposure to immigrants among natives in offshorable and nonoffshorable occupations (percentage points), by skill.

mother tongues, and religious beliefs are different from their own. As a result, low-skilled workers will find themselves squeezed by globalization whether they work in internationally exposed occupations or not. They face competition either from abroad (in the form of cheaper production costs and employers' opportunities to move production to other countries) or at home (in the form of competition from immigrant workers who are willing to work for relatively lower wages).

This means that both exposed and sheltered types of low-skilled workers may join together in a coalition opposing globalization in its different forms. This opposition should be strongest among low-skilled individuals, because these individuals face globalization-related risks no matter where they turn: As low-skilled workers who are employed in import-competing and offshorable occupations they are likely to suffer wage losses and job insecurity from the internationalization of trade and production, but if they try to move to more sheltered occupations, they are likely to experience domestic competition from immigrant workers. As a result, these individuals are likely to oppose any development that further increases any of these risks for them, such as a further trade liberalization or a lowering of barriers to immigration. Moreover, given the potential interplay between cultural fears and individuals' position in the economy, we can surmise that some – though surely not all – of the cultural concerns about immigration may not be easily divorced from economic ones as low-skilled labor often faces non-European immigrants at the workplace.[14]

---

[14] Scholars can of course isolate these two effects, especially in survey experiments (see, e.g., Brader et al. 2008; Malhotra et al. 2013). The point here is that empirically, cultural and economic threats often coincide and may reinforce one another. See also Margalit (2012) on this issue.

While low-skilled workers may therefore unite in their opposition to further globalization, with relatively small differences between exposed and sheltered individuals, there should be a larger gap in globalization-related policy preferences among high-skilled individuals. Among this group, individuals in occupations that are exposed to the international economy should be particularly interested in the gains that both free trade and production and a relatively unhindered movement of labor can generate. In terms of trade and FDI, these gains result mainly from the high returns on their labor. With respect to immigration, these individuals are likely to value the wage-compressing and hence production-cost-cutting effects of low-skilled migrants, as this increases the international competitiveness of their products and their ability to buy services provided by low-skilled labor. In contrast, the cost-saving effects on production costs are likely to play a much smaller role for high-skilled individuals who find themselves largely independent of and sheltered from global competition. Nonetheless, even these high-skilled individuals are likely to value the lower product prices and higher product varieties generated by international trade and the low-cost services low-skilled migrants can provide for them, so that high-skilled individuals overall are much more likely to support a further integration of the world economy than individuals with low levels of education.

5.4. Globalization Preferences in Fourteen European Countries: An Empirical Analysis of Attitudes toward Immigration

To test the empirical implications of this argument, we use survey data from the 2008 wave of the European Social Survey for fourteen West European countries.[15] All countries included in the analysis are advanced industrialized and open economies and have significant experience with both globalization and immigration.

The purpose of the analysis is to examine how variation in skills and off-shorability affects individual preferences about globalization-related policies, most notably their preferences on immigration. We aim to demonstrate that variation in individuals' exposure to the pressures exerted by the globalization of production is systematically related to their views about the globalization of labor. We therefore focus on immigration attitudes, although the analyses we present in the following also apply to opinions about broader aspects of globalization, namely, European integration.[16] To measure individuals' preferences

---

[15] The countries included in the analysis are Belgium, Denmark, Finland, France, Germany, Greece, Ireland, Netherlands, Norway, Portugal, Spain, Sweden, Switzerland, and the United Kingdom.

[16] Unfortunately the ESS does not include a question about trade policy or another policy regarding the internationalization of trade and production, which would allow us to test explicitly whether globalization exposure is related to preferences about these policies. In supplementary analyses we therefore used views about European integration, which are measured with respondents' self-placement on an 11-point scale ranging from the position "o – [European]

regarding the movement of labor, we use respondents' self-placement on an 11-point scale in response to the following question: "Would you say it is generally bad or good for [country]'s economy that people come to live here from other countries?" Answers range from "Bad for the economy" (0) to "Good for the economy" (10).

We have argued that we should observe differences in policy opinions regarding the globalization of labor between high- and low-skilled individuals. Moreover, we expect to see a gap between exposed and sheltered individuals, and this gap should be particularly pronounced among the highly skilled, with exposed workers holding much more favorable opinions about the economic desirability of immigration than high-skilled workers in sheltered professions. These considerations suggest three independent variables: one measuring individuals' level of skills, the second measuring their exposure to globalization, and the third an interaction term to capture the conditional effect of globalization exposure among high- and low-skilled workers. To operationalize individuals' level of skills, we use their education level and differentiate four different levels: less than lower secondary education, lower secondary education, upper secondary education, and postsecondary or tertiary education. We measure individuals' exposure to globalization as the offshorability of their job, as described previously. Finally, the conditional effect of globalization exposure on skill is captured using an interaction term between the respondents' education level and their job offshorability. We also include a number of standard variables that control for alternative explanations for variation in immigration policy preferences at the individual level. Income, measured on an ordinal 10-point scale; gender; age in years; past or present labor union membership; whether the respondent is unemployed; and whether he or she was born in his or her country of residence.

We use ordinary least squares analyses to test the different empirical predictions of our argument. To account for the fact that respondents from the same country share a common context, we include country dummies and additionally cluster the standard errors on the country level to address the related problem of within-country correlation of errors. Table 5.3 presents the results for the regression analyses of the determinants on Europeans' preferences regarding the effects of immigration on the country's economy. To facilitate the interpretation of these results, Figure 5.4 presents the marginal effects of individuals' job offshorability across different levels of education.

---

unification has already gone too far" to "10 – [European] unification should go further." Of course, European unification is a multifaceted process, which includes many more aspects than the creation of a single market. Nonetheless, economic integration is a central component of the European project. Further, given the free movement of labor within the European Union, this question also partly captures individuals' preferences about the globalization of labor. The results we obtain in this analysis (available from the authors) are broadly consistent with our argument and similar to our findings related to immigration opinions.

TABLE 5.3. *Determinants of immigration preferences*

	(1)	(2)	(3)	(4)
Job offshorability	−0.0446	−0.0948*	0.0262	0.103***
	(0.0331)	(0.0374)	(0.0422)	(0.0223)
Education level	0.468***	0.311***	0.184	0.729***
	(0.0501)	(0.0396)	(0.131)	(0.0915)
Offshorability * education level	0.0615**	0.0714***		
	(0.0160)	(0.0162)		
Age	0.00613**	0.00355	0.00486	0.00322
	(0.00183)	(0.00214)	(0.00357)	(0.00278)
Female	−0.297***	−0.360***	−0.271**	−0.297**
	(0.0551)	(0.0532)	(0.0791)	(0.0690)
Income	0.0587***	0.0390***	0.0450*	0.0556***
	(0.00920)	(0.00794)	(0.0153)	(0.0127)
Union member	0.0666	0.0452	0.0541	0.0646
	(0.0614)	(0.0559)	(0.115)	(0.0734)
Unemployed	−0.246*	−0.182	−0.129	−0.219
	(0.114)	(0.113)	(0.262)	(0.104)
Native	−1.039***	−1.070***	−1.449***	−0.920***
	(0.175)	(0.171)	(0.274)	(0.179)
Class categories				
Self-employed		0.789***		
		(0.135)		
Small business		0.129		
		(0.0885)		
Managers		0.431***		
		(0.0885)		
Office		0.119		
		(0.0683)		
Technical		0.459***		
		(0.0795)		
Production		−0.221**		
		(0.0624)		
Sociocultural professionals		0.692***		
		(0.115)		
Others		0.740*		
		(0.307)		
% Foreign-Born in Occupation			−0.00912*	0.000495
			(0.00372)	(0.00704)

(*continued*)

TABLE 5.3. (*continued*)

	(1)	(2)	(3)	(4)
Constant	4.139***	4.619***	5.195***	3.438***
	(0.237)	(0.196)	(0.0995)	(0.260)
N	15861	15861	3563	10199
R^2	0.140	0.153	0.094	0.129

Note: The dependent variable is the response to the question whether the respondent thinks immigration is good for his or her country's economy, with higher values on the 10-point scale denoting a more positive assessment of immigration. Values in parentheses are robust standard errors, clustered on country. Country dummies are included but not reported. Data are weighted by the design weight. In Models 3 and 4 (subset analyses of the low- respectively, the high-skilled) the education variable is a dummy variable differentiating between more and less low-skilled (model 3) and more and less high-skilled (model 4) individuals. Note that data on foreign-born workers at the occupation level are missing for Germany, which is therefore excluded in Models 3 and 4. $*p < 0.05$, $**p < 0.01$, $***p < 0.001$.

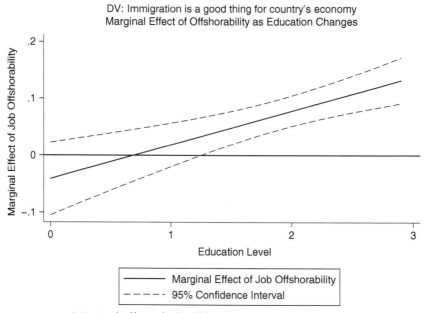

FIGURE 5.4. Marginal effect of job offshorability at different levels of education.

Most importantly, the analyses show that as expected, a) low-skilled individuals are more opposed to immigration than are high-skilled individuals, and b) the differences in opinion between individuals exposed to the global competition of production and those sheltered from such competition are much more pronounced among high-skilled than they are among low-skilled individuals.

In line with previous research, we find that more educated respondents view the economic consequences of immigration more favorably than respondents with low levels of education. The mean predicted value on the 11-point immigration question for individuals with less than lower secondary education is 4.10, whereas it is 5.69 for individuals with postsecondary or tertiary education. As low-skilled individuals face stronger competition through the increasing economic exchange across European borders as well as domestic labor market competition from low-skilled immigrants, their willingness to support further moves toward an opening of national borders is limited. Squeezed from both sides – foreign competition from international trade and production and domestic competition from migrant workers – these individuals are less likely than are high-skilled respondents to support immigration. Although individuals with low levels of education working in exposed occupations are even less supportive of proglobalization policies (mean predicted value: 4.02) than are low-skilled individuals in sheltered occupations (4.10), this difference is not statistically significant. This suggests that on a critical issue surrounding globalization low-skilled individuals tend to unite, whereas high-skilled workers, though generally in favor of globalization, show clearer splits on the basis of their exposure to global trade and production. Here, individuals in highly offshorable occupations (5.97) are significantly more supportive of the statement that immigration is good for their country's economy than equally high-skilled individuals in sheltered occupations (5.58).

To investigate the robustness of this result, we run a number of additional analyses. The first concerns the question whether our results are driven by other characteristics of workers than their exposure to globalization pressures. In particular, as Daniel Oesch has argued in Chapter 4, occupational upgrading has particularly threatened clerks and production workers. His argument suggests that these workers should oppose further competition by immigrant labor, whereas managers and professionals should be interested in the low-cost services immigrants can provide. While this argument complements our argument, it is possible that our results reflect these differences, rather than genuine effects of skills. In column 2 of Table 5.2, we therefore additionally control for Oesch's eight occupational classes (Oesch 2006), taking service workers as the base category. Consistent with Oesch's argument, we find that different types of workers vary in their views about immigration. Production workers stand out for their negative assessment of immigration, whereas individuals in more privileged employment relationships assess the consequences of immigration on the economy significantly more positively than do service workers. At the same time, controlling for occupational classes actually strengthens our original results: The effect of skills, net of occupational characteristics, remains statistically significant and positive and the interaction term between skills and offshorability rises, whereas the effect of offshorability is now more negative and significant for low-skilled workers. This result lends further support to the claim that skill and exposure to the global economy matters.

Last, we test whether concentration of foreign-born workers in respondents' occupation leads to more pessimistic assessments about immigration among those with low skills. We therefore subset our analyses by skill and include our measure of the share of foreign-born workers at the occupation level (Models 3 and 4; respondents with at most a lower secondary degree are coded as low-skill while those who have an upper secondary degree or higher are considered highly skilled). It is indeed the case that working in occupations that employ larger shares of immigrants is associated with less favorable views among the low-skilled, but this is not true among the more highly skilled. Moreover, and consistent with our argument and previous results, respondents employed in offshorable occupations are significantly more optimistic about the economic consequences of immigration when they are highly skilled, a result that does not hold among the low-skilled.[17]

Overall, these results are consistent with the argument that low-skilled workers are pressured by all forms of globalization and are therefore skeptical of a further opening of borders. In contrast, high-skilled individuals welcome the opportunities the free movement of goods, services, and labor provides. They consistently exhibit more favorable opinions about the economic desirability of immigration than do individuals with low levels of education. This favorable opinion is especially salient among individuals working in highly offshorable professions. Among respondents with a postsecondary education, those working in more exposed occupations have a significantly more positive view of the impact of immigration on their country's economy than equally educated respondents working in more sheltered occupations. This finding is in line with the idea that high-skilled individuals who are constantly exposed to the international economy are most sensitive to the beneficial effects of globalization on their national economies.

5.5. Conclusion

What are the implications of our results for the ways in which globalization shapes political cleavages in advanced capitalist democracies? On the one hand, the literature on the domestic political consequences of globalization has highlighted that economic liberalization may splinter class-based coalitions: Voters within the same skill group may derive different benefits from the free flow of goods, services, and labor depending on their sectoral or occupational profiles. Individuals who are sheltered from globalization's competitive pressures may benefit from lower prices, whereas workers employed in exposed sectors and occupations experience higher levels of competition. As we have discussed, more recent work refines these accounts, additionally differentiating the expected impacts of globalization on the basis of, for instance, firm

---

[17] This result also holds when we additionally include an interaction term between offshorability and the concentration of immigrants in a given occupation.

competitiveness and economic conditions. On the other hand, however, we consistently find that skill remains a significant determinant of preferences about the globalization of labor. To the extent that skills are a good proxy for class, our results suggest that class remains a central cleavage in the politics surrounding globalization: Low-skilled voters are more likely to voice concerns about the economic and cultural dimensions of globalization and are also more likely to flock to parties that run on antiglobalization platforms.

The persistent effect of class, we argue, stems in part from the fact that low-skilled workers are pressured by globalization in multiple ways. Such workers find it more difficult to find shelter from globalization than do individuals with higher skills. Low-skill workers employed in occupations that face few risks from offshoring because their labor has to be performed locally may be shielded from the globalization of production – but they cannot easily escape the globalization of labor. Rather, workers with few educational qualifications in advanced capitalist democracies are more likely to compete with immigrant workers, and this is especially the case when their jobs are not readily shipped abroad. By contrast, high-skill workers are less likely to encounter migrant labor in their jobs and, furthermore, tend to benefit, rather than suffer, from the internationalization of global production processes.

Last, native workers with few educational qualifications also tend to experience the potential cultural threats unleashed by globalization. These individuals may harbor more ethnocentrist attitudes to begin with. It is also the case, however, that low-skill workers are more likely than their high-skill counterparts to encounter migrant labor, and, specifically, non-European migrant workers, on the labor market. This confluence of economic and cultural threats (which may extend beyond the workplace to neighborhoods and public spaces) suggests that both dimensions may interact, have reinforcing effects on preferences, and together likely shape how globalization alters domestic cleavages.

The patterns we present here suggest that globalization should not necessarily reduce the significance of class in domestic politics – at least when we restrict our focus to individuals' exposure to economic liberalization on the labor market. Specifically, if low-skilled workers align themselves politically on the basis of how globalization influences their economic welfare they may join in a coalition opposing globalization even though these workers are exposed to different aspects of globalization. This prediction is obviously consistent with accounts that model the wage impacts of globalization on the basis of skill. However, our results show that they are also in line with sectoral accounts as low-skilled workers bear the brunt of globalization's competitive pressures from multiple fronts. We may instead observe greater variability on the part of the highly skilled.

Whether or not these labor market effects reshape political coalitions depends, of course, on a host of other factors, not the least of which is whether these labor market experiences indeed shape voter behavior at the polls (as suggested, e.g., by the findings in Walter 2015; Mughan and Lacy 2002;

Mughan et al. 2003; Margalit 2011) and whether political elites seize on these preferences. Our results suggest that low-skilled workers across occupations will likely cast ballots for parties that pledge to curb globalization, or for those that promise to soften its blow by delivering compensation. Chapters 7 and 8 in this volume will show that especially the former has become an important reality, as low-skilled workers increasingly tend to support right-wing populist parties.

6

The Return of the Family

Gøsta Esping-Andersen

Where is the family heading? The dominant view in popular debate and scientific research alike is that it is an eroding and perhaps even endangered species. The "ever-less family" scenario emerges from adherents of both Gary Becker's neoclassical economic model and theories of postmodernity. Both predict a continuous decline in marriage, more singlehood, and less binding partnerships through cohabitation or trendy "living apart together" arrangements. This, in turn, implies rising partnership instability, divorce, and repartnering. And we are said to face a long-term low fertility scenario as a growing proportion of citizens remain childless or desire fewer children.

These similar predictions emerge from diametrically opposed arguments. The Becker framework would stress the declining returns to marriage and the rising opportunity costs of motherhood that are associated with women's embrace of serious lifelong career ambitions (Becker 1960, 1981). The postmodernists see the "less family" scenario as being driven by new values that favor individualism and self-realization over long-term commitments (Lesthaeghe 1995, 1998).

I shall present an alternative interpretation of ongoing trends. The essence of my argument is that the process of family decay we have observed over the past half-century is transitory, not permanent. In my framework, the epoch of "less family" represents an *unstable equilibrium*. This implies, first, the absence of any strong, let alone hegemonic, normative coherence, and this is why it will fail to reproduce itself endogenously. Second, under such conditions family outcomes are likely to be Pareto suboptimal, exhibiting not only inefficiency but also inequities.

Rising family instability emerged in response to the decaying old normative order (equilibrium), premised on the male breadwinner-cum-housewife arrangement. This, in turn, was of course spurred by the revolution of women's roles. My core thesis is that a realignment of gender relations is a fundamental prerequisite for any new viable and stable family equilibrium to emerge.

Such a realignment has been slow in the making. I shall emphasize three reasons for this. The first is related to how much women have "masculinized" their life course in terms of employment. The key lies in the extent to which the typical woman adopts a lifelong, full-time career dedication, as opposed to the weaker commitments associated with part-time work and/or interrupted career paths. The second reason relates to the extent to which men have "feminized" their life course in terms of home production. As so much time-use research shows, male adaptation in the domestic sphere has lagged far behind the pace of women's change, resulting in blatant inequities in the distribution of work and leisure (Gershuny et al. 2005; Esping-Andersen et al. 2013). Here, the key to a new stable equilibrium lies in the move toward egalitarian partnerships. And, third, the emergence of such a new family model will be greatly facilitated by welfare state adaptation, in particular as regards policies that help reconcile motherhood and careers (McDonald 2000; Esping-Andersen 2009). This points to the importance of adopting a more investment oriented policy approach, as Gingrich and Ansell discuss in Chapter 11.

6.1. The Emergence of Multiple Family Equilibria

The early phases of the female revolution led to a profound questioning of family life as it was then defined. But in its advanced stages, the revolution will produce novel family norms that harmonize better with citizens' inherent child and partnership preferences.[1] Family values and, more specifically, preferences about having children seem not to have changed much over the past half-century. It is therefore unlikely that the fertility decline-cum-divorce boom we witnessed over the past half-century was driven by new preference sets. And, if a large share of women end up with fewer children than desired, we must conclude that outcomes are non-Paretian.

The historical dynamics can be depicted as a U-shaped curve, as shown in Figure 6.1 – here illustrated with divorce rates (TDR). Point A represents a regime dominated by the traditional male breadwinner-housewife arrangement. It should produce stable marriages (and high fertility). Point B represents a situation in which the female revolution is advanced but in which men as well as societal institutions have yet to adapt, producing marital instability. And point C depicts a regime where the female revolution has advanced to the point that gender egalitarianism has become the dominant norm.

This evolution displays features characteristic of multiple equilibria. Multiple equilibrium models have a long-standing tradition in economic analysis. Given their affinity to sociological norm theory it is surprising that the approach has rarely found its way into sociological research (see, however, Lopez-Pintado and Watts 2008).

---

[1] Goldscheider (2012) develops an argument that parallels mine in many respects.

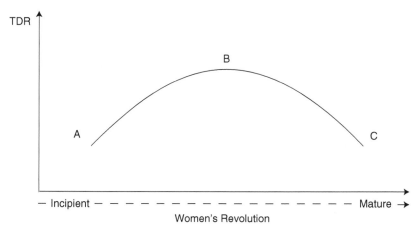

FIGURE 6.1. The revolution of women's roles and total divorce rate.

Equilibrium refers to a situation in which individuals act on well-defined expectations about others' strategies of action. It gains stability and becomes self-perpetuating when members of a community consistently abide by the same normative standards: when expectations are reconfirmed over time. In other words, equilibria exist when norms are endogenously reproduced. This logic can be exemplified by the male breadwinner family. It became an equilibrium because women invested primarily in homemaker skills in anticipation of their future role and this, of course, reproduced endogenously the self-fulfilling prophecy of comparative advantage.

A core theoretical assumption is that stable equilibria are more likely to yield Pareto optimality: They produce fair and efficient outcomes. The close links to sociological work on normative adherence are often made explicit (Blume and Durlauf 2001; Brock and Durlauf 2001; Durlauf 2001; Manski 1993; Young and Burke 2001).

Multiple equilibrium models represent a scenario in which a) there are unstable equilibria – that is, "normative confusion," and b) any number of alternative normative regimes may emerge. Finally, theory posits that the consolidation of any new stable equilibrium requires a dynamic whereby an ever-growing population adopts the novel normative standards.

In comparison to conventional sociological norm theory, multiple equilibrium models are explicitly dynamic. The dynamics are, at the outset, driven by *exogenous* "shocks" that recast expectations. If sufficiently powerful they will weaken the normative sway of how "we used to do things." But this does not mean that an alternative new normative standard will automatically emerge. For such to occur, the external "shock" must be followed by a self-reinforcing *endogenous* process of adopting a novel "self-evident way to play." This is most likely to occur via a diffusion process. Granovetter's (1978) threshold models of collective action and Krugman's (1991) theory of the Industrial Revolution offer classic examples of this logic.

The exogenous shocks that provoked the decay of traditional family norms are now well documented. Birth control allowed women to control fertility; new household technologies drastically reduced the necessary time for housework (e.g., the washing machine reduced laundry time from four hours to forty minutes); the rise of white-collar service jobs created ready-made employment opportunities for women. The upshot was that women began to invest in education rather than in homemaker skills (Goldin 2006). And this, in turn, revolutionized women's perception of what makes for Pareto optimal outcomes.

But neither societal institutions nor partnership behavior adapted itself readily to the revolution. Governments and employers often took a very long time to introduce measures to facilitate the reconciliation of motherhood and careers, and within the family women found themselves saddled with a double shift. As literally mountains of feminist writings have told us, the world ended up being unfair to women. Not surprisingly, women would conclude that the opportunity costs of marriage and having children seemed far too steep.

When men's and women's market productivities converge, traditional gender relations in the private sphere will appear both inefficient and unfair. They produce efficiency losses if women's market productivities exceed their housework productivities; they promote unfairness if wives end up with a double shift. And they promote disutilities if, because of problems of reconciling work and family, women have fewer children than desired. In non-Paretian situations there are three distinct rational responses: exit, voice, or loyalty.

The *exit* option has been well documented in terms of rising divorce and nonmarriage rates. The choice of exit was originally more prevalent among highly educated women but is now increasingly concentrated among the low educated. In the United States, for example, low-educated women are more than twice as likely not to marry (Goldstein and Kenney 2001). A very good illustration of this logic is found in Edin and Kefalas's (2005) study of unmarried mothers in the United States: Low-educated American women with strong family preferences shun marriage because of the lack of suitable male partners (McLanahan 2004). And some studies have shown that perceived unfairness leads egalitarian women to divorce (Greenstein 1996; Sayer and Bianchi 2000).

The probability of exit can be diminished via careful partner selection. There is clear evidence that assortative mating is increasing among the highly educated (Blossfeld and Timm 2003; Mare 1991; Schwartz and Mare 2005). This is no doubt the consequence of postponing marriage but also reflects higher-educated women's preference for egalitarian men. Gimenez-Nadal et al. (2012) show that partnering rates are significantly higher when men express egalitarian norms.

Loyalty implies "biting the bullet." This can take two forms. One is to resign oneself to a life of unfairness: Couples in which the wife works a double shift do not necessarily divorce. "Doing gender" may be considered a variant of this;

here couples adopt an inequitable arrangement so as to reconfirm traditional gender identities. Another is to slide back to status quo ante arrangements. Grunow et al.'s (2012) longitudinal study illustrates the loyalty scenario well: Initially egalitarian German couples revert to traditionalism once they have children – no doubt spurred also by Germany's resilient ideology of conventional motherhood roles.

The *voice* strategy implies an active effort to impose a more gender symmetric arrangement, possibly by invoking the threat of exit or by mobilizing bargaining power. When voice prevails over exit and loyalty in Pareto-suboptimal conditions, we should expect that the endogenous dynamics of a gender symmetric equilibrium will begin to accelerate. And where such a new family equilibrium begins to establish itself as a strong normative referent for how boys and girls prepare themselves for adulthood, and for how women and men perceive their natural roles in family life, that is when "the family will return."

6.2. Contradictory Evidence

The "less family" thesis faces two major contradictions. As mentioned, studies of family values show a surprising degree of stability in citizens' preferences regarding marriage, parenthood, and the desired number of children (Scott and Braun 2006).[2] It is also noteworthy that preferences hardly vary across either gender or education level. With the partial exception of Germany, we observe that the two (plus) child norm remains as strong today as in the past.

Around 1960, fertility rate (TFR) was above 2.3 in all advanced capitalist democracies. TFR then fell to levels between 1.2 and 1.7 everywhere, and over the last decades, we have, in fact, observed a bifurcated trend in national fertility rates. A growing number of countries have experienced a clear u-turn, displaying a rise in births. Both North America and Northern Europe now boast a seemingly stable fertility rate around 1.9–2.0. All the evidence suggests that the fertility reversal is positively related to development, income, and even female labor market participation (Myrskylä, Kohler, and Billari 2009; OECD 2011). However, in another group of countries, such as Germany, Japan, and the Mediterranean basin, there are no real signs of recovery. Here we observe a long-term lowest-low fertility syndrome, with TFRs below 1.4–1.5.

Even more surprisingly, the socioeconomic gradient of fertility has flip-flopped in the high-fertility countries. The most recent evidence for the

[2] As Scott and Braun (2006) show, the "postmodern" value changes are only in real evidence for issues related to sexuality. In countries as diverse as France, Italy, Sweden, and the United Kingdom the stated ideal number of children is the same for the most recent (born after 1977) cohort as it was for the pre-1947 cohorts. In Germany, however, we do see a decline (based on the 2006 Eurobarometer data from the EU Commission). Similarly, data from the World Values Surveys show that only a small minority of citizens agree that "marriage is out of date." To illustrate, in "vanguard" countries such as Denmark, Norway, and the United States, the percentage who agree is only 10–15 percent.

United States shows a U-shaped relationship between number of children and education level (Hazan and Zoabi 2011). Data from Scandinavia indicate that higher-educated women now have more children than the less educated. They are in particular more likely to have three plus children (Lappegaard and Rønsen 2005).

This means that those who should face the steepest opportunity costs of motherhood are the very same who have most children (and vice versa). In a Becker framework, this would appear irrational, and it is difficult to imagine that low-educated women are the front-runners of postmodern values.

We observe a similar reversal in marital behavior. In the United States, college educated women are more likely to marry, and their partnerships are increasingly more stable (Isen and Stevenson 2010; McLanahan 2004; Raley and Bumpass 2003). A similar trend has been identified for Scandinavia and the United Kingdom (Chan and Halpin 2008). From U.S. data[3], we know the socioeconomic divorce gap by following couples over almost twenty-five years: After twenty years of marriage, 70 percent in the top income quintile remain so, compared to less than 50 percent in the bottom income quintile.

Indeed, this trend appears to consolidate throughout the advanced world. For Denmark, I have calculated an odds ratio for union dissolution (over a ten-year period) among low-educated women of 1.27 compared to .76 for the high educated (Esping-Andersen 2009). Similar results emerge for Italy, Japan, and Spain (Bernardi and Martínez-Pastor 2011; Raymo, Fukuda, and Iwasawa 2012; Salvini and Vignoli 2011). The "less family" scenario is gradually fading within high-SES populations and is now concentrated ever more among the low-SES strata. This is nowhere more evident than in lone-mother trends, in the United States especially (McLanahan 2004).

We seem to be witnessing a demographic u-turn, and, if we are, family research requires an alternative theoretical foundation. That the resurrection of strong families is led by the highly educated is quite consistent with the multiple equilibrium framework. These are the couples who are most likely to embrace gender egalitarianism. Let us now explore the historical dynamics a bit closer.

6.3. The Erosion of the Postwar Family

The postwar male breadwinner family would be the logical starting point. Marriage occurred early in life, unions were comparably stable, and fertility high.[4] Departures from this model were spearheaded by the first wave of higher-educated women in pursuit of lifelong employment. In North America and Scandinavia, the disappearance of the housewife accelerated from the 1970s

---

[3] Population Study of Income Dynamics (PSID), waves 1980–2003.

[4] Recall, however, that high fertility in the 1940s and 1950s was also fueled by postponement due to the war.

onward. A telling statistic is the employment rate of mothers of preschool age children. In the United States it was marginal until the 1960s (<20 percent). By 1980 it had doubled, and by 2000 tripled (to 63 percent). In Scandinavia the shift was even more spectacular: For example, Danish mothers' employment rate has exceeded 80 percent for many decades now (Esping-Andersen 2009). In tandem, cohabitation (especially in Scandinavia and France) spread as an alternative to formal marriage while fertility declined and partnerships became more unstable. The prototypical unmarried, divorced, or childless Scandinavian woman in the 1970s was most likely university educated and career oriented.

Although trends moved in the same direction across all advanced countries, there are noticeable differences in terms of timing, pace, and degree. Examining fertility, some of the divergence appears simply to be lag effects: The decline starts ten to fifteen years later in laggard countries such as Italy or Spain. But there are noticeable differences in how the trajectories unfold. The Nordic countries, together with France and the Netherlands, represent a similar logic: from levels of roughly 2.5–2.8 in the 1960s, the TFR reached its nadir in the early to mid-1980s (roughly 1.5), after which it eventually recovered to a seemingly stable 1.8–2.0. Examining instead completed fertility rates we see that the most recent cohorts that can be observed do indeed reach the two-child target in these countries. That is far from the case in Italy or Spain.

In the United Kingdom and the United States, the decline culminated in the 1970s (with a low of 1.7), and then recovered back to a 2.0 level. And, in a third group, which includes Germany, Italy, Spain, and Japan, the decline begins later, bottoming out in the 1990s. This group stands out in terms of reaching lowest-low TFRs (< 1.3) and also of failing to produce, so far, any clear recovery (a number of ex-communist countries display a rather similar profile, as do a number of East Asian countries, including Singapore, Hong Kong, and Taiwan).

The fertility recovery we see in the vanguard societies squares poorly with the prediction that women's employment or postmodernism should produce a steady decline in fertility.[5] So the first question is whether the recovery is transitory or genuine. Some demographers are skeptical, arguing that the recovery may be driven by a tempo effect due to postponement and subsequent catch-up, or possibly by a surge of immigration (Goldstein, Sobotka, and Jasilioniene 2009). But for a number of countries it would be hard to maintain that the recovery is simply epiphenomenal.[6] To exemplify, in Denmark, France, Norway, and the United Kingdom the postponement process appears to have ended, and the TFR has hovered around 1.8–1.9 for more than twenty years.

---

[5] It also squares poorly with the more general prediction that fertility declines as societies become wealthier. Myrskylä et al. (2009) show that fertility recovery is especially strong in societies that score highest on the Human Development Index.

[6] Studies that adjust for the tempo effect confirm that the recovery is real for many countries (Vienna Institute for Demography, 2010).

In other words, in some countries the fertility reversal appears to be real, and, as emphasized by McDonald (2000) and Myrskylä et al. (2011), this is particularly evident in more gender-equal societies. The reversal appears similarly robust as regards marriage and divorce behavior. The latter may, in part, be driven by the logic originally argued by Goode (1962), namely, that when divorce is uncommon it will remain very much an upper-class affair; as it becomes widespread, divorce rate will rise within the lower classes. But what neither Goode nor basically anyone else had anticipated is that marital stability would rise among high-SES couples (Datta Gupta and Smith 2002; Ellwood and Jencks 2004; Esping-Andersen 2009; Härkönen and Dronkers 2006; McLanahan 2004; Salvini and Vignoli 2011). We also see in some countries that the propensity to marry (or form stable unions) in the first place is rising at the top and declining at the bottom (Goldstein and Kenney 2001). The latter, indeed, is key to Bernardi and Martínez-Pastor's (2011) argument that selection into marriage is not driving the observed rising marital stability among the higher educated. And it is also key to another, and far more troublesome argument, namely, that the growing socioeconomic gaps in marital and fertility behavior threaten to polarize society at large and, especially, the life chances of children. As Sarah McLanahan (2004) puts it, we face a situation of ever-more-diverging destinies.

6.4. Explaining the Turnaround

Why has fertility decline been so much steeper in, say, Italy and Spain, compared to France, Sweden, or the United States? And why do some countries stabilize at very low fertility rates while others recover relatively rapidly? A postmodernism explanation is hardly persuasive unless we are willing to accept that Spain is a global front-runner in terms of postmodern values, and that Sweden is now backtracking. The Becker perspective runs into similar difficulties. Lifelong female employment is the norm in Scandinavia and North America, but that is still far from the case in Germany, Italy, or Spain.

There are two striking features of the turnaround. One, it is centered in the very same countries that spearheaded the Second Demographic Transition. And, two, all indications are that it is driven by the very same social groups – higher-educated, employed women – who initially were the vanguards of "less family." All told, it would appear that the postmodernists erred profoundly as regards preference changes. As noted, the two plus child preference has remained very stable across many cohorts, in most countries, and within all social strata.

For a new and stable family equilibrium to emerge it is essential that normative dynamics toward gender egalitarianism are put into motion. As MacDonald (2004) argues, this implies adaptation to women's new roles at two levels. In the first place, public policy needs to promote family-friendly programs that further role conciliation. This means child care and adequate parental leave provisions. This dimension is explored in more detail in Gingrich and Ansell's contribution to this volume (Chapter 11).

These, however, are unlikely to be genuinely effective unless accompanied by a concomitant equalization of gender relations within couples. The key to the latter is the formation of a critical mass that promotes the diffusion of normative expectations in favor of gender egalitarian arrangements. The speed of diffusion will depend on critical thresholds. Applying a Pareto-driven decision logic, this would suggest that convergence toward a gender egalitarian family model will occur more rapidly where the cost of adopting it is perceived as lower.

I am certainly not the first to link marital behavior to gender equality. In their classical study, Brines and Joyner (1999) show that egalitarian relations promote stability within cohabiting (but not married) U.S. couples. Sevilla-Sanz (2010) finds that household formation rates are higher in countries with gender egalitarian norms. This is reconfirmed in a study that examines how gender value change over time is related to changes in the TFR (Arpino, Esping-Andersen, and Pessin 2013). Recent research also shows that couples are more stable when men contribute significantly to domestic tasks in Britain (Sigle-Rushton 2010) and the United States (Cooke 2006). But Cooke's (2006) comparison concludes that traditional specialization remains the best insurance against divorce in Germany. And yet, Bellani and Esping-Andersen (2012), also analyzing German data, reveal that gender egalitarian German couples are also increasingly stable – that is, the seeds of a new gender egalitarian family equilibrium appear to have been sown in Germany too.

The once-negative cross-national correlation between female employment and fertility turned positive by the 1990s (Ahn and Mira 2002; Billari and Kohler 2004; Brewster and Rindfuss 2000). This suggests that births may now be positively related to enhanced labor market opportunities for women, although Matysiak and Vignoli (2008) question that this relationship holds at the *microlevel*, within societies. And it is when women work that gender egalitarianism becomes a precondition for higher fertility (McDonald 2000; Neyer, Lappegård, and Vignoli 2011; Sleebos 2003). A number of studies give empirical support to this claim (Brodmann, Esping-Andersen, and Güell 2007; Cooke 2004; Craig and Siminski 2011; Myrskylä, Billari, and Kohler 2011).

And yet, female employment per se is not decisive. Scholars who examine gender relations via time-use data have been struck by one systematic finding, namely, that male adaptation exhibits huge lag effects (Gershuny, Bittman, and Brice 2005). But similar research also finds that men's contribution to domestic tasks suddenly takes off (Esping-Andersen et al. 2013). Why? All evidence suggests that the take-off in terms of equal sharing occurs when the modal woman shifts from part-timer to full-timer status. This is well illustrated by a Germany-Netherlands comparison with Scandinavia. In the former, the typical woman is a part-timer; in the latter, and in Denmark especially, she is a full-time worker for life. Women and men in the Netherlands

TABLE 6.1. *Denmark: Odds ratios of men being traditional or egalitarian*

	Men Contribute <10 Percent	Men Contribute <20 Percent	Men Contribute >40 Percent	Men Contribute >50 Percent
Log male wage	.95	1.10	.91	.95
Log female wage	1.46	.92	1.09	1.34
Nonlabor income	1.04***	1.03***	.98**	.99
Male eduction	.79*	.77***	1.14**	1.05
Homogamy	1.48	1.03	.93	.98
Number of kids	1.50	1.33*	.73**	.86
Male age	1.05	1.05**	.95***	.95***
Age difference	1.03	1.04	.97	.95
She full time	.31**	.50**	1.92***	1.80**
Mother on leave	2.37	1.88	.58	.40
Outside help	.66	1.00	.94	.88

and Germany continue to behave quite traditionally. In Denmark, the surge of men's contribution to domestic tasks coincided with the shift toward the female full-timer role. According to our latest data, more than half of all men contribute at least 40 percent of domestic work and an astounding 30 percent contribute in excess of 50 percent (Esping-Andersen et al. 2013).

The decisiveness of the shift toward lifelong, full-time commitment among women is also supported by regression analysis. As shown in Table 6.1, the only variable that really explains why male partners move toward egalitarianism in domestic work is whether the partner is a full-timer. Men are basically twice as likely to be egalitarian if the wife is a full-timer rather than part-timer (in Denmark virtually no women are housewives anymore).

As McDonald (2011) and Neyer et al. (2011) stress, we need to distinguish how gender egalitarian practices influence family behavior. Many studies seem to associate "equality" with the possibility of reconciling work and family. This leads to a focus on policies (such as child care) that should ease the inherent trade-offs between motherhood and careers (Del Boca 2002; Gornick and Meyers 2003; Gornick, Meyers, and Ross 1998; Sleebos 2003). Some studies explicitly link policies (such as father leaves) to more equal task sharing within couples (Duvander and Andersson 2006; Duvander, Lappegård, and Andersson 2010).

Reconciliation policies are very likely to promote gender egalitarian practices. For one, they should make it easier for couples to behave in egalitarian ways if they so wish; for another, they are likely to diminish the perceived cost of adopting such practices. But their causal role is ambiguous at best. First, such policies are arguably endogenous with respect to women's changing roles – they are likely to emerge only when the revolution of women's roles is already quite advanced, in particular, when full-time work becomes the norm. Second, the case of the United States suggests that egalitarian partnerships evolve also in tabula rasa contexts in terms of reconciliation policies.

It is probably at the microlevel of couple relations that gender egalitarianism becomes decisive. Obviously, fathers' involvement in child care or leave taking can only have any meaningful fertility effect on higher parities – as research shows (Brodmann, Esping-Andersen, and Güell 2007; Duvander and Andersson 2006; Duvander, Lappegård, and Andersson 2010). And as we saw, there is also growing evidence to suggest that couple stability increasingly depends on a more symmetric division of domestic tasks. All the evidence shows that this is more likely to occur among the higher educated, when women contribute a greater share of household earnings, and (again) when women are full-timers (Raley, Bianchi, and Wang 2012; Sullivan 2011).

The education effect is hardly surprising. Its influence on egalitarian values has been argued throughout the history of sociology (Durkheim 1961) – also with regard to family behavior (Oppenheim, Mason, and Bumpass 1975).

6.5. The Dynamics of Polarization

As noted, the higher socioeconomic strata pioneered family decay and now also its resurgence. Over the long haul we should expect a broad convergence around gender egalitarian family norms once the diffusion process accelerates. In the interim it is likely that the socially skewed transition will produce rising welfare dualisms in society. Sarah McLanahan (2004), in her ASA presidential address, sought to capture this with her concept of "diverging destinies." Focusing very much on the heightened concentration of lone motherhood among low-SES women, she pointed to the adverse and polarizing consequences for children's life chances.

Her point can, in fact, be generalized across a wide spectrum of family influences on child outcomes. Let us begin with the income distribution. As we all know, ongoing labor market trends are producing a burst of inequality throughout the OECD nations. Family trends have contributed additionally to the worsening distribution.

It is well established that maternal labor supply is far greater among highly educated women, and this implies of course higher household earnings. When we, additionally, take into account 1) the concentration of lone motherhood at the bottom and 2) the rising trend toward marital homogamy, especially at the top, the net effect is potential income polarization across families with children. This is illustrated for a number of EU countries in Table 6.2. Note that these data refer to couple families only.

Table 6.2 presents the ratio of earnings for the top versus bottom quintiles, separately for men's and women's earnings and, in the last column, for the couple as a whole. The figures suggest that the lower is the overall level of female employment, the more inequality will wives' earnings produce. Indeed,

TABLE 6.2. *The income distribution effects of husbands' and wives' earnings*

	Men 5th:1st Q Earnings Ratio	Women 5th:1st Q Earnings Ratio	Household 5th:1st Q Earnings Ratio
Denmark	5.8	4.3	5.2
France	5.7	8.5	6.3
Germany	4.1	4.8	4.3
Ireland	9.3	12.0	9.7
Netherlands	5.2	7.7	5.7
Spain	8.8	23.2	10.6
United Kingdom	7.0	5.3	6.4

Source: Estimated from the ECHP (European Community Household Panel).

in Denmark – where virtually all mothers work – the "wife effect" is equality producing. Where, as in Ireland or Spain, wives' employment is primarily concentrated in higher-SES households, we see huge inequality effects of their earnings contribution to household income. Hence, had only fathers worked in Spain, the top: bottom income ratio would have been 8.8; the skewed distribution of women's employment produces a top:bottom income ratio that is 10.6.

The same logic can be illustrated, now for the United States, by simulating how much the household Gini coefficient would change if women married to bottom quintile men were to adopt the labor supply behavior of women married to men in the two highest quintiles. To illustrate the magnitudes, note that among American couples, the dual-earner rate is about 80 percent within the top three quintiles, but only 45 percent in the bottom. Using the Population Study of Income Dynamics (PSID) data (for 2003), I estimated that this counterfactual would produce a 5 percent smaller Gini coefficient.

As McLanahan (2004) strongly stresses, it is the intergenerational consequence of polarization that is most worrisome. Since divorce and lone parenthood concentrate evermore in the lower-SES strata, this is likely also to add fuel to the ongoing inegalitarian trend in terms of parental investment in their children's future.

From time-use research it is well known that higher-educated parents dedicate more time to their children. The educational gradient is particularly strong when it comes to cognitively stimulating activities, such as reading and playing. In contrast, parent-child interactions in less-educated households tend to be more skewed in favor of passive activities, such as watching TV. Table 6.3 presents a profile of the gap in parental child dedication (measured in daily average hours and minutes) measured as the ratio of university educated parents over parents with less than upper-secondary education. The data refer to children less than age twelve, which is the age span when parental involvement has by far the greatest impact on children's learning.

TABLE 6.3. *Child care: Ratio of child care time of high- versus low-educated parents*

	Mothers	Fathers
Denmark	2.2	1.7
Spain	1.7	2.7
United States	1.2	1.7

Source: Danish Time Use Survey 2001; Spanish Time Use Survey 2002.

The gaps are everywhere quite substantial. To illustrate, higher-educated Danish mothers dedicate more than twice as much time to their children as do their low-educated peers. And in Spain, the paternal input among the higher educated is almost three times as great. The lower maternal ratio for the United States may be a surprise. It probably reflects the circumstance that full-time employment is much more the norm among American women than is the case elsewhere. These data, of course, measure exclusively two-parent families. Children living with only one parent will, almost by fiat, receive less time dedication.

These kinds of cumulatively produced inequalities in children's lives will, with great probability, translate into – yes – diverging destinies. That is, they should promote widening gaps in terms of children's educational attainment and later career chances. If so, the great challenge we face is how to break the Gordian knot of cumulative polarization. As far as family life is concerned, a first step must be to nurture those trends that are moving at least a segment of the population toward stronger and more stable families. We are therefore back to the earlier question, namely, What might help accelerate the emergence and consolidation of a new, workable, and stable family equilibrium?

6.6. Toward a New Family Equilibrium?

At its core, a new family model must logically be premised on a realignment of spousal relations that fits with the revolution of women's roles, that is, gender role symmetry.[7] It will gain stability if this results in greater fairness and efficiency in home production. Equity improvements will logically occur if no spouse ends up with a "double shift" and when the more and less desirable tasks are allocated fairly. The most efficient allocation of inputs depends, in the first place, on the spouses' relative productivities in paid *and* unpaid work. It goes without saying that a gender unequal allocation of domestic work ends up inefficient if both partners boast similar market productivities – and even

[7] This section draws importantly on a recent paper I coauthored with Francesco Billari.

more so when the double-shift partner's market productivities exceed those of the other partner.

In previous work, I have documented the arrival, albeit probably not the consolidation, of such an equilibrium in Scandinavia (Esping-Andersen et al. 2013). Almost half of Danish households are premised on a gender egalitarian family arrangement. For the United Kingdom we found little more than an incipient emergence of the model, and in Spain it is nowhere to be found yet.

If such a new family equilibrium represents a superior Pareto outcome, we clearly need to understand how to nurture its evolution. I have tried to make the case that it is likely to be Pareto optimal on two grounds. First, it will improve the conditions under which citizens, men and women alike, can match their family aspirations and preferences with reality as regards fertility and partnerships. Second, it should help combat the ongoing polarizing trends in terms of family effects on children's life chances.

It will be recalled that multiple equilibrium theory posits that a new hegemonic equilibrium will evolve through an endogenously self-reinforcing diffusion process. This requires broadening the clientele of susceptible women and of winning over the men. As Hakim insists, modern womanhood combines the home-centered, the careerists, and the adaptive who want both worlds (Hakim 2000). This means that change depends heavily on cascade dynamics, that is, on how rapidly and widely new preferences penetrate beyond the "elite" vanguard.

A useful starting point is Brock and Durlauf's (2001) application of utility functions and positive decision externalities. Here the social utility of adopting a new behavior increases linearly with the expected number of others doing so. This can occur under two different logics: One, the utility of choosing A over B is a direct function of the number of others also opting for A; two, people may be uncertain about the utility of A and look to others' choices in order to make the choice themselves. In both cases, the end outcome should be similar.

The assumption of a linearly accelerating increase function is quite decisive. Consider two different scenarios: In the first, any given citizen's probability of becoming converted rises in perfect tandem with the number of already affected cocitizens; in the second, the citizen's susceptibility remains unchanged until a certain number of fellow citizens have already become affected – a critical minimum is required (see also Lopez-Pintado and Watts 2008).

Sociological work on diffusion emphasizes the importance of networks and the presence of bridges from the edges of one network to another (e.g., Hedström, Sandell, and Stern 2000). Causally speaking, diffusion can occur via imitation (learning from others) or through persuasion. The feminist movement is an example of the latter. But no matter how charismatic feminist leaders may be, it is difficult to imagine that they have been a major source of diffusion beyond the confines of those who already agreed with them. In the long haul it is more likely that the process is fueled by imitation and learning. This is especially so since emulating the upper crust has been a stable feature of cultures throughout history.

In diffusion models, the speed of diffusion is given by the rate at which encounters between "affected" and "susceptible" individuals will convert someone into an affected person. The shape of the curve is the well-known logistic function that predicts an accelerating momentum of the endogenous dynamics (Fukao and Benabou 1993). Initially, the move toward a new equilibrium will be hesitant, but as the process gains strength, it will pull ever-more people toward the new way of doing things. The logic is akin to the "critical social mass" effect that Breen and Cooke (2005) describe. In the simple model, the speed reaches its maximum when half of the population is located in the egalitarian regime.

What may make ever-more individuals susceptible and subsequently affected? Here I highlight two key factors: one, the role of generalized social trust; and two, how social stratification affects diffusion.

6.6.1. Normative Cohesion and Trust

Greater certainty about others' actions evolves from trust, both interpersonally and societywide. It should be obvious how this translates into family decision making: For any given woman with career commitments, the supply of marriageable men will be larger, and the risk of entering into a partnership will be reduced. And when expectations are likely to be confirmed, couple stability should be enhanced.

Virtually by definition, a stable equilibrium will be associated with substantial trust. And the more hegemonic it becomes, the more it is likely to broaden the sphere of trust. In contrast, we should expect that unstable equilibria are associated with low levels of generalized trust – but not necessarily with localized interpersonal trust. The strong presence of familialism in Southern Europe reflects, no doubt, a social order in which trust beyond the confines of kinship is weak.

The move from localized or familial trust to generalized trust can be regarded as a prerequisite for family formation when the revolution of women's roles has advanced. To exemplify with fertility: Where the traditional male breadwinner model reigned, the decision to have children depended largely on the husband's breadwinner capacity and, perhaps, on a helping hand from relatives. As is well established in fertility research, women's decision to have children is now increasingly conditioned on their own employment status. They must place their trust in nonfamilial institutions, most obviously in the labor market and external child care. As Aassve et al. (2012) show, cross-national levels of generalized trust and fertility are positively related.

Put differently, in the traditional equilibrium it is primarily familial trust that counts. But familialism will exert a negative influence on fertility (and arguably other family related decisions) the more advanced is the revolution of women's roles. Indeed, the mix of strong familialism and weak generalized trust may help account for the lowest-low fertility syndrome observed in Southern Europe (similar reasoning is found in Livi-Bacci (2001) and Dalla Zuanna and Micheli (2004)).

This logic can also be extended to the pace of diffusion. Societies in which generalized trust is stronger are likely to experience faster diffusion while the absence of trust beyond the confines of family and friends will hinder it.

6.6.2. Social Stratification
Diffusion occurs through multiple overlapping networks that vary in density and reach (Gould 1991; Hedström, Sandell, and Stern 2000). The pace and scope of diffusion must depend on the degree of network connectedness.

Stratification influences diffusion to the extent that it shapes the ways that networks meet and overlap, that is, how the message is carried across boundaries. If the boundaries are blurred, there should be more diffusion. Additionally, the ability to receive and interpret information is key to diffusion, and this implies that educational inequalities in the population will act as barriers. More concretely, the following stratification attributes are key:

One, the degree of social fluidity in terms of intergenerational mobility is crucial. Are there strong class or racial barriers in the opportunity structure? What are the relative odds of upward mobility for working-class offspring? Overall, via the spread of education, the advanced countries have experienced a rise in social fluidity (Breen et al. 2009). Still, there are huge cross-national differences in educational inequalities and in social mobility. The proportion of youth with less than high school equivalent education is marginal (5–8 percent) in Scandinavia and the United Kingdom but is substantial (20 percent) in the United States. An even more telling statistic is the share of youngsters who fall below the PISA-defined cognitive dysfunctional threshold: a small minority in the Nordic countries and France, but almost 20 percent in Spain and the United States (Esping-Andersen 2009). Turning to mobility, the correlation between fathers' and sons' income is four times higher in the United States and United Kingdom than it is in Denmark and Norway. In Germany it is twice as high as in Denmark, and in France three times (Corak 2006). Children of families in the bottom income quintile are twice as likely to be upwardly mobile in Denmark and Sweden compared to the United States (Jäntti et al. 2006). As a general principle, intergenerational mobility is negatively related to prevailing levels of income inequality.

The characteristics of education systems will influence marriage markets and diffusion. Early tracking into vocational and academic lines creates greater social segmentation than do comprehensive systems (like the Swedish) that keep all children together through high school. Hence, early tracking should result in more stratified marital selection; late tracking, the opposite. And returning to a point made earlier, if egalitarian values are a function of levels of education, we would also expect that they will diffuse more easily the greater is the proportion of youth who complete the higher tiers of the system.

A second kind of barrier to diffusion is the presence of social segmentation, such as racial or ethnic segregation. The development of ghetto communities, be they residential or geographic, will clearly impede network bridging. Thus, the urban (black) poverty ghettos in the United States tend to be hugely distanced from mainstream society, socially, culturally, and by sheer distance (Massey and Denton 1993; Wilson 1987). A parallel case is the spread of ethnic immigrant enclaves, which, additionally, tend to produce segmented assimilation among second-generation immigrants (Portes and Manning 1986).

There are of course many other relevant expressions of social segmentation. In some societies the rich and powerful take refuge within gated communities; in others, residential social segregation is minor. And this, in turn, will also influence the degree to which children of different social backgrounds mingle in the same schools. The nature of interest organizations must also be important. Diffusion processes are likely to be far stronger where virtually the entire population is organized in large comprehensive trade unions (such as in Sweden) compared to societies built on narrow and exclusive corporativist representation, or where such mass organizations do not exist (such as in the United States).

A linearly accelerating diffusion function is far more likely to operate in societies with enhanced social fluidity and no strong segmentation. This may help explain why the egalitarian family is so much more advanced in Scandinavia compared to other nations. Where class, racial, or educational barriers are severe, one is more likely to encounter walls beyond which diffusion simply stops.

6.7. The Diffusion of Egalitarianism and Its Effect on Family Change

Whether or not diffusion is facilitated by advantageous conditions, any diffusion process will initially be slow and subsequently accelerate. The latter should occur when a critical mass of affected, or at least susceptible, people is reached, and when the social institutions adapt. But how can we identify the feedback effects from the diffusion of egalitarianism toward family change? The political economy literature typically favors a median voter logic. I suggest that a cost-benefit approach will yield a more realistic picture.

6.7.1. The Median Voter approach

The basic logic here is simple: The tipping point occurs when more than half of the relevant population favors any given change. Institutions favoring the compatibility of gender egalitarianism and family are therefore more likely to emerge as the share of gender egalitarians becomes decisive. This approach explicitly sees social institutions as endogenous to women's revolution – as do some political economists (Tabellini 2008) and welfare state scholars (Mayer 2001; Pfau-Effinger 2005).

But there are two problems if we apply a simple median voter logic. Both have their mainsprings in stratification issues. First, the model assumes that all citizens count equally – everyone's infection probability is identical. But that is unlikely to obtain for this kind of diffusion. Diffusion is likely to be far more powerful if it originates in the upper echelons of society or within highly visible substrata (rock stars or media personalities). And diffusion is likely to be much more effective if it works through networks that are large and have a long reach into other networks. Again, strong networks are more likely to be found within the upper crust. In other words, the critical mass threshold is most likely a function of *who* are the diffusers. Second, if society is highly stratified, the median voter logic is less likely to operate – at least at the aggregate level. A 51 percent majority means something very different in a society of equals than in a racially or class-torn society.

6.7.2. *The Opportunity Cost Approach*

An opportunity cost framework would appear relevant considering that Pareto efficiency and equity are integral to stable equilibria. The key issue is whether the utility of change is greater than the utility of loyalty, that is, whether the external shock has produced new opportunity costs. This, apropos, is basically how Becker et al. (1977) analyze marriage and divorce. When women acquire marketable skills and control fertility, and when the time required for domestic work is sharply reduced, the opportunity costs of full-time housewifery become obvious – especially for higher-earning women. If this is key to decision making, diffusion should accelerate when more and more women face similar utility shifts – and become susceptible to being contaminated.

The fact that ever-more women obtain marketable skills does not translate automatically into the emergence of a new "gender egalitarian" regime. As discussed earlier, the exact opposite has been the case: Women continued to be saddled with the lion's share of domestic work (the double shift) and couples engage in "doing gender" practices so as to reconfirm conventional gender roles. This of course implies the presence of novel kinds of opportunity costs. In this situation, women will be less inclined to marry and more likely to exit from relationships, and fertility will be lower (Becker, Landes, and Michael 1977; Ermisch 2003; Sevilla-Sanz 2010).

So how would a cost-benefit approach help us understand how and when a move toward gender egalitarianism becomes an endogenously accelerating process? For one, as ever-more women desire a career but find that this is bought at the price of other utilities (childbearing or good stable partnerships), they may revert to the traditional equilibrium (loyalty) – but this is clearly not Paretian. Or they may search for an alternative formula that reduces trade-offs. This search is part and parcel of the diffusion process to the extent that women will be in the market for persuasive solutions. One way would be to emulate women who seem to have succeeded. This, one would assume, will induce women to persuade their male partners to adopt a more gender egalitarian behavior, and to persuade politicians to deliver reconciliation policies.

Another way to identify thresholds via an opportunity cost framework would be to examine the perceived costs of failing to adopt gender egalitarianism compared to the perceived cost of doing so. To exemplify, women may decide against a full-time lifelong career commitment because it may prohibit them from having the number of children they aspire to have. But this opportunity-cost calculus should change radically if women have access to affordable, high-quality child care. Here we are back to our earlier conundrum: Is the welfare state endogenous or exogenous? One way to answer is that it is likely to be endogenous with regard to women's revolution (child care policy is a response to the latter), but it becomes exogenous for any given woman's utility calculus (her choices are influenced by what the welfare state delivers). This said, the critical threshold for diffusion should lie lower, and the speed of diffusion should be faster, the more family friendly is the welfare state (and labor market).

If this reflects the real historical dynamics, it is evident that the critical mass effect includes both women *and* men. In a Becker framework, the emergence of a critical mass of male adapters should, once again, be related to opportunity costs. And here the previous logic is likely to obtain once again. It is well established that men and women hardly differ in terms of their preferences for partnerships and children.

Whether driven by cost-benefit considerations or a median voter logic (or a combination of the two), it is, in the abstract, impossible to pinpoint where the critical tipping point will lie. From what we empirically know it is evident that not only the revolution of women's roles, but also the shift toward more gender egalitarian couple arrangements is spearheaded by the educated professional classes. This means that the diffusion process is driven by a population with strong trend-setting and network penetration capacities – not to forget media access and political clout. In other words, the tipping point at which the accelerator kicks in is very likely to be found way below the 50 percent-of-the-population marker. Where precisely it lies is likely to vary across societies.

6.8. Conclusion: Toward a Gender Egalitarian Equilibrium?

What will the end product of the process be? Probably everyone will agree that a viable new family equilibrium must be premised on some kind of gender symmetric arrangement. How will this become manifest? We must, to begin with, be careful about the associated fundamentals. First, gender symmetric unions are unlikely to take hold as long as women's labor market attachment is circumscribed. It is therefore unlikely to emerge as long as the prototypical woman prefers a part-time commitment and makes significant career interruptions. To put it bluntly, a new equilibrium is unlikely to gain a foothold unless the typical woman has "masculinized" her life course as far as employment is concerned.

The second fundamental regards men. As the opportunity cost hypothesis argued, the diffusion process requires also that men become contaminated. Since it is unlikely that men's earnings advantage, especially over the life course, will disappear, it is also unlikely that male adaptation involves any noticeable change in their employment careers. But the gender egalitarian equilibrium will undoubtedly require a feminization of men's domestic role. If a dual-career couple is to attain maximum efficiency and equity it will require symmetry also in terms of domestic work.

The third fundamental addresses family formation. As all available data demonstrate, the proportion of men and women who prefer to remain childless is minoritarian indeed. The two-child preference remains dominant, and a substantial number aim for three or more. If gender egalitarianism is to achieve the status of a stable equilibrium it must ensure that citizens can realistically expect to have the number of children they desire. Large gaps are the hallmark of *unstable* equilibria.

PART II

POLITICS

7

Party Alignments: Change and Continuity

Herbert Kitschelt and Philipp Rehm

Changes in the occupational structure and political economy of advanced capitalism, explained in Daniel Oesch's chapter in this volume, and related shifts in the formation of political mass preferences, examined by Silja Häusermann and Hanspeter Kriesi in the subsequent chapter, are consequential for political partisan alignments, the subject of this chapter. As previously small occupational groups with distinct political preference profiles gained numerical weight in the electorate, particularly highly educated sociocultural professionals, established party families saw their vote shares decline, unless they modified their programmatic appeals. Established parties with new strategies or new party creations went on to capture novel voter coalitions, a process that has played out in cross-nationally diverse ways.

Shifts in electoral partisan coalitions coincided with (1) a steep decline in party membership; (2) a moderate to sharp increase in electoral volatility signaling the availability of more voters to competing party appeals; (3) a decline in voter turnout, as people no longer acted simply on parental party identifications or associational ties; and (4) a corresponding rise of nonpartisan social movements and interest groups. At least three rival theoretical arguments have claimed to make sense of party system change in postindustrial democracies, all consistent with these basic facts: the postindustrial realignment; the postindustrial dealignment; and the cartel party detachment perspectives. Examining empirical trends over time and cross-national variance among party systems, we conclude that a political realignment perspective explains observable patterns best.

7.1. Three Perspectives on Postindustrial Political Alignments

The disagreements on political alignments concern facts about the nature of citizen-politician linkages and causal mechanisms that produce them in postindustrial democracies. There are three prominent perspectives on this topic:

- Postindustrial Realignment (PiR): Voters continue to coalesce around parties on the basis of durable socioeconomic interests and policy preferences, but since political-economic postindustrialization, highlighted by changing occupational profiles, has changed the distribution of preferences, established parties have been compelled to alter their appeals or tolerate the electoral success of new parties that represent voter preferences ignored by established alternatives.
- Postindustrial Dealignment (PiD): Most voters have ceased to support parties on the basis of durable and broad configurations of preferences and interests. Instead, their partisan support is motivated by specific and temporally variable issue positions, attention to which is induced by exogenous shocks or endogenous issue politics of office-seeking politicians. This process is paired with a substantial rise of partisan disaffection.
- Cartel Party Detachment (CaPaD): Faced with eroding sociodemographic moorings and organizational member affiliation, established parties move to a "cartelization" of political power that erects high barriers to the entry of outside partisan challengers and enables insider parties to converge on policy positions that disregard distinctive demands voiced by electoral constituencies.

The three theoretical frames make different predictions about the nature of and extent to which political parties express and pursue policies that reflect preferences of their electoral constituencies. They also have different implications for the programmatic appeal of political parties over time. Finally, the realignment perspective postulates durable cross-national differences in party systems configurations, whereas dealignment and cartelization theories predict convergence.

7.1.1. Realignment (PiR)

Realignment theorists hypothesize a continued capacity of democratic institutions to impose a modicum of accountability on elected politicians that creates congruence between the policy preferences of a party's electoral followers, anchored in political-economic and social experiences, and the appeals of that party's leaders. Moreover, implemented policies of the governing parties reflect elements of party appeals and are not completely washed away by imperatives resulting from global market economics or technological imperatives.

Simplifying Oesch's and Häusermann/Kriesi's description of occupational groups and preferences, in devising partisan appeals to capture bits of the electoral marketplace, political strategists have to work with the preference distributions of three major electoral constituency blocs in postindustrial society. The still largest, albeit shrinking bloc is that of *low- to intermediate-skilled blue-collar and clerical wage earners* with an ideological outlook broadly supporting redistribution (the "greed" to limit the acquisitiveness of the rich), but leaning toward conservative, authoritarian positions on sociopolitical and cultural governance (the "grid" of unquestionable, collectively enforced norms operative in a polity) and opting for culturally and economically exclusionary conceptions of citizenship and national identity as well as clear economic boundaries imposed on the flow of goods and people rather than openness and multiculturalism (the "group" aspect of political preferences).[1] A second broad group consists of *higher-skill managers and professionals in manufacturing, financial, and business services,* who tend to be market-liberal and averse to redistribution on the economic greed dimension, but more libertarian on grid/governance and inclusionary on the group/identity dimensions. The third broad group of *sociocultural professionals* is the fastest growing group since the 1960s. Its members have a tendency to combine preference for income redistribution (greed), even if they are affluent, with libertarian and inclusionary positions on governance and external boundary drawing (grid / group). A fourth group, low-skilled self-employed small business people ("petty bourgeoisie"), is minor in most postindustrial democracies but still plays an important role in Mediterranean democracies, characterized by less state intervention (capacity) and an orientation to consumption, as outlined in the introductory chapter.

Acknowledging that preference formation is intertwined with not just productive occupational roles in markets and work organizations, but also with the sociodemographics of reproduction, let us include age and gender as preference forming constitutive experiences. Women tend to be closest to the preference distribution of sociocultural professionals, particularly if they are younger, while older males tend to gravitate toward the first group, even when we control for occupation.

Abstracting from a great deal of short-term noise that affects victory or defeat in elections, in the long run strategic parties realign with the evolving preference distributions in the population, induced by changing occupational and sociodemographic group sizes. This process involves complicated trial-and-error strategizing that causes electoral volatility and voter alienation, but ultimately may produce fairly durable partisan alignments. Given the rising cognitive sophistication of many postindustrial voters who can discriminate between programmatic partisan appeals and the plausible multidimensionality of the space of salient competitive issues that politicians may strategically invoke, the old mass parties encounter severe difficulties in addressing the trade-offs among disparate elements of the electorate that are attracted by different packages of programmatic appeals. As a consequence, there is a powerful

---

[1] We adopt here the language of Douglas and Wildavsky (1982), although we believe that people's grid/group positions may often be orthogonal to their views on economic distribution (greed), thus turning a parsimonious map of preferences into a three-dimensional exercise (Kitschelt and Rehm 2014).

tendency for party systems to fragment through programmatic diversification. Some of the large, never quite "catchall" parties of the industrial era will converge on a programmatically diffuse and amorphous centrism, but they will be complemented by a proliferation of distinctive, ideologically sharply contoured smaller "boutique" parties garnering supporters in the more extreme reaches of the two- or three-dimensional policy space constituted by multiple issues of economic redistribution (greed) as well as sociopolitical governance (grid) and / or the boundaries of citizenship (group). Of course, where institutional rules of proportional representation permit the legislative representation of small parties, this process is likely to advance further than in majoritarian electoral systems.

Building on these foundations, PiR theory would expect that (1) voters gravitate to parties with programmatic appeals congruent with voter preferences. This requires that (2) at least some parties maintain their programmatic distinctiveness and do not converge on the median voter or diffuse "catchall" appeals. Moreover, if political preference profiles vary across polities, whether induced by diversity of political-economic institutions and experiences or legacies of party competition themselves, (3) postindustrial policies may generate cross-nationally quite distinctive party system configurations.

The mechanism here is that existing programmatic parties can only slowly update and change their appeals to remain credible with critical parts of the electorate and constantly face trade-offs in voter support as they move. Credibility of programmatic appeals derives from parties' past policy achievements, such as participation in shaping major political-economic arrangements, as well as the intertemporal consistency of their messages. Parties therefore cannot evolve suddenly and costlessly from any point in the political preference space to any other point. Party activists and organizations may further restrain even incremental strategic movements but thereby improve parties' programmatic credibility.[2]

Decisive evidence that partisan responsiveness still operates in democratic polities would involve showing that partisan governments still deliver diverging policies consistent with voters' preferences. The intricacies of this exploration would require another paper. But the contributions on policy choices in postindustrial capitalism and political outcomes in the current book speak to this question. While external global and EU regional constraints certainly limit policy choices, at least in the fields of economic and social policy, partisan politics still appears to encounter considerable degrees of freedom at the national level.[3]

---

[2] As efforts to think through theoretically party competition constrained by considerations of credibility and reputation, as well as activists, consider Laver and Sergenti (2011), Budge et al. (2010), and already Downs (1957, 110), who postulated that ideological immobility was imperative for rational vote-seeking party politicians, unlike contrary assumptions in the formal idealizations of spatial theories of party competition after Downs.

[3] Uplifting accounts on the responsiveness of policy to the complexion of partisan governments would include Klingemann, Hofferbert, and Budge (1994); Erikson, MacKuen, and Stimson

7.1.2. Dealignment (PiD)

The sociological and political economic moorings of dealignment theory are (1) occupational diversification that makes the organization of collective interests increasingly difficult; (2) accelerating social mobility; (3) declining vertical social differentiation ("embourgeoisement"), generating a broad and leveled "middle-class" society; and (4) educational upgrading resulting in "cognitive mobilization."[4] Furthermore, voters have gained access to a greater range of information and experiences through the advent of modern mass media and the transportation revolution of the automobile that made possible the progressive agglomeration of citizens in large metropolitan areas and the breakdown of segmental tight-knit neighborhoods and social "milieus." More cognitively and physically mobile electorates choose partisan favorites contingent upon salient issue stances that vary from election to election. Vote seeking parties therefore need less a persistent and distinct generalized ideological appeal than a generalized capacity to shape the salience of individual policy issues, thereby assembling electoral coalitions in diverse and ever-changing ways. Competence and issue ownership, not ideological reputation and persistence, count for electoral success.

In terms of political congruence between voters and politicians, PiD theory therefore predicts (1) continued representation of voter constituencies by parties, albeit (2) only on salient issues. Because the issues are disparate and varied, parties should (3) no longer map on durable underlying ideological issue dimensions. Over time, PiD theory expects (4) the erosion of generalized programmatic distinctions across partisan competitors, as partisan rivalry focuses on specific issues rather than general ideological appeals. Issue ownership and the ability to demonstrate high policy valence ("competence" to "solve" an issue) displace spatial positional markers and commitments. In general ideological terms, parties become successively more diffuse and amorphous, with both voters and politicians less and less able to indicate the overall ideological position of political parties.

For this reason, PiD does not consider it a promising or interesting exercise to explore the persistence of differences among party systems in postindustrial democracies, whether at the national, supranational, or regional and local level. The partisan competition has acquired enough flux to make these lateral differences fleeting and ephemeral.

(2002); Soroka and Wlezien (2010); and much of the literature on social policy and the welfare state. Other recent research sees parties' fulfillment of electoral promises as greater in majoritarian parliamentary systems and under conditions of economic expansion (cf. Thomson et al. 2013). More skeptical findings diagnose a systematic "right-shift" of enacted policy, when compared to responsible partisanship at the level of government declared policy and policy positions of a government's partisan constituent elements (Warwick 2011).

[4] The classic exposition of the dealignment perspective is still Dalton, Beck, and Flanagan (1984, esp. 14–17; Dalton and Wattenberg 2002; Dalton 2008).

7.1.3. Detachment (CaPaD)

CaPaD seconds the sociological analysis of PiD but adds a principal-agent and lately a political-economic argument. CaPaD sees the agents, the elected politicians, gaining independence from their voters (Katz and Mair 1995, 2009). Politicians "become self-referential, professional, and technocratic, and what substantive interparty competition remains becomes focused on the efficient and effective management of the economy" (Katz and Mair 2009: 755). Valence competition drives out positional competition.

The agents become independent of voters through mechanisms of collusion and legal protection (Katz and Mair 1995). The established parties make the entry of challengers into the party system harder through legal requirements imposed on parties' registration and internal operation and the exclusion of new contenders from the mass media, but above all through a system of public party finance by the state that excludes new entrants, while making the established parties increasingly independent of the contributions of their activist membership bases that used to serve as a check on the elected politicians' temptations to secure political survival without accountability to electoral constituencies. With less reliance on membership volunteer work and financial dues, parties then organizationally disempower the activist base by concentrating strategic discretion in leaders of the parties' legislative caucuses or cabinet members (Katz and Mair 2009: 757, 759).

Having cut off mechanisms of vertical accountability, leaders of different parties then can collude around similar policies. What emerges is a uniform "political class," whose constitutive elements resemble each other in style, appeal, and rhetoric. On the basis of self-interest, not conspiracy, interparty collusion does not require a premeditated coordination (Katz and Mair 2009: 757). Critical is that the comforts of public funding make collusion the best response of each insider party, as long as external challengers can be effectively barred from entering the electoral arena and prevented from eating into the insiders' support bases.[5]

Cartel theory has supplemented the original internal organizational-institutional argument for cartelization more recently by an external political-economic argument (Blyth and Katz 2005; Katz and Mair 2009). Globalization and European integration have undermined the parties' "room to maneuver" and deliver different policies in national or subnational settings. As positional politics with rival programmatic positions becomes devoid of credibility, politicians see cartelization as their best option for survival. Even then, they might not entirely escape the wrath of the electorate that expresses

---

[5] Blyth and Katz (2005, 39) go so far as to invoke the possibility of a Cournot-Nash type oligopolistic equilibrium in favor of cartelization. All of this depends, however, on the strong assumptions made concerning the costs of entry by new competitors (see critically Kitschelt 2000; Koole 1996).

itself in support of populist protest parties against the political class. But to a large extent, voters' preferences are products of party competition itself, thus holding the potential for rebellion at bay.

Cartel party theory radicalizes the predictions of dealignment theory. In positional terms, parties not only abandon broad ideological representation of electorates, but they are also no longer compelled to represent electoral constituencies on salient issue positions. Cartels complete the process of oligarchical control anticipated by Michels (1915) for party organization and the rise of "catchall" parties replacing ideological "parties of principle" at the systemic level. Combine Michels and Kirchheimer (1966) and infuse a political-economic postulate about the end of domestic politics through globalization – and what you get is partisan cartel theory.

7.2. Programmatic Linkage and Congruence between Voters and Parties

Do parties and their voters show preference / program congruence on overarching policy dimensions, as the realignment perspective would assert, not just on specific issues? At the *individual voter level*, citizens' policy preferences, aggregated to scores on preference dimensions of policy making, should be robust predictors of vote choice. The Häusermann/Kriesi chapter in this volume provides a reasonable benchmark to assert that people's preferences over policy dimensions indeed pattern their choices among political parties. And underlying sociodemographic conditions are substantially associated with policy preferences. Our own explorations with European Social Survey (ESS 2008) and ISSP (1996 and 2006) data permit a similar conclusion (not reported here). In the few countries where a longitudinal comparison of vote choice determinants is possible, it appears that the direct impact of sociodemographic variables, such as income, education, gender, or occupation, unmediated by preferences, has declined over time. But these experiences still work indirectly through their imprint on policy preferences, while relations between such preferences and partisan choices remain as strong as ever or actually strengthen (Knutsen and Kumlin 2005).We demonstrate this in the Online Appendix 1 to this paper with Swedish data (see http://politicalscience.osu.edu/faculty/rehm/papers.htm for the online appendix).

The focus of our analysis in this chapter is the *aggregate partisan level*, exploring the congruence between parties' programmatic appeals and their electoral constituencies' preferences. We constructed summary indices for citizens' preferences over income distribution (greed), more authoritarian or libertarian sociopolitical governance (grid), and more inclusive, multicultural or exclusive, national collective identity from the 2008 European Social Survey (see Online Appendix 2). The grid issues would be what Kriesi et al. (2008) characterize as second dimension issues of the 1970s and 1980s (law and order, civil liberties, gender roles, and family moral norms), before group issues of economic and cultural globalization shifted the attention to questions of boundary drawing between the nation and the rest of the world. While the relative emphasis of the grid / group dimension varies and currently citizens' authoritarian (libertarian) grid preferences also tend to predict their exclusionary (inclusionary) group preferences, these two dimensions may come apart and gain independent momentum. For example, lately some radical Right parties have shifted to more libertarian positions on governance, emphasizing Western individualism and libertarianism, but only to argue for an exclusionary conception of citizenship in order to defend Europe's libertarian values against the immigration of people with more collectivist and authoritarian preferences, claimed to prevail in Islam.[6]

We examine political representation by comparing the average position of a party's constituency on "3G" (greed / grid / group) issue dimensions in the 2008 European Social Survey with experts' scoring of party leaders' appeals on closely related issues in Benoit and Laver's (2006) expert survey. We explore mass-elite congruence in simple bivariate regressions of the standard form:

Position of party elite i on issue j = a + b position of party constituency i on issue j

While this is obviously not an exact science, three elements of this regression are of interest. First, there is no representation, if the *explained variance* of the relationship between mass and elite positions is nonexistent. A high correlation is a necessary, but not a sufficient condition for high representativeness (Achen 1978). Second, representation also requires that *partisan differences are similarly large* at the elite and the mass level. If positions are scaled with the same metric at both levels, a *slope coefficient* of around 1.0 would maximize representation. Smaller slope coefficients indicate that the mean positions of competing partisan elites are closer together than those of partisan voters, with very small coefficients signaling convergence among the parties' appeals, as predicted by the cartel theory. Very large coefficients, by contrast, indicate elite polarization relative to partisan electorates. Third, large regression *intercepts* imply that the representation of *most or all party elites* systematically diverge from their voters' preferred policies.[7]

Figure 7.1 displays party constituencies' positions on greed (x-axis) plotted against party elite positions on taxes versus spending, as judged by experts

---

[6] Prominent examples of this emerging fusion of elements of libertarian governance views and an exclusionary conception of citizenship and antimulticulturalism are the now-defunct party of the slain Dutch activist Pim Fortuyn and the de facto successor party led by Geert Wilders, as well as the Danish People's Party and the French National Front since Marianne LePen's ascent to the leadership position.

[7] For example, in most contemporary postindustrial democracies the issue of the death penalty may involve a large intercept, such that it predicts voters to be systematically more in favor of it than the elites of all or most political parties. In a similar vein, it has been suggested that on questions of immigration or questions of European integration the partisan elites are systematically more in favor than their electoral constituencies.

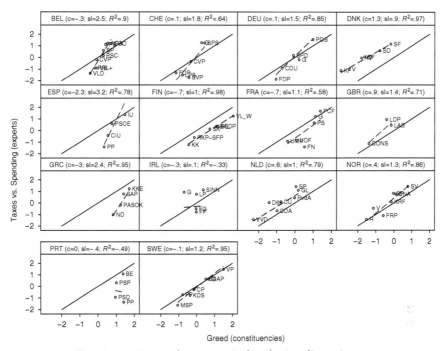

FIGURE 7.1. Representation on the economic-distributive dimension.

(y-axis). This provides a flavor of the relative positions of constituencies and parties for one particular dimension: economic distribution.

The figure suggests that party systems are generally quite representative. One can devise simple rules for scoring a party system's representativeness, requiring high R^2 and slope coefficients in the vicinity of 1.0 for full representation (Online Appendix 3). On the basis of those rules, eight of fourteen countries show close to perfect representation on the *greed dimension* (the four Scandinavians, Britain, the Netherlands, France, and Germany). Elsewhere the differences among partisan elites are more weakly reciprocated by a differentiation of party electorates corresponding to that of party elites (Belgium, Greece, Spain, and Switzerland) or almost not at all (Ireland, Portugal). Voters here ignore the parties' policy issue positions or discount what they are saying.[8]

On the *grid dimension*, representation is robust in about half of the countries (see Online Appendix 3). On the *group dimension*, the representativeness of party systems is strong in seven of fourteen countries and moderately strong in an additional four countries. As of this analysis, only Greece, Finland, and Sweden showed no representativeness of party systems on group issues, and

---

[8] On discounting and party competition, see Adams et al. (2005) and Tomz and Van Houweling (2008).

TABLE 7.1. *Patterns of representation: The full picture*

		GREED		
	No representation			Perfect representation
	←————————————————————————→			
GRID+GROUP Perfect representation ↑				Denmark
	Ireland		France Netherlands Britain	
		Spain	Germany Switzerland	
↓ No representation	Portugal	Greece	Belgium	Norway Finland Sweden

Note: See Online Appendix 3 for scoring rules and country scores on the three dimensions.

these are, of course, exactly the countries where new radical Right parties with anti-immigration appeals have succeeded in legislative elections since the 2008 data were collected.

Table 7.1 assembles a summary assessment of political representation by cross-tabling the countries' representation scores on the distributive dimension with the average score on a "second" dimension, combining sociopolitical governance and citizenship boundary issues. Before discussing cross-national differences, for now, let us observe that in most countries, except those of Southern Europe, party systems appear to be representative of their constituencies on some issue dimension(s). But which dimensions deliver representative strength varies by country (see Section 7.4).

While the data are purely cross-sectional, let us offer a possible intertemporal implication. If dealignment and cartelization theories were right, we would expect that in the countries with the longest and most durable democratic experience and with the greatest affluence and postindustrialization cartelization, or at least the unraveling of representation on ideological dimensions of policy making, has gone furthest. The evidence shows just the opposite.

7.3. Intertemporal Changes: Increasing Ideological Diffuseness and Convergence?

The theoretical literature on party system dynamics addresses intertemporal developments, but the available data are typically cross-sectional. Party realignment theory predicts persistent but substantively changing programmatic diversity among party positions. Party cartelization theory, by contrast, expects a gradual convergence of parties' policy positions. Dealignment theory sees diffuseness and convergence on broader programmatic dimensions, albeit with sharp interparty disagreements on individual highly salient issues featured by partisan entrepreneurs.

To explore changes over time, we analyzed ISSP surveys of 1990 and 2006, although their attitudinal items are far from perfect for our purposes.[9] We paired these mass-level data with the Laver and Hunt (1992) and Benoit and Laver (2006) expert scorings of party appeals for economic distribution and social permissiveness and estimated regressions as in the case of ESS 2008, with parties weighted by electoral size.

We could include twelve countries in the 1990–2006 comparison, albeit calculating regressions only on nine of them, as the United States (1990; 2006), New Zealand (1990; 2006), and Australia (2006) had only two usable parties on which scores could be constructed. Still, except in Australia, in these instances intercepts and slopes of representation can be compared. The results of this exercise are fairly similar, albeit not identical, to the results of the previous cross-sectional analysis of 2008 data.[10] Altogether, 50 percent of the cases end up with high representational congruence in 2006, as compared to 42 percent in 1990. Low representation applies to only one case in 1990 (Sweden) and only three in 2006 (Britain, Germany, Ireland). This is clearly not a pattern that would suggest the sharp decline of political representation stipulated by cartel theories of party system dynamics. We therefore conclude that patterns of static cross-sectional representation as well as the glimpses of dynamic intertemporal representation are most consistent with realignment theories.

To obtain a richer cross-sectional longitudinal design, we had to scale back measures of voter preferences and partisan appeals to simple Left-right placements. Empirical public opinion research overwhelmingly suggests that greed, grid, and group positions map onto voters' and parties' left-right positions, albeit with different weights of substantive policy content contingent upon time and country. As one plausible summary proxy for the continued distinctiveness of broad programmatic party appeals we calculate left-right party system polarization (Rehm and Reilly 2010). Here we measure polarization with

---

[9] The grid index includes survey responses to questions about (1) law and order, (2) military defense, and (3) permissibility of protest marches and demonstrations. It generates an atrocious Cronbach's alpha of .387.

[10] On *economic distribution ("greed")*, all countries but Ireland have medium to high representation in both 1990 and 2006. In seven countries, representation was very high in both periods (Australia, France, New Zealand, Spain, Switzerland, Sweden, and the United States). As is already familiar from the ESS data, Ireland defies representation on economics. On the *grid dimension*, our analysis is impaired by the somewhat inadequate mix of preference indicators at the mass level. Five of twelve cases show high representativeness in both 1990 and 2006 either because all three indicators (intercept, slope, and R^2) suggest this (France, Switzerland), or at least the first two with the third missing (United States, New Zealand, Australia 2006). Again, there is a tendency toward elite polarization such that the elites, particularly in the United States, overstate the differences that can also be found among their mass constituencies. In Norway, grid representativeness increased from intermediate to high.

party-size weighted standard deviations of party positions, with three different measures of positions: (i) a "constituency" measure, which positions parties at the average left-right self-placement of its supporters; (ii) a "perception" measure, which is based on population survey respondents' placement of parties on a left-right scale; and (iii) an "expert" measure, which is based on the average positions on a general left-right scale, as judged by experts.

Table 7.2 contains information on patterns and dynamics of party polarization, based on these three different positional measures (the data are from Rehm and Reilly 2010). Of particular interest are columns (3) and (4) for each observed group, which indicate the change in polarization before and after the fall of the iron curtain and the trend in polarization (assessed by the t-value from regressing polarization on time). While, unsurprisingly, the constituency-, perception-, and expert-based measures lead to somewhat different results, the overall conclusion remains the same: there is no universal trend. Some party systems became more polarized (such as in the United States), others less (such as in the United Kingdom and Germany), and some party systems did not change much (such as in Canada).

Of the eighteen countries for which we have pre- and post-1989 partisan left-right data in the constituency data set, six experienced a significant downward trend in polarization; nine a significant upward trend; and three had no trend (see Table 7.3). Of the ten countries for which we have pre- and post-1989 data on the perception measure, four experienced a downward trend, two an upward trend, and four no trend. Finally, of the thirteen countries for which we have pre- and post-1989 data on the expert measure, three experienced significant upward trends in polarization, three significant downward trends, and seven no trends.

Related, but not necessarily identical to a process of party convergence on indistinguishable programmatic appeals, may be a *progressively greater vagueness of positions* parties might choose when appealing to an ideologically more and more amorphous electorate. To capture the programmatic precision of partisan appeals, we calculated the standard deviations of the left-right self-placement of a party's supporters. Lower standard deviations suggest that constituencies have more homogeneous, precise preferences. There is *a substantively modest but distinctive pattern of increasing, not decreasing left-right precision in almost all countries*: Within a party, left-right self-placements by the party's supporters become increasingly similar. In fact, we find a statistically significant increase in precision (i.e., decrease in average standard deviations) in twelve countries, no significant change in seven, and significantly less precision in only two countries. One of these countries is Italy, which underwent a deep change of its party system. The other country is Norway, which started out with the highest precision in the pre-1989 period. In fact, once again there is a strong pattern of regression to the mean: systems with fuzzy party positions became increasingly crisp. The regressions for each country are in Online Appendix 4. Table 7.4 assembles levels and change

TABLE 7.2. *Party system polarization over time*

	Constituency					Perception					Experts				
	(1) <1989	(2) >1990	(3) Change	(4) Trend	(5) first-last yr (obs)	(1) <1989	(2) >1990	(3) Change	(4) Trend	(5) first-last yr (obs)	(1) <1989	(2) >1990	(3) Change	(4) Trend	(5) first-last yr (obs)
Netherlands	0.199	0.137	-0.062	-14.9	72-03 (32)	0.298	0.189	-0.109	-13.4	72-02 (31)		0.198		2.1	93-03 (4)
Iceland	0.235	0.175	-0.060	-4.3	84-03 (12)		0.244		-5.1	99-03 (5)		0.235			93-03 (2)
UK*	0.203	0.152	-0.051	-5.3	72-04 (33)	0.356	0.198	-0.158	-5.2	72-04 (33)	0.386	0.167	-0.219	-4.6	82-03 (5)
Australia*	0.141	0.095	-0.046	-5.5	72-04 (33)	0.125	0.125	0.001	0.6	84-04 (21)	0.270	0.191	-0.079	-1.9	82-03 (3)
Germany*	0.156	0.125	-0.031	-6.5	73-03 (31)	0.279	0.177	-0.102	-11.9	76-02 (27)	0.232	0.173	-0.059	-11	82-03 (5)
Belgium	0.158	0.128	-0.030	-4.8	73-03 (31)						0.211	0.149	-0.061		82-93 (2)
Greece	0.262	0.236	-0.027	-3.2	80-03 (24)							0.163		20.7	99-03 (3)
Canada*	0.055	0.051	-0.004	-0.4	72-03 (32)	0.102	0.091	-0.012	0.6	72-03 (32)	0.122	0.218	0.096	1.1	82-03 (3)
Denmark*	0.157	0.155	-0.002	1.5	73-03 (31)		0.216		-4	94-01 (8)	0.226	0.227	0.001	-0.1	82-03 (5)
Italy	0.227	0.231	0.004	-0.1	73-02 (30)						0.224	0.252	0.028	9.6	82-99 (3)
Spain	0.201	0.209	0.008	0.7	81-03 (16)							0.190		-2.4	93-02 (3)
Switzerland	0.131	0.142	0.011	3.1	72-03 (32)	0.146	0.142	-0.004	-1.3	72-03 (32)		0.329			03-03 (1)
Sweden*	0.175	0.185	0.011	3.6	72-03 (32)	0.287	0.263	-0.024	-2.4	79-02 (24)	0.243	0.234	-0.009	-0.8	82-03 (5)
France	0.198	0.214	0.016	2.7	77-03 (27)		0.136			02-02 (1)	0.266	0.199	-0.067	-1.8	82-02 (4)
New Zealand*	0.141	0.162	0.020	1.8	81-04 (22)	0.204	0.202	-0.002	0.3	81-02 (22)	0.134	0.157	0.024	1.1	82-03 (3)
USA*	0.089	0.109	0.021	7.9	72-04 (33)	0.191	0.213	0.022	3.2	72-04 (33)	0.137	0.281	0.144	4.4	82-03 (3)
Ireland	0.065	0.086	0.021	2.5	73-03 (31)		0.120			02 (1)	0.112	0.138	0.027	0.6	82-03 (5)
Norway*	0.124	0.149	0.026	3.8	73-03 (31)	0.191	0.209	0.018	2.8	73-01 (29)	0.251	0.244	-0.007	0.3	82-03 (3)
Portugal	0.147	0.177	0.031	4.5	86-04 (19)		0.180			02-04 (3)		0.160		12.4	93-03 (4)
Austria	0.082			10.1	90-03 (14)						0.181	0.212	0.031	4.8	82-03 (5)
Finland	0.184			0.1	90-03 (14)		0.157			03 (1)					

Notes: The table shows information on changes and trends in polarization based on three different Left-right measures: constituency (left-right self-placement of a party's voters), perception (left-right placement of parties by voters), and experts (expert placement of parties on general left-right scale). There are five columns for each of these measures: (1) average polarization (=weighted standard deviation) before and including 1989; (2) average polarization (=weighted standard deviation) after 1989; (3) column (2) minus column (1). This column sorts the tables. (4) t-value of regressing polarization on time. Positive [negative] t-values greater than 2 indicate that polarization went up [down] in a statistically significant way. Column (5) shows the first to last year of observations, as well as the number of years of data in parentheses (which are partially interpolated).

* indicates better data quality.

TABLE 7.3. *Diversity in cross-national changes of left-right polarization: Party constituencies*

		Levels of Polarization, Averages post-1990 (Overall Average in All Countries: .153/s.d. .054)		
		<.130	.130 – .175	>.175
Difference between pre-1990 and post-1990 averages (overall average: –.008/s.d. .031)	Less polarization: <–.023	AUS (–.046/.095) GER (–.031/.125) BEL (–.030/.128) CND (–.004/.051)	NLD (–.060/.137) UK (–.051/.132) DNK (–.002/.153)	GRC (–.027/.236) ITA (+.004/.231)
	Similar polarization: –.023 – +.007			
	Rising polarization > +.007	IRE (+.21/.086) USA (+.021/.109)	CH (+.011/.142) NZD (+.020/.162) NOR (+.026/.149)	ESP (+.008/.209) SWE (+.011/.185) FRA (+.016/.214) PRT (+.031/.177)

TABLE 7.4. *Diversity in cross-national changes of precision in left-right party positions: Party constituencies*

		Levels of Precision, Averages post-1990 (Overall Average in All Countries: .172/s.d. .017)		
		<.155 high precision	.130 – .175	>.175 low precision
Difference between pre-1990 and post-1990 averages	<–.010 increasing precision		GER (–.013/1.73)	CND (–.027/.187) BEL (–.020/.198) IRL (–.016/.199) UK (–.015/.183) NZD (–.005/.197)
	–.010 – +.010 Similar precision	USA (–.004/.142) GRC (+.009/.152)	CH (–.010/.175) FRA (–.004; .155) PRT (–.003/.165) AUT (N.D./.173) FIN (N.D./.161) SWE (+.001/.152) DNK (+.001/.158) ITA (+.009/.163)	
	> +.010 declining precision		Esp (=.015/.166) Nor (+.026/.159)	

rates in left-right precision, revealing a regional distribution we will address in section 7.4.

In sum, we find that the programmatic positions of parties in postindustrial party systems often remain rather sharply contoured, and that evidence does not support the hypothesis of an accelerating convergence and diffuseness of ideological appeals. These data provide little support for the contentions of dealignment / issue politics or party (system) cartelization postulates. To cement the superiority of the realignment perspective, however, let us see whether that analytical approach can also make sense of the diversity we observe among postindustrial party systems in terms of profiles of representation and trends in the polarization and precision of ideological appeals.

7.4. Differential Dynamics of Partisan Realignment in Postindustrial Democracies

In contrast to dealignment and cartelization theories, realignment theories of postindustrial party systems deem it possible that enduring differences persist between postindustrial party systems in different countries. For dealignment theorists, there is a great deal of volatility and issue contingency of competition within countries over time, obscuring systematic cross-national diversity. For cartelization theorists, cross-nationally postindustrial party systems should converge, and the prime variance may be the speed at which parties approach cartelization. That speed should be governed prominently by the generosity of public party finance, relieving parties of the urgency to seek approval by attracting contributions of time and money from electoral constituencies. The empirical implication of cartelization theory that more generous public funding helps existing parties to make the entry of new competitors harder and less successful, however, appears not to be borne out (Kitschelt 2000).

While the realignment perspective is generally most permissive to cross-national variance in the voter-partisan alignments and party systems of postindustrial democracies, how can they be explained? Demand-side factors (preference distributions in society) and/or supply-side factors (appeals politicians employ to rally electoral coalitions) may come into play. Variance in national preference profiles on the demand side, in turn, may be partially endogenous to long-term supply conditions: In a given polity at an earlier time the political competition among parties may have led to the creation of political-economic realities (such as social policies, trade policies, labor market regulation) that produced a lasting influence on the distribution of popular policy preferences. Moreover, on the supply side, because of their past appeals, policy activities, and competitive strategies, existing parties may credibly commit themselves only to certain stances that are by and large consistent with their past conduct or only marginally and incrementally modify such stances. Both past partisan strategies as well as political-economic institutions and resource distributions may therefore account for cross-national differences in current preference distributions and partisan realignments of postindustrial democracies.

At any given time, party systems then may not fully capture demand conditions. Debates about how to cope with electoral trade-offs and credibility problems may prevent established competitors from innovating and appealing to unrepresented interests. This, in turn, creates opportunities for fresh political entrepreneurs to launch new parties with good prospects for success. For example, for Sweden and Finland, our analysis of 2008 data for electoral constituencies and politicians discovered rather weak correspondence of voter preferences with political elites on the group (G3) dimension. It may be no accident that this void eventually enabled skillful political entrepreneurs to stage the electorally successful rise of the Swedish Democrats (2010) and the True Finns (2011), both of which take exclusionary positions on group issues, and especially on immigration none of the other parties was willing to embrace.

In order to create a bridge between past party competition and political-economic institutions in which their results have been manifested, on the one hand, and cross-national variance in postindustrial partisan realignments, on the other, let us invoke here recent behavioral modifications of spatial competition theory (Adams et al. 2005) and of agent-based behavioral modeling of spatial party competition (Laver and Sergenti 2011). Most importantly, parties cannot move around in the space of policy dimensions as they see fit, but they have to recognize and preserve what already Downs (1957) identified as an important asset of, but also constraint on parties' competitiveness, namely, reputation and consistency in their policy appeals and actions. Voters tend to discount new positions. Parties are therewith in part captives of their own past and policies. In a world with responsible partisan governments, *current* political economic institutions and resource allocations are the sediments of *past* bouts of partisan competition. In order to account for cross-national differences in partisan alignments, we have to identify the political-economic institutions and patterns of party competition that may now constrain the sets of options parties have to reconfigure their electoral coalitions under conditions of postindustrial politics and occupational structures.

Questions of economic distribution (greed) are likely to top the political agenda, where past partisan competition produced political-economic settlements in which social policy leads to sharp income redistribution, here captured not by the aggregate GINI coefficient, but the *"progressivity" of welfare states*, understood as the capacity of social policy schemes to concentrate the financial resource extraction on the wealthy, but the provision of transfers on the poor (Beramendi and Rehm 2012). Progressivity is not the same as generosity: Both generous "encompassing" as well as miserly "residual" welfare states may be progressive or not, but it is progressivity that focuses the popular attention on distributive conflict and strategic momentum of party competition on distributive issues.

Progressivity creates visibility of transfer winners and losers in household budgets. The rich will challenge generous, progressive systems and the poor will defend them. Where social transfer policies provide more of a system of insurance rather than redistribution from rich to poor, and where whatever redistribution takes place is more among different middle-income groups and across generations rather than vertical household income extremes, citizens are less disposed to give high salience to distributive partisan conflict, and parties have fewer opportunities to configure competitive strategy around making distributive issues salient through polarization.

Political economies with progressive social policies configure party systems around a free-market liberal and a redistributive pole, regardless of whether the liberal side, pushing for residual welfare states, or the redistributive side, creating comprehensive and equalizing welfare states, is winning. By contrast, party systems with insurance-based, relatively less progressive welfare states historically have featured strong "cross-class" parties running under Christian confessional or ecumenical labels or serving as focus of a national rally (such as the French Gaullists or the Japanese Liberal Democrats). Under postindustrial preference profiles, party systems with this latter trajectory are more likely to crystallize competition around dimensions of political governance (grid, $G2$) and economic and cultural boundary drawing (group, $G3$).

Not only the progressivity, but also the *generosity of welfare states* may matter for the evolution of partisan configurations. Encompassing welfare states have the tendency to provide and to subsidize a wide range of social and cultural services, in addition to dispensing more generous transfer payments in exchange for proportional taxes. In doing so, encompassing welfare states boost the growth of the occupational stratum of sociocultural professionals, particularly in education, health care, social counseling, and cultural services. While redistributive parties may push for the construction of comprehensive welfare states, they create a specter that then haunts them: the services of the welfare state are being delivered by sociocultural professionals whose intense libertarian grid / inclusionary, multiculturalist group preferences create strategic dilemmas for the old redistributive Left: if such parties do not embrace these demands for fear of losing their more authoritarian electoral bedrock support among lower-skill blue- and white-collar wage earners, postindustrial occupational groups begin to defect from their electoral coalitions in favor of new left-libertarian parties. If they do embrace the new demands, they might shed many of their old core voters, who migrate to new authoritarian and exclusionary radical right parties. In the worst of worlds, if they hesitate between both strategies, they lose core voters and remain unable to appeal to new social strata credibly.

A third element that affects the (re)shaping of partisan alignments in postindustrial democracies concerns the *extent to which party competition has been focused on programmatic politics at all, rather than clientelistic targeted benefits*, conditional on citizens' partisan vote and other partisan services.

And there may be an interaction between the two dimensions of welfare state development – progressivity and encompassingness – and clientelism: Southern European welfare states have been residual and proportional, thus not servicing the poor well at all (Ferrera 2010: 620–621). Clientelistic disbursement of benefits may have at least in part filled some of the gaps in the safety net of less well-off people that the formal welfare state left open and thus have helped to reduce the potential for a social explosion.

Where clientelistic bases of partisan competition have been prominent, they make party systems prone to breakdown, when the political-economic mechanisms that supply clientelistic resources, particularly state-governed, -subsidized, and -protected industries and discretionary social benefits (public housing, early disability retirement, etc.) experience financial crises and therefore can no longer provide the material means to sustain clientelistic networks. This has happened in heavily clientelisic party systems of middle-income countries (Greene 2007), but also in more clientelistic postindustrializing polities such as Italy, Japan, and to a lesser extent Austria in the 1980s or 1990s (Kitschelt 2007). At the same time, clientelism and its breakdown do not generate the conditions for the rise of grid / group partisan competition or even fierce party competition on the distributive dimension. Instead, faced with the breakdown of an at least partially nonprogrammatic, clientelistic party system, new political parties form around valence claims – such as quests for better governance, less corruption, and more honesty in the "political class." But these valence quests bracket people's preferences on salient policy dimensions and therefore are hard to sustain and institutionalize in partisan alternatives, thus producing highly volatile, personalistic, and programmatically amorphous parties and party systems. Where clientelistic linkages are important, party systems are not only vulnerable to breakdown, but also hard to reconstitute through new institutionalized programmatic partisan alignments, as valence competition trumps positional alignments.

Finally, as a general condition that affects the dynamics of realignment in party systems, consider *electoral systems*. Plurality single-member district systems make the successful legislative representation of new parties difficult, unless they have highly concentrated support. As long as incumbent parties have a stake and leverage to prevent a change of electoral system, postindustrial electoral realignments are less likely to occur here than in systems of proportional representation.

We now have four variables to predict party system realignments in about twenty postindustrial democracies. Rather than analyzing the relative importance of these factors (Huber and Stanig 2010; DeLaO and Rodden 2008) or their historical origins,[11] let us engage in a simple *big picture pattern*

---

[11] As indicated, behind the rise of proportional welfare schemes and encompassing, insurance oriented welfare states with subsidiary services stand cross-class parties mostly with a religious, but sometimes a national rally appeal. Greater or lesser persistence of clientelism well into the

recognition, distinguishing empirically four constellations. The objective of this more suggestive than conclusive exercise is to predict the extent to which each of four groups of countries is (1) likely to experience a crystallization of political alignments around grid/group divisions rather than primarily distributive greed divisions, and (2) the extent to which in this process rising authoritarian "rightist" parties that offensively fight globalization and multiculturalism as well as libertarian "leftist" multiculturalist counterparts begin to displace the conventional parties of the post–World War II political systems. We measure that decline of established parties by the loss of support they sustained from their combined average in the 1955–1965 decade (in Mediterranean countries: 1975–1985) to their combined average in the 2001–2011 decade. Online Appendix 5 itemizes how calculations were made for individual parties and party families in each country. Table 7.5 provides a grand summary of predictor variables; partisan dynamics as introduced in sections 7.2 through 7.3, but not yet discussed there by regional clusters; and electoral payoffs in terms of party system changes, measured by the rise and decline of party families since the 1950s.

Each partisan competitive configuration, then, is also expected to yield different socioeconomic electoral coalitions configured around partisan alternatives. For example, we would suspect that where left-libertarian and right-authoritarian parties thrive, the majority of sociocultural professionals and a large share of the remaining blue-collar working class will defect from established parties to these new alternatives. We do not, however, explore this link between micro- and macrolevel in this chapter.

In *Anglo-Saxon (settler) democracies*, partisan politics has focused on distributive conflict and resulted in narrow, but progressive welfare states. Clientelism has here been a marginal phenomenon since the early twentieth century (with the partial exception of the United States). And electoral systems make the entry of new parties hard, except in the case of New Zealand since the mid-1990s. As a consequence, we expect rather little realignment of parties around grid / group dimensions and few opportunities for new parties to enter the electoral arena successfully and in a sustained fashion. These results are generally borne out. The extreme stability of the U.S. party system, however, may mask the tremendous change the existing parties have undergone in a presidential system with decentralized parties and a growing "sorting" of voters and polarization of partisan elites according to grid / group issues inside the existing parties.

Interestingly, low levels of polarization (weak, except in the United States at the elite level recently) and feeble programmatic precision (diffuse, except

rise of postindustrial societies is related to the timing of state formation relative to democratization and industrial development, but also to the general level of economic development. Where democratization antedates the formation of professional civil services and industrialization, there is a great chance that party systems become clientelistic (Piattoni 2001; Shefter 1977).

TABLE 7.5. *Erosion and realignment of party systems in postindustrial democracies*

		Anglo-Saxon (Settler) Democracies	Scandinavia	Northern Continental Europe	Clientelistic Democracies and Economic Latecomers
Predictor variables: Where is the propensity to second dimension party alignments strong?	Proportionality of the welfare state?	Negative	Negative	Positive	Positive
	Encompassingness of the welfare state?	Negative	Positive	Positive	Negative
	Low recent importance of clientelism?	Positive	Positive	Positive/negative	Negative
	Electoral System: not plurality single member district	Negative (except NZD since 1995)	Positive	Positive	Positive
	Summary prediction	1 : 3	3 : 1	4: o or 3: 1	2 : 2
Representative-ness of party elites?	Distributive dimension?	Strong (only UK data)	Strong	Intermediate-strong	Weak
	Grid/group dimensions?	Intermediate	Weak (except Denmark)	Intermediate (except Belgium)	Weak
Dynamics of left-right polarization and precision?	Polarization levels	Weak-intermediate	Intermediate-strong	Weak-intermediate (except France)	Strong
	Polarization-change rates	Decline (AUS, UK) or rise (NZD, USA)	Increase	Stable-decline	Increase
	Precision-levels	Low (except USA)	Intermediate	Intermediate	Intermediate-high
	Precision-change rates	Increasing	Stable (except Norway)	Increasing	Stable-decreasing
Party system outcomes	Change of established parties 1955–1965 – 2001–2011	AUS, CND, UK −14.0 ; NZD −26.0 ; US −3.5	DNK, FIN, NOR, SWE −24.7	AUT, BEL, FRA, GER, NLD, SWI −24.7	GRC, IRE, POR, ESP −2.5 ; ITA, JPN −52.1
	New Left-libertarian parties (2001–2011)	4.3 ; 6.3 ; 0.7	9.2	7.7	1.0 ; 2.6
	New Right-authoritarian parties (2001–2011)	1.5 ; 5.4 ; 0.0	11.1	10.8 – 13.0	2.3 ; 2.8

recently in the United States) appear consistent with the Downsian median voter theorem in two-party systems, but the intertemporal dynamics of change in these countries is not: polarization has been increasing in the United States and the ideological precision of partisan alternatives has been increasing just about everywhere in this group (see Tables 7.2 through 7.4).[12]

In Scandinavia, the progressiveness of social policy militates against a realignment of the party system away from distributive politics, but the encompassingness of a service-oriented welfare state with an unprecedented growth of sociocultural professions has favored a postindustrial realignment around grid / group dimensions. The irrelevance of clientelism and the permissiveness of electoral systems further boost the electoral opportunities of new programmatic parties that situate themselves at polar opposites of the grid / group dimensions. These expectations are redeemed by the partisan payoffs: a sharp decline of the established parties since the 1950s (–24.7 percent), nearly matched by a rise of new parties to almost one-quarter of the electorate. The high representativeness of the party systems on all dimensions in Denmark is in line with expectations, but not the low representativeness on grid / group issues in other Scandinavian countries (Table 7.1). But those data are from 2008. As noted, the recent success of radical right parties in Finland and Sweden has corrected this picture and made party systems more accurate reflections of popular policy preferences on the grid / group dimensions in these two countries.

In the *Northern European continental party systems*, the proportionality and the encompassingness of welfare states have dampened the partisan politicization of economic distribution. These policies emerged from and were further reinforced by party systems that always incorporated cross-cutting cleavages on the grid dimension. While controversies about religious issues have faded, the old law-and-order and civil liberties agenda on the grid dimension and the questions of national identity, culture, and citizenship on the group dimension have remained alive and well and gained new salience through postindustrialization. These conditions, plus permissive electoral systems, favor partisan realignments. In a subset of these countries (Austria, Belgium, possibly France) a lingering clientelism through at least the 1980s generated a potential for protest parties invoking valence issues (corruption, quality of governance).

Examining the partisan payoffs, the Northern European continental democracies have indeed undergone as great an average postindustrial realignment as the Scandinavians (–24.7 percent). The French and the German party systems show the relatively smallest reversals (–16.3 and –14.8 percent, respectively).

---

[12] There is no room to discuss "American exceptionalism" here. The extreme narrowness and progressiveness of the American welfare state, together with sharply rising inequality and concentration of labor market risks in the poorest strata, are most likely responsible for the stability and polarization of the established parties (McCarty, Poole, and Rosenthal 2006; Rehm 2011a). Add to this that in the fragmented, decentralized American parties grid / group themes, particularly that of race, have always been incorporated and do not have to be grafted onto a primarily distribution-centered party system.

So the electoral system may not account for this relative restraint, when compared to the rest of the cohort. For the rise of radical right-wing parties, we give a range rather than a single number, because we are uncertain whether to include the *Swiss People's Party* in its entirety (higher value) or only the additional increment of support it has attracted since its programmatic reversal in the late 1980s (lower value). Also party system dynamics is broadly in line with expectations.

Finally, there is a cohort of countries we do not characterize by region, but by economic and political attributes: *clientelistic democracies and economic latecomers*. In addition to four Mediterranean polities – Greece, Italy, Portugal, and Spain – we include here Ireland and Japan. All six have proportional, if not regressive, insurance-based welfare states of a residual nature, leaving existential needs uncovered. All of them have more or less permissive electoral systems. In part because of late uneven bureaucratic professionalization and industrialization, all of them also have seen a strong or an at least intermediate impact of clientelism on their citizen-party linkage mechanism that undercuts programmatic representation and hobbles the reformation of programmatic party systems (Kitschelt 2011, 2012).

Examining the parties' electoral payoffs, we find a sharp dualism. In Italy and Japan the old party systems have partly broken down (−52.1 percent), but we see preciously little rise of grid / group based new parties (and for that matter even new parties that would take clear positions on the economic-distributive dimension). But the other four countries in the clientelistic group show much more stable party systems. In part, this may be due to the later starting observation after which party system dynamics could be observed: for the former Mediterranean dictatorships that is only the mid-1970s. More plausible, however, is the explanation that in 2008 when our data were gathered these four countries had not (yet) experienced the political-economic shock to a developmental state-centered growth strategy that precipitated the erosion, if not collapse, of clientelism in Italy and Japan. The crisis of the Eurozone since 2008 constitutes such a shock and has already begun to unravel the existing Greek and Irish party systems, with Portugal and Spain possibly following suit in prospective elections.

To sum up, the dynamics of party systems in at least three groups of postindustrial countries is quite consistent with the realignment perspective, and certainly more so than with dealignment or cartelization perspectives. Partisan politics in the fourth group – countries with a rather vigorous effort of clientelistic voter-party linkage even in post–World War II democracies until the 1990s – looks more caught up in dealignment or party system cartelization, given their weak capacity to represent the party electorates' policy preferences. Yet whereas theories of cartelization and dealignment expect these phenomena to befall the most advanced postindustrial economies, they appear to apply more accurately to relative democratic and postindustrial latecomers that, for reasons related to their pathways of political-economic development and political institutionalization (civil service, democratic regime), never articulated programmatic alignments on par with those evident in the other three groups of countries in the post–World War II era.

7.5. Conclusion

For brevity's sake, our chapter has emphasized stark contrasts between theoretical perspectives on the dynamics of party systems and between groups of countries exhibiting differential expressions of partisan realignment. With more space to develop the argument, one would show how the electoral coalitions configured around party systems have changed over time and how they vary in line with the different institutional and political-economic configurations today. Moreover, one would endogenize the differences in postindustrial realignment more rigorously in order to discern which of the four factors we itemized – progressiveness and encompassingness of welfare states, clientelism, and barriers to new party entry through electoral systems – may have the greatest leverage in affecting variants of current partisan realignment. One could then also more clearly trace back current party system dynamics to the prevailing strategic configurations of the post–World War II eras in each country. This would be helpful for exploring the extent to which party realignments in the early twenty-first century are simply a matter of affluence and development, or, as we have argued, a matter of institutions, political economy, and supply-side party strategy.

8

What Do Voters Want? Dimensions and Configurations in Individual-Level Preferences and Party Choice

Silja Häusermann and Hanspeter Kriesi

There is a contrast in the way voter preferences are conceptualized in two strands of current literature: While most of the comparative political economy literature implicitly or explicitly theorizes voter preferences on economic and social policies and their relevance for party choice in terms of – mostly unidimensional – distributive conflict, the literature on political parties and elections that deals with the determinants of party choice has always emphasized the importance of alternative, "second" dimensions of political conflict (see, e.g., Lipset and Rokkan 1967, Kitschelt 1994, Kitschelt and McGann 1995, Rokkan 2000, Bartolini 2000, Hooghe et al. 2002, Kriesi et al. 2006, 2008, Bornschier 2010, De la O and Rodden 2008).

We argue in this chapter that both strands of literature should integrate each other's insights. More specifically, we contend that in order to understand the challenges political parties face in contemporary capitalist democracies, the findings from both strands of literature need to be combined for several reasons: First of all, the European political space cannot be reduced to a single dimension of political conflict and competition, but has always been and still is structured by at least two conflict lines. The coexistence of two (or more) dimensions of conflict fundamentally alters the way we ought to view the electoral landscape and has critical implications for the way preferences are related to party choice. Moreover, the boundaries between distributional (economic) and identity-based (cultural) conflicts have become increasingly blurred: Issues such as welfare chauvinism, the unequal effects of welfare states on men and women, or the distributive balance between labor market insiders and outsiders have a clear distributive relevance, but they also relate to (more culturally connotated) considerations of a universalist versus particularist organization of the society and of social solidarity. Many economic, distributive struggles are thus inherently pluridimensional (see, e.g., Manow 2002, Manow and van Kersbergen 2009, Kitschelt and McGann 1995, Häusermann 2010, 2012).

Furthermore, the traditional Left-Right economic dimension (state intervention vs. market liberalism) itself needs to be reconceptualized in the context of welfare state maturation (Pierson 2001) and postindustrialism (Esping-Andersen 1999), and in the light of theories on the institutional configuration and rationale of capitalist regimes, such as the varieties of capitalism literature (Hall and Soskice 2001). The economic conflict dimension can no longer be analyzed in terms of "more versus less welfare spending," since postindustrial capitalism faces a range of different and distinct challenges, such as the conflicts between social insurance and redistribution, or between social protection and social investment (Häusermann et al. 2013).

The goal of this contribution is to map the structure of the political space of individual-level preferences throughout democratic Western capitalism. In the wording of the framework developed in the Introduction to this volume, we map the demand-side constraints governments face today. Our chapter follows up directly on the analysis of representation performance provided by Kitschelt and Rehm in this book. While they show that parties still represent their – changed – constituencies, we take a closer look at who these constituencies are and what they want. We address three questions. First, we ask what the key conflict lines in contemporary capitalism are. We argue that there are two fundamental dimensions of conflict structuring the individual-level preferences in European societies – a state-market dimension and a universalism-particularism dimension. We will then investigate the sociostructural factors determining the individual-level preferences with regard to these two conflict dimensions, before addressing the question of the consequences of these preferences with respect to party choice. This means that we study the extent to which the preferences on these two dimensions allow us to explain election outcomes in European societies.

For our empirical analyses, we use data from the European Social Survey (ESS 2008) and include fifteen Western European countries. These data will allow us to compare preference formation, its social structural origins, and its political implications in different types of polities as identified in the introductory chapter to this volume – countries with an institutional legacy oriented toward competitiveness, equality, status, or capture.

8.1. Theory

Religion and class have traditionally been the two conflicts structuring European politics. Arguably, both have been losing much of their structuring capacity as a result of the large-scale processes of secularization, value change, rising standards of living, and the pacification of industrial relations. In line with these societal transformations, many observers have declared the decline of cleavage politics and the rise of individualized political choices (e.g., Dalton et al. 1984, Franklin et al. 1992). Others, among whom we count ourselves, have argued that the cleavages have not disappeared. While the large-scale transformations of European societies may have weakened traditional cleavages, we argue that new cleavages have risen in their place. The new structuring conflicts that have developed since the late sixties have been embedded into the two-dimensional traditional preference structure and have thereby fundamentally transformed the meaning of both original dimensions.[1]

8.1.1. A New Universalism-Particularism Dimension

The originally religious cleavage structuring the European preference space has been profoundly transformed in several waves over the past fifty years. The first wave reaches back to the late 1960s and is the result of a set of large-scale processes that started to transform European societies profoundly in the post-war era: secularization, the educational revolution, rising living standards, tertiarization, and the establishment of the welfare states. These processes have been driving the profound value change toward "self-expression values" with an increasing emphasis on subjective well-being and quality of life (theorized above all by Inglehart (1977, 1997), Inglehart and Welzel (2005), but also by others such as Flanagan and Lee (2003) or Kitschelt (1994)). Flanagan and Lee (2003) describe the same kind of shift as a change from authoritarian to libertarian values, implying an erosion of both clerical and secular authority. Throughout the 1970s and 1980s, these new values were expressed politically mainly by the so-called new social movements. These movements mobilized in the name of human rights, peace, the emancipation of women, solidarity with the poor and the oppressed, and the protection of the environment. Their vision was one of cultural liberalism and social justice/protection. These were movements of the Left, which, in due course, spawned a new set of parties – the New Left and Green Parties – and often found close allies in the established parties of the Left (thereby deeply transforming them).

The second wave of transformative political mobilization, the wave of the 1990s and 2000s, is linked to processes, which have been conveniently summarized under the term "globalization" or "denationalization" (Kriesi et al. 2008). They have transformed the cultural-identitarian dimension through the issues of immigration, political integration, and a weakening of domestic democratic sovereignty. First, denationalization has brought about a significant increase in cultural diversity within European societies. Since the 1960s, West European societies in particular have seen massive *immigration* of groups that are in many respects distinct from the already resident population. One of

---

[1] To be sure, in the literature on political parties and elections there has also always been another strand, which argued that in West European countries, the behavior of parties and voters alike has been structured by one single ideological "left-right" dimension (e.g., Van der Eijk and Franklin 1996, Van der Eijk et al. 1999, Klingemann, et al. 1994, van der Brug and van Spanje 2009, Fuchs and Klingemann 1990). However, the meaning of the Left-Right dimension varies across countries, making it a less useful conceptualization if one wants to understand preference configurations.

the crucial questions then is how these societies cope with immigration and the resulting diversity (see Dancygier and Walter, this volume). Immigration may intensify economic competition over scarce jobs and shrinking welfare benefits. However, a growing body of empirical research shows that the actual effects of immigration flows on income, employment, and unemployment are quite small (Hainmueller and Hiscox 2007), and that "anti-immigration sentiments are far more powerfully associated with cultural values that have more to do with conceptions of national identity than they do with concerns about personal, economic circumstances" (p. 437). This means that immigration is primarily mobilized through identity-based frames, thereby transforming the libertarianism-authoritarianism dimension. The groups in the resident population who feel threatened by the increasing cultural diversity seek to defend their traditional way of life. Feelings of competitive threat from members of other ethnic or racial groups, however, have complex determinants. Among these determinants are the individuals' values and beliefs such as ethnic and racial tolerance. Crucially, such values are more widespread among the more highly educated. Education has a "liberalizing" effect; that is, it induces a general shift of political value orientations toward cultural liberalism, cosmopolitanism, and universalism (Grunberg and Schweisguth 1990: 54, 1997: 155–159, 168, Quillian 1995, Kriesi et al. 2008: 13, Stubager 2008).

The second source of conflicts related to globalization is *political integration*, that is, the transfer of political authority to institutions beyond the nation-state (Grande and Pauly 2005). This is particularly true for cases in which such a transfer jeopardizes national political sovereignty, which is obvious in the European context. As Greenfeld (1992: 10) has also pointed out, historically, the idea of democracy has been intimately tied to the idea of the nation-state. To the extent that the decision-making authority shifts to the supranational level, the individuals' democratic rights at the national level are at risk. Therefore, such shifts are bound to incite nationalist reactions among those who feel that their democratic rights are hollowed out. Individuals who identify strongly with their national community and who are attached to its exclusionary norms will perceive a weakening of the national institutions as a loss. Conversely, citizens with universalistic or cosmopolitan norms may perceive this weakening as a gain, if it implies a strengthening of a specific type of cosmopolitan political institutions (Mau 2007). Crucially again, across most advanced industrial countries, the lower classes attach greater value to the nation than the upper classes. Different authors explain this robust sociostructural correlate with mechanisms such as feelings of national belonging compensating for lower social status (Shayo 2009) or guaranteeing individual and equal dignity to all members of the nation (Greenfeld 1999, Tamir 1995).

We argue that this second wave of transformative change, linked to globalization and denationalization, was politically more consequential in its effect on the identity-related cultural dimension of political structuration than on the dimension of economic-distributive attitudes and preferences, because, as is observed by Kalmijn and Kraaykamp (2007), there is a shift from an economic to a cultural basis of stratification, worldwide. As countries modernize, cognitive skills and cultural resources such as education become more important for an individual's place in society. Education thereby becomes a more important source for politically relevant attitudes. Second, as we have argued previously (Kriesi et al. 2006, 2008), the political actors who mobilize globalization losers mainly do so in identity-based and not in economic terms. Most importantly, the new groups of "winners" and "losers" of globalization are not ideologically predefined. It is the parties of the new populist Right who have been the key promoters of the cause of voters with particularistic preferences (Bornschier 2010).

Finally, we investigate in this chapter the idea that we currently assist a third transformation of this conflict dimension into a more encompassing conflict between universalistic and particularistic preferences and attitudes. This third transformation is driven by the interaction of denationalization and financial austerity, and it moves the issue of *distributive deservingness* to the forefront of European politics. Given the transformed economic circumstances in Europe, welfare states have to be both consolidated and restructured. However, in times of scarcity, defining the scope of beneficiaries who should be entitled to benefits and services from the state becomes the most salient issue, and we suggest that this issue is more closely related to the so-called cultural dimension than to the traditional economic-distributive dimension. With this third transformation, the distinction of the two preference dimensions into one cultural and one economic becomes obsolete, as both dimensions bear clear and direct relevance for economic and social policy making.

Predominantly, the debate about distributive deservingness takes the form of welfare chauvinism (Kitschelt and McGann 1995, Andersen and Björklund 1990), that is, the idea that welfare benefits and services should be granted only to nationals, who are considered "deserving," because they are part of the community of solidarity and/or because they have contributed to social security schemes. Hence, the issue at stake here is not the level or structure of benefits or services, but the entitlement. Even though entitlement is mostly discussed with regard to immigrants, as van Oorschot (2000, 2006) has shown, narrow conceptions of welfare deservingness also exist with respect to the disabled or unemployed. Again, education turns out to be the single most important factor explaining attitudes on welfare chauvinism, deservingness, or welfare misuse (van der Waal et al. 2010, van Oorschot 2006): The lower the education level of respondents, the more they want to narrow down welfare entitlement to a limited circle of "deserving" beneficiaries. The authors consider this finding paradoxical, because the lower classes (in terms of education, income, and class) also tend to be the ones supporting welfare generosity most strongly.

It seems that welfare deservingness follows a different logic from preferences regarding traditional state-market preferences, as they – even though relevant for economic policies in the realm of welfare and labor market regulation – may be strongly linked to cultural, rather than economic mechanisms of preference formation. Van der Waal et al. (2010) indeed find – on the basis of Dutch data – that cultural mechanisms explain the link between low education and attitudes on deservingness better than mechanisms of ethnic competition.[2] Eger's (2010) and van Oorschot's (2006) finding of a strong correlation among immigration, antiimmigration attitudes, and narrow conceptions of welfare deservingness points in a similar direction: In a context of increasing cultural diversity, people with low levels of cognitive and educational resources develop feelings of insecurity and distrust, which become manifest in their beliefs that "others," that is, any kind of outgroup members, take advantage of undeserved benefits and privileges.

All these findings show that the distinction between the realm of economic and cultural politics becomes blurred, since cultural mechanisms increasingly drive preferences regarding distributive policies. Hence, as we have also argued in the introduction to this volume, the universalism-particularism dimension matters for democratic capitalism as much as the state-market dimension.

8.1.2. A Transformed State-Market Dimension

Compared to the cultural dimension, the economic dimension of voter preferences and party choice, opposing advocates of state intervention to market liberalists, has always occupied an important place in the literature on democracy and capitalism. However, there have been major controversies about the relevance and the substance of this dimension.

With regard to the *relevance* of the economic dimension of voter preferences, a key question is whether the positions of parties with regard to macroeconomic policies are still sufficiently distinct to structure voter preferences and party choice. Structural factors such as deindustrialization, reduced transportation and communication costs and the exposure of a growing number of economic sectors to international competition, the growing internationalization of finance, and the higher mobility of capital (Kitschelt et al. 1999: 445–448) might suggest that macroeconomic policies of advanced capitalist democracies tend to converge on a neoliberal consensus. Irrespective of the actual pressure toward convergence, the public may perceive the economic leeway of the national governments as being heavily constrained. This could remove macroeconomic issues from the electoral arena, since voters would refrain from basing party choices on attitudes toward issues they think their governments do

---

[2] Derks's (2004) concept of "economic populism" supports these findings. He conceives of this "syndrome" as a specific reaction against feelings of social deprivation that are prevalent among the underprivileged. Economic populists reject social achievements such as the welfare state not for their content, but because of their elitist origin. He argues that this form of "anti-welfare statism does not reflect a belief in neo-liberal market capitalism, but rather a radical expression of welfare chauvinism, inspired by a rigid form of social conservatism and a profound distrust of current social policy arrangements" (Derks 2004: 519).

not control anyway (Hellwig and Samuels 2007, Duch and Stevenson 2008). However, it would be premature to argue that the economic dimension of voter preferences and party competition has become irrelevant to the electoral dynamics of democratic capitalism, because structural and institutional factors support continued – if altered – divergence in macroeconomic policies (Kitschelt et al. 1999: 449–457, Scharpf and Schmidt 2000, Hall and Soskice 2001). It may be true that issues related to market liberalization, industrial policy, as well as monetary and fiscal policy are increasingly taken out of the hands of national governments in Europe, and that the policies of left- and right-wing governments are therefore converging on these issues (as Boix (2000), e.g., has demonstrated for fiscal and monetary policy). Nevertheless, important alternative economic issues such as labor market regulation and welfare policies remain within the discretion of national governments, and on these issues, both party policies and voter preferences continue to diverge.

This implies that, in *substantive* terms, the conceptualization of the state-market preference dimension today should focus on labor market and welfare issues, rather than on macroeconomic policies. In the wake of welfare state maturation and postindustrialism, however, the economic conflict dimension itself has been transformed. Pierson (1996, 2001) has shown that welfare state maturation has transformed the issues at stake in postindustrial capitalism: The main conflict concerns no longer simply the extent of welfare state expansion. In times of financial austerity, when cutbacks are difficult to implement and the room for expansion is limited, distributive conflict becomes more complex and the dominant issues are endogenously shaped by the institutional legacies in place (Pierson 2001: 455, Esping-Andersen 1999): While in continental Europe, for example, retrenchment, societal modernization, and insider-outsider conflicts are supposed to dominate the agenda (Häusermann 2010), welfare reform in liberal countries is expected to focus on activation policies and cost containment (Pierson 2001). The upshot of this argument is that the substance of the economic conflict dimension is altered: from the overall size of the welfare to its actual distributive design in terms of both social transfers and welfare services.

A range of theoretical work in comparative political economy and welfare state research deals with this redefinition of welfare state conflict. Three concepts are particularly relevant for our discussion of voter preferences in contemporary capitalism: redistribution, social insurance, and social investment. The first relevant distinction is between *redistribution* and *social insurance*. As the major works on the institutional design of different welfare regimes have consistently shown, the size of the welfare state does not predict its redistributive effect (see in particular Esping-Andersen 1990, Bradley et al. 2003), because the continental social insurance regimes – despite being "big" welfare states – typically distribute benefits for old age, unemployment, sickness, or disability on the basis of contributions, rather than on the basis of need. Until the 1980s, preferences toward both redistribution and social insurance could be reasonably subsumed under the heading of attitudes toward welfare generosity, since both redistributive and insurance programs were expanded. In the era of austerity, however, expansions for some groups tend to occur at the expense of cuts for others (Häusermann 2010). In this context, social insurance for labor market insiders competes with needs-based benefits for outsiders and low-income workers, and this dualization of social transfers (Palier 2010, Palier and Thelen 2010, Emmenegger et al. 2012) may lead to a weaker coherence of the overall state-market dimension.

Financial transfers are, however, only one aspect of the distributive profile of welfare states. Services – which have been strongly developed in the Nordic countries from the 1960s onward already (Huber and Stephens 2001) – play an increasingly important role in all postindustrial economies. Several analyses of the structure of social risks in postindustrial economies (Esping-Andersen 1999b, Bonoli 2005, Armingeon and Bonoli 2006) have emphasized the importance of active labor market policies, investment in human capital, and care services for the needs and demands of new social risk groups, among both the lower and the middle classes (Gingrich and Häusermann forthcoming). Rather than providing passive income replacement, social investment policies enable beneficiaries to develop human capital and participate in the labor market. Such *social investment policies* (Morel et al. 2012) have become important on the reform agendas of both liberal and continental regimes (whereas they have been prominent in the Nordic welfare states for a long time already) (Hemerijck 2013), and they may also contribute to weakening the coherence of the state-market preference dimension, because the sociostructural determinants driving social investment preferences differ to some extent and under certain institutional conditions from those driving preferences for passive income replacement. More specifically, labor market insiders are supposed to be more consumption-oriented, whereas labor market outsiders – and at times even capital – should be more favorable toward policies providing access to the labor market and investment in human capital (Rueda 2005, Schwander and Häusermann 2013, Gingrich and Ansell, this volume). Also, recent evidence shows that social investment policies – especially in the fields of care infrastructure and activation – benefit and respond to the preferences of the more highly educated middle-class voters (Van Lancker 2013, Geering and Häusermann 2013). For these reasons, it has become inadequate to conceptualize the alignment of preferences regarding the state-market dimension in terms of a mere conflict between workers and more privileged strata.

Moreover, the emergence of social investment reforms on the agenda of postindustrial welfare states also contributes to the fact that we cannot draw a clear line between cultural values and economic interests as determinants of economic-distributive policy preferences. As we have argued in the introductory chapter to this book (see Chapter 1), there is a link between universalistic attitudes and preferences for investment, which can be traced back to education and the future orientation of these policies. Hence, as for welfare chauvinism and deservingness, people's attitudes toward economic-distributive policy reforms depend not only on their position regarding the state-market dimension, but also on their universalistic versus particularistic attitudes. This is why we have to take both dimensions into account to understand both the politics and the reform of economic-distributive policies in advanced capitalist democracies.

8.2. Empirical Analysis

8.2.1. Dimensions

For the empirical analysis, we use the data of the ESS4 (2008/2009). The file includes random samples for fifteen Western European countries,[3] which we categorize into the four types of institutional legacies, as developed in the Introduction to this volume. For our analyses, the ESS4 data have the crucial advantage that they include a rotating module on attitudes toward the welfare state, which allows us to measure the state-market dimension in a sufficiently differentiated way.

To operationalize the *universalism-particularism* dimension, we create indicators for the most important issues that have defined and transformed this dimension over the past five decades. For the concerns of the new social movements, we build a scale for cultural liberalism. We use five items to build this scale (for the formulation of the items, see Appendix I): two items referring to women's emancipation, one item dealing with rights of homosexuals, and two items with authoritarianism (in school and in criminal law). Exploratory factor analysis reveals that the five items constitute a weak uniform scale (Eigenvalue of 1.23) across all countries, and in the individual regimes. For the concerns of the globalization losers, we operationalize their opposition to immigration and their Euroskepticism. For immigration, we build a scale based on six items (see Appendix I), which form a strong uniform scale (Eigenvalue of 3.40). Third, we try to operationalize that aspect of welfare conflicts in advanced capitalist democracies that we expect to be mainly associated with the universalism-particularism dimension – the question of distributive deservingness. We use two indicators for this question. First, an individual item is chosen to operationalize welfare chauvinism. This item asks whether immigrants receive more or less (in terms of social benefits and services) than they contribute. Second, we also use a set of three items to measure economic populism, welfare deservingness, or welfare misuse (see Appendix I). Although the three items only form a very weak uniform scale (Eigenvalue = .83), we still

---

[3] The countries included are Belgium, Cyprus, Denmark, Finland, France, Germany, Greece, Ireland, the Netherlands, Norway, Portugal, Spain, Sweden, Switzerland, and the United Kingdom.

use this scale for lack of a better alternative as an indicator of attitudes toward welfare state misuse.

To operationalize the *state-market* dimension, we choose indicators for all aspects of economic distributive conflict that we have discussed above. We measure preferences on redistribution with two items from the ESS survey: the question whether governments should reduce differences in income levels and the question asking respondents whether they think that for a society to be fair, the difference in standards of living should be small. For activation and social investment, we also use two items, which relate to policies promoting participation in the workforce. The first item asks respondents whether they think that governments should be responsible to provide a job to everyone who wants one, and the second item asks preferences on government responsibility for providing sufficient child care infrastructure. We also tried to operationalize social insurance preferences using two questions of the ESS survey that ask respondents how welfare benefits should be distributed – according to needs (redistribution) or according to the contributions they have made (the actuarial social insurance logic). The two items refer to unemployment insurance and pension insurance, respectively. An exploratory factor analysis (results not shown) makes it very clear that the social insurance items are very different from the indicators for redistributive or social investment preferences, which together form a weak joint factor.[4] This strikingly weak coherence of welfare preferences is, on the one hand, due to the actual multidimensionality of the welfare preference space, as theorized above. However, a certain extent of it could also be related to relatively weak indicators of social insurance. Hence, we refrain from using these indicators in the further analysis and just establish here that there is weak coherence of the economic state-market dimension.

With the nine selected indicators, we have then performed an exploratory factor analysis both including all countries and per regime. The results are presented in Table 8.1. Most importantly, we find the expected two dimensions – a universalism-particularism and a state-market dimension. Apart from two exceptions, the pattern of correlations of the original items with the two factors is very similar across all regime types. Note that, as expected, welfare chauvinism and welfare misuse/deservingness are part of the first factor. In all countries – and also in accordance with our theoretical arguments above – the universalism-particularism scale is stronger in terms of its Eigenvalue and the factor loadings than the state-market one.

---

[4] It is important to note that – in line with our theoretical expectations regarding the increasing heterogeneity of the state-market dimension – even the indicators of redistribution and social investment are rather weakly related. If one constrains the factor analysis of social policy preferences to three instead of two factors, the social investment items load on a separate factor. However, none of the resulting three factors (redistribution, social insurance, social investment) achieves an Eigenvalue higher than 1.

TABLE 8.1. *Factor analyses for preference scales: Factor loadings, rotated solutions*

Variable	Competitiveness-Oriented Countries (GB, IE)		Equality-Oriented Countries (DK, FI, NO, SE)		Status-Oriented Countries (BE, CH, DE, NL, F)	
	Universalism-particularism	State-market	Universalism-particularism	State-market	Universalism-particularism	State-market
Immigration	0.68	−0.01	0.69	−0.05	0.71	0.02
Welfare chauvinism	0.55	−0.00	0.48	−0.09	0.49	−0.01
Welfare misuse	0.44	−0.05	0.50	−0.02	0.48	0.01
Cultural liberalism	−0.39	−0.06	−0.56	−0.09	−0.49	−0.12
EU integration	−0.39	0.06	−0.32	−0.15	−0.46	0.02
Egalitarianism	−0.01	0.39	0.02	0.54	0.05	0.49
Redistribution	0.03	0.43	−0.01	0.58	0.07	0.54
Job for everyone	0.01	0.50	−0.04	0.50	0.04	0.49
Child care	−0.09	0.44	−0.13	0.32	−0.12	0.38
Eigenvalue	1.27	0.80	1.41	1.01	1.46	0.90

	Capture-Oriented Countries (ES, PT, GR, CY)		Uniform Scales	
Variable	Universalism- particularism	State-market	Universalism- particularism	State-market
Immigration	0.64	0.06	0.68	0.07
Welfare chauvinism	0.51	0.05	0.46	-0.09
Welfare misuse	0.22	-0.01	0.46	0.00
Cultural liberalism	-0.31	-0.07	-0.51	-0.19
EU integration	-0.39	0.03	-0.36	0.05
Egalitarianism	0.08	0.42	0.11	0.53
Redistribution	0.06	0.40	0.09	0.52
Job for everyone	0.06	0.54	0.06	0.55
Child care	0.02	0.55	-0.07	0.46
Eigenvalue	1.14	0.78	1.43	1.01

Note: All scales reported in the table are based on exploratory factor analysis.

In addition to the country group-specific scales, we have constructed uniform scales. While these uniform scales are not exactly identical to the group-specific scales, the two are nevertheless very highly correlated in each case (correlations between 0.96 and 0.99). Although some of the resulting dimensions are weak in terms of Eigenvalues, their pattern is remarkably similar across European societies.

8.2.2. *The Social-Structural Determinants of Political Preferences*

Tables 8.2 and 8.3 present the results of OLS-regression analyses, predicting individual levels of universalism and market-liberalism with a range of variables related to people's socioeconomic status and sociodemographic characteristics. Country dummies are included, but not shown in the tables. The overall explanatory power of our models is relatively weak, with preferences appearing least socially structured in those countries where the coherence of the preference scales is weakest (in particular the state-market scale in competitiveness- and capture-oriented countries).

Age, education, and class have clear and consistent direct effects on universalism-particularism preferences in all country groups, with younger people, the highly educated, and members of the middle class (sociocultural specialists, technicians, and managers), as well as the self-employed and office clerks being more universalistic[5]. We use Oesch's (2006) class scheme, because it allows differentiating among sections of the middle and the working class. The reference class in our analysis is the production workers, who constitute the most conservative or particularistic class in all regimes, together with service workers in state market economies, that is, Southern Europe. Since the class scheme entails a skill component, too, Table 8.2 clearly reveals the very strong effect of *education and training*. The fewer cognitive and human capital resources people have, the more they reject universalistic positions with regard to immigration, EU integration, and welfare state deservingness. Apart from this dominant effect that we see in Table 8.2, a few other variables have strong effects, but not in all regimes. *Women* have more universalistic preferences in Scandinavia, but – surprisingly so – more conservative ones in the Anglo-saxon countries. *Income* has no effect, when we control for education and class; nor has the interaction of income and education any effect at all. Overall, the strong and consistent effect of education and skill is the most important finding in this table.

Matters look different when it comes to state-market preferences. Here, *education* levels are much more weakly related to preferences than with regard to the universalism-particularism dimension. In a model estimating the

---

[5] We have calculated an additional model (not shown) without the interaction effect of education and income. The coefficients reflecting the direct effect of education on support for universalism are almost identical to the ones in Table 8.2. and they are highly significant in all country groups.

TABLE 8.2. *Determinants of preferences for universalism: OLS regression, coefficients, standard errors, and significance levels*

	Competitiveness (UK, IRE)	Equality (DK, FI, NO, SE)	Status (BE, CH, DE, NL, FR)	Capture (ES, GR, PT, CY)
Age	−0.006***	−0.005***	−0.008***	−0.003***
	(0.00)	(0.00)	(0.00)	(0.00)
Gender (female)	−0.083***	0.045**	−0.010	0.056**
	(0.03)	(0.02)	(0.02)	(0.03)
Education	0.129***	0.222***	0.213***	0.256***
	(0.03)	(0.03)	(0.03)	(0.05)
Income	0.001	0.016*	0.013	0.017
	(0.01)	(0.01)	(0.01)	(0.01)
Education*income	0.006	−0.003	0.001	−0.005
	(0.01)	(0.00)	(0.00)	(0.01)
Public sector employment	−0.071	−0.039	−0.028	−0.058
	(0.06)	(0.04)	(0.04)	(0.09)
Income*public sector	0.023**	0.019***	0.018***	−0.000
	(0.01)	(0.01)	(0.01)	(0.01)
Sociocultural professional	0.371***	0.357***	0.349***	0.126*
	(0.05)	(0.03)	(0.03)	(0.07)
Self-employed	0.461***	0.283***	0.437***	0.123
	(0.08)	(0.05)	(0.05)	(0.09)
Technical expert	0.319***	0.221***	0.250***	0.136*
	(0.07)	(0.03)	(0.04)	(0.08)
Manager	0.225***	0.259***	0.237***	0.016
	(0.04)	(0.03)	(0.03)	(0.06)
Office clerk	0.182***	0.147***	0.131***	0.100**
	(0.05)	(0.03)	(0.03)	(0.05)
Service worker	0.072*	0.084***	0.064**	0.050
	(0.04)	(0.03)	(0.03)	(0.04)
Small business owner	0.154***	0.038	0.152***	−0.002
	(0.04)	(0.03)	(0.03)	(0.04)
Production worker	*r*	*r*	*r*	*r*
Trade union member	0.070***	0.031	0.065***	0.115***
	(0.03)	(0.02)	(0.02)	(0.03)
Religiosity	0.008	−0.019***	−0.011*	−0.028***
	(0.01)	(0.01)	(0.01)	(0.01)
Constant	−0.215**	−0.090	−0.406***	−0.476***
	(0.09)	(0.08)	(0.08)	(0.11)
R^2	0.19	0.23	0.19	0.16
N	3379	6441	8066	3257

Note: *p = .05, **p = .01, ***p = .001.

TABLE 8.3. *Determinants of preferences for market liberalism: OLS regression, coefficients, standard errors, and significance levels*

	Competitiveness (UK, IRE)	Equality (DK, FI, NO, SE)	Status (BE, CH, DE, NL, FR)	Capture (ES, GR, PT, CY)
Age	0.002***	−0.003***	0.000	−0.002**
	(0.00)	(0.00)	(0.00)	(0.00)
Gender (female)	−0.070***	−0.099***	−0.100***	−0.107***
	(0.03)	(0.02)	(0.02)	(0.02)
Education	0.029	−0.020	−0.013	0.080**
	(0.03)	(0.03)	(0.03)	(0.04)
Income	0.035***	0.006	0.015*	0.033***
	(0.01)	(0.01)	(0.01)	(0.01)
Education*income	0.005	0.014***	0.017***	−0.007
	(0.00)	(0.00)	(0.00)	(0.01)
Public sector employment	−0.028	0.099**	−0.002	−0.079
	(0.06)	(0.04)	(0.04)	(0.08)
Income*public sector	−0.008	−0.033***	−0.009	0.018
	(0.01)	(0.01)	(0.01)	(0.01)
Sociocultural professional	0.056	−0.007	0.065**	0.021
	(0.05)	(0.03)	(0.03)	(0.05)
Self-employed	0.139*	0.174***	0.208***	0.154**
	(0.08)	(0.05)	(0.05)	(0.08)
Technical expert	0.131**	0.165***	0.149***	0.061
	(0.06)	(0.03)	(0.04)	(0.06)
Manager	0.201***	0.238***	0.215***	0.055
	(0.04)	(0.03)	(0.03)	(0.05)
Office clerk	0.093**	0.086**	0.104***	−0.007
	(0.05)	(0.03)	(0.03)	(0.04)
Service worker	0.005	0.013	0.078***	0.002
	(0.04)	(0.03)	(0.03)	(0.03)
Small business owner	0.076*	0.124***	0.205***	0.008
	(0.04)	(0.03)	(0.03)	(0.03)
Production worker	r	r	r	r
Trade union member	−0.100***	−0.126***	−0.128***	−0.127***
	(0.03)	(0.02)	(0.02)	(0.03)
Religiosity	−0.036***	−0.006	0.011*	0.021***
	(0.01)	(0.01)	(0.01)	(0.01)
Constant	0.048	0.675***	−0.154**	−0.468***
	(0.09)	(0.08)	(0.07)	(0.09)
R^2	0.09	0.18	0.14	0.09
N	3379	6441	8066	3257

Note: $*p = .05$, $**p = .01$, $***p = .001$.

direct effect of education (not shown), we find significant but much weaker coefficients of the relationship (below 0.08 in all country groups). Only when education goes together with a high income – as shown in Table 8.3 – do people clearly display economically more liberal (i.e. right-wing) preferences in continental and Northern Europe, an interaction that plays no role regarding preferences on universalism and particularism.

The second striking difference to the social structuring of universalism-particularism preferences is to be found in the class analysis. Contrary to what we saw in Table 8.2, the upper classes are *not* consistently more market-liberal than production workers when it comes to economic liberalism. The *sociocultural specialists*, that is, high-skilled workers in interpersonal service occupations (see Oesch 2006), do not differ significantly in their preferences from production workers, except – weakly so – in continental Europe, even though they have higher positions in the vertical stratification than production workers. The self-employed, the technical experts, small business entrepreneurs, and managers, however, are economically more clearly to the right than production workers, corresponding to the old industrial class conflict, opposing labor and capital. This result demonstrates that the new middle class has become heterogeneous with regard to the economic dimension of political conflict (Gingrich and Häusermann forthcoming). As with regard to preferences for universalism, class has very weak explanatory power for the countries of Southern Europe, which might be a result of the traditionally particularistic types of voter mobilization by parties in these countries. We also find that *trade union members* have more interventionist attitudes in all regimes.

Let us point out again: We find similar structural determinants of individual preferences throughout the country groups, with education and class showing the strongest and most consistent effects, except for Southern Europe, which has a very different legacy of party competition and institution building. Figure 8.1 locates the relevant sociostructural groups in the political space and illustrates how important they are for voter preference formation.

Despite the expected differences in levels, given the different institutional legacies, education structures preferences on the universalism-particularism dimension in all countries. Throughout all types of polities, the polarization on this dimension between different educational groups is clearly stronger than on the state-market dimension. With regard to class, differences between polarization along the state-market and the universalism-particularism dimensions become visible, too. Figure 8.1 shows only three classes: production workers (the "old" working class), as well as managers and sociocultural professionals as the two representatives of the new middle classes. When looking at the triangles per country group separately, one detects a common pattern: The state-market conflict is between production workers and managers (with sociocultural professionals in between), whereas the "new class conflict" between

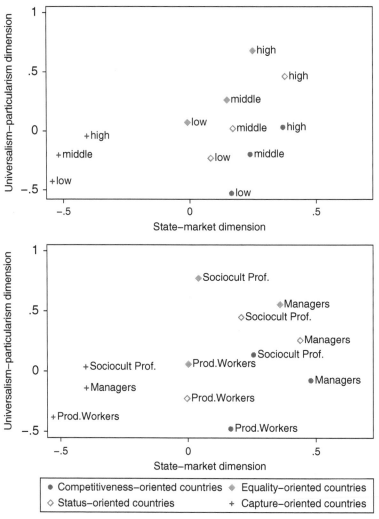

FIGURE 8.1. Political preferences by level of education and class, mean values.

production workers and sociocultural specialists differentiates these groups mainly on the universalism-particularism dimension. With regard to economic conflict in postindustrial societies, this finding is crucial, since it shows that the middle class has become divided with regard to economic-distributive policies. Therefore, economic conflict can no longer be portrayed simply as a conflict between the upper and lower classes. The upper classes have become very heterogeneous with regard to economic preferences, and this has important implications for party choice and the electoral landscape in general, to which we turn now.

8.2.3. *The Electoral Implications of Political Preferences*

In this section, we analyze the electoral implications of the political preference dimensions developed in this chapter. We explore the attitudinal correlates of party choice in the postindustrial capitalist democracies. As we have shown in the preceding sociostructural analysis, characteristics such as class and education are increasingly associated with preferences for universalism or particularism, rather than preferences for market liberalism. If this translates into party choice – and it does, as we will show – it changes not only the sociostructural profile of the constituencies these parties represent, but the entire underlying dynamic of party competition in advanced capitalist democracies (Häusermann et al. 2013).

The analysis and comparison across countries are complicated by the fact that each country has a party system of its own. To allow for cross-country and cross-regime comparisons, we have classified the parties into party families. We shall analyze preferences for the following families: the radical Left, greens, social democrats, liberals, conservative/christian democrats, and radical populist Right, based on the party the respondents voted for in the last national elections, or, if they did not participate in the last elections, the party they feel close to (see Appendix I for the operationalization). We include only parties with at least fifty respondents in our country-specific ESS samples. Given the great differences in the party systems of the European countries, we have opted for a rather simple methodology in analyzing party choice. For each party family, we analyze the contrast with the group of the nonvoters/nonpartisans. This means that we have made binary regressions for each party family in each of the four country groups. In each regression, our key independent variables are the two preference scales. In addition to these scales, which are of primary interest to us, we include a set of control variables – age, gender, education, income, public sector employment, class, union membership, and church attendance – and a set of country dummies (coefficients not shown in the tables).

Table 8.4 presents the detailed results for the countries with a status-oriented institutional legacy in the form of odds ratios (i.e., how much more likely an individual is to choose a certain party type rather than not voting/not feeling close to any party). The table shows the strong effects of universalism-particularism preferences on the choice of the green parties and the parties of the new populist Right, that is, of the main protagonists of the last two waves of political mobilization. The stronger a voter's universalistic attitudes, the greater her chance to vote for the greens; the more particularistic, the greater her chance to vote for the radical populist Right. Voters with strong universalistic attitudes are also much more likely to vote for the social democrats and for the radical Left. In these countries, the effects of the state-market preferences are considerable, too. As we would expect, state-market preferences distinguish between, on the one hand, voters of the radical and moderate (social democratic) mainstream Left, who favor more redistribution and social investment, and, on the

TABLE 8.4. *Determinants of the vote in status-oriented countries (BE, CH, DE, NL, F), for six party families, odds ratios, t-values, and significance levels*

	Radical Left	Greens / Social-Liberals	Social Democracy	Moderate Right/ Market-Liberals	Moderate Right / Christian Democrats	Right-Wing Populists
Universalism-particularism	2.101*** (8.07)	2.699*** (12.20)	1.728*** (10.32)	1.041 (0.59)	0.898 (−1.95)	0.303*** (−12.69)
State-market	0.552*** (−6.20)	0.782** (−3.23)	0.775*** (−4.79)	1.393*** (5.17)	1.242*** (4.10)	1.296** (3.02)
Age	1.016*** (3.72)	0.999 (−0.38)	1.029*** (11.97)	1.025*** (8.18)	1.032*** (13.10)	1.006 (1.55)
Gender (female)	0.832 (−1.34)	1.051 (0.43)	1.100 (1.22)	0.818* (−1.97)	0.953 (−0.59)	0.696** (−2.70)
Education	1.158 (1.35)	1.587*** (5.03)	1.140* (2.09)	1.369*** (3.95)	1.304*** (4.12)	1.229* (1.96)
Income	0.951 (−1.61)	0.966 (−1.34)	1.034 (1.93)	1.094*** (3.99)	1.111*** (5.80)	1.010 (0.35)
Public sector employment	1.206 (0.63)	0.940 (−0.23)	0.867 (−0.75)	0.634 (−1.59)	0.830 (−0.91)	0.736 (−0.81)
Income* public sector	1.019 (0.36)	1.080 (1.83)	1.077* (2.45)	1.074 (1.75)	1.044 (1.35)	1.021 (0.34)
Sociocultural professional	1.507 (1.61)	1.899** (3.09)	1.231 (1.40)	1.764** (2.85)	1.367 (1.92)	0.925 (−0.28)
Self-employed	1.046 (0.10)	3.933*** (5.01)	1.156 (0.59)	2.574*** (3.69)	1.633* (2.07)	1.110 (0.25)
Technical expert	2.078* (2.52)	1.506 (1.73)	1.527** (2.64)	1.550* (2.04)	1.936*** (3.88)	1.266 (0.85)

Manager	1.649*	1.715**	1.470**	2.459***	2.325***	1.499
	(2.11)	(2.73)	(2.95)	(5.39)	(6.33)	(1.94)
Office clerk	1.176	1.207	1.085	1.290	1.506**	1.208
	(0.73)	(0.87)	(0.64)	(1.39)	(3.10)	(0.86)
Service worker	1.594*	1.191	1.092	0.975	1.150	0.913
	(2.28)	(0.90)	(0.76)	(-0.14)	(1.10)	(-0.45)
Small business owner	1.147	2.149***	0.862	2.406***	1.814***	1.182
	(0.49)	(3.77)	(-1.00)	(5.24)	(4.32)	(0.78)
Production worker	r	r	r	r	r	r
Trade union member	2.406***	1.297*	1.569***	0.800*	1.083	1.084
	(5.99)	(2.16)	(5.57)	(-2.05)	(0.92)	(0.56)
Religiosity	0.761***	0.976	0.930*	0.972	1.361***	0.969
	(-4.80)	(-0.59)	(-2.57)	(-0.80)	(11.48)	(-0.68)
Constant	0.494	0.069***	0.118***	0.078***	0.023***	0.258***
	(-1.77)	(-7.13)	(-8.25)	(-7.75)	(-13.74)	(-3.21)
Pseudo R^2	0.19	0.2	0.14	0.19	0.19	0.17
N	1733	2690	3816	2931	3852	1971

Note: $*p = .05, **p = .01, ***p = .001$.

other hand, voters of the moderate (liberal and conservative) and radical Right, who want less of both. The more pro-market an individual is, the more likely he or she is to choose a party of the moderate Right.

For the status-oriented countries, this table also presents the effects of the control variables. While not our main preoccupation, three selected results are worth reporting. First of all, *age* is a key factor for the choice of the mainstream parties – social democrats, liberals, and conservatives/Christian democrats. The older the citizens are, the more they participate in the vote and choose mainstream parties. The age effects are of the size of magnitude of the preference scales. *Religiosity* (church attendance for the conservative/Christian-democratic parties) is the only other control variable with a similarly strong effect in this group of countries. This means that the classic religious cleavage has not faded away completely yet. Age and religion are key determinants of vote choices in all the other regime types, too (results not shown). *Class* related patterns are more complex. In the status-oriented continental European countries, the highly educated vote disproportionately for the Greens. Generally, the parties that benefit least from the highly educated are the radical Left and the radical Right, but also the social democrats. As far as income is concerned, in all regimes, voters with higher incomes disproportionately opt for the mainstream parties of the Right, to some extent also for the social democrats. Public sector employees with higher incomes are especially likely to vote for the social democrats in continental and Northern Europe, but not elsewhere. Among the new middle classes, one result clearly stands out: Relative to the production workers as the reference class, the sociocultural professionals are clearly more likely to vote for the Greens. They opt more strongly than production workers for this party family in all countries, except for the Nordic countries. Trade union members generally vote disproportionately for the Left, greens included.

After this brief account of the effect of control variables, let us return to the impact of the preference scales. Table 8.5 presents the corresponding effects for all country-groups (coefficients of controls not shown). In order to facilitate the interpretation of these results, we have drawn a figure (Figure 8.2) that situates the party families from the various country groups in the two-dimensional space, based on the combination of their dimension-specific odds ratios. In these figures, odds ratios smaller than 1 have been transformed according to a simple formula (transformed odds ratio = –1/odds ratio) so as to make them comparable to the ratios greater than 1. When looking at the overall configuration in the different country groups, it appears immediately that the overall spread of the party families on the vertical universalism-particularism dimension is generally larger than the corresponding spread on the horizontal state-market dimension. As is also immediately apparent, the extended spread on the vertical axis is due to the contrast between the green/social-liberal parties, on the one hand, and the radical populist Right parties, on the other hand. The contrast between the determinants of green and right-wing populist party choice is particularly strong in the continental status-oriented countries, which

TABLE 8.5. *Political preferences as determinants of the vote for different party families, odds ratios, t-values, and significance levels*

	Radical Left	Greens/Social-Liberals	Social Democracy	Moderate Right/Market-Liberals	Moderate Right/Christian Democrats	Right-Wing Populists
Competitiveness-oriented countries (UK, IRE)						
Universalism-particularism		1.782***	1.493***	0.747*	0.734***	
		(−4.36)	(−4.79)	(−1.97)	(−3.62)	
State-market		1.002	0.765**	0.892	1.221*	
		(−0.01)	(−2.99)	(−0.76)	(−2.38)	
N		746	1531	687	1751	
Pseudo R²		0.18	0.18	0.25	0.23	
Equality-oriented countries (DK, FI, NO, SE)						
Universalism-particularism	2.231***	3.542***	1.501***	1.362*	1.115	0.385***
	(−6.52)	(−8.08)	(−5.43)	(−2.5)	(−1.34)	(−7.62)
State-market	0.447***	0.721*	0.679***	1.667***	1.777***	1.002
	(−6.16)	(−2.14)	(−5.02)	(−4.4)	(−7.35)	(−0.02)
N	1310	1030	2909	1183	2504	1298
Pseudo R²	0.27	0.24	0.23	0.31	0.25	0.25

(continued)

TABLE 8.5. (continued)

	Radical Left	Greens/ Social-Liberals	Social Democracy	Moderate Right/ Market-Liberals	Moderate Right/Christian Democrats	Right-Wing Populists
Status-oriented countries (BE, CH, DE, NL, F)						
Universalism-particularism	2.101***	2.699***	1.728***	1.041	0.898	0.303***
	(−8.07)	(−12.2)	(−10.32)	(−0.59)	(−1.95)	(−12.69)
State-market	0.552***	0.782**	0.775***	1.393***	1.242***	1.296**
	(−6.20)	(−3.23)	(−4.79)	(−5.17)	(−4.1)	(−3.02)
N	1733	2690	3816	2931	3852	1971
Pseudo R^2	0.19	0.2	0.14	0.19	0.19	0.17
Capture-oriented countries (ES, GR, PT, CY)						
Universalism-particularism	1.256*		1.021	0.941	0.636***	0.265***
	(−2.05)		(−0.33)	(−0.34)	(−5.20)	(−3.40)
State-market	0.600***		0.899	1.262	1.172	0.82
	(−3.58)		(−1.38)	(−1.28)	(−1.58)	(−0.49)
N	1417		2178	494	1705	315
Pseudo R^2	0.17		0.04	0.09	0.17	0.2

Note: $* = .05, ** = .01, *** = .001$.

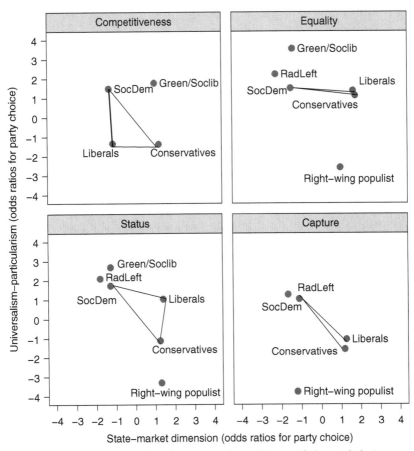

FIGURE 8.2. Odds ratios of preferences as determinants of electoral choice.
Note: Odds ratios <1 have been transformed according to the formula −1/odds in order to make them comparable to the positive odds ratios.

we have presented in more detail above, and slightly less strong for the Nordic equality-oriented countries. The Greek right-wing populist party LAOS is also strongly related to particularistic preferences of voters but also reflects more state-interventionist preferences than the other right-wing populist parties.

On the basis of these results, some readers might be tempted to argue that the relative importance of the universalism-particularism dimension is entirely due to marginal challenger parties (green and radical populist Right). Also, one might conclude that these specific challenger parties are largely irrelevant to the electoral dynamics that affect politics and policies concerned with the regulation of the capitalist economy. However, these challenger parties are not marginal anymore: Their electoral relevance has been increasing over the last couple of elections in many countries. The Greens are on the way to becoming a major party on the Left in many countries. Even more clearly, the radical populist Right has become an important party in most of the continental and Nordic countries. The Norwegian Progress Party, for example, has become one of the largest parties in Norway with around 23 percent in 2005 and 2009, and 16.3 percent in 2013. The True Finns have equally become Finlands' second largest party with 19.1 percent (2011).[6] In continental Europe, the Swiss People's Party is the country's largest with 26.7 percent (2011), the separatist Belgian New Flemish Alliance together with the radical populist Vlaams Belang take about 25 percent (2014), and the Dutch PVV has won 15.5 percent in 2010 and 10 percent in 2012. Hence, these parties have arrived at the very center of electoral competition in contemporary capitalism, with effects that transcend their original core policies, such as environmental policy or immigration. Both green and populist right-wing parties are important enough to form part of government and to shape politics and policy in contemporary capitalism. Thus, it is important to take into account that their electoral constituencies differ strongly from the ones that have traditionally been associated with left- versus right-wing electorates. Even though originally driven by cultural concerns, the shifts in their electoral constituencies affect these parties' profiles in economic and social policy making with regard to the extent of state intervention and with regard to universalistic-particularistic policies (Geering and Häusermann 2013).

In order to be able to distinguish more clearly the configuration of the *mainstream parties*, Figure 8.2 indicates a triangle among the three main party families – social democrats, liberals, and conservatives/Christian democrats. The overall orientation of the resulting triangles tells us something about the relative importance of the two dimensions for the choice among these three mainstream parties. In the equality-oriented countries of Northern Europe, the state-market dimension is clearly more important given the horizontal spread of the corresponding triangle. Here, the mainstream parties represent voter attitudes toward social investment and redistribution. By contrast, in the other country groups – competitiveness-, status- and capture-oriented countries – the triangles are more strongly spread also across the vertical dimension, reflecting universalistic versus particularistic attitudes as determinants of electoral choice.

The upshot of this discussion can be summarized succinctly by two observations: First, the universalism-particularism dimension is crucial for the distinction of the increasing number of voters who choose the new challengers in the party system. Second, this vertical – formerly purely cultural – dimension has also become important for distinguishing between the voters of the mainstream party families, except for Northern Europe. By contrast, the state-market dimension prevails for the choice of mainstream parties in Northern European,

---

[6] The Danish People's Party with 12.3 percent (2011) and the Swedish Democrats with 5.7 percent (2010) and 12.9 percent (2014) are smaller by comparison.

equality-oriented countries. Overall, the analysis of electoral configurations clearly shows that both the sociostructural profile of political parties and the motivations that drive people's vote choices cannot be analyzed in purely state-market terms. State-market preferences remain an important driver of party choice, but only for the mainstream parties (and not in Southern Europe). This transformation is also reflected in the sociostructural profile of the electorates. Education, income, and class are not related unidimensionally to party vote (anymore). The highly educated and the new middle classes are spread across the entire party spectrum, with a particular preference for the green parties. And right-wing populist parties are particularly attractive for young men with low levels of education.

8.3. Conclusion

Our goal in this contribution was to map the structure of the political space of individual-level preferences throughout Western European capitalist democracies, in order to discuss and assess its impact on party choice and electoral politics. In this conclusion, we review the findings and discuss their implications for the analysis of the politics of advanced capitalist democracies.

In line with previous analyses, we have argued theoretically and shown empirically that there are at least two fundamental dimensions of conflict structuring voter preferences. We add to the existing literature with regard to the composition and interpretation of these dimensions: The conflict line opposing universalism to particularism integrates not only the issues of immigration, EU integration, and cultural liberalism, but also questions of welfare chauvinism and welfare misuse. Even though these latter two issues refer to distributive issues, voters' attitudes toward them are clearly distinct from their attitudes toward welfare generosity more generally. At the same time, we show that attitudes regarding the traditional economic dimension have become heterogeneous. People's opinions on different distributive social policy principles have become only loosely connected. These findings show that the boundaries between both dimensions have become blurred to the extent that it does not make sense to talk about a cultural versus an economic dimension of party competition anymore. Rather, both universalistic-particularistic and state-market preferences have clear and direct implications for electoral choices, as well as for economic and social politics.

We found that the configurations of interests, that is, the sociostructural determinants of values and party choice, are very similar across countries. In terms of these sociostructural factors determining individual level preferences on both dimensions, we find clear patterns: Education, class, and age drive universalism versus particularism. The older people are and the fewer cognitive and human capital resources they have, the more they reject universalism with regard to immigration, EU integration, and welfare deservingness. Also, middle-class respondents are more likely to be open to universalistic policies than members of the working class. However, education is clearly the strongest and most consistent predictor of universalism. Matters are different when it comes to the state-market preference scale. Here, we find a stronger relationship with income (direct or in interaction with education). This difference is due to a split within the new middle class: Sociocultural specialists, that is, high-skilled service workers in interpersonal occupations, have more economically interventionist preferences than managers or technical specialists. Hence, these sociocultural specialists differ only weakly from the (lower-skilled) working class in their preferences for redistribution and social investment, a finding that implies that the new middle class has become heterogeneous with regard to the state-market dimension of political conflict. Distributive conflict can no longer be portrayed simply as a conflict between the upper and the lower classes (even though income continues to play a role in differentiating among the highly educated). Rather, parts of the new middle class have aligned with lower classes with regard to economic preferences and have become an important support base for the welfare state in postindustrial times.

These (re)configurations of sociostructural groups and their preferences have important electoral implications, as they translate into party choice, by changing both the sociostructural profile of party constituencies and the underlying dynamic of party competition in contemporary capitalism. Two major findings result from our analysis of party choice: First, attitudes on the universalism-particularism axis explain the vote choice for green and radical right-wing populist parties. Also, the spread of party families across this dimension is generally more polarized than the corresponding spread across the state-market dimension, except for the United Kingdom and Ireland. Hence, green and radical right-wing populist parties are reshaping the European party systems profoundly. In some countries, they receive up to 30 percent of the votes and more, making them likely to enter government coalitions. The second finding is that state-market preferences have an overall more limited effect on electoral choice, but they still distinguish mostly between the choice of moderate right-wing parties and (radical and moderate) left-wing parties. In Northern Europe, this dimension is clearly more important in differentiating moderate right- from moderate left-wing parties than the universalism-particularism dimension. In the rest of Western Europe, however, the choice between these mainstream parties is equally strongly structured by both preference dimensions.

Overall, our analysis of electoral dynamics shows that both dimensions need to be taken into account in order to understand party politics in contemporary capitalist democracies. Challenger parties alter the dynamics of party competition, even with regard to the moderate parties that still distinguish themselves with regard to state-market issues. This state-market dimension itself has been transformed: parties today compete with regard to specific welfare policies such as redistribution and social investment.

Appendix I. List of Variables

Indicators	Original ESS Variables	Survey Question
Immigration	imsmetn	… allow many/few immigrants of the same ethnic group/race as majority
	imdfetn	… allow many/few immigrants of different ethnic group/race as majority
	impcntr	… allow many/few immigrants from poorer countries outside Europe
	imbgeco	… immigration bad or good for country's economy
	imueclt	… countries cultural life undermined/enriched by immigrants
	imwbcn	… immigrants make country better/worse place to live
Cultural liberalism	wmcpwrk	… women should be prepared to cut down on paid work for sake of family
	mnrgtjb	… men should have more right to job than women when jobs are scarce
	freehms	… gays and lesbians free to live life as they wish
	schtaut	… school teach children obey authority
	hrshsnt	… people who break the law much harsher sentences
Welfare misuse	uentrjb	… most unemployed people do not really try to find a job
	bennent	… many manage to obtain benefits/services not entitled to
	prtsick	… employees often pretend they are sick to stay at home
Welfare chauvinism	imrccon	… immigrants receive more or less than they contribute
EU integration	euftf	… European unification go further/gone too far
Egalitarianism	smdfslv	… for fair society, differences in standard of living should be small
Redistribution	gincdif1	… governments should reduce differences in income levels
Job for everyone	gvjbevn	… government should be responsible to provide a job to everyone who wants one
Child care	gvpdlwk	… government should be responsible to ensure sufficient child care services for working parents
Pension insurance	earnpen	… higher or lower earners should get larger old age pensions
Unemployment insurance	earnueb	… higher or lower earners should get larger unemployment benefits

(continued)

Indicators	Original ESS Variables	Survey Question
Church attendance	rlgatnd	How often attend religious service apart from special occasions
Catholicism	rlgdnm	Religion belonging to at present: catholicism
Party choice	prtvt	... for which party did you vote in the last election?
	prtcl	... which party do you feel close to?

Note: Immigration, cultural liberalism, welfare misuse: constructed by factor analyses for the entire file, based on the corresponding original ESS variables; missing values on the original variables have been imputed on the basis of the other original variables of the respective set.

9

Trade Unions and the Future of Democratic Capitalism

Anke Hassel

During the twentieth century, trade unions and employers' organizations had a firm place in modern market economies. Union organizations were the counterweight to business, striving to compensate for the vulnerability of the individual worker to the risks of the market. As economic and political organizations, trade unions could raise wages, improve working conditions, and promote center-left political parties, which represented their interests in the political arena. Social insurance and redistribution, employment protection, health and safety, and the expansion of the middle class over the last hundred years were directly connected to the presence of trade unions. Their organizations and functions emerged in the process of industrialization in the late nineteenth century parallel to employers' organizations.

From the vantage point of the second decade of the twenty-first century, twentieth century industrial organization has been undergoing tremendous change. These developments have impacted on political parties' and industrial interest associations' capacities to make and affect public policies and ultimately to affect economic outcomes, such as economic growth, unemployment, and inflation. Nevertheless, the stark cross-national diversity in industrial relations and political mobilization of labor, crystallized through long struggles, has not simply disappeared without a trace in contemporary postindustrial capitalism. Some critical elements linger on and separate in particular the Scandinavian from the Continental European polities, even though they are often combined under the rubric of "coordinated" market economies. These two, in turn, are still, in some ways, set apart from both the Anglo-Saxon liberal political economies, where the decline of organized labor has been most pronounced, as well as from the Mediterranean "mixed-market" capitalisms, with rather strong state intervention. As asserted in this book's introduction, there are common shocks and directions of change, albeit without entirely removing the cross-national diversity of industrial relations systems and their capacities to cope with the challenges of market allocation.

Since the mid-1980s trade unions are rapidly losing members and influence in almost all industrialized countries. The loss of employment in manufacturing, the rise of service sector employment, the emergence of global value chains, as well as political and policy changes have altered the way employment is organized in advanced industrialized economies today. Instead of steady wage gains in line with productivity increases for the standard worker, wages for the majority of workers are stagnant; instead of highly regulated employment relationships, labor markets are liberalized, centralized collective bargaining structures are dismantled, and social inequality has been continuously rising. In many countries trade unions have almost completely retreated into the public sector.

Only two decades ago, no observer would have expected trade unions to disappear from the scene. The contribution by Golden, Wallerstein, and Lange (1999) in the volume *Continuity and Change in Contemporary Capitalism* (Kitschelt et al. 1999) painted a worried, but still confident, scenario. They nevertheless argued that persistent diversity between countries would refute any general theory as to why unions are in decline. This left hope that erosion of union organization was just a temporary phenomenon. Moreover they stated that "the current weakness of unions appears, in most countries, to be more a product of sustained unemployment (and occasional political assault) than an increase of institutional decay" (Golden, Wallerstein, and Lange 1999: 225). Institutions were found to be significantly more stable compared to union membership.

However, only two years later, a research report for the Fondazione Rodolfo Debenedetti in 2001 reached a more skeptical conclusion. The authors assumed that union membership would continue to decline, alongside changes in labor market institutions. The most likely scenario would be a long-term decentralization of collective bargaining, which would weaken attempts to coordinate wage bargaining at a national level. National coordination of bargaining would be replaced by wage bargaining in large firms, which might or might not transcend national boundaries (Boeri et al. 2001: 117).

More recent assessments are even more outspokenly pessimistic. Baccaro and Howell (2011) state that there is a general direction of change in virtually all industrialized countries toward trade union decline, differentiated collective bargaining, and increasing firm-level diversity. Avdagic and Baccaro argue that the current trends point to a decrease in the relevance of trade unions everywhere with no credible sign of reversal in the future (Avdagic and Baccaro 2012). If this assessment is correct – and there is no reason to fundamentally doubt it – the question arises as to what the likely implications of these transformations for the future of democratic capitalism are. How will an ongoing decay of labor market institutions and union representation affect the workings of advanced industrialized economies?

Three theoretical approaches give us some information on the role of trade unions and labor market institutions in democratic capitalism: power resource, neocorporatist, and varieties of capitalism (VoC) theories. Let us consider here what implications they might have for the development of industrial organization, when exposed to the shocks of technological change in the occupational structure and globalization experienced by postindustrial capitalism since the 1980s. How much are the preexisting industrial relations organizations of business and labor capable of withstanding the new shocks? How will their bargaining systems fare – in terms of coverage of wage earners, centralization, and coordination of negotiations? Are these institutional fabrics still associated with distinctive macroeconomic outputs and outcomes?

In the spirit of *power resource theory of labor union power* (Korpi 1989; Esping-Andersen 1985; Palme 1990), employers are expected to take advantage of the job displacements precipitated by external shocks. But where unions are strong, this theory may expect them to remain tenacious and hold on to some power even under the impact of shocks. The decline of union organization, as well as the decline of centralized bargaining, may therefore be directly proportional to the union power at the beginning of the 1980s.

Two other perspectives, the *neo-corporatism theories* and *varieties of capitalism* theories, may have somewhat different expectations. They stipulate a bifurcation of viable industrial relations regimes. At one extreme, there are highly organized, centralized systems of symmetrical power of business and labor associations that are able to coordinate through elite accommodation (corporatist governance/interest intermediation, coordinated market economies [CMEs]).[1] At the other extreme, there are less organized, decentralized, divided sectors of economic interest associations with little capacity to engage in coordinated bargaining (pluralist interest intermediation, liberal market economies [LMEs]).

In general, both neocorporatist and varieties of capitalism perspectives consider "pure" cases of either corporatist coordination-centralization or liberal competition-decentralization as more efficient equilibria than "mixed" cases of partial centralization and coordination (cf. Calmfors and Driffil 1988; Hall and Gingerich 2009). Whereas the former are likely to sustain a resilient fabric of associations and associated economic performance, the latter see weak associations further degrade, but with little harm to economies that are anyway relying on market allocation. A difficult question is, therefore, what happens to this intermediate group with partially centralized industrial relations organizations and a lack of coherence of liberal or coordinated market institutions that

---

[1] As references for the corporatism literature, see Lange and Garrett 1985; Pizzorno 1978; Schmitter 1974. For the varieties of capitalism literature, see especially Soskice 1999 and Hall and Soskice 2001. The varieties of capitalism perspective develops out of the corporatism literature, adding onto a close consideration of firm-level corporate governance and industrial training regimes. The predictions of both perspectives about the fortunes of industrial interest associations are, therefore, very similar.

encompasses industrial relations, corporate governance, occupational training systems, and research and development (Hall and Soskice 2001)? One might venture a guess that these incoherent sets of political-economic institutions are particularly hard-hit by the exogenous technological and globalization shocks. Since it is less costly to let interest associations disintegrate than to build centralized interest associations, it is likely, therefore, that incoherent systems converge on the disorganized state of affairs in liberal market economies (LMEs) through a rapid decline of capital and labor associations and a disintegration of centralized wage bargaining. They will continue to deliver a worse economic performance.

In other words, while the power resource perspective may expect a gradual decline of interest associations proportional to the peak of mobilization in the 1970s and 1980s, the corporatist/varieties of capitalism perspective expects a bifurcation: Highly organized corporatist systems stay put, while in intermediate incoherent systems and in liberal market systems industrial interest associations disintegrate and centralization, as well as coordination of bargaining, implode. In macroeconomic terms, the power resource perspective makes predictions primarily concerning distributive outcomes (strong leftist mobilization leads to more redistribution) and, to a lesser extent, economic performance. The corporatist/varieties of capitalism perspectives also predict that "congruent" institutional systems approximating either the coordinated market economy (corporatist) type or the liberal market economy type, rather than a mix of the two, perform better.

As a matter of fact, however, the data for the last twenty years show patterns that imply that a mixture of both theoretical perspectives is at work. National institutional configurations adjust to new power constellations that derive from economic and societal changes. Most importantly, the process of the disintegration of organized economic interests is asymmetrical and multidimensional, as discussed in Section 9.1. Apparently consistent with power resource perspectives, labor organizations decline more steeply than business associations, and especially where the former were weaker to begin with.

But wage bargaining coordination and even centralization do not change in lockstep. The simple dichotomies of the varieties of capitalism literature, and even the addition of intermediate incoherent cases, do not entirely reflect the diversification of industrial organization and wage bargaining in the 1990s and 2000s. Consequently, at the macroeconomic level, as discussed in Section 9.2, it has become harder to detect an impact of the more complicated and multidimensional industrial relations regimes on macroeconomic outcomes, such as inflation, growth, and employment. Nevertheless, as the financial crisis and the crisis of European integration – particularly in the Euro currency union – since 2007 demonstrate, distinctive industrial relations regimes plausibly leave some imprint on economic performance, albeit without validating the old unidimensional models and dichotomies.

9.1. The Decline and Transformation of Labor Market Institutions

Strong labor market institutions dominated much of the Western world throughout the twentieth century and particularly during the four decades after World War II. National economies were largely characterized by manufacturing industries, whose workers were likely to be unionized and whose wages would be set in negotiation with these unions. Unionized manufacturing firms were trendsetters for wage setting in other parts of the economy, and trade unions played an important role in national politics and welfare expansion

In this section, I analyze the changes of key indicators of labor market institutions over the last three decades, on the basis of aggregate country-level indicators of union density rates and institutional characteristics of wage setting, which are the standard data used to characterize industrial relations systems (see Table 9.A1). They cover the affluent Western countries of the OECD. In order to sharpen the analysis, in line with theoretical assumptions about different types of market economies discussed in the Introduction to this volume, I group the countries in the extended VoC framework into liberal market economies (LMEs) (Australia, Canada, Ireland, New Zealand, the United States, the United Kingdom), coordinated market economies (CMEs) (Austria, Belgium, Germany, Luxembourg, the Netherlands), Nordic CMEs (Denmark, Finland, Norway, Sweden), and mixed market economies (MMEs) (France, Greece, Italy, Portugal, Spain), a group referred to as state "capture" – political economies based on the terminology of the Introduction. In addition I use data from the European Social Survey on the composition of union membership.

Following standard VoC arguments, coordinated market economies are defined by decision making in key economic activities that are not market based but rely on strategic interaction (coordination) of large firms, their interest associations, and trade unions. Nordic CMEs have additional features of coordination, such as a strong public sector, high levels of centralization, and strong institutional support for trade unions. Liberal market economies primarily rely on market exchanges.

Mixed market economies, as defined by Molina and Rhodes (2007), are characterized by the central role of the state in facilitating coordination and compensating for the lack of autonomous self-organization of business and labor. Labor and business have traditionally used their access to state resources to maintain their position in the political economy. Mixed market economies can be seen as part of the family of coordinated market economies, in the sense that the economic actors, trade unions and business organizations, have similar organizational features to CMEs. Business organizations often hold monopolies or quasi-monopolies over membership domains and have privileged access to state resources. Unions are frequently politically divided and compete strongly over political influence. However, the actors do not have similar capacities to CMEs; nor do they use these capacities for autonomous

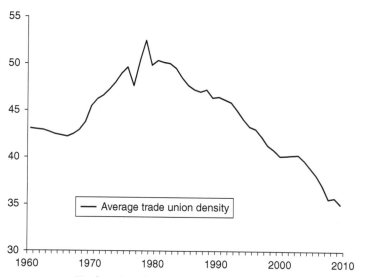

FIGURE 9.1. Trade union density in selected OECD countries (LMEs, CMEs, Nordic CMEs, and MMEs).
(Data based on ICTWSS.)

coordination as CMEs do. Rather, organized interests use their resources to lobby the state for protection or compensation.

9.1.1. Union Membership

A quick glance at union membership data reveals the diversity of unionization rates in Western Europe. The discrepancy between membership rates in different countries is far more pronounced than, for instance, party affiliations or voting patterns. This already indicates that there is no "natural" pattern of unionization in advanced industrialized countries, but that institutional factors shape union organizations to a great extent. Over time, unionization patterns have not converged, but rather diverged, even though most followed roughly similar trends of rising membership strength during the 1970s and decline since the early 1990s.

However, there is a clear and expected trend of declining union density rates across the OECD (Figure 9.1). Overall density rates declined from 45 percent (1980s average) to 30 percent (2000s average) (Table 9.1). A significant difference exists between unions in Nordic CMEs and all other groups. While the average union density rate in all other groups stands at around 24 percent, Nordic CME countries still have a density rate of over 70 percent in the 2000s, mainly because they administratively tie unemployment insurance coverage to union membership, with this so-called Ghent system thus providing an additional membership incentive (Lind 2009; Rothstein 1992).

TABLE 9.1. *Union density, employers' density, wage bargaining coordination, centralization, and coverage by type of market economy and decade*

	Union Density				Employers' Organization Density				Collective Bargaining Coverage				Collective Bargaining Centralization				Collective Bargaining Coordination			
	1980s	1990s	2000s	change	1980s	1990s	2000s	change	1980s	1990s	2000s	change	1980s	1990s	2000s	change	1980s	1990s	2000s	change
Nordic	73.14	76.58	72.21	−1%	65	68.83	68.92	+6%	79	85.16	85.24	+8%	3.8	3.48	2.79	−27%	3.98	3.6	3.1	−22%
CME	36.37	31.98	27.03	−25%	100	87	79	−21%	88.25	88.14	86.72	−2%	3.25	2.9	2.78	−14%	4.28	3.64	3.64	−15%
MME	34.20	27.87	25.10	−27%	—	—	59.85	—	76.7	78.85	72.25	−6%	3.1	3.13	3.05	−2%	3.4	3.33	3.18	−6%
LME	43.89	33.20	25.22	−43%	—	—	48.75	—	54.28	43.18	32.30	−41%	2.17	1.80	1.58	−27%	2.13	1.87	1.83	−14%

Source: ICTWSS.

TABLE 9.2. *Correlations of union density, employers' density, wage bargaining coverage, centralization, and coordination (2000s)*

		Employers Density	Coverage	Centralization	Coordination
Union density	Correlation coefficient	.434*	.589**	.493**	0.331
	N	23	33	32	30
Employer density	Correlation coefficient		.806**	.521*	.593**
	N		22	22	22
Coverage	Correlation coefficient			.817**	.614**
	N			32	30
Centralization	Correlation coefficient				.823**
	N				30

Source: ICTWSS.

The strongest decline in unionization took place in LMEs, where union density rates decreased from 44 percent to 25 percent over three decades. In both Continental CMEs and mixed market economies, where unionization was weaker to begin with (roughly 35 percent in the 1980s), a drop by about one-quarter of union density took place over a twenty to thirty year period. In general, this pattern confirms expectations of the power resource perspective, but is mildly inconsistent with the other perspectives. The weakest labor unions in the 1980s took the biggest hit ever. The hit was also pretty substantial in a number of CMEs, whether coherent or not.

9.1.2. *Employers' Organizations and Collective Bargaining Coverage*
Collective bargaining coverage and employers' density rates are highly correlated (.806**; Table 9.2). This is due to the fact that firms that belong to employers' organizations participate in collective bargaining that covers the workforce of those firms. High levels of employers' density thereby almost automatically translate into high levels of bargaining coverage. Discrepancies occur when collective agreements are extended to firms that do not belong to employers' organizations or when firms are members of an employers' organization without participating in collective bargaining.[2]

---

[2] This is a relatively recent phenomenon in Germany, where employers' organizations set up subsidiaries for firms that did not want to be bound by collective agreements: OT (without agreement status).

Comprehensive data on employers' organizations are only available for the most recent period, and, for most countries, no trend can be established. As expected, CMEs have the highest level of employers' density: 87 percent, on average, for the whole period. This has declined from 96 percent in the 1980s to 82 percent in the 2000s. In comparison, the lowest level of employers' organization is to be found in LMEs with 51 percent and – also as expected – followed by Central and Eastern Europe (CEE) with 60 percent and MMEs with 74 percent.

As with union density, we find a strong stratification of developments since the 1980s (Table 9.1). In Nordic CMEs, both employers' organizational density and bargaining coverage have increased from high levels, while in Continental CMEs they have maintained the very same high level. Starting from a slightly lower level, they declined slightly in MMEs, but virtually collapsed in LMEs. This pattern appears to be most consistent with the corporatist/varieties of capitalism perspective.

The coincidence of an institutional stability of bargaining coverage and employers' organization with an ongoing decline of union density rates in CMEs supports the assumption that coordination does not depend on trade unions' power resources but might be due to employers' preferences for coordination and a function of the fabric of political-economist coordination as a whole, as asserted by the varieties of capitalism perspective.

9.1.3. Wage Bargaining Centralization and Coordination

Theoretically, employers' density rate or coverage does not predict the centralization of collective bargaining. Empirically, however, both are significantly correlated (Table 9.2). Higher levels of employers' density and bargaining coverage relate positively to higher levels of wage bargaining centralization.

The country type averages reveal interesting diversity. Starting from low or very high levels, the drop in collective wage bargaining centralization is precipitous in both LMEs and Nordic CMEs. It is substantial, but less pronounced, in Continental CMEs, and MMEs have sustained a level of centralization that makes them the set of countries with the highest average centralization in the 2000s. Wage bargaining decentralization either took place through proactive institutional reforms such as in Sweden, Australia, or New Zealand or occurred more gradually and informally through an increasing amount of company level bargaining, which eroded collective bargaining at a regional or national level.

Wage bargaining coordination may proceed with less than perfect centralization, for instance, when companies or sectors take wage leadership. Yet, the last columns of Table 9.1 reveal that coordination fell into roughly similar patterns differentiating the four groups of countries as far as centralization is concerned: From low levels, the decentralization is greatest among LMEs, followed by Nordic and Continental CMEs, with MMEs sustaining rather high levels of coordination.

Overall, the CME category, highlighted in the varieties of capitalism literature, shows little internal similarity of members. The pressure for decentralization and liberalization is great in Nordic CMEs, but tempered by continuing high levels of labor and business organization and collective bargaining coverage. Conversely, Continental CMEs sustain higher, albeit eroding, levels of coordination, as well as high coverage, but at lower levels of union and employer density. This may be an indicator of growing divides between wage bargaining insiders and outsider companies and wage earner categories. MMEs see declining union and employer density, yet continued solid collective bargaining centralization and coordination. Political leverage may have kept unions at the bargaining table, despite declining leverage, in order to stave off worse outcomes implemented without their participation.

Taken together, the evidence from macrolevel indicators shows that, over time, unionization rates have significantly declined in all groups of countries. A more detailed discussion of unionization rates will be provided in the following section. However, other institutional indicators such as employers' organizations, collective bargaining coverage, coordination, and centralization have shown a more nuanced pattern of some resilience in CMEs and MMEs while LMEs and CEEs have drifted more toward a largely unregulated system of collective bargaining and employers' coordination and organization.

Institutional resilience can be due to the lack of appropriate indicators to measure change. Baccaro and Howell have argued that creeping changes of the content of collective bargaining at a national level might change the dynamic of the system, while leaving formal institutions intact. These changes cannot be detected by formal indicators that measure only the predominant bargaining level (Baccaro and Howell 2011).

However, ongoing collective bargaining, carried out by highly organized employers' confederations and covering large numbers of employees, continues to install an element of harmonization and standardization of pay grades across industries. The degree of standardization of working conditions that occurs in CMEs, and to some extent MMEs, through wage bargaining should not be underestimated for the regulation of the labor market. This could imply that coordination persists among businesses, while union organization continues to decline. Coordination of business, therefore, outlives trade union organization and trade union strength.

9.1.4. *Unionization of Insiders and Outsiders*

A different aspect of the changing nature of trade unionism points to the increasing trend toward labor market segmentation. Recent research on dualization has explored the process in which policies differentiate between rights, entitlements, and services for different groups or categories of entitled citizens. Labor market insiders are in a secure employment position, while those without or with insecure employment are labor market outsiders.[3] Dualization occurs when differential treatment of insiders and outsiders increases, when parts of the insiders are shifted to become outsiders, and with the development of new institutional distinctions among different groups of workers (Emmenegger et al. 2012: 10).

Dualization particularly affects "new" and nontraditional groups entering the labor market such as women, young employees, or migrant workers, who are at risk of being clustered in the outsider group, as the probability of their entering stable and skilled standard employment relationships is, by trend, smaller than for older men (Schwander and Häusermann 2013; Barbieri and Scherer 2009). Until the 1970s, the precarious situation of women was not visible on a political level, as family and marriage policies provided protection. The past few decades have increasingly politicized this problem. The same also applies to the outsider group of migrant workers (Emmenegger and Careja 2012), who are considered the overrepresented group in nonstandard, precarious working conditions (Emmenegger and Careja 2012: 128).

The emerging increasing cleavage between labor market insiders and outsiders has accentuated the question how trade unions mediate potential conflicts of interest. In most of the literature, it is assumed that unions organize labour market insiders (Becher and Pontusson 2011; Rueda 2007). This implies that union preferences are dominated by labor market insiders. If unions have to choose between the two groups, it is likely that they side with that of the insiders, even at the expense of labor market outsiders.

The data on unionization rates of insiders and outsiders are from the European Social Survey (ESS), which include trade union membership data and some information on the employment status of the respondent. This includes data about age, gender, full-time/part-time employment, and income, as well as permanent/temporary employment (see Table 9.A2 in annex).

The insider-outsider ratio is the weighted average of density ratios in various employment segments (gender, age, income, unemployment protection, working hours, sector). As an example, for the insider-outsider ratio, I calculated the ratio of trade union density of female over male members, the ratio between members below the age of 25 and above (25–65), the ratio of trade union (TU) members holding a limited term contract or no contract at all over the ratio of TU members having an unlimited contract, TU members having a monthly income categorized as lower median over TU members having an income categorized as upper median, and so on. The mean of these ratios is the io ratio.

Table 9.3 reports the ESS-based data on the unionization of various subcategories of workers. Small unionization ratios in Table 9.3 indicate a large deficit in outsider unionization compared to that of insiders. On the whole, as assumed in the literature, trade unions in almost all countries are focused

[3] Definitions of insiders and outsiders vary. See Schwander and Häusermann (2013) and Rueda (2007).

TABLE 9.3. *Union density ratios of selected employment segments, 2008*

Country group		LME	MME	CME	Nordic CME
Gender	Female/Male	1.09	.77	.60	1.10
Age	<25/25–65	.20	.14	.19	.23
Contract	Limited term/Unlimited term	.55	.39	.61	.73
Income	Lower than median/ higher than median	.49	.48	.80	.83
Unemployment (last 5 years)	Yes/No	.25	.54	.72	.84
Unemployment (long-term more than 12 months)	Yes/No	.36	.66	.93	.84
Working hours	<17/>17 hours	.47	.45	.51	.52
Sector	Service/Manufacturing	.65	.63	.96	.77
Sector	private/public	.26	.25	.63	.67

Source: ESS.
Note: LME: UK, IRE; MME: ESP, FR, GR, PT; CME: BE, GE, NL, SWI; Nordic CME: DK, FI, NO, SW.

on labor market insiders rather than outsiders. Unionization rates of those with above-average incomes, standard working hours, unlimited contracts, and a history of steady employment are higher than those of workers who are part-time, with limited contracts and below average pay. The widest gap is between younger and older workers.

In 2008, in fourteen Western European countries, the unionization rate of young workers was only one-fifth that of older workers. This was partly due to the generational difference that young workers combine several factors of labor market insecurity: They are more likely to be in insecure employment and work in the service economy, factors that make unionization less likely. But it could also be a sign of what the future of trade unions will look like in two decades: Only in Denmark and Finland were the unionization rates of those less than twenty-five-year-olds above 20 percent. In eight countries, unionization of young workers was below 10 percent. Big gaps also exist for part-timers who work less than seventeen hours a week. On average, their unionization rate is only half that of full-time workers.

The smallest gap is between men and women. In six out of fourteen countries, female unionization rates are higher than male unionization rates – despite the fact that women, like young workers, often work in areas of less secure employment and are often seen, by definition, as labor market outsiders. Gender equality in unionization is most pronounced in LMEs and Nordic countries. Continental CMEs and MMEs have larger gender gaps. In other dimensions, notably regarding income, unemployment, and fixed-term contracts, LMEs and MMEs are more segmented in comparison to CMEs and the Nordic countries, where unionization rates between the groups differ less. This is, however, partly due to the fact that Belgium shows unionization patterns of Nordic CMEs.

When all employment segments are combined, a pattern of an average unionization ratio of labor market outsiders versus insiders emerges. We can identify two distinct groups of countries: those countries where unionization amounts to a significant share of the overall workforce and those countries where unionization is confined to a particular segment of the workforce. I label the two groups "universalist" and "segmented," respectively. The first group of countries comprises the Nordic countries plus Belgium; the second group is made up of all other Western European countries. All countries with unionization rates above 40 percent, with the exception of Norway, have a Ghent system in which trade unions administer state-subsidized unemployment funds. Only four Western European countries – Sweden, Denmark, Finland, and Iceland – have real Ghent systems. Belgium has a hybrid system; even though unions do in fact exercise a great deal of administrative control, it is often considered a de facto Ghent system (Scruggs 2002). All other countries, with the exception of Austria, have unionization rates of considerably less than 30 percent.

Belgium turns out to have the most universal union system in Western Europe, followed by the Nordic countries and then by Northern Continental Europe, Germany, the Netherlands, Ireland, and France. At the bottom are the United Kingdom, Portugal, and Spain.

In addition to having higher membership levels overall, universalist trade union systems are also less exclusionary for labor market outsiders. In other words, universalist unions attract both a relatively higher share and higher absolute numbers of labor market outsiders. Figure 9.2 compares unionization rates between insiders and outsiders. The data again show that in all countries but Belgium outsiders are less likely to be union members than insiders.

Segmentalist (insider-focused) unions, on the other hand, recruit, and reproduce their membership from existing strongholds. Depending on employers' attitudes, collective bargaining institutions and production regimes can be in either manufacturing sectors or the public sector. There are very few examples of trade union strongholds in private services industries. Organizational developments of segmentalist trade unions are, therefore, more strictly path-dependent and opportunity-driven. These processes are born of the necessity to legitimize the use of membership funds, which restrict investments in new membership areas, as well as organizational boundaries and the distribution of power within the organization.

Disaggregated by our four groups of countries, the Nordic CMEs have the least insider/outsider division, as they include most Ghent systems. They are followed by the Continental CMEs, the averages of which only resemble

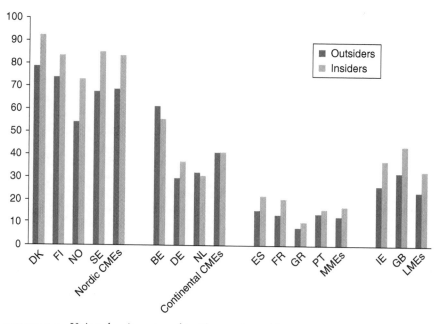

FIGURE 9.2. Union density rates of insiders and outsiders, 2010.
Source: EES, own calculations.

the Nordic countries because they include Belgium with its Ghent system, while the other Continental CME countries take a middle position between Nordic countries and MMEs. LMEs appear to have the greatest insider/outsider division, but we have to mention that, as protection for labor market insiders is low, the distinction between insiders and outsiders carries less meaning. The divide between insiders and outsiders thus tends to be most acute in CMEs and MMEs, both of which still have moderately high levels of unionization and wage bargaining coordination but exclude substantial proportions of the labor market from such representation.

Overall, the traditional liberal market economies constituted one extreme pole of fragmented, disorganized industrial relations systems in the 2000s, even more so than ever before. At the same time, however, the identity of coordinated market economies, or even of a gradation of power resources across political economies, has broken up to such an extent as to make the existing unidimensional theoretical frameworks for understanding the processes of change more problematic. While there are correlations between union and employer density, collective bargaining coverage, and wage bargaining coordination and centralization, they are sufficiently loose as to crystallize subgroups of clusters with rather distinct profiles of industrial relations systems.

9.2. Industrial Relations and Economic Management and Performance

There is a long and rich list of literature on the role of unions and labor market institutions for economic management and performance. The aim here is not to summarize all the evidence and literature but to point out some of the recent trends and the most remarkable developments, as they relate to the changes of industrial relations in the four groups of countries.

Regarding our theoretical expectations, power resource theory would expect a linear relationship between the strength of unions and labor market institutions and outcomes. Weaker unionization and weaker institutions translate into less involvement for unions in economic decision making and ultimately greater social inequality. Neocorporatism and VoC assume that particular institutional configurations have beneficial effects for unions, governments, and businesses alike, which are, in principle, self-sustainable. Higher levels of coordination and centralization provide opportunities for central decision making on wages, which can be traded with policy adjustments. The decline of unions and labor market institutions, therefore, does not automatically imply a weaker role of unions in economic management, nor greater wage inequality in itself, but might endanger central decision making if coverage declines dramatically. The evidence shows that higher levels of coordination and centralization are still associated with better economic outcomes. However, as unionization declines, these benefits are increasingly restricted to specific economic sectors.

9.2.1. Trade Unions and Economic Management

Trade unions played an important role in the Keynesian welfare state. They were key actors in economic management, primarily regarding wage expectation, but also in a wider sense of political influence over economic policy. Adjustments during the business cycle were constrained by the fact that nominal wages were rigid rather than flexible and expansive fiscal policies were used to counteract business downswings. Deflation or budget balancing, on the one hand, generally added to a fall in prices but not wages; expansive monetary and fiscal policies, on the other, empowered workers in tight labor markets, who might be tempted to turn their bargaining power into nominal wages. Therefore, during the 1960s and 1970s, a mechanism was needed to enable macroeconomic control over nominal wage developments. Governments employed various kinds of "incomes policies" either to induce wage restraint or to negotiate it (Hassel 2006; Braun 1975). As labor markets were tight, governments and businesses did not have any other policy tool to force unions to discipline wage expectations than to achieve trade union cooperation.

This model of economic management gradually eroded as a result of slower growth in advanced industrialized countries during the 1960s, inflationary shocks in the 1970s, and the subsequent liberalization of capital markets.

A crucial component of the shift in economic policy moving away from a "mixed economy," as described by Shonfield, to an overwhelmingly liberal and private economy, was a new political understanding that put a premium on market mechanisms in contrast to state correction (Shonfield 1965).

The policy shift also occurred in economic theory, which now claimed that – contrary to Keynesian assumptions – demand-side policies led to price increases but had no effect on the real economy. Monetary policy aimed at controlling inflation and not at accommodating wage expectations by trade unions. Only supply-side policies could promote economic growth in mature national economies. Supply-side policies targeted market regulation and subsidies. Rather than accommodating and facilitating regulated markets, governments were keen to eradicate regulations that were prone to rent seeking and inefficiencies. State failure, rather than market failure, moved into the center of attention, and the state itself became a key target for policy reform.

In that context, trade unions were forced to assume a different role. Instead of being the key institutional pillars for underwriting stability, protection, and egalitarian wages, trade unions were increasingly perceived by policy makers and business as rent seekers. They presented obstacles for supply-side reforms, flexible adjustment, and competitiveness. Restrictive monetary policy punished high settlements with higher unemployment and, therefore, attacked trade unions directly and intentionally.

Trade unions met increasing political opposition, not just from center-right governments, initially the Thatcher and Reagan administrations, but subsequently also from the center-left. Policies of the "Third Way," as initiated and developed by the government of Tony Blair in the United Kingdom after 1997, embraced supply-side policies as well as public service reforms and had a similarly skeptical view of trade unions to the center-right. Trade unions, therefore, not only met increasing opposition from business but also in the political arena. Fritz Scharpf concluded that, in a neoliberal setting, the cooperation of trade unions was not required anymore (Scharpf 1991).

However, the move toward supply-side policies and restrictive monetary and fiscal policies did not initially diminish the importance of trade unions. Austerity and deregulation policies were politically costly for governments. In many countries, where proportional representation dominated and governments were in coalitions, there was still a tendency to cooperate with trade unions over wages and social policy reforms. The 1990s in particular saw a new wave of tripartite agreements between government and unions over wage restraint in the context of economic restraints by the European Monetary Union (EMU) (Hassel 2006; Hancké and Rhodes 2005). Governments realized that the economic costs of negotiated adjustment were lower than forcing trade unions to accept new realities of high interest rates and higher unemployment. These tripartite negotiations largely vanished once EMU set in and governments could temporarily relax over public deficits and inflation differentials. This also showed that social pacts were not intended as

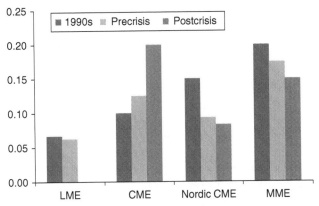

FIGURE 9.3. Number of social pacts signed per year.
Source: ICTWSS.
Note: precrisis: 2000–2007; postcrisis: 2008–2012.

a permanent policy tool but rather a temporary and unstable phenomenon (Avdagic et al. 2011) (see Figure 9.3).

Over time, a new economic and political reality set in. Flexible labor markets, activating social policies, and supply-side economic policies have largely succeeded as policy blueprints – even after the financial crisis of 2008. They were reinforced by policy recommendations from international organizations, such as the OECD, the World Bank, and IMF, and became part of the policy agenda of the EU Commission. Today, they are part of the parcel of Troika recommendations in the conditionality section of bailout programs (Armingeon and Baccaro 2011).

Globalization and the rise of the service economy added to the policy change. The opportunity of offshoring altered the conditions under which manufacturing firms were willing to invest in advanced industrialized countries. Concession bargaining and vigorous cost cutting became standard management practices in big manufacturing firms. Permanent core workers remained largely protected, but an increasing share of manufacturing workers moved into fringe employment, which was temporary and insecure. In the service sectors, where unions remained weak and underrepresented, working conditions and employment protection were below manufacturing standards in many areas and remained as such.

Therefore, the wave of tripartite concertation during the 1980s and 1990s, which gave European trade unions a new temporary lease of life, did not solve the fundamental dilemma trade unions found themselves in with the end of the Keynesian welfare state. The new economic policy paradigm focused on liberalization, deregulation, and supply-side reforms. Trade unions benefited from regulation and Keynesian demand policies and were, therefore, a natural target of policy makers who were seeking change. The financial crisis did not change this. While governments continue to hold on to a neoclassic macroeconomic paradigm that recommends constant supply-side reforms, trade unions did not gain from the rise of critical perspectives on financial capitalism. Neither were unions generally consulted over austerity policies; nor did social pacts or policy concertation revive during the financial crisis.

Power resource theory can explain neither the rise nor the decline of policy concertation over the last three decades. Rather, neocorporatist theory assumes a return to policy concertation to lure trade unions into cooperation during an economic boom. New attempts to utilize the beneficial effects of neocorporatist policy making drove governments to engage in social pacts. This is the case even under conditions of increasing union weakness. The decline of social pacts after the crisis, however, shows the limits of neocorporatism as a policy tool.

9.2.2. *Effects of Industrial Relations on Economic Performance*

In the literature, the effect of industrial relations institutions on economic performance is widely established (Traxler et al. 2000). Different types of bargaining institutions and unionization have affected nominal wage changes and unemployment levels. In terms of basic assumptions about union behavior in different institutional settings, this literature embeds the assumptions of neocorporatism and assumes that trade unions face a trade-off of choosing between pay and employment. Union bargaining strategies can favor one over the other. Industrial relations institutions enable trade unions to exercise nominal wage restraint, while making wages less flexible and generally more compressed. In the VoC literature, comprehensive wage bargaining institutions ensure that companies do not compete for skilled workers by leapfrogging. Either way, centralized wage bargaining provides a dampening effect on wages, which in turn contributes positively to economic performance.

Economywide coordination mechanisms have been identified as the most important factor influencing wage bargaining behavior. Several authors have pointed out that the coordination of wage bargaining can take place even in organizationally decentralized wage bargaining institutions (Soskice 1990; Traxler et al. 2000). The lack of formal centralization can be compensated by a wage bargaining structure that is organized around a pattern-setter mechanism or replaced by other mechanisms such as government intervention.

Without coordination of wage bargaining behavior, local wage bargaining will reflect the local conditions on the labor market and not the wider economic constraints. Local bargaining can encourage leapfrogging, with highly profitable companies influencing the expectations of workers in other companies. Local trade unions that are not embedded in a national bargaining system tend to exploit their bargaining power, since they do not have any reason not to do so (Soskice 1990; Flanagan 1999).

However, centralization of wage bargaining might contribute to the power of trade unions. As union bargaining power increases, wage settlements can, therefore, be less responsive to economic constraints. In decentralized bargaining structures, unionized firms might be outcompeted by nonunionized firms (Flanagan 2003). The result is a hump-shaped relationship, where highly centralized and highly decentralized wage bargaining institutions outperform intermediate levels of centralization (Calmfors and Driffil 1988).

With regard to empirical evidence, research has shown mixed results. Many studies covering the OECD countries between the 1960s and today find that labor market rigidities are related to institutional variables. For instance, in a comprehensive empirical study, labor market institutions were seen as a major explanation for differences in economic performance, accounting for 55 percent of the variation in unemployment; the generosity of the unemployment benefit system was the most important factor, followed by taxes and union density (Nickell et al. 2005).

The OECD Employment Outlook concluded in 2006:

> Overall, recent empirical research suggests that high corporatism bargaining systems tend to achieve lower unemployment than do other institutional set-ups. Nevertheless, the evidence concerning the impact of collective bargaining structures on aggregate employment and unemployment continues to be somewhat inconclusive. The overall non-robustness of results across studies probably reflects, at least in part, the difficulty of measuring bargaining structures and practices, as well the fact that the same institutional set-up may perform differently in different economic and political contexts. One exception to this pattern is the robust association between higher centralisation/ co-ordination of bargaining and lower wage dispersion. Evidence is mixed, however, about whether the compressed wage structures associated with corporatist bargaining reduce employment by pricing low-skilled workers – or those residing in economically disadvantage regions – out of work. (OECD, 2006: 86)

Which institutions are responsible for rigidities and to what extent do these institutions matter? Baker presented a comparison of findings from eleven econometric studies between 1997 and 2005 and focused on a number of institutional variables, such as employment protection, unemployment benefit replacement rates, union density, a bargaining coordination index and the magnitude of the tax wedge, unemployment benefit duration, collective bargaining coverage, and expenditures in active labor market policies. The review shows that so far no single institutional variable is consistently found to be significantly different from zero across all studies (Baker et al. 2007).

Another recent study by Baccaro and Rei focused on the same set of variables and data concluded that there was no robust evidence of labor market institutions' effects on the unemployment rate. The authors concluded that the within-country variation of bargaining coordination is not associated with lower unemployment and that bargaining coordination does not moderate the impact of other institutions (Baccaro and Rei 2007). Similarly, a report by the EU Commission shows that encompassing labor relations have some moderating effects on nominal wage developments. Stronger labor relations

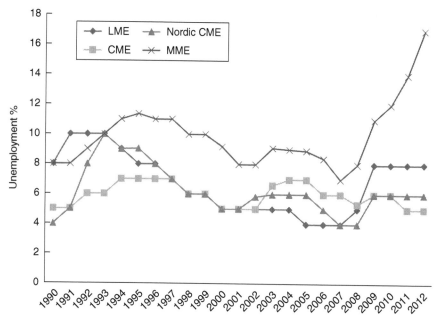

FIGURE 9.4. Unemployment rates 1990–2012.
(OECD Statistics.)

contribute to positive economic outcomes on the labor market and have a robust dampening effect on wage inequality, poverty, and gender pay inequality. It also argues that the effect of labor relations on economic performance seems to have become weaker in recent years (EU Commission 2008).

On the other hand, when assessing the periods before and after the financial crisis, the data are more supportive of a return to the positive effects of coordinating institutions. While economic performance during the years of the financial bubble, in the early 2000s, favored LMEs, the postcrisis years again show a pattern of slightly better economic performance in countries with higher levels of wage bargaining coordination. CMEs as a group outperform LMEs after 2008, even when Ireland is taken out of the group of LMEs. In particular the Continental CMEs (Austria, Germany, Belgium, Luxembourg, and the Netherlands) all had lower unemployment rates in the postcrisis years (2008–2013) compared to the precrisis years (2001–2007) (see Figure 9.4). MMEs have been hit hard by the financial crisis and the subsequent sovereign debt crisis. This implies that higher levels of coordination, combined with articulate trade unions, still carry some weight for crisis adjustment. As performance has diverged among the different groups of countries after 2008, we might expect a return to a bifurcated development of coordinated (corporatist) institutions versus liberal ones.

9.2.3. Wage Inequality

During the golden years of democratic capitalism, centralized wage bargaining institutions and trade union strength have been key factors for explaining different patterns of wage and income distributions (Baccaro 2011; Bradley et al. 2003; EU Commission 2008; Pontusson 1996; Pontusson et al. 2003; Rowthorn 1992; Wallerstein 1999). Centralized trade union organizations pushed up wages for the low paid, and centralized wage bargaining institutions ensured that standard pay scales were applied across all industries. As a result, countries with centralized bargaining institutions and strong trade unions tended to have more compressed wage structures as well as more egalitarian income distribution. Power resource theories would expect that a decline in union strength would be associated with an increase in wage inequality. Neocorporatism and VoC, on the other hand, would assume that as long as bargaining centralization and coordination held, there would be sufficient incentive for employers to maintain a compressed wage structure.

In recent years, the effects of labor market institutions on wage compression have been far weaker than in earlier decades (Baccaro 2011). Baccaro suggests that unions began to abandon egalitarian wage policies during the 1980s, as a result of increasing resistance by high-skilled workers (Baccaro 2011). Wage compression made it harder for employers to recruit high-skilled workers, but also created competition between blue- and white-collar unions in Sweden, which contributed to the demise of centralized bargaining. In other cases, centralized bargaining lost its distributive function. "While income inequality increased in almost all countries in the sample, this increase does not seem to have been caused by the deterioration in industrial relations institutions (trade union decline and collective bargaining decentralization)" (Baccaro 2011).

Baccaro does not find any statistical correlation between union decline or other labor market institutions and growing inequality (except in the Central and Eastern European countries). Instead, economic factors such as technology-induced shifts for the demand of skilled labor and increasing globalization seem to be better predictors. Similarly, Golden and Wallerstein report that the determinants of wage inequality were different in the 1980s and in the 1990s. While in the 1980s, growing wage dispersion was due to changes in the institutions of the labor market, including declining unionization and a decline in the level at which wages were bargained collectively, in the 1990s, increases in pay inequality were due to increasing trade with less developed nations and a weakening of social insurance programs (Golden and Wallerstein 2011).

Moreover, as the literature assumes, there is evidence that more insider-oriented unions are correlated to higher levels of wage inequality compared to more universal trade unions. As the scatterplot in Figure 9.5 shows, countries where unions are more universal are also countries where wage inequality is comparatively lower. While the causality can, in principle, work both ways, with more egalitarian wages propping up union membership

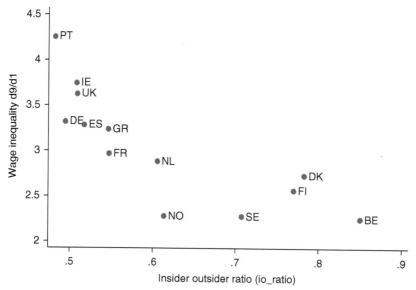

FIGURE 9.5. Insider/outsider ratio of unionization and wage inequality, selected countries, 2008.
Source: ESS.

among outsiders, this might also hint at a process of social closure of some trade unions against labor market outsiders.

9.3. Conclusion

In this chapter, I have looked at trends of union and business organizations and their implications for the future of democratic capitalism. As in earlier assessments, the results concentrated on a steady union decline within much more stable wage bargaining institutions (Golden et al. 1999; Avdagic and Baccaro 2012). Given the rapid economic changes of deindustrialization and globalization, business coordination and wage bargaining centralization showed remarkably high levels of institutional resilience.

We can draw several conclusions from the observation that unions weaken while institutions remain relatively stable:

- Stability of wage bargaining institutions does not guarantee unionization rates. High levels of union density are almost exclusively due to the "Ghent" system of linking union membership with unemployment insurance administration. Wage bargaining centralization or wage bargaining coverage does not prevent unions from declining. While union density rates are still positively related to centralized wage bargaining institutions, they cannot prevent union density rates from falling.

- Wage bargaining coordination can persist without union strength. Existing institutions have important benefits for employers as well as for unions. Coordination capacities can be exercised through employers' organizations, bargaining coverage, and bargaining centralization, even though trade unions are very weak. Coordination and liberalization of labor markets can, therefore, go hand in hand. The decline of trade unions is, therefore, not in itself an indication that coordination also declines. It is not trade unions who push employers into coordinated wage bargaining institutions.
- While the unionization rates of women are catching up with those of men in a number of countries, unionization rates of young workers are worryingly low. In 2008, in no country in our sample, were unionization rates of young workers more than a quarter of those of older workers. Seen in this light, the future of unions appears pretty bleak.
- Union organizations that operate under Ghent systems have high coverage rates for labor market outsiders. They are generally universal. Countries with universal trade unionism are Denmark, Finland, Belgium, and Sweden. LMEs have dualist union structure while CMEs become more segmented.
- Policy concertation reemerged in Western Europe during the 1980s but is in secular decline since the early 1990s, as supply-side policies continue to dominate the policy agenda even after the financial crisis.
- Postcrisis economic performance indicates a return to positive effects of coordination and wage bargaining centralization. CMEs have outperformed both LMEs and MMEs in the postcrisis era.
- Moreover, wage inequality remains greater in countries with decentralized bargaining systems and segmented trade union structures. The corporatist/coordinated economies have still lower levels of wage inequality.

The trends that are described in this chapter imply that with the decline of unionization labor market institutions have become somewhat less important for economic management and the performance of modern economies. Governments pursue less policy concertation and the impact of institutions on performance has weakened.

Labor market institutions in *all* economic models are in a process of transformation. LMEs continue to liberalize and increase flexibility. MMEs have been hit hard by the sovereign debt crisis, and labor market institutions are undergoing fundamental policy reforms. CMEs utilize their own comparative institutional advantages when responding to economic shocks and the rise of the service economy. In particular, dualization of labor markets with an increase of labor market outsiders has been a common trend.

However, labor market institutions are still relevant for the patterns of coordination of economies as VoC/neocorporatist theory suggests. Rather than converging on a model of liberal market economies, CMEs (both Continental and Nordic countries) continue to develop along their own trajectories based on business coordination and a more negotiated political economy. Continental and Nordic coordinated market economies pursue distinct paths and might, over time, diverge from each other into different models of coordination when coping with economic shocks (Thelen 2014). But the main finding is that their economies are still governed by different rules compared to both LMEs and MMEs.

Moreover, the observed trends of union decline do not have to persist. Change is possible at any time, and social movements and political unrest can reverse the current decline. Nobody expected the outburst of social activism in the late 1960s before it occurred. Similarly, a new wave of activism might still follow the austerity policies of the financial crisis. However, there has been no sign that trade unions have benefited from the financial crisis or that the current wave of austerity policy has increased trade union influence over governments.

Appendix

TABLE 9.A1. *Industrial relations indicators, 1980s, 1990s, 2000s, OECD*

	Union Density			Employers' Organization Density			Collective Bargaining Coverage			Collective Bargaining Centralization			Collective Bargaining Coordination		
	1980s	1990s	2000s	1980s	1990s	2000s	1980s	1990s	2000s	1980s	1990s	2000s	1980s	1990s	2000s
Australia	45.00	33.34	21.33			100	85.0	66.7	45.0	3.70	2.40	1.80	3.50	2.40	1.80
Austria	52.12	41.72	32.80	100	100		95.0	98.0	98.8	3.30	2.90	2.50	4.30	4.00	4.00
Belgium	52.29	54.45	51.88			74	96.5	96.0	96.0	3.40	3.40	3.40	4.50	4.20	4.20
Canada	34.71	33.96	29.97				37.5	36.4	31.9	1.00	1.00	1.00	1.00	1.00	1.00
Denmark	77.87	76.21	71.62		58	62.50	82.5	84.0	82.3	3.00	2.90	2.50	3.80	3.20	3.30
Finland	69.89	78.19	72.03	65	62.50	68.57	78.0	89.8	90.0	3.90	4.20	3.75	3.60	3.70	3.60
France	14.38	8.96	7.84		74.00	74.50		92.0	90.0		2.00	2.00		2.00	2.00
Germany	34.24	29.85	21.72			61.50	76.5	70.2	64.4	3.00	3.00	2.70	4.00	4.00	4.00
Greece	37.62	32.20	25.03			43.73	70.0	67.5	65.0	4.00	3.50	3.50	4.00	4.00	4.00
Ireland	60.26	51.80	37.50			60.00	61.8	60.0	49.5	2.50	4.40	3.70	2.20	4.60	4.70
Italy	43.72	37.70	38.68			60.67	84.5	81.8	80.0	2.40	3.00	2.90	3.50	2.90	2.40
Netherlands	28.84	24.91	20.91			85.00	85.0	84.5	84.4	3.30	3.20	3.30	4.30	4.00	4.00
New Zealand	58.56	30.99	21.42					39.9	18.8	3.40	1.00	1.00	4.10	1.20	1.50
Norway	57.51	56.99	54.40			61.00	70.0	71.5	73.5	4.30	3.50	2.20	4.50	4.00	2.50
Portugal	44.48	25.62	21.08			61.50	72.5	79.0	56.2	2.20	3.00	2.80	2.50	3.40	2.60
Spain	10.99	15.97	15.60			73.50	79.8	87.1	87.8	3.80	3.00	3.00	3.60	3.00	3.70
Sweden	81.23	84.14	75.63		86.00	83.60	85.3	90.7	92.8	4.00	3.30	2.70	4.00	3.50	3.00
United Kingdom	46.34	34.60	28.94			37.50	65.5	39.2	34.6	1.40	1.00	1.00	1.00	1.00	1.00
United States	18.46	14.48	12.14				21.6	16.9	14.0	1	1	1	1	1	1
Average	45.4	39.0	30.6	63.6	73.4	57.4	70.2	69.1	56.2	2.6	2.3	2.1	3.2	2.9	2.7

Source: ICTWSS.

TABLE 9.A2. *Unionization rates, selected countries, 2008*

Country		BE	DE	DK	ES	FI	FR	GB	GR	IE	NL	NO	PT	SE	SW
Age	15–25	16.00	3.41	26.26	2.08	25.76	1.74	5.86	2.40	4.71	5.73	12.74	1.18	17.51	2.53
	26–65	45.08	13.91	79.06	9.76	63.32	9.70	20.35	11.03	19.03	19.76	52.45	8.82	66.00	12.89
Gender	Male	0.43	0.15	0.71	0.09	0.56	0.10	0.18	0.13	0.17	0.21	0.44	0.08	0.56	0.15
	Female	0.36	0.10	0.75	0.08	0.63	0.08	0.19	0.08	0.19	0.14	0.49	0.08	0.60	0.07
Contract	Unlimited	0.44	0.15	0.70	0.12	0.61	0.09	0.22	0.13	0.25	0.21	0.52	0.09	0.58	0.12
	Limited	0.36	0.07	0.59	0.06	0.45	0.03	0.09	0.07	0.17	0.07	0.38	0.04	0.36	0.10
	No contract	0.17	0.05	0.33	0.02	0.35	0.02	0.06	0.04	0.08	0.06	0.22	0.03	0.06	0.03
Income	Upper median	0.42	0.16	0.80	0.10	0.67	0.11	0.25	0.15	0.25	0.20	0.51	0.13	0.63	0.15
	Lower median	0.44	0.12	0.72	0.09	0.55	0.07	0.13	0.07	0.15	0.15	0.39	0.05	0.50	0.10
Unemployment (last 5 years)	Yes	0.57	0.08	0.71	0.06	0.57	0.03	0.05	0.05	0.04	0.12	0.30	0.04	0.48	0.11
Unemployment (long-term more than 12 months)	No	0.50	0.13	0.69	0.14	0.65	0.10	0.25	0.10	0.21	0.26	0.41	0.08	0.64	0.18
	Yes	0.54	0.09	0.59	0.07	0.57	0.05	0.07	0.08	0.07	0.20	0.30	0.05	0.55	0.14
Working hours	No	0.52	0.13	0.76	0.11	0.66	0.07	0.23	0.07	0.15	0.19	0.40	0.05	0.58	0.14
	<17 hours	29.58	5.65	33.98	4.55	31.25	7.58	10.96	7.14	9.03	8.45	19.66	2.44	29.23	8.55
	>17 hours	40.08	13.39	76.32	8.70	60.75	9.12	19.73	10.55	18.94	18.73	48.76	8.29	59.27	12.01
Sector	Manufacturing	0.48	0.17	0.65	0.11	0.57	0.07	0.13	0.08	0.12	0.16	0.45	0.05	0.61	0.08
	Services	0.34	0.07	0.56	0.04	0.49	0.05	0.12	0.06	0.07	0.14	0.30	0.02	0.43	0.04
	Public, etc.	0.34	0.14	0.71	0.18	0.67	0.13	0.29	0.20	0.31	0.25	0.68	0.15	0.63	0.16

Source: ESS, own calculations.

PART III

POLICIES

Postindustrial Social Policy

Evelyne Huber and John D. Stephens

In the past three decades, the systems of social consumption in advanced industrial countries have undergone significant changes. Economic and demographic changes have necessitated adaptations to cover new risks in addition to the old while making the welfare states fiscally sustainable (Armingeon and Bonoli 2006). In the period of welfare state expansion, partisanship strongly manifested itself in the battles over the introduction of welfare state programs and their expansion. Expenditures were a reasonably good proxy for generosity, and scores of quantitative studies showed strong effects of partisanship. Quantitative analyses also demonstrated the depressing impact of veto points on expenditures (Huber and Stephens 2001). In the era of retrenchment and recalibration, problem pressures and policy legacies have added to the complexity of policy-making processes and raised the question whether partisanship continues to matter. In line with the argument in this book, this chapter is the first of three studying the political determinants of consumption and investment policies and their distributive effects. We focus on the political determinants of social consumption policies across advanced industrial societies. Ansell and Gingrich (this volume) develop a similar analysis of social investment policies. Finally, Beramendi (this volume) analyzes the distributive impact of different combinations of these two sets of policies.

We analyze the determinants of extensive or far-reaching reforms, and we focus in particular on the impact of partisanship on the reform process. Our argument in its briefest form is that partisan preferences on the Left and the Right as to the kinds of reforms to be implemented remain quite distinct, but

A previous version of this paper was delivered at the conference "The Future of Democratic Capitalism," Duke University, October 2012. We would like to thank Pablo Beramendi, Silja Häusermann, Herbert Kitschelt, Hanspeter Kriesi, Joakim Palme, and the participants at the conference at Duke and the earlier conference in Zürich, June 2011, for comments on previous drafts of the chapter or help with data.

that the translation of these preferences into policies is shaped by the interaction of the magnitude of economic and demographic problems, policy legacies, constitutional veto points, and coalitional pressures.

Most parties have accepted the need to restrict some benefits (e.g., raise the retirement age) and to reevaluate the merits of public and private participation in the provision of social services (e.g., employment agencies). However, Left parties continue to favor inclusive coverage, equality in access to and quality of social services, and public responsibility for direct provision or extensive regulation. Right parties, in contrast, favor more room for private insurance and provision of social services in step with a retreat of public provision and regulation, with predictable results of rising inequalities of coverage, access, and quality.

The severity and timing of economic pressures, in particular levels of unemployment, account for the timing of reform attempts and shape their extent. Prolonged high levels of unemployment force more extensive adaptations. Policy legacies shape the costs of alternative paths of reforms. Programs with wide and generous coverage are popular and politically costly to cut. Programs with privileges for well-organized groups are difficult to reform. Programs with extensive public participation or a public monopoly are more amenable to cost controls than programs with extensive private participation.

Constitutional veto points, that is, presidentialism, bicameralism, judicial review, and provisions for popular referenda, privilege the status quo (Immergut 1992) and thus obstruct translation of partisan preferences into outcomes. They make reforms in any direction more difficult. In addition, where party systems are fragmented and encourage coalitions across the Left-Right divide, reform policies will reflect a compromise between diverging partisan preferences.

Given the number of factors that interact in shaping policy reforms, and given the complexity of reforms themselves, statistical models of the impact of partisanship hide as much as they reveal. We provide estimates of partisan effects on various dimensions of welfare state effort in the retrenchment period later in this chapter, but we caution that they rather underestimate the role of party differences in the policy-making process. The reforms themselves are extremely difficult to measure, as one would have to construct composite measures and assign weights to changes in retirement age, changes in credits for childbearing or education, changes in calculations of benefit formulas, years over which the reform is phased in, and others, just to take the example of pensions. And the models would have to include more than two-way interactions of determinants.[1] Ideally, one would do a systematic comparative analysis of, say, pension reform, in the universe of advanced industrial democracies. This is way beyond the limits of this chapter. Instead, we choose a number of countries that vary in our independent variables and a set of reforms that were extensive,

---

[1] The contributions to Bonoli and Natali (2012) profile the multidimensional nature of welfare state reforms and the complexity of their determinants.

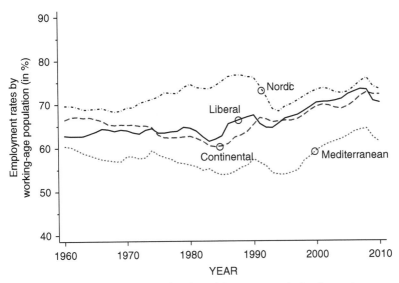

FIGURE 10.1. Employment levels of working-age population by regime type. (Brady et al. 2014.)

and we trace the translation (or failure of translation) of partisan preferences into reform policies. We begin by reviewing common constraints and some common trends in responses, before turning to our cases. For this general overview, we group countries by welfares state regime type, because these types represent similar policy legacies. In the case selection we choose countries from three regime types.

10.1. Economic and Demographic Constraints

Economic growth underwent cyclical variations, but the correlations in the annual pooled data between growth rates and unemployment ($r = -.16$) and employment levels ($r = -.05$) are surprisingly low. The employment and unemployment indicators tell one much more about stress on the welfare state: Switzerland, with average per capita growth rates below 1 percent but with very high levels of employment and low levels of unemployment in the period 1990–2007, is under much less economic stress than Greece, which has growth above 2 percent but unemployment at 10 percent and employment at 55 percent.

The differences in employment (Figure 10.1) and unemployment by welfare state regime type are striking though not surprising. The Nordic countries already had very high employment levels in 1990 with 76 percent of the population fifteen to sixty-four employed, well above the target set by the EU in the European Employment Strategy (EES) seven years later. The

Finnish and Swedish banking crisis hit those two countries very hard in the early 1990s, resulting in steep drops in employment and increases in unemployment (see the online appendix for graphs of individual countries at http://www.unc.edu/~jdsteph/common/articles-common.html). By the eve of the 2008 financial crisis, the Nordic countries' employment levels were up to 75 percent and unemployment stood at 5.1 percent. The Anglo-American welfare states rivaled the performance of the Nordic countries with increases in employment and decreases in unemployment, with precrisis averages of 73 percent of the working age population employed and 4.8 percent unemployed.

One can clearly see the effect of labor reduction strategies and their reversal in the continental welfare states in Figure 10.1. Though employment levels improve, these countries, with the exception of Switzerland, are still below the EES 70 percent target in 2007, primarily because of low levels of women's employment. Austria and the Netherlands are outliers in different ways. Austria never has had an unemployment problem, and its employment performance is second only to Switzerland's among the continental countries until the Netherlands surpasses it in the late 1990s. Thus, economic stress is unlikely to produce as much social policy change in Austria as it does in all of the other continental countries. As of the early 1980s, the Netherlands had one of the poorest records in Europe on both employment indicators but subsequently carried through a number of labor market and social policy reforms, which are widely credited for its stellar performance on both indicators by 2007, with employment levels of 76 percent and an unemployment rate of 4.5 percent.

The Mediterranean countries are clearly the poorest performers on both indicators. Portugal is an outlier in this group with higher employment levels and lower unemployment levels. In the other three countries, economic stress has been a motivating force in social policy reform.

In terms of demographic stress, the regimes vary somewhat with respect to the currently aged population, with the Anglo-American regimes with 13 percent of the population older than sixty-five in 2007 compared to 16–18 percent in the other welfare state regimes. More important for future pressures related to aging are fertility rates, which vary strongly across the regimes: The total fertility rates in Anglo-American and Nordic regimes are just below population reproduction at 1.9, while the continental regimes have low fertility rates (1.6) and the Mediterranean regimes yet lower rates (1.4). This has important implications for future pension and health care costs that we discuss later. With regard to family structure change, the Nordic and Anglo-American welfare states had higher proportions of single mother households than the continental welfare states in 1980, but the rate of change since then has been the same across the regimes (Huber and Stephens 2001).

Labor force change reinforces the decline of the male breadwinner industrial worker family. Though there is variation in the percentage of the working age population employed in industry, by the 2000s, it is very low everywhere, only 14 percent in the liberal welfare states and 17 percent in the other welfare state regimes. The decline of unions aggravates the problem because, by the 2000s, workers in private services are only protected by prevailing labor market institutions in the Nordic countries, as indicated by average union density rates of 68 percent in Nordic welfare states and less than 27 percent in the other welfare state regimes. Without union protection, the social policy regime is called upon to meet yet more needs.

10.2. Policy Responses

Under the weight of these economic and demographic pressures, the two dominant responses of all governments in the 1990s were efforts to contain costs and to raise levels of employment. The former set of efforts was directed with particular emphasis at pension systems and health care, but it also included unemployment and sickness compensation programs. The latter set of efforts had two main components, activation policy and work/family reconciliation policies (Gingrich and Ansell, this volume).

10.2.1. Cost Containment and Pension Reforms

Beginning in the 1980s, all the fully matured PAYGO pension systems were under pressure from a combination of aging populations, slower wage growth, and declining standard employment (Myles and Pierson 2001). Aging populations and slower wage growth meant that the revenue growth of the pension funds would not keep pace in the future with the growth in pension expenditures. Either the contributions would have to increase or the benefits would have to decrease, or both, if the systems were to be kept viable. Declining standard employment meant that fewer people would accumulate sufficient pension credits for a regular pension. This called for the introduction or improvement of minimum pensions, or social assistance pensions.

Every single advanced industrial country undertook some kind of pension reform, ranging from small adjustments in contributions and benefits to major cuts in benefits and structural changes in the systems. The most common reforms concerned the formula for calculating benefits and the qualifying conditions. Governments lengthened the base years for calculating the replacement rate and switched from indexation to wage growth to indexation to inflation. They lengthened the contribution period for pension entitlements, raised the retirement age, and tightened penalties for early retirement. More far-reaching changes entailed a switch from defined benefit to defined contribution systems, and the introduction of demographic factors into the calculation of the benefits. Structural changes led to the introduction of supplementary second and third pillars in the form of collective occupational and individual private schemes, in some countries mandatory, in others collectively negotiated or voluntary, but supported through the tax system. A further common trend was toward moving privileges of public sector employees into greater alignment with the lower benefits of private sector employees.

The trend toward defined contribution rather than defined benefit systems and toward greater reliance on private savings increased the probability of ending up with insufficient pensions for people with nontraditional employment histories. It also could work to the disadvantage of women, who are more likely to suffer career interruptions. To deal with these problems, some governments introduced pension credits for child rearing and elderly care and/ or improved access to minimum pensions or means-tested noncontributory pensions.

Clearly, pension reforms have been politically very difficult to implement. Of all the social programs other than health care they have widest coverage and impact in the sense of affecting the largest number of people for long periods and in important ways. The difficulty has been aggravated where trade unions have played roles in the administration of pension funds. As a result, successful reformers tended to rely on two main strategies: First, they phased in reforms over a long period. Second, they proceeded in a stepwise fashion rather than proposing sweeping overhauls.

The purpose of phasing in reforms over a long period was to neutralize opposition from the people who would be most likely to engage in major protest actions – those relatively close to retirement. People below forty years of age tend not to think a lot about retirement. Thus, raising the retirement age and/ or lowering benefits over ten years would affect people fifty-five years of age and younger, and the closer to fifty-five, the more people would have thought about the issue. Raising the retirement age and benefits over twenty-five years would only affect people forty years of age and younger – a constituency for whom the issue is much less salient. Indeed, the time lag between the year of the major pension reforms and their projected full implementation in Germany ranges from twenty-three to approximately twenty-six years, and in Italy it is a full forty years (Bonoli and Palier 2008: 33).

Proceeding in a stepwise fashion can again serve to reduce the size of the potential opposition because reforms can be limited to certain categories of people. However, as Bonoli and Palier (2008) emphasize, it can serve yet another function: Initial reforms can prepare the ground for later ones. For instance, changes that lower the value of pensions from the first pillar will create a demand for supplementary pensions and thus ease the way for the introduction of second and third pillars.

Table 10.1 illustrates the extent of and cross-national variability in change in the replacement rates in pensions as a result of pension reforms in the past two decades. The figures in the first column are Scruggs's (2013) data for the replacement rate of a single newly retired average production worker in 1995 and thus represent the benefits in the old systems before the recent reforms took effect. The figures in the second and third columns are the OECD's (2011) estimates of the replacement rates that can be expected by

TABLE 10.1. *Average pension replacement rates by welfare state regime (worker with an average wage)*

	Scruggs 1995 Newly Retired Worker	OECD New Worker 2008	
		Public Only	Public and Private Mandatory
Nordic welfare states			
Denmark	53.3	32.6	89.8
Finland*	66.3	65.2	65.2
Norway*	60.0	52.4	60.3
Sweden*	69.4	46.8	62.5
Mean	62.3	49.3	69.5
Continental European welfare states			
Austria*	81.6	89.9	89.9
Belgium*	68.2	52.1	52.1
France*	60.3	60.4	60.4
Germany*	75.4	56.0	56.0
Netherlands	46.0	33.1	99.8
Switzerland	38.6	38.2	64.1
Mean	61.7	55.0	70.4
Mediterranean welfare states			
Italy*	85.7	71.7	71.7
Portugal*	65.7	69.2	69.2
Spain*	106.60	84.9	84.9
Mean	86.0	75.3	75.3
Anglo-American welfare states			
Australia	32.2	14.8	58.9
Canada	53.3	50.4	50.4
Ireland	40.3	31.3	31.3
New Zealand	41.8	41.1	41.1
United Kingdom	50.2	37.4	37.4
United States	57.2	47.3	47.3
Mean	45.8	37.1	44.4
Japan	51.3	39.7	39.7

Note: *Mature defined benefit earnings related PAYGO system providing retirement wage for most retired persons, including higher income individuals.

a single worker with the average wage who begins work in 2008 and works a full career.[2] Unfortunately, the figures are not fully comparable. Scruggs's figures include only statutory plans while the OECD figures also include negotiated plans provided the coverage is near-universal. These negotiated plans

[2] The Swedish figures are corrections to the OECD figure issued by the Swedish pension authority (Lowen and Settegren 2011).

were an important part of the retirement income of workers in Denmark and the Netherlands already in 1995 and will be increasingly important in Sweden. The 1995 figures do include statutory individual account tiers of Switzerland and Australia, which later were also features of the reformed schemes in Sweden and Norway. These plans are included in the OECD's figures for "Private Mandatory" along with the negotiated plans previously mentioned. The asterisks indicate the countries that had mature defined benefit earnings related PAYGO systems providing an adequate retirement wage for most retired in 1990. All of them reformed their system, and in many cases this involved adding or strengthening a funded mandatory private tier. In fact, the table shows that significant cuts in replacement rates occurred in countries that did not introduce compulsory funded plans, such as Germany and Belgium.[3] Both countries introduced voluntary tax subsidized plans. Note that the Mediterranean countries did cut the replacement rates but did not introduce a funded tier and that even the reduced replacement rates are still comparatively high. Given the low fertility of these countries, these pension commitments almost certainly are not sustainable and these pension systems will have to undergo further reform.[4] The OECD provides figures (not shown) that show that existing replacement rates would be maintained or even increased after the reforms because of greater reliance on the private voluntary systems not only in these two countries, but in all other countries with such systems, Canada, Ireland, New Zealand, the United Kingdom, and the United States (that is, all of the liberal welfare states save Australia) *provided that there is a full take-up rate in the voluntary systems at all income levels.* Of course, it is very unlikely that the take-up rate will be nearly that high at low or even moderate income levels; thus, all of these countries are very likely to develop high levels of income stratification among the retired once the new systems fully mature.

10.2.2. *Cost Containment in Health Care*
Health care costs have been escalating across OECD countries, driven primarily by advances in medical technology but also by the rising aged proportion of the population (Hacker 2004). Since governments foot the major part of the medical bill in every country except the United States (see Figure 10.2 and online appendix), governments have attempted to contain costs. As Bambra (2005) and Freeman and Rothgang (2010) argue, public health care systems do not follow Esping-Andersen's three worlds classification. Our

---

[3] The OECD figures for Austria are not consistent with Schulze and Schludi's (2006: 594) assessment of "a 10 percent retrenchment in pension benefits."

[4] This applies doubly to Greece, which is not in the table because Scruggs (2013) provides no data for Greek pension replacement rates. The OECD (2011) figure for the future pension of a Greek worker beginning work in 2008 is a replacement rate of 111.2%, an astounding figure that says much about current Greek economic difficulties.

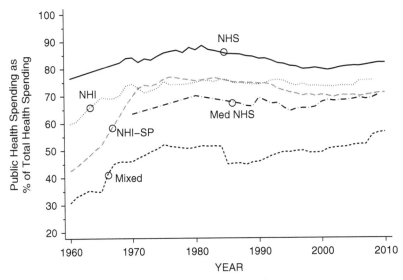

FIGURE 10.2. Public health care spending by health care regime.
(Brady et al. 2014.)

classification in the figures is based on Hacker (2004) with some differences
in a few cases: We classify the Nordic countries, the Mediterranean countries,
the United Kingdom, and New Zealand as National Health Services (NHS);
Canada as national health insurance (NHI) with a single government payer;
continental Europe and Australia as decentralized National Health Insurances;
and the United States and Switzerland as mixed private and public health
insurance systems.[5] For reasons outlined in the next paragraph, we place the
Mediterranean countries in a separate category. In his analysis of these same
data up to 2000, Hacker (2004) argues that governments with NHSs in countries with veto free constitutional structures (which turns out to be all of the
non-Mediterranean NHSs) were uniquely equipped to control costs (as is supported by our updated figures) and that one way they managed to do that was
to reduce the public share of total health spending (which does not appear to
be the case since 2000).

With the benefit of more recent data and adding the Mediterranean countries[6] we can considerably nuance Hacker's analysis while maintaining the
spirit of his explanation. Hacker's main point is that governments with NHSs
in veto free systems have both a high degree of control over the medical care
system and the political ability to make large changes in the system and he

---

[5] In 1996, Switzerland made health insurance mandatory, similar to the Obama reform of 2010.
This would still argue for a separate category for these two countries.
[6] Only Italy was included in Hacker's analysis.

hints that these changes could take different directions (2004: 708). This would include the ability to limit costs but also to increase spending if the government deemed that desirable and the economic situation permitted it. The Mediterranean NHSs are of more recent origin (established in the late 1970s or 1980s) and are incomplete in that they control much less of total cost than the other NHSs. Moreover in Spain the health care system is highly decentralized and financing is uneven (Osterkatz 2013). They have not been very effective at controlling cost increases though some of the increases in these countries certainly represent efforts to catch up to the rest of Europe in delivering good-quality public health care.

The figures for public percentage of total health care spending suggest no diminution of governments' role in health care. However the spending figures hide a rise in private provision of health care in many countries and/or an introduction of competition in health care provision in which public providers compete with private providers (Gingrich 2011a). For example, if a government introduces a voucher system in which the citizen can choose between a public or private provider, the government share of total health care spending may stay the same while private provision of health services increases. In her study of markets in the provision of health care, education, and long-term care, Gingrich (2011a) cautions that this trend cannot be seen as an unambiguous victory for neoliberal preferences over traditional social preferences for state provision. Rather, on the basis of her research on Sweden, the United Kingdom, and the Netherlands, she develops a typology of different types of markets and argues that the different types have quite different distributive implications and thus should map onto the traditional policy preferences of the Left and Right.

10.2.3. Cost Containment, Activation, and Work/Family Reconciliation Policies

Unemployment replacement rates moved to the center of the debate about both cost containment and activation. Accordingly, they changed considerably between 1971 and 2010 in many countries (Scruggs 2013; van Vliet and Caminada 2012). The Nordic countries saw a general decline after the mid-1980s, to between 60 and 70 percent after 2000 (see Figure 10.3 and online appendix). The unemployment replacement rates were stable in continental countries so they ended up somewhat higher than in the Nordic countries. In the liberal welfare state regimes, the picture is also one of general decline. The Southern European countries defy the general trend, moving upward and converging with the Nordic and continental groups. The data on which the graphs are based are for a worker (single or married with a non-working spouse) with average earnings and a full contribution period. Thus, they do not reveal changes in the replacement rate across income categories. Clasen and Clegg (2011) argue that unemployment compensation underwent a process of homogenization of benefits and of programs in many countries.

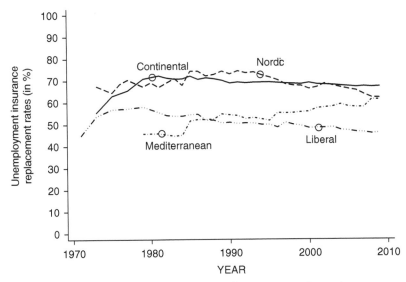

FIGURE 10.3. Unemployment insurance replacement rates by regime type. (Scruggs 2013.)

Therefore, the replacement rates for higher income groups fell more steeply, and for lower income groups less steeply, than those shown in Figure 10.3.

Sickness insurance replacement rates were also the target of cost containment efforts, but they played less of a role in the activation discussion than disability pensions. A very similar picture emerges to the trajectory of unemployment replacement rates, with considerable variation among countries and over time, but an overall downward trend in the social democratic and liberal regimes in contrast to an overall flat trajectory in the continental countries. The waiting periods for both unemployment and sickness insurance benefits show similar regime differences to the generosity in replacement rates, but there is no uniform tendency toward lengthening the waiting periods. The qualifying conditions for the two insurance schemes also do not show a uniform pattern toward making them more stringent.

Governments took other measures to promote activation that are not as easily quantifiable (Huo 2009). In some but not all cases they shortened the duration of regular unemployment insurance benefits and thus moved up the transition into programs with lower unemployment assistance or social assistance benefits. Almost ubiquitous was the imposition of stricter activation requirements to continue to receive the benefits. Recipients were required to participate in training, look for a job, and accept a job even if they were overqualified or the job paid a lot less than the job that was lost.

The main innovations and the only welfare state expansions since 1990 have occurred in activation and in work/family reconciliation policies. Specifically,

TABLE 10.2. *Effect of a two-standard-deviation change in partisan government on selected measures of welfare state effort*

	Left Cabinet		Christian Democratic Cabinet	
	Pre-1986	Post-1985	Pre-1986	Post-1985
Nonaged spending (sd = 3.9)	3.2		2.6	
Social spending (sd = 5.2)	4.3	1.4	4.0	
Public health spending, percentage total (sd = 13.1)	8.3	−2.9	6.6	
Parental leave replacement rate (sd = 21.3)	22.6	7.0		
Unemployment replacement rates (sd = 21.5)	22.8		14.5	
Sick pay replacement rates (sd = 26.1)	21.8		26.1	
Minumum pension replacement rates (sd = 13.6)	11.5		6.1	
Standard pension replacement rates (sd = 14.7)			7.6	−3.7

Source: Brady (2014); Scruggs (2013). Blank cell indicates insignificant coefficient.

most countries introduced or expanded paid parental leave and/or preschool education and day care, and some countries introduced or strengthened long-term care insurance and services for the elderly. The social democratic regimes could build on a strong foundation, whereas the continental and liberal regimes charted predominantly new territory.

10.3. The Politics of Reforming Social Consumption

Table 10.2 demonstrates how much less significant and substantively important partisanship has been in statistical analyses of the post-1985 period than the earlier period. We constructed the political variables to measure cumulative record of cabinet seats held by Left, Christian democratic, and secular center or Right parties before 1986, and for 1986 and later. The table summarizes results for indicators of social consumption from multiple regressions with the usual control variables. In the pre-1986 period, only two variables are not significant; in the later period ten variables are not. Moreover, the magnitude of a two standard deviation change in the significant partisan variables on the dependent variables shrank to half or less, with only one exception. As noted, these are only measures of expenditures and replacement rates, and they do not capture dimensions such as qualifying conditions, which can be quite important. In the case of pensions, these are only replacement rates in the mandatory public systems for a newly retired worker and thus underestimate already legislated cuts for future retirees. They also do not include negotiated occupational pensions, as in the Dutch and Danish second tier, nor the optional but publicly subsidized systems, which will play increasingly important roles. The data on public spending on health care are a good example of the limitations of the quantitative indicators; the reductions in the public share of total health spending since 1985 in social democratic governed countries, from a very high initial level, are real (see online appendix graphs), but they do not tap the most important dimension of health care reform, which is changes in how public health care is delivered (see our discussion of Gingrich 2011a earlier).

Nevertheless, Left partisanship continues to be significant and substantively important for one-year unemployment replacement rates and for parental leave replacement rates, and Christian democratic partisanship has an even somewhat stronger expansionary effect on unemployment replacement rates, making up for a negative effect in the earlier period. The effect on parental leave squares with our argument that the Left continued to lead the way in work/family conciliation policies. Again, the muted effects do not indicate disappearance of differences in partisan preferences; they indicate stronger constraints from problem pressures, policy legacies, veto points, and coalitional pressures.

Table 10.3 summarizes the key variables shaping the problem pressures and the context for the translation of partisan preferences into reform policies in four countries: the United Kingdom, Sweden, Germany, and the Netherlands. These cases represent three different welfare state regime types and thus have different policy legacies. They also differ in the presence of constitutional veto points and in the degree of parliamentary fragmentation, both of which condition the ability of parties in government or participating in government to shape the design and implementation of policy reforms according to their preferences.

As we argued elsewhere, in the era of welfare state retrenchment, the effect of partisanship became somewhat muted. By the 1990s the changes in the world economy and demographic changes subjected the welfare state to strong fiscal pressures, which constrained the Left. At the other end of the spectrum, the broad social coalitions that had come to support the welfare state once it was established constrained the Right in efforts to cut expenditures (Huber and Stephens 2001). Economic pressures, specifically high levels of unemployment for extended periods, became very powerful drivers of both expenditures and reform initiatives, regardless of the party in power. Nevertheless, parties maintained different preferences regarding the types of reforms. Their ability to translate these preferences into policy, of course, depended on their participation in government, the necessity to compromise with coalition partners, and the presence of veto points in the political system.

Though every government has to address the issue of cost controls, and every government is concerned with reducing unemployment and raising employment levels, there are different ways to reach these goals. The Left

TABLE 10.3. *Welfare state problem pressures and constraints on partisan politics*

	United Kingdom	Sweden	Germany	Netherlands
Welfare state problem pressures				
Economic pressure – unemployment crisis (8%+)	82–88, 91–96	93–97	94–	82–87
Demographic pressure fertility decline 1980–2007	1.9→1.9	1.7→1.9	1.4→1.4	1.6→1.7
Demographic pressure percentage aged 1980–2007	15→15	16→17	16→20	12→15
Family change, percentage of children living with single mother	10→21	13→18	6→16	7→9
Deindustrialization 1980–2007 (percentage working age population)	20→15	26→17	28→21	17→15
Union decline 1980–2007	50→28	78→71	35→20	35→19
Constraints on partisan politics				
Veto points	Low	Low	High	Low
Coalition constraints	Low	Low	Increasing	High
Policy legacies – mature PAYGO	No	Yes	Yes	No
Policy legacies health care NHS	Yes	Yes	No	No

consistently favors more redistributive and solidaristic policy designs, which require a strong state role as payer, provider, and regulator. This may entail higher levels of taxation. The Right consistently favors closer links between contributions and benefits and a lowering of commitments and expenditures in public programs, opening the way for private payers and providers and for more reliance on the market. This may entail a preference for tax cuts over strengthening the financial basis of existing programs. When it comes to the structure of provisions, the Left prefers to rely on public transfers and services, whereas the Right prefers to rely on tax incentives and private services. These preferences are clearly visible in proposals for pension reforms and health care reforms (Gingrich 2011a; Häusermann 2010).

We can find similar differences in policy preferences regarding unemployment compensation and positive and negative activation (Nelson 2013). Again, virtually every country has imposed stricter work requirements, but different governments have chosen different paths. Proposals from the Right prioritize negative activation – cutting replacement rates and reducing the duration of benefits – whereas preferences from the Left prioritize inclusion of non-traditional workers and positive activation – emphasis on training and job placement. During deep and lasting economic downturns, when employment creation takes center stage, the Left prefers to create public sector jobs and the Right prefers to subsidize low wage work in the private sector.

Such policy preferences and proposals are rarely fully reflected in policy. Only in situations of one-party majority government without veto points might one even expect them to be. Yet, even in these situations, policy legacies shape reform options. Cutbacks in public transfers and services are easier where they are less universalistic to begin with. Moreover, parties are likely to encounter internal resistance against radical measures and end up with policy packages that are multidimensional and offer some compensation to some groups that are negatively affected. In coalition governments and systems with veto points the reliance on complex policy packages is particularly pronounced (Bonoli and Mach 2000). In fact, as Häusermann (2010) puts it, the very capacity to bring about significant reforms depends on coalitional engineering and flexibility. Moreover, at times governing parties in countries with a tradition of involvement of unions and employers in social policy making sought a compromise with the opposition and the social partners, in the interest of devising viable long-term solutions for major reforms.

The timing and intensity of economic pressures varied across countries, shaping the timing and depth of reforms. Denmark, the Netherlands, and Belgium, along with Spain and Ireland, were the first countries to face steeply rising unemployment, in the early 1980s. Accordingly, they became the first countries to engage in serious welfare state reforms.[7] The reforms became particularly far reaching in the Netherlands, because the Netherlands had started from a comparatively low level of total employment, and that level sank to the lowest point of just barely above 50 percent, along with that of Ireland (see online appendix). Only in Spain did total employment sink even lower – to 45 percent. Though Spain was a laggard in welfare state development at that point, the country was already forced to undertake painful reforms in the mid-1980s, which led to a break between the Socialist government and the unions.

Unemployment in Germany and France peaked in the 1990s, as in Finland and Sweden. In Germany, the main underlying reason was unification; in Finland and Sweden it was the financial crisis of the early 1990s. Unemployment in the East has remained a serious problem for Germany and has forced a series of deep-going reforms, under Christian Democratic led and Social Democratic

---

[7] The United Kingdom also reached the high unemployment threshold of three years over 8% that we use in Table 10.2 in the mid-1980s, but the Thatcherite cuts to the welfare state began earlier. They were motivated by government ideology not an employment crisis.

led governments alike. Finland and Sweden responded to the crisis with serious austerity measures as well, under governments with different political colorings.

While all postindustrial welfare states faced the same problem pressures, the degree of pressure varied greatly, as one can see for our four cases in Table 10.2.[8] The employment crisis was least in Sweden and greatest in the United Kingdom. The demographic pressures on the pension system are greatest in Germany and least in Sweden and the United Kingdom. In addition, Germany has a mature PAYGO pension system, which is both a problem pressure and policy legacy constraint on partisan politics. Postindustrial family structure change is most advanced in the United Kingdom and Germany, creating greater pressures for reform to address new social risks. The decline of industry is another marker for the decline of the industrial age male breadwinner family, which was well served by old social risk policies. While there is variation in the level of industrial employment at the end of the time series, the overwhelming majority of employees are working in services in all countries. The unionization figures indicate that, except in Sweden, few workers outside the industrial core are unionized and thus the labor markets are certainly dualized, putting an extra burden on the welfare state to protect these vulnerable workers.

10.3.1. The United Kingdom

Britain is one of the countries where partisanship is particularly visible in reform outcomes because the electoral system mostly produces majority governments and there are no veto points. In fact, there is little doubt that the differences between Thatcher/Major and Blair/Brown are the largest partisan differences in social policy in any OECD country. In the early 1980s, the Conservatives under Thatcher proposed to abolish the State Earnings-Related Pension Scheme (SERPS), which complemented the flat-rate Basic State Pension. When this proposal generated very strong opposition and a decline in the approval ratings of the government, the government instead lowered replacement rates in the SERPS and introduced subsidies for contracting out to individual pension plans in 1986 (Schulze and Moran 2006). Here policy legacies in the form of broad coverage were responsible for the government's retreat from a straight pursuit of its preferences. Employers already had the option of contracting out, as long as their occupational pension plan offered benefits at least equal to the SERPS. The modified proposal was opposed by the Labour Party and some backbenchers of the Conservatives but passed. In the mid-1990s the Conservatives under Major eliminated the requirement that occupational pension plans offer the same minimum protection as the SERPS, and they changed the formula to

---

[8] The problem pressures in our four cases are fairly representative of the welfare state regime to which they belong.

lower SERPS benefits again. In 1997, shortly before losing the election, they developed a new plan that would have resulted in a gradual elimination of the entire state pension system (Schulze and Moran 2006).

New Labour's main concern was with low income earners and irregular workers who were not able to build up occupational pensions and for whom individual pensions were too expensive (as the Conservatives had not put any ceilings on administrative charges). They proposed to replace SERPS with a new State Second Pension that would improve benefits for low income earners and slowly transition to a flat-rate benefit structure while maintaining earnings-related contributions. In order to make it more attractive for lower income earners to build up private pensions, a new kind of Stake Holder Pensions was established, with charges limited to a percentage of the contributions, not flat fees. These reforms were passed in 1999 and 2000, and they were followed by a reform in 2004 that established a Pension Protection Fund that would compensate people if their occupational pension fund were to become insolvent. In sum, New Labour radically changed course from the Conservatives' reforms aimed at eliminating the state pension system toward strengthening that system and the role of the state in guaranteeing occupational pensions as well, and making the system more inclusive and equitable.

In the United Kingdom governments were also able radically to change course in the health care sector and put a clear partisan imprint on these reforms. The Conservatives under Thatcher and Major and New Labour differed dramatically in terms of the resources devoted to the National Health Service. Under the Conservatives, the NHS along with public education was starved for funds, a policy that led to high levels of public dissatisfaction with these public services. By the turn of the century, very large majorities responded to pollsters saying that they were willing to pay more taxes for better public health care and education. In the 2001 election, the Liberal Democrats outflanked Labour on the Left on the issue and Labour responded by greatly increasing spending in these areas and others, implementing the largest increase in social spending in the post–World War II era. In the case of health care, Labour doubled real expenditure between 2000 and 2008, and as a result waiting lines for outpatient procedures fell from fourteen to four weeks (Gingrich 2011a: 91–92).

Hacker (2004) notes that it is somewhat counterintuitive that countries with the most statist health care systems, National Health Services, were also the ones that were most active in introducing market oriented reforms. Gingrich's (2011a) work on health care reform makes this paradox more understandable as she shows that Left and Right governments differed greatly in how they shaped health care markets. In the case of the United Kingdom (Gingrich (2011a: 86–101), the Conservatives created a system of hospital competition with a cost conscious governmental purchaser, which may have controlled costs but did not improve care, and they created new risks for individuals by reducing coverage of some procedures and introducing tax breaks for the purchase of private insurance. By contrast, Labour moved to restore stronger collective guarantees and introduced competition in a fashion that gave hospitals incentives to be responsive to consumer demands for high-quality services and timely delivery. In her analyses of the development of health care markets in Sweden and the Netherlands, Gingrich finds similar difference between the approaches of Left parties and Right parties.

In the area of labor markets and activation, New Labour's New Deals signaled another sharp departure from Conservative policy. The government promoted and subsidized work for targeted groups, starting with youth. New Labour set and then raised the minimum wage; it cut taxes on low income groups; it greatly expanded the negative income tax; it increased the universal child allowance significantly; and it increased support for lone parents (Waldfogel 2010: chapters 2 and 3). Child poverty measured in relative terms, which had risen from 9 percent to 20 percent of children under the Conservatives, fell to 14 percent by 2004 (LIS key figures). Measured in absolute terms, child poverty was cut in half (Waldfogel 2010: 2).

10.3.2. Germany

In Germany, the 1989 pension reform (to be effective in 1992) was limited. It introduced an increase in the retirement age for women, the unemployed, and disabled, and penalties for early retirement and a change of indexation. It was supported by both major parties and the social partners (Hinrichs 2000). Unification greatly increased fiscal pressures and complicated the political scene, and from then on pension politics became highly contentious, and the party in opposition – when they controlled the Bundesrat – used it to block reforms or at least extract major concessions. The result was that actual policies passed did not fully reflect the underlying partisan differences. After gaining power in 1998, the SPD-Green coalition rolled back important parts of the cutbacks imposed by the 1997 reform under the CDU/CSU-FDP coalition. One of the issues the SPD had insisted on but failed to incorporate in the 1997 reform was an extension of pension coverage to the marginally employed and the self-employed, which was blocked by the FDP (Schulze and Jochem 2006). The Red-Green coalition then put pension coverage for the marginally employed into law in 1999.

The Red-Green government's pension reform adopted in 2001 boldly addressed the intensified fiscal constraints by moving from a defined benefit to a defined contribution plan, a move that was expected to lower replacement rates from 70 to 64 percent over a number of years. In addition, it introduced a voluntary capitalized individual savings plan supported by tax incentives. On these two issues, the government had moved toward the center, but it did not go as far as the CDU/CSU and the FDP would have wanted (Häusermann 2010). Moreover, the reform contained improvements for the elderly with insufficient resources, who were moved to a basic means tested minimum pension scheme. More cutbacks followed in 2004, expected to lower the replacement rate in the public scheme to about 52 percent by 2030 and increasing the retirement age for the unemployed to sixty-three. At the same time, the abolition of credit points for periods of higher education and the introduction of taxation of pension benefits worked in an egalitarian direction. A reform measure that had long been under discussion but never implemented because of the danger of political backlash was the increase in the general retirement age from sixty-five to sixty-seven; it was implemented under the Grand Coalition in 2007. In sum, the intense fiscal pressures forced all parties to undertake retrenchment, and the veto points in the system forced movement toward the center, but the differences in commitment to equity and solidarity continued to have an impact on concrete policies.

The high and persistent unemployment levels after unification prompted a first wave of labor market deregulation under the center-right coalition in the 1990s. After a temporary recovery of job growth in the first years of the Red-Green coalition, renewed growth in unemployment induced the government to embark on a series of significant reforms in unemployment insurance and activation policy. The Hartz legislation had four parts and involved changes in the Federal Labor Agency to improve services, new instruments of labor market policy, stricter activation rules, and curtailment of benefits for the long-term unemployed. Benefit duration for the unemployed aged fifty-five and older was reduced to a maximum of eighteen from thirty-two months. Most controversial was Hartz IV, with lower benefits for the long-term unemployed and a fusion of contribution-related unemployment assistance with social assistance. After exhausting unemployment insurance benefits (or ALG I), recipients are shifted to ALG II, which depends on a comprehensive means test and requires activation. It provides a low cash benefit and in addition housing and other supplements, including supplements for children. ALG II can also be paid to the working poor, if their earnings do not meet needs of the household.

This was a heavy dose of negative activation, and it was accompanied by a series of measures to stimulate job creation. Subsidies were provided for start-ups by unemployed people; temporary agency work was liberalized; and fixed term contracts for older workers were liberalized as well. In the Hartz reforms, partisanship was muted by the problem pressure, on the one hand, and the existence of veto points, on the other hand. The reforms were widely seen as necessary, and they were the result of a compromise with the CDU/CSU who controlled the Bundesrat (Hinrichs 2010; Eichhorst and Marx 2011).

10.3.3. Netherlands
The Netherlands constitutes a case of muting of partisan effects in pension policy by the requirements of coalition formation. All governments were coalition governments that involved the center (the Christian Democrats) or stretched the whole spectrum (the Purple coalitions), so compromises had to be found

internally. The Netherlands has a general flat-rate residency-based pension that provides a replacement rate of about 55 percent of the average wage and a system of publicly regulated occupational pensions negotiated by the labor market partners that cover about 90 percent of employees (Anderson and Immergut 2006). The dominant austerity tool employed by governments of all stripes was suspension of indexation in the general pension scheme. In 1992 indexation was made conditional by law on the labor market participation rate. In order to strengthen the financial base of the general pension scheme, the PvdA-led Purple Coalition introduced a tax-financed reserve fund in 1997. This mode of financing is a good example of internal compromise: The PvdA had suggested financing through higher contributions from higher income earners but had to abandon this plan because of opposition from coalition partners. The center-right government in power in 1987 had improved the portability of occupational pensions, and the Purple Coalition passed a reform including part-time workers in the occupational pension schemes in 1994.

The Netherlands confronted a major unemployment problem combined with low employment levels beginning in the 1970s, and reforms continued over some thirty years. The logic of coalition governments kept partisan effects small here also, but the changes in the composition of these coalitions nevertheless revealed some partisan effects. The center-right Lubbers I government (1982–1986) embarked on significant cuts in the unemployment replacement rate from more than 90 percent to less than 80 percent and in disability pensions (see online appendix), but it was not until 1987 that it passed a major systemic reform. This reform integrated unemployment assistance into unemployment insurance; that meant a significant shortening of the benefit period before the recipient would be shifted onto social assistance. At the same time, eligibility was widened to nontraditional workers and activation obligations were imposed, and the easy route from unemployment into the disability scheme was closed. In 1991 the center-left Lubbers III government (1989–1994) attempted to improve job placement by strengthening the tripartite administration of job placement agencies.

With the formation of the Purple Coalition, the Christian Democrats were ousted from government, and thus the most steadfast defenders of the participation of the social partners in social insurance administration. The government concluded that the social partners were unwilling to enforce activation and thus embarked on removing them stepwise from the administration of the insurance schemes. The Left and the Right compromised on further flexibilization of the economy and the labor market, stricter activation, and an effort to protect benefit levels as much as possible (Hoogenboom 2011). On the one hand, the government continued to tighten eligibility conditions for unemployment and disability benefits, but, on the other hand, it also improved the position of atypical workers (Vis, van Kersbergen, and Becker 2008). In contrast, the center-right government that assumed power in 2002 continued the tightening of conditions and lowered benefit levels and duration (Hoogenboom 2011).

10.3.4. *Sweden*

The Swedish pension reform of 1994–2001, which transformed a mature DB PAYGO earnings-related pension system into a defined contribution PAYGO with an individual account tier, is an example of partisan bargaining to achieve a broad compromise acceptable to all bargaining partners, in this case, the political parties. By the early 1990s, the major political parties and interest groups in Sweden recognized that the existing DB PAYGO pension system was not viable.[9] The first-order preference of the bourgeois parties would have been a funded individual account system, but they recognized that that was not politically possible because of the transition costs. The core solution to the demographic and economic problems of the existing DB PAYGO system was a notional defined contribution PAYGO system that adjusted actual pension levels to changes in wage growth and life expectancy at retirement. Within these parameters, the pension benefit would depend on lifetime contributions to the system. Two smaller parties, the Left Party and the Right populist New Democracy Party, were unwilling to sign on to the basic parameters of the reform. In negotiations between the Social Democrats and the four mainstream bourgeois parties, a number of disputes arose with the two main ones being whether to divert part of the contributions to the system to an individual account funded system, as the bourgeois parties wanted, and whether contributions should be levied on income above the benefit ceiling, which would introduce a redistributive element into the system, as the Social Democrats wanted. The compromise was to designate 2.5 percent of the total 18.5 percent payroll contribution to an individual account system and levy contributions on earnings above the benefit ceiling but only at a rate of 50 percent of the normal rate.

As we argued previously, the absence of veto points should enable governments to implement their preferences and effect rapid change motivated by partisan preferences, economic necessity, or both. One can see this in the case of Sweden in the wake of the early 1990s economic crisis, where a coalition of bourgeois parties in the early 1990s cut health spending and then social democratic governments continued these cuts until 2000 before increasing spending again. In this case, the absence of veto points enabled governments of different partisan colors to respond aggressively to the economic crisis and turn double-digit budget deficits into budget surpluses in less than a decade.

One can see a similar development in labor market policy. The development of unemployment replacement rates is indicative of overall labor market policy (see online appendix). During the crisis years of the 1990s both the Social Democrats and the bourgeois coalition agreed that the replacement rate had to be cut as a cost saving measure. The bourgeois government of 1991–1994 reduced the replacement rate from 90 percent to 80 percent. The following

---

[9] This account is based on Schludi (2005), Palme (2003), Anderson and Immergut (2006), and interviews by the authors with interest group and party representative in May 1992.

Social Democratic government further reduced it to 75 percent. Once the budget balance was restored, the Social Democrats raised the replacement rate back to 80 percent. The bourgeois government elected in 2006 lowered the replacement rate to 70 percent. This action was not motivated by economic distress; the budget surplus in 2006 was 4 percent of GDP and GDP per capita had grown 4 percent per annum in 2004–2006. The bourgeois coalition motivated the change by an appeal to market liberal principles arguing that "it has to pay to work."

The partisan divide can be seen in other changes to the unemployment benefit system in this period. The ceiling in Swedish unemployment benefits is not indexed to inflation, much less to wage developments, and, in the period under examination, the income of the average production worker (the basis for Figure 10.3 and the figures in the online appendix) periodically pushed above the ceiling. The social democratic governments increased the ceiling in 1997 and 2001, in contrast to the bourgeois governments of 2006 to the present. The social democratic government also raised the ceiling for the first one hundred days of unemployment; this was promptly reversed by the new bourgeois government in 2007 (Ferrarini et al. 2012: 36).

10.4. Conclusion

We have demonstrated that problem pressures have forced welfare state reforms designed to put programs on a fiscally sound basis by controlling costs and raising employment levels in all countries. Yet, these reforms have differed markedly in their inclusiveness and distributive impact. We have argued that partisanship has continued to play an important role in shaping policies, despite the weight of policy legacies and problem pressures and the obstacles to translation of partisan preferences into policies presented by veto points and the necessity of coalition formation. In fact, in our earlier work we may well have underestimated the continuing strength of partisan influences (Stephens, Huber, and Ray 1999; Huber and Stephens 2001), in part because we focused on policy output and consequences, and in part because the Nordic economic crisis seemed to endanger the strongest cases for the impact of Left strength. In addition, efforts to meet the qualifying conditions for the European Monetary Union constrained policy choices in many European countries. With the benefit of hindsight, we can see that in the aftermath of the Nordic economic crisis and of New Labour's rise to power in Britain, partisan differences reasserted themselves visibly in the shape of new welfare state policies.

By focusing more on the process than the outcome of policy making, we have been able to identify multiple paths to the muting of partisan preferences in outcomes. In some cases, governments were forced to drop ideologically inspired plans by popular resistance to cuts of broad-based programs (Conservatives in the United Kingdom on SERPS). In other cases, partisan preferences were molded into compromise measures internally within coalition governments that spanned political blocs (Netherlands; Grand Coalition in Germany). In still other cases, they were modified through bargaining between governments and opposition where veto points provided the opposition with leverage (Germany). In countries with clear partisan majorities and an absence of veto points, though, the differences between Left and Right governments continued to leave a strong mark on the generosity, inclusiveness, and distributive character of social consumption. The next chapter shifts the focus to social investment policies.

The Dynamics of Social Investment: Human Capital, Activation, and Care

Jane Gingrich and Ben W. Ansell

In recent decades, the language of "social investment" has entered the vocabularies of policy makers and academics alike. Social investment policies stand in sharp distinction to two alternatives: social consumption policies and neoliberal economic policies. Whereas social consumption policies, such as unemployment benefits and pensions, aim to mitigate the economic risks of income loss by providing redistributive transfers and insurance, social investment policies emphasize the supply side of the economy. By providing education, employment, and training services to citizens, from the very young through to the working age population, they promise to halt the proliferation of low-end jobs, to reduce inequality and poverty, and to underpin long-run economic growth. In the language of many prominent advocates of social investment, these policies deliver a "win-win": addressing the poverty and dislocation of neoliberal labor markets, while harnessing these markets' potential for growth in a postindustrial global economy (Esping-Andersen 2000).

However, as is often the case, the reality of social investment policies has been more varied than the enthusiasm around them might suggest. This chapter focuses on the political determinants of social investment policies. Over the past three decades, while the overall percentage of GDP that OECD countries devote to education, family policy, and active labor market policy has grown, it has remained relatively constant as a percentage of total spending. Moreover, the countries at the top of the social investment league, the Nordic countries, have a history of such spending that long predates the current emphasis on investment. Indeed, recent assessments of social investment policies, while lauding their potential, have advanced more pessimistic conclusions (Jenson 2009; Morel, Palier, and Palme 2012).

This pattern raises several questions: Why have social investment policies emerged more forcefully in some contexts than others? What explains the particular patterns of investment? What are the implications of these trends for economic and political life across advanced capitalist economies?

To answer these questions, we make several claims. First, we conceptualize social investment policies as a set of distributive policies that have both individual and collective consequences. Social investment policies deliver specific benefits to individuals that can be more or less egalitarian or fiscally progressive. However, social investment policies also alter the structure of labor markets. Whereas social consumption policies "decommodify" workers, social investment policies "recommodify" them by supporting market competition rather than replacing it. This recommodification can collectively increase wages and improve working conditions for workers, but it can also create more competition among workers and benefit employers. The emphasis on social investment as a "win-win" policy obscures how different forms of social investment create sharply different winners. Second, we argue that policies alone do not have set distributional consequences. Whether a policy is progressive or regressive, or collectively prolabor or proemployer depends on a given national context: in particular the structures of existing policy provision and of the labor market. Third, we argue that political parties seize on these differences, engaging in social investment policies that serve both ideological and electoral ends by attracting new voters while shoring up existing support coalitions.

We begin by briefly outlining the history of social investment policies and then develop our key claim that social investment policies are distributive policies whose relative attractiveness to political parties depends on the preexisting shape of the policy area and labor market. We then move to examining three core areas of social investment: family policy, education, and active labor market policies for working-age adults. For each case we present statistical findings, and a brief case examining how politicians employed social investment policies to achieve electoral and ideological aims. We conclude with a discussion of the likely future of the social investment agenda.

11.1. Social Investment: What It Is and Where It Comes From

The language of social investment grew out of both academic and policy research looking to "modernize" advanced welfare states. Through the 1980s and 1990s, the growing costs of maturing social programs, combined with fiscal constraints, high unemployment, global competition, and slowing productivity growth, prompted concerns about the sustainability of social spending. These concerns dovetailed with an emerging critique of the impact of social spending on job creation and unemployment (OECD 1994). In response, neoliberal prescriptions for cutting benefits and liberalizing labor markets became commonplace. Yet, next to these pressures for cutbacks, scholars and advocates were also pointing to "new social risks" such as long-term unemployment, divorce, and child poverty that many welfare states failed to cover (Taylor-Gooby 2004).

Social investment policies emerged, in part, to address these new challenges. These policies aimed to achieve social goals – lower poverty, social inclusion, gender equity – through longer-term investments in individual skills rather than direct income transfers. Most social investment policies aimed to enhance general skills (through formal education from preschool to university and retraining programs) and promote an adaptable labor market able to absorb newly skilled entrants. In emphasizing women's labor force participation, benefits for young children, and work incentives for working-age adults, these policies targeted groups marginalized by traditional social programs.

These policies shifted away from Esping-Andersen's (1990) ideal of "decommodification." In contrast to high spending on labor market insiders, social investment policies aimed at a broader strategy of "flexicurity" that harnessed greater labor market flexibility, the transition from manufacturing to services, and the wage premium from "skill biased technological change" to achieve social ends. As such, these policies emphasized a "recommodification" of workers that moved beyond the neoliberal vision of the market, calling for an activist state that could enable workers in the short run and transform markets to promote better jobs in the long run. To borrow Kathleen Thelen's (2012) term, the model promoted "embedded flexibilization": promoting more competitive markets while harnessing the benefits of competition for workers themselves (Boix 1998; Morel, Palier, and Palme 2012).

There is substantial evidence that social investment policies worked as intended. At the individual level, a large body of economic literature confirms the private returns to human capital investment (Goldin and Katz 2009). At the country level, Nelson and Stephens (2012) find a positive relationship among a range of social investment policies, the consequent level of general skills, and both overall employment and employment in high skilled jobs. Indeed, through the late 1990s and 2000s, the highly educated Nordic countries experienced high growth without the dramatically rising inequality plaguing other parts of the OECD (Pontusson 2005).

Despite these apparent benefits, OECD countries have not adopted social investment policies wholesale. Table 11.1 displays total public spending, as a percentage of GDP, for twenty-one advanced industrial countries on the three core social investment policies examined in this paper: family policy, education, and active labor market policy. We sort countries into four groups based on their historic welfare and labor market structures: liberal countries (Australia, Canada, Ireland, New Zealand, the United Kingdom, the United States, and Japan), Nordic countries (Denmark, Finland, Norway, and Sweden), continental European countries (Austria, Belgium, France, Germany, the Netherlands, and Switzerland), and Southern European countries (Greece, Italy, Portugal, and Spain).[1]

---

[1] We group Japan with the Liberal countries, despite its commonalities with Continental labor markets, because of its limited levels of social spending in both social consumption and investment.

TABLE 11.1. *Social investment spending*

	Social Investment Spending (Percentage GDP)		Social Investment (Percentage Govt. Spending)		Family Policy (Percentage GDP/Govt.)	Education (Percentage GDP/Govt.)	ALMP (Percentage GDP/Govt.)
	1985–1989	2000–2005	1985–1989	2000–2005	2007	2006	2005
Australia	6.3	8.0	37.0	35.8	2.4 / 10.7	4.8 / 21.5	0.4 / 1.8
Canada	7.5	.	32.6		1.0	.	0.3
Ireland	8.0	7.9	31.4	36.7	2.6 / 12.1	4.8 / 22.3	0.6 / 2.8
New Zealand	8.7	9.2	35.4	36.8	3.0 / 12.0	6.2 / 24.8	0.4 / 1.6
United Kingdom	7.7	8.0	32.6	31.3	3.2 / 12.5	5.6 / 21.9	0.5 / 2.0
United States	6.0	6.2	32.6	28.8	0.7 / 3.3	5.7 / 26.5	0.1 / 0.5
Japan	.	4.6	.	21.7	0.8 / 3.8	3.5 / 16.5	0.3 / 1.4
Denmark	10.7	14.1	34.2	40.0	3.3 / 9.4	7.9 / 22.4	1.7 / 4.8
Finland	8.7	10.1	31.0	32.1	2.8 / 8.9	6.1 / 19.4	0.9 / 2.9
Norway	9.3	10.5	32.9	36.9	2.8 / 9.8	6.5 / 22.8	0.7 / 2.5
Sweden	12.8	11.9	35.2	32.5	3.4 / 9.3	6.9 / 18.8	1.3 / 3.6
Austria	8.8	9.1	29.7	27.9	2.6 / 8.0	5.4 / 16.6	0.6 / 1.8
Belgium	8.8	9.3	28.8	28.7	2.6 / 8.0	6 / 18.5	1.1 / 3.4
Germany		7.9		25.1	3.0 / 9.5	5.6 / 17.8	0.9 / 2.9
France	8.6	9.2	27.7	26.7	1.8 / 5.2	4.4 / 12.8	1.0 / 2.9
Netherlands	9.4	8.3	30.3	31.2	2.0 / 7.5	5.5 / 20.7	1.3 / 4.9
Switzerland	6.1	7.1	31.2	29.8	1.3 / 5.5	5.5 / 23.1	0.7 / 2.9
Greece	2.7	4.8	15.1	20.4	1.1 / 4.7	4 / 17.0	0.1 / 0.4
Italy		6.2		21.3	1.4 / 4.8	4.7 / 16.1	0.6 / 2.1
Portugal		7.1	30.8	26.5	1.2 / 4.5	5.3 / 19.8	0.7 / 2.6
Spain	4.3	5.6	20.3	22.5	1.2 / 4.8	4.3 / 17.3	0.8 / 3.2

Across all four groups we see a slight rise in social investment spending from 1985 through 2005, even as the number of younger citizens has remained stable. More striking, however, are the ongoing differences among countries. Since 2000, each of the Nordic countries has spent more than 10 percent of GDP on social investment policies, a figure no other country reaches. Moreover, despite increasing spending, the Southern European countries still spend just half the level of the Nordic countries. Finally, the liberal countries (excluding Japan) and the continental countries spend around 8 percent of national income, with the former slightly below and the latter slightly above that threshold. These cross-national patterns hold up not just in the aggregate but also individually for family policy, education, and active labor market policy spending.

Furthermore, social investment has not displaced traditional social consumption. Table 11.1 shows relatively constant ratios of social investment spending as a percentage of total public spending, as increases in more traditional consumption items – particularly health and pensions – have offset absolute spending increases on social investment.

11.2. The Distributive Politics of Social Investment

What explains these cross-national and temporal differences in social investment spending? Why have social investment policies not displaced social consumption policies? To understand why and when social investment is attractive to politicians, we argue that we need to theorize the individual and collective distributive consequences of a given policy in a given environment. Political parties build on these differences; thus policies will be more or less favorable to left- and right-wing parties across contexts. This multifaceted distributive nature of social investment helps explain the often-piecemeal policy adoption within and across countries.

Our theoretical approach begins with a simple premise. In selecting a policy, parties do not just follow the preferences of existing constituents, but look to create new coalitions around their broader distributive goals. All parties would like to introduce policy that aligns the interests of new voters with those of the party while also delivering benefits to the base. That is, parties are both opportunistic and ideological.

In general terms we can identify two main categories of parties: the "Left," which historically draws on a working-class base and tends to prefer policies that distribute resources toward lower-income voters (progressive policies), and the "Right," which draws on the support of employers and wealthier voters and tends to prefer policies that distribute resources toward high-income voters (regressive policies).

Parties, however, do not face a stable configuration of potential voters. Instead, demographic and economic shifts have upset old cleavages, presenting parties with both threats – declines in their traditional voting base – and opportunities – new unattached groups of potential voters (Dalton 2000; Kitschelt and Rehm, this volume). For the Left, globalization and deindustrialization have reduced both the size of the manufacturing workforce and the political strength of unions while greater public fiscal constraints have slowed the growth in the public sector workforce – shrinking two of its traditional bases. At the same time, new groups, possibly sympathetic to the Left, have emerged: working women, sociocultural professionals, and nonunionized labor market "outsiders" (Häusermann 2010). For the Right, particularly Christian Democrats, social change has also eroded some traditional support bases – stay-at-home mothers, farmers, small businesses – but again there are potentially sympathetic rising groups: managerial professionals and socially conservative blue-collar workers.

The policies that parties used to attract and retain traditional supporters have also often lost economic or political efficacy. Through the postwar era, the Left promoted activist macroeconomic management and full employment policies. In response to both the stagflationary 1970s and broader deindustrialization, the Left first turned toward public employment and social consumption policies. However, such policies imply high rates of taxation and centralized wage restraint by unions, both of which became more politically challenging for the Left as its working-class base shrank. For the Right, particularly Christian Democrats, the massive entry of women into the workforce created new demands for previously unprovided social goods – child care, maternity benefits, and higher education access for women – destabilizing traditional "male breadwinner" models of social provision. Furthermore, high-income individuals, previous bedrocks of the Right's support, began to turn away from its calls for tax and spending cuts, or stratifying social consumption policies, in favor of postmaterialist Left parties.

Social investment policies both deliver specific goods to individuals (e.g., parental leave, training, higher education) and can reshape the labor market. As such, parties can use them both to attract voters and to compensate for the reduced efficacy of traditional social consumption policies. A "win-win" policy for the Left would deliver benefits tilted toward lower-income voters and improve labor market conditions for unions and workers more generally, allowing it to provide specific benefits to new voting groups while improving working conditions for its base. A "win-win" policy for the Right, by contrast, would deliver benefits tilted to higher-income voters, while also making labor market conditions more flexible or beneficial for employers.

However, "win-win" social investment policies are not always politically possible: Existing policy and labor market structures can limit the ability of a given party to target new constituents or negotiate change with existing constituents. Two features of the existing environment shape the capacity of policy makers to achieve their goals. First, the existing policy structure shapes whether parties can target benefits progressively or regressively, and thus align new voters with their core goals. Second, the existing labor market structure – whether it is integrated or dualized – shapes whether a given policy will increase wage dispersion (thus hurting existing workers but helping employers) or will support high wages across the labor market (helping workers but potentially costing employers).[2]

Where expanding social investment will both be fiscally progressive and homogeneously increase the wages of workers, the Left has a strong incentive to introduce it. By contrast, where expanding such programs will both be fiscally regressive and increase wage heterogeneity, the Right is more likely to do so (although, the Right is generally more cautious about increasing public spending).

However, oftentimes parties face cross-pressuring environments. Where policies benefit low-income individuals but may increase wage dispersion, the Left's base (labor market "insiders") are likely to push against expanding social investment policies, while its broader ideological and electoral interests push for more spending (Rueda 2007). Symmetrically, the Left is also cross-pressured when social investment policies support homogeneous wage structures but are fiscally regressive.

By contrast, policies that are regressive but place costs on employers cross-pressure the Right – expanding such programs could attract voters and further the Right's broader goals, but also hurt employers by increasing labor costs (through taxes or wages). Where spending is progressive but promises to weaken labor market insiders, the Right is also cross-pressured between aligning the interests of new voters with the party's overall goals and delivering benefits to their base.

Thus to understand its individual and collective distributive consequences, we need to look at how a social investment policy works in a given context. First, to distinguish whether increased spending is progressive or not, we need to examine the distributive impact of an additional Euro of spending. Sometimes that Euro will be spent on a relatively poorer citizen, making the policy more fiscally progressive and hence preferable for left-wing parties. Programs such as preschool for low-income children, employment and training services for unemployed workers, and universal education tend to have this impact. Conversely, sometimes the next Euro of spending will go to relatively richer citizens, making the policy fiscally regressive, and more attractive to the Right, for instance, public spending on higher education in countries with limited enrollment (Ansell 2008), maternity benefits tied to income, and training programs targeted at employers.

Second, the collective consequences of social investment policies also vary across labor markets. Where social investment programs increase training or skills in a high-participation "integrated" labor market, they may increase the "reservation wage" at the low end of the labor market. In this situation,

---

[2] Thelen (2012) makes a similar argument about how existing institutional structures shape coalitions and change political strategies.

TABLE 11.2. *Social investment policies and partisan preferences*

Type of Labor Market	Impact of Policy Expansion on Individuals	
	Progressive	Regressive
Integrated	LEFT: EXPAND SI RIGHT: LIMIT SI	CROSS-PRESSURE
Dualized	CROSS-PRESSURE	LEFT: LIMIT SI RIGHT: EXPAND SI

spending benefits labor as a whole by increasing the skill set of existing and future workers. Iversen and Stephens (2008) argue that skill formation and wage coordination are interlinked components of more egalitarian welfare states. This potential for complementarity between egalitarian wage policy and human capital is likely to be especially attractive for Left parties. Conversely, for the Right, new benefits in these labor markets are likely to deliver straight costs to employers without necessarily providing gains. Even where expanding some benefits – such as parental leave – may be regressive at the outset, these policies place high costs on employers (through higher taxes) without increasing the marginal productivity of workers. This spending then, can collectively harm the Right's constituents in the labor market even where the beneficiaries of spending are upper-income voters.

By contrast, where these same programs activate large numbers of existing outsiders in "dualized" labor markets, they may create more wage competition at the low end of the labor market, potentially undermining the protections of existing workers. In more dualized labor markets, social investment policies can collectively threaten labor, even if spending is progressive, by undercutting the wage premium to labor, particular "insiders" (Rueda 2007). In such situations, left-wing parties feel cross-pressured. Employers, however, do stand to gain from activation (through a more competitive labor market) in a more dualized economy even if they face some new tax costs, making such shifts more attractive for the Right.

Thus, the Left and the Right face different trade-offs depending on the existing policy and labor market structure. Where policies offer a "win-win" or a "lose-lose" set of outcomes for a given party, the predictions are relatively clear. Table 11.2 suggests that the Left will expand fiscally progressive policies in integrated labor markets while the Right will expand regressive policies in dualized labor markets. Where parties are cross-pressured, we expect less overall reform and less clear partisan effects, as cross-cutting coalitions are likely to mobilize around change (Häusermann 2010). However, since the argument is conditional, these more incremental expansions can create an impetus for future change – for instance, the expansion of funding for higher education could tip a system from being regressive to progressive.

We show how these conditional partisan dynamics play out in the following sections. We first examine the conditioning effect of the labor market in family policy, followed by the conditioning effect of the progressivity of spending in education, and finally, the joint effects of the labor market and spending progressivity in shaping active labor market policy.

11.3. Family Policy

Family policy, in particular early childhood education and care, is a central component of the social investment agenda. Family policies include transfers to families through child allowances and tax breaks, provision and subsidization of child care and early childhood education, and paid and unpaid leaves for parents (Jenson 2009). Family policy coincides with the social investment agenda in two ways: It promotes the human capital of women by encouraging them to stay in the labor force, and it promotes the development of children by reducing poverty and developing their cognitive skills. Historically, only a few countries engaged in mass family policies (Morgan 2006). However, in recent years, the EU, individual countries, and a range of policy experts have advocated family policies (e.g., Heckman and Masterov 2007; Esping Andersen 2000).

Moreover, in many countries, there is substantial, often untapped, public demand for these policies. Figure 11.1a shows the average responses among women to two questions in the 2008 European Social Survey: how much responsibility should the government have to provide child care and respondents' assessment of overall provision of affordable child care (running from very poor to very good). The Nordic countries fall in the top right corner with female respondents both preferring government support for child care and feeling satisfied with family policies. By contrast, women in liberal welfare states (the United Kingdom, Ireland, and Switzerland) are less supportive of both (albeit, with still relatively high levels of support). The most interesting cases, however, are those in which women desire government spending on child care but do not feel existing policies support it. These cases of mismatch present an opportunity for politicians to attract female voters.

Why do some policy makers take advantage of growing demand for family policy while others do not? Understanding these choices requires examining how Left and Right parties' generic goals fit with the existing labor market structure. Where female labor force participation is already relatively high (in an integrated labor market) supporting women's employment is unlikely to reduce the wages of existing insiders but is likely to place new costs on employers. By contrast, in dualized labor markets where women's employment is low, policies that activate female workers can harm existing workers by expanding competition for jobs, potentially benefiting employers. Referring to Figure 11.1, we see that the gap between respondents' preferences and policy evaluations is greatest in countries with highly dualized labor markets, where such policies

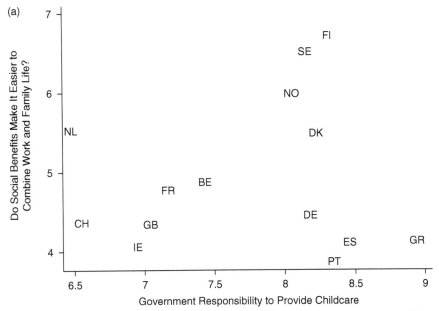

FIGURE 11.1a. Female preferences over child care and judgments over social policy and work/family balance.
(European Social Survey 2008)

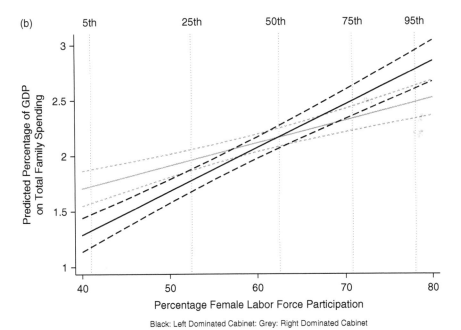

b. Estimated effects of partisanship on parental leave at different levels of female labor force participation.

create difficult trade-offs for politicians on the Left and opportunities for those on the Right.[3]

We now test more broadly how the labor market conditions party strategy over family policy. We examine family policy spending for twenty-one OECD countries between 1980 and 2006, using data drawn from the OECD Social Expenditures database. We examine the impact on family policy of political partisanship – using a 5 point scale of cabinet partisanship developed by Armingeon et al. (2008), increasing in left-wing control – *conditional* on the labor market context: the level of female labor force participation. For ease of interpretation, we present graphical simulations of our key results in Figure 11.1b.[4] This graph displays both the predicted levels of spending for Left- and Right-dominated cabinets at differing levels of female labor force participation and 95 percent confidence intervals. The in-sample distribution of female labor force participation is indicated by dotted vertical lines.

Figure 11.1b demonstrates that under both Left- and Right-dominated cabinets family spending rises as female labor force participation rises. However, the effect is far larger for Left parties than for Right parties – indeed at levels below the median female labor force participation, we estimate that Right-dominated cabinets are likely to have higher family policy spending than Left parties, with this pattern reversing for above-median female labor force participation.[5]

Put simply, in dualized labor markets with accordingly fewer women in the workforce, right-wing parties appear more interested in this form of social investment policy, whereas as the labor market becomes more integrated, left-wing parties are higher family policy spenders. Indeed, in dualized labor markets it may not be in the interest of left-wing parties to provide further spending *even if* they would be happy to do so in a more integrated labor market. This pattern helps to explain the "lock-in" effect of social investment policy

---

[3] Family policies also have varied distributive consequences. Although much family spending flows to low-income users, certain policies can be regressive. For example, low-income women are often less likely to take an unpaid or low-paid leave, skewing the benefits of these leaves to higher-income women. Equally, child allowances can be targeted regressively, for example, with large tax deductions for high earners or 'cash for care' schemes. Finally, although daycare spending can be targeted to low-income users (such as Head Start in the US), higher income women, who are more likely to be in the labor force, are often the first to take advantage of daycare at low levels of spending. As spending expands, however, it becomes more redistributive, extending to lower-income women who begin to work.

[4] We conducted a series of dynamic specifications, first a pooled regression with a lagged dependent variable and year dummies, second a Prais-Winston regression with an AR1 error term, and third an error-correction model including lags and changes of each variable. We control for income and other social spending as well as the interactive effects of partisanship and the conditioning variables Results are broadly consistent across these dynamic specifications.

[5] In a separate analysis (not shown) we also find that left-wing governments are more likely to increase spending on daycare provision when enrollment rates are higher and hence spending is likely to be more fiscally progressive, whereas right-wing governments do not increase spending as enrollment rises.

regimes. By contrast, in these situations, right-wing parties may be attracted to family policy. The case of Germany demonstrates this dynamic.

11.3.1. Case Study: Family Policy in Germany

The example of the family policy reforms of the Christian Democratic Union–Social Democratic Party (CDU-SPD) grand coalition, led by Angela Merkel, effectively demonstrates how once-anathema policies have been used to attract new constituencies while achieving the broader redistributive and labor market goals of the center-right. Although the grand coalition of 2005 to 2009 included both the Christian Democratic Union and the Social Democratic Party, one of the CDU's rising stars, Ursula von der Leyen – minister for family affairs, senior citizens, women and youth, pushed forward family policy. The policy both responded to partisan objectives to reduce fiscal progressivity and labor market rigidities, and to electoral objectives in terms of developing CDU support among working women.

By the 1990s, the CDU's traditional support base, like that of the SPD, had been undergoing serious erosion. The party risked losing higher-income socially liberal voters to the Greens or FDP, and their traditional constituency of religious women, in particular wives and mothers outside the labor force, was shrinking. Rising female labor force participation was creating new, as yet unfulfilled, demands for family policy. Referring to Figure 11.1a, Germany's position in the bottom right corner suggests women had strong preferences for government supported child care but were dissatisfied with the degree to which government policies offered it. The CDU could rely on neither traditional policies of welfare-state stratification nor a neoliberal turn to deregulation to address these demands. Family policy provided a means of attracting these new groups of voters by both benefiting higher-income voters and stimulating the labor market *outside* the unionized working-class base of the SPD.

The von der Leyen reforms consisted of four core reforms: tax allowances for child care, family allowances tied to income (*Elterngeld*), paternity leave, and the mass expansion of day care facilities. These policies in combination greatly facilitated the entry and reentry of mothers into the workforce through the subsidization of both maternity leaves and child care. As such the reforms clearly targeted female voters, especially those entering the workforce for the first time. By encouraging female labor-market "outsiders" to participate in the labor force (through the now reduced costs of maternity and child care), the CDU were able to weaken further the predominant role of male working-class unionized insiders in structuring wage and benefit levels in the German labor market – potentially benefiting employers (Fleckstein and Seeleib-Kaiser 2011).

Moreover, the distributive balance of these reforms met the CDU's ideological goals. The *Elterngeld* provided up to 67 percent of previous income as postpartum support, replacing a flat payment that had disproportionately benefited poorer families. Erler (2009) notes that left-wing critics castigated the

Elterngeld as being disproportionately targeted toward high earners. Indeed, the original idea had emerged from the Green Party (von Wahl 2008), whose higher-income socially liberal constituents the CDU was keen to catch. To be sure, the policy was not without in-party critics – in particular there was vociferous opposition from religious conservatives and supporters of the traditional male breadwinner model. Nonetheless, the CDU was able to build family policy in ways favorable to its ends in the labor market (and in distributive terms). Wiliarty (2010) notes that even though family policy "began as an SPD policy, it is now very clearly the domain of the CDU."

11.4. Education

The single largest element of the "social investment agenda" is a policy area that long predates it: public education. Most advanced industrial countries spend more than 5 percent of national income on education and increasingly define it as a core component of the welfare state. In contrast to the threat of cutbacks that many "social consumption" policies – namely, pensions and unemployment benefits – face, education has been spared from aggressive cuts by policy makers. Indeed, policy makers across the political spectrum have often touted investment in "human capital" as key to postindustrial production, with improved education of workers contributing to raising wages for workers and to meeting the ever-growing demand of business for educated workers in an increasingly skill-based economic structure (Goldin and Katz 1998).

The public, too, has demanded more investment in education, pushing governments' spending. Figure 11.2a demonstrates the close connection between citizens' preferences for greater education spending and increases in actual spending. Using survey data from the International Social Survey Program in 1990, 1996, and 2006, the x-axis shows the average national support in a given year for greater education spending (on a 5 point survey scale), and the y-axis shows the annualized change in per student education spending following the survey for 1990–1995, 1995–2000, and 2005–2008. Two points are worth noting. Figure 11.2a shows a close fit between preferences for more spending and actual spending following the survey: a correlation of 0.56. The greatest changes have occurred in the liberal countries – indicating that education has been the key area of social investment expansion in these countries, whereas the Nordic countries, which already were already major investors in education, have stability. Despite a close fit between public demands and government activity, the relationship is not unambiguous, as the case of the United Kingdom shows. During the Conservative governments of 1990 and 1996 citizens expressed a strong preference for greater education spending but it was only under New Labour that spending increased substantially.[6] This pattern suggests important partisan effects in education spending.

---

[6] British public opinion had thus been 'mismatched' with policy in the 1990s – indeed, removing the UK from the data increases the correlation to 0.72.

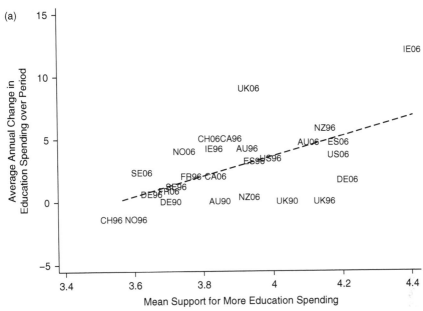

FIGURE 11.2a. Preferences over education spending and changes in spending.

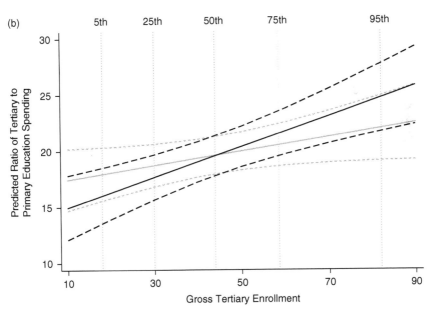

Black: Left Dominated Cabinet; Grey: Right Dominated Cabinet

b. Effect of partisanship (Armingeon) on tertiary/primary spending ratio at various gross tertiary enrollment levels.

Indeed, a substantial literature has emerged arguing precisely this point: Public education spending is not solely a function of public (or expert) demands, but also of the preferences of partisan actors (Castles 1989; Boix 1998; Busemeyer 2009; Ansell 2008, 2010). The underlying assumption in much of this work is that in aggregate education spending is fiscally progressive and hence favored by the Left. However, whether spending is progressive or not depends on the existing program structure. When spending is directed toward a program that is universal in nature – for example, primary education – it will typically be fiscally progressive and favored by the Left. However, in some cases – higher education in systems with limited enrollments – the spending may in fact be regressive (Ansell 2008; but see Busemeyer 2009; and Iversen and Stephens 2008). In this case, it is unlikely that left-wing parties will support expansion, as such spending is likely to benefit wealthier citizens.[7]

In order to test the conditioning effect of policy progressivity, Figure 11.2b demonstrates how the existing structure of higher education policy shapes the strategies of political parties. It shows the predicted ratio of public spending on tertiary education vis-à-vis primary education between 1970 and 2006, for Left- and Right-dominated governments, conditional on the level of enrollment in higher education.[8] When higher education enrollment is low, below 25 percent – Right parties are more likely to increase spending than Left parties, whereas once higher education spending becomes mass – above gross enrollments of 60 percent – left-wing governments appear to favor increased spending. Thus, this element of the social investment agenda may remain unfulfilled *even though* were higher education enrollments to be larger the Left would certainly favor increased spending. However, as higher education systems increase in their enrollment size, public spending on higher education moves from regressive to progressive (Ansell 2008, 2010). This shift in the distributive consequences of spending helps to explain varying patterns of support across parties, as parties' strategies are conditional on the existing structure.

11.4.1. Case Study: Higher Education in the United Kingdom

New Labour's reforms to the British higher education system between 1997 and 2003 provide a telling example of how partisan preferences changed in response to changes in the economy and potential coalitions of political support. In the 1990s, Britain was at the forefront of the broader transition to postindustrial economic structures. Manufacturing had collapsed during the 1980s to be replaced by a growing high value-added service sector, centered on business and financial services, and a large low-skilled service sector, centered

---

[7] There are also potential labor market costs to doing so. More limited higher education systems are more common in countries with dualized labor markets, in which the Left is generally more concerned with supporting labor market insiders with vocational, not higher, education.

[8] This figure shows the same pattern found in Ansell 2008 but extends the endpoint from 1999 to 2006. As with Figure 11.1b, predicted effects come from a Prais-Winston regression with AR1 errors.

on retail and hospitality. This transition produced an increased bipolarity in Britain between "lovely" and "lousy" jobs, in Goos and Manning's (2007) evocative terms. Facing this economic transition, a New Labour government elected in 1997, seeking to reduce the inequality of the Thatcher years, focused on social investment policies in education that provided general skills both in compulsory schooling and at university. This pattern is quite clear in the analysis of responsiveness to public opinion in Figure 11.2a. The aim was jointly to increase the returns to basic education and to provide opportunity for working- and middle-class children to attend university and take advantage of the growing demand for degrees in the service sector. In the meantime New Labour had also shifted its electoral base away from the shrinking working class and toward a coalition of university-educated sociocultural professional and labor market outsiders – women, ethnic minorities, and unskilled service sector workers. Along with investment in basic education, higher education policy provided a means to tie these new groups to New Labour.

Higher education, however, was traditionally a tricky policy area for the Labour Party. Before the 1980s it had been limited to fewer than 10 percent of the population, most of whom were upscale Conservative voters. Labour had expressed little interest in expanding universities during its governments of the 1960s and 1970s. The Conservative Party, in fact, had been the proponents of expansion in the 1980s. As enrollments became larger and the working-class base became smaller, Labour viewed universities differently. No longer the preserve of the elite they might instead reach swing middle-class voters, urban ethnic minorities, and above all women – entering the labor force and university at ever larger numbers. The problem Labour faced was that even though there were attractive labor market consequences of expanding higher education, overall its funding was regressive, taxing all wage earners to provide free tuition and maintenance to wealthier citizens.

New Labour's higher education reforms of 1998 and 2004 appeared paradoxical on the surface – here was an ostensibly left-wing party introducing, then raising, tuition fees. However, New Labour viewed tuition fees as a way to *increase* progressivity of higher education, while mitigating their incidence on lower-income students. The introduction of fees meant resources were provided by wealthier citizens (students and their families) rather than general revenues. Moreover, a series of bursaries were created for poorer students, access promotion requirements were established for universities, and a conditional loan repayment system was created such that graduates who earned less had lower repayments. Meanwhile a 50 percent enrollment figure was established to encourage expansion of student numbers. Putting these parts together New Labour was able to expand the university system to attract new constituencies and simultaneously increase the progressivity of the policy. Social investment allowed Labour to achieve its usual objectives in unusual fashion.

11.5. Active Labor Market Policy

Active labor market policies (ALMP), including job search services, training, employment incentives, and support, aim to achieve the underlying promise of social investment: to develop a near fully employed workforce with marketable and adaptable skills with appropriately substantial remuneration. Many contrast these policies with so-called passive labor market policies that protect the jobs and income of individuals who currently have jobs (Rueda 2007). Whereas passive labor market policies decommodify workers by reducing their exposure to labor market risk, arguably active labor market policies *recommodify* those outside the labor market by providing them with subsidized temporary employment and training to make them more marketable to employers.

As Bonoli (2010) notes, ALMP policies predate the "social investment" agenda by several decades. In particular, Nordic countries, above all Sweden, have long promoted policies intended to increase the size and quality of labor supply (Stephens 1979). As the social investment agenda emerged in the 1990s, however, policy makers shifted their attention to two key areas of active labor market policy: training and employment services. Training policies aim to provide employers with a subsidized skilled workforce, make unemployed workers more likely to find work, while also boosting wages of employed workers. Employment services aim to discourage workers from passive reliance on tax-funded benefits, boost the incomes of unemployed workers, and provide employers with a cheap subsidized workforce.

As with family policy and education, though, underneath this seeming "win-win" for economic growth and workers lie real trade-offs. First, at the collective level, active labor market policies often have ambiguous, even negative, effects on labor market insiders. Despite their small size in terms of funding, they can act as the "thin end of the wedge" of greater liberalization.

Figure 11.3a shows this difference in support for passive versus active labor market policies between industrial insiders and the growing group of "sociocultural professionals" (SCPs) in the service sector. This graph uses two questions on the International Social Survey Program "Role of Government" module (1996, 2006) asking citizens whether they support "aid to declining industries" (passive spending) and "government financing projects for new jobs" (active spending).[9] It shows the percentage of respondents who express a higher level of support for declining industries than job creation, compared to those who prefer job creation. While the latter is not a perfect measure of ALMPs, in almost every country we see that blue-collar workers are more positively inclined toward passive policies than SCPs. We also see sharp cross-national differences – with ALMPs more relatively popular in liberal market economies and Nordic countries than in the dualized labor markets of continental Europe and Japan. Since their core support group is labor market insiders,

---

[9] Coding of blue collar and SCPs comes from Häusermann (2010).

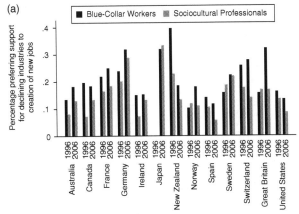

FIGURE II.3a. Support for declining industries versus government creation of jobs.

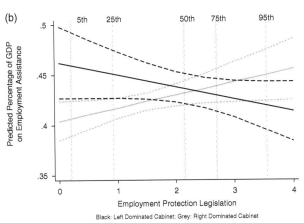

b. Effects of partisanship on spending on employment assistance conditional on EPL.

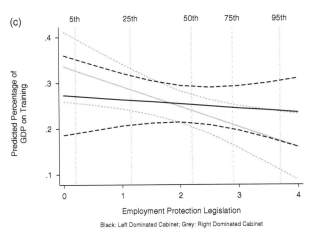

c. Effects of partisanship on spending on training conditional on EPL.

left-wing governments need to take into account the fact that some ALMP policies potentially undermine insiders by encouraging low-wage competition from the previously unemployed.

Second, at the individual level, the distributive consequences of policies vary depending on how they are targeted. Here, progressivity may be less important per se than whether benefits are largely to insiders or outsiders. Personal employment services are almost always fiscally progressive since they are focused directly on the unemployed, but are also prooutsider. Subsidies to employers supporting hiring new workers, by contrast, may be regressive if the subsidy is deadweight loss given employers who might have hired without subsidization. Equally, for some forms of training, unions might harness them and target them to labor market insiders, producing a regressive fiscal effect.

These dynamics suggest trade-offs for parties based on the existing labor market and policy structure. The most comprehensive quantitative work on the determinants of ALMP policies is from Rueda (2006, 2007), who argues for precisely such a *conditional* effect of government partisanship. Whereas Rueda expects left-wing governments to expand passive labor market policies, he argues that their preferences over active labor market policies are likely to be ambiguous and depend on the policy environment. Where such policies help poor "outsiders" but hurt unionized "insiders," left-wing parties will be cross-pressured. In general, the extent of the insider-outsider trade-off will be highest where labor markets are the most dualized by high levels of employment protection legislation (EPL) (Emmenegger et al. 2012). Here, the competitive threat of activation on insiders is highest, creating cross-pressures for left-wing parties for most types of ALMP spending. Hence, in high EPL environments, left-wing parties may want lower spending on activation. Right parties, by contrast, will be more supportive of activation policies the higher is the level of employment protection, as this undermines insider power. However, there are some types of ALMP that can be targeted more extensively to insiders. Training is a good example. In low EPL environments, such training is likely to be aimed at those out of the workforce. However, in high EPL environments upskilling often implies spending on insiders and is typically run with participation by unions. Thus, we expect right-wing parties to be less supportive of training expenditures than left-wing parties in high EPL environments, where insiders can capture them.

Figures 11.3b and 11.3c examine the predicted levels of spending for Left- and Right-dominated cabinets on, respectively, employment services and training, at different levels of EPL.[10] Figure 11.3b begins with employment assistance policies. Here we find confirmation of Rueda's hypothesis, albeit on a larger and more recent data set. At low levels of EPL Left cabinets are predicted to spend substantially more on employment assistance spending. However, as EPL rises, this pattern flips, with Left parties spending marginally

---

[10] As before, we run Prais-Winsten AR1 regressions on twenty-one countries from 1986 to 2006. EPL data comes from the OECD's employment protection index (OECD, 2008).

less than Right parties at the highest levels of EPL. Left-wing parties may broadly favor employment assistance spending because of its fiscal progressivity. However, at high levels of EPL, spending on employment assistance threatens to weaken the position of labor market insiders by providing employers with cheap alternative sources of labor.

Figure 11.3c shows a striking difference when we examine training spending. At low levels of EPL Left parties are not associated with higher training spending than Right parties. In low EPL environments, training may not be controlled by unions and thus constitutes a prooutsider policy that undermines insiders. Conversely, at high levels of EPL, Left parties spend substantially more than do Right parties (significant at the 5 percent level). The proinsider nature of training policies where unions are powerful and employees have less risk of unemployment is more attractive to the Left seeking insider support in such countries. By contrast, training policies are unattractive to the Right in high EPL environments as they reinforce high labor costs for employers.

These patterns are thus broadly supportive of Rueda's conjecture and our discussion of the varied distributive politics of ALMP. Most ALMP policies are, per Rueda, collectively prooutsider and thus only in the Left's interest where EPL is low. However, training policies are arguably proinsider, especially in high EPL environments, and here we see a reversal of the pattern for employment assistance. Thus, the choice of governments to focus on some ALMP policies at the expense of others has been predicated on their particular collective and individual distributive outcomes. As elsewhere, this has often produced piecemeal adoption, with the potentially complementary logic of these policies at the mercy of partisan changes in government.

11.5.1. Case Study: Active Labor Market Policy in the Netherlands
The political coalitions underpinning active labor market policy programs in the Netherlands have shifted over the past few decades as a postindustrial flexibly employed services workforce has replaced the postwar unionized manufacturing workforce. Before the mid-1980s, Dutch policy makers struggled with responding to the collapse in effectiveness of wage setting during the Dutch Disease of the 1970s and the ensuing mass unemployment (Visser and Hemerijk 1997). While a series of bargains struck in the 1980s reduced these macroeconomic struggles, they ushered in new debate over the microeconomics of Dutch labor markets. In particular, policy makers turned their attention to the pathologies of the Dutch public employment services system, which they increasingly saw as a monolithic state bureaucracy serving the chronically unemployed. Dutch politicians during the 1990s sought to shift employment services to an activation-based model to aid job search and training for the newly unemployed, citizens looking to switch jobs, and underserved youth and minority populations. However, the political parties approached this classic

social investment policy area with distinct goals and strategies that responded to the more dualized Dutch labor market.

The first of the major reforms of employment services were introduced by the Christian Democrat (CDA)/Social Democrat (PvDA) coalition government led by Ruud Lubbers (CDA) from 1989 to 1994. CDA ministers also led the Ministry of Social Affairs and Employment during this period, and the 1990 Employment Services Act reflected the party's ideological preferences. The bill decentralized and privatized the existing service and placed it under the administration of the social partners. At the same time, it maintained a trend of increased spending on employment services that began in Lubbers's previous cabinet – a total increase of spending on active labor market policy from 0.7 percent of GDP in 1982 to almost 1.4 percent by 1993 (Rueda 2007). Why did a center-right party drive forward this expansive labor market policy? Despite its nominally progressive fiscal structure, the policy fell into line with the CDA's broader preferences for restructuring the labor market. Whereas the previous service had focused on the chronically unemployed, the new service focused on individuals entering and reentering a more flexible, liberalized labor market. Furthermore, emphasis was placed on employer demand to drive placement and information provision. Finally, the act permitted private agencies to take on placement and advisory roles.

The new structure, however, did not last long. The official van Dijk review of 1995 castigated its administration and performance, accusing the social partners of "rent-seeking" and failing to operate the system on behalf of the unemployed (Visser and Hemerijck 1997). The incoming Purple coalition government led by the PvDA and reformist parties of the Left (D'66) and Right (VVD) removed the social partners from control and recalibrated the system through the Employment Services Act of 1996. The focus of employment policy shifted back to the most marginalized groups and a particular focus on ethnic minorities and the unemployed in major cities. This included creation of so-called Melkert jobs, named after the PvDA minister of social affairs and employment, which were created in large cities with social dislocation problems (Visser and Hemerijck 1997). The scathing van Dijk review partially motivated this policy change. Nonetheless, it also met the electoral goals of Purple coalition partners. The PvDA and D'66 were able to target resources to labor market outsiders in the cities and to ethnic minorities, helping to secure an increasingly urban constituency for both parties. Prooutsider policies such as these had become more electorally viable for the Left as the strength of Dutch employment protection declined over the late 1990s (the OECD EPL indicator declined from 2.73 to 2.12 between 1995 and 1999).

The development of this "flexicurity" labor market model exemplifies the difficulties in expanding social investment policies under single governments. ALMPs expanded dramatically under the Right, partly as a way to weaken insiders in a highly dualized labor market. Once, however, dualization and employment protection had begun to decline, left-wing parties became more interested in using ALMPs to help outsiders since their insider base had become weaker. In this sense, it took the Right to start "flexicurity" but the Left to finish it.

11.6. The Future of the Social Investment Agenda

What are the prospects for the social investment model given our findings? We have argued that the partisan politics of social investment often prevent a comprehensive adoption of the full panoply of social investment policies since their distributive effects are often cross-cutting. These distributive politics are shaped by the existing labor market and policy context, which vary substantially across advanced industrial countries.

In the Nordic countries, a mix of long-standing integrated labor market structures and the unintended consequences of policy choices to activate women created fertile conditions for the Left to push a social investment policy. Here, policies tend to be progressive and push for better conditions for workers as a whole. By contrast, in Southern European countries, the Left gained less from these policies – as they did little for its base or its short-term distributive or labor market goals. In the continental European and liberal countries, the Left has been more cross-pressured, generally engaging in these policies only once broader changes in the labor market or policy environment made social investment more progressive or less threatening to traditional support bases.

The Right, by contrast, has been generally less supportive of spending, but it has spent under favorable circumstances – where it could target the benefits of higher education, training, and vocational training to its voters or its base among employers. While our theory predicts the Right may have a stronger interest in social investment in places like Spain, where a more dualized labor market or regressive policy structures suggest it could gain from these policies, its support of lower taxes likely makes it more cautious overall. In countries with dualized labor markets undergoing substantial transformation, as in the case of female labor force participation in Germany, the Right has, however, employed social investment policies as an opportunistic electoral strategy.

In general, it appears that "path breakers" (Morgan 2009) have emerged in the cases when cross-pressuring has been the greatest and the political logjam has been broken by broader economic and societal shifts that undermine old policies, destabilize existing labor market institutions, and create novel potential electoral coalitions.

More broadly, what does the piecemeal adoption of the social investment model imply for the future of democratic capitalism? The social investment agenda originated as a bridge between the twin imperatives of solidaristic democracy and free market capitalism. By employing the market to attain the ends that democratically elected governments might otherwise try to engender by fiat – full employment, high and equally dispersed wages, and an end to the marginalization of particular groups – social investment promised to make seemingly antagonistic forces work symbiotically. This suggests that even at the time when free market capitalism has placed democratic governance under most duress, policies looking to bridging the tensions inherent in modern democratic capitalism will remain on the agenda. How these policies play out, however, will depend on their distributive consequences (Beramendi, this volume) and is likely to remain politically determined.

12

Stability and Change in CMEs: Corporate Governance and Industrial Relations in Germany and Denmark

Gregory Jackson and Kathleen Thelen

12.1. Introduction

By now it is conventional in the literature on the political economy of the rich democracies to distinguish between "liberal" and "coordinated" varieties of capitalism (Hall and Soskice 2001). These two models are widely seen as representing alternative paths to economic efficiency. However, the liberal market economies (LMEs) have traditionally been strongly associated with high levels of inequality, while the coordinated market economies (CMEs) have been more successful in combining economic growth with greater social solidarity (e.g., Acemoglu and Robinson 2012). A large body of scholarship suggests that the capacity of CMEs to support these more egalitarian outcomes is closely related to the way in which distributional compromises between labor and capital have been institutionalized.

Two institutions featuring most prominently in understanding capitalist diversity are those for corporate governance and industrial relations. Corporate governance in CMEs is characterized by "patient capital" involving stable and committed shareholders who hold large ownership blocks of shares and insulate firms from hostile takeovers. These arrangements allow managers to take a long-term view that reflects a broad set of stakeholder interests. LMEs, by contrast, are associated with corporate governance institutions characterized by dispersed ownership, greater liquidity and arm's length modes of finance, and an active market for corporate control. Organized around an institutional logic of shareholder value and seeking to maximize short-term returns on investment, this pattern of corporate governance is thought to exhibit greater

The authors thank James Conran, Sabrina Fischenich, Tom O'Grady, and Soeren Salzwedel for research assistance. We also are grateful for helpful comments and suggestions from Peter Gourevitch, Silja Häusermann, Martin Höpner, Herbert Kitschelt, Jette Steen Knudsen, Brett Meyer, Andreas Rasch, and Steen Thomsen. All errors remain our own.

agility, for example, in mobilizing risk capital for new ventures and facilitating restructuring via mergers and acquisitions.

Different corporate governance institutions are typically seen as supporting distinct industrial relations regimes (Höpner 2005: 16, figure 5; Aoki 2001; Aoki and Jackson 2008). Patient capital in CMEs underpins cooperative relations with unions by supporting investments in human capital and allowing firms to retain workers through economic downturns. Europe's coordinated market economies thus traditionally have featured social partnership with strong unions, centralized collective bargaining, strong employment protections, generous welfare benefits, and robust investment in worker training. More market-oriented finance and shareholder-value orientation in LMEs, by contrast, reinforces adversarial industrial relations. By placing priority on shareholder value, corporations make greater use of fluid "hire and fire" labor market institutions and are less inclined to undertake firm-specific investments in worker training. Accordingly, industrial relations in LMEs feature patchy collective bargaining coverage and weak unions, flimsy employment protections, meager social benefits, low firm (or state) investment in training, and decentralized, largely individualized wage setting.

Most scholars see the fate of egalitarian capitalism in CMEs as strongly tied up in the resilience of complementary sets of corporate governance and industrial relations institutions. Yet disagreements remain about how current pressures are playing out in these realms and in what ways they are interrelated. The varieties of capitalism (VoC) approach embraces an equilibrium view that emphasizes positive feedback and points mostly to continued stability (Hall and Soskice 2001). Where comparative advantage depends on incremental innovation and requires institutional support for relational assets, political coalitions of firms, employees, and governments are likely to defend CME institutions. An alternative "liberalization" thesis argues that past institutional arrangements are undergoing serious erosion (see especially Streeck 2009; also Howell 2003; Glyn 2006). Changes in global finance have weakened ties between "patient capital" and industry, and growing competition and union decline have created pressures for greater flexibility in all aspects of labor relations.

These disagreements over the extent and direction of change notwithstanding, however, VoC and liberalization theorists alike tend to view corporate governance and industrial relations institutions as highly complementary, meaning that developments in one domain are strongly conditioned by those in the other (Höpner 2005). The core difference is that VoC predicts stability in both institutional realms based on a coalition to preserve past comparative advantages, whereas liberalization theories predict a weakening of support for past coordinated institutions due to growing pressures and new exit options for investors and firms in the globalized economy.

In this chapter, we assess these arguments by comparing developments in corporate governance and industrial relations in two cases usually described as

CMEs: Germany and Denmark. In line with a major theme of this volume, we find that current trends in these countries support neither the VoC arguments around stability nor the liberalization arguments for convergence. Germany and Denmark have experienced institutional change in both realms but followed divergent paths of liberalization.[1] Specifically, Germany combines relative stability of coordination in industrial relations (at least within the core manufacturing sector) with significant liberalization in corporate governance among large corporations.[2] Denmark presents an almost mirror image: significant labor market liberalization despite continued stability of corporate governance based on patient capital by concentrated owners. The resulting institutional configurations are a more mixed or hybrid pattern seemingly at odds with dominant theoretical frameworks. As such, these developments are consistent with another core message of this volume, that most advanced political economies are less coherent than frequently assumed (Beramendi et al. Introduction).

To explain these divergent trajectories of liberalization, we advance a political coalitional argument that emphasizes the interaction of producer group politics and partisan coalitions. Unlike other policy arenas considered in this volume such as social policy, electoral politics have a weaker direct effect on corporate governance and industrial relations. In the area of corporate governance, voters do not typically have well-articulated preferences, and policy develops more as "quiet politics" between political parties and organized interests (Culpepper 2011). Likewise, electoral politics do not directly affect most aspects of industrial relations, and many of the developments analyzed in the following emerged out of bargaining between unions and employers. Nevertheless, we will show that the role of partisan politics in these arenas has been heavily influenced by producer groups as "intense policy demanders" representing important constituencies (Bawn et al. 2012), and that state policy has therefore played an important role in channeling developments in both realms.

As noted in the editors' Introduction, political outcomes are shaped by strategic interactions within institutional constraints that define what is technically feasible and politically viable. In the case of corporate governance and industrial relations reforms in Denmark and Germany, differences in the way coordination has historically been achieved have had important consequences for the interest orientations of key actors vis-à-vis liberalization and the resulting political coalitions for or against institutional change. In Germany, banks were the key actors providing patient capital and labor relations relied on sectorally based negotiations. In Denmark, by contrast, foundations and families

---

[1] The arguments we develop here extend previous work (Thelen 2014) by exploring the realm of corporate governance and its interactions with labor relations.

[2] The trends we analyze in this paper have been pursued and adapted with greatest vigor by Germany's large corporations listed on the stock exchange and engaged in global business operations. Elsewhere in the German economy, corporate governance has been less affected.

played a greater role in corporate governance and labor relations involved more encompassing national level bargaining. These divergent identities and interests of key actors have created different coalitions around liberalization, pushing institutional change along different paths. In Germany, liberalization has created more heterogeneous corporate governance arrangements and produced a less encompassing and more bifurcated pattern of labor relations – thus promoting the kind of intense "risk dualization" the editors of this volume associate with "status-oriented" capitalism (Beramendi et al., this volume; see also Palier and Thelen 2010). In Denmark, by contrast, a more encompassing coalition has introduced more "universalistic" liberalizing moves in labor relations, although at the same time preserving the kind of patient capital long associated with coordinated corporate governance. We characterize the resulting pattern as involving a more "embedded" pattern of liberalization – one that corresponds to what the editors describe as "cushioned risk differentiation" associated with "equality oriented" capitalism. In short, in both cases we observe liberalization, but occurring under the auspices of different coalitions and associated as well with rather different distributional consequences (see also Huber and Stephens; Gingrich and Ansell; Hassel; and Rueda et al., this volume).

12.2. Trajectories of Liberalization: Situating the Cases of Germany and Denmark

We begin by situating our two countries in a broad cross-national context.[3] In the area of *corporate governance*, we observe a general trend toward liberalization across several common measures shown in Table 12.1 – the dispersion of corporate ownership, the formal legal rights of shareholders, and value of mergers and acquisitions (M&A) activity. Corporate ownership has become substantially more dispersed across all CMEs, as the presence of large block holders with "patient" investments has declined and more diversified institutional investors play a greater role. Still, as a group CMEs remain far behind the LMEs on this measure. Of the two countries analyzed here, Germany is the more liberal on this score: Dispersed ownership among this country's largest firms increased between 1995 and 2008 from 35 percent to 50 percent. While the level also increased in Denmark, it remains much lower, at 25 percent. In terms of formal shareholder rights, Scandinavian counties have started to converge toward levels more commonly associated with LMEs, with Denmark actually in the lead. A similar movement can be observed among many continental CMEs, including Germany. Finally, in terms of M&A activity most

---

[3] We present data on three groups of countries for which comparable data are available. The Scandinavian CME group includes Denmark, Finland, Norway, and Sweden. The continental CME group includes Austria, Belgium, France, Germany, Italy, the Netherlands, and Switzerland. LME countries include Australia, Canada, the United Kingdom, and the United States.

TABLE 12.1. *Corporate governance indicators, 1990s and 2000s*

	Percentage of Large Firms with Dispersed Share Ownership			Shareholder Protection Index (0 to 5)			M&A Deal Value as Percentage GDP	
	1995	2008		1993	2003		1991	2007
Scandinavian	0.08	0.30	**Scandinavian**	3.0	3.6	**Scandinavian**	2.4	7.1
Denmark	0.10	0.25	Denmark	2.0	4.0	Denmark	1.4	5.8
Finland	0.15	0.50	Finland	3.0	3.5	Finland	1.5	1.8
Norway	0.05	0.15	Norway	4.0	3.5	Norway	1.4	12.4
Sweden	0.00	0.30	Sweden	3.0	3.5	Sweden	5.4	8.3
Continental	0.24	0.36	**Continental**	1.6	2.9	**Continental**	1.2	7.1
Austria	0.05	0.15	Austria	2.0	2.5	Austria	0.3	2.0
Belgium	0.00	0.20	Belgium	0.0	3.0	Belgium	1.6	3.5
France	0.30	0.35	France	3.0	3.5	France	0.7	5.3
Germany	0.35	0.50	Germany	1.0	3.5	Germany	0.9	3.9
Italy	0.15	0.25	Italy	1.0	2.0	Italy	1.2	7.7
Netherlands	0.30	0.55	Netherlands	2.0	2.5	Netherlands	1.5	20.5
Switzerland	0.50	0.50	Switzerland	2.0	3.0	Switzerland	2.4	6.7
Liberal	0.69	0.75	**Liberal**	4.8	4.0	**Liberal**	5.0	11.3
Australia	0.55	0.70	Australia	4.0	4.0	Australia	3.3	11.1
Canada	0.50	0.75	Canada	5.0	4.0	Canada	3.3	11.9
United Kingdom	0.90	0.75	United Kingdom	5.0	5.0	United Kingdom	8.5	11.4
United States	0.80	0.80	United States	5.0	3.0	United States	5.1	10.8
Japan	0.50	0.70	Japan	4.0	4.5	Japan	0.1	1.6

Notes: Percentage of top 20 firms by sales without a block holder owning greater than 10% of shares.
Sources: Percentage of Large Firms with Dispersed Share Ownership: La Porta et al. 2003; and Thomson Banker One, own calculations; Shareholder Protection Index (0 to 5): Djankov et al. 2008; M&A Deal Value as Percentage GDP: Thomson Banker One, own calculations.

TABLE 12.2A. *Bargaining level, 1970–2010*

Country	1970	2010	Change
Denmark	5	3	−2
Finland	5	3	−2
Norway	4	3	−1
Sweden	5	3	−2
Austria	3	3	No chg
Belgium	4	4	No chg
France	3	2	−1
Germany	3	3	No chg
Italy	3	3	No chg
Netherlands	3	3	No chg
Switzerland	3	3	No chg
Australia	4	2	−2
Canada	1	1	No chg
United States	1	1	No chg
United Kingdom	3	1	−2
Japan	1	1	No chg

Note: 5 = national or central level; 4 = national or central level, with additional sectoral/local or company level; 3 = sectoral or industry level; 2 = sectoral or industry level, with additional local or company level; 1 = local or company level.
Source: Jelle Visser (http://www.uva-aias.net/208).

CMEs (including both Germany and Denmark) still lag substantially behind the LME countries – even if the market for corporate control clearly plays a growing role in the CMEs as well. In sum, despite some institutional change in corporate governance, particularly liberalization aimed at strengthening the legal rights of shareholders, patterns of ownership and takeover markets have so far not converged on LME countries.

In terms of *industrial relations institutions*, we again observe a mixed pattern. Tables 12.2a and 12.2b record changes between 1970 and 2010 with reference to two common indicators of liberalization: the level at which collective bargaining occurs and trends in bargaining coverage. In terms of bargaining level, most LME countries were already very decentralized to begin with, but those that previously had exhibited some degree of coordination became more decentralized over this period. Continental CMEs (including Germany) overall demonstrate a higher degree of stability in formal bargaining arrangements, whereas Denmark clusters with the other Nordic countries in having experienced significant formal decentralization over this period. Turning to Table 12.2b, we see that collective bargaining coverage in Denmark and other Nordic countries remains very high, slightly higher in fact than it was in 1970. By contrast, all of the LME countries register (sometimes dramatic) declines

TABLE 12.2B. *Collective bargaining coverage, 1970–2010*

Country	1970	2010	Percentage Change
Denmark	80	85*	+6
Finland	73	90***	+23
Norway	65	74**	+14
Sweden	84	91	+8
Austria	95	99	+4
Belgium	85	96	+13
France	70	92**	+31
Germany	85	61	−28
Italy	85	85	−0
Netherlands	76	84	+11
Switzerland	50	49	−2
Australia	90	45*	−50
Canada	34	32***	−7
United States	30	13	−56
United Kingdom	73	31	−58
Japan	32	16**	−50

Note: Bargaining (or union) coverage measures the proportion of employees covered by wage bargaining agreements as a proportion of all wage and salary earners in employment with the right to bargaining, adjusted for the possibility that some sectors or occupations are excluded from the right to bargain (removing such groups from the employment count before dividing the number of covered employees over the total number of dependent workers in employment).
* indicates data from 2007 (latest available).
** indicates data from 2008.
*** indicates data from 2009.
Source: Jelle Visser (http://www.uva-aias.net/208).

since then. Continental countries show more mixed results, with Germany recording the most significant loss.

Here again, the picture that emerges does not comport entirely with either VoC or liberalization theories. Against VoC theories that predict stability in CMEs, we see significant formal decentralization, not just in LMEs but also in the highly coordinated market economies of Scandinavia. But against liberalization theories, we see high stability of formal bargaining coordination in Germany despite shrinking coverage, as well as continued high coverage of collective bargaining in Denmark and other Scandinavian countries despite decentralization.

The rest of this chapter examines the dynamics of institutional change in corporate governance and industrial relations in Germany and Denmark. We shall argue that the differences in how coordination was institutionalized have shaped both the producer group and partisan coalitions around liberalization and the resulting trajectories of change. In corporate governance, we contrast the prominent role played by banks in Germany's model of "patient capital" to the more stable role of foundations and the emerging role of pension funds in Denmark. In industrial relations, we emphasize differences in Germany's more sectorally organized system relative to the more centralized national-level pattern in Denmark (see also, especially, Martin and Swank 2012). The different starting points in how coordination was institutionalized have influenced the subsequent patterns of liberalization in each country and have also shaped how developments in the two institutional domains relate to one another.

12.3. The Politics of Liberalization in Germany

Germany has undergone significant liberalization in both corporate governance and labor relations. Institutional change in both domains has fallen short of convergence on LME style institutions but has produced a more complex and heterogeneous institutional landscape. "Patient capital" by banks has undergone substantial erosion, giving way in the manufacturing sector to a hybrid form of corporate governance based on a version of shareholder value that is "negotiated" with labor and that continues to support competitive advantage based on high skill production. The pattern of organization in industry, however, is becoming less representative of the economy as a whole; alongside this negotiated shareholder-value model, the emerging service economy is mostly based on very different institutions of corporate governance and labor relations. The pattern of liberalization we observe for Germany is thus a growing dualization, associated with the negative distributional consequences documented elsewhere in this volume (e.g., Rueda et al.; Hassel, this volume).

12.3.1. *Corporate Governance in Germany*

Banks historically formed the core of Germany's corporate governance regime, providing patient capital through credit finance, ownership stakes, seats on company supervisory boards, and the exercise of proxy votes. As pivotal players in the country's dense intercorporate network, banks had a central role in managing competition and promoting industrial restructuring at the sectoral level (Windolf and Beyer 1996). However, since the 1990s, large private banks have exited their traditional role and lobbied for financial market reforms as a response to diminishing returns of their former *Hausbank* model. In the face of low interest rates and slowed lending, they reorientated their business strategies toward more arm's length investment banking. Private banks, such as Dresdner and Commerzbank, were central in driving the diffusion of new corporate governance practices oriented toward shareholder value in Germany (Fiss and Zajac 2004).

Legislation enacted by governments of both the Left and the Right actively promoted these changes. The CDU-FDP government privatized major state-owned enterprises in the energy and telecommunications sectors in the early 1990s and later adopted legal reforms increasing shareholder rights and liberalizing the use of corporate equity. Their centerpiece 1998 reform Law on Control and Transparency (KonTrag) improved auditor independence and required disclosure of multiple supervisory board memberships and ownership stakes exceeding 5 percent (see especially Ziegler 2000). The law also reduced the power of large owners by eliminating multiple voting rights and voting rights restrictions, barring banks from using proxy votes in conjunction with direct shareholding exceeding 5 percent, and requiring banks to solicit proxy instructions from shareholders. Finally, KonTrag removed restrictions on share swaps, share buybacks, and stock options, thus giving firms greater opportunities to engage with equity markets.

While KonTrag was pushed by the CDU-FDP coalition, the politics of corporate governance reform did not follow a standard Left-Right logic. In the debates on KonTrag, the SPD favored an even more radical reform. As Höpner and others have shown, Germany's unions had signaled support for many of these reforms, viewing them as useful in limiting the power of German banks (Cioffi and Höpner 2006). This provided the SPD with an opportunity to show itself as proliberalization on an issue that would not antagonize a key electoral constituency. Once in office, therefore, the SPD-Green government (1998–2005) continued along the same lines, promoting the tax-free sale of long-term equity stakes in 2002. Large commercial banks such as Deutsche Bank responded eagerly, by selling shares and reducing their presence on the supervisory boards of industrial firms (Höpner and Krempel 2004).

Germany's large corporations had little interest in actively defending traditional arrangements. On the contrary: Changes in corporate governance played into the self-interests of managers themselves, most importantly through rapidly rising levels of executive compensation. Moreover, many large manufacturing firms had anyway become largely self-financing and thus were less dependent on bank credit. At the same time, the proportion of shares owned by foreign institutional investors had grown among the DAX30 companies, thus increasing pressures for transparency and engagement with shareholders. Most importantly of all, German industry favored liberalization as a way to globalize their business operations as new opportunities opened up to expand into European markets through mergers and acquisitions. The value of M&A grew during the merger wave of 1998–2005; around three-quarters of this activity involved cross-border transactions, especially diversification into new and growing industries (Jackson and Miyajima 2007).[4]

Unions, for their part, were supportive of those aspects of corporate governance reforms that increased transparency and information disclosure (Höpner 2003). Reforms along these lines enhanced the importance of board-level

---

[4] Prominent cases included the Daimler Chrysler merger in 1998 and the fusion of Hoechst with French Rhône-Poulenc to form Aventis in 1999.

codetermination vis-à-vis management. They also presented opportunities for works councils and unions to influence company decision making related to M & A activities and, especially, to negotiate over the consequences of corporate structuring. These developments formed the foundation for what we have elsewhere termed "negotiated" shareholder value (Jackson 2003; Vitols 2004).

Parties of the Left and Right alike steered clear, however, of corporate governance reforms on which unions and industry presented a unified front against banks. Regarding hostile takeover bids, for example, German managers sided with labor in opposing liberalization. The takeover of Mannesmann by Vodafone in 2000 was a symbolic moment in shifting managers' attention to the importance of maintaining share prices to hold off unsolicited bidders (Höpner and Jackson 2006). Thus, in debates over the European Takeover Directive, both the SPD and the CDU opposed the initiative, following the cues of a unified coalition of unions and employers in industry (Callaghan and Höpner 2005; Culpepper 2011; Callaghan 2009). As a result of intense joint lobbying, the Schröder government opted out of EU proposals in favor of board "neutrality" during hostile bids, allowing the shareholders' meeting to utilize a 75 percent majority vote to empower management regarding defensive actions for an eighteen-month period (Culpepper 2011).[5] Despite some high profiles cases (Mannesmann and later Hochtief), the number of hostile takeover bids in Germany has remained low.

A similar constellation of interests allowed unions successfully to resist changes that would have compromised their influence on company supervisory boards. The Social Democrats had little to gain by attacking an institution of intense interest to labor, and which anyway continued to enjoy the support of large corporations in the core of the German manufacturing economy (Jackson 2003; Höpner and Waclawczyk 2012; Paster 2012). Thus, German unions were able to fend off proposed reductions in the size of these boards that would have limited the number of seats available to external labor unions relative to worker representatives from inside the company. They also lobbied successfully for various provisions in the new European corporate form (SE) aimed at protecting the status quo levels of board-level employee codetermination (Keller and Werner 2010; Kluge and Stollt 2006).

Taken together, corporate governance liberalization in Germany, while extensive, has fallen well short of a straightforward convergence on U.S.-style deregulation. Instead, corporate governance arrangements have become more heterogeneous over time. Many German firms, such as Robert Bosch, ZF Friedrichshafen, Carl Zeiss, Bertelsmann, and Deichmann, remain privately owned or enjoy patient capital through foundation ownership and therefore have not been strongly affected by the aforementioned changes. Germany's

---

[5] Nonetheless, the scope for defensive actions is effectively limited to share buybacks, engaging in alternative acquisitions, and searching for a white knight. Deviations from one share–one vote principles have become very rare in Germany (Deminor Rating 2005).

important *Mittelstand* sector has also successfully retained a modified form of *Hausbank* relationship with German savings bank and cooperative banking sectors, which have been partially shielded from full-scale liberalization (Deeg 2009; Schmid 2013). Family owners have remained central for *Mittelstand* firms and largely protected them from the full effects of capital market pressures (Lubinski 2011).

Meanwhile, as we have seen, firms that were most directly affected by corporate governance reforms developed a hybrid approach based on "negotiated" shareholder value (Vitols 2004; Jackson 2003). In this model, codetermination does not impede new shareholder-value management practices but does shape and adapt them to fit with existing commitments to core employees. In the face of intensified international competition, labor and management in Germany's core industrial firms have thus largely sought to take advantage of new possibilities (e.g., through mergers and acquisitions to increase market share) while continuing to nurture the skills and competencies of their core workforces in order to maintain German industry's long-standing comparative institutional advantage. But as we shall see, these firms also adapted themselves to having a leaner core set of employees and relied to a greater extent on strategies of externalizing cost-sensitive tasks to other sectors of the economy (see also Palier and Thelen 2010).

12.3.2. *Industrial Relations in Germany*
The trends in corporate governance cited previously have had a paradoxical effect on labor relations: both intensifying cooperation between unions and employers within the industrial core and simultaneously fueling dualization. This section elaborates both aspects.

As we saw, "negotiated" shareholder value often consolidated social partnership between managers and unions in Germany's large industrial firms as many of these firms used M&A possibilities to strengthen their market position and shore up the employment security of their core workers. In line with the expectations of VoC theory, these firms continue to rely on high levels of employee cooperation and skills to support their success in export markets, which is based on strategies of high quality production and incremental innovation (Schneider and Paunescu 2012b). While the emerging configuration – more liberal capital markets but continued cooperative labor relations – seems to contradict the notion of institutional complementarities, the situation offers large firms the option of a dual strategy – allying with worker representatives to preserve those aspects of coordination that continue to generate comparative advantage in the market, but also using capital market pressures to force certain concessions and adjustments.[6] In industrial relations, these trends are reflected, for example, in the growth since the 1990s of company-level

---

[6] For a theoretical discussion, see the alternative framework based on the notion of essentiality in Aoki and Jackson (2008).

"Pacts for Employment and Competitiveness" (*betriebliche Bündnisse zur Beschäftigungs- und Wettbewerbssicherung*) in large industrial firms (Rehder 2003). Such deals involve trade-offs in which managers commit themselves to job security for employees in exchange for flexibility, especially regarding working times.[7]

A similar desire to maintain competitive advantage lies behind manufacturing employers' continued support for coordinated industrywide bargaining, albeit, as we will see later, for a shrinking number of workers. Although apparently inconsistent with their otherwise vocal demands for "flexibility," these firms continue to negotiate industry-level wage scales that limit wage differentiation both within and across companies. They continue to value sectoral bargaining for imposing "order" and "predictability" on the labor market and for keeping distributional issues and associated conflict off the shop floor.[8] For many of the same reasons German employers prefer not to stir up conflict by promoting union fragmentation. Unions and employers thus spoke with one voice in denouncing a 2010 Labor Court ruling that gave rival unions the right to operate alongside the dominant industrial unions. Together they argued that that collective bargaining autonomy and branch agreements remain centrally important supports for the country's industrial competitiveness (see also "Grundsatzbeschluss" 2010).[9]

The continued reliance on social partnership by core industrial firms was evident in how business used short-time work policies *(Kurzarbeit)* as a response to the recent financial crisis. Short time work policies cater very specifically to firms and (skilled) workers in the industrial core, providing subsidies to firms that are that are experiencing a cyclical downturn to allow them to avoid laying off their most valued employees. In this way firms can weather downturns while "preserving the human capital specific to the firm and reducing the costs of turnover" (Arpaia et al. 2010: 3; also Sacchi et al. 2011: 5). Such policies have always enjoyed support from both the SPD and CDU/CSU, and unions and employers in export industries successfully lobbied the government for legislation to twice extend these subsidies in parliament as the crisis unfolded. At its peak, 3.2 percent of German workers – overwhelmingly employed in industrial sectors, and primarily in metalworking – were being supported

---

[7] In addition, shareholder-value management is strongly associated with adoption of performance-based pay schemes linking salaries to business and/or individual performance (Jackson et al. 2005). The new layer of pay schemes represents a controlled but de facto decentralization of collective bargaining.

[8] Industrywide coordination on wage issues was reaffirmed in the engineering industry in the 2000s when engineering employers acceded to the metalworking union's long-standing demand for unified wage scales for white- and blue-collar workers.

[9] The managing director of the Metal Employers Association (Gesamtmetall) held up the British example as a warning against the kind of union fragmentation and competition that his organization sees as having contributed to the demise of British industry ("Ende der Tarifeinheit" 2010). See also Lesch (2010).

by short-time work arrangements (Schmitt 2011; Bundesagentur für Arbeit 2009). Wage negotiations in 2009 complemented these policies, as bargaining centered on how much firms would top up the state subsidies.

However, this intensification of cooperation within manufacturing firms has been bundled with declining union coverage and the erosion of solidaristic institutions outside the industrial core (Jackson and Sorge 2012; Palier and Thelen 2010). In fact, the local-level agreements described previously that have stabilized employment in these companies have almost always been accompanied by measures of "vertical disintegration" in which services previously performed internally – from cafeterias to cleaning – have been outsourced to lower-cost producers (Doellgast and Greer 2007). In addition, large firms have often adopted more complex subsidiary structures strategically to place lower-skill work outside the arrangements governed by social partnership (Casey et al. 2012). They have also increasingly turned to temporary agencies to cover unskilled work, at considerable savings considering the fact that the wages of agency workers are on average 25–30 percent lower than those of permanent employees (Mitlacher 2007: 582; Eichhorst and Marx 2012: 23). As an example, corporate restructuring after privatization in telecommunications decreased collective bargaining coverage, as companies created call centers staffed by atypical workers to perform low-skill tasks (Doellgast 2012; Sako and Jackson 2006).

These trends have combined with much lower rates of unionization outside Germany's industrial core, contributing to the erosion in collective bargaining coverage noted at the outset and fueling the emergence of a significant low-wage sector. The resulting pattern in German industrial relations is increasingly bifurcated, featuring strong coverage and collective representation in the (still-significant) core economy, but alongside an emerging "patchwork" (*Flickenteppich*) of regional- and sector-specific arrangements and "large unregulated zones" outside the ambit of the formal bargaining structures (Weinkopf and Bosch 2010: 2; also Bosch et al. 2009: 45; Bispinck 2010).

On this less organized periphery, corporate governance models often associated with "patient capital" have not been sufficient to promote cooperative labor relations. This applies above all in the growing low-wage service sector, where employers do not view investments in worker training and stable organizational routines as important to competitive advantage. Thus, in businesses such as retailing, family owners often do not support social partnership with unions but actively pursue low-road employment models. For example, prior to their 2012 bankruptcy, the family-owned drugstore chain Schlecker founded its own temporary work agency, laying off workers and rehiring them at substantially reduced levels of wages and benefits – prompting a major scandal in 2010. Similarly, the family-owned supermarket chain Lidl has been notoriously hostile to works councils. In sectors like this where firms are following low-cost strategies, family owners have little interest in developing more collaborative relationships with labor representatives.

The erosion of collective bargaining via strategies of downsizing and through the long-term shift in employment out of manufacturing has, of course, not been a matter of explicit public policy or electoral politics in any straightforward sense. But this de facto drift toward liberalization outside the industrial core received a massive de jure boost in the context of the Social Democratic Party's turn toward labor market activation in the Hartz reforms of the early 2000s. The editors of this volume characterize this episode as a failed experiment to extend the party's appeal "to an alliance of educated middle class voters and business" that, however, ultimately foundered on the "strong pivotal position of organized labor" (Beramendi et al., this volume). Business associations were deeply involved in the effort to mobilize public opinion in favor of these reforms. In 2000 they launched a large-scale public relations campaign, the so-called Initiative Neue Soziale Marktwirtschaft (New Social Market Initiative, INSM), aimed at extolling the virtues of freer labor markets (Kinderman 2014).[10] Acting as classic "intense policy demanders" in the sense of Bawn et al. (2012), the INSM devised the motto "just is whatever creates employment" ("sozial ist was Arbeit schafft"), which was subsequently picked up by the CDU/CSU and FDP before being adopted by the Social Democratic Minister of Labor and Economy Wolfgang Clement, "as the more or less official slogan of the Agenda 2010 labor market reforms" (Kinderman 2014: 11–12).

Whatever the precise combination of electoral motives and business interests that lay behind it, the Hartz reforms represented a massive liberalization of labor markets. By all accounts, these measures contributed to the rapid growth of a low-wage sector that had reached 6.5 million by 2008 (Bispinck 2010: 1). Some of this employment involves so-called minijobs, a form of part-time work promoted under the Hartz reforms that involves limited working hours and low pay and that does not carry the usual social benefits. But even among full-time workers low-wage employment had increased to more than 20 percent by 2010 ("Hungerlohn" 2010). For comparative perspective, this put Germany at a level similar to LMEs such as the United Kingdom (20.7 percent) and United States (25 percent), and well above all other CMEs, including Denmark (13.4 percent) (see Thelen 2014: figure 4.4; also Bosch et al. 2009: 7–8).

As an electoral gambit, Hartz backfired, generating widespread protests in 2004 that directly contributed both to the SPD's defeat in 2005 and, more importantly, to the emergence of Die Linke as a significant electoral challenge. Thus in the meantime, both SPD and CDU have distanced themselves from this harsh approach.[11] The Social Democratic Party's subsequent insistence on

---

[10] Enlisting the services of a major advertising company, they also poured 10 million euros per year into this effort between 2000 and 2008.

[11] As Kinderman (2014) notes, even the INSM moderated its rhetoric. The campaign lives on, however, and in fact Wolfgang Clement himself – who remained convinced of the agenda even after the SPD abandoned it – currently serves as head of its board of trustees (Kinderman 2014: 18).

a statutory minimum wage in its coalition negotiations with the CDU can thus be seen as a move on the part of the party to recapture working-class votes as part of its historic core constituency. In the meantime, however, the trends in collective bargaining toward reduced coverage show no signs of ending and continue to fuel very significant dualization dynamics in Germany.

12.4. The Politics of Liberalization in Denmark

The Danish case is in some ways a mirror image of Germany. Corporate governance is characterized by greater stability of "patient capital" due to the ownership role of foundations and cooperatives. Danish corporations have also successfully adapted their stakeholder-oriented corporate governance style – albeit in a more liberal guise under the banner of corporate social responsibility (CSR). This pattern reflects a key difference in how patient capital was constituted in Denmark, with banks historically absent from corporate governance and industrial foundations and cooperatives more significant.[12] Unlike private banks in Germany, Danish foundations and cooperatives had little to gain from liberalization, being essentially nonprofit entities in perpetuity.

Meanwhile, labor relations have undergone significant liberalization through decentralization of collective bargaining and labor market policies focused on broad-based flexibilization and the promotion of general skills. In contrast to events in Germany, however, compromises over liberalization have often involved negotiated trade-offs between more privileged segments of the labor movement that welcomed some aspects of liberalization and lower-skill workers who were more directly threatened by these moves. The result has been a less dualized (more "embedded" or "cushioned") variety of liberalization (see also Hassel; Rueda et al.; and /Gingrich and Ansell, this volume).[13]

12.4.1. Corporate Governance in Denmark

In Denmark, changes in corporate governance were introduced through both legal reforms and voluntary codes. While reforms under both Social Democratic and center-Right governments generally involved liberalization, neither side attempted to overturn employee representation. Moreover, liberalization had weaker effects than in Germany because of the very different composition of "patient capital" in Denmark – rooted less in banks and anchored more in foundations and cooperative associations.

---

[12] In the 1990s, foundation ownership existed in 19 of the largest 100 firms in Denmark, compared to just 5 in Germany (Thomsen 1996).

[13] While some authors classify Denmark as now having converged with LME economies (Schneider and Paunescu 2012a) or stress convergent pressures of liberalization, we see the Danish case as moving toward a less institutionally "coherent" and more hybrid pattern that combines liberal and coordinated elements in new ways (Campbell and Pedersen 2007), albeit in an inverse pattern relative to Germany.

The Social Democratic government (1993–2001) adopted only minor legal changes by implementing various EU measures around transparency, disclosure, and capital requirements. A wider public debate on corporate governance was sparked with its 1999 Green Paper on Active Ownership.[14] The report was never intended to inform legislation but reviewed international developments related to Denmark's existing stakeholder model and concluded that greater shareholder protection was needed. The resulting debates triggered the then-outgoing Social Democratic minister of economic and business affairs to appoint a committee composed of four prominent business leaders[15] to report on ethical conduct by supervisory boards, resulting in the Nørby Committee's Report on Corporate Governance in Denmark.

Nørby advocated stronger liberalization, including restrictions on dual class shares widely used by Danish foundations,[16] changes in supervisory board practices, and greater openness to takeovers (Andersen 2003). Still, the Nørby report notably did not promote stock options for managers and argues more generally that "it is insufficient that the management focuses solely on the interests of shareholders" and that "the interests of other stakeholders must be considered" (p. 37). Nørby was again not designed to propose legislation but outlined voluntary principles of self-regulation by companies inspired by the UK Cadbury Code. The Copenhagen Stock Exchange adopted these recommendations in its code on a comply-or-explain basis, but only somewhat later, in 2005, under the subsequent center-right government (2001–2011) led by Venstre (Liberal Party of Denmark). Venstre continued on this very gradual path of liberalization with measures aimed at simplifying corporate law and promoting the formation of new companies.[17]

Despite liberalization, patient capital remained more stable, relative to Germany, because of its distinctive institutional makeup. In Denmark, patient capital is anchored above all in the role of enterprise foundations and cooperative associations. While these forms of ownership are not unique to Denmark, they remain much more prevalent there than in other countries, including Germany (Thomsen and Pedersen 1996). A study of the largest twenty-five corporations between 1973 and 2008 confirms that 40–45 percent of these firms are majority owned by foundations and cooperative associations (Iversen and

---

[14] See http://www.fm.dk/publikationer/1999/debatoplaeg-om-aktivt-ejerskab/
[15] The committee was chaired by Lars Nørby Johansen, a board member of the foundation-owned company Falck, and composed of three other top corporate managers.
[16] A position advocated by Danish institutional investors such as LD (Employees Capital Pension Fund) and ATP (Danish Labour Market Supplementary Pension Fund).
[17] Measures included establishing new rules on shareholder voting in 2003 (Andersen 2003), implementing EU directives of capital requirements in 2006, and merging the legal framework for public and private limited companies in 2010 (Neville 2014). After returning to office in 2011, the Social Democratic government continued to follow this same path in its 2013 reform, by simplifying regulations for setting up small private limited companies.

Larsson 2011; see also Binda and Iversen 2007).[18] Foundations have almost never sold their stakes in Danish corporations, apart from one prominent exception.[19]

Enterprise foundations (*erhvervsdrivende fond*) have remained stable and patient owners as a result of their status as nonprofit entities governed by charter. Historically, many foundations were created by company founders or their families to administer a large ownership stake in a particular company (Hansen 2010). Foundation ownership thus moves the company out of direct family control and typically codifies a dual objective that combines the successful operation of the business with a charitable social purpose of some kind. A prominent example is the Carlsberg Foundation, which was set up in 1882 and currently owns 30 percent and controls 75 percent of votes in Carlsberg, as well as holding five of fourteen seats on the board. Similar foundations were created for the ship container firm A. P Møller-Mærsk and the pharmaceuticals firms Novo Nordisk and Coloplast. Foundation directors are usually Danish citizens, have very long tenures as directors (an average of 9.8 years), and receive modest fixed salaries devoid of performance-driven incentives (Hansmann and Thomsen 2013). While their charters sometimes include provisions for supporting family members, foundations are profitable (Thomsen and Rose 2004) but reinvest these profits in voluntary corporate social responsibility (CSR) activities such as through charitable activities, supporting stable employment (Lausten 2002) or long-term projects.

Unlike in Germany, neither the corporate sector nor the financial community pushed strongly for more far-reaching liberalization. First, banks have historically played only a minor role in Danish corporate governance because of restrictions on bank holdings of corporate shares (Rose and Mejer 2003). Second, foreign institutional investors play a small role in the average listed firm (Rose 2007), being concentrated among the twenty blue chip companies that account for 76 percent of market value and 79 percent of turnover on the Copenhagen Stock Exchange (Petersen and Plenborg 2006). Third, Denmark has few listed companies, at least half of which are SMEs. Rather, a high proportion of large firms remain privately owned: Of the top fifty Danish companies (by sales) 34 percent are nonlisted privately held corporations compared to just 16 percent in Germany (own calculations, Thomson Banker One).

Further support for patient capital – and CSR – has arisen from Danish pension funds, unlike in Germany, where domestic pension funds are still negligible.[20] The total assets of pension funds grew steadily from 36.8 percent of

---

[18] Cooperatives are dominant in Denmark's agricultural sector, including very large-scale cooperatively owned conglomerates: Arla Foods, Danish Crown, and DLG.

[19] The House of Prince cigarette firm was an indirect holding of two foundations via a pyramid structure and was sold to British-American Tobacco as part of efforts to consolidate their business portfolio.

[20] In Denmark, pension funds are rooted in the second pillar of fully funded flat-rate supplementary pensions for all wage earners (ATP) and the third pillar of occupational pensions introduced

GDP in 1981 to 152.5 percent of GDP in 2008 (Andersen 2011). In 2003, ATP alone owned 8 percent of stocks listed in Denmark (Neumann and Voetmann 2003). While Danish pension funds have promoted liberalization, major Danish pension funds such as LD (Employees Capital Pension Fund) and ATP (Danish Labour Market Supplementary Pension Fund) are governed by joint representation of employers and unions. The ATP and LD have advocated liberal reforms to eliminate dual class voting rights and increase transparency around foundation ownership but found few political allies. Moreover, ATP and LD pursue this agenda within a largely enlightened and long-term approach to companies stressing CSR as a means toward shareholder value. For example, ATP was an early adopter of CSR-related investment screens in 2006, and Pension Denmark adopted the UN Principles of Responsible Investment in 2008.

Consequently, parallel to liberalization, corporate governance reform in Denmark has also focused significantly on CSR. In LMEs, CSR often serves as a substitute for state regulation (Jackson and Apostolakou 2010; Kinderman 2012), but in Denmark it developed through government campaigns designed to involve the social partners. The support of foundations, pension funds, and unions for CSR creates a broad political coalition and transcends a purely business-driven approach. CSR was initially promoted in 1994 by the Social Democratic government, in a campaign inspired by one (foundation-owned) firm's efforts to promote workplace integration of migrants. Under the title "it concerns us all" the campaign sought to ensure that companies upheld their responsibilities of having an inclusive labor market (e.g., integration of persons with disabilities, unemployed, or otherwise at risk). After regaining power in 2001, the center-right Venstre government started a second wave of CSR initiatives to include "sustainable growth" (climate aspects and governance of the supply chain). Their 2008 CSR action plan promoted the adoption of CSR as a means of supporting Danish competitiveness in global markets. Supported by large corporations and Danish pension funds, the Venstre government introduced a 2008 amendment to the financial reporting laws to include disclosure of nonfinancial activities related to CSR on a comply-or-explain basis.[21] Since 2011, the Social Democratic government maintained this approach by initiatives in 2012 to promote companies' adoption of international standards of CSR certification, which were used by 76 percent of listed companies in 2011.[22]

In sum, patient capital has remained a stable core of Danish corporate governance, despite some more active role of the stock market and M&A activity at the margins. Consequently, the inroads of shareholder value at the level of

---

through collective bargaining in the early 1990s (Andersen 2011). These third-pillar funds are under joint control by representatives of employers and unions.

[21] See section 2.2 in http://csrgov.dk/file/319999/proposal_report_on_social_resp_december_2008 .pdf.

[22] See http://csrgov.dk/file/374342/csr_rapport_2011.pdf. In comparative terms, 69 percent of Danish firms were members of Global Compact in 2012, compared to 44 percent in Germany and 14 percent in the United Kingdom (own calculations, ASSET4 database).

corporate governance practices have remained modest. For example, despite increasing use of performance-related pay schemes for executives (Rose and Mejer 2003), compensation for Danish CEOs is modest in international comparisons, and few of them enjoy high-power equity-based incentives. As in Germany, the center-right government made no significant political move against employee codetermination on the board. Consequently, a majority of employee directors report high or reasonable levels of influence and continue to prioritize stakeholder interests over shareholder value and the stock market (Rose 2008). And despite the growth in M&A activities, hostile takeover battles have remained absent. Whereas Germany eliminated many of its takeover protections and experienced a few major hostile takeover cases, around half of listed Danish firms retain dual class shares as a form of takeover defense, particularly among foundation owned firms (Rose 2005). We shall discuss several exceptional cases of privatization and friendly takeovers by foreign investors in the next section.

12.4.2. *Industrial Relations in Denmark*

In Germany, we saw that liberalization in corporate governance accompanied continued coordination in labor relations – at least within large industrial firms. Against this backdrop, Denmark presents a near-mirror image, combining greater stability in patient capital with considerable decentralization in industrial relations. A major difference between the two countries, however, concerns the broader context of politics – a difference we have characterized as "dualizing" (Germany) versus "embedded" (Denmark) liberalization. While Germany has seen an erosion in collective bargaining coverage outside an institutionally stable but shrinking core, Danish unions enjoy a much broader reach – encompassing larger numbers of low-skill workers in services but also extending into the ranks of higher-skilled salaried workers. Danish unions also organize large numbers of women, especially in the public sector, and as noted in the Introduction, such constituencies often favor investment over consumption policies and universalistic over particularistic schemes (Beramendi et al. Introduction, this volume). In many ways negotiations worked out in Danish industrial relations over the past twenty years represent a balancing act as the peak trade union confederation LO has sought to accommodate the interests of a broader spectrum of members – spanning white- and blue-collar, salaried and manual, public and private sector workers – who are very differently positioned to benefit – and lose – from different liberalizing moves. Although partially worked out directly in collective bargaining between unions and employers, this balancing act has also relied in important ways on a supportive state. Thus, as we will show, the shift to a right-wing government in 2001 introduced changes that posed a considerable threat to the model.

Collective bargaining in Denmark has undergone very significant decentralization as wage negotiations have been successively pushed "out to the enterprises" (Due and Madsen 2008). Peak level "solidaristic" wage bargaining famously broke down in the 1980s when a coalition of employers and skilled unions in industry engineered the decentralization of bargaining from the peak to the industry level (Due et al. 1994: 150; Iversen 1996: 422–423). But bargaining decentralization did not stop at the industry level. Further changes in the 1990s virtually eliminated the previously quite widespread "normal" system of pay (in which the wages set in industry-level bargaining were applied with no flexibility at lower levels) in favor of the expansion of more flexible arrangements. While this development clearly responds to firm preferences for more wage flexibility, salaried professionals and semiprofessionals often supported more flexible arrangements that would recognize their competencies and reward investments in education. In some sectors dominated by such workers, industry contracts involve so-called figureless agreements that simply establish basic principles to which local bargainers are meant to adhere, without stipulating a minimum increase of any kind. In 1989, just 4 percent of all employees worked under "figureless agreements," but by 2010 this had increased to nearly one-third (see also Due and Madsen 2008: 517; see also Arbejdsgiverforening n.d.: 5). In contrast to the "noisy realignments and political conflicts" of the 1980s that brought solidaristic wage policy to an end, these further moves in Denmark in the direction of a more flexible wage formation system mostly unfolded quietly "without much pomp and ado" (Vartiainen 2011: 12; see also Due and Madsen 2008: 519–520).

In Germany dualizing liberalization has created a strongly bifurcated pattern in which some workers (particularly in low-end services) find themselves entirely outside the realm of collective bargaining and union coverage. By contrast, Danish bargaining continues to cover a broader spectrum of workers at different skill and education levels. Negotiated minimum wages (the so-called minimum wage system) that prevail in lower-skill sectors share with the figureless agreements just described increased room for local bargaining, but these contracts also set firm floors beneath which no worker can fall. While more flexible than before, the resulting system is still quite different from that in Germany, where larger swaths of the labor market are outside the regulated zone and the lowest-wage workers (e.g., in minijobs) are also outside the traditional benefit structure. So while wage inequality has risen in both countries, in Denmark this is due more to increases at the high end than to slippage at the low end of the income spectrum. One sees this in a comparison of changes in the ratio of the median income to the lowest decile (the 50/10 ratio). The D50/D10 ratio rose in Germany by 23 percent between 1990 and 2008, from 1.57 to 1.93. In Denmark the 50/10 ratio rose less (about 14 percent) and by 2008 had just reached the 1990 level for Germany at 1.57 (OECD figures).[23]

---

[23] Relatively more generous unemployment benefits also set a higher floor (reservation wage) for low-skilled workers in Denmark.

Not just collective bargaining, but other labor market institutions in Denmark have also experienced significant liberalization. In employment protections and training measures as well, we observe a broad difference between dualizing and embedded flexibilization. Whereas the dominant pattern in Germany combines the stabilization of employment within the industrial core with flexibilization and activation on the periphery, Denmark famously pursued more broad-based liberalization – both in labor market policies and in accompanying training initiatives (see also Martin and Swank 2012; Martin and Thelen 2007b; Thelen 2014: chapter 4). Denmark has traditionally featured higher levels of labor market fluidity than most other CMEs (Estevez-Abe et al. 2001), but major policy innovations in the 1990s enhanced labor-market flexibility while also, however, providing significant subsidies to promote skill development on a broad scale (Madsen 2006). In this period, Denmark's Social Democratic government doubled its expenditures on active labor market policies (ALMP), to nearly 2 percent of GDP, a level that exceeded that in other countries. Parallel reforms also established the most comprehensive system of adult (continuing) vocational education and training in all of Europe, offering training courses free of charge and available to anyone eighteen years old or older (Nielsen 1995; Schulze-Cleven 2009). Because these training measures are designed to promote labor market mobility, the content of the skills is also general – which is to say, training is also aligned with the portable skills traditionally associated with the LME model (chapter 3 in Thelen 2014; see also Anderson and Hassel 2013).

Such policies were a crucial accompaniment to the politics of labor market liberalization and collective bargaining decentralization noted previously. A key moment occurred in 1998 when the Social Democratic government intervened to end a general strike prompted by low-skill unions protesting against a wage agreement worked out in the export sector. The government was able to broker a deal through targeted concessions to lower-skilled constituencies. Concretely the deal compensated the new risks associated with labor market liberalization and wage flexibilization with an "expansion in the scope of collective bargaining" to incorporate "other forms of security" (particularly skills and training for low-skill workers) into central contracts (Ibsen 2012: 2, 16; Andersen and Mailand 2005: 3). In the context of this volume this move can be seen as a strategy to shore up the coalition between two core Social democratic constituencies – higher educated salaried employees favoring investment strategies and lower-skill white- and blue-collar interests concerned about the impact of liberalization.

State support for social investment policies (including, especially, those that support training) has been crucial to sustaining this deal, and the Danish model has by no means been immune to shifting political winds. Notably, the center-Right government of the 2000s reduced organized labor's role and implemented significant cuts in social spending (Jørgensen and Schulze 2012). ALMP in this period tilted decisively in the direction of activation, as the share

of funds devoted to training declined. Supported by the radical populist Danish
Peoples Party, this government crafted an austerity coalition based on a double
shift – broadly speaking, away from the "state" to the "market" and away
from "risk pooling" to "risk differentiation" especially though welfare chauvinism and the targeted exclusion of immigrants (see also Beramendi et al.,
Introduction, this volume). In an effort to undermine the power of a key Social
Democratic constituency, the right-wing government also sought to undermine
union power by breaking up the Ghent system of administering unemployment
insurance – an effort that was, however, only partially successful.

The changes in Denmark in the 2000s were significant but conform nonetheless to a pattern of "constrained partisanship." Constituencies that support
high levels of social investment appear still to be quite robust, so that even
after ten years of center-right control (2001–2011) and significant cutbacks,
social investment in Denmark remains strong in comparative perspective (see
Figure 1.1 in Beramendi et al., Introduction; also Gingrich and Ansell, this
volume). Thus while spending on ALMP declined very significantly (from
0.35 percent of GDP in 2000 to 0.18 percent by 2010 according to Rathgeb
(2014: 17)), Denmark still spends more on these measures than most other
countries. On training specifically, Denmark has declined from internationally unique heights in 2000 to much lower levels of spending, but still invests
more in training per unemployed person than all other countries save Austria,
Finland, and Norway (Rathgeb 2014: 16, figure 5). Moreover, and thanks also
to (state-facilitated) collective bargaining deals on training, low-skill workers
are receiving much more training in Denmark than in the rest of the European
Union. Recent figures indicate that almost a quarter of Danes with the lowest educational achievement levels (levels 0–2 of the International Standard
Classification of Education, ISCED) participate in adult education and training
programs (the EU average is 3.8 percent) (CEDEFOP 2012).[24]

Patient capital has also been important in sustaining a model that channels wage flexibility and reembeds liberalizing moves in compensatory social
and social-investment policies. Thus the most adversarial labor relations in
Denmark can be found in foreign-owned companies. Such firms have often
adopted more unalloyed shareholder-oriented management practices and
been reluctant to engage fully with Danish unions – resulting in a minimal-
ist interpretation of their legal obligations toward worker representatives and
declining firm investments in training (Navrbjerg and Minbaeva 2009; see also
Rocha 2009). For example, when the Danish telecommunications giant TDC
was taken over by U.S. private equity investors, the new management discon-
tinued apprenticeship programs, increased supervision of low-skilled work,
and introduced variable pay schemes at call centers – often leading to less

---

[24] The Right government had also abandoned previous tripartite practices, but these appear
to have been restored under the Social Democrats, at least in the area of vocational training
reforms (Mailand 2014).

favorable wage rates. Yet even in these somewhat extreme cases, Denmark's institutional infrastructure has an effect. For example, TDC has retained more compressed wage differentials at the bottom of the salary scale and between incumbent and outsourced work than in Germany or several other European economies (Doellgast et al. 2013).

For the majority of Danish firms, corporate governance reforms in fact reinforced adoption of new concepts of CSR, which have arguably opened new areas for union participation. The "it concerns us all" initiative that was adopted in 1994 occurred at precisely the same time as the major Social Democratic push in training described earlier. The CSR initiative, actively supported by the trade union federation LO, also promoted a "social index" to evaluate company CSR activities. As labor relations and welfare reforms progressed, the social partners became increasingly involved and a very dense policy network of overlapping initiatives emerged (Morsing 2004). Subsequent CSR initiatives have likewise been promoted with a broad consensus of the social partners. For example, in 2009, the government created a new Danish Council on CSR, a group that includes major companies, business associations, pension fund representatives, NGOs, and union representatives. CSR initiatives have been used to promote responsibility for labor issues along the supply chain, and in some cases (e.g., Carlsberg) explicitly to extend union-management cooperation overseas to developing countries.

12.5. Discussion

Pressures for liberalization are ubiquitous across the rich democracies but rarely take the form of an outright dismantling of institutional support for coordination in CMEs. Moreover, patterns of stability and change across different sets of institutions are complex. In this chapter, we have emphasized how different trajectories of liberalization are influenced by the political coalitions that channel these pressures and translate them into concrete institutional reforms.

In Germany, the politics of liberalization in corporate governance and labor relations redounded above all to the benefit of large listed firms in the manufacturing sector. These firms have been able to benefit from selective liberalization in both realms – taking advantage of new M&A opportunities that accompanied corporate governance reforms and higher executive salaries, while also benefiting from the growth of a less regulated labor-relations periphery through lower-service prices and lower taxes. The declining influence of patient capital and pressure for shareholder value has intensified cooperation with labor in the industrial core but at the same time created new and longer-term political problems related to labor market dualization. For now, large firms have been able to use these less institutionally coherent "hybrid" arrangements to underwrite the continued success of the German export model based on high skills and coordinated labor relations. At the same time, though, these trends have fueled processes of dualization that German unions – only weakly anchored outside the industrial core – have been largely unable to counteract.

Denmark illustrates an alternative pattern of change. Despite greater stability in corporate governance, institutional changes in labor relations have produced more flexible – though still more encompassing – arrangements that depart from the logic underpinning "traditional" coordinated capitalism. Danish institutions now allow for wage decentralization, even wage individualization; support general (as opposed to firm- or industry-specific) skills; and organize around employment (rather than job) security. They also, however, provide more durable protections than in Germany for the most vulnerable groups in the labor market. This very different pattern of politics prevails here because emerging new interests (low-skill service sector workers but also larger numbers of women and salaried employees) are well organized by unions and thus represented both in bargaining with employers and in politics. While by no means immune to shifting political winds, organized labor's continued relative strength and broader presence has more often than in Germany produced encompassing reforms based on negotiated trade-offs between liberalization and measures that collectivize the resulting labor market risks through various social investment policies (above all, training) (Levy 1999; Bonoli 2005: 442ff.; Martin and Thelen 2007a; Martin and Swank 2012; Gingrich and Ansell, this volume).

These empirical results are illuminating in light of dominant theories in two important respects. First, both VoC theorists and their critics tend to see corporate governance and industrial relations as interconnected, whereby "patient capital" and coordinated collective bargaining reinforce one another, on the basis of either their coherence around a similar logic of coordination (VoC) or their shared vulnerability to global market pressures (liberalization theories). By contrast, we have argued that changes in corporate governance and industrial relations are interrelated, but in a more politically contingent fashion. Both Germany and Denmark have evolved toward less institutionally coherent combinations, but in different ways that reflect the distinctive political coalitions in each country and result in new "hybrid" logics of interaction between these two institutional arenas.[25] In Germany, a negotiated model of shareholder value has emerged that seeks to reconcile continued coordination in labor relations within the industrial core with a more shareholder-oriented type of corporate governance. However, as we have seen, the resulting intensification

---

[25] Another interesting paradox that cannot be pursued further here is the interplay between formal-institutional and informal change in the two countries. Germany combines rather significant formal-institutional changes in corporate governance (but alongside strong informal continuities in large swaths of the economy outside the large export-oriented firms, e.g., among the *Mittelstand*) with low levels of formal-institutional change in industrial relations (but as we have seen significant informal erosion).

of cooperation in these parts of the economy has been at the expense of the growth of a less regulated periphery in wide swaths of the labor market where unions are much weaker and collective bargaining coverage spottier. In Denmark, the stability of patient capital through foundation ownership has helped soften or even constrain (e.g., through CSR) how firms utilize their more liberal labor market institutions. Indeed, we might speculate that the degree of freedom from the capital market created via patient capital remains a necessary condition for the more solidaristic type of embedded liberalization found in Denmark.

Second, these case studies show that political intermediation plays a more complex role in liberalization than often assumed. Our case studies show that the politics of liberalization defy simple Right/Left categorizations, whereby Left parties are usually considered "defenders" of coordination and liberalization is hypothesized as negatively correlated with Left party power. On the contrary, Left parties have played a crucial role in pushing liberalization in German corporate governance as well as in some aspects of Danish labor relations. These "paradoxical" party positions reflect the wider political alignments of parties with organized groups whose identities and interests differed between the two countries in politically consequential ways. In terms of patient capital, German banks – unlike Danish foundations– supported liberalization and shareholder value. In terms of labor relations, Germany's industrial unions more strongly supported labor market insiders, whereas more centrally organized Danish unions pursued more encompassing approaches to labor market liberalization.

These different pathways matter for the future competitiveness of these economies, as well as for the distributional consequences of liberalization that will continue to shape the politics of the political economy. The German trajectory of dualistic liberalization is likely to become increasingly unsustainable, as core manufacturing employment continues its very slow decline and labor relations in the service sector do not deliver a more egalitarian alternative. Meanwhile, the Danish trajectory of embedded liberalization clearly relies on significant state support to underwrite a "higher-road" transition to service sector employment. In this context, an important and often neglected keystone of the Danish flexicurity model may be corporate governance – where barriers to hostile takeovers remain in place, and managers are held accountable to a wider range of interests than those of shareholders. In fact, patient capital in Denmark may be an important testing ground for theories that see financialization as a driving force in the overall convergence of capitalisms.

PART IV

OUTCOMES

13

Constrained Partisanship and Economic Outcomes

Pablo Beramendi

The *relative autonomy of politics*, to use an expression slightly out of fashion, as a determinant of social and economic outcomes is yet again in the eye of the beholder. While some see processes such as globalization, deindustrialization, and more recently the Great Recession as a sign of structural factors overruling the ability of incumbents to pursue their agenda and shape the distribution of winners and losers across society, others see the responses to the financial crisis as reflecting the differences among well-oiled and persistent institutional organizations of capitalism. In the former tale, which we refer to in this volume as *economic structuralism*, incumbents quickly turn into irrelevant witnesses of a process of convergence in economic and distributive outcomes. In the latter tale, visible in various forms in the literature on *varieties of capitalism*, incumbents adjust their strategy to preserve coalitions articulated around the needs of organized interests, both producers and labor. Economic outcomes are affected by policies that reflect divergent distributions of interests among producers and workers stratified by skill level. Earlier contributions to the volume have already discussed how our approach relates to these accounts.[1] This chapter focuses on the evolution of economic outcomes in advanced industrial democracies and assesses whether the model of constrained partisanship developed in this book lends any analytical power to understand them.

In what follows, I make four points. First, while there is some empirical basis to substantiate the notion of relative convergence in economic outcomes among advanced industrial societies, a careful scrutiny reveals deep-rooted differences in terms of economic inequality and labor market opportunities. Second, these differences reflect to a large extent the balance between

For extensive feedback on a previous version of this chapter I thank my coeditors as well as Ben Ansell, Jonas Pontusson, David Soskice, and David Rueda. The usual disclaimer applies.

[1] For a more extensive discussion, see the Introduction to the volume ("The Politics of Advanced Capitalism").

investment and consumption policies: Investment oriented economies generate in the long run more egalitarian societies and better labor markets. Third, those parties ideologically inclined to pursue these goals are constrained by two institutional features largely overlooked by previous explanations: the level of revenue collection by the state and the ability of organized labor to capture a large share of the budget via consumption policy. Less fiscal capacity and pro-insiders regulations jointly limit the scope of investment policies, thereby shaping the distribution of outcomes and opportunities in society. Fourth, the same conditions mediate the impact of policy choices on income inequality and the distribution of labor market opportunities.

To develop this argument, the rest of the chapter is organized as follows. First, I present an overview of economic outcomes in advanced capitalist societies. Thereafter, in Section 13.2, I present the theoretical argument linking partisan strategies, policy choices, and distributive outcomes. Section 13.3 analyzes empirically the link between policy choices and distributive outcomes. Section 13.4 concludes.

13.1. Growth and Allocation: Beyond the Illusion of Convergence

A first look at the evolution of growth rates among industrialized democracies seems to lend some support to the structuralist view that advanced economies are undergoing a process of convergence, at least in relative terms. Figure 13.1 plots average annual rates of economic growth for two periods, 1970–1990 and 1990–2010. I choose here long periods to capture the long-term development of growth patterns, rather than more short-term business cycle effects. The cross-national average growth rate has indeed lowered between the two periods from about 2.1 to 1.9 percent, suggesting that weaker performers in the earlier period tend to perform better in more recent ones. However, Figure 13.1 also shows that the trend has been far from uniform across countries. Clearly, forces other than structuralist transformations are also at work. Moreover, countries in categories as those suggested by the *varieties of capitalism* approach (Hall and Soskice 2001) differ sharply in their evolution. Put simply, the variation in growth trajectories among coordinated market economies is larger than that between coordinated and liberal market economies. Countries such as Sweden or the Netherlands had rather weak growth performance before the 1990s but show higher-than-average growth in the later period. At the same time, several relatively high-performing coordinated market economies such as Italy, France, Norway, Germany, or Finland performed above average between 1970 and 1990 but developed into completely opposite dynamics after the 1990s. While Finland and Norway experienced high levels of growth post 1990, Italy, Japan, France, and Germany performed poorly. Hence, in terms of pre-crisis growth trajectories, we certainly do see a large amount of variation that remains unexplained by previous accounts.

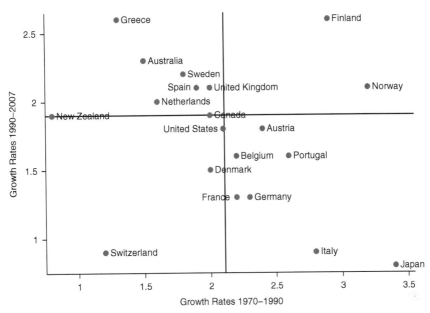

FIGURE 13.1. GDP growth rates, 1970–1990 and 1990–2007. (UN Data)

More importantly, this cross-national variation in *changes in the size* of the pie becomes even starker when we focus on changes in the *distribution of the pie* in advanced industrial economies. Much has been written on the age of rising inequality in the OECD countries and its potential social, institutional, and political consequences (2011; Bartels 2008; Gilens 2013; Stiglitz 2012). Figure 13.2 plots the level of income inequality in the mid-1980s against the change in inequality from the mid-1980s to the mid-2000s. Again, Figure 13.2 could support the structuralist notion of a convergent trend driven by the unleashing of capitalism. After all, in all but five countries, income inequality has increased over the period in question. Only France, Switzerland, and Belgium maintained the same or slightly lower levels of income inequality, while Ireland reduced inequality substantively. In all other countries, inequality has increased, particularly in those countries that were below average levels in the 1980s. However, a more careful scrutiny reveals that variation in outcomes performance remains very large. The Nordic countries Sweden, Norway, Denmark, and Finland, for instance, which had very low rates of inequality in the 1980s, remain at the lower end of the distribution: Despite increases of 10 to 30 percentage points, none of these countries' level of Gini income inequality exceeds 0.3. The other coordinated market economies of continental and Southern Europe are – again – strongly disparate. Austria, Germany, and the Netherlands to some extent close up to the (stable) level of inequality France

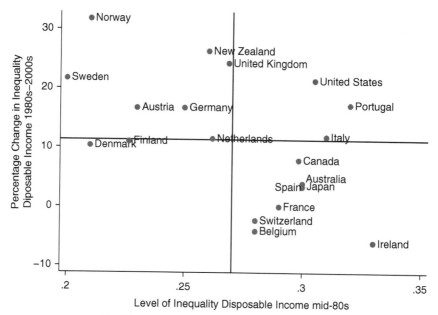

FIGURE 13.2. Levels of inequality in disposable income in the mid-1980s and percentage change in inequality between the 1980s and 2000s.
(LIS data)

had in the 1980s already, whereas the Southern European countries start at rather high levels of inequality and increase them moderately. While the coordinated countries thus indeed show some signs of convergence, the liberal market economies have developed in different ways. The United Kingdom, United States, and New Zealand increase inequality strongly from an already rather high level, whereas Canada and Australia remain stable at relatively high rates of inequality.

Reviewing these distributions of outcome indicators, I find little evidence for either convergence or regime stability across forms of organized capitalism. This conclusion is further reinforced when one relates the current level of inequality in disposable income (as captured in Figure 13.2) to measures that, albeit indirectly, tap into the distribution of economic opportunities and the working of labor markets. Figure 13.3 explores the relationships among income inequality; the size of the intergenerational income elasticity, that is, how well parents' income predicts their children's position in the income distribution (Corak 2012a); and the incidence of long-term unemployment (average levels for the period 1990–2010). A high correlation of income across generations suggests that income mobility levels are low and therefore the distribution of opportunities to improve the relative position within the income distribution is also very unequal. Likewise, high average levels of long-term unemployment

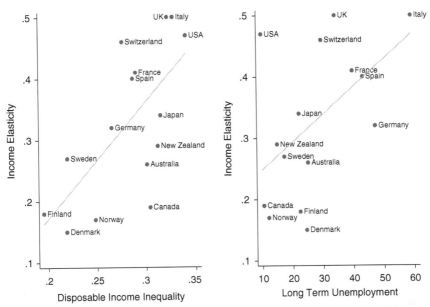

FIGURE 13.3. Income inequality, intergenerational income elasticity, and long-term unemployment.

indicate that people who fall into unemployment in that society will find it harder to resume work and improve their economic situation. Unsurprisingly, as shown in Figure 13.3 (right panel), this is closely related to the size of the intergenerational income elasticity.

The patterns displayed in Figure 13.3 reinforce earlier findings. First, there is a great deal of variation across countries in terms of the correlation among inequality, the intergenerational income elasticity, and long-term unemployment. Second, the variation does not conform with the distinction between liberal and coordinated economies, nor with any other standard conceptualization/categorization in the field. Among the countries with high inequality and high elasticity, we find political economies as diverse as Italy and the United States. At the lower end of the correlation, in turn, we find a more familiar cluster of Scandinavian societies, but the middle range is again populated by countries as diverse as Canada, Australia, Germany, and New Zealand. Even more intriguing are the patterns in the association between the income elasticity and the average levels of long-term unemployment throughout the period: Canada seems to have more in common with Scandinavia than with the other liberal market economies, whereas countries as diverse as Italy and the United Kingdom seem to have medium to high levels of long-term unemployment along with a rather high intergenerational income elasticity.

Overall, the evidence shown in Figures 13.1–13.3 poses an important puzzle about the evolution of economic outcomes in advanced democracies: Why are some societies able to combine low levels of income inequality, low intergenerational income elasticities, and low levels of long-term unemployment, whereas others display either highly unequal results in terms of both outcomes and opportunities or mixed results, combining moderate levels of income inequality with high levels of long-term unemployment and intergenerational income elasticities? In the rest of this chapter I contend that these outcomes link back directly to government's politico-economic strategies in terms of consumption and investment. I proceed in two steps. I begin by presenting a theoretical argument linking partisan strategies, policies, and outcomes. Thereafter, the next two sections offer systematic empirical evidence on the linkages between different politico-economic strategies and distributive outcomes in terms of income and opportunities. Finally, I briefly outline the core implications of my findings.

13.2. Political Strategies and Economic Outcomes

In line with the rest of the chapters in this volume, I conceptualize the fundamental choice by incumbents as one between investment and consumption. I reason from the premise that the relative balance between investment and consumption links back to different growth strategies.[2] An investment or innovation based strategy builds on skills upgrading in the medium run and aspires to increase productivity level, and to sustain growth through "leading edge innovations" in Aghion and Howitt's (2006) terms. In contrast, for countries behind the technology frontier growth occurs primarily via capital investments, the import of technologies developed elsewhere, and consumption oriented policies aimed at sustaining high levels of aggregate demand (Acemoglu et al. 2006). In line with this logic and the rest of the volume, I define "investment" widely as the combination of fiscal policy and regulations that contributes to increase the overall productivity of the economy, and that of labor and capital in particular.[3] The term "investment" refers to the future orientation of these measures in the fields of education, research and development, child care, activation, and public infrastructure. The goal is to maximize future returns through increases in productivity. On the other hand, I consider consumption expenditures and regulations as policy measures (again, including fiscal

---

[2] By politico-economic strategy I refer to a combination of employment policy (regulations), fiscal policy (taxes and transfers), and public service provision. In terms of regulation, governments must choose the level of internal protectionism of organized interests there is to be. This has direct implications for the real levels of economic competition and innovation within political economies. In terms of fiscal policy and public service provision, governments must choose how much to privilege consumption expenditure at the expense of future returns via investments in education, research and development, and child care.

[3] A slightly narrower distinction between consumption and investment oriented expenditures has also developed in the welfare state literature (Esping-Andersen 1999; Bonoli and Natali 2012; Morel et al. 2012; Hemerijk 2013).

policy and regulations) devoted to boost citizens' ability to purchase goods and services in the short run. The balance between these two sets of policy instruments is critical to understand economic and distributive outcomes in the postindustrial world.

To establish the logic ruling the connections among parties, policies, and outcomes, my argument builds on the following premises. First, parties use policy to build and sustain stable electoral coalitions (Esping-Andersen 1985). In doing so, parties face an intertemporal dilemma that underpins all consumption and investment policies. Consumption provides voters with tangible and quantifiable benefits today. Investments, in turn, generate a significant opportunity cost in terms of consumption and offer benefits that are risky and often accrue to voters well after the election has passed. Second, at the microlevel, I assume that when making political choices, citizens care about their net benefits from both the market and the state (final income), including the value they derive from public goods that are often not accounted for in standard fiscal policy measurements (Beramendi and Rehm 2015). Third, in grappling with the dilemma between consumption and investment, parties face supply and demand constraints when choosing the combination of consumption and investment policy that maximizes their electoral and political returns. The analysis moves beyond conceptions of partisanship focused exclusively on a unidimensional definition of Left-Right ideology (Bartels 2008; Dixit and Londregan 1998; Hibbs 1977; Alt 1985; Huber and Stephens 2001) to understand preferences and strategies as responses to preference sets that include distributive and nondistributive elements (Hausermänn and Kriesi, this volume) and preexisting legacies that limit incumbents' options. I argue that the variance in economic outcomes identified in the previous section reflects the conditional impact of partisan strategies in terms of consumption and investment under different sets of constraints. Most prominently, I focus on two types of constraints: the legacy of past policy commitments and the state's revenue collection capacity. The interaction works as follows.

Investment policies are costly in the short run and generate uncertain political returns in the medium to long run. They also imply an opportunity cost in terms of the *current* capacity to consume. It is precisely because of these two features that the state's capacity of revenue collection plays, I argue, such a central role as a constraint on the supply side of politics. Critically, the intensity of the trade-off between investment and consumption policies depends on the level of available resources: When political coalitions allow very large levels of revenue generation, there is less of a trade-off, and egalitarian efforts combining both consumption and investment become feasible. By contrast, without enough revenues to ensure consumption and then entertain investment policy initiatives, the latter do not rank high in the incumbent's list of policy priorities. In turn, at any given time, this list captures preexisting commitments in terms of the balance between consumption and investment, and their feedback effect on voters' predispositions toward different policy reforms.

TABLE 13.1. *The structure of political constraints*

		Revenue Collection	
		High	Low
Dualization	High	Status	Capture
	Low	Equality	Competitiveness

In societies where hegemonic political coalitions rest on consumption policy expenditures (most prominently, status and capture oriented ones), the room of maneuver to detract resources from transfers and devote them to investment policies is very small. This is particularly the case in highly dualized labor markets. More dualization implies a stronger commitment of policy (both fiscal and regulatory) toward insiders (Rueda 2007; Gingrich and Ansell, this volume), leaving relatively fewer resources available for investment policy at any given level of revenue collection. In turn, less dualization, whether via policy, institutions, or regulation, implies that incumbents' hands are less tied by prior policy commitments. In other words, governments have more room to maneuver to alter their policy strategies. The point is not to use policy legacies to predict policy, as this could quickly become circular; the point is to think of the balance between consumption and investment as the outcome of past political struggles acting as a constraint today.[4]

To develop the argument in detail, Table 13.1 summarizes the structure of political constraints faced by parties and links back to the model developed earlier in the book. In what follows I outline how different sets of constraints shape both the ability of parties to pursue different combinations of investment and consumption and, more importantly for the purposes of this chapter, the differential distributive impact of these choices.

Earlier analyses (Kitschelt and Rehm, this volume) suggest that to achieve a sustained presence in office, left-wing parties must successfully forge a coalition of manufacturing workers, low skilled service workers, and high skilled, normatively liberal, service workers (the so-called sociocultural professionals). By contrast, the ideal coalition of conservative parties includes both workers with traditional values, high wage earners and liberal professionals, and employers, particularly owners of businesses with traditional values. Left parties must design policy, both distributive and normative, to attract and retain high skilled, high paid workers. In turn, conservative parties must use policy, often second-dimension politics, to attract a portion of low income voters. A key insight throughout many of the chapters in this book is that the nature

---

[4] Clearly, such a balance captures past parties' strategies and channels, indirectly, the impact of electoral institutions and the organization of labor markets. For earlier contributions along these lines: Hicks and Kenworthy 1998; Lange and Garrett 1985; Alvarez et al. 1991; Rueda and Pontusson 2000; Beramendi and Cusack 2009.

of political competition in each of these quadrants mediates the gap between the parties' ideal political strategies and what they can actually achieve. To the extent that policies are the tool to build and sustain feasible political coalitions (Esping-Andersen 1985), the constraints outlined in Table 13.1 matter not only because they condition the amount of resources available but also because they feed back into the structure of political demand. That is, the pivotal groups to which parties respond when competing electorally are themselves a function of previous policy (Esping-Andersen 1993; Oesch, this volume). As a result, the politics of inequality varies within each of the four configurations in Table 13.1, shaping, in combination with the supply side constraints, the balance between consumption and investment and their distributive effects.

Let us consider first the choices over consumption and investment in high revenue, low dualization contexts. To become self-enforced and electorally sustainable, large levels of revenue generation must be understood as part of a broader political exchange between incumbents and highly organized labor and employers. High wage earners and sociocultural professionals only endorse a strategy of equality insofar as the benefits they receive via public goods and the fiscal system exceed the costs they pay through different tax tools.[5] Moreover, the strategy's sustainability requires the implicit consent of private investors, as it rests on high levels of both public and private employment. To secure high levels of private investment, governments must reduce the relative share of capital and corporate taxes in the economic policy strategy.[6] In turn, the low levels of dualization reflect the past success of social democracy in forging a complex coalition across classes and sectors (Moene and Wallerstein 2002). Once the fiscal resources were in place, social democrats enjoyed enough resources to forge the coalition between manufacturing workers and sociocultural professionals via multidimensional policy strategy: Wage compression and progressive and universalistic fiscal transfers ensure the support of the bottom half of the wage distribution; high levels of public employment to absorb the surplus of deindustrialization are tailored

---

[5] A large share of the sociocultural professionals (health and education workers, for instance) are actually public sector employees. This, in turn, facilitates the task of revenue collection. By contrast, a pure transfer state with less public service provision has a harder time sustaining the support of high wage earners.

[6] In addition, the political support of wage earners, in particular high wage earners, requires tax policy tools not to be too progressive. Otherwise, the net benefits for this pivotal group of voters would be negative, and they would withdraw their political support. The implication is clear: Taxes on labor not only bear a larger share of the cost of redistribution, thus reducing the level of progressivity between factors (Cusack and Beramendi 2006); they also become less progressive in their design. Moreover, as the relative importance of labor taxes increases, the internal stability of the social democratic coalition comes into question and governments shift the burden from producers to consumers (Kato 2003; Beramendi and Rueda 2007; Steinmo 2010). In this context, capital commits to stable investment and long-term growth in return for the government's promise not to tax their benefits to finance the welfare state (Przeworski and Wallerstein 1988).

TABLE 13.2. *Policy configurations across different sets of constraints*

		Revenue Collection	
		High	Low
Dualization	High	High consumption	Low consumption
		Low investment	Low investment
	Low	High consumption	Low consumption
		High investment	High investment

to sociocultural professionals; active and passive labor market policies to ease labor market transitions thus reinforce low levels of labor market dualization; and public investments in higher education and early child care demonstrate to high wage earners a return on their taxes. Over time, wage earners meet the cost of a system from which, in the long run, they emerge as net beneficiaries. Such an egalitarian strategy targets both outcomes and opportunities and secures equality as much via the long-term effects of public investments and taxes on wage compression as through the short-run redistributive impact of consumption transfers (Boix 1998; Pontusson 2005; Steinmo 2010; Esping-Andersen 2010; Huber and Stephens 2014).

This strategy is built on the combination of high levels of both investment and consumption effort, as summarized in Table 13.2, and has provided the basis for the long- term electoral hegemony of Social Democracy in Scandinavia. Only recently, when the fiscal constraints have become tighter, immigration is paving the way for increased levels of dualization (Lindvall and Rueda 2014), and export oriented high wage service workers are revisiting the balance between their earnings potential and their disposable income, have conservative forces been able to forge alternative coalitions based on the restriction of consumption and progressivity and the limitation of access to services and insurance to nationals. These recent transformations aside, societies able to mobilize large levels of revenue in labor markets with low levels of dualization remain those where the intertemporal trade-off between effort on consumption and effort on investment seems less acute.

This policy regime translates directly into the distributive outcomes that concern this chapter. Wage compression in the labor market and progressive consumption policies contribute to an egalitarian distribution of disposable income. In turn the extensive investment in active labor market policies eases labor market transitions for the unemployed, thus reducing the scope of long-term unemployment. Finally, large scale, universally accessible educational investments facilitate the equalization of opportunities early on, thus reducing the size of the income elasticity. In sum, when revenues are high and dualization is low, consumption and investment operate as complementary mechanisms that reinforce each other to reduce inequalities of both outcomes and economic opportunities. By contrast, as politicians operate under alternative sets of constraints, both the relative effort in terms of investment and consumption policies and the distributive impact of incumbents' policy choices change significantly.

Consider, for instance, societies where past political struggles have yielded a scenario characterized by relatively lower levels of revenue collection and flexible labor markets (a scenario we refer to as *competitiveness* throughout the volume). Under these conditions long-term commitments by organized economic actors are neither feasible nor credible. Parties approach consumption and investment policies as a realm of its own, relatively less constrained by intertemporal exchanges, and use them to target the core elements of their constituencies, urban workers in manufacturing and urban sociocultural professionals for the Left, and business owners, rural workers, and high paid service workers for the Right. Supporters of the Left demand expansions in coverage and effort, particularly targeted toward liberal urban professionals (Ansell 2010; Kitschelt and Rehm, this volume). Supporters of the Right demand policies, such as higher education tax deductions accruing to the upper end of the wage distribution, that ultimately exacerbate preexisting inequalities of income and opportunities. In terms of consumption, Left parties will pursue higher levels of progressivity in both transfers and taxes, and Right parties will oppose them. In terms of investment, the Left will pursue the spread of opportunity to middle and low income voters, whereas the Right will underfund public education throughout for the benefit of market alternatives that reproduce and enhance existing income and wealth inequalities. Because progressivity implies a higher share of overall revenue collection on the shoulders of capital (progressivity between factors or classes) and a more targeted allocation of benefits to the lower strata and of the tax burden to the upper strata of the pre-fisc distribution, polarization over redistribution is stronger and the size of the consumption budget is bound to be smaller. Moreover, labor is not organized enough to capture a large share of the budget for consumption transfers, and high wage earners and capital coalesce to limit its use to boost investment oriented expenditures. By adjusting policy to their electoral constituencies, parties generate policy portfolios that include lower overall revenues, well-targeted and relatively small consumption expenditures, and significant investment efforts (i.e., *low consumption, high investment* in Table 13.2).

In terms of distributive impact, this policy regime generates a different set of outcomes: The fact that both taxes and consumption transfers are progressive limits the size of the budget at the effectiveness in containing inequality (Korpi and Palme 1998). More interestingly, higher efforts in investment policy may boost rather than reduce income inequality. In democracies with universalistic public services across the life course, access to enhanced opportunities facilitated by larger investment efforts is effectively universal and highly redistributive (Ansell 2010). By contrast, in democracies where the revenue pool is politically constrained, access to investment opportunities is restricted to those able to pursue a full educational career, while flexible labor markets for low skilled workers open exit options along the way. To the extent that the actual access to expanded investment opportunities remains de facto an option mostly for the upper half of the wage distribution, a stronger investment effort will cause an increase in inequality. At the same time, I expect it to reduce the levels of long-term unemployment by facilitating a better match between the supply and demand of skills. Finally, to the extent that enhanced opportunities are accessed by the children of the well-off, I expect it to fail to reduce the size of the intergenerational income elasticity.

I turn now to consider partisan strategies and distributive outcomes for the other two scenarios in Table 13.1, those we refer to as *status* and *capture* earlier in the volume. Policy regimes in both in these contexts reflect the legacy of political struggles where parties have been tailored to the interests of either industry level unions in the manufacturing sector (the Left) or prone-to-order wage earners, self-employed, and small business owners (the Right). For the latter, typically Christian Democratic Parties, the goal was to secure the wage earner coalition without disrupting society's order. In the spirit of nineteenth century social Catholic and Protestant movements, Christian Democrats see corporatism and social policy as mechanisms both to pool (across industries) and to stratify risks (within industries) via insurance systems (Mares 2003; Van Kersbergen 1995). For them, the ideal-type political strategy consists in reproducing market inequalities over the life course via insurance mechanisms. This implies a large system of transfers with replacement rates such that the inequality of benefits approximates the inequality in earnings, and a design of investment policy of smaller size and with much lower redistributive clout. By contrast, the Left typically defends more progressive designs of both transfers and revenues (i.e., reducing the importance of social security contributions vis-à-vis income taxes) for insider manufacturing workers and, over time, larger and more accessible investments in education. The fundamental parameters of the system, though, build a strong consumption bias relative to investment efforts.

Of course, the scope of this tension, and the associated distributive consequences, is conditional on the level of revenue collection. And this is no accident of history, but the consequence of different sequences in the formation of welfare states and revenue systems, and the incidence of dualization. As argued previously, high revenues result from the working of a cross-class agreement that limits the burden of capital relative to that of workers and consumers, an agreement typically enforced via corporatist arrangements and coalition bargains in the legislature. The Christian Democratic version of this agreement places more emphasis on payroll and social security contributions as opposed to income taxes, but it follows a similar logic.

For a long time, the amount of revenue generated was enough to guarantee very generous insurance schemes for permanent workers and fund investment efforts in education. Social Democracy would have a more progressive emphasis than Christian Democracy, but the tension between consumption and investment was muted by a generous purse. Interestingly, as the sociodemographic transformations analyzed earlier in the book (aging, deindustrialization, and the incorporation of women into the labor force) unfolded, budgetary demands for both investment and consumption increased, as did labor market pressures. Dualization emerges then as a response both to try to maintain the privileges of the core of the labor force, a pivotal electoral group for both the Left and the Right, and at the same time to alleviate the mismatch between supply and demand caused by deindustrialization. Over time, partisan struggles turn into conflicts about the scope and design in the adjustment of consumption expenses (Huber and Stephens, this volume), the degree of deregulation of labor markets, and the size and coverage of various investment efforts, but the fundamental balance between consumption and investment remains in place (*high consumption, low investment* in Table 13.2). In terms of distributive outcomes, I expect increasing efforts in investment to translate into lower levels of income inequality through the redistributive effect of public services, but I also expect these effects to be muted by the relative power of insiders in the labor market. The higher the ability of a core of the labor force to monopolize access to public investments, the lesser their egalitarian impact on the distribution of both income and economic opportunities. By contrast, I expect increasing efforts in consumption to contribute very little, because of the minimally progressive nature of insurance based policies, to the reduction of income inequality. Indeed, as the ability of insiders to capture policy in the labor market grows strong, I predict higher efforts in consumption policy to cause marginal increases (rather than decreases) in the levels of income inequality. At the same time, I suggest that high consumption, low investment societies will show relatively higher levels of long-term unemployment and income elasticity, reflecting the fact that economic opportunities remain highly stratified across generations and sectors in the labor market.

By contrast, in those countries where the protection of insiders precedes the expansion of the welfare state, policy constraints become particularly stringent. By and large, these countries undertook industrialization via import substitution under autocracy in the late sixties, which in turn imposed early on a core of heavily protected and well-organized labor market insiders (Rueda 2007; Wibbels 2012), achieved democratization comparatively late; and only began the construction of the welfare state after the oil crisis, the abandonment of Keynesianism, and the rise of fiscal and monetary orthodoxy (Maravall 1996a; Boix 1998). Born in this new international and ideological environment, these welfare states feature lower levels of state and fiscal capacity by comparative standards (Persson and Besley 2011). This in turn limits considerably the feasibility of large-scale public interventions to correct market outcomes via consumption policy. It also constrains the ability to sustain public investment over time. Social Democrats do pursue public investments (Boix 1998) but to a much lower extent, as they cannot engage in long-term reform strategies with market actors. The Right in turn courts small business and the self-employed with favorable regulations and tax treatments. Accordingly, employment gains occur via reforms that exploit the business cycle to generate large amounts of low skill, low quality jobs, with the resulting emergence of extremely dualized labor markets via high levels of employment protection (Rueda et al., this volume), further empowering organized workers to maximize their consumption share via transfers and small business to secure favorable tax treatment. As the latter are left untouched by the fiscal system, a disproportionate share of the fiscal burden falls, again, on payroll workers and consumers.

With no resources, rulers' hands are tied and no feasible economic policy strategy is feasible beyond the satisfaction of basic consumption needs. In this situation incumbents have very little room for maneuver, and policy features low levels of both consumption and investment. Families and the informal sector emerge, or indeed remain, as functional equivalents, further undermining the fiscal capacity of the state. Born under a rather adverse international and ideological environment, these state structures constrain the scope and success of egalitarian interventions. Both tax progressivity and redistributive scope are low by comparative standards, and inequalities in the labor market remain extremely pronounced, only to increase over time. The combination of high levels of employment protection, weak financial capacity, and a relatively underdeveloped and insider oriented welfare state yields a scenario in which we observe very low levels of redistribution and progressivity. The fiscal state tends to be both small and regressive, constraining equalization via either investment or consumption by both lack of revenue and design (*low consumption low investment* in Table 13.2). The resulting pattern of distributive outcomes is one in which the marginal effects of increasing efforts in consumption if anything exacerbate inequality and increasing efforts in investment, while egalitarian in nature, are hardly feasible because of budgetary constraints. As a result, inequality and long-term unemployment reach peak levels, and the intergenerational income elasticity remains high over time.

To summarize, the argument developed throughout this section suggests that the distributive impact of consumption and investment policies on income inequality and the distribution of economic opportunities in the labor market is mediated by the amount of resources available to incumbents and the relative power of insiders within the labor market.

13.3. Empirical Evidence: Consumption, Investment, and Distributive Outcomes

To evaluate this claim, this section proceeds in three steps. First, I focus on the role of consumption and investment as determinants of the distribution of disposable income in advanced industrial societies. Second, I analyze the impact that these policies have on the long-term unemployment rate, which is taken as

TABLE 13.3. *The distributive implications of consumption and investment policy on inequality*

		Revenue Collection	
		High	Low
	High	$\dfrac{\partial DPI}{\partial C} > 0$	$\dfrac{\partial DPI}{\partial C} > 0$
		$\dfrac{\partial DPI}{\partial I} < 0$	$\dfrac{\partial DPI}{\partial I} < 0$
Dualization	Low	$\dfrac{\partial DPI}{\partial C} < 0$	$\dfrac{\partial DPI}{\partial C} < 0$
		$\dfrac{\partial DPI}{\partial I} < 0$	$\dfrac{\partial DPI}{\partial I} > 0$

Note: I, investment; C, consumption; *DPI*, disposable income inequality; *LTU*, long-term unemployment.

a proxy of the difficulty of unemployed citizens in reentering the labor market within a year. Third, I close the section by analyzing the role of consumption and investment policies in shaping the size of the intergenerational income elasticity across advanced democracies.

Table 13.3 summarizes the empirical implications of the argument on the relationships among consumption, investment, and disposable income inequality. To evaluate the conditional effect of consumption and investment on inequality across different scenarios in Table 13.3 I use a time series cross-sectional analysis with twenty-one OECD countries over the period 1990–2007. The limited time range of the data set reflects the availability of data for the different elements incorporated in the definition of investment.[7] Given the imbalance and short nature of the panel, I estimate the models using OLS with robust standard errors clustered by country. The results are robust to the use of alternatives such as panel corrected standard errors as well as to the inclusion of additional assumptions about the error term showing processes of serial correlation of order 1. I have also performed analyses including country and year fixed effects, and the results are robust across specifications.[8]

---

[7] Investment refers to the per GDP expenditures on public and private research and development, tertiary education, child care services, and active labor market policies, 1992–1995, 2003–2007, OECD data. Investment data are lacking for Switzerland and Norway for the 1992–1995 period. Consumption refers to the sum of per GDP expenditures on old age pensions, survivors' pensions, unemployment benefits, and incapacity pensions, 2003–2007, OECD data.

[8] These additional specifications are available from the author upon request.

The dependent variable for the analyses is the GINI coefficient for disposable income inequality for the age group eighteen to sixty-five, as reported by LIS and the OECD (2011).[9]

Critically, the identification of the conditional effects of consumption and investment require modeling the interaction among the policy terms, our variables of primary interest, and the conditional variables in a way that most closely resembles the conditioning factors highlighted in Table 13.3. To this end, the specifications include, for each set of policy tools (consumption and investment), the estimation of a three-way interaction among the level of effort in that particular policy realm and two contextual variables: the degree of employment protection of full-time workers, which we take as a proxy for the existing level of dualization, and the level of revenue as a share of the economy, which we take as a proxy of the level of resources available to incumbents. These two indicators approximate the two variables that define the set of constraints under which incumbents operate (Table 13.1).

In addition, the specification includes a number of standard controls. The level of pretax and transfers income inequality controls for the effect on redistribution of existing grievances associated with the distribution of market outcomes (Lupu and Pontusson 2011) as well as for possible second-order effects associated with previous policy interventions (Ringen 1987). The level of union density controls for the power of labor within the polity (Huber and Stephens 2001). A dummy variable distinguishing federal and nonfederal countries and Gallagher's index of disproportionality capture the confounding impact of institutional constraints on redistributive platforms (Iversen and Soskice 2006; forthcoming).[10] Finally, the estimation of the effect of either policy tool includes a control for the budgetary effort on the other. Thus, the analysis of the conditional effect of investment on inequality includes a control for consumption, and vice versa.

The findings reported in Figure 13.4 lend support to our theoretical expectations.[11] When enacted in a context of low employment protection and low revenue collection, that is, an environment where resource allocation occurs primarily through market competition, a marginal increase in investment policy is positively associated with income inequality. This suggests that access to investment opportunities is unevenly distributed: The same people who perform well in the labor market gain access to investment policies such as higher education, which ultimately generate a regressive distributive outcome. By contrast, investment policies in scenarios where public resources allow the provision of services to be enjoyed nearly universally by a majority of the population

[9] The exclusion of pensioners is motivated by the need to control for market income inequality and the distortive effect the latter have, by virtue of having a market income of 0, on cross-national analyses focusing on the gap between market and disposable income inequalities.
[10] Data for union density, federalism, and disproportionality were taken from the Comparative Political Database (Armingeon et al. 2012).
[11] The corresponding tables for Figure 13.4 are reported in the Appendix.

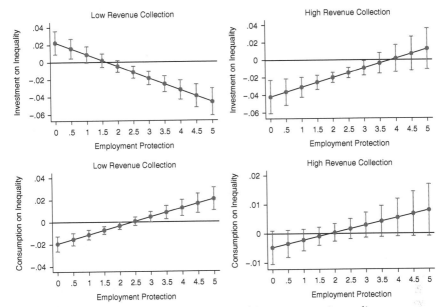

FIGURE 13.4. The impact of consumption and investment on inequality.

have a strong egalitarian effect (top right panel in Figure 13.4). Interestingly, though, the scope of this egalitarian effect is muted as employment protection increases, suggesting that the access to investment opportunities becomes part of the insiders' privileges. In rich, dualized, status-oriented societies, the egalitarian impact of investment policies is muted by the segmentation of access to the very resources provided by these policies.

The bottom two panels in Figure 13.4 focus on the impact of consumption policies on disposable income inequality. Marginal increases in welfare state transfers reduce income inequality at low levels of revenue collection, but only in societies with relatively low levels of employment protection. More transfers imply less inequality in competitiveness oriented political economies.[12] This is hardly surprising as these are the societies where transfer policies tend to be more progressive in their design. By contrast, as employment protection increases, the impact of consumption on inequality reverses. In status oriented and capture oriented societies more consumption implies a stronger effort on either neutral or outright regressive policy tools geared to benefit labor market insiders, thus marginally contributing to the spread of the income distribution.[13] Stated briefly, by altering the constraints faced by politicians to pursue

---

[12] A similar finding applies to societies with high fiscal capacity and low dualization, even though the results barely reach the threshold of statistical significance.

[13] This is consistent with recent findings on the nature of insider-outsider inequalities in these regimes (Häusermann and Schwander (2012)).

more progressive policy designs, and privileging insiders as the core of any successful electoral coalition, dualization reverses the distributive impact of welfare state transfers, especially in those societies where the fiscal trade-offs faced by politicians are more acute.

I turn now to analyze the joint impact of investment and consumption policy on a different form of inequality, namely, the availability of economic opportunities for those worse off in the labor market. I proxy this concept through the long-term unemployment rate, that is, the share of unemployed who have not found new employment after a year seeking it. Regarding the specification, I approach the problem with a similar three-way interaction to that employed before, but rather than treating each policy component separately, I employ the ratio of investment to consumption as the main independent variable of interest. I am less interested in identifying the marginal impact of each policy tool on labor market opportunities and more on the impact of adjustments to the relative balance between them, given existing levels of consumption commitments. Accordingly, the current level of consumption expenditures is a critical control variable in the specification. In addition, I control for the level of unemployment and the existing level of consumption expenditures. The former effectively controls for all other determinants of labor market outcomes (Daveri and Tabellini 1997) and focuses the attention on the gap between the unemployment and the long-term unemployment rate. The latter allows me to explore the impact on economic opportunities of increasing the relative effort of investment for a given level of effort in consumption.

Figure 13.5 reports the core findings.[14] Consistent with the argument in this book, both the level of fiscal resources and the degree of dualization jointly mediate the impact of the investment to consumption balance on the economic opportunities available to the unemployed. In polities with less effective revenue collection systems, increasing marginally the effort on investment makes no difference. The scope for budgetary adjustment is too limited, and this in turn has very little bearing on actual labor market outcomes. By contrast, an increase in the relative importance of investment vis-à-vis consumption generates significant labor market consequences in high revenue collection societies.

In line with our theoretical argument, these consequences are mediated by the level of dualization under which potential reforms take place. In less regulated, insider oriented contexts, more investment translates, for instance, via higher efforts in active labor market policies, into better labor market matching, thereby reducing the scope of long-term unemployment. Interestingly, as was the case with the impact of investment on inequality, these positive effects become significantly smaller the higher the incidence of dualization. At the

---

[14] Again, findings are robust to the inclusion of country and year fixed effects.

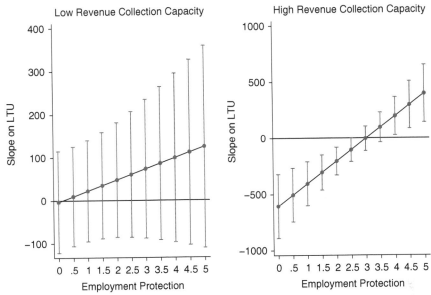

FIGURE 13.5. The impact of the I/C ratio on long-term unemployment.

extreme, when the protection of insiders is very high, and the latter can secure for themselves access to the benefits provided by increasing investment efforts, increasing investment works to enhance further the preexisting patterns of segmentation in the labor market.

Overall, Figures 13.4 and 13.5 bring out one central message: Ceteris paribus, the distributive effects of investment and consumption policy are mediated by the preexisting legacies on the basis of which these policies are pursued. These findings lend strong support to the theoretical argument developed in this chapter and the volume.

Finally, Figure 13.6 analyzes the predicted income elasticity in the late 2000s as a function of two variables:[15] the average levels of, respectively, investment and consumption for the period 2003–2007 relative to total effort. The idea is to explore the marginal effect of investment policies on mobility, holding the level of income inequality constant. The income elasticity reflects the extent to which parents' income predicts that of their children. As such it provides a preliminary and imperfect measure of the extent to which opportunities to earn income remain, on average, stacked across generations.

---

[15] Because I am using the data computed by Corak (2012b) there is only one cross section of observations available for this analysis. The relationship reported in Figure 13.6 controls for the level of disposable income inequality.

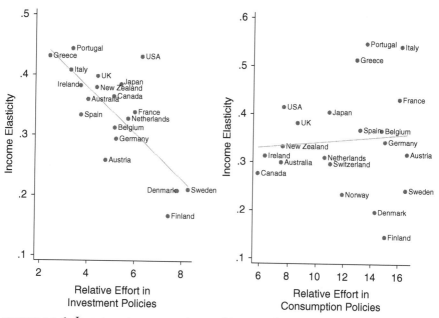

FIGURE 13.6. Investment, consumption, and income elasticity.

The combined effects of investment and consumption policies on inequality and long-term unemployment translate quite directly into the cross-national variation in terms of the size of the income elasticity, as revealed by the geographic patterns displayed in Figure 13.6. In line with the findings in Figures 13.4 and 13.5, investment, by reducing the levels of both income inequality and long-term unemployment, has a strong negative effect on the size of the income elasticity. Accordingly, the elasticity is particularly low in societies with limited dualization and high fiscal capacity, such as Finland, Sweden, and Denmark; extremely high in capture oriented societies such as Portugal and Greece; and mixed in political economies where incumbents are constrained by either status or competitiveness. In status oriented economies, the positive effects of investment on the income elasticity are downgraded by dualization. In economies oriented towards competitiveness, the virtuous consequences of investment in the labor market cancel out with the exacerbation of income inequalities and the uneven access to opportunities for income mobility (Corak 2012b).

Similarly aligned with previous results are our findings on the relationship between consumption policy and the size of the income elasticity. An overview of the patterns displayed in the right panel of Figure 13.6 suggests that, to the extent that it becomes an important budgetary item, consumption effort increases the size of the income elasticity in status and capture oriented societies, providing further evidence of the segmented nature of the distribution of economic opportunities. By contrast, stronger efforts in consumption policies complement investment in reducing the size of the income elasticity in nations with low levels of dualization and high levels of revenue collection. Universal access to services and progressive transfers reinforce each other in limiting the scope of inequality, long-term unemployment, and the size of the income elasticity.

13.4. Discussion

This chapter has analyzed the relationship between policy strategies and distributive outcomes in advanced capitalism. I have shown that the balance between consumption and investment policies, as developed under different sets of supply and demand constraints, is a major predictor of the observable differences across democracies in terms of income inequality, long-term unemployment, and the size of the income elasticity. These findings lend considerable support to the model of constrained partisanship developed in this volume. Additional explorations of the relationship between policy choices and income mobility exploiting microlevel data source is a natural next step in this research agenda.

Appendix

Throughout this section Model 1 refers to OLS with robust standard errors; Model 2 refers to standard PCSE; and Model 3 refers to PCSE with an assumed common serial correlation on order 1 in the error term. All models include a constant.

TABLE 13.A1. *Determinants of disposable income inequality (investment)*

	Model 1	Model 2	Model 3
Investment	0.0868***	0.0868***	0.0775***
	(0.024)	(0.022)	(0.0227)
Employment protection	0.1328**	0.1328***	0.1309***
	(0.060)	(0.050)	(0.0448)
Tax revenue	0.0085**	0.0085**	0.0082**
	(0.0040)	(0.0034)	(0.0034)
Investment × employment protection	−0.0382***	−0.0382***	−0.034***
	(0.0103)	(0.0086)	(0.0083)
Investment × tax revenue	−0.0026***	−0.0026***	−0.0022***
	(0.00069)	(0.0006)	(0.0006)
Employment protection × tax revenue	−0.0035*	−0.0035**	−0.0036***
	(0.0017)	(0.0015)	(0.0013)
Employment protection × investment × tax revenue	0.001***	0.001***	0.0009***
	(0.00029)	(0.0003)	(0.0002)
Federalism	−0.0065***	−0.0065***	−0.0077***
	(0.0018)	(0.0018)	(0.0022)
Disproportionality	−0.00001	−0.00001	−0.0002
	(0.0002)	(0.0002)	(0.0002)
Union density	−0.0005***	−0.005***	−0.0008***
	(0.0001)	(0.0001)	(0.0001)
Consumption	−0.0012*	−0.0012**	−0.0017**
	(0.0006)	(0.0006)	(0.0007)
Market income inequality	0.1928***	0.1928***	0.1164***
	(0.0515)	(0.0315)	(0.0240)
N	212	212	212
R^2	0.8628	0.8628	0.9485

TABLE 13.A2. *Determinants of income inequality (consumption)*

	Model 1	Model 2	Model 3
Consumption	−0.0340***	−0.0340***	−0.0250**
	(0.0090)	(0.0081)	(0.0115)
Employment protection	−0.1552***	−0.1553***	−0.0804
	(0.0483)	(0.4673)	(0.0554)
Tax revenue	−0.0074***	−0.0074***	−0.0047
	(0.0025)	(0.0023)	(0.0031)
Consumption ×employment	0.0134***	0.0135***	0.0083*
protection	(0.0040)	(0.0038)	(0.0051)
Consumption × tax revenue	0.0006***	0.0006***	0.0004
	(0.0002)	(0.0002)	(0.0003)
Employment protection × tax	0.0025*	0.0025*	0.0009
revenue	(0.0013)	(0.0013)	(0.0015)
Employment protection ×	−0.0002**	−0.0002**	−0.0001
consumption × tax revenue	(0.0001)	(0.0001)	(0.0001)
Federalism	−0.0066***	−0.0066***	−0.0091***
	(0.0020)	(0.0020)	(0.0024)
Disproportionality	−0.0006**	−0.0006**	−0.0005
	(0.0002)	(0.0003)	(0.0003)
Union density	−0.0005***	−0.0005***	−0.0009***
	(0.0001)	(0.0001)	(0.0001)
Investment	−0.0169***	−0.0169***	−0.0076***
	(0.0019)	(0.0019)	(0.0014)
Market income inequality	0.2114***	0.2114***	0.1299***
	(0.0477)	(0.0317)	(0.0250)
N	212	212	212
R^2	0.8537	0.8537	0.9432

TABLE 13.A3. *Determinants of long-term unemployment*

	Model 1	Model 2	Model 3
Investment to consumption ratio	599.7142***	382.0214**	599.7142**
	(105.1133)	(133.6511)	(220.0094)
Employment protection	66.4182***	50.5716**	66.4182**
	(13.9073)	(17.1535)	(24.1705)
Tax revenue	6.8308***	5.0243*	6.8308***
	(1.0419)	(1.3379)	(2.3104)
Investment to consumption ratio × employment protection	−149.7843**	−89.9625***	−149.7843**
	(44.5155)	(53.7871)	(71.2623)
Investment to consumption ratio × tax revenue	−24.1191***	−16.0576***	−24.1192***
	(3.3203)	(4.2275)	(6.9620)
Employment protection × tax revenue	−2.413***	−1.7929**	−2.4128***
	(0.4209)	(0.5007)	(0.7673)
Employment protection × investment to consumption ratio × tax Revenue	7.0126***	4.6459***	7.0127***
	(1.4013)	(1.6282)	(2.2606)
Unemployment	1.6907***	1.6263***	1.6907**
	(0.2250)	(0.2368)	(0.6090)
Consumption	−0.2828	−0.7584	−0.2828
	(0.5063)	(0.5085)	(1.3697)
N	259	259	259
R²	0.6402	0.6706	0.6402

14

Happiness and the Welfare State: Decommodification and the Political Economy of Subjective Well-Being

Christopher J. Anderson and Jason D. Hecht

Do welfare states make people happy? In this chapter, we argue that the answer depends critically on how we conceptualize welfare states and the logics that underpin their presumed connection with well-being. In particular, we contend that understanding the relationship between welfare states and happiness requires that we distinguish between the "how much" protection welfare states offer and "what kind" of labor market opportunities they provide to go along with that protection. Welfare states are about more versus less protection, but they also are about whom they protect and in what way. This matters for happiness; more protection produces more happiness for those at risk, but having more flexible labor markets produces more happiness, too, even if a country's overall levels of protection are lower.

To make our argument and organize the empirical analysis, we rely critically on two concepts. The first is that of decommodification, taken from Gøsta Esping-Andersen's (1985) work. Decommodification means that people's access to basic resources needed to sustain their lives is protected from market risks to which they would be exposed if illness, old age, and unemployment would disrupt market-based resource flows. Decommodification supplies life satisfaction by granting peace of mind. The second concept is that of human capacities to choose one's own life and competently cope with challenges, which we take from Armatya Sen's (2011) *The Idea of Justice*. People's happiness depends on their capabilities and ability to make choices. This requires freedoms but also investments in their capabilities, skills, and competences.

The experience of freedom and choice, particularly in labor markets, provides fulfillment that translates into life satisfaction. In this vein, a highly regulatory welfare state, conferring little freedom of choice on people, for example,

We are grateful to Ben Ansell, Pablo Beramendi, and Herbert Kitschelt, as well as the organizers of and participants in the Future of Democratic Capitalism Workshops held at the University of Zurich and Duke University, for their comments on previous versions of this paper.

in labor markets, may generate less life satisfaction than a freedom-inducing welfare state, even if decommodification is equally high. So instead of more decommodifying welfare states simply making all or most citizens a bit happier than less decommodifying ones, different kinds of welfare states also create distinct sets of more or less happy citizens across countries. As a result, variations in aggregate happiness are driven by both the quantity of social protection and the extent to which they allow flexibility for workers seeking opportunities in the labor market.

The two-dimensional account of the welfare state and its implications for life satisfaction resonates directly with the scheme developed in the editors' Introduction to this volume. Political economies vary in the extent to which governments intervene in market processes, for example, by building encompassing welfare states, and thus absorb risks, with the potential to improve the life satisfaction of those most exposed to market risks. But political economies also allocate differential resources to people's investment in capabilities to innovate and adjust to future developments (especially education and research), when compared to the effort that supports people's current consumption and replacement of market income (unemployment and sickness benefits, pensions). And it is more investment-oriented polities that also tend to have lighter regulation of employment, as they empower citizens to deploy their skills in coping with the risks of the market economies in which they live.

We take it, therefore, that where polities make greater investments in citizens' skills that allow them to make occupational and lifestyle choices people are likely to be happier. In other words, life satisfaction should be highest in polities that combine encompassing welfare states (state intervention) with light regulation of labor markets and people's empowerment through skill formation (investment orientation), while it should be lowest where welfare states are residual and combined with tightly regulated labor markets (consumption orientation).

We begin with a careful look at correlations among decommodification, employment regulations, and happiness at the macrolevel, and then proceed with a more rigorous account of how welfare states shape reports of subjective well-being at the microlevel – a question that has received relatively little attention in previous comparative research on the welfare state and happiness. To make our argument, we first provide a brief overview of research on the connection between decommodification and happiness.[1] Second, we attempt to reproduce macrolevel relationships among decommodification, employment regulations, and happiness. We find evidence of a positive correlation between decommodification and happiness, as well as a negative correlation between strict employment regulations and happiness. Third, in an effort to highlight the specific mechanisms at work that connect welfare states to happiness, we

---

[1] To our knowledge, no previous scholarship has specifically examined the link between employment regulations and happiness.

turn our investigation to reports of subjective well-being at the individual level. We find that the interaction of decommodification and employment regulations with specific individual-level characteristics can have marked effects on reports of subjective well-being. Fourth and finally, we conclude with a discussion of happiness research in comparative politics, as well as the implications of our results in light of the recent economic misfortune that has plagued Western Europe and the OECD.

14.1. Welfare States and Happiness: Is More Better?

Citizen support for the welfare state is at least partially reflective of the degree to which people demand social protection. Extensive comparative politics research on support for the welfare state suggests a host of factors that potentially shape demand for the welfare state at both the individual level (e.g., Kitschelt 1994; Iversen and Soskice 2001; Moene and Wallerstein 2001; Rueda 2005; Rehm 2011b) and the macrolevel (e.g., Korpi 1983; Iversen and Soskice 2006; Brooks and Manza 2007; Lupu and Pontusson 2011; Beramendi 2012; Rehm, Hacker, and Schlesinger 2012). Each of these accounts provides its own story of why support for the welfare state varies, but a common thread concerns the various forms of social risk, in particular, the risk of income loss individuals or groups of individuals confront.

Speaking generally, individuals at a higher risk of income loss demand higher levels of social protection from the state and therefore express higher levels of support for the welfare state. Presumably if or when those demands are met, however extensive they may be, individuals experience an increased sense of well-being because of the security provided by the extension of a social safety net. This version of the story of the relation between welfare states and happiness answers that welfare states make people happy when social risks are mitigated, although the level of happiness is contingent on a number of factors at the individual, group, and even national levels.

A related logic supporting a link between the welfare state and happiness concerns the capacity for the welfare state to "decommodify" citizens from the perils of the modern marketplace. Defined more precisely, labor can be considered decommodified to "the degree to which individuals, or families, can uphold a socially acceptable standard of living independent of market participation" (Esping-Andersen 1990: 37). In a strong view of this perspective, where labor force participation essentially reduces individuals to nothing more than commodities, the idea that the welfare state can make individuals happier by shielding them from this fate can be considered self-evident (Pacek and Radcliff 2008).

Work in this area has focused correlations at the macrolevel and is chiefly concerned with the deleterious effects that economic insecurity can foist on citizens competing in the labor market (Radcliff 2001). A long and illustrious line of political economists including Marx, Polanyi, and Lindblom has discussed this negative externality of wage labor under capitalism. The relationship between decommodification and happiness can therefore be interpreted as stemming from welfare states' function as an antidote to the stress and anxiety caused by work in the modern world (Radcliff 2001; Pacek and Radcliff 2008).

Consequently, states that provide higher levels of decommodification (et ceteris paribus) through their welfare states should possess citizenries that are on average happier than states providing lower levels of decommodification. Consistent with these ideas, and regardless of the logic one may prefer, an emerging macrolevel literature on the relationship between welfare states and happiness has found a correlation between welfare state effort and happiness (Radcliff 2001; Pacek and Radcliff 2008; DiTella, MacCulloch, and Oswald 2003).

These empirical findings and the theoretical priors that underpin them are not without critics. Veenhoven (2000) in particular doubts the relationship between the welfare state and happiness, arguing that, after controlling for a country's affluence, higher levels of social protection fail to equalize happiness outcomes among a country's citizenry, with countries that provide higher levels of decommodification possessing no more equal happiness distributions than countries with lower levels of decommodification (Veenhoven 2000).

Veenhoven's primary argument posits a kind of crowding out effect when it comes to social protections provided by the state. He contends that greater social protections do not necessarily imply greater social protections for society as a whole because state-provided protections may not be of higher quality than those provided by private organizations (Veenhoven 2000). In addition, he argues that the security gained from increased welfare provisions may be offset by a loss in individual freedoms, or by diminished economic growth that he finds elsewhere to be correlated with higher levels of happiness (Hagerty and Veenhoven 2003).

We take Veenhoven's critique seriously and agree that welfare states that offset higher levels of protection with restrictions on individuals' freedoms in the labor market may ultimately have a negligible impact on citizens' life satisfaction. The trouble with Veenhoven's critique is in the empirical testing of the argument; his results hinge critically on the use of raw social security expenditure data as a proxy for welfare state effort, an approach that has fallen out of favor with scholars of the welfare state[2] (Pacek and Radcliff 2008). In addition, he fails to test his hypothesis explicitly regarding the deleterious effect of

---

[2] Social spending (i.e., welfare state effort) as a measure of welfare state generosity has been critiqued for its inability to paint an accurate picture of the welfare state's influence on citizens' life chances (e.g., Scruggs and Allan 2006). For example, social spending tends to increase during periods of economic downturn. This does not necessarily mean that a welfare state has become more generous. Rather, it may simply indicate that social spending has risen as more and more people come to rely on entitlements because of unemployment or income loss.

flexibility loss on expressions of life satisfaction. We remedy these empirical shortcomings in two ways. First, we utilize Scruggs's decommodification index (Scruggs 2004), which quantifies and updates Esping-Andersen's (1990) original decommodification formulation and provides more precise measures for separable welfare state institutions (see also Scruggs and Allan 2006). This exercise is similar to that performed by Pacek and Radcliff (2008), who reassess the relationship between decommodification and happiness with Scruggs's data and find a positive and statistically significant relationship between welfare states and happiness. Second, we test the flexibility loss hypothesis by utilizing a measure of employment regulation strictness developed by the OECD and made available in the Comparative Political Data Set I (Armingeon et al. 2012). By controlling for employment regulations and decommodification simultaneously, we enable ourselves to evaluate better how social welfare protections and labor market flexibility combine to shape expressions of life satisfaction cross-nationally.

Our chapter then tackles both an empirical as well as a theoretical question. On an empirical level, the question is this: How robust is the relationship between welfare states and happiness? The theoretical question follows: Why is (or is not) there a correlation between decommodification and happiness? Moreover, if it does exist, are decommodification and labor market flexibility two of the primary mechanisms responsible for connecting welfare state institutions to happiness? We take up each of these questions in turn.

14.2. Exploring the Welfare State–Happiness Link Empirically

The dependent variable examined in this paper is a measure of people's quality of life in the form of subjective well-being (i.e., happiness). Psychologists also variously refer to this construct as life satisfaction or happiness, while economists on occasion also have labeled it "experienced utility" (for reviews, see Diener, Suh, Lucas, and Smith 1999; Frey and Stutzer 2002). The literature on subjective well-being is wide and deep and covers a wide variety of social sciences (e.g., Radcliff 2001).[3] Suffice it to say, for present purposes,

---

[3] Given the varied social science traditions that have explored the foundations of subjective well-being, it should be no surprise that happiness has been attributed to myriad different sources by researchers, although these sources have been debated and evolved over time. Wilson's (1967) study on the correlates of "avowed happiness," one of the earliest significant works of happiness scholarship, stressed that happiness is largely driven by psychological factors within individuals. For Wilson, a happy person is "young, healthy, well-educated, well-paid, extroverted, optimistic, worry-free, religious, married person with high self-esteem, job morale, modest aspirations, of either sex and of a wide range of intelligence" (Wilson 1967: 294). Today research on subjective well-being tends to focus less directly on the correlates of happiness, and more on the processes and environments that tend to lead to happiness (Diener et al. 1999).

Still, factors found to influence subjective well-being vary from hypertension (Blanchflower and Oswald 2008a), to religious devotion (Ellison 1991), to goal setting behavior (Brunstein

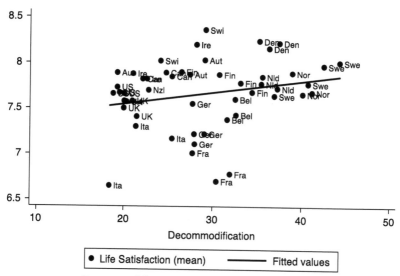

FIGURE 14.1. Decommodification and life satisfaction in seventeen OECD democracies, 1981–2000.

that the validity and reliability of indicators measuring subjective well-being (SWB) have been extensively researched.[4] In the following, we use two standard indicators measuring life satisfaction (one on a 1–10 scale, the other on a 1–4 scale) (for question wording, see Appendix) from the World Values Surveys and Eurobarometer surveys, respectively.

To begin our assessment of the robustness of the relationships among decommodification, employment regulations, and happiness, we first examine the correlation between decommodification and happiness with the help of World Values Survey data for seventeen countries from 1981 to 2000[5] in a scatterplot presented in Figure 14.1. We have superimposed a linear trend line to orient the reader.

___

1993). Material conditions have been shown to influence subjective well-being, with people in richer countries reporting higher levels of happiness, all else equal (Cantril 1965; Inglehart 2000; DiTella and MacCulloch 2008: Pacek and Radcliff 2008). Reports of subjective well-being also seem to follow a U-shaped pattern throughout the course of individuals' lives (Blanchflower and Oswald 2008; Anderson and Hecht 2011), with the trials and tribulations of middle age apparently depressing happiness during those years.

[4] For well more than two decades, psychologists have extensively researched the validity and reliability of different happiness indicators (for a review, see Frey and Stutzer 2002; see also Sandvik, Diener, and Seidlitz 1993). In an earlier survey of research on subjective well-being, Diener (1984) concluded that "[the] measures seem to contain substantial amounts of valid variance" (p. 551) (see also the survey about various measures of subjective well-being by Andrews and Robinson 1991).

[5] We are prevented from extending our analysis past 2002 by the lack of availability of decommodification data beyond that point in time.

A careful inspection of Figure 14.1 reveals a couple of notable characteristics of the relationship between decommodification and happiness. First, there is a moderately strong and positive correlation between them. Second, certain countries fit this relationship better than others. While countries at the high end of happiness such as Norway and Sweden seem to fit relatively well, others such as Ireland, Italy, France, and Canada seem to fit relatively poorly. In the case of Ireland and Canada, which can be located toward the middle- to upper-left portion of the scatterplot, individuals are happier given the level of decommodification than the regression line would predict. In contrast, for France, Italy, and Germany, which can be located toward the lower-left and lower-center portions of the scatterplot, individuals are somewhat less happy given the level of decommodification.

While these two groups of outliers do not diverge enough to obviate the positive correlation between decommodification and happiness, they are of particular note because they group nicely along Esping-Andersen's worlds of welfare capitalism: Ireland and Canada are prototypical examples of liberal welfare states in Esping-Andersen's classification scheme, while France, Germany, and Italy represent conservative welfare states. Thus the continental European democracies such as France, Germany, Austria, and Switzerland defy the positive trend between decommodification and happiness. While this result is puzzling at first, it becomes less so when we investigate scatterplots that demonstrate the relationship between employment regulations and happiness at the country level.

Figure 14.2 plots the same World Values Survey life satisfaction data against employment regulation strictness data from the OECD discussed previously. Here we observe a relatively strong negative correlation between employment regulations and life satisfaction, with the United States, United Kingdom, Ireland, and Canada locating in the upper left, combining low levels of employment regulation with moderate levels of happiness. In contrast, countries such as France, Germany, and Italy locate in the lower right, indicating high levels of employment regulation paired alongside low levels of happiness.

This finding may provide initial insight as to why the continental European countries fit the decommodification-happiness trend so poorly. Specifically, although this group of countries provides a relatively high level of decommodification for its citizens, that decommodification appears to be offset by strict employment regulations that are correlated with lower expressions of happiness. While this evidence is merely descriptive, it does indicate that there is not a "one size fits all" story with regard to the relationship between welfare states and happiness. Although welfare states providing higher levels of decommodification seem to lead to happier citizens, those that simultaneously restrict labor market flexibility through strict employment regulations appear to offset those gains as a result of stringent employment regimes. We proceed to a more robust assessment of these correlations in the next section of the chapter.

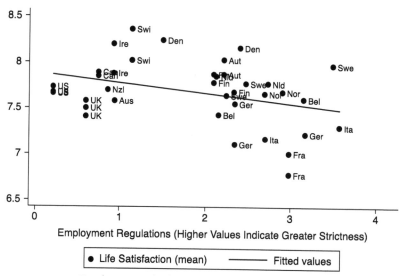

FIGURE 14.2. Employment regulations and life satisfaction in seventeen OECD democracies, 1985–2000.

14.3. The Welfare State and Happiness at the Macrolevel

The true test of the connection between welfare states and happiness, and our ability to judge the debate that has evolved regarding the dual mechanisms of decommodification and flexibility reduction, requires a more sophisticated analytic strategy. Thus, utilizing Eurobarometer data we proceed with a replication of previous analyses of the relationships among decommodification, employment regulations, and happiness, where we investigate the correlation between the two phenomena while controlling for GDP growth, the unemployment rate, the rate of inflation, a year counter to control for any time trend that might be present, and population. To gain additional confidence in these macrolevel findings, we also estimate models with the addition of dummies accounting for Esping-Andersen's three worlds of welfare capitalism.[6] We utilize ordinary least squares (OLS) regression to estimate our model, calculating robust standard errors due to heteroskedastic errors caused by repeated country observations (e.g., Hamilton 2009). The results are reported in Table 14.1.[7]

[6] Our assignment of countries to Esping-Andersen's worlds of welfare capitalism is as follows. We classify Ireland and the United Kingdom as liberal welfare states. We classify Denmark, Finland, Norway, and Sweden as social democratic welfare states. Finally, we classify Austria, Belgium, France, Germany, Italy, and the Netherlands as conservative welfare states. See Esping-Andersen 1990, chapter 2 and Esping-Andersen 1999, chapters 4 and 5.

[7] Our analysis here closely mirrors that of Pacek and Radcliff (2008). Our analysis has a slightly lower number of observations (215 vs. 242). However we include twelve rather than eleven countries (Norway being the addition), and our analysis extends back five more years (to 1970 rather than 1975).

TABLE 14.1. *Country-level determinants of life satisfaction in twelve European democracies: Eurobarometer data*

Independent variables	Life Satisfaction							
	Model 1	Model 2	Model 3	Model 4	Model 5	Model 6	Model 7	Model 8
Decommodification	.029*** (.002)	.016*** (.003)	.019*** (.003)	.005 (.004)	.019*** (.003)	.005 (.004)		
Employment regulations	-.183*** (.013)	-.133*** (.015)	-.11*** (.030)	-.074** (.027)	-.110*** (.030)	-.074** (.027)		
GDP growth	.002 (.005)	-.006 (.005)	-.000 (.005)	-.007 (.005)	-.000 (.005)	-.007 (.005)	-.008 (.006)	-.016** (.005)
Unemployment rate	-.017*** (.004)	-.024*** (.004)	-.024*** (.003)	-.031*** (.003)	-.023*** (.003)	-.031*** (.003)	-.025*** (.003)	-.027*** (.003)
Inflation rate	.009 (.007)	-.001 (.007)	.002 (.006)	-.08 (.006)	.002 (.006)	-.008 (.006)	-.021*** (.003)	-.020*** (.003)
Year	-.007*** (.002)	-.008*** (.002)	-.008** (.002)	-.009*** (.002)	-.008* (.002)	-.009*** (.002)	-.003† (.002)	-.005** (.001)
Population		-.003*** (.001)		-.003*** (.000)		-.003*** (.000)		-.004*** (.000)
Liberal			-.084 (.071)	-.129† (.068)	.117 (.077)	.073 (.069)	-.198*** (.031)	-.062* (.031)
Conservative			-.202*** (.038)	-.202*** (.036)			-.444*** (.028)	-.288*** (.030)
Social Democratic					.202*** (.038)	.202*** (.036)		
Constant	17.7*** (.128)	19.7*** (3.783)	18.6*** (4.514)	22.1*** (3.976)	18.4*** (4.522)	21.9*** (3.980)	10.5*** (3.498)	13.8*** (2.835)
Number of observations	163	163	163	163	163	163	215	215
R²	0.67	0.73	0.73	0.79	0.73	0.79	0.65	0.78

Note: The results are OLS regression estimates and their robust standard errors (in parentheses): †$p < .10$, *$p < .05$, **$p < .01$, ***$p < .001$.

The first notable finding is that the results demonstrate a strong and positive correlation between decommodification and happiness even after the inclusion of the employment regulation variable and the other controls. This correlation is somewhat stronger in Model 1 than in Model 2 after the inclusion of the population variable, an unsurprising result given that decommodification and population are correlated (–0.51 level). In addition, the negative relationship between employment regulations and happiness we observed earlier continues to be robust. The unemployment rate shows a statistically significant and negative correlation with happiness in both models, a result that fits with our expectations about the effect of rising unemployment on happiness at the macrolevel. The time trend parameter is also statistically significant and negative, indicating a slight decline in happiness over time during our sample period. Finally, the population parameter in Model 2 is negatively correlated with happiness. This fits with patterns that we observed previously with regard to Scandinavia, which routinely demonstrated the highest levels of happiness but are countries with relatively low populations. Thus far then our intuitions about the relationships among decommodification, employment regulations, and happiness have proven correct. States that provide higher levels of social protection tend to have happier citizens, while states that restrict labor market flexibility tend to depress reports of life satisfaction somewhat.

In Models 3 through 8 decommodification and employment regulation again take their positive and negative respective signs and are generally highly statistically significant. The lone exception to this is Models 4 and 6, where the decommodification parameter takes the appropriate sign but fails to achieve conventional levels of significance, a result that can be attributed to the highly correlated population parameter in these model specifications. Consistent with Models 1 and 2, Models 3 through 8 also demonstrate that the unemployment rate, time trend, and population parameters are negatively correlated with happiness. Overall, the models including worlds of welfare capitalism dummies produce no significant deviations from the results observed in Models 1 and 2 in terms of the parameters that are constant across the set of models.

Turning our attention to the worlds of welfare capitalism dummies themselves, two points salient to our analysis become apparent. First, of the three welfare worlds, social democratic welfare state types perform the best. In Models 3, 4, 7, and 8 social democratic welfare states serve as the reference category, and both the liberal and conservative parameters take negative signs and are statistically significant, with the exception of the liberal welfare state parameter in Model 3. When social democratic dummies are included in the model specification and conservative welfare states serve as the reference category (Models 5 and 6), the social democratic dummies both take positive signs and are significant at the $p < .001$ level.

The second notable point concerning the welfare state dummies included in Table 14.1 is that controlling for decommodification and employment regulations at the country level appears to account for a substantial amount of the happiness-producing capacities of the various welfare state types. This can be observed most clearly by comparing the welfare state parameter estimates of Models 3 and 4 with those of Models 7 and 8. Model specifications 7 and 8 omit the decommodification and employment regulation parameters, and within these models the welfare state dummies nearly double in magnitude[8] and are all significant at the $p < .05$ level or better.

In particular, the decommodification and employment regulation parameters appear to do an especially good job of accounting for discrepancies in happiness between liberal regimes and the other two welfare state types. In Models 3 and 4, the liberal dummy, which provides a comparison between liberal and social democratic welfare states, is only significant at the $p < .10$ level in Model 4, and insignificant in Model 3. In contrast in Models 7 and 8, which omit the decommodification and employment regulation parameters, the liberal dummy is significant (at $p < .05$ or better) in both models. This denotes that there is a significant difference between the liberal and social democratic welfare state types in terms of happiness, but that difference is only manifested clearly when decommodification and employment regulations are not accounted for. Liberal regimes also exhibit no statistically significant difference from conservative regimes when controlling for decommodification and employment regulations, as is the case in Models 5 and 6.

Beyond these results based on Eurobarometer data, we also reestimated identical models with the help of data from the World Values Survey (WVS). This allows us to evaluate the decommodification–happiness, employment regulation–happiness relationships using an alternate measure of happiness that has a different scale (10 point versus 4 point). Moreover, the WVS data provided a wider cross section of countries that can be evaluated, as countries from North America and the Asia-Pacific region are included. As the results in Table 14.2 show, the negative employment regulation–happiness correlation remains consistently strong across these models. This employment regulation parameter approaches conventional levels of significance in Models 9 through 14 and is statistically significant at the $p < .01$ level in four of the six specifications. The decommodification parameter performs somewhat less well, only reaching conventional levels of significance when both the population and welfare state parameters are omitted in Model 9. Still, these results do little to detract from our confidence in the robustness of our welfare state relationships of interest, as the number of observations for these WVS data is extremely low (an average of thirty-one observations per model).

---

[8] The lone exception to this is the liberal welfare state parameter in Model 8, which decreases in magnitude but improves in terms of its statistical significance.

TABLE 14.2. *Country-level determinants of life satisfaction in seventeen oecd countries: World Values Survey data*

Independent variables	Life Satisfaction							
	Model 9	Model 10	Model 11	Model 12	Model 13	Model 14	Model 15	Model 16
Decommodification	.033** (.010)	.000 (.012)	.014 (.016)	−.004 (.018)	.014 (.016)	−.004 (.018)		−.028 (.026)
Employment regulations	−.293** (.077)	−.161* (.058)	−.439** (.110)	−.233 (.137)	−.439** (.110)	−.233 (.137)		−.012 (.011)
GDP growth	.045** (.016)	−.006 (.024)	.066** (.021)	.010 (.026)	.066** (.021)	.010 (.026)	.029 (.020)	−.012 (.011)
Unemployment rate	−.007 (.020)	−.014 (.011)	−.017 (.021)	−.018 (.015)	−.017 (.021)	−.018 (.015)	−.040* (.016)	−.013 (.022)
Inflation rate	.059* (.016)	.032 (.018)	.060* (.027)	.035 (.025)	.060* (.027)	.035 (.025)	−.021 (.026)	−.013 (.013)
Year	.003 (.016)	.012 (.013)	−.008 (.014)	.006 (.015)	−.008 (.014)	.006 (.015)	−.012 (.013)	.003 (.011)
Population		−.009* (.003)		−.008† (.004)		−.008† (.004)		−.011** (.003)
Liberal			−.678* (.294)	−.290 (.292)	−.528* (.223)	−.214 (.251)	−.146 (.098)	.211 (.149)
Conservative			−.150 (.194)	−.077 (.178)			−.451** (.128)	−.118 (.125)
Social democratic					.150 (.193)	.077 (.178)		
Constant	1.753 (30.829)	14.980 (26.480)	23.295 (28.771)	−3.850 (30.479)	23.144 (28.789)	−3.927 (30.456)	31.571 (26.415)	2.248 (21.458)
Number of observations	28	28	28	28	28	28	47	35
R^2	0.55	0.71	0.62	0.72	0.62	0.72	0.39	0.68

Note: The results are OLS regression estimates and their robust standard errors (in parentheses): $†p < .10$, $*< .05$, $**< .01$, $***< .001$.

Taken together then, these macrolevel results suggest that both decommodification and labor market flexibility serve as two avenues that connect welfare states to happiness. Specifically, while higher levels of decommodification are associated with greater expressions of happiness at the country level, stricter employment regulations that reduce labor market flexibility in terms of the ability to change firms or move in and out of employment tend to depress happiness. With these findings in mind, we can now proceed to evaluate not only how these two mechanisms combine to produce patterns of happiness across welfare state types, but also how they create distinct sets of winners and losers once we turn to examining happiness at the microlevel.

14.4. Revisiting Happiness and the Welfare State at the Macrolevel

Our analysis thus far has uncovered two possible mechanisms that connect welfare states to happiness in the forms of decommodification and labor market flexibility. However, we are left with a multitude of questions concerning how these mechanisms manifest themselves at the individual level. Previous research, including Radcliff (2001) and Pacek and Radcliff (2008), discusses how more generous welfare states tend to lead to happier citizenries. According to their logic, this stems from the added protection that individuals living under such generous welfare states enjoy from the fickleness of the modern marketplace. This sounds completely plausible, and it represents one possible avenue for connecting welfare states and happiness, which we explored through our investigation of the relationship between decommodification and happiness earlier.

At the same time, we are less certain that it is the sole way by which the welfare state can shape individuals' well-being. Similar to Veenhoven, we expect that certain types of welfare states may indeed possess some flexibility-reducing characteristics, while others do a better job of allowing workers flexibility in their employment options. For example, conservative welfare states tend to pair benefits tied to employment with a lack of workforce mobility, making the job market less flexible relative to liberal or social democratic welfare states. Consequently, we expect that such circumstances may reduce happiness levels for workers looking to transition across firms, across the public and private sectors, or moving from unemployment to employment, or vice versa. This implies that the debate between the Radcliff and Veenhoven camps may not be a debate at all. In fact, we argue that both are correct, and that the trade-offs implicit in modern welfare states have distinct impacts on different types of citizens. While some may benefit primarily from the increased security provided by higher levels of decommodification, others may prefer the flexibility that more dynamic labor markets entail. This also is directly related to why Scandinavians routinely report such high levels of happiness, as the universality of social democratic welfare states obviates such a trade-off, combining high levels of decommodification with flexible labor markets.

Specifically, we anticipate that the mechanisms of decommodification and flexibility will manifest themselves at the individual level across variables for which welfare states create distinct sets of winners and losers. Given the available data, we expect that gender, age, unemployment, and education are all variables that will allow us to highlight how the protection provided by decommodification, and the relative flexibility provided by employment regulations, work to shape happiness at the individual level. These variables exemplify how the manner in which these mechanisms combine can encourage or reduce happiness within specific groups, and how happiness winners and losers are shaped by the manner in which welfare state institutions structure both social protections and labor market dynamism.

We are especially interested in the possibility that decommodification and employment regulations shape happiness across distinct time horizons. For employment regulations, we hypothesize that this is most likely to matter over the medium to long term, meaning that we expect it to interact most crucially with factors such as education and gender that remain fixed once an individual has entered the labor market. In contrast, decommodification is likely to be more relevant for individuals over the short to medium term. As a result, we anticipate that it will shape happiness most directly through variables such as age and unemployment that can more immediately produce anxiety and stress among vulnerable workers. While the logic for unemployment in this case is evident, we expect that a country's level of decommodification is also particularly relevant for young workers preparing to enter the labor market or at the early stages of their working life, as well as older workers who are preparing to or have just retired. We investigate these possibilities in the following.

14.5. Exploring Sources of Happiness at the Microlevel

Our microlevel investigation assesses how the worlds of welfare capitalism interact with individual-level characteristics to shape happiness across different groups of people. Table 14.3 initiates that investigation in reporting the results for our baseline, multilevel model of life satisfaction.

As can be seen in Table 14.3, the large number of observations included in our analysis yield extremely precise estimates of our parameters, with each one demonstrating statistical significance at the $p < .001$ level in our baseline regression, with the exception of the housework as primary responsibility parameter. The results show that age and age squared, respectively, are negatively and positively correlated with life satisfaction. Consistent with previous research, this indicates a U-shaped pattern of happiness over an individual's life course – a result we explore in greater detail later. Women, individuals with higher levels of education, and individuals who are married report higher average levels of happiness, as do individuals who are more ideologically conservative. Finally, the year variable indicates that individuals are becoming slightly less happy

TABLE 14.3. *Microlevel Determinants of life satisfaction in twelve European democracies: Baseline model*

Independent variables	Life Satisfaction
	Baseline Model
Age	−.381***
	(.010)
Age squared	.052***
	(.001)
Woman	.087***
	(.008)
Education	.060***
	(.001)
Married	.483***
	(.008)
Unemployed	−1.167***
	(.016)
Housework as primary responsibility	−.019
	(.012)
Retired	−.095***
	(.014)
Left-Right ideology	.064***
	(.002)
Year	−.012***
	(.001)
Decommodification	.083***
	(.001)
Employment regulations	−.320***
	(.012)
Social democratic welfare state	.534***
	(.013)
Liberal welfare state	.500***
	(.030)
Number of observations	295,160
Pseudo R^2	.07

Note: The results are ordered logit regression estimates and their standard errors (in parentheses): $^{\dagger}p < .10$, $^{*}< .05$, $^{**}< .01$, $^{***}< .001$. The data for our analysis are from an update of the Eurobarometer Trend File, which permit us to evaluate the drivers of happiness for 295,160 individuals across twelve West European countries between 1985 and 2002. As before, our dependent variable is measured on a scale from 1 to 4, with 1 denoting respondents who are "not at all satisfied" with their lives, while 4s denote respondents who are "very satisfied" with their lives. We estimate ordered logit regressions to explore correlations between our dependent variable and the explanatory variables in our model, and then proceed to calculate predicted probabilities in order to provide more substantive interpretations of our results.

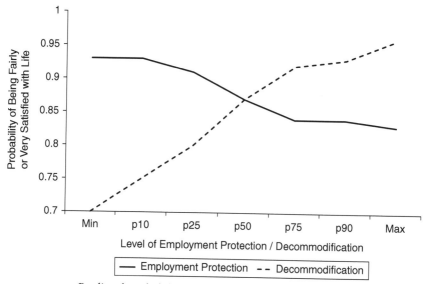

FIGURE 14.3. Predicted probability of life satisfaction by level of employment protection and decommodification.

over time, although the effect is rather small. Conversely, unemployment and retirement both have a deleterious effect on happiness.

Turning to welfare state estimates of interest, the decommodification and employment regulation parameters take positive and negative signs, respectively, as they did previously in our macrolevel analyses. This suggests that higher levels of decommodification and less strict employment regulations do tend to have a positive influence on reported levels of life satisfaction at the microlevel. The social democratic and liberal welfare state dummies are also both positive and possess similar magnitudes. This indicates not only that individuals are better off in terms of happiness living under social democratic and liberal regimes than under conservative regimes, but also that once decommodification and employment regulations are controlled for, citizens living under these two regime types tend to benefit similarly with regard to life satisfaction. Having reviewed our baseline output, we turn to Figure 14.3 for a more substantive interpretation of the effect of our dual mechanisms, decommodification and labor market flexibility. Figure 14.3 displays the predicted probabilities of an individual's reporting that she is "fairly satisfied" (3) or "very satisfied" (4) with her life across the range of values for decommodification and employment regulations present in our data.

Figure 14.3 reveals that both welfare state mechanisms are capable of exerting substantial influence over happiness at the microlevel. Beginning with decommodification, the results reveal that moving from the minimum to the maximum level of decommodification yields an improvement in predicted happiness of just above 25 percent. Holding the other explanatory variables at their mean values, individuals living with the minimum level of welfare state protection have a slightly better than 70 percent chance of reporting that they are at least fairly satisfied with their lives, while individuals living with the maximum level of welfare state protections have nearly a 96 percent chance of reporting that they are at least fairly satisfied with theirs. The results for labor market flexibility are not quite as impressive, but still quite considerable. Individuals living under regimes with the minimum level of employment regulations have about a 93 percent chance of reporting that they are happy, while those living under regimes with the strictest regulations enjoy only an 83 percent chance of reporting happiness. Combined, these results suggest that both our welfare state mechanisms of interest play an important role in shaping happiness at the individual level; however, they reflect averages across our sample overall. To achieve a better understanding of the precise manner in which each of these mechanisms operates, we next turn to evaluating how they shape happiness for specific groups within our sample.

14.6. Examining Microlevel Heterogeneity

As we discuss previously, we expect that decommodification and employment regulations may influence microlevel happiness through separate time horizons. While employment regulations are likely more relevant for medium- to long-term happiness considerations, decommodification has the capacity to shape happiness over the short to medium term through the mitigation of work-related pressure and anxiety. While our data do not permit us to adjudicate specifically between short- and long-term dimensions of happiness, we proceed in this section to interact each of the mechanisms with both individual-level characteristics that have the capacity to change over the short to medium term, as well as those that remain more or less fixed over the medium to long term. In doing so, we are able to examine our intuition that our dual welfare state mechanisms may be influential over distinct time horizons. Table 14.4 reports the results of our interaction specifications.

We begin with medium- to long-term happiness considerations and evaluate two sets of interactions with our employment regulations parameter. First, we investigate the interaction of education level with employment regulations. While individuals can clearly change their level of education over time, here we treat it as essentially fixed over the medium to long term since most individuals do not dramatically alter their level of education once they enter the labor market. The interaction parameter between education and employment regulations reported in Table 14.4 is statistically significant ($p < .001$), negative, but of relatively low magnitude. The negative sign indicates that returns on education in terms of happiness are slightly greater in strict employment regulation regimes than relaxed regimes. However, given the low magnitude of the parameter estimate, this difference is likely to be small. We investigate this more closely in Figure 14.4.

TABLE 14.4. *Microlevel determinants of life satisfaction in twelve European democracies: Interaction models*

Independent variables	Life Satisfaction			
	Education × Employment Regulations	Woman × Employment Regulations	Age × Decommodification	Unemployment × Decommodification
Age	-.381***	-.381***	-.574***	-.383***
	(.010)	(.010)	(.047)	(.010)
Age squared	.052***	.052***	.092***	.053***
	(.001)	(.001)	(.006)	(.001)
Age × decommodification			.006***	
			(.002)	
Age squared × decommodification			-.001***	
			(.000)	
Woman	.087***	.185***	.086***	.085***
	(.008)	(.020)	(.008)	(.008)
Woman × employment regulations		-.043***		
		(.008)		
Education	.070***	.060***	.060***	.060***
	(.003)	(.001)	(.001)	(.001)
Education × employment regulations	-.004**			
	(.001)			
Married	.483***	.483***	.486***	.482***
	(.008)	(.008)	(.008)	(.008)
Unemployed	-1.166***	-1.164***	-1.165***	-1.977***
	(.016)	(.016)	(.016)	(.078)
Unemployed × decommodification				.028***
				(.003)

Housework as primary responsibility	-.020 (.013)	-.022† (.013)	-.016 (.013)	-.020 (.013)
Retired	-.096*** (.014)	-.095*** (.014)	-.089*** (.014)	-.094*** (.014)
Left-Right ideology	.064*** (.002)	.064*** (.001)	.064*** (.002)	.064*** (.002)
Year	-.012*** (.001)	-.012*** (.001)	-.012*** (.001)	-.012*** (.001)
Decommodification	.083*** (.001)	.083*** (.001)	.080*** (.003)	.081*** (.001)
Employment regulations	-.299*** (.013)	-.298*** (.013)	-.318*** (.012)	-.322*** (.012)
Social democratic welfare state	.532*** (.013)	.533*** (.013)	.539*** (.013)	.533*** (.013)
Liberal welfare state	.506*** (.030)	.500*** (.030)	.501*** (.030)	.499*** (.030)
Number of observations	295,160	295,160	295,160	295,160
Pseudo R^2	.07	.07	.07	.07

Note: The results are ordered logit regression estimates and their standard errors (in parentheses): †$p < .10$, *$p < .05$, **$p < .01$, ***$p < .001$.

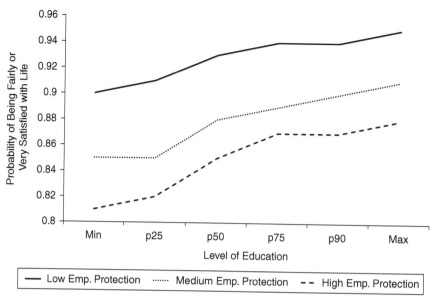

FIGURE 14.4. Predicted probability of life satisfaction by level of education across employment protection regimes.

Figure 14.4 reports the predicted probability of happiness across levels of education and employment regulations. Most apparent from a quick investigation of the figure are the differences across employment regulation regimes, which are equivalent to intercept differences among low, medium, and high regulation regimes. Individuals living under low regulation regimes are much more prone to reporting at least a fair level of happiness than individuals living under high regulation regimes. These effects are consistent across education levels, although the differences are slightly more pronounced among those with only minimal levels of education than those with higher levels of education. In addition, as anticipated on the basis of the sign of the interaction parameter, the slope of the strict employment protection curve is slightly steeper than that of the other two curves. Overall, though, Figure 14.4 reveals that employment regulation regimes are important shapers of happiness regardless of one's level of education.

Turning to the gender–employment protection interaction model specification, we again observe that the interaction parameter is highly significant and negatively signed. The negative sign indicates that stricter regimes tend to have a more harmful effect on women's happiness than men's. This is particularly interesting because women, on average, report higher levels of life satisfaction than men. It is also logical when one considers the dual roles that working women play at home and in the office. For many women, motherhood may dictate having to shift between full- and part-time employment, or in and out

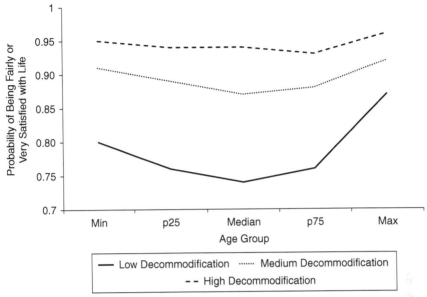

FIGURE 14.5. Predicted probability of life satisfaction by age group across decommodification regimes.

of the workforce. Consequently, it makes sense that employment regulation regimes that make such transitions more difficult for women would also tend to depress happiness in women living under such regimes relative to those living under more flexible labor market setups. We can infer then that, although both men and women are happier living in countries with more dynamic labor markets (ceteris paribus), countries with the most stringent employment regulations have an especially negative influence on the happiness of women. Or, perhaps more appropriately, especially strict employment regimes have a less harmful influence on men's happiness than on women's happiness.

We now proceed to investigate short- to medium-term happiness considerations and evaluate interactions among age, unemployment, and our decommodification parameter. Whereas the significant interaction effects we observed with regard to employment regulations were of relatively modest magnitude, we anticipate that the potentially shorter-run impact of decommodification on happiness will yield slightly more dramatic effects across various groups within our sample. Starting with the age-decommodification interaction model specification, we can see that both the age and age squared interactions are statistically significant, suggesting that the effect of age on happiness is contingent on the level of decommodification that an individual enjoys from her welfare state. Figure 14.5 provides a more substantive interpretation.

Similar to the education–employment regulations interaction effects we investigated in Figure 14.4, there are intercept-type differences across decommodification regimes with respect to happiness. Individuals living under high decommodification regimes report substantially higher levels of life satisfaction than those individuals living under medium or low decommodification regimes. However, perhaps the more interesting feature of Figure 14.5 is the differences in the slopes of the U-shaped curves across the various decommodification regimes. In the case of high decommodification regimes, returns to happiness are highly consistent over the life course. In fact, the predicted probability of being at least fairly satisfied with life only fluctuates between 0.93 and just above 0.95 for individuals living under high decommodification regimes. This can be contrasted with the U-shaped probability curve for individuals living under low decommodification regimes. For these individuals, the predicted probability of being happy varies greatly throughout the life course, hitting a low point of 0.74 at the median age group, and reaching levels of 0.80 and 0.87 for the lowest and highest age groups, respectively. This dramatic low point makes a great deal of sense for individuals living under low decommodification regimes. These are individuals who are in the midst of their careers and face pressures not only at the workplace, but also as breadwinners expected to support their family within the context of being the relevant locus of social protection in states that do not provide much of a safety net.

Last we turn to the results for unemployment, which truly highlight the impact that high levels of decommodification can have in terms of happiness for vulnerable workers. In this case the interaction term is statistically significant and positively signed. Consistent with previous results, we find that employed individuals tend to be happier as the level of decommodification increases. While approximately 70 percent of employed respondents report being at least fairly satisfied with their lives under low decommodification regimes, about 95 percent offer this response at the maximum level of decommodification. This difference is considerable, but it pales in comparison to that for the unemployed. Our calculations show that unemployed individuals living under the lowest level of decommodification have *only a* 31 percent chance of reporting that they are at least fairly satisfied with their lives. However, when we move up to the highest level of decommodification, we observe that unemployed individuals enjoy a better than 90 percent chance of being happy. That is, an unemployed individual's probability of reporting being at least fairly satisfied for her life nearly triples under the highest level of decommodification relative to the lowest. Another way of looking at this is noticing the difference in levels of happiness between employed and unemployed individuals under the highest levels of decommodification, which is quite trivial (0.2), and that under the lowest levels of decommodification, which is quite large (0.39). This analysis makes quite clear that for individuals living under the (ideally) short- to medium-term stress of unemployment, the level of social protection provided by the state makes a great deal of difference in terms of the happiness reported by those who are out of work.

Taken together, the multilevel regression evidence presented further demonstrates not only that decommodification and labor market flexibility serve as dual mechanisms that connect welfare states to happiness at the individual level, but also that the relative magnitude of these effects is contingent on individuals' personal characteristics and labor market status. In addition, these analyses provided some indication that decommodification and labor market flexibility may work through distinct dimensions of happiness; while decommodification matters more for happiness in the short to medium term, labor market flexibility has the capacity to shape happiness over more medium- to long-term time horizons. Although further research is required to confirm this finding, this has clear implications for the impact of shifts in welfare state policy on the public mood. Specifically, while increases in spending aimed at boosting social protections can be expected to improve the life satisfaction of a country's citizenry over the shorter term, the effect of labor market reforms aimed at making labor markets more dynamic likely requires a greater amount of time to improve the well-being of citizens.

14.7. Conclusion

Our analysis shows that the link between welfare states and happiness is real, but also complex. In particular, we highlighted two mechanisms that connect welfare states to happiness in the form of decommodification and labor market flexibility and demonstrated that these mechanisms work differently for different kinds of people. In sum, welfare regimes have the capacity to shape happiness through multiple means, with a high level of decommodification and flexible labor markets serving as but two of those means that we have identified within this chapter. As a consequence, prior debates over the impact of welfare states on happiness require correction. Social protections and labor flexibility both matter for happiness, and to the extent that some welfare states provide more of one but less of the other, we can expect those welfare state setups to have a kind of neutral effect on happiness through these offsetting mechanisms.

Speaking more generally, this chapter is an exploration into the mechanisms that connect social policy institutions to the level of life satisfaction enjoyed by those individuals who rely on them. While happiness may seem to be an unusual variable for political economists to devote analytical attention to, we believe this is a promising area for future research, especially given the state of threat that welfare states are experiencing as a result of the global economic crisis. Austerity, budget slashing, and cutbacks have all seen a rise in prominence within the political lexicon across the OECD in recent years. This illustrates the paradox of social policy: It is hardest to deliver during periods when citizens need it most.

There are two primary reasons why adopting happiness as an alternative metric by which to evaluate the effects of political-economic arrangements in postindustrial democracies is a good idea: One is theoretical and one is policy-based. From a theoretical perspective, life satisfaction shows how the outcomes of different institutional legacies and arrangements experienced by individual citizens vary across countries. In the language of the Introduction, where strong state intervention with encompassing welfare states is combined with an investment-oriented policy that provides flexibility for individuals, life satisfaction is greatest. This combination prevails in Nordic countries. In Anglo-Saxon liberal market economies, there is a fair amount of emphasis on investment and flexibility, but too little encompassing protection to achieve similar levels of happiness. Conversely, many continental European welfare states deliver encompassing protection, but little flexibility, combined with limited investments, particularly in education. Finally, in Southern European welfare states that exemplify the combination of limited encompassingness with highly rigid labor markets and consumption orientation of their social policies, our data reveal the lowest levels of life satisfaction.

From a practical perspective, happiness as a measure of policy effectiveness makes sense because it is not necessarily maximized through increased spending, at least not spending on social consumption. Our analysis suggests that higher levels of decommodification do not necessarily produce reports of higher levels of life satisfaction among a country's citizenry. As a result, a shift in attention to reported life satisfaction might provide a tool for policy makers to search for effective policy solutions that have the capacity to improve the well-being of citizens, while minding governments' bottom lines.

As a consequence, a deeper understanding of the social sources of happiness matters. If the transformations described here do not leave a trace in people's happiness, policy makers may wish to focus on those that do. But if they do, we need to know *who* is affected and *in what way* in order to manage the structural transformations in a manner that will satisfy the citizenries of capitalist democracies.

Appendix

Question wording for reports of life satisfaction:

Eurobarometer:
"On the whole, are you very satisfied, fairly satisfied, not very satisfied, or not at all satisfied with the life you lead?"

World Values Survey:
"All things considered, how satisfied are you with your life as a whole these days?" Responses range from "1" (dissatisfied) to "10" (satisfied).

15

Conclusion: Advanced Capitalism in Crisis

Pablo Beramendi, Silja Häusermann, Herbert Kitschelt,
and Hanspeter Kriesi

We began this project spurred by our skepticism of diagnostics proclaiming the convergence in terms of outcomes and policy among advanced industrial societies, a view only invigorated by the financial crisis that began in the fall of 2007. In this interpretation, the crisis operates as the catalyst of a long-expected return of capitalism to its pre-1945 normalcy, marred by extremely slow improvements of people's quality of life and by a structural determinism asserting the power of capital and sweeping away the importance of institutional differences (cf. Schäfer and Streeck 2013; Streeck 2014). In this process, the key mechanisms at work are global trade openness, labor migration to rich countries, and especially the free and speculative movement of capital. Jointly, they unravel preexisting industrial relations systems and exert downward pressures on wages and standards of living. The decline in aggregate demand, in turn, contributes to slowing economic growth, rising long-term unemployment, and a dualization of labor markets with a rapidly eroding core of protected insiders. This process coincides with an increasing concentration of wealth and incomes at the individual and household levels, reinforced by a switch to less progressive forms of taxation (Piketty 2014). Faced with this specter, electoral elites engage in a defensive insulation ("cartelization"), trying to shelter themselves from populist challengers who call upon the incumbents to listen to the citizens' grievances. The breakdown of political representation, in turn, fuels popular dissatisfaction and cynicism with democracy and partisan competition, an erosion of public trust and civic-mindedness, as well as a decline of political participation in all of its expressions.

Our volume has challenged the claim that there is increasing uniformity and convergence in the processes, outputs, and outcomes of politics in postindustrial capitalist democracies. There is a continuous stream of challenges originating from the realms of demographics, technology (and related patterns of consumption), and the global system of production and finance.

Politicians' responses to these challenges are refracted through the lens of domestic political-economic institutions as well as shifting partisan alignments. In developing this logic, we have also questioned the idea that observable cross-national differences reflect the functional adaptation – via politics but functional nonetheless – of previously configured politico-economic equilibria around producers' interests.

In closing our study, this conclusion addresses two sets of questions. First, we take stock of the core lessons of our comparative analysis of the dynamics of democratic capitalism. How much path-dependent continuity is there, to what extent are the challenges contingent on past trajectories, to what extent are they common? Are policy responses constrained by past trajectories, exogenous shocks, and domestic configurations of preferences and power? Second, we link our results to the financial and economic crisis that has been shaping the political economy of the advanced capitalist countries since 2008 and draw the main implications of our analysis about the medium- to long-term consequences of this critical juncture. Contrary to earlier distinctions among different regime types, we argue that the key distinction for the current development of advanced capitalism is that between the (Northwestern) core countries and the (Southern) periphery. Compared to the gap between these two sets of countries, all other distinctions that have dominated comparative political economy so far pale to relative insignificance.

15.1. Lessons from the Comparative Analysis

15.1.1. Long-Term Structural Transformations

In taking stock of what we have learned, we follow the structure of this volume. The first two chapters have documented the importance of long-term developments that set the Southern European countries apart – Carles Boix's account of the development of the structure of advanced economies and David Rueda's, Erik Wibbels's and Melina Altamirano's account of the two types of industrialization and the related approaches to compensate for market risks. Boix's chapter documents the process of economic growth and its variation across countries. He essentially makes two points: First, overall growth has slowed in the recent decades; second, the catch-up process of latecomers only narrowed the gap with the earlier industrializers up to the stagflation crisis of the mid-1970s and early 1980s. However, it did not erode the long-run differences across countries rooted, on the one hand, in processes of urbanization and protoindustrialization reaching back to medieval times and, on the other hand, in the corresponding timing of industrialization. In the last four decades, intercountry equalization has slowed and intracountry inequality has widened in several countries. As Boix argues, the overall decrease of the growth rate across OECD economies can essentially be explained by a shift of jobs from the manufacturing sector (with high productivity) to the service sector (characterized by low productivity). To explain the different trajectories of the industrial core (Northwestern Europe and North America) and the industrial periphery (mainly Southern Europe), Boix refers to the differences in their internal sectoral composition: Generally speaking, the industrial core has developed a sizable high-value-added industrial sector, while the periphery is lacking such sectors. Moreover, Southern European countries have been clear laggards in the generation of service jobs. As a result, their employment ratios have remained much lower than those in other countries.

While Boix's analysis points to the Southern European countries' relative lack of high-value-added sectors, he does not identify any specific institutional factors accounting for it. The argument of Rueda et al. complements Boix's account. Rueda, Wibbels, and Altamirano distinguish between two models of industrialization – one characterizing the industrial core, and one characteristic of the industrial periphery in Southern, Central and Eastern Europe, but also in Latin America and other developing economies. Their point is that the two models induced different institutional mechanisms for the compensation of the working class: The early core industrializer countries, which adopted an export-oriented model of industrialization, introduced social policy in order (ex post) to compensate the risks of open markets for their working class (Katzenstein 1985; Cameron 1978). By contrast, later and faster industrializing countries of the industrial periphery followed a model of import substitution that combined the protection of domestic product markets with the (ex ante) protection of labor-market insiders in these protected sectors. In this model, the collusion between capital and labor to capture the rents associated with protection was possible because the costs of this model could be externalized to captive consumers.

Rueda et al. claim that the labor-market institutions that have been built by late industrializers for an era of protectionism have persisted and now serve to block the labor market adjustments needed in a world of increasingly open markets. They argue that, in the countries of the industrial periphery, proinsider labor market policies have become a source of social exclusion and segmented labor markets. Confronted with the challenge of increasingly open product and financial markets, the export-oriented industrializers enjoy a comparative advantage: Their strong value-added-industrial sectors make them highly competitive and relatively more capable of adjustment to the new challenges. For the protectionist industrializers of the industrial periphery, however, together with technological change, the new challenges have eroded their low-value-added industries and exacerbate the already existing dualization of their economies, by expanding the informal sector (work that occurs outside the legal system of taxing, spending, and regulating) and promoting a large pool of labor market outsiders with heterogeneous preferences and stark limitations for collective action. As the following parts of this volume show, the implications of the different trajectories of early and late industrializers for domestic politics, the future of the welfare state, as well as the current state of the European integration process have been quite dramatic.

15.1.2. Transformations of the Social Structure

Large-scale structural shifts are also occurring in the social structure with important implications for political alignments. In this respect, the contributions to this volume have focused on occupational groups embodying different skill levels, with the middle losing the most: Technological change has eroded the semiskilled and vocationally trained occupations predominant among middle-income blue- and white-collar wage earners in manufacturing and services. As Daniel Oesch's chapter shows, employment in five West European countries with different welfare regimes has since 1990 expanded most at the top of the occupational hierarchy. Occupational upgrading has been driven by two categories – managers and sociocultural professionals. On the other hand, large numbers of semi- and low-skilled jobs have vanished, together with the unskilled people: Educational expansion and occupational upgrading went hand in hand – except in Spain (the example of Southern European countries in this chapter), where educational expansion over the last two decades was particularly strong and outpaced occupational upgrading, not least because of the institutional barriers to structural change discussed previously. Two categories in particular lost out from occupational change – office clerks and production workers. Within Europe, only Britain shows signs of the polarized pattern of structural change that has been found in the United States before: employment growth both at the top and at the bottom of the occupational hierarchy.

Even if it does not appear to be necessary to create low-paid service jobs to achieve full employment in advanced industrial countries, all is not well with the changing occupational structure. In fact, what seems to be shaping up is a dualized social structure. As is pointed out by Oesch, the changing occupational structure makes it more difficult for the low skilled to move up in the employment hierarchy. Without higher education, it becomes increasingly difficult to secure a job that provides a middle-class lifestyle. Moreover, low skilled workers are threatened by the implications of globalization. As Dancygier and Walter demonstrate, the low skilled are "squeezed by globalization whether they work in internationally exposed occupations or not." They face competition either from abroad (in the form of offshoring of their jobs) or at home (in the form of competition from immigrants). As far as competition by immigrants is concerned, Oesch shows that the polarization of the occupational structure in Britain and the Spanish experience have been shaped by immigration into the bottom ranks of the occupational structure. Without immigration, the trend toward upgrading in these two countries would have been even stronger.

The shifts in the occupational structure are complemented by the emerging shifts in the family structure, as analyzed by Esping-Andersen's chapter. His core thesis is that while the early phases of the revolution of gender roles led to a profound questioning of family life, in its advanced stages, the revolution is about to produce novel family norms that match better people's fertility and partnership preferences. According to this argument, a new and dominant family equilibrium, buttressed by the norms of gender egalitarianism, is emerging in the very same social groups – higher-educated, employed women – and countries – Scandinavia, the United States, France – that spearheaded the second demographic transition. This new family equilibrium needs to build on family-friendly public policies that facilitate role conciliation and on the formation of a critical mass of equalized gender relations within couples. The fact that the emergence of this new equilibrium is more advanced in the core countries (the United States and the European Northwest) than in the periphery (Southern Europe) and that it is more advanced among the highly skilled than among the low skilled in each country contributes to and reinforces the structural differences that we have already observed in the chapters on industrialization patterns and occupational structures. The kinds of cumulatively reinforced inequalities in children's lives produced by the different pace of the development toward the new family pattern will, according to Esping-Andersen, most probably translate into diverging destinies.

What emerges from the chapters on the structural transformations in advanced capitalist countries is *a double process of differentiation within and between nations*: Within nations, the gap in terms of basic life chances between growing (high-skilled) professional occupational categories and a shrinking vocationally skilled stratum of manufacturing wage earners is widening.[1] Equally widening is the gap between the early industrializers of Northwestern Europe and the Anglo-Saxon countries and the late industrializers of Southern Europe and other emerging economies. It is well known that the inequality within the advanced capitalist countries has been increasing over the past decades. Moreover, if anything, the Great Recession has boosted the heterogeneity between the members of the Eurozone (see later discussion). The analyses presented throughout this volume confirm these well-known facts.

15.1.3. Politics

What are the implications of these structural changes for political alignments? Two chapters address party politics; one chapter deals with the mobilization by trade unions. While the first two insist on the continued importance of party politics, the chapter on unions tells a story of union decline combined with a decreasing relevance of labor market institutions for the performance of the economy more generally.

Herbert Kitschelt and Philipp Rehm's chapter on party politics provides evidence to the effect that political parties and elected politicians continue to "impose a modicum of accountability." The two authors side with realignment

---

[1] Note that this gap is not equal to the gap between labor market insiders and outsiders. Outsiders are defined by their risk of becoming unemployed or atypically (temporarily, precariously) employed. Skill levels and labor market risk are, however, not strongly correlated, as there are both high skilled outsiders and low skilled insiders.

theorists and against theorists of postindustrial dealignment or cartel party detachment, who either predict the erosion of generalized programmatic distinctions between parties and/or insist on the parties' and politicians' becoming increasingly self-referential, technocratic, and hard to distinguish from each other. Realignment theory, instead, predicts that the structural transformations analyzed in the previous chapters generate a fundamental restructuring of the established party systems. It expects large catchall parties to shrink in favor of increasingly distinctive, ideologically differentiated new or reconstituted established parties that appeal to voters in the more distant reaches of the political space.

The evidence assembled by Kitschelt and Rehm allows us to confirm three points. First, except for Southern Europe, party systems appear to be representative of their constituencies on key, but country-specific issue dimensions. Second, the programmatic positions of parties remain rather distinct, and there is no evidence of an accelerating convergence or diffuseness of ideological appeals. Three, except again in Southern Europe (plus Japan and Ireland), the dynamics of party systems have been quite consistent with the realignment perspective. These systems have either polarized (the case of the United States) or undergone a realignment to accommodate new conflict structures (Northern and continental Europe). In contrast, cartelization and dealignment have befallen those Southern European countries where the structural transformations were most limited and clientelism remains a relatively prevalent party-voter linkage mechanism.

Häusermann and Kriesi's contribution specify these realignments and to link them back to the changing social structure. The existing conflict structure in the partisan space is shown to be two-dimensional across Europe. These two dimensions correspond to the dimensionality of the preference space we have introduced in the Introduction to this volume: the classic state-market dimension and what we have called the "universalism-particularism" dimension. In addition, they find that the configuration of interests, that is, the social-structural determinants of the political preferences, is structured by education, class (occupation), and age, as expected in the Introduction. Thus, education, class, and age drive the contrast between universalism and particularism. The low-skilled, production, and service workers and older people reject universalism with regard to immigration, EU integration, and welfare deservingness. Education turns out to be clearly the strongest predictor of universalism. With respect to the state-market dimension, by contrast, education does not have any effect, as a result of the greater heterogeneity of what used to be called the "middle" class: Sociocultural professionals, despite their higher SES, tend to side with the interventionist preferences of production workers, while managers tend to side with the promarket preferences of the self-employed.

The political implications of this configuration of preferences for partisan realignments are important. First of all, preferences on the universalism-particularism dimension are crucial for the realignment processes. They explain the vote choice for green and populist parties of the radical Right. On the one hand, the universalist-interventionist part of the highly educated constitutes a structural potential for the Left in general and for the green parties in particular. On the other hand, the particularism of the low or vocationally skilled clerical and blue-collar working class induces them increasingly to turn away from the traditional parties of the Left, because these parties continue to adhere to the universalistic dispositions of both highly educated professionals as well as the intellectuals of the labor movement. As the life chances of the low skilled deteriorate in comparative terms (or, alternatively, as their relative deprivation increases), they increasingly form the core constituency of the radical populist Right, which is diametrically opposed to the greens on the universalist-particularist dimension. Second, if the state-market preferences have a more limited effect on electoral preferences, they still determine the choices between the parties of the moderate Right and the moderate Left – parties that are generally losing ground to parties that choose to compete above all on the universalism-particularism dimension. Again, and in line with the analysis of Kitschelt and Rehm, the countries of Southern Europe turn out differently: Compared to the other country groups, they show the least distinctive pattern of reconfigured preferences, which results in a weaker predictive power of preferences for partisan choice.

The universally shrinking share of manual production workers reduces the traditional base for working-class politics in general and for labor unions in particular. In most countries, unions have not been able to make up for a shrinking pool of wage earners in their best-organized sectors by inroads into new occupational segments and boosting rates of organizing in new sectors. The result, as documented in Hassel's chapter, is a trend of declining union density rates and centralization as well as coordination of wage bargaining across the advanced capitalist countries, albeit without entirely wiping out differences. At one extreme, there are Nordic countries exhibiting relatively little decline of union density, predicated on the continued existence of the Ghent system of union management of unemployment insurance and wage bargaining coverage. At the other extreme, there are market-liberal systems exhibiting a collapse of union density and all manner of collective wage bargaining. In between, however, are systems that, while showing considerable declines of union density, preserve either wage bargaining centralization or at least coordination. Hassel calls the union systems in the first group of countries "universalist," and those in all the other countries "segmented." The "universalist" systems not only have higher membership levels, but are also less exclusionary; that is, they also tend to cover typical labor market outsiders. By contrast, the "segmented" systems recruit and reproduce their membership from existing strongholds of labor market insiders.

Hassel's review of the literature suggests that both labor market institutions and unionization rates lose their explanatory power to account for varying economic performance and wage inequality. With weakening economic interest group capacity to engage in collective bargaining, the mediating role of partisan politics may undermine what is left of a match between labor market regimes and economic performance.

We come away from these three chapters on politics with the impression that – even before the financial and economic crisis set in – the traditional configuration of forces shaping these policies has undergone significant change and considerably modified the premises of economic and social policy making in advanced capitalist countries. On the one hand, the unions and the corporatist channels in general seem to have lost an important part of their past relevance for determining these policies. On the other hand, the party systems have been undergoing a process of realignment driven by issues that were initially not centrally related to social and economic policy making. As a result, governments are now confronted with a deeply transformed configuration of preferences and power relations, which constrains the set of feasible policy options even in the fields of social and economic policies.

15.1.4. Policies
The three chapters in this section analyze how the structural transformations outlined previously, in interaction with strongly transformed political parties and declining unions, affect policy outputs in advanced capitalist countries. Moreover, they all emphasize the highly important effect of institutional legacies on the political dynamics of policy reform and eventually policy outputs: Institutions condition the effect of partisanship and interest group politics on policy outputs. The first two chapters focus on both consumption- (Huber and Stephens) and investment-related (Gingrich and Ansell) social policies, while Jackson and Thelen focus on regulatory policy in the fields of corporate governance and labor relations.

By the 1990s, the welfare state had largely been built in the advanced industrial countries. This simple fact has had profound consequences for the margin of maneuver for policy making. As Evelyne Huber and John Stephens observe at the outset of their chapter on social policy, problem pressures and policy legacies have added to the complexities of policy-making processes and raised the question whether partisanship continues to matter. They argue that under the weight of economic (rising unemployment) and demographic (aging) pressures, governments of all advanced capitalist countries had to make efforts to contain costs (in pension systems, health care, and unemployment) and to raise levels of employment. Nevertheless, they show that parties continue to matter within the constraints imposed by these pressures: The Left consistently favors more redistributive and risk pooling policy designs, while the Right promotes risk differentiation through closer links between contributions and benefits, cuts in public expenditures, and the introduction of private solutions. The parties' ability to translate these preferences into policies depended crucially on their capacity to compromise with coalition partners, and on the presence of veto points in the system.

The diversity of contingent partisan governance, when faced with similar challenges of structural occupational and demographic change in "mature" welfare states, unfolds both within sets of countries that share similar institutional parameters, as well as across such sets. Huber and Stephens's case studies of structural adjustment policies in the United Kingdom, Sweden, Germany, and the Netherlands as incarnations of different institutional configurations and legacies of welfare capitalism demonstrate this continued diversity. Let us add that – while Huber and Stephens do not incorporate a case study of a Mediterranean country – their evidence, and that in Gingrich and Ansell's chapter, shows persistent divergence of policy-making trajectories, setting the Southern countries apart from the rest of the club of affluent democracies. Southern European countries have consistently spent less than other OECD countries on investment-oriented social policies, while having relatively high consumption-related expenditures, especially in the field of pensions. A lack in electoral realignment and responsiveness, together with strong, clientelistic policy legacies, power asymmetries, and weak state structures, seem to account for this locked-in pattern.

As Huber and Stephens argue, the main innovations and the only welfare state expansions since 1990 have occurred in social investment policies (activation and family policies). Jane Gingrich and Ben Ansell have analyzed these policies in more detail. They first observe a slight rise in social investment spending from 1985 through 2005 across countries, but also significant differences in the level of spending between countries: The Nordic countries continue to be the leaders with respect to social investment, while the Southern European countries still spend just half the level of the Nordic countries, with the continental and liberal countries taking intermediary positions. Within this context, their main claim is that the parties' positions with respect to social investment depend on two context factors – the domain-specific policy legacies and the inclusiveness of labor market structure and labor market regulation. From their perspective, social investment policies are distributive policies that, conditional on these two factors, may either be risk pooling and progressive (enhancing the labor market opportunities of the low skilled and their earnings power) or risk differentiating and regressive (increasing wage competition through the expansion of labor supply, while distributing resources toward middle- and high-income voters). Their results show for three different types of social investment policies – family, education, and active labor market policies – that, in line with their expectations, partisanship, indeed, continues to matter: Under progressive distributive conditions, the Left clearly outperforms the Right in social investment, while under regressive conditions, there is no distinction between Left and Right governments.

When it comes to social investment strategies, as opposed to issues of taxation or fiscal austerity, it is the conservative parties and their choices that drive partisan differences. Conservatives may resist investing in public higher education, when they gain sufficient leverage (as in the Anglo-Saxon world or in the Mediterranean countries). By contrast, in the realm of family policy reform, conservatives in Northern Europe are relenting under the impact of public opinion, electoral competition for the female vote, and demographic constraints that urge the inclusion of women in labor markets (see Figure 11.1 in the chapter of Gingrich and Ansell) and agreeing to family policy reform, such as in the case of the German Christian Democrats. In spite of similar demographic and opinion pressure, no such reversal appears to be forthcoming on the Southern European Right, even though a certain flexibility in this policy realm may be electorally advantageous. To be sure, Southern European countries cannot afford a substantial extension of public child care at this time. But parties might reasonably engage in regulatory and symbolic measures that reassess women's position in economy and polity. With the exception of Zapatero's failed attempt to regulate and expand social services in Spain, precious little along those lines is expressed by recent social policy reforms in the region.

As these contrasts suggest, prospects of electoral vote maximization may not necessarily trigger the mechanism that turns around parties to pursue policy reform in an environment heavily constrained by power asymmetries, policy legacies, and organizational inertia. Such environments make leaders most concerned about the integrity and continuity of their political organizations, undercutting their effectiveness in their efforts to pursue short-term vote maximization. Parties have trouble building up the stock of trust and perception of consistency and accountability that makes voters embrace them, even when they change their policy appeals. This problem is particularly virulent in a context of low administrative and fiscal administrative capacities where politicians' promises of public goods appear to be cheap talk.

The chapter by Gregory Jackson and Kathleen Thelen shifts our attention away from welfare state reforms to regulatory policies for which the dynamics of partisanship are less relevant than the dynamics of interest group and producer group politics, even if they assert themselves at times in indirect ways, contributing to the modification of existing industrial relations regimes. These authors show that the differences in the organization and coordination of producer's interests between Denmark and Germany have fostered different coalitions and "liberalizing strategies" in the fields of corporate governance and labor market regulation: In Germany, a strong sectorally based coalition, anchored in large financial and manufacturing firms, has successfully lobbied for liberalization in corporate governance regulations, while intensifying coordination in labor relations. This intensified coordination benefited the core workers in the manufacturing industry, though at the expense of a growing share of labor market outsiders (increasing dualization). In Denmark, by contrast, a more encompassing national level coalition has presided over changes that have liberalized labor market coordination and regulation, while preserving patient capital–oriented corporate governance. In some sense, we can read Jackson and Thelen's chapter as an application of Hassel's distinction between segmented and universalist systems of interest organization. The more segmented institutions of coordination and interest representation – both among labor and among capital – in Germany have led to a more dualizing strategy of liberalization than the encompassing, less sectorally differentiated institutional framework of coordination in Denmark. Hence, even though both countries underwent strongly liberalizing reforms, the distributional effects of these reforms differ, with the costs being more concentrated in Germany and more equally spread in Denmark.

This takes us to the dynamic relationships among policies, economic outcomes, and the political process, and to the implications of our analysis for the evolution of advanced democratic capitalism.

15.1.5. Outcomes
Our analysis of policy differences points to one major determinant of the distribution of economic resources and opportunities across democracies: whether political parties pursue investment, consumption, or a combination of both as their main strategy to shape the distribution of economic resources and opportunities in society (Beramendi, this volume). Political parties choose social and economic policy strategies against the backdrop of past politico-economic strategies and the state's ability to generate revenues. Four such strategies have been distinguished in the Introduction and are taken up in Beramendi's contribution. High levels of fiscal capacity make it affordable to pursue a joint strategy of high consumption and high investment, generating sustainable growth, low inequality, high mobility, and low long-term unemployment, provided there is a partisan configuration available that pushes for such policies. Some countries have strong revenue capacities but lack the political partisan configurations to push for more than primarily consumptive policies. This applies especially to the continental welfare states with strong cross-class parties. Other countries have strong revenue capacities, yet a predominance of big business interests in partisan politics that favors sparse consumptive spending, combined with a modicum of investment spending, particularly if they can draw elements of the sociocultural professionals into the governing coalition. This applies especially to the Anglo-Saxon welfare states. Only in some Northern European countries does strong revenue capacity coincide with a partisan coalition of low-skilled wage laborers together with sociocultural professionals that pushes for both social consumption and investment. Finally,

there are countries that lack both state capacity to extract revenue and partisan coalitions of political-economic forces that would promote investment policies, as they are dominated by petty bourgeois interests hostile to both state investment and comprehensive universalistic social consumption programs. The latter subvert effective taxation and tolerate particularistic and often regressive social consumption patterns that shore up partisan coalitions perpetuating the weakness of state capacity. This pattern, in turn, has been dominant in Mediterranean Europe, especially Italy, Greece, Portugal, and, to a lesser extent, Spain and even France. In polities with weak states, where fiscal capacity is low and regressive patterns of social consumption dominate investment as a result of insiders' power to secure their privileges, bad outcomes accumulate and concentrate: low growth, high unemployment and long-term unemployment, little to no mobility, and high levels of inequality. Interestingly, at the extreme, these different distributive scenarios translate quite directly into people's perceptions of happiness and life satisfaction.

In their chapter, Christopher Anderson and Jason Hecht introduce happiness or life satisfaction as an impact measure of effective social and economic policy. In practical terms, this kind of yardstick makes sense, because it also takes into account qualitative consequences of policies that are not easily measured by traditional expenditure data. Indeed, as Anderson and Hecht show, life satisfaction is not necessarily maximized through increased spending. In political terms, party politicians may pay attention to the (changes in) life satisfaction of their voters in order to assess their chances of (re-)election. Anderson and Hecht's analyses show that there are two aspects of social and economic policy, which contribute significantly to the life satisfaction of voters: universalist social protection as provided by the Nordic welfare states, and labor market flexibility, as provided by the Anglo-Saxon and the "flexicurity"-oriented Scandinavian countries. Flexibility boosts life satisfaction by maximizing people's opportunities to make productive contributions to society. Interpreting investment in education and skills as enabling mechanisms to respond flexibly to labor market changes, their results are directly compatible with the fourfold distinction of political-economic trajectories (consumptive and investive policies and economic outcomes in terms of inequality and growth) and partisan configurations we outlined in our Introduction to this volume. At one extreme, labor market inclusion through policies of social investment combined with comprehensive social insurance and progressive redistribution to the worst off nurture life satisfaction. At the other extreme, labor market dualization through failed efforts of investment and particularistic, often regressive welfare states depress life satisfaction. In other words, the dualizing path to liberalization of the Southern European countries in particular, which combines social protection for insiders with labor market flexibility for outsiders, is a recipe for citizens' unhappiness, as it fuels uncertainty and existential anxieties. As analyzed earlier, these dynamics were present before the crisis and have only been reinforced ever since.

15.2. Advanced Capitalism and the Great Recession

Many have presumed that the Great Recession, just as the Great Depression of the 1930s, has been a momentous "critical juncture" that enables politicians to realign electoral constituencies around new formulae for sustained economic growth and the allocation of its rewards (Gourevitch 1986; Luebbert 1991; Bermeo and Pontusson 2010). While it is unclear how profound the impact of the Great Recession will be on the institutions and political-economic coalitions shaping policy in postindustrial capitalism, the crisis is an external shock, a catalyst enhancing preexisting tendencies and exacerbating challenges and performance problems that beset countries already before its impact became operative. In closing this book, we turn to the question of how the politico-economic dynamics outlined previously feed back into the patterns of political conflict in advanced democratic societies today. In doing so, we pay some attention to the implications of our argument to the understanding of the Great Recession. Our analysis focuses on two levels of conflict: political contentions *within nations*, that is, how the politico-economic outcomes outlined earlier shape domestic conflict across political economies; and political contentions *between nations*, especially in the context of the European sovereign debt crisis.

15.2.1. Political Conflict within Nations

In assessing how the dynamics analyzed throughout this book feed back into domestic patterns of conflict, we follow again the stylized division of four different trajectories against the backdrop of which partisan conflict unfolds. We have conceptualized the space of partisan conflict in terms of two dimensions of conflict, one over the level of state intervention versus market liberalism and a second dimension relative to universalistic as opposed to particularistic values and policies. Patterns of partisan conflict at the national level are defined by the relative saliency of these dimensions, which shapes key issues and strategies of distributive policy reform.

Let us consider first the Anglo-Saxon countries, that is, competitiveness-oriented polities with a policy legacy of narrow, albeit quite progressive welfare states that have developed only moderate levels of consumption spending, but are at least intermediately generous in terms of social investment policies. Given the high and exacerbating income and wealth inequality in these countries, it is likely that economic-distributive conflicts regarding the extent of market-correcting state intervention are kept alive between the parties, even though the center-left parties make concessions to the market-liberalizing Right, first in Australia, New Zealand, and the United States and, more recently, under Blair in Britain. Key questions concern the extension of public social protection versus claims for increased privatization. This partisan polarization along the state-market dimension may be reinforced with second-dimension politics in the realms of political governance and identity. Economically declining sectors of the dominant national, cultural, or ethnic groups may – rather than demanding stronger state intervention – embrace and settle for exclusionary and repressive cultural and citizenship policies that ensure that *"others"* – identified in terms of cultural practices (e.g., non-Christians) and/or national origins (immigrants) – are treated worse or entirely excluded from partaking in the benefits of either social consumption or social investment policies. This mobilization of nationalistic-particularistic policy goals creates an opening for politicians from the new populist, but also from the mainstream Right to rally support, even though their economic policy proposals to privilege small and affluent minorities are unlikely to resonate with the pivotal voting groups. Hence, we expect polarized conflict between market-liberal and particularistic parties and parties that advocate an extension of risk pooling, especially with regard to investment-related social policies that have been a traditional focus of policy efforts in these countries.

By contrast, in polities that have a policy legacy of proportional, consumptive social policies with little redistributive effort and a weak emphasis on social investment, that is, continental European status-oriented countries, a certain depolarization of the partisan conflict over state intervention versus market liberalism takes place: On the moderate Right, the established mainstream parties have historically been strongly implicated in the construction of the consumption-oriented social policies. They neither can, nor want to backtrack from these welfare states drastically. On the Left, the convergence of the mainstream parties toward the defense of the existing levels of social protection is reinforced by electoral realignment: As their electoral constituencies' socioeconomic status increases, these parties tend toward more moderate positions regarding redistribution. Partisan conflict, therefore, is likely to focus intensely on questions related to the universalism-particularism dimension. Nationalistic-particularistic right-wing populist parties, supported primarily by the working class, have emerged in most countries, as a reaction to the rise of the left-wing multicultural parties who spearhead the universalistic demands of sociocultural professionals in favor of social investment, cultural liberalism, and openness. In terms of economic and social policy reforms, this pattern of domestic conflict implies that key issues will revolve around reforms not primarily of the *size*, but of the *profile* of the welfare state. Particularistic demands resonate with selective retrenchment strategies at the margins of the welfare state and labor market (i.e., choosing a strategy of increasingly dualized social protection systems; see Emmenegger et al. 2012; and Schwander 2012), while universalistic appeals embrace more investment-oriented policies (i.e., a strategy of universalistic and redistributive social investment and flexicurity).

As the divide between universalism and particularism unfolds, the politicians of the erstwhile electorally hegemonic center-left and center-right parties are attacked as a "political class," a "cartel" unable to respond to popular preferences. Interestingly, these criticisms ignore that these established parties cater to their voters' anxieties not to rock the boat of the welfare state and not to expose those currently protected from the new vagaries of capitalist labor markets.

Third, in polities that combine strongly developed policies of social investment with comprehensive, universalistic, and progressive policies of social consumption, both dimensions of conflict are likely to remain salient: The traditional economic partisan conflict between proponents of strong state intervention versus market liberalism is unlikely to wither, especially when the particularly high levels of total public social expenditures move questions of fiscal viability to the foreground. At the same time, the very development of these strong, universalistic welfare states has created a particularly sizable and politically relevant group of sociocultural professionals and public sector employees, who support universalistic values and policies. However, particularistic, exclusionary "populists" open up a second partisan battlefront fighting against libertarian, culturally inclusionary "elitists." In terms of partisan conflict over economic and social policies, this second dimension is likely to materialize most strongly in the form of welfare chauvinist appeals, that is, a dualization of social protection along particularistic lines.

Finally, fourth, in the capture-oriented polities with very weak social investment policies, combined with particularistic, often residual and regressive social policies of consumption, processes of dualization, elite insulation, and path-dependent power asymmetries trigger a profound crisis of the entire party systems. It is these countries in which new populist citizens' tribunes have the most reason to complain about the policy nonresponsiveness and irresponsibility of their politicians, caught in networks of clientelistic reciprocity, dependency, and corruption. It is here where the notion of "party cartel" (Katz and Mair 2009) may approximate the practice of multiparty political competition most closely, since clear programmatic patterns of conflict along either dimension are blurred.[2]

In some instances, the strains of this system of governance could until recently be papered over by economic windfalls from the European monetary integration and structural funds. Here the sovereign debt crisis then swiftly triggered a powerful earthquake in the party system (Ireland, Greece) or promises to do so in the near future (Portugal, Spain). But because in all of these

---

[2] Not by accident, the affluent OECD countries that have incorporated elements of clientelistic political accountability even under conditions of advanced economic development – Italy, Japan, and Austria above all, but more arguably also Belgium, Greece, Ireland, Portugal, and Spain – have for the most part experienced significant challenges (and in some cases overhauls) of their post–World War II party systems since the early 1990s.

countries programmatic partisanship has been weak and has even weakened over the past decades – even though politicians often staged ideological conflict in the parliamentary arenas and the mass media – it has been difficult for political entrepreneurs to build new parties on a programmatic base and coordinate large numbers of activists and aspiring elected politicians around common partisan platforms. As a consequence, parties are politically weak and unstable, with fragmented and multiple leadership, which has detrimental effects on the stability of governments and their capacity to form coalitions in favor of sustained policy reform, thereby further undermining the credibility and legitimacy of the established partisan actors. Political mavericks featuring new partisan labels may quickly rise to electoral notoriety but are equally quickly subsequently being dismantled and exposed as political snake oil salesmen and fraudsters who are no better than the preceding post–World War II "political class." The rapid churning of political elites and the widespread dissatisfaction, if not ennui and disgust, with democracy may well trigger a profound crisis of democratic governance in at least some of these polities, Accordingly, the gap between Northern and Southern democracies in terms of trust and satisfaction with democracy has grown exponentially since the beginning of the crisis (Alonso 2014), thus constraining the feasibility of supranational political integration.

15.2.2. *Political Conflict between Nations: The Euro Crisis*

This growing political gap in terms of satisfaction with democracy reflects institutional and structural differences that predate the crisis and whose consequences have only become apparent with the scarcity of resources triggered by the Great Recession. While this volume is not about the European Union members or the Eurozone crisis, as a last step in this analysis, we approach Europe's coordination problems by analyzing the centrifugal forces that emerge from combining different politico-economic models under a common economic space. We contend that the way the EU has experienced the global financial crisis, originated in the United States, ultimately reflects the tensions resulting from integration into a common economic space (and for a large subset of countries a common currency) of very diverse national political-economic policy and coalitional regimes. In what follows we exploit our analytical framework to illuminate the nature and the range of possible solutions to the Euro crisis.

By assembling members with all these different political-economic configurations in advanced capitalism, the EU constitutes a microcosm reflecting the full heterogeneity of the advanced capitalist world writ large. The importance of examining the EU also results from the fact that its members constitute a nontrivial subset of the universe of the world's advanced capitalist democracies, namely, two-thirds of the countries with more than $25,000 purchasing power parity adjusted per capita income and more than 2 million inhabitants in 2010. Members of Euroland alone amount to about one-half of the entire global set of countries meeting these criteria. We find EU members in all possible combinations of political-economic capacities and institutions we have analyzed in this volume (in terms of Figure 1.4. of the Introduction: configurations with performance features abbreviated as equality, status, competitiveness, capture).[3] The challenges of coordination as a response to the crisis among the full set of EU members provide a sort of testing ground for the analytical distinctions among political-economic regimes against the backdrop of which national governments have varying room to maneuver ("constrained partisanship") that we have developed in this volume.

Arguably, there is much to gain from integrating fiscally in common currency areas, and much to lose from not doing so. Analysts of the Euro have pointed out as much since the 1990s (Krugman 1991; Eichengreen et al. 1995; Casella 2005) and their assessments appear today vindicated: A fragmented fiscal authority within a common currency area generates macroeconomic imbalances that ultimately worsen economic and social outcomes (De Grauwe 2013; Hall and Franzese 1998; Iversen and Soskice 2012; Schimmelfennig 2013; Hall 2012; Krugman 2012). To be sure, economic theory and past historical experiences provide enough grounds to justify an institutional response in the form of countercyclical activation measures and the institutionalization, via fiscal integration, of a larger redistributive effort among EU members. Several proposals have given concrete form to this general idea (Pisani-Ferry et al. 2013; De Grauwe 2013). These proposals vary in ambition, design, and redistributive impact,[4] but they tend to share a similar political fate: the oblivion of archives. Further fiscal integration is regarded as both the reasonable response to the crisis and politically unfeasible. Why?

Our analytical framework has some purchase in addressing this question. The EMU drew together under a common currency countries with different political-economic institutions and levels of fiscal capacity, as measured, indirectly and imperfectly, by the amount of revenue they are capable of collecting

---

[3] Add to this diversity the further variance contributed by the unique endowments and challenges faced by the poorer postcommunist members of the EU. We will, however, ignore this subject here.

[4] A common European budget would imply a standard system of automatic stabilizers and massive redistributive transfers across the territories of the union. A second, slightly more realistic, approach would involve the mutualization of default risks through the so-called Eurobonds. Again, an actual default would imply, under such a system, a significant transfer of resources among members of the union. Finally, from a nuanced understanding of the specific constraints at work in the EU crisis, the Tommaso Padoa-Schioppa group proposed an automatic cyclical adjustment insurance fund to make palatable internal devaluations through intertemporal, countercyclical management (Enderlein et al. 2012): The idea is to accumulate buffers in good times and use them *automatically* (i.e., independently of political controversies) in bad times. In addition, a European Debt Agency will manage according to clear criteria and strict procedures the trade-off between access to bailouts and the preservation of budgetary sovereignty. Again, the adoption of such a system would imply a major step up in the level of fiscal federalism and redistribution among the EU members.

relative to the size of their economy. In addition, these countries also differ in their propensities to cope with market challenges through investment (e.g., through education, skill formation, research) and/or consumption (e.g., through pensions, sickness and unemployment benefits). The strategic room to maneuver for governments is circumscribed by the institutions and policies that support these legacies, as well as the mobilized interest coalitions that built and defend them.

The inscription of different political economies in the EU in general, and Euroland more narrowly, is at the fore in Figure 15.1, reflecting countries' investment orientations and tax revenues before the collapse of Lehman Brothers marked the beginning of the end of the new Gilded Age. Euroland members have intermediate to high total spending levels. In terms of the composition of their spending, they cover the full range of options: A number of countries, such as the Netherlands or Finland, feature large investment efforts; a second group feature intermediate investment efforts and tax capacities (Austria, Belgium, Germany, and even France); finally, a third cluster, consisting mainly of the Mediterranean EU members, shows low investment and low tax capacity levels. In addition, a number of EU members with high investment effort remain outside Euroland, though they diverge according to whether they exhibit low social consumption (the United Kingdom and Ireland) or high social consumption (Nordic countries), paired with differential tax revenues.[5]

In understanding Europe's struggles today, the patterns displayed in Figure 15.1 are relevant in three respects. First, the differences in growth strategies, as captured by the investment to consumption ratio, shape the coordination problems in terms of monetary policy very early on in the process. Second, the way these coordination problems were dealt with polarized even further the gap between investment- and consumption-oriented countries that had existed already before the crisis, setting the stage for differing responses to the common shock. Third, the interplay between past strategies and the crisis determined the elasticity of labor markets and public purses to the common shock, fueling heterogeneity on both dimensions further and adding to the preexisting constraints on the possibility of fiscal coordination in the union.

The diversity of growth strategies translates into a divergence of approaches to monetary policy. Investment-oriented Northern European economies exercised strong pressure to sustain low interest rate policies, not only because of the lingering costs of German reunification, but also because of labor market

---

[5] Arguably, Euroland, when compared to those on the agenda among the EU members as a whole, may face relatively simpler coordination problems among member states. But in reality, the EU and Euroland are integrated also with respect to monetary policy. Key currencies linked to larger areas are safer bets for investors, and this de facto reduces the monetary policy autonomy of outsiders within the union. For a full analysis of this phenomenon, see (Pluemper and Troeger 2008).

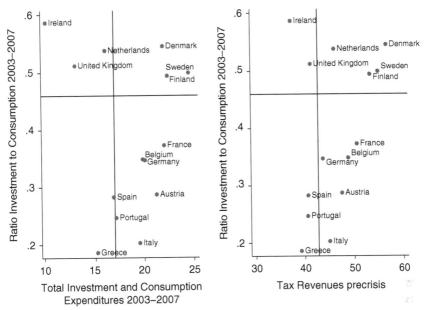

FIGURE 15.1. The EU before the crisis.

(Consumption refers to the sum of per GDP expenditures on old age pensions, survivors' pensions, unemployment benefits, and incapacity pensions, 2003–2007, OECD data; Investment refers to the per GDP expenditures on public and private research and development, tertiary education, child care services, and active labor market policies, 2003–2007, OECD data. The data for Total Tax Revenue as a percentage of GDP were obtained from the OECD National Accounts, 2003–2007.)

regimes (coverage and coordination) that tend to deliver wage restraint. As a result these economies become more competitive in international markets relative to economies where the management of labor costs was less centralized. At the other end of the spectrum, consumption-oriented economies benefited from the monetary union in two ways: first, by way of direct compensation via structural funds, as a necessary side payment to accept the very adoption of a common market; and, second, by facilitating an excessive supply of credit that allows countries with relatively lower levels of fiscal capacity to engage in fast growing growth strategies. The latter involved a focus on low skill low productivity sectors such as construction and infrastructural spending oriented toward tourism. These in turn fueled wage inflation, in sharp contrast with the labor market strategies in the North.

These dynamics have reinforced the gaps between divergent long-term economic trajectories. In addition to the disadvantages of low state tax capacity and absence of self-restraining industrial relations coverage and coordination, the Southern Euroland countries continue to rely primarily on an industrial structure with small sectors of high value added manufacturing (cf. Boix, this

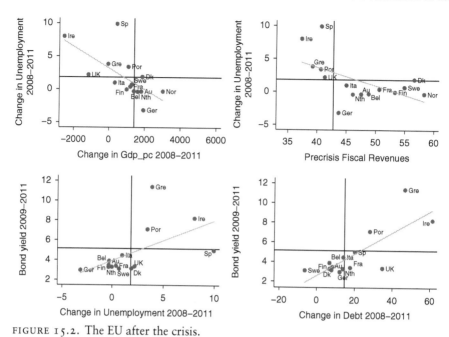

FIGURE 15.2. The EU after the crisis.
(GDP data from OECD National Accounts. Unemployment, bond yield data, and Debt
data were downloaded from the EUROSTAT database.)

volume). This trajectory originates in the capture of economic development
policies by sectional interests and clientelistic partisan politics. And it has contributed to a deep dualization of labor markets that protects insiders and makes
outsiders victims of rapidly surging unemployment, as economies enter recession. In the Northern continental economies the insider/outsider dualism is also
real, but mitigated by more competitive industries, higher total factor productivity, and the presence of still more inclusive labor and social policy regimes.

Unsurprisingly, the interaction between these divergent policy strategies and
the financial crisis translates into a polarization of economic fortunes in three
dimensions: labor markets, fiscal resources, and creditworthiness in international markets. Figure 15.2 presents evidence on each of these fronts.

The labor market responses to the crisis reflect prior politico-economic
strategies. In the case of investment-oriented political economies, we anticipate
a lower elasticity of labor markets to economic downturns. Well-established
systems of active labor market policies in the context of less rigid labor markets facilitate a better adjustment and ameliorate the response of the unemployment rate to economic slowdowns. Countries with an innovation based
strategy and high levels of fiscal capacity (such as Finland, Netherlands, and,
to a lesser extent, Germany) are capable of better absorbing the negative consequences of the shock not only because the demands for budgetary intervention

will be smaller, but also because their automatic stabilizers are more effective. Accordingly, aggregate demand holds its ground, citizens' levels of welfare decrease to a lesser degree, and the fiscal sustainability of the state does not come into question.

As the level of fiscal capacity and the investment/consumption balance shifts, the situation reverses. We expect consumption-oriented countries to show a much higher elasticity of unemployment relative to GDP. Two reasons, one economic, one political, substantiate this expectation. Economically, by virtue of the low investment rates themselves, consumption-oriented economies feature a larger share of low skill, low productivity labor (see the chapters by Boix and Oesch, this volume). Politically, the structure of the labor force also reflects the capture of regulatory policy by organized interests during the process of industrialization and is, as a result, highly dualized. In those circumstances, Left parties and unions cater to the interests of insiders (Saint Paul 1996; Rueda 2007), while less protected outsider workers provide a buffer during economic downturns. The presence of the latter group enhances the elasticity of the unemployment rate with respect to GDP. The situation becomes particularly untenable in consumption countries with low fiscal capacity, as they confront large and rapid increases in their budgetary demands with very limited margin to cope with them. This is hardly surprising as there is a clear feedback loop linking capacity and production/employment, namely, the organization of tax structures and its interplay with the dualization of labor markets. Low fiscal capacity states tend to be highly regressive as well. That is, they have both regressive tax structures (high reliance on labor and consumption taxes) and not very progressive tax designs. These, in turn, hinder the performance of labor markets, particularly in countries with dualized, highly rigid, labor markets (for a more detailed discussion of this link see Daveri and Tabellini 2000; Rueda 2007).

Unsurprisingly, debt has skyrocketed in precisely those countries with the lowest fiscal capacity and the highest labor market elasticities to changes in GDP, in no small part as a result of the transformation of private financial debt (banking liabilities associated with the collapse of the housing boom) into public debt commitments (often through the funding of European rescue packages). Moreover, the implications of the specific distributions of risks and capacity are further reinforced by the reaction of international markets and investors (bottom panels in 15.2). Higher unemployment and lower fiscal resources (as captured by debt in the right panel) imply a higher risk for investors, who flee to safer, fiscally sounder economies. As a result, the divergence in economic fortunes translates into differential opportunities to obtain resources in international financial markets, which further reinforce the process.

As both types of Northern and Southern European economies became more closely intertwined through growing financial flows from North to South (Hale and Obstfeld 2014), the private and/or public indebtedness of

Southern European economies began to spin out of control. Add onto this the United States–induced shock of the Great Recession beginning in 2007/8, and the Southern Euroland economies descended into a deep private and public debt crisis. The interaction among structural productivity disparities within Euroland, endogenously caused by different economic institutional configurations, differential tax capacities, and the U.S. finance-induced Great Recession, has promoted a polarization of economic fortunes within Euroland. With growing state indebtedness in the South, bond markets began to perceive Northern Euroland members as much better bets, rendering them less subject to hostile bond market speculation.[6]

The dual crises generated by Euroland's inherent disparities and by the Great Recession, therefore, resulted in surging unemployment in the Mediterranean countries, combined with rapidly rising private and public indebtedness, creating a vicious circle of financial deterioration, as international bond speculators targeted these countries. Exemplified by the Spanish experience, former economic miracles quickly turned into nightmares for policy makers and citizens alike. The picture emerging is clear: The geography of economic fortunes among EU members has become more polarized in terms of income, fiscal resources, and unemployment incidence.

The patterns outlined in Figure 15.2 have direct consequences for the political management of the Euro crisis. As the geography of labor market risks and the inequality of resources become more heterogeneous, the political feasibility of integration declines. The specific concentration of risks and low capacity at work in Europe only make the trade-offs associated with political and economic integration starker (Beramendi 2012, 2014). The European sovereign debt crisis has hit particularly hard those countries with large numbers of self-employed market participants operating in retail, services, and crafts production, countries where tax avoidance is common political currency, and clientelism a prominent mode of political exchange. At the other end, Northern- and continental-oriented economies have grown stronger, have reduced their debt commitments through favorable financing conditions, and face lesser budgetary needs. In the absence of a common economic fate, there is little incentive for these countries to tie their political future to the struggling South.

The Eurozone is involved in a giant struggle: The Northern continental countries – led by Germany because of its size, but ardently supported by Austria, Finland, and the Netherlands – try to impose their will on the Southern countries and remake their political economies without, in obvious ways, violating their peoples' political sovereignty. France is a bystander oscillating between Northern and Southern perspectives. Britain – as nonmember of the Eurozone – is disengaging, as the stakes of and struggles over the intra-Eurozone political economy are increasingly alien to its liberal market economy. Likewise, the

---

[6] For a more exhaustive, detailed account of the crisis generating mechanisms in Euroland, consult Scharpf (2011).

Nordic countries Denmark and Sweden see no reason to put their economies and political-economic compacts at risk by joining Euroland.

Whether and how the conflict within Euroland is resolved depends on the economic performance of the Northern EMU members. If Northern austerity backfires and the Northern export-oriented economies slow down as a result, a large-scale institutional reform of the EU will become more feasible.[7] If, as seems more likely, the North and the South continue to experience divergent economic, social, and political trajectories, the future of the European project is likely to be reshaped, and possibly compromised, by the propensity of disaffected voters to listen to a panoply of political messiahs and the collapse of programmatic politics in the South.

The May 2014 European legislative elections began to supply the electoral mediation for the deepening institutional disparities within Euroland and the EU writ large. For the first time in European electoral history, parties in just about all of the larger European countries – most starkly in Britain, France, and Italy, but for the first time even in Germany, hitherto the anchor of European federalism – have politicized the costs of European integration for national trajectories of political-economic choice. The electoral turn of political economy is finally also coming to European integration. The framework developed in this volume offers a fruitful analytical strategy to approach this process.

---

[7] Insofar as the European bailouts succeed in reducing the systemic risks for the Union, this scenario becomes less likely. It is very telling that the only system and transfers that the core countries have been willing to consider are those specifically targeted to contain specific financial risks affecting financial institutions in the creditor countries (Beramendi 2014; Copelovitch and Enderlein 2014). For more systematic microevidence on the determinants of preferences for bailouts among German voters, see Bechtel et al. (2014).

References

Aassve, Arnstein, Francesco C. Billari and Léa Pessin. 2012. "Trust and Fertility Dynamics." In *Population Association of America Annual Meeting.* San Francisco, CA.

Åberg, R. 2003. "Unemployment Persistency, Over-education and the Employment Chances of the Less Educated." *European Sociological Review* 19(2):199–216.

Abramson, Scott and Carles Boix. 2014. "*The Roots of the Industrial Revolution: Political Institutions or (Socially Embedded) Know-How?*" Princeton University. Unpublished manuscript.

Acemoglu, Daron, Philippe Aghion and Fabrizio Zilibotti. 2006. "Distance to Frontier, Selection, and Economic Growth." *Journal of the European Economic Association* 4(1):37–74.

Acemoglu, Daron and James A. Robinson. 2012. *Why Nations Fail: The Origins of Power, Prosperity and Poverty.* London: Profile Books.

Achen, Christopher H. 1978. "Measuring Representation." *American Journal of Political Science* 22(3):475–510.

Adams, James F., Samuel Merrill III and Bernard Grofman. 2005. *A Unified Theory of Party Competition: A Cross-National Analysis Integrating Spatial and Behavioral Factors.* Cambridge: Cambridge University Press.

Adsera, A. and C. Boix. 2002. "Trade, Democracy, and the Size of the Public Sector: The Political Underpinnings of Openness." *International Organization* 56(2):229–262.

Agell, J. 2002. "On the Determinants of Labour Market Institutions: Rent Seeking vs. Social Insurance." *German Economic Review* 3(2):107–135.

Aghion, Philippe and Peter Howitt. 2006. "Appropriate Growth Policy: A Unifying Framework." *Journal of European Economic Association* 4(2–3):269–314.

Ahlquist, John S. and Christian Breunig. 2012. "Model-Based Clustering and Typologies in the Social Sciences." *Political Analysis* 20(1):92–112.

Ahn, Namkee and Pedro Mira. 2002. "A Note on the Changing Relationship between Fertility and Female Employment Rates in Developed Countries." *Journal of Population Economics* 15(4):667–682.

Aitken, Brian J. 1992. "Measuring Trade Policy Intervention: a Cross-Country Index of Relative Price Dispersion." Vol. 838. *Policy Research Working Papers*. Washington, DC: World Bank.

Albertos, Jose Fernandez and Dulce Manzano. 2008. "Business and Labor Market Policies." *Estudios/Working Papers (Centro de Estudios Avanzados en Ciencias Sociales)* (237).

Aleksynska, Mariya and Martin Schindler. 2011. "Labor Market Regulations in Low-, Middle-and High-Income Countries: A New Panel Database." *IMF Working Papers*: 1–76.

Allard, Gayle. 2005. "Measuring Job Security over Time: In Search of a Historical Indicator for EPL (Employment Protection Legislation)." *Instituto De Empresa, Spain. Working Paper WP05-17.*

Alonso Sonia. 2014. "You Can Vote But You Cannot Choose: Democracy and the Sovereign Debt Crisis in the Eurozone." *Juan March Institute, Working Paper, Feburary.*

Alt, James. 1985. "Political Parties, World Demand, and Unemployment: Domestic and International Sources of Economic Activity." *American Political Science Review* 79:1016–1040.

Alvarez, Michael, Geoffrey Garrett and Peter Lange. 1991. "Government Partisanship, Labor Organization and Macro-Economic Performance." *American Political Science Review* 85(2):539–556.

Andersen, Jørgen Goul. 2011. "Denmark: The Silent Revolution towards a Multipillar Pension System." In *The Varieties of Pension Governance: Pension Privatization in Europe*, ed. B. Ebbinghaus. Oxford: Oxford University Press.

Andersen, Jørgen Goul and Tor Björklund. 1990. "Structural Changes and New Cleavages: The Progress Parties in Denmark and Norway." *Acta Sociologica* 33(3):195–217.

Andersen, Paul Krüger. 2003. "Corporate Governance in Denmark." In *Company Law*, ed. P. Wahlgren. Stockholm: Stockholm University, Stockholm Institute for Scandinavian Law.

Andersen, Søren Kaj and Mikkel Mailand. 2005. "The Danish Flexicurity Model: The Role of the Collective Bargaining System." In *FAOS*, ed. FAOS. Copenhagen: University of Copenhagen.

Anderson, Christopher J. and Jason D. Hecht. 2011. "Living Happily Ever After? Demographic Dynamics and Subjective Quality of Life in Capitalist Democracies." Paper prepared for presentation at the conference on "The Future of Democratic Capitalism," June 16–18, Swiss Federal Institute of Technology, Zürich.

Anderson, Karen and Ellen Immergut. 2006. "Sweden: After Social Democratic Hegemony." In *The Handbook of West European Pension Politics*, eds. Ellen Immergut, Karen Anderson and Isabelle Schulze. Oxford: Oxford University Press: 349–295.

Anderson, Karen M. and Anke Hassel. 2013. "Pathways of Change in CMEs: Training Regimes in Germany and the Netherlands." In *The Political Economy of the Service Transition*, ed. A. Wren. Oxford: Oxford University Press: 171–194.

Andrews, Frank M. and John P. Robinson. 1991. "Measures of Subjective Well-Being." In *Measures of Personality and Social Psychological Attitudes*, eds. John P. Robinson, Philip R. Shaver and Lawrence S. Wrightsman. San Diego: Academic Press: 61–114.

Ansell, Ben W. 2008. "University Challenges: Explaining Institutional Change in Higher Education." *World Politics* 60(2):189–230.

Ansell, Ben W. 2010. *From the Ballot to the Blackboard. The Redistributive Political Economy of Education.* Cambridge: Cambridge University Press.

Antonczyk, D., B. Fitzenberger and U. Leuschner. 2009. "Can a Task-Based Approach Explain the Recent Changes in the German Wage Structure?" *IZA Discussion Paper* No. 4050.

Aoki, Masahiko. 2001. *Toward a Comparative Institutional Analysis.* Cambridge, MA: MIT Press.

Aoki, Masahiko and Gregory Jackson. 2008. "Understanding an Emergent Diversity of Corporate Governance and Organizational Architecture: An Essentiality-Based Analysis." *Industrial and Corporate Change* 17(1):1–27.

Arbaci, S. and J. Malheiros 2010. "De-Segregation, Peripheralisation and the Social Exclusion of Immigrants: Southern European Cities in the 1990s." *Journal of Ethnic and Migrant Studies* 36(2):227–255.

Arbejdsgiverforening, Dansk. n.d. "*Flexicurity in Denmark.*" ed. D. Arbejdsgiverforening. Copenhagen.

Armingeon, Klaus and Giuliano Bonoli. 2006. *The Politics of Post-Industrial Welfare States.* London: Routledge.

Armingeon, K., M. Gerber, P. Leimgruber and M. Beyeler. 2008. "Comparative Political Data Set 1960–2006." *Institute of Political Science, University of Berne.*

Armingeon, Klaus and Lucio Baccaro. 2011. "The Sorrows of Young Euro: Policy Responses to the Sovereign Debt Crisis." *Paper presented at the CES conference in Barcelona.*

Armingeon, Klaus, Laura Knöpfel, David Weissstanner, Sarah Engler, Panajotis Potolidis and Marlène Gerber. 2012. *Comparative Political Data Set.* Bern: Institut für Politikwissenschaft.

Arpaia, A., N. Curci, E. Meyermans, J Peschner and F. Pierini. 2010. "*Short Time Working Arrangemetns As Responses to Cyclical Fluctuations.*" ed. D.-G. f. E. a. F. Affairs. Brussels: European Commission.

Arpino, Bruno, Gosta Esping-Andersen, and Lea Pessin, 2013. "Changes in Gender Role Attitudes and Fertility." Unpublished paper, Demosoc Unit, Pompeu Fabra University.

Arzheimer, Kai. 2009. "Contextual Factors and the Extreme Right in Western Europe, 1980–2002." *American Journal of Political Science* 53(2):259–275.

Attewell, P. 1987. "The Deskilling Controversy." *Work and Occupations* 14(3):323.

Autor, D., F. Levy and R. J. Murnane. 2003. "The Skill Content of Recent Technological Change: An Empirical Exploration." *Quarterly Journal of Economics* 118(4):1279–1333.

Autor, D., L. Katz and M. Kearney. 2008. "Trends in U.S. Wage Inequality: Revising the Revisionists." *The Review of Economics and Statistics* 90(2):300–323.

Autor, David. 2010. "The Polarization of Job Opportunities in the U.S. Labor Market: Implications for Employment and Earnings." Paper jointly released by The Center for American Progress and The Hamilton Project.

Avdagic, Sabina, Martin Rhodes and Jelle Visser, eds. 2011. *Social Pacts in Europe: Emergence, Evolution, and Institutionalization.* Oxford: Oxford University Press.

Avdagic, Sabina and Lucio Baccaro. 2012. "The Future of Employment Relations in Advanced Capitalism: Inexorable Decline?" *Unpublished manuscript*, April 2012.

Baccaro Lucio and Rei, Diego. 2007. "Institutional Determinants of Unemployment in OECD Countries: Does the Deregulatory View Hold Water?" *International Organization* 61(2):527–569.

Baccaro, Lucio and Chris Howell. 2011. "A Common Neoliberal Trajectory: The Transformation of Industrial Relations in Advanced Capitalism." *Politics & Society* 39(4):521–563.

Baccaro, Lucio. 2011. "Labor, Globalization and Inequality: Are Trade Unions Still Redistributive?" In *Comparing European Workers Part B: Policies and Institutions* (Research in the Sociology of Work, Volume 22), ed. David Brady. Bingley: Emerald Group:213–285.

Baker, Dean, David R. Howell, Andrew Glyn and John Schmitt. 2007. "Are Protective Labor Market Institutions at the Root of Unemployment? A Critical Review of the Evidence." *Capitalism and Society* 2(1):1–71.

Balassa, Bela. 1981. *The Newly Industrializing Countries in the World Economy.* New York: Pergamon Press.

Bambra, Clare. 2005. "Worlds of Welfare and the Health Care of Discrepancy." *Social Policy and Society* 4(1):31–41.

Barbieri, Paolo and Stefani Scherer. 2009." Labour Market Flexibilization and Its Consequences in Italy." *European Sociological Review* 25(6):677–692.

Barro, Robert J. 1997. *Determinants of Economic Growth.* Cambridge, MA: MIT Press. 2008. "Inequality and Growth Revisited." Working Paper Series on Regional Economic Integration no. 11, Asian Development Bank.

Bartels, Larry M. 2008. *Unequal Democracy: The Political Economy of the New Gilded Age.* Princeton, NJ: Russel Sage Foundation.

Bartolini, Stefano. 2000. *The Political Mobilization of the European Left, 1860–1980: The Class Cleavage.* Cambridge: Cambridge University Press.

Bawn, Kathleen, Martin Cohen, David Karol, Seth Masket, Hans Noel and John Zaller. 2012. "A Theory of Political Parties: Groups, Policy Demands and Nominations in American Politics." *Perspectives on Politics* 10(03):571–597.

Beaulieu, Eugene. 2002. "Factor or Industry Cleavages in Trade Policy? An Empirical Analysis of the Stolper-Samuelson Theorem." *Economics and Politics* 14(2):99–131.

Becher, Michael and Jonas Pontusson. 2011. "Whose Interests Do Unions Represent? Unionization by Income in Western Europe." *Research in the Sociology of Work* 22:181–211.

Bechtel, Michael M., Jens Hainmueller and Yotam Margalit. 2014. "Preferences for International Redistribution: The Divide over the Eurozone Bailout." *American Journal of Political Science* 58(4):835–56.

Becker, Gary S. 1960. "An Economic Analysis of Fertility." In *Demographic and Economic Change in Developed Countries*, ed. Gary S. Becker. Princeton, NJ: Princeton University Press: 209–231.

Becker, Gary S., Elisabeth M. Landes and Robert T. Michael. 1977. "An Economic Analysis of Marital Instability." *Journal of Political Economy* 85(6):1141–1187.

Becker, Gary S. 1981. *A Treatise on the Family.* Cambridge, MA: Harvard University Press.

Bell, D. 1973. *The Coming of Post-Industrial Society.* New York: Basic Books.

Bellani, Daniela and Gösta Esping-Andersen. 2012. "Applying a Multiple Equilibrium Framework to Divorce Risks in Germany." *European Population Conference*, Stockholm.

Bengston, Niklas, Bertil Holmlund and Daniel Waldenström. 2012. *Lifetime versus Annual Tax Progressivity: Sweden, 1968–2009*. Uppsala Center for Fiscal Studies. Department of Economics. Working Paper 2012:8.

Benner, Mats and Torben Bundgaard Vad 2000. "Sweden and Denmark: Defending the Welfare State." In *Welfare and Work in the Open Economy. Vol. II. Diverse Responses to Common Challenges*, eds. Fritz Scharpf and Vivien Schmidt. Cambridge: Cambridge University Press: 399–466

Benoit, Kenneth and Michael Laver. 2006. *Party Policy in Modern Democracies*. London: Routledge.

Bentolila, Samuel and Giuseppe Bertola. 1990. "Firing Costs and Labour Demand: How Bad Is Eurosclerosis?" *The Review of Economic Studies* 57(3):381–402.

Beramendi, P. and D. Rueda. 2007. "Social Democracy Constrained: Indirect Taxation in Industrialized Democracies." *British Journal of Political Science* 37:619–641.

Beramendi, Pablo and Thomas R. Cusack. 2009. "Diverse Disparities." *Political Research Quarterly* 62(2):257–275.

Beramendi, Pablo. 2012. *The Political Geography of Inequality: Regions and Redistribution*. New York: Cambridge University Press.

Beramendi, Pablo and Philipp Rehm. 2012. "Redistribution and Preference Formation." *Manuscript*.

Beramendi, Pablo and Philipp Rehm. 2015. "*Who Gives, Who Gains? Progressivity and Preferences.*" Mimeo: Duke University and Ohio State University.

Beramendi, Pablo and David Rueda. 2014. "Inequality and Institutions: The Case of Economic Coordination." *Annual Review of Political Science*, 17:13.1–13.21.

Beramendi, Pablo. 2014. "Economic crises and fiscal unions: understanding Europe's crisis." Paper prepared for presentation at the Meetings of the European Political Science Association, Barcelona June 20–22, 2013 and at the CES Meetings, Amsterdam June 25–27, 2013.

Berman, E., J. Bound and S. Machin. 1998. "Implications of Skill-Biased Technological Change: International Evidence." *Quarterly Journal of Economics* 113(4):1245–1279.

Bermeo, Nancy and Jonas Pontusson 2010. *Coping with the Crisis*. New York: Russel Sage Foundation.

Bernardi, Fabrizio and Luis Garrido. 2008. "Is There a New Service Proletariat? Post-Industrial Employment Growth and Social Inequality in Spain." *European Sociological Review* 24(3):299–313.

Bernardi, Fabrizio and Juan-Ignacio Martínez-Pastor. 2011. "Divorce Risk Factors and Their Variations over Time in Spain." *Demographic Research* 24(31):771–800.

Besley, Timothy and Torsten Persson. 2011. *Pillars of Prosperity: The Political Economics of Development Clusters*. Princeton, NJ: University Press.

Billari, Francesco C. and Hans-Peter Kohler. 2004. "Patterns of Low and Lowest-Low Fertility in Europe." *Population Studies* 58(2):161–176.

Binda, Veronica and Martin Jes Iversen. 2007. "Towards a 'Managerial Revolution' in European Business? The Transformation of Danish and Spanish Big Business, 1973–2003." *Business History* 49(4):506–530.

Bispinck, Reinhard. 2010. "Niedriglöhne und der Flickenteppich von (unzureichen-dend) Mindestlöhnen in Deutschland." *WSI Report*.

Blanchard, Olivier J. and Lawrence H. Summers. 1986. "Hysteresis and the European Unemployment Problem." *NBER Macroeconomics Annual,* Volume 1. Cambridge, MA: MIT Press: 15–90.

Blanchflower, David G. and Andrew J. Oswald. 2008. "Is Well-Being U-Shaped over the Life Cycle?" *Social Science & Medicine* 66(8):1733–1749.

Blauner, R. 1964. *Alienation and Freedom: The Factory Worker and His Industry.* Chicago: University of Chicago Press.

Bleses, Peter and Martin Seeleib-Kaiser. 2004. *The Dual Transformation of the German Welfare State.* Basingstoke: Palgrave Macmillan.

Blinder, Alan. 2007. "How Many U.S. Jobs Might Be Offshoreable." *CEPS Working Paper* No. 142.

Blossfeld, Hans-Peter and Andreas Timm, eds. 2003. *Who Marries Whom? Educational Systems As Marriage Markets in Modern Societies.* Dordrecht: Kluwer.

Blume, Lawrence E. and Steven N. Durlauf. 2001. "The Interactions-Based Approach to Socioeconomic Behavior." In *Social Dynamics,* eds. Steven N. Durlauf and H. Peyton Young. Washington, DC: Brookings Institution Press: 15–44.

Blyth, Mark. 2001." The Transformation of the Swedish Model. Economic Ideas, Distributional Conflict, and Institutional Change." *World Politics* 54(October):1–26.

Blyth, Mark and Richard Katz. 2005. "From Catch-all Politics to Cartelisation: The Political Economy of the Cartel Party." *West European Politics* 28:33–60.

Boeri, Tito, Agar Brugiavini and Lars Calmfors. 2001. *The Role of Trade Unions in the Twenty-First Century: A Study for the Fondazione Rodolfo Debenedetti.* Oxford: Oxford University Press.

Boix, Carles. 1998. *Political Parties, Growth and Equality: Conservative and Social Democratic Strategies in the World Economy.* Cambridge: Cambridge University Press.

Boix, Carles. 2000. "Partisan Governments, the International Economy, and Macroeconomic Policies in Advanced Nations, 1960–93." *World Politics* 53:38–73.

Bonoli, G. 2010. "The Political Economy of Active Labor-Market Policy." *Politics and Society* 38(4):435.

Bonoli, Giuliano. 2005. "The Politics of the New Social Policies: Providing Coverage against New Social Risks in Mature Welfare States." *Policy and Politics* 33(3):431–449.

Bonoli, Giuliano and André Mach. 2000. "Switzerland: Adjustment Politics and Institutional Constraints." In *Welfare and Work in the Open Economy. Volume II. Diverse Responses to Common Challenges,* eds. Fritz W. Scharpf and Vivien A. Schmidt. Oxford: Oxford University Press: 131–174.

Bonoli, Giuliano and Bruno Palier. 2008. "When Past Reforms Open New Opportunities: Comparing Old-Age Reforms in Bismarckian Welfare Systems." In *Reforming the Bismarckian Welfare Systems,* eds. Bruno Palier and Claude Martin. Oxford: Blackwell: 21–39.

Bonoli, Giuliano and David Natali. 2012. *The Politics of the New Welfare State.* Oxford: Oxford University Press.

Borjas, George, Jeffrey Grogger and Gordon H. Hanson. 2008. "Imperfect Substitution between Immigrants and Natives: A Reappraisal." *NBER Working Paper* No. 13877.

Bornschier, Simon and Hanspeter Kriesi. 2012. "The populist right, the working class, and the changing face of class politics." In *Class Politics and the Radical Right,* ed. Jens Rydgren. Abingdon: Routledge: 10–30.

Bornschier, Simon. 2010. *Cleavage Politics and the Populist Right: The New Cultural Cleavage in Western Europe*. Philadelphia: Temple University Press.

Bosch, Gerhard. 2009. "Low Wage Work in Five European Countries and the United States." *International Labour Review* 148(4):337–356.

Bosch, Gerhard, Claudia Weinkopf and Thorsten Kalina. 2009. "Mindestlöhne in Deutschland." Friedrich Ebert Stiftung.

Botero, Juan C., Simeon Djankov, and Rafael La Porta. 2004. "Florencio Lopez-de Silanes and Andrei Shleifer. 2004. 'The Regulation of Labor.'" *The Quarterly Journal of Economics* 119(4):1339–1382.

Brader, Ted, Nicholas A. Valentino and Elizabeth Suhay. 2008. "What Triggers Public Opposition to Immigration? Anxiety, Group Cues, and Immigration Threat." *American Journal of Political Science* 52(4):959–978.

Bradley, David, Evelyne Huber, Steaphie Moller, François Nielsen and John D. Stephens. 2003. "Distribution and Redistribution in Postindustrial Democracies." *World Politics* 55:193–228.

Bradley, David, Evelyne Huber and John D. Stephens. 2014. *Comparative Welfare States Data Set*. Chapel Hill and Durham, NC: University of the North Carolina and Duke University.

Braun, Anne Romanis. 1975. "The Role of Incomes Policy in Industrial Countries since World War II." *IMF Staff Papers* 23(1):1–36.

Braverman, H. 1974. *Labor and Monopoly Capitalism*. New York: Monthly Review Press.

Breen, Richard and Lynn Prince Cooke. 2005. "The Persistence of the Gendered Division of Domestic Labour." *European Sociological Review* 21(1):43–57.

Breen, Richard, Ruud Luijkx, Walter Müller and Reinhard Pollak. 2009. "Nonpersistent Inequality in Educational Attainment: Evidence from Eight European Countries." *American Journal of Sociology* 114(5):1475–1521.

Brewster, Karin L. and Ronald R. Rindfuss. 2000. "Fertility and Women's Employment in Industrialized Nations." *Annual Review of Sociology* 26:271–296.

Brines, Julie and Kara Joyner. 1999. "The Ties That Bind: Principles of Cohesion in Cohabitation and Marriage." *American Sociological Review* 64(3):333–355.

Brock, William A. and Steven N. Durlauf. 2001. "Discrete Choice with Social Interactions." *The Review of Economic Studies* 68(2):235–260.

Brodmann, Stefanie, Gösta Esping-Andersen and Maia Güell. 2007. "When Fertility Is Bargained: Second Births in Denmark and Spain." *European Sociological Review* 23(5):599–613.

Brooks, Clem and Jeff Manza. 2007. *Why Welfare States Persist: The Importance of Public Opinion in Democracies*. Chicago: University of Chicago Press.

Brunstein, J. C. 1993. "Personal Goals and Subjective Well-Being." *Journal of Personality and Social Psychology* 65:1061–1070.

Budge, Ian, Lawrence Ezrow and Michael D. McDonald. 2010. "Ideology, Party Factionalism and Policy Change: An Integrated Dynamic Theory." *British Journal of Political Science* 40(04):781–804.

Bundesagentur für Arbeit. 2009. "*Der Arbeitsmarkt in Deutschland: Kurzarbeit, Aktuelle Entwicklungen*." Berlin: Bundesagentur fürr Arbeit.

Busemeyer, M. R., 2009. "Social Democrats and the New Partisan Politics of Public Investment in Education." *Journal of European Public Policy* 16(1):107–126.

Butler, T., C. Hamnett and M. Ramsden. 2008. "Inward and Upward: Marking out Social Class Change in London, 1981–2001." *Urban Studies* 45(1), 67–88.

Callaghan, Helen and Martin Höpner. 2005. "European Integration and the Clash of Capitalisms. Political Cleavages over Takeover Liberalization." *Comparative European Politics* 3(3):307–332.

Callaghan, Helen. 2009. "Insiders, Outsiders and the Politics of Corporate Governance: How Ownership Structure Affects Party Positions in Britain, Germany and France." *Comparative Political Studies* 42:733–762.

Calmfors, Lars and John Driffill. 1988. "Bargaining Structure, Corporatism and Macroeconomic Performance." *Economic Policy* 3(6):14–47.

Cameron, David R. 1978. "The Expansion of the Public Economy: A Comparative Analysis." *American Political Science Review* 72(4):1243–1261.

Cameron, David. 1984. "Social Democracy, Corporatism, Labour Quiescence and the Representation of Economic Interest in Advanced Capitalist Society." In *Order and Conflict in Contemporary Capitalism*, ed. John H. Goldthorpe. Oxford: The Clarendon Press: 143–78.

Campbell, John L. and O. K. Pedersen. 2007. "The Varieties of Capitalism and Hybrid Success: Denmark in the Global Economy." *Comparative Political Studies* 40(3):307–332.

Campbell, John L. and John A. Hall. 2009." National Identity and the Political Economy of Small States." *Review of International Political Economy* 16(4):547–572.

Cantril, Hadley. 1965. *Pattern of Human Concerns*. New Brunswick, NJ: Rutgers University Press.

Card, D., F. Kramarz and T. Lemieux. 1999. "Changes in the Relative Structure of Wages and Employment: A Comparison of the United States, Canada, and France." *Canadian Journal of Economics* 32(4):843–877.

Card, David. 2001. "Immigrant Inflows, Native Outflows, and the Local Labor Market Impacts of Higher Immigration." *Journal of Labor Economics* 19(1):22–64.

Casella, Alessandra. 2005. "Redistribution Policy: A European Model." *Journal of Public Economics* 89:1305–1331.

Casey, Catherine, Antje Fiedler and Ljiljana Erakovic. 2012. "Liberalising the German Model: Institutional Change, Organisational Restructuring and Workplace Effects." *Industrial Relations Journal* 43(1):53–69.

Castells, M. and Y. Aoyama. 1994. "Paths toward the Information Society: Employment Structure in G-7 Countries, 1920–1990." *International Labour Review* 133(1):5–33.

Castles, Francis G. 1978. *The Social Democratic Image of Society*. London: Routledge and Kegan Paul.

Castles, Francis G. 1989. "Explaining Public Education Expenditure in OECD Nations." *European Journal of Political Research* 17(4):431–448.

CEDEFOP. 2012. *Vocational Education and Training in Denmark*. Luxembourg: European Centre for the Development of Vocational Training.

Centeno, Miguel A. and Alejandro Portes. 2006. "The Informal Economy in the Shadow of the State." In *Out of the shadows: Political Action and the Informal Economy in Latin America*, eds. Fernández-Kelly, Patricia and Shefner, Jon. University Park: Penn State University Press: 23–48.

Chan, Tak Wing and Brendan Halpin. 2008. "*The Instability of Divorce Risk Factors in the UK.*" Oxford: University of Oxford.

Chandler, Alfred D. 1990. *Scale and Scope*. Cambridge, MA: Harvard University Press.

Cioffi, John W. and Martin Höpner. 2006. "The Political Paradox of Finance Capitalism: Interests, Preferences, and Center-Left Party Politics in Corporate Governance Reform." *Politics and Society* 34(4):463–502.

Citrin, Jack, Donald P. Green and Cara Wong. 1997. "Public Opinion toward Immigration Reform: The Role of Economic Motivations." *Journal of Politics* 59(3):858–881.

Clasen, Jochen and Daniel Clegg. 2011. "The Transformation of Unemployment Protection in Europe." In *Regulating the Risk of Unemployment: National Adaptations to Post-Industrial Labour Markets in Europe*, eds. Jochen Clasen and Daniel Clegg. Oxford: Oxford University Press: 333–345.

Collier, Ruth Berins and David Collier. 1991. *Shaping the Political Arena*. Princeton, NJ: Princeton University Press

Constant, Amelie and Klaus F. Zimmermann. 2005. "Immigrant Performance and Selective Immigration Policy: A European Perspective." *National Institute Economic Review* 194(1):94–105.

Conway, Paul, Veronique Janod and Giuseppe Nicoletti. 2005. "Product Market Regulation in OECD Countries: 1998 to 2003." *Technical report* OECD Economics Department Working Paper (419).

Cooke, Lynn Prince. 2004. "The Gendered Division of Labor and Family Outcomes in Germany." *Journal of Marriage and Family* 66(5):1246–1259.

Cooke, Lynn. 2006. "'Doing' Gender in Context: Household Bargaining and Risk of Divorce in Germany and the United States." *American Journal of Sociology* 112(2):442–472.

Copelovitch, Mark and Henrik Enderlein. 2014. "*Preference Heterogeneity and Systemic Relevance: Understanding Variation in EU/IMF Responses to the Euro Crisis.*" (Mimeo). Madison: University of Wisconsin.

Corak, Miles. 2006. "Do Poor Children Become Poor Adults? Lessons from a Cross-Country Comparison of Generational Earnings Mobility." In *Dynamics of Inequality and Poverty*, eds. John Creedy and Guyonne Kalb. Oxford: JAI Press: 143–188.

Corak, Miles. 2012a. "Inequality from Generation to Generation: The United States in Comparison." In *The Economics of Inequality, Poverty, and Discrimination in the 21st Century*, ed. Robert S. Rycroft. Santa Barbara, CA: ABC-CLIO.

Corak, Miles. 2012b. "Income Inequality, Equality of Opportunity, and Intergenerational Mobility." *Journal of Economic Perspectives* 27(3):79–102.

Crafts, N. and G. Toniolo, eds. 1996. *Economic Growth in Europe since 1945*. Cambridge: Cambridge University Press.

Craig, Lyn and Peter Siminski. 2011. " If Men Do More Housework, Do Their Wives Have More Babies?" *Social Indicators Research* 101(2):255–258.

Culpepper, Pepper D. 2011. *Quiet Politics and Business Power: Corporate Control in Europe and Japan*. New York: Cambridge University Press.

Cusack, Thomas R. and Pablo Beramendi. 2006. "Taxing Work." *European Journal of Political Research* 45(1):43–75.

Czada, Roland. 2005. "Social Policy: Crisis and Transformation." In *Governance in Contemporary Germany*, eds. Simon Green and William E. Paterson. Cambridge: Cambridge University Press: 165–189.

Dalla Zuanna, Gianpiero and Giuseppe A. Micheli. 2004. *Strong Family and Low Fertility: A Paradox? New Perspectives in Interpreting Contemporary Family and Reproductive Behaviour*. Dordrecht, London: Kluwer Academic.

Dalton, Russell, Paul Allen Beck and Scott C. Flangan. 1984. *Electoral Change in Advanced Industrial Democracies*. Princeton, NJ: Princeton University Press.

Dalton, Russell. 2000. *The Decline of Party Identification*. Oxford: Oxford University Press.

Dalton, Russell and Martin P. Wattenberg. 2002. *Parties without Partisans: Political Change in Advanced Industrial Democracies*. Oxford: Oxford University Press.

Dalton, Russell. 2004. *Democratic Challenges, Democratic Choices: The Erosion in Political Support in Advanced Industrial Democracies*. Oxford: Oxford University Press.

Dalton, Russel. 2008. *Citizen Politics: Public Opinion and Political Parties in Advanced Industrial Democracies*. 5th ed. Washington, DC: Congressional Quarterly Press.

Dancygier, Rafaela. 2010. *Immigration and Conflict in Europe*. New York: Cambridge University Press.

Dancygier, Rafaela and Michael J. Donnelly. 2013. "Sectoral Economies, Economic Contexts, and Attitudes Toward Immigration." *Journal of Politics* 75(1):17–35.

Datta Gupta, Nabanita and Nina Smith. 2002. "Children and Career Interruptions: The Family Gap in Denmark." *Economica* 69(276):609–629.

Daveri, Francesco and Guido Tabellini. 1997. "Unemployment, Growth and Taxation in Industrial Countries." CEPR Discussion Papers 1681, CEPR Discussion Papers.

Daveri, Francesco and Guido Tabellini. 2000. "Unemployment, Growth and Taxation in Industrial Countries." *Economic Policy* 15(30):47–104.

Davidsson, Johan and Marek Naczyk. 2009. "The Ins and Outs of Dualisation: A Literature Review." REC-WP Working Paper (02).

De Grauwe, Paul. 2013. "The Political Economy of the Euro." *Annual Review of Political Science* 16:153–170.

De La O, Ana L. and Jonathan A. Rodden. 2008. "Does Religion Distract the Poor?" *Comparative Political Studies* 41(4–5):437–476.

De Soto, Hernando. 1989. "*The Other Path: The Invisible Revolution in the Third World.*" Perennial Library.

Deeg, Richard. 2009. "The Rise of Internal Capitalist Diversity? Changing Patterns of Finance and Corporate Governance in Europe." *Economy and Society* 38(4):552–579.

Del Boca, Daniela. 2002. "The Effect of Child Care and Part Time Opportunities on Participation and Fertility Decisions in Italy." *Journal of Population Economics* 15(3):549–573.

Deminor Rating. 2005. "*Application of the One Share – One Vote Principle in Europe.*" Brussels: Deminor Rating.

Derks, Anton 2004. "Are the Underprivileged Really That Economically Leftist? Attitudes towards Economic Redistribution and the Welfare State in Flanders." *European Journal of Political Research* 43(4):509–521.

Di Tella, Rafael, MacCulloch, Robert J. and Andrew J. Oswald. 2003. "The Macroeconomics of Happiness." *The Review of Economics and Statistics* 85(4):809–827.

Di Tella, Rafael and Robert J. MacCulloch. 2008. "Gross National Happiness as an Answer to the Easterlin Paradox." *Journal of Development Economics* 86(1):22–42.

Diener, Edward F. 1984. "Subjective Well-Being." *Psychological Bulletin* 95(3):542–575.

Diener, Edward F., Eunkook M. Suh, Richard E. Lucas and Heidi L. Smith. 1999. "Subjective Wellbeing: Three Decades of Progress." *Psychological Bulletin* 125(2):276–302.

Dixit, A. and John Londegran. 1996. "The Determinants of Success of Special Interests in Redistributive Politics." *Journal of Politics* 58:1132–1155.

Dixit, Avinash and John Londregan. 1998: "Ideology, Tactics, and Efficiency in Redistributive Politics." *Quarterly Journal of Economics* 113:497–529.

Doellgast, Virginia and Ian Greer. 2007. "Vertical Disintegration and the Disorganization of German Industrial Relations." *British Journal of Industrial Relations* 45(1):55–76.

Doellgast, Virginia Lee. 2012. *Disintegrating Democracy at Work: Labor Unions and the Future of Good Jobs in the Service Economy*. Ithaca, NY: ILR Press.

Doellgast, Virginia, Katja Sarmiento-Mirwaldt and Chiara Benassi. 2013. *Alternative Routes to Good Jobs in the Service Economy: Employment Restructuring and Human Resource Management in Incumbent Telecommunications Firms*. London: London School of Economics.

Doeringer, P. and M. Piore. 1971. *Internal Labor Markets and Manpower Analysis*. Lexington, MA: Heath.

Donzelot J. 2004. "La ville à trois vitesses: relégation, périurbanisation, gentrification." *Esprit* 303:14–39.

Douglas, Mary and Aaron Wildavsky. 1982. *Risk and Culture: An Essay on the Selection of Technical and Environmental Dangers*. Berkeley: University of California Press.

Downs, Anthony. 1957. *An Economic Theory of Democracy*. New York: Harper.

Duch, Raymond M. and Randolph T. Stevenson. 2008. *The Economic Vote: How Political and Economic Institutions Condition Election Results*. Cambridge: Cambridge University Press.

Due, Jesper, Jørgen Steen Madsen, C. Strøby Jensen and L. K Petersen. 1994. *The Survival of the Danish Model*. Copenhagen: DJØF Forlag.

Due, Jesper and Jørgen Steen Madsen. 2008. "The Danish Model of Industrial Relations: Erosion or Renewal?" *Journal of Industrial Relations* 50:513–529.

Durkheim, Emile. 1961. *Moral Education: A Study in the Theory and Application of the Sociology of Education*. New York: The Free Press.

Durlauf, Steven N. 2001. "A Framework for the Study of Individual Behavior and Social Interactions." *Sociological Methodology* 31(1):47–87.

Dustmann, C., J. Ludsteck and U. Schönberg. 2009. "Revisiting the German Wage Structure." *Quarterly Journal of Economics* 124:843–881.

Duvander, Ann-Zofie and Gunnar Andersson. 2006. "Gender Equality and Fertility in Sweden." *Marriage & Family Review* 39(1–2):121–142.

Duvander, Ann-Zofie, Trude Lappegård and Gunnar Andersson. 2010. "Family Policy and Fertility: Fathers' and Mothers' Use of Parental Leave and Continued Childbearing in Norway and Sweden." *Journal of European Social Policy* 20(1):45–57.

Edin, Kathryn and Maria J. Kefalas. 2005. *Promises I Can Keep: Why Poor Women Put Motherhood before Marriage*. Berkeley: University of California Press.

Eger, Maureen A. 2010. "Even in Sweden: The Effect of Immigration on Support for Welfare State Spending." *European Sociological Review* 26(2):203–217.

Ehrlich, Sean and Cherie Maestas. 2010. "Risk, Risk Orientation, and Policy Opinions: The Case of Free Trade." *Political Psychology* 5(31):657–684.

Eichengreen, Barry, Jeffry Frieden and Jürgen von Hagen, eds. 1995. *Monetary and Fiscal Policy in an Integrated Europe*. New York: Springer Verlag.

Eichhorst, Werner and Paul Marx. 2011. "The Labor Market and Social Protection in Germany." Paper presented at the workshop on "New Trends in Social Protection: Western Europe in Comparative Perspective." Center for European Studies, University of North Carolina, Chapel Hill, April 7–8.

Eichhorst, Werner and Paul Marx.2012. "Non-Standard Employment across Occupations in Germany: The Role of Replaceability and Labor Market Flexibility." IZA and SDU.

Ellison, Christopher G. 1991. "Religious Involvement and Subjective Well-Being." *Journal of Health and Social Behavior* 32(1):80–99.

Ellwood, David T. and Christopher Jencks. 2004. "The Uneven Spread of Single-Parent Families: What Do We Know? Where Do We Look for Answers?" In *Social Inequality*, ed. Kathryn M. Neckerman. New York: Russell Sage Foundation: 3–77.

Emmenegger, Patrick 2010. "The Long Road to Flexicurity: The Development of Job Security Regulations in Denmark and Sweden." *Scandinavian Political Studies*. 33(3):271–294.

Emmenegger, Patrick. 2011. "Job Security Regulations in Western Democracies: A Fuzzy-Set Analysis." *European Journal of Political Research* 50(3):336–364.

Emmenegger, Patrick and Romana Careja. 2012. "From Dilemma to Dualization: Social and Migration Policies in the 'Reluctant Countries of Immigration' " In *The Age of Dualization: The Changing Face of Inequality in Deindustrializing Societies*, eds. Patrick Emmenegger, Silja Häusermann, Bruno Palier and Martin Seeleib-Kaiser. Oxford: Oxford University Press: 124–148.

Emmenegger, Patrick, Silja Häusermann, Bruno Palier and Martin Seeleib-Kaiser. 2012. *The Age of Dualization: The Changing Face of Inequality in Deindustrializing Countries*. Oxford and New York: Oxford University Press.

Enderlein, Henrik, Peter Bofinger, Laurence Boone, Paul De Grauwe, Jean-Claude Piris, Jean Pisani-Ferry, Maria Joao Rodrigues, André Sapir and Antonio Vitorino. 2012. "Completing the Euro: A Road Map Towards Fiscal Union in Europe." *Report by the Tommaso-Padoa-Schioppa Group*.

Erikson and J. H. Goldthorpe. 1992. *The Constant Flux. A Study of Class Mobility in Industrial Societies*. Oxford: Clarendon Press.

Erikson, Robert, Michael B. Mackuen and James A. Stimson. 2002. *The Macro Polity*. Cambridge, MA: Cambridge University Press.

Erler, Daniel. 2009. "Germany: Taking a Nordic Turn?" In *The Politics of Parental Leave Policies*, eds. S. Kamerman and P. Moss. Bristol: Policy Press.

Ermisch, John. 2003. *An Economic Analysis of the Family*. Princeton, NJ: Princeton University Press.

Espina, Alvaro. 2007. *Modernizacion y Estado del Bienestar en España*. Madrid: Siglo XXI.

Esping-Andersen, Gösta. 1985. *Politics against Markets: The Social Democratic Road to Power*. Princeton, NJ: Princeton University Press.

Esping-Andersen, Gösta. 1990. *The Three Worlds of Welfare Capitalism*. Cambridge: Polity Press.

Esping-Andersen, Gösta. 1993. *Changing Classes: Stratification and Mobility in Post-Industrial Societies*. London: Sage.

Esping-Andersen, Gösta. 1996. "Welfare States without Work: The Impasse of Labour Shedding and Familialism in Continental European Social Policy." In *Welfare States in Transition: National Adaptations in Global Economies*, ed. Gösta Esping-Andersen. London: Sage: 66–88.

Esping-Andersen, Gösta. 1999. *Social Foundations of Postindustrial Economies*. Oxford and New York: Oxford University Press.

Esping-Andersen, Gösta 1999b. "Politics without Class? Post-industrial Cleavages in Europe and America." In *Continuity and Change in Contemporary Capitalism*, eds. Herbert Kitschelt, Peter Lange, Gary Marks and John D. Stephens. Cambridge: Cambridge University Press.

Esping-Andersen, Gösta. 2000. "A Welfare State for the 21st Century." Report to the Portuguese Presidency of the European Union, Lisbon.

Esping-Andersen, Gösta. 2009. *The Incomplete Revolution: Adapting Welfare States to Women's New Roles*. Cambridge, UK: Polity Press.

Esping-Andersen, Gösta. 2010 "*Equality with a Happy Bourgoisie: Social Democratic Egalitarianism*." (Mimeo). Juan March Institute.

Esping-Andersen, Gösta, Diederik Boertien, Jens Bonke and Pablo Garcia. 2014. "Couple Specialization in Multiple Equilibria." *European Sociological Review* 30(2):137–150.

ESS. 2008. "European Social Survey Round 4 Data." Data file edition 4.0. Norway: Norwegian Social Science Data Services. http://ess.nsd.uib.no/ess/conditions.html (accessed March 25, 2011).

Estevez-Abe, Margarita, Torben Iversen and David Soskice. 2001. "Social Protection and the Formation of Skills: A Reinterpretation of the Welfare State." In *Varieties of Capitalism: The Institutional Foundations of Comparative Advantage*, eds. P. A. Hall and D. Soskice. Oxford: Oxford University Press.

EU Commission. 2008. "Industrial Relations in Europe 2008." Brussels.

Eurostat. 2012a. "Population by Country of Birth." http://epp.eurostat.ec.europa.eu/tgm/table.do?tab=table&init=1&plugin=1&language=en&pcode=tps00178 (accessed on August 28, 2012).

Eurostat. 2012b. "Population Projections." http://epp.eurostat.ec.europa.eu/tgm/table.do?tab=table&init=1&plugin=1&language=en&pcode=tps00002 (accessed on August 28, 2012).

Evans, Geoffrey, ed. 1999a. *The End of Class Politics? Class Voting in Comparative Context*. Oxford: Oxford University Press.

Evans, Geoffrey and James Tilley. 2012. "How Parties Shape Class Politics: Explaining the Decline of the Class Basis of Party Support." *British Journal of Political Science* 42(1):137–161.

Evans, Geoffrey and Nan Dirk de Graaf. 2013: *Political Choice Matters: Explaining the Strength of Class and Religious Cleavages in Cross-National Perspective*. Oxford: Oxford University Press.

Felstead, A., D. Gallie, F. Green and Y. Zhou. 2007. "Skills at work, 1986–2006." *Working paper*, ESCR Centre on Skills, Knowledge and Organisational Performance, Universities of Oxford and Cardiff.

Fernández Macías, E. 2012. "Job Polarization in Europe? Changes in the Employment Structure and Job Quality, 1995–2007." *Work and Occupations* 39(2):157–182.

Ferrarini, Tommy, Kenneth Nelson, Joakim Palme and Ola Sjöberg. 2012. *Sveriges Socialförsäkringar in Jämförande Perspectiv: En Institutionell Analys av Sjuk-, Arbetsskade- och arbetslöhersförsäkringarna in 18 OECD-länder 1930 till 2010.* Stockhom: Statens Offentliga Utredningar.

Ferrera, Maurizio and Anton Hemerijck. 2003. "Recalibrating Europe's Welfare Regimes." In *Governing Work and Welfare in a New Economy – European and American Experiments,* eds. Jonathan Zeitlin and David M. Trubek. Oxford: Oxford University Press: 88–128.

Ferrera, Maurizio 1993. *Modelli della Solidaritá.* Milano: Il Mulino.

Ferrera, Maurizio. 1996. "Il Modelo sud-europeo di welfare state." *Rivista Italiana di scienza politica* 1:67–101.

Ferrera, Maurizio and Elisabetta Gualmini. 2004. *Rescued by Europe?* Amsterdam: Amsterdam University Press.

Ferrera, Maurizio. 2010. "The South European Countries." In *The Oxford Handbook of the Welfare State,* eds. Francis G. Castles et al. Oxford Handbooks Online: 616–629.

Findlay, Ronald and Henryk Kierzkowski. 1983. "International Trade and Human Capital: A Simple General Equilibrium Model." *The Journal of Political Economy* 91(6):957–978.

Fiss, Peer C. and Edward Zajac. 2004. "The Diffusion of Ideas over Contested Terrain: The (Non)adoption of a Shareholder Value Orientation among German Firms." *Administrative Science Quarterly* December (49):501–534.

Flanagan, Robert J. 1999. "Macroeconomic Performance and Collective Bargaining: An International Perspective." *Journal of Economic Literature* 37(3):1150–1175.

Flanagan, Robert J. 2003. "Collective Bargaining and Macroeconomic Performance." In *International Handbook of Trade Unions,* eds. John T. Addison and Claus Schnabel. London: Edward Elgar: 172–196.

Flanagan, Scott C. and Aie-Rie Lee. 2003. "The New Politics, Culture Wars, and the Authoritarian-Libertarian Value Change in Advanced Industrial Democracies." *Comparative Political Studies* 36:235–270.

Fleckstein, Timo and Martin Seeleib-Kaiser. 2011. "Business, Skills and the Welfare State: the Political Economy of Employment-Oriented Family Policy in Britain and Germany." *Journal of European Social Policy* 21(2):136–149

Franklin, Mark, Thomas Mackie and Henry Valen. 1992. *Electoral Change: Responses to Evolving Social and Attitudinal Structures in Western Countries.* Cambridge: Cambridge University Press.

Freeman, Richard and Heinz Rothgang. 2010. "Health." In *The Oxford Handbook of the Welfare State,* eds. Francis G. Castles, Stephan Leibfried, Jane Lewis, Herbert Obinger and Christopher Pierson. New York: Oxford University Press: 367–377.

Frey, Carl Benedikt and Michael A. Osborne. 2013. "The Future of Employment: How Susceptible Are Jobs to Computerisation?" *Paper presented at the Machine and Employment Workshop.* September 17, 2013. Oxford University Engineering Sciences Department and the Oxford Martin Programme on the Impacts of Future Technology.

Frey, Bruno S. and Alois Stutzer. 2002. *Happiness and Economics: How the Economy and Institutions Affect Human Wellbeing.* Princeton, NJ: Princeton University Press.

Frieden, Jeffry. 1991. "Invested Interests: The Politics of National Economic Policies in a World of Global Finance." *International Organization* 45(4):425–451.

Frieden, Jeffry A. and Ronald Rogowski. 1996. "The Impact of the International Economy on National Policies: An Analytical Overview." In *Internationalization and Domestic Politics*, eds. Robert Keohane and Helen Milner. Cambridge: Cambridge University Press.

Fuchs, Dieter and Hans-Dieter Klingemann. 1990. "The Left-Right Schema." In *Continuities in Political Action*, eds. M. K. Jennings and J. Van Deth. Berlin: DeGruyter.

Fuchs, Victor R. 1968. *The Service Economy*. National Bureau of Economic Research, New York: Columbia University Press.

Fukao, Kyoji and Roland Benabou. 1993. "History versus Expectations: A Comment." *Quarterly Journal of Economics* 108(2):535–542.

Galasso, Vincenzo. 2008. *The Political Future of Social Security in Aging Societies*. Cambridge: Cambridge University Press.

Garrett, Geoffrey. 1998. *Partisan Politics in the Global Economy*. Cambridge: Cambridge University Press.

Geering, Dominik and Silja Häusermann. 2013. "Transformed Party Electorates and Economic Realignment in Western Europe." Manuscript.

Gelman, Andrew. 2008. *Red State, Blue State, Rich State, Poor State. Why Americans Vote the Way They Do*. Princeton, NJ: Princeton University Press.

Gerschenkron, Alexander. 1962. *Economic Backwardness in Historical Perspective*. Cambridge, MA: Belknap Press of Harvard University Press.

Gershuny, Jonathan, Michael Bittman and John Brice. 2005. "Exit, Voice, and Suffering: Do Couples Adapt to Changing Employment Patterns?" *Journal of Marriage and Family* 67(3):656–665.

Gerxhani, K. 2004. "The Informal Sector in Developed and Less Developed Countries: A Literature Survey." *Public Choice* 120(3):267–300.

Gibson, Martha Liebler and Michael D. Ward. 1992. "Export Orientation: Pathway or Artifact?" *International Studies Quarterly* 36(3):331–343.

Gilens, Martin. 2012. *Affluence and Influence: Economic Inequality and Political Power in America*. New York and Princeton, NJ: Russell Sage Foundation and Princeton University Press.

Gilens, Martin. 2013. *Affluence and Influence: Economic Inequality and Political Power in America*. Princeton, NJ: Princeton University Press.

Gimenez-Nadal, J., Jose Molina and Almudena Sevilla-Sanz. 2012. "Social Norms, Partnerships and Children." *Review of Economics of the Household* 10(2):215–236.

Gingrich, Jane. 2011a. *Making Markets in the Welfare State: The Politics of Varying Reforms*. New York: Cambridge University Press.

Gingrich, Jane. 2011b. *The Politics That Markets Make*. New York and Cambridge: Cambridge University Press.

Gingrich, Jane and Ben W. Ansell. 2012. "Preferences in Context. Micro Preferences, Macro Contexts, and the Demand for Social Policy." *Comparative Political Studies* 45(12):1624–1654.

Gingrich, Jane und Silja Häusermann. Forthcoming. "The Decline of the Working Class Vote, the Reconfiguration of the Welfare Support Coalition and Consequences for the Welfare State," *Journal of European Social Policy*.

Glyn, Andrew. 2001. "Inequalities of Employment and Wages in OECD Countries." *Oxford Bulletin of Economics and Statistics* 63:697–713.

Glyn, Andrew. 2006. *Capitalism Unleashed: Finance Globalization and Welfare.* Oxford: Oxford University Press.

Golden, Miriam A., Michael Wallerstein and Peter Lange. 1999. "Postwar Trade-Union Organization and Industrial Relations in Twelve Countries." In *Continuity and Change in Contemporary Capitalism,* eds. Herbert Kitschelt, Peter Lange, Gary Marks and John D. Stephens. Cambridge: Cambridge University Press: 194–230.

Golden, Miriam A. and Michael Wallerstein. 2011. "Domestic and International Causes for the Rise of Pay Inequality in OECD Nations between 1980 and 2000." In *Comparing European Workers Part A* (Research in the Sociology of Work, Volume 22), ed. David Brady. Bingley: Emerald Group: 209–249.

Goldin, Claudia and Lawrence Katz. 1998. "The Origins of Technology-Skill Complementarity." *The Quarterly Journal of Economics* 113(3):639–732.

Goldin, Claudia. 2006. "The Quiet Revolution That Transformed Women's Employment, Education, and Family." *American Economic Review* 96(2):1–21.

Goldin, Claudia and Lawrence Katz, 2007. "The Race between Education and Technology: The Evolution of U.S. Educational Wage Differentials 1890 to 2005." NBER Working Paper 12984.

Goldin, Claudia. 2009. *The Race between Education and Technology.* Cambridge, MA: Harvard University Press.

Goldscheider, Frances. 2012. "The Gender Revolution and the 2nd Demographic Tranisition." Paper presented at the European Population Council meeting, Stockholm, June 13.

Goldstein, Joshua R. and Catherine T. Kenney. 2001. "Marriage Delayed or Marriage Forgone? New Cohort Forecasts of First Marriage for U.S. Women." *American Sociological Review* 66(4):506–519.

Goldstein, Joshua R., Tomáš Sobotka and Aiva Jasilioniene. 2009. "The End of 'Lowest-Low' Fertility?" *Population and Development Review* 35(4):663–699.

Goldthorpe, John H. and Abigail McKnight. 2006. "The Economic Basis of Social Class." In *Mobility and Inequality: Frontiers of Research from Sociology to Economics,* eds. S. Morgan, D Grusky and G Fields. Stanford, CA: Stanford University Press: 109–136.

Goode, William J. 1962. "Marital Satisfaction and Instability: A Cross-Cultural Class Analysis of Divorce Rates." *International Social Science Journal* 14(3):544–567.

Goos, M. and A. Manning. 2007. "Lousy and Lovely Jobs: The Rising Polarisation of Work in Britain." *Review of Economics and Statistics* 89(1):118–133.

Goos, M., A. Manning and A. Salomons. 2009. "Job Polarization in Europe." *AEA Papers and Proceedings* 99(2):58–63.

Gornick, Janet C., Marcia K. Meyers and Katherin E. Ross. 1998. "Public Policy and the Employment of Mothers: A Cross-National Study." *Social Sciences Quarterly* 79(1):35–54.

Gornick, Janet C. and Marcia K. Meyers. 2003. *Families That Work: Policies for Reconciling Parenthood and Employment.* New York: Russell Sage Foundation.

Gould, Roger V. 1991. "Multiple Networks and Mobilization in the Paris Commune, 1871." *American Sociological Review* 56(6):716–729.

Gourevitch, Peter. 1986. *Politics in Hard Times: Comparative Responses to International Economic Crises.* New York: Cornell University Press.

Grande, Edgar and Louis W. Pauly, eds. 2005 *Complex Sovereignty. Reconstituting Political Authority in the 21st Century.* Toronto: Toronto University Press.

Granovetter, Mark. 1978. "Threshold Models of Collective Behavior." *American Journal of Sociology* 83(6):1420–1443.

Greene, Kenneth F. 2007. *Why Dominant Parties Lose: Mexico's Democratization in Comparative Perspective.* Cambridge: Cambridge University Press.

Greenfeld, Liah. 1992. *Nationalism: Five Roads to Modernity.* Cambridge, MA: Harvard University Press.

Greenfeld, Liah. 1999. "Is Nation Unavoidable? Is Nation Unavoidable Today?" In *Nation and National Identity: The European Experience in Perspective*, eds. Hanspeter Kriesi, Klaus Armingeon, Hannes Siegrist and Andreas Wimmer. Chur: Rüegger: 37–54.

Green-Pedersen, Christoffer. 2001. "Minority Governments and Party Politics: The Political and Institutional Background to the 'Danish Miracle.'" *Journal of Public Policy* 21(1):53–70.

Greenstein, Theodore N. 1996. "Gender Ideology and Perceptions of the Fairness of the Division of Household Labor: Effects on Marital Quality." *Social Forces* 74(3):1029–1042.

Gregory, Mary, Wiemer Salverda and Stephen Bazen, eds. 2000. *Labour Market Inequalities.* Oxford: Oxford University Press.

Grossman, Gene and Helpman, Elhanan. 1994. "Protection for Sale." *American Economic Review* 84:833–850.

Grunberg, Gérard and Schweisguth, Etienne. 1990. "Libéralisme culturel et libéralisme économique." In *L'électeur français en question*, ed. CEVIPOF, Paris: Presses de la Fondation Nationale de Sciences Politiques: 45–69.

Grunberg, Gérard and Schweisguth, Etienne. 1997. Recompositions idéologiques. In *L'électeur a ses raisons*, eds. D. Boy and N. Maye. Paris: Presses de la Fondation Nationale de Sciences Politiques:130–178.

Grunow, Daniela, Florian Schulz and Hans-Peter Blossfeld. 2012. "What Determines Change in the Division of Housework over the Course of Marriage?" *International Sociology* 27(3):289–307.

Guillen, Ana. 2010. "Defrosting the Spanish Welfare State: The Weight of Conservative Components." In *A Long Good-Bye to Bismarck? The Politics of Welfare Reform in Continental Europe*, ed. Bruno Palier. Amsterdam: Amsterdam University Press: 183–206.

Gwartney, J., R. Lawson and J. Hall. 2012. "Economic Freedom of the World." *Annual Report.* Fraser Institute.

Hacker, Jacob S. 2004. "Dismantling the Health Care State? Political Institutions, Public Policies and the Comparative Politics of Health Reform." *British Journal of Political Science* 34:693–724.

Hacker, Jacob S. and Paul Pierson. 2010. *Winner Take All Politics: How Washington Made the Rich Richer – and Turned its Back on the Middle Class.* New York: Simon & Schuster.

Hagerty, Michael R. and Ruut Veenhoven. 2003. "Wealth and Happiness Revisited: Growing Wealth of Nations Does Not Go with Greater Happiness." *Social Indicators Research* 64(1):1–27.

Hainmueller, Jens and Michael J. Hiscox. 2006. "Learning to Love Globalization: Education and Individual Attitudes toward International Trade." *International Organization* 60(2):469–498.

Hainmueller, Jens and Michael J. Hiscox. 2007. "Educated Preferences: Explaining Attitudes toward Immigration in Europe." *International Organization* 61(2): 399–442.

Hainmueller, Jens and Michael J. Hiscox. 2010. "Attitudes toward Highly Skilled and Low-skilled Immigration: Evidence from a Survey Experiment." *American Political Science Review* 104(1):61–84.

Hakim, Catherine. 2000. *Work-Life-style Choices in the 21st Century: Preference Theory*. Oxford: Oxford University Press.

Hale, Galina and Maurice Obstfeld. 2014. "The Euro and the Geography of International Debt Flows." *Federal Reserve of San Francisco WP Series* 10.

Hall, Peter A. and Robert Franzese. 1998. "Central Bank Independence, Coordinated Wage bargaining, and European Monetary Union." *International Organization* 52:505–535.

Hall, Peter A. and David Soskice. 2001. *Varieties of Capitalism: The Institutional Foundations of Comparative Advantage*. New York: Oxford University Press.

Hall, Peter and Katheleen Thelen. 2009." Institutional Change in Varieties of Capitalism." *Socio Economic Review* 7:7–34.

Hall, Peter and Daniel W. Gingerich. 2009. "Varieties of Capitalism and Institutional Complementarities in the Political Economy: An Empirical Analysis." *British Journal of Political Science* 39:449–482.

Hall, Peter A. 2012. "The Economics and Politics of the Euro Crisis." *German Politics* 21(4):355–371.

Hamilton, Lawrence C. 2009. *Statistics with Stata*. Belmont, CA: Brooks/Cole.

Hancké, Bob and Martin Rhodes. 2005. "EMU and Labor Market Institutions in Europe: The Rise and Fall of National Social Pacts." *Work and Occupations* 32(2):196–228.

Hansen, Soren Friss. 2010. "Nonprofit Organizations and Enterprises: Danish Foundation Law as an Example." In *Comparative Corporate Governance of Nonprofit Organizations*, eds. K. J. Hopt and T. von Hippel. Cambridge: Cambridge Universy Press.

Hansmann, Henry and Steen Thomsen. 2013. "Managerial Distance and Virtual Ownership: The Governance of Industrial Foundations." Working paper.

Hanson, Gordon H. 2009. "The Economic Consequences of the International Migration of Labor." *Annual Review of Economics* 1:179–207.

Härkönen, Juho and Jaap Dronkers. 2006. "Stability and Change in the Educational Gradient of Divorce. A Comparison of Seventeen Countries." *European Sociological Review* 22(5):501–517.

Hassel, Anke. 2006. *Wage Setting, Social Pacts and the Euro: A New Role for the State*. Amsterdam: Amsterdam University Press.

Hassel, Anke 2014. "The Paradox of Liberalization – Understanding Dualism and the Recovery of the German Political Economy." *British Journal of Industrial Relations* 52(1):57–81.

Häusermann, Silja. 2006. "Changing Coalitions in Social Policy Reforms: The Politics of New Social Needs and Demands." *Journal of European Social Policy* 16 (1):5–21.

Häusermann, Silja and Palier, Bruno. 2008. "The State of the Art: The Politics of Employment-Friendly Welfare Reforms in Post-Industrial Economies." *Socio-Economic Review* 6:1–28.

Häusermann, Silja and Hanna Schwander. 2009. "Who Are the Outsiders and What Do They Want? Welfare State Preferences in Dualized Societies." Paper prepared for the Panel 'Security, Freedom and the Varieties of Welfare Capitalism', 5th General Conference of the European Consortium for Political Research, 10 – 12 September, Potsdam, Germany.

Häusermann, Silja. 2010. *The Politics of Welfare State Reform in Continental Europe: Modernization in Hard Times.* New York: Cambridge University Press.

Häusermann, Silja and Stefanie Walter. 2010. "Restructuring Swiss Welfare Politics: Post-Industrial Labor Markets, Globalization and Attitudes Toward Social Policy." In *World Value Change in Switzerland*, eds. Simon Hug and Hanspeter Kriesi. Lanham, MD: Lexington Press: 143–68.

Häusermann, Silja and Hanna Schwander. 2012. "Varieties of Dualization: Identifying Insiders and Outsiders across Regimes." In *The Age of Dualization. The Changing Face of Inequality in Deindustrializing Societies*, eds. Patrick Emmenegger, Silja Häusermann, Bruno Palier and Martin Seeleib-Kaiser. Oxford and New York: Oxford University Press.

Häusermann, Silja. 2012. "The Politics of Old and New Social Policy." In *The New Welfare State in Europe*, eds. Guliano Bonoli and David Natali. Oxford: Oxford University Press: 111–134.

Häusermann, Silja, Georg Picot and Dominik Geering. 2013. "Partisan Politics and the Welfare State: Recent Advances in the Literature." *British Journal of Political Science* 43(1):221–240.

Häusermann, Silja, Thomas Kurer and Hanna Schwander. 2014. "High-Skilled Outsiders? Labor Market Vulnerability, Education and Welfare State Preferences," *Socio-Economic Review.* doi: 10.1093/ser/mwu026

Hays, Jude, Sean Ehrlich and Clint Peinhardt. 2005. "Government Spending and Public Support for Trade in the OECD: An Empirical Test of the Embedded Liberalism Thesis." *International Organization* 59(2):473–494.

Hays, Jude. 2009. *Globalization and the New Politics of Embedded Liberalism.* Oxford: Oxford University Press.

Hazan, Moshe and Hosny Zoabi. 2011. "Do Highly Educated Women Choose Smaller Families?" in *CEPR Discussion Paper 8590.* London: Centre for Economic Policy Research.

Heckman, J. J. and D. V. Masterov. 2007. "The productivity argument for investing in young children." *Applied Economic Perspectives and Policy* 29(3):446.

Hedström, Peter, Rickard Sandell and Charlotta Stern. 2000. "Mesolevel Networks and the Diffusion of Social Movements: The Case of the Swedish Social Democratic Party1." *American Journal of Sociology* 106(1):145–172.

Helbling, Marc. 2011. "Why Swiss-Germans Dislike Germans: Opposition to Culturally Similar and Highly Skilled Immigrants." *European Societies* 13(1):5–27.

Helbling, Marc and Hanspeter Kriesi. 2014. "Opposing Low-Skilled Immigrants: Labor Market Competition, Welfare State and Deservingness." *European Sociological Review* 30(5):595–614.

Hellwig, Timothy and David Samuels. 2007. "Voting in Open Economies: The Electoral Consequences of Globalization." *Comparative Political Studies* 40(3):283–306.

Helpman, Elhanan, Oleg Itskhoki and Stephen Redding. 2008. "Inequality and Unemployment in a Global Economy." *NBER Working paper* 14478.

Hemerijck, Anton. 2013. *Changing Welfare States*. Oxford: Oxford University Press.

Hibbs, Douglas A. 1977. "Political Parties and Macroeconomic Policy." *American Political Science Review* 71(4):1467–1487.

Hicks, Alexander and Lane Kenworthy. 1998. "Cooperation and Political Economic Performance in Affluent Democratic Capitalism." *American Journal of Sociology* 103:1631–1672.

Hinrichs, Karl. 2000. "Elephants on the Move: Patterns of Pension Reform in OECD Countries." *European Review* 8:353–378.

Hinrichs, Karl. 2010. "A Social Insurance State Withers Away: Welfare State Reform in Germany." In *A Long Goodbye to Bismarck? The Politics of Welfare Reform in Continental Europe*, ed. Bruno Palier. Amsterdam: Amsterdam University Press: 45–73.

Hiscox, Michael J and Scott L Kastner. 2004. "A General Measure of Trade Policy Orientations: Gravity-Model-Based Estimates for 76 Nations, 1960 to 2000." (*Mimeo*). Cambridge MA: Harvard University.

Hix, Simon. 1999. "Dimensions and Alignments in European Union Politics: Cognitive Constraints and Partisan Responses." *European Journal of Political Research* 35(1):69–106.

Hobolt, Sara and Patrick Leblond. 2009. "Is My Crown Better Than Your Euro? Exchange Rates and Public Opinion on the Single European Currency." *European Union Politics* 10(2):202–225.

Hoffmann-Nowotny, Hans-Joachim. 1973. *Soziologie des Fremdarbeiterproblems*. Stuttgart: Enke.

Hoogenboom, Marcel. 2011. "The Netherlands: Two Tiers for All." In *Regulating the Risk of Unemployment: National Adaptations to Post-Industrial Labour Markets in Europe*, eds. Jochen Clasen and Daniel Clegg. Oxford: Oxford University Press: 75–99.

Hooghe, Lisbeth, Gary Marks and Carol J. Wilson. 2002. "Does Left/Right Structure Party Positions on European Integration?" *Comparative Political Studies* 35:965–989.

Höpner, Martin. 2003. *Wer beherrscht die Unternehmen? Shareholder Value, Managerherrschaft und Mitbestimmung in großen deutschen Unternehmen*. Frankfurt am Main: Campus.

Höpner, Martin and Lothar Krempel. 2004. "The Politics of the German Company Network." *Competition & Change* 8(4):339–356.

Höpner, Martin. 2005. "What Connects Industrial Relations and Corporate Governance? Explaining Institutional Complementarity." *Socio-Economic Review* 3(331–358).

Höpner, Martin and Gregory Jackson. 2006. "Revisiting the Mannesmann Takeover: How Markets for Corporate Control Emerge." *European Management Review* 3:142–155.

Höpner, Martin and Maximilian Waclawczyk. 2012. "Opportunismus oder Ungewissheit? Mitbestimmte Unternehmen zwischen Klassenkampf und Produktionsregime." *MPIfG Discussion Paper* 12(1): Köln: Max-Planck-Institut fuer Gesellschaftsforschung.

Howell, Chris. 2003. "Varieties of Capitalism: And Then There Was One?" *Comparative Politics* 36(1):103–124.

Huber, Evelyne and John D. Stephens. 1998. "Internationalization and the Social Democratic Model: Crisis and Future Prospects." *Comparative Political Studies* 31(3):353–397.

Huber, Evelyne and John D. Stephens. 2001. *Development and Crisis of the Welfare State: Parties and Policies in Global Markets*. Chicago: University of Chicago Press.

Huber, John. 2006. "Combating Old and New Social Risks." In *The Politics of Post-Industrial Welfare States: Adapting Post-War Social Policies to New Social Risks*, eds. Klaus Armingeon and Giuliani Bonoli. New York: Routledge: 143–169.

Huber, John and Piero Stanig. 2010. "Individual income and voting for redistribution across democracies." Unpublished Manuscript.

Huo, Jingjing. 2009. *Third Way Reforms: Social Democracy after the Golden Age*. New York: Cambridge University Press.

Hurley, J. and E. Fernández Macías. 2008. *More and Better Jobs: Patterns of Employment Expansion in Europe*. Dublin: European Foundation for the Improvement of Living and Working Conditions (Eurofound).

Ibsen, Christian Lyhne. 2012. *The "Real" End of Solidarity?* Cambridge MA: MIT.

Ilg, R. and S. Haugen. 2000. "Earnings and employment trends in the 1990s." *Monthly Labor Review* 123:21.

Immergut, Ellen. 1992. *The Political Construction of Interests: National Health Insurance Politics in Switzerland, France and Sweden, 1930–1970*. New York: Cambridge University Press.

Inglehart, Ronald. 1977. *The Silent Revolution – Changing Values and Political Styles among Western Publics*. Princeton, NJ: Princeton University Press: 19–71.

Inglehart, Ronald. 1997. *Modernization and Postmodernization: Cultural, Economic, and Political Change in 43 Societies*. Princeton, NJ: Princeton University Press.

Inglehart, Ronald. 2000. "Globalization and Postmodern Values." *The Washington Quarterly* 23(1):215–228.

Inglehart, Ronald and W. E. Baker. 2000. "Modernization, Cultural Change and the Persistence of Traditional Values." *American Sociological Review* 65:19–51.

Inglehart, Ronald and Christian Welzel. 2005. *Modernization, Cultural Change, and Democracy: The Human Development Sequence*. Cambridge: Cambridge University Press.

Isen, Adam and Stevenson, Betsey. 2010. "Women's education and family behavior." *NBER Working Paper* no. 15725.

Ivarsflaten, E. 2005. "The Vulnerable Populist Right Parties: No Economic Realignment Fuelling Their Electoral Success." *European Journal of Political Research* 44(3):465–492.

Iversen, Torben. 1996. "Power, Flexibility and the Breakdown of Centralized Wage Bargaining: The Cases of Denmark and Sweden in Comparative Perspective." *Comparative Politics* 28(4):399–436.

Iversen, T. and A. Wren. 1998. "Equality, Employment, and Budgetary Restraint: The Trilemma of the Service Economy." *World Politics* 50:507–546.

Iversen, Torben and Thomas R. Cusack. 2000. "The Causes of Welfare State Expansion: Deindustrialization or Globalization?" *World Politics* 52(03): 313–349.

Iversen, Torben and David Soskice. 2001. "An Asset Theory of Social Policy Preferences." *American Political Science Review* 95(4):875–894.

Iversen, Torben. 2005. *Capitalism, Democracy, and Welfare.* New York: Cambridge University Press.

Iversen, Torben and David Soskice. 2006. "Electoral Institutions and the Politics of Coalitions: Why Some Democracies Redistribute More than Others." *American Political Science Review* 100(2):165–181.

Iversen, T. and J. D. Stephens. 2008. "Partisan Politics, the Welfare State, and Three Worlds of Human Capital Formation." *Comparative Political Studies* 41(4–5):600.

Iversen, Torben and David Soskice. 2009. "Distribution and Redistribution: The Shadow of the Nineteenth Century." *World Politics* 61(3):438–486.

Iversen, Torben and Frances Rosenbluth. 2010. *Women, Work and Politics: The Political Economy of Gender Inequality.* New Haven, CT: Yale University Press.

Iversen, Martin Jes and Mats Larsson. 2011. "Strategic Transformations in Danish and Swedish Big Business in An Era of Globalisation, 1973–2008." *Business History* 53(1):119–143.

Iversen, Torben and David Soskice. 2012. "A Structural-Institutional Explanation of the Eurozone Crisis." *(Mimeo).* Harvard University and London School of Economics.

Iversen, Torben and David Soskice. forthcoming. "Dualism and Political Coalitions: Inclusionary versus Exclusionary Reforms." *World Politics.*

Jackson, Gregory. 2003. "Corporate Governance in Germany and Japan: Liberalization Pressures and Responses." In *The End of Diversity? Prospects for German and Japanese Capitalism*, ed. K. Yamamura and W. Streeck. Ithaca, NY: Cornell University Press.

Jackson, Gregory, Martin Hoepner and Antje Kurdelbusch. 2005. "Corporate Governance and Employees in Germany: Changing Linkages, Complementarities, and Tensions." In *Corporate Governance and Labour Management: An International Comparison*, ed. H. Gospel and A. Pendleton. Oxford: Oxford University Press.

Jackson, Gregory and Hideaki Miyajima. 2007. "Varieties of Takeover Markets: Comparing Mergers and Acquisitions in Japan with Europe and the USA." RIETI Discussion Paper Series 07-E-054.

Jackson, Gregory and Androniki Apostolakou. 2010. "Corporate Social Responsibility in Western Europe: An Institutional Mirror or Substitute?" *Journal of Business Ethics* 94(3):371–394.

Jackson, Gregory and Arndt Sorge. 2012. "The Trajectory of Institutional Change in Germany, 1979–2009." *Journal of European Public Policy* 19(8):1146–1167.

Jäntti, Markus, Berndt Bratsberg, Knud Røed, Oddbjørn Raaum, Robin Naylor, Eva Österbacka, Anders Björklund and Tor Eriksson. 2006. "American Exceptionalism in a New Light: A Comparison of Intergenerational Earnings Mobility in the Nordic Countries, the United Kingdom and the United States." *IZA Discussion Paper* No. 1938. Bonn.

Jean, Sebastien and Giuseppe Nicoletti. 2002. "Product market regulation and wage premia in Europe and North-America: An empirical investigation." *OECD Economics Department Working Papers* No. 318. OECD.

Jenson, J. 2009. "Lost in Translation: The Social Investment Perspective and Gender Equality." *Social Politics: International Studies in Gender, State & Society* 16(4):446.

Jessoula, Matteo and Tiziana Alti. 2010. "Italy: An Uncompleted Departure from Bismarck." In *a Long Good-Bye to Bismarck? The Politics of Welfare Reform in Continental Europe*, ed. Bruno Palier. Amsterdam: Amsterdam University Press: 157–182.

Jørgensen, Henning and Michaela Schulze. 2012. "A Double Farewell to a Former Model? Danish Unions and Activation Policy." *Local Economy* 27(5–6):637–644.

Juhn, C. 1999. "Wage Inequality and Demand for Skill: Evidence from Five Decades." *Industrial and Labor Relations Review* 52(3):424–443.

Jupille, Joseph and David Leblang. 2007. "Voting for Change: Calculation, Community, and Euro Referendums." *International Organization* 61(4):763–782.

Kahhat, Jaime. 2007. "Markets and the Dynamics of Inequality." Background paper prepared for the project "Markets, the State and the Dynamics of Inequality: How to Advance Inclusive Growth." UNDV, Bureau of Development Policy, Poverty Group.

Kalmijn, Matthijs and Gerbert Kraaykamp. 2007. "Social Stratification and Attitudes: A Comparative Analysis of the Effects of Class and Education in Europe." *The British Journal of Sociology* 58(4):547–576.

Kaltenthaler, Karl, Ronald Gelleny and Stephen Ceccoli. 2004. "Explaining Citizen Support for Trade Liberalization." *International Studies Quarterly* 48:829–851.

Kato, Junko. 2003. *Regressive Taxation and the Welfare State*. New York: Cambridge University Press.

Katz, L. F. 1999. "Technological Change, Computerization, and the Wage Structure." Working Paper, Department of Economics, Harvard University.

Katz, Richard S. and Peter Mair. 1995. "Changing Models of Party Organization and Party Democracy." *Party politics* 1(1):5.

Katz, Richard S. and Peter Mair. 2009. "The Cartel Party Thesis: A Restatement." *Perspectives on Politics* 7(4):753–766.

Katzenstein, Peter J. 1985. *Small States in World Markets: Industrial Policy in Europe*. Ithaca, NY: Cornell University Press.

Kayser, Mark. 2007. "How Domestic Is Domestic Politics? Globalization and Elections." *Annual Review of Political Science* 10:341–362.

Keller, Berndt and Frank Werner. 2010. "Industrial Democracy from a European Perspective: The Example of SEs." *Economic & Industrial Democracy* 31(4):40–54.

Kerr, C., J. T. Dunlop, F. H. Harbison and C. A. Meyers. 1960. *Industrialism and Industrial Man*. Cambridge, MA: Harvard University Press.

Kinderman, Daniel. 2012. "'Free Us up So We Can Be Responsible!': The Co-Evolution of Corporate Social Responsibility and Neo-Liberalism in the UK, 1977–2010." *Socio-Economic Review* 10(1):29–57.

Kinderman, Daniel. 2014. "Challenging Varieties of Capitalism's Account of Business Interests: The New Social Market Initiative and German Employers' Quest for Liberalization, 2000–2014." Max-Planck Institut für Gesellschaftsforschung Discussion Paper.

King, Desmond and David Rueda. 2008. "Cheap Labor: The New Politics of 'Bread and Roses' in Industrial Democracies." *Perspectives on Politics* 6(2):279–297.

Kirchheimer, O. 1966. "The Transformation of the Western European Party Systems." In *Political Parties and Political Development*, eds. Joseph LaPalombara and Myron Weiner. Princeton, NJ: Princeton University Press.

Kitschelt, Herbert 1994. *The Transformation of European Social Democracy*. New York: Cambridge University Press.

Kitschelt, Herbert. 2000. "Citizens, Politicians, and Party Cartellization: Political Representation and State Failure in Post–Industrial Democracies." *European Journal of Political Research* 37(2):149–179.

Kitschelt, Herbert. 2007. "The Demise of Clientelism in Affluent Capitalist Democracies." In *Patrons, Clients, and Policies: Patterns of Democratic Accountability and Political Competition*, eds. Herbert Kitschelt and Steven Wilkinson. Cambridge, MA: Cambridge University Press: 298–321.

Kitschelt, Herbert. 2007. "Growth and Persistence of the Radical Right in Postindus – Trial Democracies: Advances and Challenges in Comparative Research." *West European Politics* 30(5):1176–1206.

Kitschelt, Herbert. 2011. "Clientelistic Linkage Strategies. A Descriptive Exploration." Duke University: Workshop on Democratic Accountability Strategies.

Kitschelt, Herbert. 2012. "*Research and Dialogue on Programmatic Parties and Party Systems.*" Final Report. International IDEA (Institute for Democracy and Electoral Assistance). Stockholm: International Institute for Democracy and Election Assistance.

Kitschelt, Herbert and Anthony J. McGann. 1995. *The Radical Right in Western Europe*. Ann Arbor: The University of Michigan Press.

Kitschelt, Herbert, Peter Lange, Gary Marks and John D. Stephens. 1999. *Continuity and Change in Contemporary Capitalism*. New York: Cambridge University Press.

Kitschelt, Herbert, Peter Lange, Gary Marks and John D. Stephens. 1999. "Convergence and Divergence in Advanced Capitalist Democracies." In *Continuity and Change in Contemporary Capitalism*, ed. H. Kitschelt et al. Cambridge: Cambridge University Press: 427–460.

Kitschelt, Herbert and Philipp Rehm. 2013. "What's the Matter with America? American Voter-Party Alignments in Comparative Perspective." Prepared for Delivery at the Annual Meeting of the American Political Science Association, Chicago: August 28–31, 2013.

Kitschelt, Herbert and Philipp Rehm. 2014. "Occupations as a Site of Political Preference Formation." *Comparative Political Studies* 47(2)(2014):1670–1706. DOI: 10.1177/0010414013516066

Klingemann, Hans-Dieter, Richard Hofferbert and Ian Budge. 1994. *Parties, Policies, and Democracy*. Boulder, CO: Westview Press.

Kluge, Norbert and Michael Stollt, eds. 2006. *The European Company – Prospects for worker board-level participation in the enlarged EU*. Brussels: ETUI.

Knutsen, O. 2004. *Social Structure and Party Choice in Western Europe: A Comparative Longitudinal Study*. Basingstoke: Palgrave- Macmillan.

Knutsen, Oddbjorn and Staffan Kumlin. 2005. "Value Orientations and Party Choice." In *The European Voter: A Comparative Study of Modern Democracies*, ed. Jaques Thomassen. Oxford: Oxford University Press: 125–166.

Kohler, Hans-Peter, Francesco C. Billari and José A. Ortega. 2002. "The Emergence of Lowest-Low Fertility in Europe during the 1990s." *Population and Development Review* 28(4):641–680.

Kohli, M. forthcoming. "Generations in aging societies: inequalities, cleavages, conflicts." In *Challenges of Aging: Retirement, Pensions, and Intergenerational Justice*, ed. Torp, C. Basingstoke: Palgrave Macmillan.

Koole, Ruud. 1996. "Cadre, Catch-all or Cartel?" *Party Politics* 2(4):507–523.

Korpi, T. and M. Tåhlin. 2009. "Educational Mismatch, Wages, and Wage Growth: Overeducation in Sweden, 1974–2000." *Labour Economics* 16(2):183–193.

Korpi, Walter. 1983. *The Democratic Class Struggle*. New York: Routledge & Kegan Paul.

Korpi, Walter. 1989. "Power, Politics, and State Autonomy in the Development of Social Citizenship: Social Rights during Sickness in Eighteen OECD Countries since 1930." *American Sociological Review* 54(3):309–328.

Korpi, Walter and Joakim Palme. 1998. "The Paradox of Redistribution and Strategies of Equality: Welfare State Institutions, Inequality, and Poverty in the Western Countries." *American Sociological Review* 63(5):661–687.

Kravdal, Oystein and Rindfuss, R. 2008 "Changing Relationship between Education and Fertility. a Study of Men and Women Born 1940 to 1964." *American Sociological Review* 73:854–873.

Kriesi, Hanspeter. 1998. "The Transformation of Cleavage Politics: The 1997 Stein Rokkan Lecture." *European Journal of Political Research* 33(2):165–185.

Kriesi, Hanspeter, Edgar Grande, Romain Lachat, Martin Dolezal, Simon Bornschier and Tim Frey. 2006. "Globalization and the Transformation of the National Political Space: Six European Countries Compared." *European Journal of Political Research* 45(6):921–956.

Kriesi, Hanspeter, Edgar Grande, Romain Lachat, Martin Dolezal, Simon Bornschier and Timotheus Frey. 2008. *West European Politics in the Age of Globalization*. Cambridge: Cambridge University Press.

Krugman, Paul. 1991. "History versus Expectations." *Quarterly Journal of Economics* 106(2):651–667.

1991. *Geography and Trade*. Leuven: Leuven University Press.

Krugman, Paul. 1994. "Past and Prospective Causes of High Unemployment." *Economic Review* 79:23–43.

Krugman, Paul. 2008. "Trade and Wages, Reconsidered." *Brookings Papers on Economic Activity* 2:103–138.

2012. *End This Recession Now*. Norton: New York.

Kurth, James R. 1979. "The Political Consequences of the Product Cycle: Industrial History and Political Outcomes." *International Organization* 33(Winter):1–34.

La Porta, Rafael and Andrei Shleifer. 2008. "The unofficial economy and economic development." *National Bureau of Economic Research Working Paper*.

Landes, David S. 2003. *The Unbound Prometheus*. New York: Cambridge University Press.

Lange, Peter and Geoffrey Garrett. 1985. "The Politics of Growth: Strategic Interaction and Economic Performance in Advanced Industrial Democracies, 1974–1980." *Journal of Politics* 47(3):792–827.

Lappegaard, Trude and Rønsen, Marit 2005 "The Multifaceted Impact of Education on Entry into Motherhood." *European Journal of Population*, 21:31–49.

Lausten, Mette. 2002. "CEO Turnover, Firm Performance and Corporate Governance: Empirical Evidence on Danish Firms." *International Journal of Industrial Organization* 20(3):391.

Laver, Michael and Ben W. Hunt. 1992. *Policy and Party Competition*. New York: Routledge.

Laver, Michael. 2005. "Policy and the Dynamics of Political Competition." *American Political Science Review* 99(2):263–281.

Laver, Michael and Ernest Sergenti. 2011. *Party Competition: An Agent-Based Model*. Princeton, NJ: Princeton University Press.

Leblang, David, Joseph Jupille and Amber Curtis. 2011. "The Mass Political Economy of International Public Debt Settlement." Presented at the Political Economy of International Finance (PEIF) meeting 2011, Berlin.

Lesch, Hagen. 2010. "TArifeinheit: BDA und DGB mit einer Stimme." In *Gewerkschaftsspiegel*. Köln: Institut der deutschen Wirtschaft.

Lesthaeghe, Ron. 1995. "The second demographic transition in Western countries: An interpretation." In *Gender and Family Change in Industrialized Countries*, eds. Karen Oppenheim Mason and Ann-Magritt Jensen. Oxford: Clarendon: 17–62.

Lesthaeghe, Ron. 1998. "On Theory Development: Applications to the Study of Family Formation." *Population and Development Review* 24:1–14.

Levy, Jonah. 1999. "Vice into Virtue? Progressive Politics and Welfare Reform in Continental Europe." *Politics and Society* 27(2):239–273.

Levy, Santiago. 2008. *Good Intentions, Bad Outcomes: Social Policy, Informality, and Economic Growth in Mexico*. Washington, DC: Brookings Institute Press.

Lind, Jens. 2009. "The End of the Ghent System as Trade Union Recruitment Machinery?" *Industrial Relations Journal* 40(6):510–523.

Lindbeck, Assar, and Dennis, J. Snower. 1986. "Wage Setting, Unemployment and Insider-Outsider Relations." *American Economic Review* 76(2):235–239.

Lindblom, Charles. 1977. *Politics and Markets*. New York: Basic Books.

Lindvall, Johannes and David Rueda. 2013. "The Insider-Outsider Dilemma." *British Journal of Political Science* 44(2):460–475.

Lipset, Seymour M. and Stein Rokkan 1967 (1985). "Cleavage Structures, Party Systems, and Voter Alignments." In *Consensus and Conflict: Essays in Political Sociology*, ed. Seymour M. Lipset, New Brunswick, NJ: Transaction Books:113–185.

Livi-Bacci, Massimo. 2001. "Too Few Children and Too Much Family." *Daedalus* 130(3):139–156.

Lopez-Pintado, Dunia and Watts, Duncan 2008 "Social Influence, Binary Decisions and Collective Dynmaics." *Rationality and Society* 20:399–443

Lora, Eduardo. 2001. "A Decade of Structural Reform in Latin America: What Has Been Reformed and How to Measure It." *IDB Working Papers*.

Loveless, Tom. 2006. *The Peculiar Politics of No Child Left Behind*. New York: The Brookings Institution.

Lowen, Tommy and Ole Settegren. 2011. *Kommentar till OECD's skattning av framtida pensionsnivå i Sverige*. Stockholm: Pensionsmyndigheten.

Lubinski, Christina. 2011. "Path Dependency and Governance in German Family Firms." *Business History Review* 85(4):699–724.

Luebbert, Gregory M. 1991. *Liberalism, Fascism or Social Democracy*. New York: Oxford University Press.

Lupu, Noam and Jonas Pontusson. 2011. "The Structure of Inequality and Politics of Redistribution." *American Political Science Review* 105(2):316–336.

Madsen, Per Kongshøj 2006. "How Can It Possibly Fly? the Paradox of a Dynamic Labour Market in a Scandinavian Welfare State." In *National Identity and the Varieties of Capitalism: The Danish Experience*, eds. J. A. Campbell, J. A. Hall and O. K. Pedersen. Montreal: McGill-Queen's University Press.

Maier, Friederike. 1994. "Institutional Regimes of Part-Time Working." In *Labor Market Institutions in Europe: A Socioeconomic Evaluation of Performance*, ed. Gunther Schmid. New York: ME Sharpe: 151–183.

Mailand, Mikkel. 2014. "Tripartite Agreement on Vocational Education Reform." EIRO: Eurofound. http://www.eurofound.europa.eu.eiro/dk13110191.

Mair, Peter. 2006. "Ruling the Void? The Hollowing of Western Democracy." *New Left Review* 42:1–27.

Malhotra, Neil, Yotam Margalit and Cecilia Hyunjung Mo. 2013. "Economic Explanations for Opposition to Immigration: Distinguishing between Prevalence and Conditional Impact." *American Journal of Political Science* 57(2):391–410.

Maloney, W. F. 1999. "Does Informality Imply Segmentation in Urban Labor Markets? Evidence from Sectoral Transitions in Mexico." *The World Bank Economic Review* 13(2):275–302.

Manning, A. 2004. "We Can Work It Out: The Impact of Technological Change on the Demand for Low-Skill Workers." *Scottish Journal of Political Economy* 51(5):581–608.

Manow, Philip. 2002. "The Good, the Bad, and the Ugly." *Kölner Zeitschrift für Soziologie und Sozialpsychologie* 54(2): 203–225.

Manow, Philip. 2010. "Trajectories of Fiscal Adjustment in Bismarckian Welfare Systems." In *A Long Goodbye to Bismarck? The Politics of Welfare Reform in Continental Europe*, ed. Bruno Palier. Amsterdam: Amsterdam University Press: 279–300.

Mansfield, Edward and Diana Mutz. 2009. "Support for Free Trade: Self-Interest, Sociotropic Politics, and Out-Group Anxiety." *International Organization* 63(2):425–457.

Manski, Charles F. 1993. "Identification of Endogenous Social Effects: The Reflection Problem." *Review of Economic Studies* 60(3):531–542.

Manza, Jeff and Clem Brooks. 1999. *Social Cleavages and Political Change: Voter Alignments and U.S. Party Coalitions*. Oxford University Press.

Maravall, José Maria. 1996a. *Regimes, Politics, and Markets*. Oxford: Oxford University Press.

1996b. *Los Resultados de la Democracia*. Madrid: Alianza Editorial.

Mare, Robert D. 1991. "Five Decades of Educational Assortative Mating." *American Sociological Review* 56(1):15–32.

Mares, Isabela. 2003. *The Politics of Social Risk: Business and Welfare State Development*. Cambridge: Cambridge University Press.

2006. *Taxation, Wage Bargaining, and Unemployment*. New York: Cambridge University Press.

Margalit, Yotam. 2011. "Costly Jobs: Trade-related Layoffs, Government Compensation, and Voting in U.S. Elections." *American Political Science Review* 105(1):166–188.

Margalit, Yotam. 2012. "Lost in Globalization: International Economic Integration and the Sources of Popular Discontent." *International Studies Quarterly* 56(3):484–500.

Martin, Cathie Jo and Kathleen Thelen. 2007. "The State and Coordinated Capitalism: Contributions of the Public Sector to Social Solidarity in Postindustrial Societies." *World Politics* 60(1):1–36.

Martin, Cathie Jo and Kathleen Thelen. 2007a. "The State and Coordinated Capitalism: Contributions of the Public Sector to Social Solidarity in Post-Industrial Societies." *World Politics* 60 (October 2007):1–36.

Martin, Cathy Jo and Kathleen Thelen. 2007b. "Varieties of Coordination and Trajectories of Change: Social Policy and Economic Adjustment in Coordinated

Market Economies." *Presented at the Annual Meeting of the American Political Science Association.* Chicago.

Martin, Cathie Jo and Duane Swank. 2012. *The Political Construction of Business Interests: Coordination, Growth, and Equality.* Cambridge: Cambridge University Press.

Massey, Douglas S. and Nancy A. Denton. 1993. *American Apartheid: Segregation and the Making of the Underclass.* Cambridge, MA: Harvard University Press.

Massey, Douglas S., ed. 2008. *New Faces in New Places: The Changing Geography of American Immigration.* New York: Russell Sage Foundation.

Matysiak, Anna and Daniele Vignoli. 2008. "Fertility and Women's Employment: A Meta-analysis." *European Journal of Population* 24(4):363–384.

Mau, Steffen. 2007. *Transnationale Vergesellschaftung. Die Entgrenzung sozialer Lebenswelten.* Frankfurt a.M.: Campus.

Mayda, Anna Maria and Dani Rodrik. 2005. "Why Are Some People (and Countries) More Protectionist Than Others?"*European Economic Review* 49(6): 1393–1430.

Mayda, Anna Maria. 2006. "Who Is against Immigration? A Cross-Country Investigation of Individual Attitudes toward Immigrants." *The Review of Economics and Statistics* 88(3):510–530.

Mayda, Anna Maria. 2008. "Why Are People More Pro-Trade Than Pro-Migration?" *Economics Letters* 101(3):160–163.

Mayer, Karl Ulrich. 2001. "The Paradox of Global Social Change and National Path Dependencies: Life Course Patterns in Advanced Societies." In *Inclusions and Exclusions in European Societies*, eds. Alison E. Woodward and Martin Kohli. London: Routledge: 89–110.

McCarty, Nolan, Keith T. Poole and Howard Rosenthal. 2006. *Polarized America: The Dance of Ideology and Unequal Riches.* Boston: MIT Press.

McDonald, Peter. 2000. "Gender Equity in Theories of Fertility Transition." *Population and Development Review* 26(3):427–439.

McLanahan, Sara. 2004. "Diverging Destinies: How Children Are Faring under the Second Demographic Transition." *Demography* 41(4):607–627.

Melitz, Marc. 2003. "The Impact of Trade on Intra-Industry Reallocations and Aggregate Industry Productivity." *Econometrica* 71(6):1695–1725.

Michels, Robert. 1915. *Political Parties: A Sociological Study of the Oligarchical Tendencies of Modern Democracy.* Kessinger.

Mitlacher, Lars W. 2007. "The Role of Temporary Agency Work in Different Industrial Relations Systems." *British Journal of Industrial Relations* 45(3): 581–606

Moene, Karl Ove and Michael Wallerstein. 2001. "Inequality, Social Insurance, and Redistribution." *American Political Science Review* 95(4):859–874.

Moene, Karl Ove and Michael Wallerstein. 2002. *Social Democracy as a Development Strategy.* Oslo: IDEAS.

Molina, Oscar and Martin Rhodes. 2007. "The Political Economy of Adjustment in Mixed Market Economies: A Study of Spain and Italy." In *Beyond Varieties of Capitalism: Conflict, Contradictions, and Complementarities in the European Economy*, eds. Bob Hancké, Martin Rhodes and Mark Thatcher. Oxford: Oxford University Press: 223–252.

Morel, Nathalie, Bruno Palier and Joakim Palme. 2012. *Towards a Social Investment Welfare State? Idea, Policies and Challenges.* Bristol: Policy Press.

Moreno, Luis. 1997. *La Federalizacion de España*. Madrid: Siglo XXI.

Moreno Luis. 2007. "The Nordic Path of Spain's Mediterranean Welfare." *Center for European Studies Working Paper* 183 (2008).

Morgan, Kimberly J. 2006. *Working Mothers and the Welfare State: Religion and the Politics of Work-Family Policy in Western Europe and the United States*. Sanford, CA: Stanford University Press.

Morgan, Kimberly J. 2009. "Promoting Social Investment Through Work-Family Policies: Which Nations Do It and Why?" In *Child Care and the Social Investment Model: Political Conditions for Reform*, eds. Morel, Palier and Palme. Bristol: Policy Press.

Morsing, Mette. 2004. "Denmark: Inclusive Labour Market Strategies." In *Corporate Social Responsibility across Europe*, ed. A. Habisch, J. Jonker, M. Wegner and R. Schmidpeter. Berlin: Springer.

Mosley, Hugh. 1994. "Employment Protection and Labor Force Adjustment in EC Countries." In *Labor Market Institutions in Europe: A Socioeconomic Evaluation of Performance*, ed. Gunther Schmid. New York: ME Sharpe: 59–81.

Mudde, Cas. 2007. *Populist Radical Right Parties in Europe*. Cambridge: Cambridge University Press.

Mughan, Anthony and Dean Lacy. 2002. "Economic Performance, Job Insecurity and Electoral Choice." *British Journal of Political Science* 32(3):513–533.

Mughan, Anthony, Clive Bean and Ian McAllister. 2003. "Economic Globalization, Job Insecurity and the Populist Reaction." *Electoral Studies* 22(4):617–633.

Murillo, Maria V and Andrew Schrank. 2009. "Labor Unions in the Policymaking Process in Latin America." In *Institutions, Actors and Arenas in Latin American Policymaking*. London: Palgrave.

Myles, John and Paul Pierson. 2001. "The Political Economy of Pension Reform." In *The New Politics of the Welfare State*, ed. Paul Pierson. Oxford: Oxford University Press: 305–333.

Myrskylä, Mikko, Hans-Peter Kohler and Francesco C. Billari. 2009. "Advances in Development Reverse Fertility Declines." *Nature* 460(7256):741–743.

Myrskylä, Mikko, Francesco C. Billari and Hans-Peter Kohler. 2011. "*High Development and Fertility: Fertility at Older Reproductive Ages and Gender Equality Explain the Positive Link*." Max Planck Institute for Demographic Research, Rostock, Germany.

Navrbjerg, Steen E. and Dana B. Minbaeva. 2009. "HRM and IR in multinational corporations in Denmark: uneasy bedfellows?"*International Journal of Human Resource Management* 20(8):1720–1736.

Nelson, M. and J. D. Stephens. 2012. "Do Social Investment Policies Produce More and Better Jobs?" In *Towards a Social Investment Welfare State? Ideas, Policies and Challenges*, eds. Morel, Palier and Palme. Bristol: Policy Press.

Nelson, Moira. 2013. "Making Markets with Active Labor Market Policy: The Influence of Political Parties, Welfare State Regimes, and Economic Change on Spending on Different Types of Policies." *European Political Science Review* 5(2):255–277.

Neumann, Robert and Torben Voetmann. 2003. "Does Ownership Matter in the Presence of Strict Antiactivism Legislation? Evidence from Equity Transactions in Denmark." *International Review of Financial Analysis* 12(2):157.

Neyer, Gerda, Trude Lappegård and Daniele Vignoli. 2011. "Gender Equality and Fertility: Which Equality Matters?" in *Stockholm Research Reports in Demography* 2011:9. Stockholm: Department of Sociology, Stockholm University.

Nicholas, David. 1997. *The Growth of the Medieval City: from Late Antiquity to the Early Fourteenth Century.* London: Longman.

Nickell, S. and B. Bell. 1996. "The Distribution of Wages and Unemployment. Changes in the Distribution of Wages and Unemployment In OECD Countries." *American Economic Association Papers and Proceedings* 86:302–308.

Nickell, S., L. Nunziata and W. Ochel. 2005. "Unemployment in the OECD since the 1960s. What Do We Know?" *Economic Journal* 115(500):1–27.

Nielsen, Søren. 1995. *Vocational Education and Training in Denmark.* Brussels: CEDEFOP.

Nomi, Tomoaki. 1997. "Determinants of Trade Orientation in Less Developed Countries." *Policy Studies Journal* 25(1):27–38.

Norris, Pippa. 2005. *Radical Right: Voters and Parties in the Electoral Market.* New York: Cambridge University Press.

North, Douglass C. 1990. *Institutions, Institutional Change and Economic Performance.* Cambridge: Cambridge University Press.

OECD. 1998. *"Employment Outlook."* Paris: OECD.

OECD. 1999. "Employment Outlook, July 1999." The Organisation for Economic Cooperation and Development.

OECD. 2011. *Pensions at a Glance 2011: Retirement Income Systems in OECD and G20 Countries.* Paris: OECD.

OECD. 1994. *The 1994 Jobs Study.* Paris: OECD.

OECD. 1999. *Employment Protection and Labour Market Performance."* *Employment Outlook*, Chapter 2. Paris: OECD.

OECD. 2006. *Employment Outlook 2006.* Paris: OECD

OECD. 2007. *OECD Workers in the Global Economy: Increasingly Vulnerable? Employment Outlook*, Chapter 3. Paris: OECD: 105–155.

OECD. 2008. *A Profile of Immigrant Populations in the 21st Century: Data from OECD countries.* OECD: Paris.

OECD. 2008. *Employment Protection in the OECD 2008.* Paris: OECD.

OECD. 2011. *Doing Better for Families.* Paris: OECD.

OECD. 2011. *International Migration Outlook.* Paris: OECD.

OECD. 2012. *Education at a Glance.* Paris: OECD.

OECD. 2012a. "Dataset: International Migration Database." http://stats.oecd.org/ (accessed on August 28, 2012).

OECD. 2012b. "Dataset: Population." http://stats.oecd.org/ (accessed on August 28, 2012).

OECD. Various Years. *Economic Outlook.* Paris: OECD

OECD. Various Years. *Labor Force Statistics.* Paris: OECD.

Oesch, Daniel. 2006. "Coming to Grips with a Changing Class Structure: An Analysis of Employment Stratification in Britain, Germany, Sweden and Switzerland." *International Sociology* 21(2):263–288.

Oesch, Daniel. 2006. *Redrawing the Class Map: Stratification and Institutions in Germany, Britain, Sweden and Switzerland.* London: Palgrave Macmillan.

Oesch, Daniel. 2008. "Explaining Workers' Support for Right-Wing Populist Parties in Western Europe: Evidence from Austria, Belgium, France, Norway and Switzerland." *International Political Science Review* 29(3):349–373.

Oesch, Daniel. 2012. "The Class Basis of the Cleavage between the New Left and the Radical Right: An Analysis for Austria, Denmark, Norway and Switzerland." In *Class Politics and the Radical Right*, ed. J. Rydgren. London: Routledge: 31–51.

Oesch, Daniel. 2013. *Occupational Change in Europe: How Technology and Education Transform the Job Structure*. Oxford: Oxford University Press.

Oesch, Daniel and J. Rodriguez Menes. 2011. "Upgrading or Polarization? Occupational Change in Britain, Germany, Spain and Switzerland, 1990–2008." *Socio-Economic Review* 9(3):503–532.

Offe, Claus. 1972. *Strukturprobleme des kapitalistischen Staates*. Frankfurt/ Main: Suhrkamp.

O'Neil, Kevin and Marta Tienda. 2010. "A Tale of Two Counties: Natives' Opinions toward Immigration in North Carolina." *International Migration Review* 44(3):728–761.

Oppenheim Mason, Karen and Larry L. Bumpass. 1975. "U.S. Women's Sex-Role Ideology, 1970." *American Journal of Sociology* 80(5):1212–1219.

O'Rourke, Kevin and Richard Sinnott. 2002. "The Determinants of Individual Trade Policy Preferences: International Survey Evidence." In *Brookings Trade Forum*, eds. Susan Collins and Dani Rodrik. Washington DC: Brookings Institution Press.

Osterkatz, Sandra Chapman. 2013. "Commitment, Capacity, and Community: The Politics of Multi-level Health Reform in Spain and Brazil." PhD dissertation, University of North Carolina at Chapel Hill.

Ottaviano, Gianmarco I. P. and Giovanni Peri. 2008. "Immigration and National Wages: Clarifying the Theory and the Empirics." *National Bureau of Economic Research Working Paper* 14188.

Pacek, Alexander and Benjamin Radcliff. 2008. "Assessing the Welfare State: The Politics of Happiness." *Perspectives on Politics* 6(2):267–277.

Palier, Bruno and Kathleen Thelen. 2010. "Institutionalizing Dualism: Complementarities and Change in France and Germany." *Politics and Society* 38(1):119–148.

Palier, Bruno. 2010. "The Dualizations of the French Welfare State." In *A Long Good-Bye to Bismarck? The Politics of Welfare Reform in Continental Europe*, ed. Bruno Palier. Amsterdam: Amsterdam University Press: 73–100.

Palme, Joakim. 1990. "*Pension Rights in Welfare Capitalism: The Development of Old-Age Pensions in Eighteen OECD Countries, 1930 to 1985*." Stockholm: Swedish Institute for Social Research.

Palme, Joakim. 2003. "Pension Reform in Sweden and the Changing Boundaries between Public and Private." In *Pension Security in the 21st Century*, eds. Gordon L. Clark and Noel Whiteside Oxford. Oxford: Oxford University Press: 144–167.

Paster, Thomas. 2012. "Do German Employers Support Board-Level Codetermination? The Paradox of Individual Support and Collective Opposition." *Socio-Economic Review* 10(3):471–495.

Peri, Giovanni, and Chad Sparber. 2009. "Task Specialization, Immigration, and Wages." *American Economic Journal: Applied Economics* 1(3):135–69.

Persson, Torsten and Timothy Besley 2011. *Pillars of Prosperity: The Political Economics of Development Clusters*. Princeton, NJ: Princeton University Press.

Petersen, Christian and Thomas Plenborg. 2006. "Voluntary Disclosure and Information Asymmetry in Denmark." *Journal of International Accounting, Auditing and Taxation* 15(2):127–149.

Pfau-Effinger, Birgit. 2005. "Culture and Welfare State Policies: Reflections on a Complex Interrelation." *Journal of Social Policy* 34(1):3–20.

Piattoni, Simona. 2001. *Clientelism, Interests, and Democratic Representation: The European Experience in Historical and Comparative Perspective.* Cambridge: Cambridge University Press.

Pieper, Ute. 2000. "Deindustrialisation and the Social and Economic Sustainability Nexus in Developing Countries: Cross-country Evidence on Productivity and Employment." *The Journal of Development Studies* 36(4):66–99.

Pierson, Paul. 1994. *Dismantling the Welfare State? Reagan, Thatcher and the Politics of Retrenchment.* Cambridge: Cambridge University Press.

Pierson, Paul. 1996. "The New Politics of the Welfare State." *World Politics* 48(2):143–179.

Pierson, Paul. 2001. "Coping with Permanent Austerity: Welfare State Restructuring in Affluent Democracies." In *The New Politics of the Welfare State*, ed. Paul Pierson. Oxford and New York: Oxford University Press.

Piketty, Thomas. 2014. *Capital in the Twenty-First Century.* Cambridge, MA: Harvard University Press.

Piore, Michael and Charles Sabel. 1984. *The Second Industrial Divide.* New York: Basic Books.

Pisani-Ferry, Jean, Erkki Vihriälä and Guntram B. Wolff. 2013. Options for a Euro-area Fiscal Capacity, *Bruegel Policy Contribution* 2013/1.

Pizzorno, Alessandro. 1978. "Political Exchange and Collective Identity in Industrial Conflict." In *The Resurgence of Class Conflict in Western Societies since 1968*, eds. C. Crouch and A. Pizzorno. London: Macmillan: 277–298.

Plümper, Thomas and Vera Troeger. 2008. "Fear of Floating and the External Effects of Currency Unions." *American Journal of Political Science* 52(3):656–676.

Pontusson, Jonas and Peter Swenson. 1996. "Labor Markets, Production Strategies and Wage Bargaining Institutions: The Swedish Employer Offensive in Comparative Perspective." *Comparative Political Studies* 29(2):223–250.

Pontusson, Jonas. 1996. "*Wage Distribution and Labor Market Institutions in Sweden, Austria and Other OECD Countries.*" Institute for European Studies.

Pontusson, Jonas, David Rueda and C. R. Way. 2003. "Comparative Political Economy of Wage Distribution: The Role of Partisanship and Labour Market Institutions." *British Journal of Political Science* 32:281–308.

Pontusson, Jonas. 2005. *Inequality and Prosperity: Social Europe Vs. Liberal America.* Century Foundation. Ithaca, NY: Cornell University Press.

Pontusson, Jonas and David Rueda. 2010. "The Politics of Inequality: Voter Mobilization and Left Parties in Advanced Industrial States." *Comparative Political Studies* 43(6):675–705.

Pontusson, Jonas. 2011. "Once Again a Model: Nordic Social Democracy in a Globalized World." Pp. 89–115. In *What's Left of the Left? Futures of the Left*, eds. James Cronin, George Ross and James Shoch. Durham, NC: Duke University Press.

Porter, Michael E, Augusto Lopez-Claros, Klaus Schwab, Xavier Sala-I-Martin et al. 2007. "The Global Competitiveness Report 2006–2007." *World Economic Forum.* Geneva, Switzerland 2006.

Porter, Michael. 1990. *The Competitive Advantage of Nations.* New York: Simon & Schuster.

Portes, Alejandro and Robert D. Manning. 1986. "The Immigrant Enclave: Theory and Empirical Examples." In *Competitive Ethnic Relations*, eds. Susan Olzak and Joane Nagel. New York: Elsevier: 47–68.

Poulantzas, Nicos. 1973. *Political Power and Social Classes*. London: New Left Review.

Progressivity: Sweden, 1968–2009. Uppsala Center for Fiscal Studies. Department of Economics. Working Paper 2012: 8.

Przeworski, A. and H. Teune. 1970. *The Logic of Comparative Social Inquiry*. New York: Wiley.

Przeworski Adam und John Sprague. 1986. *Paper Stones: A History of Electoral Socialism*. Chicago: University of Chicago Press.

Przeworski, Adam and Michael Wallerstein. 1988. "Structural Dependence of the State on Capital." *American Political Science Review* 82:11–29.

Quillian, L. 1995. "Prejudice as a Response to Perceived Group Threat: Population Composition and Anti-Immigrant and Racial Prejudice in Europe." *American Sociological Review* 60, 586–611.

Radcliff, Benjamin. 2001. "Politics, Markets, and Life Satisfaction: The Political Economy of Human Happiness." *American Political Science Review* 95(4):939–952.

Raley, Kelly R. and Larry L. Bumpass. 2003. "The Topography of the Divorce Plateau: Levels and Trends in Union Stability in the United States after 1980." *Demographic Research* 8(8):245–260.

Raley, Sara, Suzanne M. Bianchi and Wendy Wang. 2012. "When Do Fathers Care? Mothers' Economic Contribution and Fathers' Involvement in Child Care." *American Journal of Sociology* 117(5):1422–1459.

Rathgeb, Philip. 2013. "A viable model of egalitarian capitalism? Danish 'Flexicurity' and the Political Right." Joint NordWel & REASSESS Summer School, Reykjavik, Iceland, August 15–20.

Rathgeb, Philip Markus 2014. "A Viable Model of Egalitarian Capitalism? Danish "Flexicurity" and the Political Right." Paper for Joint NordWel & REASSESS International Summer School, Reykjavik, Iceland.

Ray, Debraj. 2010. "Uneven Growth: A Framework for Research in Development Economics." *The Journal of Economic Perspectives* 24(3):45–60.

Raymo, James M., Setsuya Fukuda and Miho Iwasawa. 2012. "Educational Differences in Divorce in Japan." *CDE Working Paper No. 2012-01*. Madison, WI: Center for Demography and Ecology.

Rehder, Britta. 2003. *Betriebliche Bündniss für Arbeit in Deutschland: Mitbestimmung und Flächentarif im Wandel*. Frankfurt: Campus.

Rehm, Philipp. 2009. "Risks and Redistribution. An Individual-Level Analysis." *Comparative Political Studies* 42(7):855–881.

Rehm, Philipp. 2011a. "Risk Inequality and the Polarized American Electorate." *British Journal of Political Science* 41(2):363–387.

Rehm, Philipp. 2011b. "Social Policy by Popular Demand." *World Politics* 63(2):271–299.

Rehm, Philipp and Timothy Reilly. 2010. "United We Stand: Constituency Homogeneity and Comparative Party Polarization." *Electoral Studies* 29(1):40–53.

Rehm, Philipp, Jacob S. Hacker and Mark Schlesinger. 2012. "Insecure Alliances: Risk, Inequality, and Support for the Welfare State." *American Political Science Review* 106(2):386–406.

Ringen, Stein. 1987. *The Possibility of Politics*. Oxford: Clarendon Press.

Rocha, Robson Sø. 2009. "The Impact of Cross-Border Mergers on the Co-Decision-Making Process: The Case of a Danish Company." *Economic & Industrial Democracy* 30(4):484–509.

Rodrik, Dani. 1998. "Why Do More Open Economies Have Bigger Governments?" *Journal of Political Economy*, 106(5) October.

2011. *The Globalization Paradox: Democracy and the Future of the World Economy.* New York: Norton.

Rogowski, Ronald. 1989. *Commerce and Coalitions: How Trade Affects Domestic Political Alignments.* Princeton, NJ: Princeton University Press.

Rokkan, Stein. 2000. *Staat, Nation und Demokratie in Europa. Die Theorie Stein Rokkans aus seinen gesammelten Werken rekonstruiert und eingeleitet von Peter Flora.* Frankfurt: Suhrkamp.

Rose, Caspar and Carsten Mejer. 2003. "The Danish Corporate Governance System: From Stakeholder Orientation Towards Shareholder Value." *Corporate Governance: An International Review* 11(4):335.

Rose, Caspar. 2005. "Takeover Defenses' Influence on Managerial Incentives." *International Review of Law & Economics* 25(4):556–577.

Rose, Caspar. 2007. "Can Institutional Investors Fix the Corporate Governance Problem? Some Danish Evidence." *Journal of Management & Governance* 11(4):405–428.

Rose, Caspar. 2008. "The Challenges of Employee-Appointed Board Members for Corporate Governance: The Danish Evidence." *European Business Organization Law Review (EBOR)* 9(02):215–235.

Rosenstein-Rodan, Paul N. 1943. "Problems of Industrialisation of Eastern and South-Eastern Europe." *The Economic Journal* 53(210/211):202–211.

Rothstein, B. 1992. "Labor Market Institutions and Working-Class Strength." In *Structuring Politics: Historical Institutionalism in Comparative Analysis*, eds. Sven Steinmo, Kathleen Thelen and F. Longstreth. New York: Cambridge University Press: 33–56.

Rowthorn, B. 1992. "Corporatism and Labour Market Performance." In *Social Corporatism: A Superior Economic System?* eds. J. Pekkarinen, M. Pohjola and B. Rowthorn, Oxford: Clarendon Press: 82–131.

Rowthorn, Robert and Ramana Ramaswamy. 1997. "Deindustrialization: Causes and Implications." Washington, DC: *International Monetary Fund Working Paper 42*

Rowthorn, Robert and Ramana Ramaswamy. 1999. "Growth, Trade, and Deindustrialization." *International Monetary Fund Staff Papers* 46 (March).

Rowthorn, Robert and Ken Coutts. 2004. "De-industrialisation and the Balance of Payments in Advanced Economies." *Cambridge Journal of Economics* 28(5):767–790.

Rueda, David and Jonas Pontusson. 2000. "Wage Inequality and Varieties of Capitalism." *World Politics* 52(3):350–384.

Rueda, David. 2005. "Insider-Outsider Politics in Industrialized Democracies: The Challenge to Social Democratic Parties." *American Political Science Review* 99(1):61–74.

Rueda, David. 2006. "Social Democracy and Active Labour-Market Policies: Insiders, Outsiders and the Politics of Employment Promotion." *British Journal of Political Science* 36(3):385.

Rueda, David. 2007. *Social Democracy Inside out: Partisanship and Labor Market Policy in Industrialized Democracies.* New York: Oxford University Press.

Rueda, David. forthcoming. "The State of the Welfare State: Unemployment, Labor Market Policy and Inequality in the Age of Workfare." *Comparative Politics.*

Sacchi, Stefano, Federico Pancaldi and Claudia Arisi. 2011. "The Economic Crisis as a Trigger of Convergence? Short-Time Work in Italy, Germany and Austria." In *Carlo Alberto Working Papers*. Milan: University of Milan.

Saint Paul, Gilles. 1996. "Exploring the Political Economy of Labour Market Institutions." *Economic Policy* 11(23):265–315.

Sako, Mari and Gregory Jackson. 2006. "Strategy Meets Institutions: The Transformation of Management-Labor Relations at Deutsche Telekom and NTT." *Industrial and Labor Relations Review* 59(April 3):347–366.

Salvini, Silvana and Daniele Vignoli. 2011. "Things Change: Women's and Men's Marital Disruption Dynamics in Italy during a Time of Social Transformations, 1970–2003." *Demographic Research* 24(5):145–174.

Sandvik, Ed, Ed Diener and Larry Seidlitz. 1993. "Subjective Well-Being: The Convergence and Stability of Self-Report and Non-Self-Report Measures." *Journal of Personality* 61(3):317–342.

Sayer, Liana C. and Suzanne M. Bianchi. 2000. "Women's Economic Independence and the Probability of Divorce." *Journal of Family Issues* 21(7):906–943.

Schäfer, Armin and Wolfgang Streeck, eds. 2013. *Politics in the Age of Austerity*. Cambridge: Polity Press.

Schäfer, Armin and Wolfgang Streeck. 2013. *Politics in the Age of Austerity*. Cambridge: Polity Press.

Schank, Thorsten, Claus Schnabel and Joachim Wagner. 2007. "Do Exporters Really Pay Higher Wages? First Evidence from German Linked Employer-Employee Data." *Journal of International Economics* 72(1):52–74.

Scharpf, Fritz W. 1991. *Crisis and Choice in European Social Democracy*. Ithaca, NY: Cornell University Press.

Scharpf, Fritz W. and Vivien A. Schmidt. 2000. *Welfare and Work in the Open Economy*. 2 Volumes. Oxford: Oxford University Press.

Scharpf, F. 2000. "Economic Changes, Vulnerabilities, and Institutional Capabilities." In *Welfare and Work in the Open Economy*. Vol. I. *From Vulnerability to Competitiveness*, eds. F. Scharpf and V. Schmidt. Oxford: Oxford University Press: 21–124.

Scharpf, Fritz. 2011. "Monetary Union, Fiscal Crisis and the Preemption of Democracy." *MPIfG Discussion Paper* 11/11.

Scheve, Kenneth and Matthew J. Slaughter. 2001a. "What Determines Individual Trade-Policy Preferences?" *Journal of International Economics* 54(2):267–292.

Scheve, Kenneth and Matthew J. Slaughter 2001b. "Labor Market Competition and Individual Preferences over Immigration Policy." *The Review of Economics and Statistics* 83(1):133–45.

Scheve, Kenneth and Matthew Slaughter. 2004. "Economic Insecurity and the Globalization of Production." *American Journal of Political Science* 48(4):662–674.

Schimmelfennig, Frank. 2013. "European integration in the Euro crisis: the limits of postfunctionalism." Paper for MZES workshop 'Coping with Crisis: Europe's Challenges and Strategies,'" Mannheim June 2013.

Schludi, Martin. 2005. *The Reform of Bismarckian Pension Systems: A Comparison of Pension Politics in Austria, France, Germany, Italy, and Sweden*. Amsterdam: Amsterdam University Press.

Schmid, Thomas. 2013. "Control Considerations, Creditor Monitoring, and the Capital Structure of Family Firms." *Journal of Banking & Finance* 37(2):257–272.

Schmidt, Vivien A. 2009. "Putting the Political Back into Political Economy by Bringing the State Back in Yet Again." *World Politics* 61(3):516–546.

Schmitt, John. 2011. *Labor Market Policy in the Great Recession: Some Lessons from Germany and Denmark.* Washington DC: Center for Economic and Policy Research.

Schmitter, Philippe C. 1974. "Still the Century of Corporatism?" *Review of Politics* 36:85–131.

Schneider M. and M. Paunescu. 2012. "Changing Varieties of Capitalism and Revealed Comparative Advantage from 1990 to 2005." *Socio Economic Review* 10:731–753.

Schneider, F., A. Buehn and C. E. Montenegro. 2010. "Shadow Economies all over the World: New Estimates for 162 Countries from 1999 to 2007." *World Bank Policy Research.*

Schneider, Martin R. and Mihai Paunescu. 2012. "Changing Varieties of Capitalism and Revealed Comparative Advantages from 1990 to 2005: A Test of the Hall and Soskice Claims." *Socio-Economic Review* 10(4):731–753.

Schulze, Isabelle and Martin Schludi. 2006. "Austria: From Electoral Cartel to Competitive Coalition Building." In *The Handbook of West European Pension Politics*, eds. Ellen Immergut, Karen Anderson and Isabelle Schulze. Oxford: Oxford University Press: 555–604.

Schulze, Isabelle and Michael Moran. 2006. "United Kingdom: Pension Politics in an Adversarial System." In *The Handbook of West European Pension Politics*, eds. Ellen Immergut, Karen Anderson and Isabelle Schulze. Oxford: Oxford University Press: 49–96.

Schulze, Isabelle and Sven Jochem. 2006. "Germany: Beyond Policy Gridlock." In *The Handbook of West European Pension Politics*, eds. Ellen Immergut, Karen Anderson and Isabelle Schulze. Oxford: Oxford University Press: 660–710.

Schulze-Cleven, Tobias. 2009. "Flexible Markets, Protected Workers: Adjustment Pathways in Europe's New Economy." *Political Science*, University of California, Berkeley, Berkeley.

Schwander, Hanna. 2012. "The Politicization of the Insider-Outsider Divide in Western Europe: Labour Market Vulnerability and Its Political Consequences." *Unpublished PhD Thesis*, University of Zurich.

Schwander, Hanna and Silja Häusermann. 2013. "Who Is In and Who Is Out? A Risk-Based Conceptualization of Insiders and Outsiders." *Journal of European Social Policy* 23(3):248–269.

Schwartz, Christine and Robert Mare. 2005. "Trends in Educational Assortative Marriage from 1940 to 2003." *Demography* 42(4):621–646.

Scott, Jacqueline and Braun, M 2006. "Individualization of Family Values?" In *Globalization, Value Changes and Generations*, eds. P. Ester, M. Braun and P. Mohler. Tokyo: Brill Academic.

Scruggs, Lyle. 2002. "The Ghent System and Union Membership in Europe, 1970–1996." *Political Research Quarterly* 55(2):275–297.

Scruggs, Lyle. 2004. "Welfare State Entitlements Data Set: A Comparative Institutional Analysis of Eighteen Welfare States." Version 1.2.

Scruggs, Lyle. 2013. "Comparative Welfare Entitlements Dataset 2." Department of Political Science, University of Connecticut. http://cwed2.org.

Scruggs, Lyle and James Allan. 2006. "Welfare-State Decommodification in 18 OECD Countries: A Replication and Revision." *Journal of European Social Policy* 16(1):55–72.

Seeleib-Kaiser, Martin, Adam Saunders and Marek Naczyk. 2012. "Shifting the Public-Private Mix: A New Dualization of the Welfare States." In *The Age of Dualization. The Changing Face of Inequality in Deindustrializing Societies*, eds. Patrick Emmenegger, Silja Haeusermann, Bruno Palier and Martin Seeleib-Kaiser. Oxford: Oxford University Press: 151–175.

Sen, Armatya. 2011. *The Idea of Justice*. Cambridge, MA: Harvard University Press.

Sevilla-Sanz, Almudena. 2010. "Household Division of Labor and Cross-Country Differences in Household Formation Rates." *Journal of Population Economics* 23(1):225–249.

Shayo, Moses. 2009. "A Model of Social Identity with An Application to Political Economy: Nation, Class, and Redistribution." *American Political Science Review* 103(2):147–174.

Shefter, Martin. 1977. "Party and Patronage: Germany, England, and Italy." *Politics & Society* 7(4):403–451.

Sheldon, G. 2005. "*Der berufsstrukturelle Wandel der Beschäftigung in der Schweiz 1970–2000: Ausmass, Ursachen und Folgen.*" Neuchâtel: Bundesamt für Statistik: 1–68.

Shonfield, Andrew. 1965. *Modern Capitalism: The Changing Balance of Public and Private Power*. Oxford: Oxford University Press.

Sides, John and Jack Citrin. 2007. "European Opinion about Immigration: The Role of Identities, Interests and Information." *British Journal of Political Science* 37(3):477–504.

Sigle-Rushton, Wendy. 2010. "Men's Unpaid Work and Divorce: Reassessing Specialization and Trade in British Families." *Feminist Economics* 16(2):1–26.

Silver, Beverly J. 2003. *Forces of Labor: Workers' Movements and Globalization since 1870*. New York: Cambridge University Press.

Skaksen, J. and A. Sørensen. 2002. "Skill Upgrading and Rigid Relative Wages: The Case of Danish Manufacturing." *IZA Discussion Paper 664*.

Sleebos, Joëlle. 2003. "Low Fertility Rates in OECD Countries: Facts and Policy Responses." In *OECD Labour Market and Social Policy Occasional Papers 15*. Paris: OECD.

Solow, Robert M. 1956. "A Contribution to the Theory of Economic Growth." *Quarterly Journal of Economics* 70(1)(February 1956): 65–94.

Sniderman, Paul M., Peri, P., de Figueiredo, R. J. P. and Piazza, T. 2000. *The Outsider: Prejudice and Politics in Italy*. Princeton, NJ: Princeton University Press.

Sniderman, Paul M. and Louk Hagendoorn. 2007. *When Ways of Life Collide*. Princeton, NJ: Princeton University Press.

Sniderman, Paul M., Michael Bang Petersen, Rune Slothuus, Rune Stubager. 2014. "Crosswinds: a Study of a Clash between Liberal Democratic and Islamic Values." Princeton University Press.

Soroka, Stuart Neil and Christopher Wlezien. 2010. *Degrees of Democracy: Politics, Public Opinion, and Policy*. Cambridge University Press.

Soskice, D. 1990. "Wage Determination – The Changing Role of Institutions in Advanced Industrialized Countries." *Oxford Review of Economic Policy* 6(4):36–61.

Soskice, D. 1999. "Civergent Production Regimes: Coordinated and Uncoordinated Market Economies in the 1980s and 1990s." In *Continuity and Change in Contemporary Capitalism*, eds. Herbert Kitschelt, Peter Lange, Gary Marks and John D. Stephens. Cambridge: Cambridge University Press: 101–135.

Spence, Michael and Sandile Hlatshwayo. 2011. "The Evolving Structure of the American Economy and the Employment Challenge: Council for Foreign Relations." *Comparative Economic Studies* 54:703–738.

Spitz-Oener, A. 2006. "Technical Change, Job Tasks and Rising Educational Demands: Looking Outside the Wage Structure." *Journal of Labor Economics* 24:235–270.

Steinmo, Sven. 1988. "Social Democracy vs. Socialism: Goal Adaptation in Social Democratic Sweden." *Politics and Society* 16(4):403–446.

2010. *The Evolution of Modern States: Sweden, Japan and the United States.* Cambridge: Cambridge University Press.

Stephens, John. 1979.*The Transition from Capitalism to Socialism.* Urbana: University of Illinois Press.

1996. "The Scandinavian Welfare States: Achievements, Crisis, and Prospects" In *Welfare States in Transition,* ed. Gösta Esping-Andersen. London: Sage.

Stephens, John D., Evelyne Huber and Leonard Ray. 1999. "The Welfare State in Hard Times." In *Continuity and Change in Contemporary Capitalism,* eds. Herbert Kitschelt, Peter Lange, Gary Marks and John D. Stephens. New York: Cambridge University Press: 164–193.

Stiglitz, Joseph. 2012. *The Price of Inequality: How Today's Divided Society Endangers Our Future.* New York: W. W. Norton.

Streeck, Wolfgang. 2005. "Industrial Relations: From State Weakness as Strength to State Weakness as Weakness: Welfare Corporatism and the Private Use of the Public Interest." In *Governance in Contemporary Germany,* eds. Simon Green and William E. Paterson. Cambridge: Cambridge University Press: 138–164.

Streeck, Wolfgang. 2009. *Re-Forming Capitalism.* Oxford: Oxford University Press.

Streeck, Wolfgang. 2011. "The Crisis of Democratic Capitalism." *New Left Review* No. 71 (September–October):5–29.

Streeck, Wolfgang. 2014a. *Buying Time: The Delayed Crisis of Democratic Capitalism.* London: Verso Books.

Streeck, Wolfgang. 2014b. "How Will Capitalism End?" *New Left Review* 87(May–June):35–64.

Stubager, R. 2008. Education Effects on Authoritarian-Libertarian Values: A Question of Socialization. *British Journal of Sociology,* 59(2), 327–350.

Sullivan, Oriel. 2011. "An End to Gender Display through the Performance of Housework? A Review and Reassessment of the Quantitative Literature Using Insights from the Qualitative Literature." *Journal of Family Theory & Review* 3(1):1–13.

Tabellini, Guido. 2008. "Institutions and Culture." *Journal of the European Economic Association* 6(2–3):255–294.

Tåhlin, M. 2007. "Skills and Wages in European Labour Markets: Structure and Change." In *Employment Regimes and the Quality of Work,* ed. D. Gallie. Oxford: Oxford University Press.

Tamir, Yael. 1995. "The Enigma of Nationalism." *World Politics* 47:418–440.

Taylor-Gooby, P. 2004. *New Risks, New Welfare: The Transformation of the European Welfare State.* Oxford University Press

Thelen, Kathleen. 2012. "Varieties of Capitalism: Trajectories of Liberalization and the New Politics of Social Solidarity." *Annual Review of Political Science* 15:137–159.

Thelen, Kathleen. 2014. *Varieties of Liberalization and the New Politics of Social Solidarity*. New York and Cambridge: Cambridge University Press.

Thomassen, Jacques. 2005. *The European Voter: A Comparative Study of Modern Democracies*. Oxford: Oxford University Press.

2009. "The European Voter Database." Updated version. ZA-Nr. 3911.

Thomsen, Steen. 1996. "Foundation Ownership and Economic Performance." *Corporate Governance: An International Review* 4(4):212–221.

Thomsen, Steen and Torben Pedersen. 1996. "Nationality and Ownership Structures: The 100 Largest Companies in Six European Nations." *Management International Review* 36(2):149–166.

Thomsen, Steen and Caspar Rose. 2004. "Foundation Ownership and Financial Performance: Do Companies Need Owners?" *European Journal of Law and Economics* 18(3):343–364.

Thomson, Robert, Terry Royedb, Elin Naurinc, Joaquín Artésd, Mark Fergusonb, Petia Kostadinova and Catherine Moury. 2013. "The Program-to-Policy Linkage: A Comparative Study of Election Pledges and Government Policies in Ten Countries." Paper prepared for the Annual Meeting of the American Political Science Association, Chicago, August 28-September 1.

Tokman, V. E. 1992. *Beyond Regulation: The Informal Economy in Latin America*. Boulder, CO, and London: Lynne Rienner.

Tomz, Michael and Robert P. Van Houweling. 2008. "Candidate Positioning and Voter Choice." *The American Political Science Review* 102(3):303–318.

Toniolo, G. 1998. "Europe's Golden Age, 1950–1973: Speculations from a Long-run Perspective." *Economic History Review* 2:252–267.

Traxler, Franz, Sabine Blaschke and Bernhard Kittel. 2000. *National Labor Relations in Internationalized Markets*. Oxford: Oxford University Press.

Turnham, D., B. Salome and A. Schwarz. 1990. "The Informal Sector Revisited." Organization for Economic Cooperation and Development.

Vail, Mark I. 2010. *Recasting Welfare Capitalism. Economic Adjustment in Contemporary France and Germany*. Philadelphia: Temple University Press.

Van der Brug, Wouter and Joost van Spanje. 2009. "Immigration, Europe and the 'New' Cultural Dimension." *European Journal of Political Research* 48:309–334.

Van der Eijk, Cees and Mark N. Franklin. 1996. *Choosing Europe? The European Electorate and National Politics in the Face of Union*. Ann Arbor: University of Michigan Press.

Van der Eijk, Cees, Mark N. Franklin and Wouter Van der Brug. 1999. "Policy preferences and party choice." In *Political Representation and Legitimacy in the European Union*, eds. H. Schmitt and J. Thomassen. Oxford: Oxford University Press.

Van der Waal, Jeroen, Peter Achterberg, Dick Houtman, Willem de Koster and Katerina Manevska 2010. "'Some Are More Equal than Others': Economic Egalitarianism and Welfare Chauvinism in the Netherlands" *Journal of European Social Policy* 20:350–363.

Van Kersbergen, Kees. 1995. *Social Capitalism: A Study of Christian Democracy and the Welfare State*. London and New York: Routledge.

Van Lancker, Wim. 2013. "Putting the Child-Centered Investment Strategy to the Test: Evidence for the EU27." *European Journal of Social Security*, 15(1):4–27.

Van Oorschot, Wim. 2000. "Who Should Get What and Why? on Deservingness Criteria and the Conditionality of Solidarity among the Public." *Policy and Politics* 28(1):33–48.

2006. "Making the Difference in Social Europe: Deservingness Perceptions Among Citizens of European Welfare States." *Journal of European Social Policy* 16:23–42.

Van Vliet, Olaf and Koen Caminada. 2012. "Unemployment Replacement Rates Dataset Among 34 Welfare States, 1971–2009: An Update, Extension, and Modification of the Scruggs Welfare State Entitlements Data Set." *NEUJOBS special report* no. 2, January 2012.

Vartiainen, Juhana. 2011. "Nordic Collective Agreements: A Continuous Institution in a Changing Economic Environment." In *The Nordic Varieties of Capitalism* (Comparative Social Research, Vol. 28), ed. Lars Mjøset. Emerald Group: 331–363

Veenhoven, Ruut. 2000. "Wellbeing in the Welfare State: Level Not Higher, Distribution Not More Equitable." *Journal of Comparative Policy Analysis* 2(1):91–125.

Venn, Danielle. 2007. "Legislation, Collective Bargaining and Enforcement: Updating the OECD Employment Protection Indicators." *OECD Social and Migration Working Paper*.

Vienna Institute for Demography. 2010. "European Demographic Data Sheet." Vienna: VID

Vis, Barbara, Kees van Kersbergen and Uwe Becker. 2008. "The Politics of Welfare State Reform in the Netherlands: Explaining a Never-Ending Puzzle." *Acta Politica* 43:333–356.

Visser, Jelle and Anton Hemerijck. 1997. *A Dutch Miracle: Job Growth, Welfare Reform, and Corporatism in the Netherlands*. Amsterdam: Amsterdam University Press.

Vitols, Sigurt. 2004. "Negotiated Shareholder Value: The German Version of an Anglo-American Practice." *Competition and Change* 8(4):1–18.

Von Wahl, Angelika. 2008. "From Family to Reconciliation Policy: How the Grand Coalition Reforms the German Welfare State." *German Politics and Society* 26(3):25–49.

Wagner, Joachim. 2007. "Exports and Productivity: A Survey of the Evidence from Firm-level Data." *The World Economy* 30(1):60–82.

Waldfogel, Jane. 2010. *Britain's War on Poverty*, New York: Russell Sage.

Wallerstein, Michael. 1999. "Wage-Setting Institutions and Pay Inequality in Advanced Industrial Societies." *American Journal of Political Science* 43(3):649–680.

Walter, Stefanie and Linda Maduz. 2009. "How Globalization Shapes Individual Risk Perceptions and Policy Preferences. a Cross-National Analysis of Differences between Globalization Winners and Losers." WCFIA Working Paper Series.

Walter, Stefanie. 2010. "Globalization and the Welfare State: Testing the Microfoundations of the Compensation Hypothesis." *International Studies Quarterly* 54(2):403–426.

Walter, Stefanie. 2013. *Financial Crises and the Politics of Macroeconomic Adjustments*. Cambridge: Cambridge University Press.

Walter, Stefanie. 2015. "Globalization and the Demand-Side of Politics: How Globalization Shapes Individual Perceptions of Labor Market Risk and Policy Preferences." In *IPES Annual Conference*. Cambridge MA: Harvard University.

Warwick, Paul V. 2011. "Voters, Parties, and Declared Government Policy." *Comparative Political Studies* 44(12):1675–1699.

Weinkopf, Claudia and Gerhard Bosch. 2010. "The Minimum Wage System and Changing Industrial Relations in Germany (Executive Summary)."

Wibbels, Erik. 2006. "Dependency Revisited: International Markets, Business Cycles, and Social Spending in the Developing World." *International Organization* 60 (02):433–468.

Wibbels, Erik. forthcoming. *Trade, Development and Social Insurance.* Cambridge: Cambridge Unviersity Press.

Wilensky, Harold. 1975. *The Welfare State and Equality: Structural and Ideological Roots of Public Expenditures.* Berkeley and Los Angeles: University of California Press.

Wiliarty, Sara. 2010. *The CDU and the Politics of Gender in Germany.* Cambridge: Cambridge University Press.

Wilson, Warner R. 1967. "Correlates of Avowed Happiness." *Psychological Bulletin* 67(4):294–306.

Wilson, William J. 1987. *The Truly Disadvantaged: The Inner City, the Underclass, and Public Policy.* Chicago: University of Chicago Press.

Windolf, Paul and Jürgen Beyer. 1996. "Cooperative Capitalism: Corporate Networks in Germany and Britain." *British Journal of Sociology* 2:205.

Wood, Adrian. 1995. *North-South Trade, Employment, and Inequality.* Oxford: Oxford University Press.

Wren, Anne and Philipp Rehm. 2013. "Service Expansion, International Exposure, and Political Preferences." In *The Political Economy of the Service Transition*, ed. A. Wren. Oxford: Oxford University Press.

Wright, E. O. and J. Singelmann. 1982. "Proletarianization in the Changing American Class Structure." *American Journal of Sociology* 88:176–209.

Wright, E. O. and R. Dwyer. 2003. "The Patterns of Job Expansions in the USA: A Comparison of the 1960s and 1990s." *Socio-Economic Review* 1:289–325.

Young, H. Peyton and Mary Burke. 2001. "Competition and Custom in Economic Contracts: A Case Study of Illinois Agriculture." *American Economic Review* 91(3):559–573.

Ziegler, J. Nicholas. 2000. "Corporate Governance and the Politics of Property Rights in Germany." *Politics and Society* 28(2):195–221.

Index